Pra   Airport
Operations, Safety, and
Emergency Management

Practical Airport Operations, Safety, and Emergency Management
Protocols for Today and the Future

Jeffrey C. Price

Jeffrey S. Forrest

AMSTERDAM • BOSTON • HEIDELBERG • LONDON
NEW YORK • OXFORD • PARIS • SAN DIEGO
SAN FRANCISCO • SINGAPORE • SYDNEY • TOKYO

Butterworth-Heinemann is an imprint of Elsevier

Acquiring Editor: Sara Scott
Editorial Project Manager: Hilary Carr
Project Manager: Punithavathy Govindaradjane
Designer: Vicky Pearson

Butterworth-Heinemann is an imprint of Elsevier
The Boulevard, Langford Lane, Kidlington, Oxford OX5 1GB, UK
50 Hampshire Street, 5th Floor, Cambridge, MA 02139, USA

Notices
Knowledge and best practice in this field are constantly changing. As new research and experience broaden our
understanding, changes in research methods, professional practices, or medical treatment may become necessary.

Practitioners and researchers must always rely on their own experience and knowledge in evaluating and using any
information, methods, compounds, or experiments described herein. In using such information or methods they should be
mindful of their own safety and the safety of others, including parties for whom they have a professional responsibility.

To the fullest extent of the law, neither the Publisher nor the authors, contributors, or editors, assume any liability for any
injury and/or damage to persons or property as a matter of products liability, negligence or otherwise, or from any use or
operation of any methods, products, instructions, or ideas contained in the material herein.

ISBN: 978-0-12-800515-6

British Library Cataloguing-in-Publication Data
A catalogue record for this book is available from the British Library.

Library of Congress Cataloging-in-Publication Data
A catalog record for this book is available from the Library of Congress.

For Information on all Butterworth Heinemann publications
visit our website at http://store.elsevier.com/

Working together
to grow libraries in
developing countries

www.elsevier.com • www.bookaid.org

Contents

Foreword

The global aviation industry is a complex and interconnected network of airports, airlines, manufacturers, and air traffic control systems, all working closely together to connect people with each other and to facilitate the transportation of goods. In 2015, it was estimated that the global aviation industry provided over 56 million jobs globally and over $2 trillion of global GDP (gross domestic product). As global connections grow closer every year, the aviation industry must meet and exceed the demands of current travelers, shippers, and commerce.

Airports are, of course, critical to the success of the global aviation industry. Airports provide the needed infrastructure to safely and successfully facilitate air commerce and air travel. Unfortunately, many of our nation's airports are in dire need of upgrade and expansion, so the need for increased funding, creative personnel, and innovative ideas is a "must" in order to sustain an effective and efficient U.S. air transportation system. Like any successful industry, airport operators understand they must continually adapt in order to survive. Managing an airport just five years ago involved many different demands than the demands of today, and that trend of change will continue into the future. Airport operators have learned that they must now think, talk, and operate as entrepreneurs—especially as entrepreneurship relates to exceeding the overall passenger experience! Today's Airport Manager must continuously balance the challenges of regulatory requirements with offering the right amount of amenities and growth. These challenges are what make the profession of managing airports very exciting and rewarding.

I would like to introduce you to an exciting career field that is neither highly known nor well-advertised, but is rewarding, challenging, and integral to the success of the Aviation Industry—specifically, a career in Airport Operations, Safety, and Emergency Management. No matter the size or complexity of your airport, the components of operations (Ops), safety, and emergency management are always present. If you are running a small airport, these functions may be performed by one or two people. In contrast, large-hub certificated airports may employ up to 100 staff to ensure that duties are performed correctly. As airports continue to grow and air travel increases, airports will be looking for qualified candidates who can help face the many related challenges that are coming.

The material in this book has been carefully researched and reviewed. It is presented in a way that enables the reader to achieve maximum retention. Whether this is your first course in airport management or you are a seasoned professional, you will find the material in each chapter very helpful in preparing you for an amazing career or enhancing your current abilities in the field. The chapters and their order have been carefully selected to help readers build their base knowledge and understand what is needed to run a safe, secure, and efficient airport operation—an airport operation that current and future travelers will expect.

If you have ever wondered how airports are owned, how they fit together into a larger system, how they are funded, how airports are regulated, or how safety is incorporated into the airport environment, then this book is perfect for you. You will learn about the role the Federal Aviation Administration (FAA) plays in airports, the different components of an airfield, including taxiway, runway, and supporting navigational aids used for the safe operation of aircraft.

Some of the topics identified in this book have evolved from recent events, changes in technology, or federal mandates and are important to understand and keep abreast of. For example, Safety Management Systems (SMS) is something that has been around for many years in various industries, including aviation. However, the FAA is now mandating SMS-related efforts into the airport operating environment and is requiring new skills and knowledge of the airport employee. The integration of technology and process improvement into Emergency Management is something that continues to evolve, whether it is coordinating the response of firefighters to a burning aircraft or supporting a response to a natural disaster in the community. In addition, the use of the National Incident Management System and Incident Command System is rather new for airports. This book also discusses technologies that are innovative to the industry, like the use of Unmanned Aeronautical Vehicles (UAVs) or Unmanned Aerial Systems (UASs) on or near airports; responses to laser sightings; and NextGen improvements.

As an aviation professional, I am excited and encouraged to see students and industry professionals learning the contents of this textbook. The topics and supporting material are relevant to the issues we face today in the airport industry. The field of Airport Operations, Safety, and Emergency Management is becoming a highly desired career choice and one that is well embraced and supported in the aviation industry. I have enjoyed a very rewarding and challenging career in this field and look forward to the excitement and viability of Airport Operations in the coming years. This textbook will not only assist students in learning the basic methods, techniques, and systems used to run an airport, but will also be a reference guide for those who, like myself, are currently in the industry.

The authors of this textbook, Jeffrey Price, M.A., C.M., and Jeffrey Forrest, Ph.D., have done a fabulous job researching and writing in preparation for writing this text. They are both extremely credible professionals within the industry and have a history of producing relevant, meaningful, and educational publications that have been used throughout the world. For example, together they authored *Practical Aviation Security: Predicting and Preventing Future Threats, Second Edition* (2013), a widely used and well-referenced text in the aviation industry. They also authored the American Association of Airport Executive's (AAAE) *Certified Member Body of Knowledge* modules, which have assisted aviation professionals throughout the United States in obtaining their professional rating as a Certified Member of AAAE. The contribution made to the industry by these two skilled authors is invaluable. The air transportation industry is thankful to have well-written material that is relevant, meaningful, and useful in everyday settings.

Finally, I support *you* in expanding your knowledge about the great career of Airport Operations, Safety, and Emergency Management. The journey ahead is rewarding and I want to personally thank you for reading this text. The industry is in need of individuals with this knowledge, and we anxiously await an increased pool of qualified and motivated people to join us in running the world's airports.

Dan Sprinkle, A.A.E., MBA
Vice President—Airport Operations
Denver International Airport

Preface

In 1968, author Arthur Hailey's novel, *Airport*, went to the top of the *New York Times* Best Sellers list. *Airport* described a fictional "day-in-the-life" of an Airport Manager trying to keep the airport running safely and efficiently despite a huge variety of operational, security, and emergency problems. Hailey's work depicted 12 hours of Airport Operations that could easily serve as a menu of typical problems airport operators continue to face to this day, including: blizzards, internal airline and airport politics, noise complaints, air traffic control challenges, stowaways, disgruntled passengers and impatient pilots, aircraft operational problems, personality issues, and threats to security. To some extent, modern Airport Operations Managers might refer to many of the situations presented in *Airport* as perhaps a "typical Monday"!

Airport Operations was not especially well-known as a career opportunity when *Airport* was published. Early Airport Operations personnel were typically staffed, by default, with former pilots. There were few aviation or airport management training or educational programs during this era, and pilots were the best qualified resource for serving in airport management and operations. It was also common for most to assume that the Federal Aviation Administration (FAA) or the airlines operated public airports. To this day, many individuals are surprised to learn that usually a city or county serves as the employers of airport operational personnel and is responsible for the day-to-day operations of their local airport(s).

Today, there are dozens of colleges and universities offering varying levels of degree programs designed for those seeking a career in aviation operations or aviation management. Correspondingly, there is a growing body of published work, including textbooks, certification training programs, and industry publications addressing the many aspects and challenges of **Airport Operations**, or **"Ops."**

In modern educational and professional Airport Operations training programs, and other texts on the subject, much emphasis has been placed on "passenger throughput modeling." Modeling is extremely useful in Ops, especially in aiding in the development of efficient terminal design. However, much of this effort focuses on terminal or airfield design concepts as related to operations. In contrast, this text addresses the day-to-day practical requirements of Airport Operations needed to ensure the efficient and effective flow and air transportation of passengers, baggage, and cargo.

Practical Airport Operations, Safety, and Emergency Management targets the current and future Airport Operations professional charged with ensuring that all functions of an airport are safely, securely, and effectively executed. Airport Operations personnel are on the "front lines" at our nation's airports, solving safety and security problems, ensuring compliance with regulations, being ambassadors to the general public, serving as peacemakers between tenants and airlines, and responding to human-made and natural disasters. These and many more operational responsibilities are described in this book, and in ways that enhance the reader's ability to protect passengers, and to protect the airport from risk and liability. While several chapters of this book relate to the operation of Part 139 commercial service "certificated" airports, the information presented is also highly relevant to general aviation airport operators who want to be informed about best practices and regulatory requirements of operating an airport. Regardless of airport size or classification, understanding how to implement effective operational processes helps all airport authorities to comply with FAA grant assurances, while also reducing operating costs and legal exposure. Most importantly, effective and safe operational policies and processes save lives. Therefore, *Practical Airport Operations, Safety, and Emergency Management* explores these policies and processes in great detail, providing the reader with foundational knowledge necessary for operating a safe and effective airport service.

Chapters 1 to 3 provide the context for Airport Operations personnel, addressing the physical, regulatory, and political environment that Ops personnel must understand to be successful.

Chapters 4 and 5 focus on Safety Management Systems (SMS) as an international safety standard that is being adopted by airports throughout the world. SMS is now considered an essential element to an airport safety culture. SMS can help reduce accidents and the severity of accidents and identify the highest priority risks and hazards so that funding for operations and safety can be more effectively budgeted.

Chapters 6 to 8 focus on Part 139 operations and relate to commercial airfield safety. More than just a recital of the regulations, these chapters are combined with best practices from a variety of areas including the Airport Cooperative Research Program (ACRP), the National Fire Protection Association (NFPA), and other references to form a construct for developing an effective airfield safety program.

Chapter 9 focuses on terminal and landside operations. While airfield safety is a regulatory responsibility, it is the terminal and landside operations that bring in a tremendous amount of revenue to the airport and are also important touchpoints to the passenger experience.

Chapters 10 to 12 focus on emergency management at airports. The Airport Emergency Plan, incident management systems, and handling specific hazards, such as aircraft crashes, natural disasters, and hazardous materials, are addressed.

Chapter 13 discusses future operational challenges to Airport Operations, including Unmanned Aerial Vehicles and spaceports.

Ultimately, it is our desire that this text be used to increase overall efficiency and safety in operations at airports. We also strongly believe that this text provides the aspiring student of aviation management a solid foundation for understanding and embracing Airport Operations as a profession. *Practical Airport Operations, Safety, and Emergency Management* is highly accessible to the new or aspiring airport management professional. The text is also of great value to the experienced Airport Operations Manager as a day-to-day reference for administering effective and safe Airport Operations.

(Note: *Practical Airport Operations, Safety, and Emergency Management* is a companion to our first textbook, *Practical Airport Security: Predicting and Preventing Future Threats, Second Edition* [Butterworth-Heinemann, 2013].)

Jeffrey C. Price and Jeffrey S. Forrest
Denver, Colorado, 2016

Acknowledgments

As with any extensive and challenging team project, there are numerous people to thank for their assistance and dedication. Our fear is that someone will be forgotten, so here is our best effort at including everyone who assisted in the production of this book. Our sincerest thanks and appreciation go to all these individuals and any that may have been inadvertently unnamed.

We would like to acknowledge, first and foremost, our wives, Jennifer Price and Betsy Forrest, who suffered tremendously, particularly in the final months as we were up against deadlines. They not only had to take on the extra load of getting things done, but also "putting up" with us. Jeff Price would like to thank his kids, Austin, Alex, and Ashton, who graciously gave up a lot of dad time this past year so he could get the book done, and to his parents, Zig and Dianne Price, who did a lot of the heavy lifting in filling in for dad when the kids and Jen needed help. And to Marion Shelley (Nana) who helped foster a love of airports in JP.

A huge thanks goes out to Megan Jones and Dawn Escarcega, who were critical to the entire process, working on edits, reviews, citations, chasing down photos, and just about anything else we asked them to do on short notice and always with a deadline of yesterday. Special thanks also goes to Chris Hardaway, J.D., for his critical analysis of many of our passages and pointing out viable legal resources to integrate into the text. Without Megan, Dawn, and Chris, this book would not have been possible. Also, a very special thanks to our team at Elsevier, including Hilary Carr, Sara Scott, Pam Chester, and Punithavathy Govindaradjane for your flexibility, encouragement, and patience!

For this book, we wanted to include industry essays to provide the reader with "real-world" perspectives. As a result, many professionals took time out of their busy schedules to write for us or to give us one-on-one interviews. Thank you to our contributors, Tim Barth, Martha Edge, Meredith Champlin Eaton, Alex Gertsen, Robert Olislagers, Tim O'Krongley, Justin Overholt, John Paczkowski, Zechariah Papp, Jim Payne, Jim Schell, Rosemary Rizzo, Dave Ruppel, Dan Sprinkle, Jason Taussig, and Steve Thompson, and to Jessica Birnbaum, Nick Meacher, and William Payne for their contributions of time and expertise.

A very special thanks to Alfonso Denson, President/CEO-Birmingham Airport Authority Board, and Jim Payne, Director of Operations & Planning at the Birmingham/Shuttlesworth International Airport (BHM). BHM is very progressive in the training and development of its operations and maintenance staff and a lot of the material in the operations and emergency management sections of this text was either developed, trained, or tested during training sessions conducted by J. Price at BHM. Both Alfonso and Jim are true leaders in our industry!

Thank you also to the American Association of Airport Executives for its long-standing support of airport training at airports throughout the United States, and to Airports Council International.

We would also like to thank Shaun Sederberg and Alex Gertsen for sharing some of their excellent photography. Additional thanks go out to Kim Day and Stacey Stegman at Denver International Airport, who gave permissions to use photographs and also allowed several members of the Denver International Airport team to contribute their personal essays.

Others who contributed in ways they may not even have realized, but did so through support, side work, friendship, and professional guidance, are: Sherilyn Kadel (JP's source of inspiration and encouragement, may she never be forgotten), J. David Rigsby, Starla Bryant, Alex Sweetman, Greg Donovan, Kevin Matthews, Steve Runge, Steve Davis, Dawson Frank, Ron Fano, and Stephen Flynn—and Arthur Hailey, author of the novel *Airport*, for inspiring a generation of Airport Managers and operators. Finally, we would like to thank Dr. Sandra Haynes, Dean of the College of Professional Studies at Metropolitan State University of Denver, for providing support and latitude to our already busy schedules as we produced this book.

AIRPORT OPERATIONS, SAFETY, AND EMERGENCY MANAGEMENT

Airport airside "Ops" at Denver International Airport, CO, Terminal A.

Image by Shahn Sederberg, courtesy Colorado Division of Aeronautics, 2013.

Airport landside construction and operations at Denver International Airport's South Terminal Development Project.

Image by Shahn Sederberg, courtesy Colorado Division of Aeronautics, 2014.

Centennial Airport ATCT and Administration Building, CO.

Image by Shahn Sederberg, courtesy Colorado Division of Aeronautics, 2007.

The prime function of **Airport Operations** is the effective and efficient planning, implementation, and control of the production of air service at an airport. Those familiar with Airport Operations management know that "every successful flight begins and ends at an airport." In that sense, Airport Operations focuses on providing quality services that ensure safe air service at the airport and effective operational support of all arriving and departing passengers and aircraft. As a distinct function within airport management, Airport Operations is also strategically comprised of policies, regulations, resources, and methods that are committed to supporting safety management and emergency management within the airport environment. Within Airport Operations, **safety management** is charged with planning, implementing, and controlling processes for identifying and reducing potential hazards or risks associated with providing air service at the airport. In contrast, **emergency management** focuses on planning, implementing, and controlling actions that mitigate or respond to crises in ways that reduce risk to life and property at the airport.

Although related and systematically integrated, Airport Operations[1] is not directly responsible for **Airport Security**, which is a duty shared by airport management, law enforcement, and many governmental agencies. Airport Security personnel are responsible for identifying and eliminating threats or risks that are deliberately initiated against the populace interacting within the airport environment, as well as property and infrastructure. In this textbook, Airport Operations, along with safety and emergency management, are examined in relation to threats or risks derived from incidents, accidents, or natural hazards.

Federal, state, and local regulations permeate many concerns in Airport Operations, safety management, and emergency management. Airport Operations is responsible for managing and complying with these regulations as they apply to supporting the movement of passengers and cargo on the airport. Airport Operations is not directly responsible for managing safety regulations that apply to the operation of aircraft for the purpose of flight.

Airport Operations management must ensure safe air service in variable conditions to thousands of passengers, airport employees, vendors, cargo shipments, and other stakeholders and resources. The **primary objective** for Airport Operations is to safely move departing passengers (and other stakeholders), bags, and cargo from **landside**[2] (public access and transportation areas), through the terminal or other related facilities, and then to **airside**[3] (Secured Areas and flight operations) sections of the airport. This process is reversed for arriving passengers. This objective must be sustained while operating in many dynamic and high-risk operating conditions, such as greatly

---

[1]*Note:* When referring to Airport Operations or titles such as "Airport Operations Manager," this text refers to personnel who work directly for the airport sponsor. Some airlines and other airport tenants may also have job titles called "Airport Operations Manager," but in those contexts they mean that that individual is in charge of the operation of that air carrier or that tenant facility at that particular airport. They do not have any responsibilities related to actually operating the airport itself, which is the focus of this text. Similarly, some titles within the Transportation Security Administration (TSA) may include "Airport Security manager," which is not to be confused with the actual Airport Security Coordinator or the airport's director of security. TSA has variously used the security manager title for checkpoint managers or supervisors, but they have zero jurisdiction beyond the checkpoint area, nor do they have any responsibility for the Airport Security Program. Unless otherwise noted, Airport Operations and Airport Security personnel work for the airport sponsor and have direct responsibilities for the operation of the airport.

[2]*Landside* commonly refers to Ground Transportation areas such as the highway, light rail, or other intermodal connections, e.g., the parking structure, and passenger pickup and dropoff locations.

[3]*Airside* commonly refers to those areas within the perimeter fence of an airport and other security access points leading to access to aircraft or movement areas for aircraft operations.

varying weather conditions and continuous variations in passenger frequency and related demands or needs. Additionally, Airport Operations must provide these services in ways that allow the airport to continuously function as a "system-within-systems" of complex regulatory, security, and National Airspace concerns.

The profession of Airport Operations, along with all areas of aviation management, must be conducted within a framework of strong **ethics** and regulatory requirements. Many professional aviation organizations and airport authorities publish standards of ethical conduct and methods for instilling ethical values in airport employees. The business of aviation is laden with high risks to many members of the global community. Therefore, all stakeholders in Airport Operations management systems must conduct business at an airport within a shared value of professional ethics.

MANAGING AIRPORT OPERATIONAL SYSTEMS

Airport Operations Managers frequently refer to their airport and runway systems as the "most expensive piece of pavement in the city." This adage highlights the importance of the airport as a system of relatively high expense that must support and integrate safely and reliably into the **National Airspace System (NAS)** and the local community infrastructure. Airport Operations must continuously maintain and inspect a plethora of airport infrastructure all related as a **system-of-systems** designed to ensure the safety of millions of passengers per year. When a runway is out of operational service at a hub or major airport, the flow of aircraft within the NAS can be affected regionally, nationally, and in some cases internationally. The "domino effect" of delayed traffic throughout the NAS as caused by a single operational slowdown at a single airport demonstrates how most airports must be designed and operated in a way to seamlessly integrate with some of the busiest airspace systems in the world (Sharghi, 2012). Any flight delay can easily cost tens of thousands of dollars to multiple airlines. These concerns of operational costs must balance with the ability of the airport to function safely, within regulatory compliance, and in an ethical manner. All stakeholders affected by airport operational issues must be treated with the highest regard for their safety and also be considered fairly in terms of their concerns and specific needs. Furthermore, the traveling public has a social expectation of the airport to provide adequate and effective resources for emergency management and response should an incident, accident, or hazard occur. This expectation is not unreasonable, given the high intensity of security barriers and related systems that air travel passengers have to contend with in comparison to other modes of travel.

Providing effective and ethical operational services in response to emergency situations is a universal principle in Airport Operations management. At a macro level, these values and processes also extend to the planning of systems that enable the airport to adapt to advances in technology, such as new types of aircraft, ranging from the large "heavy" Airbus 380 to the Cessna Mustang-Very Light Jet. Additionally, new innovations and applications, such as those associated with **Unmanned Aerial Vehicles (UAVs)**,[4] are currently creating significant operational and regulatory concerns for airports and the NAS. Concurrently, the United States is also advocating the development of commercial spaceports in conjunction with commercial air service at various airports.

---

[4]Federal Aviation Administration. (2015). *Unmanned aircraft systems (UAS) regulations & policies.* Retrieved from: http://www.faa.gov/uas/regulations_policies

Presently there are more than 12 Federal Aviation Administration (FAA) designated spaceports, as well as other categories of airport-related facilities that support various types of space vehicle launch and landing operations.[5]

As a strategy for helping ensure compliance and effectiveness of Airport Operations, FAA encourages airport authorities to increase or develop ancillary revenue sources. In addition to revenue earned from aircraft or airline operations, airport authorities seek to stimulate sources of nonflight (known as non-aeronautical)-related revenue as a way to help sustain airport infrastructure and operating requirements necessary to remain in compliance with federal and local requirements, including policies and regulations. For example, many airports now offer services to the public that are similar to shopping mall environments or other similar concentrations of retail and service businesses. The many services of a shopping mall and other passenger or visitor services, including restaurants, health spas, and business centers, must integrate with airport functional areas, such as security-screening operations, cargo acceptance and processing facilities, and aircraft services (e.g., fueling, maintenance and ground handling). While these for-profit or service-fee entities and facilities contribute significantly to the revenue of an airport, they must also be provided operational and emergency response services by the airport authority.

AIRPORT OPERATIONS AND COMMERCE

Much like a small town, an airport is a place where multiple types of business and commerce are conducted. Generally, there are two primary operational activities taking place at an airport: aeronautical and nonaeronautical. Aeronautical-related activities include the commercial air carriers, Fixed Base Operators (FBOs), Specialized Aviation Service Operators (SASOs) (flight schools, maintenance shops), and other types of flying-related activities, such as charter flights, skydiving, banner towing, and recreational flying. Airports also commonly have large corporate flight departments, aircraft based and operating through the facility, or aircraft manufacturers; in some cases, airports are colocated with military bases. Non-aeronautical-related activities include concessions, Ground Transportation (parking, commercial and private vehicle pickup and dropoff), vendors who provide supplies and services to the tenants and concessions, and contractors who provide services and construction activities at the airport.

THE AEROTROPOLIS: A MAJOR CHALLENGE FOR AIRPORT OPERATIONS

Various metropolitan areas are now developing integrated business and industrial parks that feature an airport as the center node for supporting commerce. This concept is frequently referred to as an "airport city" or **aerotropolis**.[6] An aerotropolis is similar to the more traditional geographic designation of a "central business district," or CBD. In contrast to a CBD, the aerotropolis is developed from land-use strategies and tactics centered on the airport as the foci for commerce (Price & Forrest, 2014). The integrated nature of the aerotropolis with the community and commerce places significant new demands on airport management and operational personnel.

---

[5]Federal Aviation Administration. (2013). *Active licenses*. Retrieved from: http://www.faa.gov/data_research/commercial _space_data/licenses/#operatorLicenses

[6]Kasarda, J. (2015). *About the aerotropolis*. Retrieved from: http://www.aerotropolis.com/airportCities/about-the -aerotropolis

An aerotropolis bonds the airport and related operational concerns more directly to the geography, culture, and sociology of the surrounding community than most traditional airport settings. The prime airport within an aerotropolis is a significant asset to the community in (a) supporting law enforcement activities within and external to the airport, (b) providing responses to emergency or natural disaster situations, and (c) facilitating the effective and efficient flow of passengers, cargo, and other stakeholders throughout the aerotropolis' region and within the NAS. An aerotropolis creates new concerns related to security, as it is potentially a significant target for potential criminal and terrorist activity. Providing safe, effective, and efficient passage of travelers, cargo, and other visiting stakeholders to the aerotropolis is emerging as the most significant future challenge to Airport Operations and emergency response services (Kasarda, 2015).

AIRPORT OPERATIONS MANAGEMENT

As described above, Airport Operations (or "Ops") and emergency management are primarily responsible for managing the airport to sustain the safe, effective, and efficient flow of passengers and cargo. Airport Ops is charged with keeping the airport functional during all hours of operation and under greatly varying conditions. Managers of Airport Operations and emergency response must *routinely plan, schedule, direct, control, and evaluate airport personnel and other resources in an environment of high stress and high risk.* Airport Operations is concerned with managing the stress of and risk to a populace similar to a small city, within tightly controlled boundaries and under highly regulated procedures.

Ops
   Airport Operations is commonly referred to as "Ops" in the domain of airport management. In this textbook, Ops is used interchangeably with Operations, as is experienced in the profession.

The breadth and depth of an Airport Operations division can vary greatly among airports. However, while there are more than 5,000 public-use airports in the United States,[7] including more than 450 commercial service airports of all sizes, the mission of Airport Operations stays essentially the same. Large airports usually have operational departments or divisions consisting of hundreds of personnel. In contrast, operations management at small **general aviation (GA)** airports may be assigned to an individual with other responsibilities, such as maintenance or overall airport management.

Depending on the size of the airport, Ops personnel may also fulfill the roles of firefighter, paramedic, police officer, ambassador to passengers, and customer service agent, and in nearly all cases act as a representative of the airport authority. As a department, Airport Operations is often structured around areas of functional responsibility, such as (a) airfield Ops, (b) terminal Ops, (c) landside or Ground Transportation Ops, (d) police, fire, emergency, and medical services Ops, and (e) communication Ops. Although staffing, functional areas, and organizational structures of Airport Operations vary greatly among airports, the types of concerns routinely addressed by

---

[7]United States Department of Transportation. (2014). *Table 1-3: Number of U.S. airports(a).* Retrieved from: http://www.rita.dot.gov/bts/sites/rita.dot.gov.bts/files/publications/national_transportation_statistics/html/table_01_03.html

operations and emergency response personnel remain the same at many airports. For example, common concerns and responses include:

1. Is it snowing: Make sure the snow is removed from all operational areas and that surfaces meet operational and regulatory requirements. Notify pilots of the condition of the runway.
2. A passenger slipped and fell in the terminal: Ensure paramedics are responding and immediately begin to address airport liability issues.
3. A suspicious item was found on an airplane: Begin working with federal, state, and local agencies to mitigate risk and resulting effects on Airport Operations.
4. Construction is being conducted onsite: Ensure contractors are not driving on operational runways and taxiways without proper authorization.
5. An aircraft accident or incident has occurred: Above all, focus on saving lives, stabilizing the scene, and protecting property and the environment. Notify all relevant stakeholders, coordinate response to inquiries, manage the media, and return the airport back to routine operations as soon as possible.
6. An automobile has stalled on an entrance road within the airport's landside area: Ensure that the vehicle is attended to and is not a safety or security hazard. Rapidly develop a course of action to ensure the vehicle does not impede the flow of passengers to and from the airport.

Managing an airport safely, effectively, and efficiently requires attention to numerous functional areas. For example, when airport planners, engineers, and architects design and build new facilities or renovate existing facilities, airport Ops personnel provide extensive feedback to the design team. Ops also assists in overseeing the construction as a way to ensure safety and compliance with regulatory concerns. During construction, operational personnel also handle rerouting of aircraft for airfield projects, passenger movement for terminal projects, or vehicle movement for landside projects. Airport Operations may also enforce leases for concessions or tenants. Ops personnel routinely audit and inspect tenants to make sure they are in compliance with provisions in the lease and airport rules, regulations, and business standards.

Airport Operations helps to ensure that airline boarding and arrival gates are managed in accordance with FAA and **Transportation Security Administration (TSA)** policies and regulations. This duty also includes monitoring use agreements established between the airport authority and the airline. At various airports, Ops personnel may also conduct ramp control of aircraft movements and related revenue collection functions, such as the logging of aircraft registration ("N-number" or "tail numbers") so that landing fees can be tracked and assessed.

OPERATIONS THROUGHOUT THE AIRPORT LAYOUT

Even though there are some differences between commercial service and GA airports, all airports have three major areas requiring operations management: (a) landside, (b) terminal, and (c) airside (Figure 1.1). Each area has unique characteristics in terms of operational and emergency response requirements.

Landside areas represent the initial arrival or terminus of the passenger's air travel and interaction with the airport. Landside operations include parking lots, Ground Transportation (private and commercial), and intermodal connections, such as subway, light rail, or roadways. Commercial vehicle fees from taxis, limos, and other forms of Ground Transportation generate

FIGURE 1.1

Operations, safety, and emergency management are core functions of aviation management within the airport or aerotropolis environment.

significant revenue for the airport. Safe, effective, and efficient landside services can increase the benefits to travelers of the airport as a desired node for travel. Therefore, providing operational support to landside infrastructure and entities operating in those areas is vital.

The **terminal** area is where passenger check-in and security screening take place. Even at small airports, the terminal area can generate significant revenue to the airport through the leasing of space and commissions on concession sales. Therefore, terminal operations management is concerned with handling resources and personnel such that passengers receive at least satisfactory customer service within a healthy, safe, and secure facility. Upon arriving from landside, passengers check-in with their airlines, process through the Security Screening Checkpoint, and proceed to the boarding gates. When they land at the airport, they return through the terminal, including the concourses, to be reunited with their luggage, and then proceed back out to landside and on to other destinations.

Airside is a heavily regulated portion of the airport where aircraft takeoff, land, receive service, and conduct other forms of flight-related operations. Airside operations address: (a) the airfield environment, (b) core elements of Airport Operations, including weather, communications, security systems, and personnel, and (c) integration and management of air carriers, vendors, tenants, contractors, and other affiliates.

REGULATORY REQUIREMENTS AND AIRPORT OPERATIONS

The FAA has statutory authority under Title 49, U.S. Code (U.S.C.) § 44706 to issue **Airport Operating Certificates (AOCs)**[8] to airports serving passenger-carrying operations of certain air

---

[8]Airport Operating Certificates, 49 U.S.C. § 44706 (2010).

carriers and to establish minimum safety standards for the operation of those airports. The FAA uses this authority to issue requirements for the certification and operation of certain land airports through Part 139 of Title 14, Code of Federal Regulations.[9] These regulations call for the development of safety program emergency plans, snow removal and wildlife hazard plans, and airfield driver training programs, as well as that certain maintenance and safety standards are maintained.

GA airports that do not serve scheduled and nonscheduled air carriers exceeding various seat capacities[10] are generally exempt from the Part 139 requirement for an FAA operational authorization. However, all GA airports that receive federal grant monies are still bound (as are commercial service airports) by the FAA's **Grant Assurances (Obligations)** programs. When airport operators accept funds from the FAA-administered **Airport Improvement Program (AIP)**,[11] the airport sponsor or operating agency must agree to certain grant assurances (or obligations). These obligations require the recipients to maintain and operate their facilities safely and efficiently and according to specified conditions. Even though the GA community does not have to adhere to the same standards as a commercial service airport, Grant Assurance #19 requires airports to be operated in a safe and serviceable condition.[12] Therefore, GA operators often attempt to maintain the "139 standard" as a matter of best practice and to fulfill the requirements of the grant assurances. Regardless of Part 139 in relation to various airport categories, all civilian airports are subject to local legislative laws, policies, or other requirements for operation as stipulated by local government agencies.

A common misconception is that the FAA operates U.S. airports. Instead, civilian airports are operated by a city, county, or **airport authority** (or operator[13]), or, in some cases, a state or port authority. An airport authority is usually established as an independent entity by local legislative process and serves under the authority of a government or legislative board. At most airports, FAA air traffic control (ATC) controls the movement of aircraft and vehicles in the **Airport Movement Area (AMA)**. The AMA, usually referred to as the "movement area," includes runways, taxiways, and other areas mutually agreed on by the airport operator and the FAA. Also, the airport authority, rather than the FAA, must open or close an airport, as warranted by varying operational circumstances or conditions.[14]

Airport Ops personnel must work closely and synergistically with ATC to move aircraft into and out of the airport's airspace. Ops personnel must also work with TSA security screening personnel to ensure the efficient flow of arriving and departing passengers. Operations personnel are expected to respond to many other matters concerning safety, security, or efficiency, such as a tenant driving

---

[9]Certification of Airports, 14 CFR Part 139 (2004).

[10]Air carrier aircraft with more than 30 seats and scheduled operations of air carrier aircraft with 10 to 30 seats.

[11]When a public-use airport accepts money from the U.S. federal government through the Airport Improvement Program (AIP), it must adhere to grant or sponsor assurances. These assurances allow the federal government to enforce certain requirements, such as (a) the airport being operated in a safe and serviceable condition, (b) the airport operator being responsible for hazards to airspace on and around the airport, and (c) the airport operator not unjustly discriminating against an airport user (along with other assurances).

[12]Federal Aviation Administration. (2014). *Grant assurances (obligations).* Retrieved from: http://www.faa.gov/airports/aip/grant_assurances/

[13]U.S. civil airports are managed by entities that are commonly and interchangeably referred to as "operators," "authority," or "provider." Sometimes these terms are combined, e.g., "operating authority."

[14]During an airfield emergency, the FAA commonly closes the active runway or denies other flights permission to land while personnel are addressing the emergency, but unless articulated in an agreement, airport management has the authority to open or close the airport. The TSA's Federal Security Director also has this authority, but not the FAA.

recklessly on the airfield, an aviation employee[15] not wearing a security identification display badge, or a maintenance issue, such as a broken escalator.

A primary long-term goal for Airport Operations is to sustain and facilitate the effective and efficient deployment of emergency response services at an airport. For example, the crash of Asiana Flight 214 at the San Francisco International Airport in 2013 demonstrated various aspects of the industry's focus on operational safety and airport emergency response (Figure 1.2). In the

FIGURE 1.2

Top, Crash of Asiana Flight 214 at San Francisco International Airport. *Bottom*, Congresswomen N. Pelosi and J. Speier, Mayor E. Lee, Fire Chief J. Hayes-White, and San Francisco International Airport (SFO) Police Chief D. Schmidt touring crash site led by the National Transportation Safety Board (NTSB) Chairman D. Hersman and SFO Director J. Martin.

Courtesy of Morrow, J. (2013) Crashed Asiana Flight 214 [digital image]. Retrieved from: https://www.flickr.com/photos/donotlick/ 9490536515/. Courtesy of Nancy Pelosi. (2013). Congresswoman Pelosi tours the crash site of Asiana 214 [digital image]. Retrieved from: https://flic.kr/p/g9fF4j.

---

[15]Airports are usually comprised of employees from a variety of companies. The reference "airport employee" means an employee of the airport operator. Airline employees work for a commercial air carrier. Tenant employees work for a company that leases property at the airport. Contractors and vendors are service providers to the airport and its tenants. Government employees that work at an airport can include TSA personnel, Border Protection, Immigration and Customs Enforcement personnel, state and local law enforcement, FAA personnel, and others. Collectively, these groups are typically referred to in the industry as "aviation employees."

case of Flight 214, Airport Operations personnel, police, fire, and emergency medical service (EMS) responded immediately. Fatalities and injuries resulting from the crash included a passenger death caused by the operation of a responding fire truck subsequent to the accident. Despite the horrific conditions of the crash, only three people lost their lives. Had it not been for U.S. safety standards and regulatory requirements supported and implemented by Airport Operations and emergency response services at San Francisco International Airport, the Asiana Flight 214 accident could have been much worse.

AIRPORT MANAGEMENT AND AIRPORT OPERATIONS

Airport Operations is comprised of regulations, policies, procedures, resources, and personnel that provide the infrastructure and organization integrated within and across four primary concerns of airport management: (a) airport safety, (b) Airport Operations, (c) airport emergency management and response, and (d) airport planning. These areas are explored in-depth within this textbook, and are introduced below (Figure 1.3).

Part 1: Airport Operations and the Airport Environment

Essentially all entities within the airport environment rely on a well-functioning Airport Operations department. This section of the textbook addresses the overall organization and assignment of duties and the role Ops plays in each of those factors within the airport environment. Airport Operations is commonly subdivided into structures focused on landside, terminal, and airside functions.

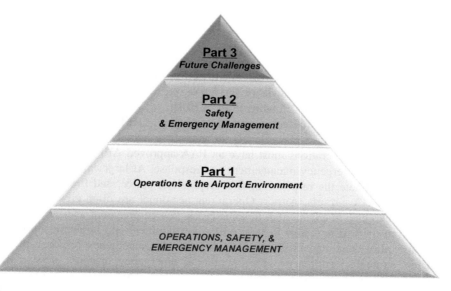

FIGURE 1.3

Primary topics addressed in this textbook as related to Airport Operations, safety, and emergency management.

Regardless of the size or level of service, all public airports have operational functions or requirements. For many small GA airports this may require that operations be conducted by one or two individuals. As airports grow, they typically first add maintenance and other administrative personnel to their operational staff. Maintenance personnel are usually cross-trained in operational duties and perform such until the airport sponsor can justify the creation of an independent Ops department. Part 1 addresses the "how-to" of planning and organizing an Airport Operations department.

Part 2: Airport Operations and Safety and Emergency Management

This section of the textbook addresses overall Airport Operations with an emphasis on safety and emergency management processes. Special topics such as Safety Management Systems (SMS) and Title 14 CFR Part 139 are featured. SMS is the formal, top-down business approach to managing safety risk, which includes a systemic approach such as necessary organizational structures, accountabilities, policies, and procedures. The four elements of SMS described in this section of the textbook are: (a) safety policy, (b) safety risk management, (c) safety assurance, and (d) safety promotion.

Title 14 Aeronautics and Space, Chapter I—Federal Aviation Administration, Department of Transportation Subchapter G—Air Carriers and Operators for Compensation or Hire: Certification and Operations, Part 139—Certification of Airports (typically referred to as "Part 139"), addresses the safety and certain operational requirements of commercial service airports. Part 139 focuses on three areas: (a) safety self-inspection, (b) safety programs, and (c) maintenance programs. The safety self-inspection requires that Airport Operations personnel ensure that FAA standards are maintained on a daily basis. Federal regulators certify the airport for operation and make periodic inspections; however, it is the duty of Airport Operations to inspect areas where aircraft operate and to ensure that elements such as pavement, navigational aids, signs, markings, and lighting systems are in proper working order. Examples of routine Airport Operations maintenance include ensuring fencing and jet blast deflectors are in place, pavement repair, navigational aid care, and airport snow and ice control.

Other safety programs supported by Airport Operations include, (a) the **Airport Emergency Plan (AEP)**, (b) the **Wildlife Hazard Management Plan (WHMP)** program, (c) the **Notices to Airmen (NOTAM)** program (pilot advisory service of, e.g., hazardous or nonstandard conditions), (d) the **Construction Safety and Phasing Plan (CSPP)**, (e) various **ground vehicle operations and regulations**, and (f) **Aircraft Rescue and Firefighting (ARFF)** requirements.

Many Aircraft Accidents take place during the takeoff or landing phase, often on or adjacent to airport property. Airport Operations must have an FAA-approved AEP that follows federal regulations and guidance for emergency management and response. At larger airports, Airport Operations personnel often coordinate the response of first responders, police, and fire assets. At small, commercial service and GA airports, Airport Operations personnel are often cross-trained in the areas of firefighting, emergency medical, and, in some cases, law enforcement and security.

This section of the textbook also focuses on the development and implementation of the **emergency response plan** contained in the AEP. Included in the emergency response plan are regulations, policies, strategies, and tactics for operational emergency response personnel to address related core functions, such as: (a) command-and-control, (b) communications, (c) alert and warning, (d) emergency public notification, (e) Protective Actions, (f) law enforcement and security, (g) firefighting rescue, (h) health and medical, (i) overall resource management, and (j) Airport Operations and maintenance. Specific hazards are also addressed, including Aircraft Accidents, natural disasters, security incidents, and hazardous material incidents. This section also describes airport requirements to utilize and integrate with the **National Incident Management System (NIMS)** and related Incident Command System.

Part 3: Future Airport Operational Challenges

Airport operators are now embracing new challenges as research and development into the civilian and commercial use of UAVs and **spaceport operations** brings these concepts to reality. Integration of the **Next Generation Air Transportation System (NextGen)** ATC system will also bring new challenges to the industry.

The development and integration of UAVs for personal use by citizens and commercial industries is now a global demand. UAVs have a wide range of civilian applications, including agriculture, Search and Rescue, law enforcement, surveillance, power line patrol, and wildfire spotting, among many other applications. Regulations are currently being proposed and evaluated by the FAA for the operation of UAVs in the civilian and commercial sectors. Civilian UAVs currently require line-of-sight operations by the pilot of the vehicle, but are nonetheless flown from a remote location. This aspect alone will require new ways of managing operations at airports that may eventually integrate UAV activity within their airspace or ground movement areas. Launch and recovery operations will have to be integrated into the airside environment of the airport. UAV operations will also require special runway use considerations, pavement maintenance standards, and other issues, such as emergency recovery operations.

The advent of the horizontal takeoff to **low Earth orbit (LEO)** space vehicle operations has created a viable commercial spaceflight industry. Several U.S. airports have already submitted applications to be certificated as commercial **spaceports** (or commercial space facilities) by the FAA under 14 CFR Part 413.5.[16] The licensing an FAA 14 CFR Part 139 airport uses for space operations must be coordinated with the FAA's **Office of Commercial Space Transportation (AST)**. Spaceport designation results in new security and safety issues for airport operators. There will be new aircraft rescue and firefighting equipment and new maintenance and personnel training requirements for handling a craft that has departed to, or arrived from, LEO. Other operational concerns being developed and evaluated include medical facilities onsite to handle new types of physiological problems that may develop in passengers visiting the space environment, airside transportation to areas where commercial space operations are conducted, and overall emergency response requirements unique to space vehicles and travel.

Another future challenge to Airport Operations is the extensive FAA transition of the ATC system from a land-based to a satellite-based system. This effort is referred to as the FAA's **NextGen**[17] program, and it significantly enhances the flow of aircraft into the traffic area of an airport and throughout the NAS. NextGen also uses onboard weather and traffic avoidance technologies, further enhancing the ability of aircraft to fly more efficiently in the NAS. With increased effectiveness and efficiencies in ATC resulting from NextGen, airports will likely have to increase

---

[16]License Application Procedures, 14 CFR Part 413 (2001).

[17]For more information on NextGen (signifying the FAA's next generation of ATC technology), see https://www.faa .gov/nextgen/programs/

their ground operations services and incorporate many new and related procedures and technologies to safely, effectively, and efficiently deal with an increase in arrivals, departures, and passenger flow.

Airport Manager Wanted
Reflections on the Responsibilities of Airport Management and Operations

by Robert P. Olislagers
Executive Director, Centennial Airport (APA), Englewood, CO

(Adapted from a Speech by Foster Smith[18])

Airport Manager Wanted: Must have extensive experience and background in aviation—must not be too old or too young—and, as someone else once added, *old enough to know better and young enough to enjoy it!*

The successful candidate must have experience managing municipal or county-owned airports, airport districts, airport authorities, joint-use airports or privately owned airports. Must be proficient in all Airport Operations functions, including, but not limited to, Parts 139 and 1542 compliance; be certificated, accredited, licensed, and vetted; be familiar with National Incident Management System (NIMS), emergency management; have first-hand knowledge and be familiar with first-responder equipment and how they are deployed during incidents and accidents on and off the airport. The candidate must be able to predict snow and ice storms, and know at all times when to plow, when to broom, and when to deice while simultaneously giving braking action reports comprehensible to Alaska bush pilots and sun-belt pilots alike!

Must have engineering experience and practical know-how in all phases of constructing runways, taxiways, roads, hangars, fuel farms, terminals, baggage systems, sewer systems, IT systems, utility systems, security systems, storm drainage systems, deicing systems, LEED [Leadership in Energy and Environmental Design] and HVAC [heating, ventilating, and air conditioning]; be able to read and understand blueprints, legal descriptions, GIS [geographic information system] maps, rights-of-way, longitude/latitude coordinates, GPS [Global Positioning System] coordinates, Airport Layout Plans (ALPs), and Part 77 imaginary surfaces.

Must be familiar with all laws, including, but not limited to, local land use and zoning laws; state, territorial, tribal, and federal laws; grant assurances, especially those pertaining to revenue diversion; fire codes, electrical codes, water, plumbing, and gas codes; property leases; easements including navigation easements; civil rights and civil service rules; Disadvantaged Business Enterprise (DBE) and Women Owned Businesses Certification (WBE) participation; Airport Improvement Program (AIP) grants, budgets, accounting, and finance, including cash management, Generally Accepted Accounting Principles (GAAP),

(Continued)

---

[18]"Airport Manager Wanted" was originally presented in a speech by Foster Smith, Chairman of the Rockford Airport Authority at the AAAE (American Association of Airport Executives) Annual Conference in Fort Worth, Texas, April 27, 1965. Adapted by Robert P. Olislagers, Chief Executive Officer of Centennial Airport.

(Continued)

Governmental Accounting Standards Board (GASB), and the rules within the Sarbanes-Oxley Act (SOX), leveraged financing, Passenger Facility Charge Program (PFC), investments, single and annual audits, and be able to explain the same in layman's terms so everyone can understand them.

Must be proficient in psychology and sociology; must understand the intricacies of local, state, national and world geo-politics, as well as matters of national security; must have extensive experience in air service development (ASD), labor relations, public speaking, public relations, marketing, aeronautical and nonaeronautical development, farming, mineral exploration, pest eradication, and wildlife management (without offending anyone).

Must be able to work closely with elected officials, including county supervisors and commissioners, mayors, city council members, sheriffs, and assessors, as well as city managers, chief county administrators, chiefs of staff, chiefs of police, state police, public works directors, building inspectors, health inspectors, Fire Chiefs, fire marshals, zoning officers, and planners; and must also have an excellent working relationship with the FAA Flight Standards District Office (FSDO), FAA Airport District Office (ADO) managers and engineers, FAA regional administrators, Terminal Radar Approach Control Facilities (TRACON) staff, FAA Washington, DC, staff, including the heads of all the FAA divisions, as well as state aviation officials and aeronautics boards and staff. The ideal candidate is not required to like these people, just be able to get along and work with them.

The candidate should be well-connected and favorably known to the governor, members of congress (on both sides of the aisle), including having access to email addresses of their respective staffers, state senators and representatives, and all local newspaper editors and TV Station Managers; be able to contribute to political action committees (PACs) of key elected officials that are not bosses (or could become bosses); be proficient with social media and manage at least two smartphones 24/7 to answer any questions that may and will arise at any time of the day or night. Must be on a first-name basis with at least one well-connected and informed state and/or federal lobbyist, preferably Todd Hauptli.[19]

Must be willing to work under challenging budget conditions with little or no job security, be available 24 hours a day, seven days a week—and, be able to go without sleep for several days at a time during snow storms, hurricanes, VIP [very important person] visits, Super Bowls, airshows, and national security events. Being tactful while sitting through aeronautical proposals requiring free rent, tax incentives, and economic development capital is highly desirable.

Must have the requisite security clearances and possess visionary and prophetic powers concerning the future of Next Generation Air Transportation System (NextGen), Area Navigation (RNAV), Metroplex, unmanned aeronautical vehicles and systems (UAV/UAS), spaceports, airline expansion/contraction and consolidation plans, TSA playbook scenarios, and Temporary Flight Restrictions (TFRs); as well as being able to anticipate FAA and TSA policy decisions and directives next week and next month regarding land uses, general aviation issues, tall structures, airport closures, access lanes, Airport Security responsibilities, TSA

(Continued)

---

[19]At the time of this writing (2015), Todd Hauptli was the current president and CEO of the AAAE.

(Continued)

Screening Partnership Programs (SPPs), TSA Airport Security Program (ASP) and TSA staffing; and be able to keep up with TSA staff changes that happen faster than a rollout of the next smartphone!

The ideal candidate should be able to envision the airport from the point-of-view of the community including noise complainants, tenants, tax payers, AOPA [Aircraft Owners and Pilots Association], passengers, policy makers, FAA, state DOT [Department of Transportation] and aeronautics divisions, city councils and county boards, as well as airport commissions and advisory boards.

Must be able to get along with and motivate the Greatest Generation, Baby Boomer, Millennial, and GenX employees all working in the same space and time toward the same goals as outlined above and below. The ideal candidate must also have a good understanding of and be able to operate with police and fire departments; know about prevailing and living wages, affordable housing, salaries, overtime rules, collective bargaining agreements, right to work regulations, benefits, 401(k), 457(f), and other retirement and pension programs, vacation time accrual cost, healthcare and benefits programs and associated costs, insurance premiums, directors and officers liability insurance, risk management and safety management systems.

The ideal candidate should be very familiar with cost recovery, prevailing contract and lease terms and prices for landing fees, floor and office space, gates, parking space, fuel flowage, car rentals, concessions, liquor licenses, and in-house and outsourced labor costs for custodial and other services, while complying with nondiscriminatory provisions required in all FAA-regulated contracts—except transactions involving the mayor's cousin.

The successful candidate will also be skilled in obtaining surplus equipment "for nothing," and be able to rebuild and rehabilitate such equipment, including manufacturing parts no longer available, without cost to the airport. Furthermore, the candidate will be able to educate the public and elected officials of the value of the airport through economic impact studies, direct, indirect, and induced multipliers and explain to every man, woman, child, and business within the airport's taxing district why every dollar spent is actually worth more than a dollar.

He or she should be especially skilled at diplomacy in dealing with all local organizations requesting the use of airport property, runways and taxiways as drag strips, temporary car parking lots, 5K and 10K runs, exotic and hotrod car events, picnics, free gravel and the occasional flight instructor's wedding. Likewise, the ideal candidate must display empathy with representatives of charities seeking donations for the policeman's benevolent association, sheriff's cookout, firemen's ball, Boy Scouts, Girl Scouts (love those cookies), and other not-for-profit charitable organizations and foundations for cancer, MS [multiple sclerosis], wayward boys and girls, the homeless, and churches looking for a Sunday home.

Above all, he or she must have a thick skin and a sense of humor. A recommendation from AAAE or ACI-NA [Airports Council International—North America], but preferably both, is helpful but offers no guarantee.

Please send your cover letter, application, and resume to P.O. Box 13 and do not contact the current manager—he doesn't know he's leaving.

Vignette
Airport Operations—A Day in the Life

Denver International Airport (DEN) is the fifth busiest airport in the United States and the thirteenth busiest in the world. It sits on 53 square miles of land in eastern Colorado. More than 53 million passengers pass through its doors every year, along with robust cargo operations and 16 commercial airlines.

The operations department includes operations support (emergency management and related functions), airside Ops, security, police, fire, emergency medical services (EMS), and terminal and customer services. Ops personnel are divided between working terminal, airside, or in the B-Tower, which provides ramp control for aircraft as they transition to and from FAA control to their ramp gates.

The Airport Operations Manager (AOM) would typically start a morning with a briefing by the off-going AOM to exchange any relevant information about the airfield, upcoming activities, such as construction, and any relevant maintenance or security issues.

DEN is too large to have one individual conduct airfield inspections, so several assistant operations managers assist the AOM with this function. In addition to inspecting the airfield to ensure it is safe for operation and in compliance with the Part 139 standard, the AOM will check-in with the firefighting personnel, the airport police commander, and personnel in the communications and maintenance centers.

The AOM will also check the weather and any NOTAMs, which reference areas of the airfield that may be out of compliance with Part 139 or any hazardous conditions, such as the appearance of construction cranes or airfield signs or lighting outages.

Once the morning checklists are complete, much of the AOM's job is similar to that of a police officer. The AOM patrols the airfield and terminal building looking for problems or issues and responding to calls for assistance. Throughout the day the AOM may respond to situations similar to the following examples:

- An issue at the screening checkpoint causing the lines to back up.
- A traffic altercation at the passenger pickup and dropoff areas.
- An aircraft incident, such as a faulty landing gear indication.
- A maintenance issue, such as a problem with the underground automated guideway transit system.
- A security issue, such as an individual failing to display their identification badge.
- A call from a regulatory agency, such as the FAA or TSA, to discuss or resolve an operational discrepancy.

By the end of the day, the AOM is wrapping up their logbook entries and getting ready to brief the incoming AOM for the next shift. The AOM will turn over their vehicle, radio, and cell phone and conclude their shift.

REFERENCES

Kasarda, J. (2015). *About the aerotropolis*. Retrieved from: http://www.aerotropolis.com/airportCities/about-the-aerotropolis.

Price, J. C., & Forrest, J. S. (2014). Securing the aerotropolis: city-centric airport security. *Aviation Security International, 20*(5), 28–31.

Sharghi, K. (2012). *Congested airspace*. Retrieved January 21, 2015, from: http://svs.gsfc.nasa.gov/cgi-bin/details.cgi?aid = 11147.

OPERATING AIRPORTS AS COMPLEX AND REGULATED GLOBAL RESOURCES

2

General Aviation (GA) and corporate aircraft operations at Centennial Airport, Denver, CO. View from the APA Air Traffic Control Tower (ATCT). Centennial Airport routinely hosts GA and corporate flight operations from around the world on a daily basis.

Image by Shahn Sederberg, courtesy Colorado Division of Aeronautics, 2007.

Passenger terminal-to-terminal crossover bridge at Denver International Airport, CO, between Main Terminal and Terminal A.

Image by Shahn Sederberg, courtesy Colorado Division of Aeronautics, 2013.

Baggage handler off-loading an Allegiant Airlines MD-80 at Fort Collins-Loveland Airport, CO.

Image by Shahn Sederberg, courtesy Colorado Division of Aeronautics, 2010.

"When you've seen one airport, you've seen one airport."
Industry adage

THE ADVENT OF AIRPORT OPERATIONS

For some years, I have been afflicted with the belief that flight is possible to man. My disease has increased in severity and I feel that it will soon cost me an increased amount of money, if not my life....

Wilbur Wright, personal correspondence to Octave Chanute, May 13, 1900

Orville and Wilbur Wright are credited with the first powered, controlled, and sustained piloted flight. Some argue that the Wright brothers created the world's first airport at Ohio's Huffman Prairie Flying Field. Their efforts in using this field to develop, build, takeoff, and land aircraft set the earliest foundation for modern Airport Operations. At the Huffman Prairie Flying Field, the Wright brothers pioneered issues similar to modern Airport Operations, for example, animal and wildlife control, snow on the field, and control of visitors and, eventually, passengers. Wilbur Wright's prophecy that his passion to seek human flight "will soon cost me an increased amount of money, if not my life" was a salient foreshadowing of the future of global aviation, especially as related to the complexity of Airport Operations.

In the early stages of controlled flight, pilots learned that they could land in varying conditions, irrespective of property usage. With time, pilots, landowners, and government officials recognized that a designated and prepared landing surface increased flight safety while reducing operational costs. Established and maintained areas for flight operations also quickly became locations for pilots to secure and service their aircraft. In these early settings, barns and other farming structures were commonly used as makeshift terminals and aircraft repair centers. Runways were roughed circular or rectangular areas, usually clear-cut and somewhat graded. Tanks or fuel trucks for fuel storage and dispensing were usually placed in a convenient location for servicing aircraft. Thus, a patch of cleared land used as a runway, a nearby barn used for service and storage, and tanks for fueling became the iconic infrastructure for the emergence of the airport (or aerodrome[1]) and associated Airport Operations (Figures 2.1 and 2.2). In modern times, a **landing surface**, **terminal facility**, and **fuel storage/dispensing** areas still remain as core operational elements of most commercial and general aviation (GA) airports.[2]

As commercial aviation advanced, and paying passengers and freight such as mail and cargo started arriving, larger buildings were needed to keep passengers out of the weather while they waited for their flight, and to sort incoming and outgoing cargo and bags. Soon, the symbolic barn

---

[1]Airports are also commonly referred to as "aerodromes" in various parts of the world.

[2]Even in modern times, not all airports have operational infrastructure as described. For example, established airports that are remotely located may consist of little more than a cleared area of land serving as a runway—with no infrastructure, fuel, or personnel. In these cases, it is especially burdensome on the pilot to determine the operational viability of the airport for the purpose of flight.

FIGURE 2.1 Pre-World War I (1908) military operations of a Wright flyer.

Note the "barn-styled" hanger and cleared runway area in background. Visitors are standing close to operational areas, which was a common practice at airports during this era.

Source: http://history.nasa.gov/SP-4406/chap1.html (in public domain).

FIGURE 2.2 Two U.S. Army Jennys, undergoing fueling operations.

Note the open operational field and individuals sitting in grass area (background). Although difficult to discern in the image, along the top edge of both aircraft upper wings is a ridge dotted with observing visitors along with their parked cars.

Source: http://vintageairphotos.blogspot.com/search/label/Jenny (in public domain).

evolved to become a terminal building, and the cleared landing surfaces became defined runways, often paved and maintained by the operator or landowner of the facility.

Early passenger airports flourished in geographies juxtaposed to areas containing wildlife or roaming farm stock. Additionally, early visitors to airports would often arrive by horse or car and usually park, sit, or traverse in areas close to the runway for better observation of aircraft arrivals and departures. Airport overseers or landowners soon recognized the increased risk to safety posed by humans and animals near runways or other airport operational areas. As a result, fencing was erected to prevent individuals and most wildlife from inadvertently breaching operational areas.

As passenger traffic grew, so did the need to provide passengers and the "meeters and greeters,"[3] with food service, restrooms, and parking, among many other common needs. Infrastructure that could support the effective and efficient flow of passenger pickup and departure became essential to meeting higher frequencies of aircraft arrivals and departures.

With the advent of larger and more complex passenger aircraft, pilots demanded improved and safer operating environments. Emergencies, accidents, and incidents began to increase at airports, requiring the presence of individuals and equipment that could more rapidly respond to related safety issues.

The aforementioned concerns were indicative of the need to organize and staff airports with individuals who could manage the flow of visitors, passengers, cargo, and aircraft while ensuring the support for and implementation of operational safety measures. From these demands grew the need for formalized *airport management focused on operational control, safety assurance, and emergency response*.

OPERATING AIRPORTS AS SOCIETAL ICONS

Airports serve as gateways to communities throughout the nation and the world. Airports often typify the initial images or impressions a traveler makes when visiting a new destination. Consequently, airports have evolved to become societal icons, representing intrinsic and extrinsic statements of value to surrounding communities, as well as to the travelers using the airport. In this regard, many cities and counties place artwork, unique architectural features, or informative exhibits in their airport passenger areas as strategies for establishing or branding social and community values. Therefore, *an additional mission of Airport Operations is to establish strategies and tactics to ensure the viability of the airport's image to the public*. Paramount to these efforts is ensuring the public safety of all stakeholders interacting with the airport's operating environment.

DEVELOPMENT OF AIRPORT OPERATIONS

The early days of aviation were virtually unregulated and comprised of mostly transient pilots flying from city to city and landing in farms or any other area that would enable takeoff and landing operations. These pilots frequently set up temporary camps to offer airplane rides and flight lessons

---

[3]A term often ascribed to those bringing people to the airport for departure or greeting them on arrival.

that were unregulated by local or national government agencies. By the late 1920s, aviation evolved from a novelty to a national form of commercial activity. The passing of the **Airmail Act of 1925 (Kelly Act)** allowed the U.S. Postmaster to contract for private air service, and the **Air Commerce Act of 1926** required pilot, mechanic, and aircraft licensing. These Acts subsequently created a need for air service providers at fixed locations throughout the country. These locations would eventually become known as **Fixed Base Operators (FBOs).**[4] FBOs became ingrained in the earliest forms of airport terminal buildings. FBOs are now prolific and are essential to sustaining the demand for airports around the world. FBOs are discrete forms of operations that collaborate extensively with overall Airport Operations and a multitude of regulatory and safety agencies on a daily basis.

The Airmail Act of 1925, which authorized the Postmaster General to transfer the delivery of airmail from government air service to commercial entities, initiated the need for more encompassing and structured air transportation regulation. Correspondingly, three U.S. federal agencies held power over air transportation and the delivery of airmail: the (a) U.S. Post Office Department, (b) U.S. Commerce Department, and (c) U.S. Interstate Commerce Commission.[5] This disjointed organizational structure for regulatory control over air travel and airmail delivery led to the need for oversight by a central agency. In response, the **Civil Aeronautics Act of 1938** established the **Civil Aeronautics Authority (CAA)**, the precursor to the **Federal Aviation Administration (FAA)**.

By 1928, the first airport management trade organization was also established. The first meeting of the **American Association of Airport Executives (AAAE)** consisted of 10 Airport Directors attending the National Air Races at Mines Field (now Los Angeles International Airport).[6] By 1954, AAAE adopted the first professional accreditation standards for their **Accredited Airport Executives (AAE)** program. AAAE currently offers training for airport employees through its **Certified Member (CM)** program. The CM program offers training and knowledge manuals essential to airport management and Airport Operations personnel and is a precursor to Accredited Airport Executive status.[7]

World War I and World War II significantly advanced technologies and capabilities of aircraft, moving the world from small, propeller-driven airplanes to the advent of the "Jet Age"[8] and high-capacity passenger flights.

Faster aircraft and global increases in commercial air travel required states and nations to build new airports with longer runways and larger terminal facilities. Along with these developments

---

[4]Desert Jet-Aircraft Charter. (2012, July 5). "What is a fixed base operator?" Retrieved February 2, 2015, from http://www.desertjet.com/what-is-a-fixed-base-operator/

[5]Wensveen, J., & Wells, A. (2011). *Air transportation a management perspective* (7th ed., p. 39). Farnham, England: Ashgate.

[6]American Association of Airport Executives. (n.d.). Retrieved February 4, 2015, from http://www.aaae.org/about_aaae/history/

[7]See Price, J. C., & Forrest, J. S. (2013). *Body of knowledge: Mod. 3. Airport Operations, security & maintenance* (New rev. ed.). Alexandria, VA: American Association of Airport Executives. For additional AAAE training information, see http://www.aaae.org/training_professional_development/professional_development/accredited_airport_executive_program/program_study_materials/bodyofknow.cfm

[8]The Jet Age is commonly referenced as beginning in 1958 and extending to modern times. It is marked by the development of turbine jet engines employed for commercial air service (e.g., the Pan American Boeing 707 in 1958).

came the need for greater operational abilities to store in hangers or park,[9] service, fuel, and maintain aircraft. Most importantly, the public and air service passengers developed a high expectation that commercial air service would be continuously safe, that the government would issue policies and regulations to ensure safety, and that other entities and agencies—especially airports—would also respond to emergencies, accidents, or incidents.

AIRPORT OPERATIONS AND FEDERAL SUBSIDIES

After World War II, the United States was left with a surplus of airports that had been constructed for the war effort but were no longer needed by the military. In a model that would be repeated throughout U.S. history, whenever a large-scale military conflict ended, a military drawdown of personnel, equipment, and resources followed, and World War II was no different. In 1946, the federal government transferred the ownership of these surplus airports to local cities and counties. However, along with the transfer came certain requirements, such as (a) the airport would remain open and available for public use, (b) aeronautical users would not be unjustly discriminated against, and (c) the airport operator would maintain a safe and serviceable airport and runway environment. Eventually, these "promises" became known as **grant assurances** or sponsor assurances.[10] Airport operators are required to follow Grant Assurances when accepting federal grant monies, originally allocated for airport development and operations through the Federal Airport Act of 1946.

Since 1946, government legislation has greatly enhanced the operational viability of airports across the United States. In 1982, the **Airport and Airway Improvement Act** was established to further improve airport infrastructures, operating environment, and safety. This Act led to what is now known as the **Airport Improvement Program** (AIP). Regardless of whether an airport operator is required to adhere to Title 14 CFR Part 139 (see Chapter 1), any airport accepting AIP funds must adhere to grant assurances.[11] Grant assurances fundamentally explain how a federally subsidized airport must be operated in order to continue to receive federal subsidies. Although there are 39 grant assurances, the ones that most closely relate to the function of Airport Operations are:

#11 Pavement Preventative Maintenance
#17 Construction Inspection and Approval
#19 Operation and Maintenance
#20 Hazard Removal and Mitigation

---

[9]Parking an aircraft is commonly referred to as "chalking" (i.e., wheel stops) or "tie-down" (i.e., lashing tie points of aircraft to the ground with rope).
[10]FAA Airport Compliance Manual Order 5190.6b, which is discussed in greater detail throughout subsequent sections of the text.
[11]Grant assurance requirements last for 20 years from the date of acceptance of the AIP monies, unless the money was used to acquire property, in which case the requirements are indefinite, or until the property is purchased back from the FAA. Although the FAA doesn't own the land per se, it does represent an ownership interest in the land because federal dollars were used to purchase it.

AIRPORT OPERATIONS, SAFETY, AND SECURITY

Other airport departments are also responsible for elements of AIP grant assurance categories. However, Airport Operations is unique in that its mission includes supporting operational viability across all functions of the airport. In this regard, operations is, by necessity, the foundation for supporting airport safety and security throughout the airport environment. Introduced in Chapter 1, but expanded upon here, the airport environment is divided into three operational categories: (a) landside, (b) terminal, and (c) airside.

1. The **landside** portion of an airport begins with the airports' intermodal connections, the private and commercial vehicles, light rail, and subway systems that connect the airport to the community-at-large. Landside also includes the parking structure and the passenger pickup and dropoff locations on the curb.
2. The **terminal** portion of an airport begins at the transition point between the curbside and the ticket counter areas. The terminal also includes the baggage claim areas and various passenger amenities such as rest rooms, information booths, and concessions. The terminal is bisected at the passenger Security Screening Checkpoint, between public areas and **Sterile Areas** (areas requiring security screening for access).[12]
3. The **airside** portion of an airport includes all runways and taxiways and other locations such as ramp[13] areas, where aircraft move, park, or are serviced. The internal boundary of the airside typically begins at the doors leading from the Sterile Area. The external boundary of airside is the airport perimeter fence. From an airport planning perspective, the "airside" is also considered to be the Sterile Area, but from a practical standpoint, when one thinks of airside, one usually relates that to outside the buildings, *that is, the places where the planes move.* The term *airside* is not an officially defined term within either the FAA regulations or the Transportation Security Administration (TSA) regulations, but is commonly used throughout the aviation industry to denote the area within the airport perimeter fence.

Several legislative actions formed the baseline for how airports today operate in regard to safety and security. The passage of the **Airport and Airway Development Act of 1970** and the creation of **Title 14 CFR Part 139—Airport Certification** together established minimum operational safety standards for airports. Additionally, **Title 14 CFR Part 107**[14]**—Airport Security** outlined the minimum security guidelines and requirements for Airport Operation.

As mentioned earlier, airports are valued and held in varying frames of reference by society. To communities, they are a source of economic stimulus but also noise and environmental pollution. To the hotel, restaurant, taxicab, and tourist industries, airports are the pathway to their revenue streams. To the government, airports are essential facilities that help ensure the viability of the **National Airspace System (NAS)**. The government also views airports as critical resources for national defense and a key element of safety management and community support during natural disasters. To airlines, airports are a necessity that must operate for them to keep making money.

---

[12]The Sterile Area is considered to be that area of the airport where screening is required to be conducted before access is allowed. Generically, it's the area beyond the Security Screening Checkpoint up to any door that accesses the airfield.
[13]The term *ramp* is used synonymously with the terms *tarmac* and *apron.*
[14]Now known as Title 49 CFR Part 1542 (Airport Security).

Regardless of how an airport is valued, the top priority of the airport operator is to run the airport in a **safe, secure, and efficient** manner. These objectives must be met while (a) maximizing revenues for the airport authority, (b) keeping costs down for the aircraft operator, (c) meeting the needs of the traveling public, and (d) facilitating the flow of air commerce (e.g., passengers, cargo, mail). Airports are expected to operate safely in a variety of weather conditions, while accommodating many different types of aircraft and aircraft traffic patterns. Airports represent a system of assets and services that must be kept safe and secure on a full-time basis.[15]

AIRPORT OPERATIONS AND COMMUNICATIONS

"Regardless the span of responsibilities, it is the job of someone in a raider jacket with 'AIRPORT OPERATIONS' emblazoned across the back, carrying a cell phone and a radio, to communicate and keep the place running."

Tim Barth, director of Cheyenne Regional Airport, WY

A cornerstone to operating a safe, secure, and efficient airport is the management and operation of effective and efficient communications and related infrastructure. Airport Operations is usually charged with implementing and managing airport communications and systems. For example, Airport Operations manages essential communication services such as the airport paging office and the operations and emergency "communications (comm) center," or "operations (Ops) center." Operations personnel typically staff these facilities 24 hours a day, 365 days a year. The Ops communications center often supports the collecting and disseminating of information from (a) police, fire, and emergency medical dispatch personnel, (b) weather monitoring and reporting services, (c) security and fire alarm systems, (d) heating, ventilation, and air conditioning/environmental control systems, and (e) train or passenger movement status reporting systems. Personnel in the Ops center also monitor the airport's overall status and dispatch Ops, security, and other personnel to solve problems as needed. The Ops and communications center is commonly located near the Emergency Operations Center. Personnel in the Ops communications center are expected to staff and support the **Emergency Operations Center (EOC)** during airport incidents.

Many functional types of communications used at large airports are also needed and conducted at smaller airports, but usually by an operations officer who is also responsible for other duties, such as airfield inspection and response.

Comm
    Airport and flight communications is commonly referred to as "comm" in the domain of aviation. In this textbook, comm is used interchangeably with communications, as is experienced in the profession.

[15]Hoerter, S. (2001). *The airport management primer* (2nd ed., p. 36). Mount Pleasant, SC: S. Hoerter.

AIRPORTS AS A SYSTEM-OF-SYSTEMS

Airports can be simple systems, with a small runway and a few hangars, often operated by a city or county official, or perhaps a locally contracted individual. In some cases the local "Airport Manager," is often also a tenant and a pilot. Airports can also be highly complex systems, with millions of passengers, millions of tons of cargo, and billions of bags pushing through the system on an annual basis (Figure 2.3).

According to the FAA's **National Plan of Integrated Airport Systems (NPIAS)**[16] there are 19,360 landing facilities in the United States (FAA, 2015). However, 14,212 of these facilities are closed to the public (private) and are not eligible for federal funding. The NPIAS identifies 5,148 total public-use airports, with 3,331 eligible for federal grant monies. As of 2015, there are 3,345

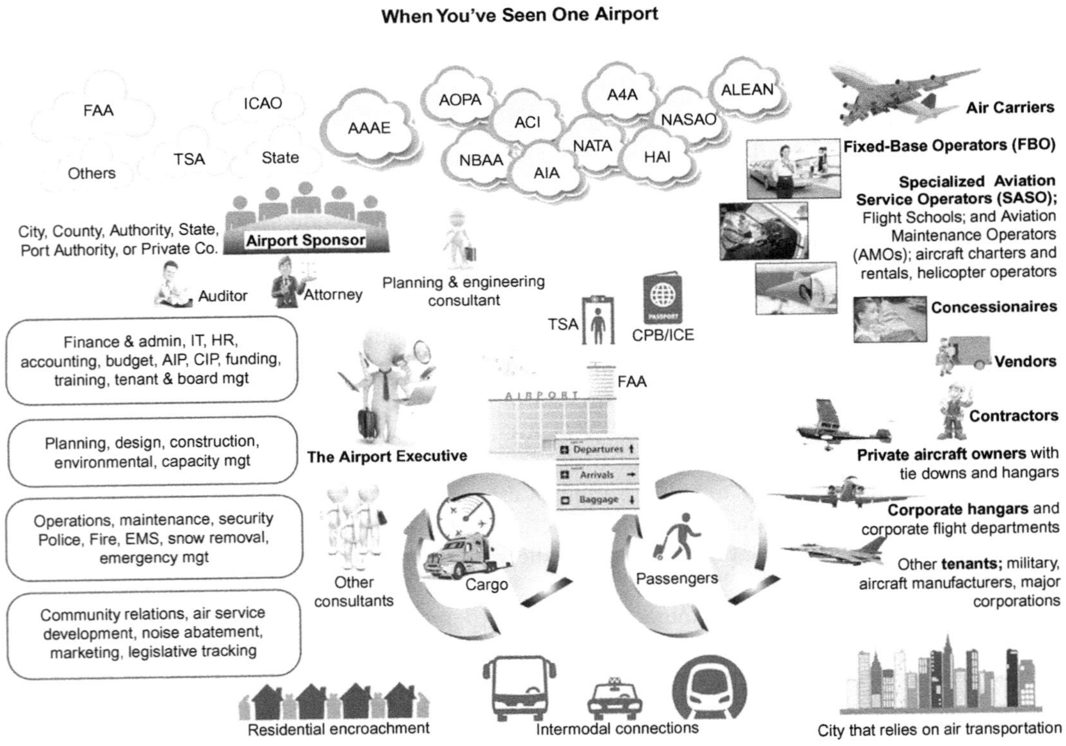

FIGURE 2.3

Complex systems-of-systems representing operational areas of airport management.

---

[16]The NPIAS identifies airports in the United States that are eligible for federal funding by the role they serve and the amounts and types of development eligible for federal funding under the AIP in 5-year increments.

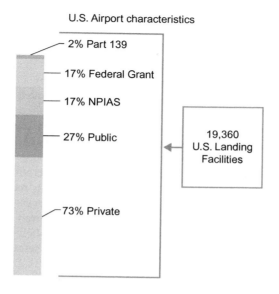

U.S. Airport characteristics

2% Part 139

17% Federal Grant

17% NPIAS

27% Public

19,360 U.S. Landing Facilities

73% Private

FIGURE 2.4

Relative percentages of U.S. airport characteristics in relation to all U.S. landing facilities.

existing or proposed airports in the NPIAS (Figure 2.4). Some airports, such as Branson, Missouri, are privately owned but publicly operated. Of the NPIAS airports, 450 are commercial service and are regulated under Title 14 CFR Part 139. The remainder are GA airports. GA airports predominantly conduct private flights such as business and corporate travel, flight training, and charter operations. GA airports might also have low levels of commercial service activity, but if that activity does not exceed 2,500 enplanements (a passenger boarding a commercial operation), then the airport remains classified as GA.

AIRPORT AUTHORITIES AND ORGANIZATIONAL MANAGEMENT

The **airport sponsor** is a common reference to the legal entity that operates an airport. The airport sponsor could be a city, county, airport authority, port authority, state, or private company. Nearly as many variations of airport sponsor structures exist as airports in the United States. The FAA does not mandate that an airport sponsor operate under any particular airport organizational structure.

The FAA regulates the operation of commercial service airports and National Airspace. For airports with a control tower, the FAA controls air and ground traffic on runways and taxiways, *but the FAA does not operate airports*. With the exception of military airports, the federal government also does not operate airports. For the most part, local governments run airports.

Municipalities (cities or counties) operate nearly all public-use airports in the United States. Some municipalities have created an **airport authority**, or governing board responsible for operating a single airport, or system of airports, within a regional area. Some airports are operated by a state, such as in Alaska, or by a port authority,[17] such as the Port Authority of New York and New Jersey (PANYNJ).

At a city-operated airport, the **Airport Director**, also known as the **airport executive** or **director of aviation**, is often appointed by the mayor, or may be hired by a division or department head, such as the city manager or public works director. At county-operated airports, the executive may be hired and report directly to the board of commissioners, or be hired by the county administrator or manager, or a department or division head. When an airport executive is a direct political appointment, they may find themselves in the position of campaigning for their bosses reelection or risk losing their job.

The support of the airport sponsor is critical to Airport Operations. The airport sponsor is key to (a) securing funding for necessary equipment and materials required to properly maintain the airport in a safe and secure condition, (b) supporting necessary rules and regulations, and (c) supporting minimum business Operating Standards (referred to as minimum standards). An airport sponsor that focuses on sustaining processes and policies that follow rules, regulations, and at least minimum standards contributes greatly to safety and security throughout the airport.

In some cases, the city or county (collectively referred to as a municipality) will create an airport authority. An authority may be created to run one airport, or a system of airports, such as the Los Angeles World Airports, which operates Los Angeles International Airport, Palmdale, and Van Nuys airports. Authority board members are usually appointed by a city or county, but operate largely independently of the elected officials. An authority can only be dissolved by the entity that created it through similar legislation (i.e., resolution).

In some cases, the authority operates other transportation-related systems, such as the PANYNJ, which operates the subway, rail, tolls, bridges, and shipping ports, in addition to five airports: John F. Kennedy International Airport (JFK), Newark Liberty International Airport, LaGuardia Airport, Stewart International Airport, and Teterboro Airport, and recently agreed to perform certain management functions at the Atlantic City International Airport. Various states operate airports, with examples including the State of Alaska, which operates all public-use airports in the state; the State of Washington, which operates 16 airports throughout its state; and, Hawaii, which also operates all of its public-use airports.

Private companies operate some airports, or certain operational elements of the airport are contracted out, such as in Teterboro. Under the PANYNJ, Teterboro's operational staff is contracted to a private company. Similarly, certain terminals at JFK and LaGuardia are contracted to private companies, and master concessionaires commonly manage concessions at many commercial service airports in the United States.

The Airport Manager, referred to variously as the **Airport Manager**, the **Airport Director**, or, in some cases, the **Director of Aviation**,[18] is responsible for the safe, secure, and efficient

---

[17]A port authority is similar to an airport authority, but a port authority often includes other forms of transportation such as maritime, rail, trucking, bridges, and tolls, or in the case of PANYNJ, the operation of the World Trade Center.

[18]Each airport organizational structure is slightly different as are Airport Director titles. There is no regulatory distinction between the titles Airport Manager, Airport Director, Director of Aviation, Deputy Manager for Aviation, and so forth; each municipal structure, however, may distinguish these terms in-house.

operation of the airport. The Airport Manager must supervise all of the functions of an airport and, depending on the size of the facility, can do this through a variety of means. At small airports, one individual may comprise the entire airport staff and serve as the Airport Manager, leaving that individual to seek city and county resources and personnel to accomplish certain functions, such as snow removal, airfield maintenance, engineering, and Public Information.

As airports develop, larger and dedicated staffs are needed to fulfill many management and operational functions. Large commercial service airports often have a staff of several thousand employees fulfilling a variety of roles, including (a) operation and maintenance of the airport, (b) administrative and finance, including generating revenue for the airport, (c) short- and long-term capital planning, (d) financing large projects through bonds or AIP funds, (e) handling environmental and noise abatement issues, (f) human resource management, and (g) public relations. Airport Managers are also property managers, marketing and developing the airport, and enticing new tenants and air carriers to the facility, then negotiating and managing leases that can be worth millions of dollars per year. All of these (and many more) functions must be managed while keeping the airport sponsor routinely informed about the activities of the airport and briefed on upcoming issues, regulations, and legislation.

The airport executive must balance the needs of all stakeholders while still ensuring that planes, people, and cargo continuously move through the facility in a safe, effective, and efficient manner. To reach these objectives, it is not unusual for the Airport Manager to retain external managerial support staff and services. Examples of these types of external staff members include (a) auditors, (b) attorneys, and (c) engineer/planning consulting firms—to name just a few.

1. The airport **auditor** is usually an outside agent, reporting directly to the airport sponsor, or sometimes is a third party engaged to perform auditing services to ensure that airport funds are properly managed.
2. The airport **attorney** is also usually an outside agent, reporting directly to the airport sponsor, or is retained as outside counsel to provide legal advice and guidance to the Airport Manager. Attorneys are also involved in negotiating aeronautical use agreements (airline/airport contracts), leases, and contracts and in providing legal perspectives to the airport sponsor.
3. Nearly every public-use airport engages the services of an **aviation engineering and planning** firm. Because airport construction and master planning are complex and heavily regulated functions, airports engage such companies to be the experts in these fields. Small airports may engage one company to provide for all airport planning and engineering needs, while large airports may contract with several companies, in addition to their own in-house staff of planners and engineers.

Airport Operations personnel must collaborate with airport engineers and planners during airfield construction projects. Airport operators must ensure safety on the airport during construction and minimize disruption to flight operations. Airport Ops personnel are frequently involved in the planning stages of airport construction projects to provide guidance and counsel on safe, airfield-movement practices. Ultimately, the Airport Manager must referee conflicts between airport operational personnel, who desire to maintain the safest aircraft-operating environment possible, and airport engineers and planners, who also desire to maintain a safe environment, but strive to keep construction costs down.

Airport Management Divisions

- Finance & Administration
- Marketing & Air Service Development
- Operations, Maintenance, Safety, & Security
- Planning & Design

FIGURE 2.5

Rudimentary airport management functional areas found at many U.S. airports.

With each airport being operated by various forms of cities, counties, and authorities, airport organizational charts vary widely from one airport to the next. The organizational chart shown in Figure 2.5 is rudimentary and reflects four managerial divisions typically found at most airports.

1. The **finance and administration** functions of an airport typically include human resources, accounting, budget, revenue and property management, concession management, leasing and legal, and risk management.
2. The **marketing and air service development (ASD)** functions relate to bringing business to the airport. ASD is a functional area focusing on recruiting new air carriers to the airport and motivating existing air carries to increase or improve service at a commercial service airport.
3. The **operations, maintenance, safety, and security** functions of an airport relate directly to the safety and security of the traveling public. Operational functions are discussed throughout this text, but primarily address ensuring that all airport infrastructure, systems, and personnel are operating in a safe and secure manner. Maintenance personnel within operations perform in three main areas: (a) airfield maintenance, which is focused on airfield signs, markings, lighting, and certain aids to navigation; (b) building maintenance, which is focused on heating, ventilation, and air conditioning systems and the overall maintenance of the terminal building (lights, plumbing, etc.); and (c) fleet maintenance, which is concerned with keeping airport vehicles such as snowplows and other essential vehicles in good operation. Emergency management also usually comes under the operation function of an airport. Security functions are related to TSA security requirements under Title 49 CFR Part 1542 (Airport Security) for commercial service airports and GA security guidance for GA airports. A mix of police, unarmed security officers, and Airport Operations personnel usually fulfill these functions.
4. The **planning and design** functions of an airport relate to capital improvement projects, airfield design elements, master planning, noise abatement, construction projects, and environmental management.

AIRPORTS, FEDERAL AVIATION ADMINISTRATION, AND TRANSPORTATION SECURITY ADMINISTRATION

Airports are regulated by the FAA, an agency under the **U.S. Department of Transportation (DOT)**. Most FAA regulations relate to airport safety or management processes prescribed by grant assurances. Until 2001, the FAA was responsible for aviation security regulations, but after the terrorist attacks on September 11, 2001, the security regulations were transferred to the newly created **TSA**.

The TSA regulates commercial service airports under Title 49 CFR Part 1542—Airport Security and commercial aircraft operators in aircraft used in commercial carriage that exceed a **maximum gross takeoff weight** of 12,500 pounds.[19] Most GA airports in the United States, public-use or otherwise, are not regulated by the TSA, with the exception of three airports within the Flight Restriction Zone of Washington, DC (College Park, Washington Executive, and Potomac Airfield).

Airports are also required to follow a variety of other regulations from government agencies. Examples include the **Environmental Protection Agency (EPA)**, **Customs and Border Protection and Immigration**, and **Customs Enforcement**, particularly for those airports with **ports of entry** into the United States, and other state and local laws and organizations. A major responsibility of Airport Operations is to ensure regulatory policies and laws are strictly followed. This facet of Airport Operations is not only important in terms of compliance, it is critical to the safety and security of all airport stakeholders and the NAS.

AIRPORT OPERATIONS AND STATE AERONAUTICAL DIVISIONS

States commonly have divisions within their transportation departments that act as advocates for promoting, developing, or otherwise supporting airport operational needs within their state boundaries. Objectives and levels of support vary greatly from state to state and within each aeronautics division. However, it is common to find state aeronautical divisions facilitating licensing, grant funding, and subcontracting of services directly related to the improvement of Airport Operations. State aeronautical divisions can be a viable resource for Airport Operations personnel seeking expert advice and potential funding for airport improvement needs, especially as related to enhanced safety and security. For example, the Tennessee Department of Transportation's Aeronautics Division describes its role as follows:

> This division is responsible for licensing public airports, monitoring compliance with federal grants and providing flight services for branches of state government. It performs engineering services, aviation planning studies, airport improvement, and project design consultation to local airports. It insures the operational safety and efficiency of the state aviation facilities system.[20]

The Colorado Division of Aeronautics features the robust Colorado Discretionary Aviation Grant Program[21] (Figure 2.6). Colorado's Division of Aeronautics routinely awards grant funding through this program to airports seeking support for effective air transportation systems in Colorado. These awards are applied to operational functions such as runway extensions, airport environment repair, airport safety enhancements, and sustainability programs.

---

[19]Also known as *maximum design takeoff weight* (MDTOW), which is the maximum total weight of the aircraft allowed for takeoff operations. This limitation is established using a specific aircraft's Airworthiness requirements and structural capability.
[20]See http://www.tdot.state.tn.us/aeronautics/
[21]See https://www.codot.gov/programs/aeronautics/AviationGrants

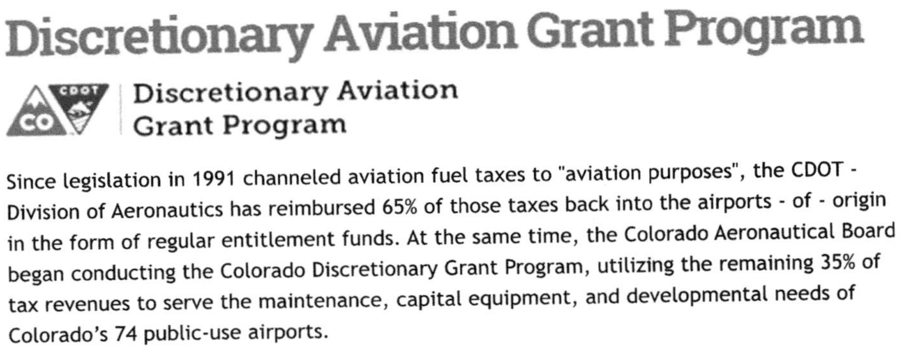

Discretionary Aviation Grant Program

Discretionary Aviation Grant Program

Since legislation in 1991 channeled aviation fuel taxes to "aviation purposes", the CDOT - Division of Aeronautics has reimbursed 65% of those taxes back into the airports - of - origin in the form of regular entitlement funds. At the same time, the Colorado Aeronautical Board began conducting the Colorado Discretionary Grant Program, utilizing the remaining 35% of tax revenues to serve the maintenance, capital equipment, and developmental needs of Colorado's 74 public-use airports.

FIGURE 2.6

The Colorado Department of Transportation's Division of Aeronautics supports its Discretionary Aviation Grant Program, which is nationally recognized for its support of airport operational concerns.

Source: Colorado Department of Transportation (CDOT).

AIRPORT OPERATIONS AND INDUSTRY TRADE ORGANIZATIONS

"When the flights arrive and depart on time, everyone's happy—That's the mission of Airport Operations."

John Selden, former general manager, Port Authority of New York and New Jersey

Helping to make sense of and comply with the variety of regulations governing Airport Operations are industry trade organizations. Trade organizations provide services to airport operators, usually in the form of lobbying efforts, assisting with regulatory issues, and providing training and information on industry topics, best practices, and trends. **AAAE** and the **Airports Council International (ACI)** are the two leading airport management trade associations. Both provide certification and training programs to airport personnel in most areas of airport management and operations.

In addition to the airport management industry having its own trade organizations, so does almost every other airport tenant. Airlines have **Airlines 4 America** and the **International Air Transportation Association (IATA)**; corporate aircraft operators have the **National Business Aviation Association (NBAA)**; GA pilots have the **Aircraft Owners and Pilots Association (AOPA)**; FBO operators and specialized aviation service operators have the **National Air Transport Association (NATA)**; and helicopter operators (**Helicopter Association International [HAI]**) and flight instructors (**National Association of Flight Instructors [NAFI]**) have their own industry groups.

Whenever an Airport Manager or other stakeholder desires to make policy changes at the airport that may affect the tenants, the manager can expect that representatives from the above organizations will also have varying perspectives on the issue(s). In some cases, the tenant group or trade organization may help the airport operator, but in other cases they may actively oppose the policy or procedure sought and leverage political pressure or community support to modify or eliminate the proposed measure. State aeronautical departments also have their own organization for national representation, known as the **National Association of State Aviation Officials (NASAO).**[22]

Government and nonprofit, nongovernmental organizations (NGOs) also lobby or advocate for public needs in air travel, such as on-time-service and safety.[23] In addition to these organizations, the public has access to the most influential policy and rulemaking body in aviation—the U.S. Congress. For example, pressure from citizens (and their related groups) eventually caused Congress to legislate **14 CFR 259.4–Contingency Plan for Lengthy Tarmac Delays**. Otherwise known as "the tarmac rule," this regulation provides relief for airline passengers who are stuck on an airplane for lengthy periods of time. Although this regulation is most beneficial to passengers, it is important to realize that it is the Airport Manager who is burdened with the responsibility of taking care of unexpected surges in passengers returning to the terminal as a result of airlines exceeding tarmac time delays.

SUMMARY

The fundamental mission of Airport Operations is to provide a safe, secure, and efficient environment for the conduct of flight operations and all associated elements. Soon after the advent of the airplane came the creation of the first airport. As commercial flying grew in popularity, so did the formalization of airport management and Airport Operations, as the flying public had a certain expectation of safety while flying. Airport Managers ensured that the landing field was prepared for flight operations. As World War II ended, many municipalities accepted airports from the federal government that were already constructed in their jurisdictions for the war effort. However, the transfer of the airport from military to municipal use also came with the assurance that the municipality would operate the airport in a safe and secure manner, thus formalizing the role of Airport Operations. The term **airport sponsor** was also introduced and is still used to this day to denote the legal entity responsible for the operation of the airport.

Makeshift terminals were constructed around landing fields, creating the first FBOs. Many of these early FBOs would later be replaced by commercial airline terminals and formalized structures designed to accommodate passenger and landside traffic to and through the facility, such as parking lots, passenger arrival and departure lanes for vehicle traffic, and concessions to allow passengers to eat and relax in comfort while waiting for their flight. Through these additional demands on the facility came additional needs to ensure the safety of the public, not just on the runways and taxiways, but through the entire passenger supply chain—landside-to-terminal-to-airside and back. The role of operations expanded beyond the airfield to all elements of the airport.

Airports are costly facilities, so through the use of operating agreements with the airlines, and land leases with concessionaires, and other tenants, Airport Managers sought to provide additional revenue streams. Airport Operations personnel are often charged with lease enforcement. As hijackings and airline and airport bombings began occurring in the 1960s and 1970s, the role of Airport Operations expanded to include security enforcement.

---

[22]See http://www.nasao.org/
[23]See http://www.dot.gov/airconsumer and http://www.thirtythousandfeet.com/organ.htm

Today, many airports are operated by a city or county, or an authority, which is an independent level of government created through a legislative process, such as a state law or municipal resolution. Airports are heavily regulated entities, with the FAA and TSA being the agencies with the most influence on Airport Operations. Several trade associations certify, train, and assist airport executives in their job duties, but the trade associations also represent other aviation organizations and interest groups that may find themselves in conflict with the airport operator from time-to-time. Despite the friction or competing agendas between airports and other aviation entities, Airport Operations personnel still must ensure that the public continues to move in a safe, secure, and efficient manner.

Reflections on Airport Ops by a Newly Appointed GA Airport Manager

by Zechariah Papp
Airport Manager, Salida Harriet Alexander Airport, Chaffee County, CO

It has been an amazing opportunity and challenge to take over as the Airport Manager at Harriet Alexander Airfield (ANK) (Figure 2.7) in Salida, Colorado.[24] When I was enrolled at Metropolitan State University of Denver, I never thought that I would be running an airport in less than four years, let alone in my hometown.

I am the only employee at this small, publically owned, and uncontrolled airport. As the manager, I am in charge of all ground maintenance including snow removal, mowing, fixing broken equipment, and maintaining runway and lighting systems. Along with those responsibilities, I deal with hangar leases, new construction at the airfield, billing, and ordering for the facility. Since we are jointly owned by the City of Salida and Chaffee County, I am required to attend city and county meetings to inform the boards about the activities of the airport.

We have been moving forward on two FAA grant-funded projects for our facility. We are planning to fog seal and restripe the entire airfield. This will help preserve all the pavement surfaces so they last longer in the extreme weather shifts we have in this mountain valley. We are also working on a new Airport Master Plan that will be instrumental in developing our vision for the future of ANK.

Running an airport can be extremely overwhelming and I have had to mentally train myself to break tasks apart, prioritize, and work on them one by one.

When I saw the county was accepting applications for a new Airport Manager, I thought I had a decent idea of everything that goes into running an airport. To my surprise, I stepped into a facility that was in need of a lot of attention. It has been a challenge just to fix the broken equipment, and get all the maintenance current. I have felt on certain days like Sisyphus at the bottom of the hill. I learn more about the position with each passing day, and can see that hill getting smaller. I have no doubt in my mind that soon enough this airport's potential will truly shine.

(Continued)

---

[24]See https://www.codot.gov/programs/aeronautics/PDF_Files/AirportDirectory/2015_2016COArptDir.pdf

(Continued)

SALIDA   Harriet Alexander Airport   ANK

LATITUDE	LONGITUDE	ELEVATION
38-32.296667N	106-02.918333W	7523' MSL

Navigation

VOR	GPS	ILS
114.9 (BLUE MESA)	YES	NO

Runway Data

Runway	Length	Width	Surface	Lights	VGSI	App Lgts
6/24	7348'	75'	ASPH	MIRL	P2L/P2L	NONE
H1	36'	36'	CONC	NONE	NONE	NONE

Communications

CTAF/UNICOM	Lights	Weather	ATIS	APP/DEP	Tower	Ground	RCO
122.7	122.7	AWOS 133.85 719-539-5263	--	--	--	--	--

SALIDA   Harriet Alexander Airport   ANK

FIGURE 2.7 Harriet Alexander Airfield (ANK) in Salida, Colorado.

ANK supports GA operations, including hang-gliding and traditional glider operations (depicted data not for navigation).

Courtesy of the Colorado Department of Transportation (CDOT).

REFERENCE

Federal Aviation Administration (FAA). (2015). *National plan of integrated airport systems.* Washington, DC: U.S. Dept. of Transportation, Federal Aviation Administration.

OPERATIONS AND THE AIRPORT ENVIRONMENT

3

Technicians with the Colorado Governor's Office of Information Technology (OIT) perform maintenance and repairs to the Berthoud Pass–Mines Peak Automated Weather Observing System (AWOS). Elevation 12,493′.

Source: MSL Image by Shahn Sederberg, Colorado Division of Aeronautics, 2014.

An Automated Weather Observing System (AWOS) located at the Steamboat Springs Municipal Airport, Steamboat Springs, CO. In background: wind sock and segmented circle. Steamboat Ski Resort and Mt. Werner also can be seen in the background.

Source: Image by Shahn Sederberg, Colorado Division of Aeronautics, 2014.

"Airports are a portal to the planet."
Harrison Ford, Living in the Age of Airplanes, IMAX

The complexities of the airport environment for a typical, public-use airport drive the plethora of functions and roles inherent to Airport Operations. A U.S. public-use airport is essentially a federally regulated and locally owned facility, responsible for creating an active business environment while simultaneously fulfilling a critical role in the National Airspace System. A public airport is neither a 100% public facility nor 100% business enterprise, as it routinely must serve both demographics. While airports are operated by a local government entity (municipality, authority, or some other state organization; see Chapter 2), the airport sponsor must establish operational plans and capabilities that meet federal regulations, the needs of the public, and demands of commerce. As previously described, public-use airports that accept federal grant funding through the Airport Improvement Program (AIP) must comply with sponsor assurances, as defined in the **Federal Aviation Administration (FAA) Airport Compliance Manual—Order 5190.6b**. As we shall discover in this chapter, the FAA Airport Compliance Manual is the baseline operating handbook that Airport Managers and sponsors use to address operational needs for their airport.

AIRPORT COMPLIANCE MANUAL (ORDER 5190.6b) AND GRANT (SPONSOR) ASSURANCES

All airports operating under Part 139 must maintain specific safety standards and related programs. Airports that are awarded AIP grant money must also adhere to those safety standards but usually are granted AIP support to further enhance existing Part 139 (a) safety, (b) security, (c) reconstruction, and (d) capacity Operating Standards. Written grant or sponsor assurances[1] are contractual promises an airport sponsor makes to the FAA in exchange for AIP financial awards. Although not specifically stated as such in grant assurances, the conditions within each grant assurance contract provide what is, in essence, a management manual containing guidelines and requirements for Airport Operations.

Conditions specified in sponsor assurances ordinarily have a 20-year life span, which renews every time the airport accepts another AIP grant. For example, if an airport accepts AIP monies in 2016, the airport is obligated under grant assurances until the year 2036. If the airport then accepts another AIP grant, say in the year 2020, then the airport is obligated under grant assurances until the year 2040. Also, any airport that falls under the **Surplus Property Act of 1944**,[2] or has received AIP money to buy real property under the Act, is usually obligated to meet conditions set forth in the grant assurances for (a) the lifetime of the airport in the case of real property and (b) useful life for the purchase of equipment or infrastructure.[3] In either case, the airport must buy the federally funded property (real or equipment/infrastructure) back from the FAA in order to be released early from the conditions of the grant assurances.[4]

GRANT ASSURANCE REQUIREMENTS

Grant assurances typically require that the airport receiving AIP funding follow numerous federal laws, executive orders, and specific federal regulations (among many other requirements). Airport Operations is often charged with oversight, to ensure the airport and its tenants comply with these assurances. Some assurances that connect directly to the Airport Operations function are:[5]

1. **Pavement Preventative Maintenance (Grant Assurance 11):** Airports are required to have a preventative maintenance management program, and it is often the function of Airport Operations to report pavement deterioration. Part 139 airports require daily pavement inspections so this function is inherent within the regulation, but grant assurances also make it applicable to non-Part 139 airports (mostly general aviation [GA] airports) that accept federal funding.

---

[1]"Grant assurances" and "sponsor assurances" are synonymous terms, commonly used interchangeably by Airport Operations and management personnel.
[2]Surplus Property Act of 1944: Public Airports, 50 U.S.C. §§ 1611–1646 (2006). Retrieved from: http://disposal.gsa.gov/SurplusAct
[3]Federal Aviation Administration (FAA) (2009). *Lifetime of airport real property or useful life of equipment under Surplus Property Act of 1944. Order 5190.6b.* Washington, DC: Federal Aviation Administration. Retrieved from: http://www.faa.gov/airports/resources/publications/orders/compliance_5190_6/media/5190_6b_chap3.pdf
[4]Some airport sponsors attempt to avoid grant obligations to close the airport for other uses.
[5]FAA (2014). *Airport Improvement Handbook. Order 5100.38D.* Washington, DC: Federal Aviation Administration. Retrieved from: http://www.faa.gov/airports/aip/aip_handbook/media/AIP-Handbook-Order-5100-38D.pdf. (Refer to the AIP Handbook for a listing of all grant assurance categories, along with applicability.)

2. **Conformity to Plans and Specifications (Grant Assurance 16):** Airport Operations personnel are often charged with overseeing the safety of construction on airports, but may also be charged with ensuring that contractors on federally funded projects stay within the approved plans and specifications.

3. **Construction Inspection and Approval (Grant Assurance 17):** Airports are required to maintain competent, technical supervision of the construction site and to ensure that any project work complies with regulations and procedures prescribed by the FAA. Airport Operations personnel typically are charged with the responsibility to daily and periodically inspect airport construction projects. *Note:* Airport planners and engineers are usually not directly responsible for compliance with Grant Assurances 16 and 17, as they are not always onsite or available when construction issues come up, as projects can be scheduled for weekends and after-hours.

4. **Operations and Maintenance (Grant Assurance 19):** Airport operators are required to operate the airport in a safe and serviceable condition. Chapter 7 of the *Airport Compliance Manual* directly addresses the nature of Airport Operations (FAA, 2009) and focuses on the sponsor responsibilities for operation and maintenance of the airport. *Note:* When the FAA refers to areas within Airport Operations, it frequently refers to areas of maintenance. For our purposes, we will consider that maintenance issues and standards are airport operational in nature, unless otherwise specified. While much is encompassed in Grant Assurance 19, the core elements include: (a) operating the airport's aeronautical facilities, when required; (b) marking and lighting hazards to air navigation; and (c) notifying pilots of any condition affecting the aeronautical use of the airport. In order to effectively accomplish this requirement, Airport Operations personnel must continuously inspect the airport and the airspace surrounding the airport to look for hazards to navigation.

5. **Hazard Removal and Mitigation (Grant Assurance 20):** Airports are required to take appropriate action to protect the airspace, which includes the **Airport Movement Area (AMA)**, from obstructions or hazards to air navigation. The "movement areas" (AMA)[6] include the runways, taxiways, and other areas of an airport that are used for taxiing, takeoff, and landing of aircraft, exclusive of loading ramps and aircraft parking areas. Airport Operations personnel must continuously monitor and inspect the airfield in the airspace around the airport for hazards that may appear throughout operations. For example, construction cranes are often erected overnight and without warning. Therefore, under Grant Assurance 19 Operations and Maintenance, the airport operator must issue a **notice to airmen (NOTAM**[7]) (Figure 3.1) to warn pilots of the aeronautical hazard, and then follow up with the operator of the construction (hazard) to ensure they have properly notified the FAA. Another example of a hazard to aviation can be **foreign object debris (FOD)**, including live or deceased wildlife, aircraft or vehicle parts that have fallen onto the ramp, and loose, ground-service equipment. If the object cannot be immediately removed, then a NOTAM must be issued. This grant assurance speaks directly to the core function of Airport Operations, which is to provide a safe operating environment for aeronautical operations and to notify pilots if there is an unsafe condition on the airport.

---

[6]Sometimes referred to as either the Airport Movement Area or simply the movement area.

[7]Prock, G. (2010). *Notice to Airmen (NOTAM): Procedures update: Issuing a NOTAM today digital NOTAM tomorrow.* Retrieved from: https://www.faa.gov/about/office_org/headquarters_offices/arc/programs/pacific_aviation_directors _workshop/2010/media/0415_10am_prock.pdf

> **NOTAM** - *a notice or advisory distributed by means of telecommunication containing information concerning the establishment, conditions or change in any aeronautical facility, service, procedure or hazard, the timely knowledge of which is essential to personnel and systems concerned with flight operations.*

FIGURE 3.1 NOTAM (Notice to Airmen).

NOTAM—a notice or advisory distributed by means of telecommunication containing information concerning the establishment, conditions, or change in any aeronautical facility, service, procedure, or hazard, the timely knowledge of which is essential to personnel and systems concerned with flight operations.

Source: Prock, G. (2010). FAA AIM NOTAM Operations.

6. **Economic Nondiscrimination (Grant Assurance 22):** The airport is required to be available for public use on reasonable terms and without unjust discrimination to all types of aeronautical activities. This requirement results in the airport producing a key document for Airport Operations, referred to as the "minimum standards." Minimum standards are addressed in **FAA Advisory Circular 150/5190-7,** *Minimum Standards for Commercial Aeronautical Activities*.[8] Minimum standards are business Operating Standards that all aeronautical businesses on the airport are required to adhere to and maintain. Often the minimum standards relate to items such as amount of space required to be leased by a tenant for certain functions. Many of the minimum standards also relate to operational requirements for the air carriers or aeronautical tenants, such as **Fixed Base Operators (FBOs)**, flight schools, air charters, commercial hangar tenants, and maintenance operations on the airfield. Usually, it is the responsibility of Airport Operations to ensure that the tenants are in compliance with the published minimum standards.

7. **Fee and Rental Structure (Grant Assurance 24):** The FAA requires airports to set a fee and rental structure to make the airport as self-sustainable as possible. *Self-sustainable*, within this context, means that the airport relies on its own operational revenue stream rather than local, municipal, tax funding to operate. *Self-sustainable* does not imply that the airport may not accept AIP grant funds. Operations personnel are sometimes charged with ensuring that landing fees are collected, writing down the **N-number**[9] of aircraft that use the facility so that they may be charged for the use (where applicable), or verifying that the FBOs or air traffic control tower is properly logging airport use for revenue-generating purposes.

Airports often create and publish a set of "rules and regulations" for all airport users in order to fulfill the requirements of applicable grant assurances. Airport operators also create and publish minimum standards that apply to the aeronautical businesses on their airport. While not regulated by the FAA, most commercial service airports have business standards for concessions, and, frequently, it is the responsibility of Airport Operations personnel to ensure that concessionaires are also following these minimum standards.

---

[8]FAA (2006). *Advisory Circular 150/5190-7-Minimum standards for commercial aeronautical activities*. Retrieved from: https://www.faa.gov/regulations_policies/advisory_circulars/index.cfm/go/document.information/documentID/22332
[9]FAA aircraft registration number.

RULES, POLICIES, AND REGULATIONS/MINIMUM STANDARDS

The following are primary rules, policies, and regulations commonly described in minimum standards as published by airport operators:

1. **Security:** These rules commonly relate to the security requirements under Title 49 CFR Part 1542 Airport Security. Part 1542 includes policies and regulations for (a) access to Secured Areas and Sterile Areas of the airport, (b) the requirement that airport personnel wear an approved access/identification badge, (c) the requirement that airport personnel challenge individuals who are not wearing the proper badge (or any badge) in Security Areas, and (d) the requirement that individuals maintain a proper escort of other individuals who do not have access/ID in a Security Area. Other security-related regulations may include: (a) ensuring airport entrances, gates, and doors are properly secured and responding to alarms at these access points, (b) controlling the airfield to ensure there have not been penetrations of the perimeter fence, and (c) maintaining a clear zone so that vehicles or other items are not placed close enough to the fence to allow someone access over the fence. Airport Operations personnel also commonly respond to security incidents to represent the airport, or, in some cases, assume Incident Command, or otherwise make decisions on behalf of the airport sponsor.

2. **Conduct of persons and tenants using the airport:** These policies and regulations typically relate to the: (a) conduct of businesses and concessions, (b) unauthorized advertising or leafletting, (c) travel or movement of passengers in authorized areas, (d) regulations addressing bicycles, roller blades, or skateboards or other conveyances within the airport, and (e) safety measures, including the use of reflective clothing in certain areas, such as traffic control or construction sites. This category tends to be a catchall for a variety of regulations; for example, regulations at Denver International Airport prohibit bringing marijuana on site. Airport Operations personnel are frequently charged with enforcing these regulations and either taking direct action to intervene when there is a violation or notifying the proper police agency for response. These rules may also address the lawful distribution of newspapers, flyers, or other materials at the airport and the requirements for individuals to protest at the facility.

3. **Vehicle operations:** These regulations typically address traffic and public safety issues on both the land- and airside. Items such as (a) speed limits, (b) licensing of drivers who operate vehicles on airport property, (c) permits and markings for airside vehicles, and (d) reporting of accidents are all typically included in this section. While vehicle operations in the public area (landside) are the jurisdiction of law enforcement, airport operational personnel must often enforce vehicle movement violations on the airfield. Airside violations, depending on severity, are sometimes handled within the airport Violation Notice system, or sometimes as a civil infraction, requiring a court appearance and possible penalties, fiscal repercussions, and points on the license.

   Airports often establish "Violation Notice" systems to enforce rules and regulations. Employees who fail to follow security or airport safety and operational regulations may be given a Violation Notice that requires a response from their employer. Common penalties include a formal letter notifying the individual's employer of the violation and requiring

(a) counseling by either the supervisor for the airport's safety or security manager, (b) requiring the employee to repeat security- or safety-related training, or (c) suspending the employee's access to the airport for a period of time, such as revoking their Airport Identification Badge. In some cases, airport sponsors have codified their rules and regulations to make them civil ordinances and have attached fines to the list of penalties. Airport Operations personnel typically handle violation issues that deal with employees of the air carriers and attendance at the airport. However, if an individual who does not work at the airport accesses the airfield illegally, this action requires law enforcement action, with the potential of prosecution by local or federal authorities.

4. **Landside-related regulations:** Landside areas include the parking garage, passenger pickup and dropoff locations, and commercial passenger operations. Regulations often relate to: (a) where individuals are allowed to park and for how long, (b) access for taxicabs and other commercial vehicle operators, such as limousine services to the airport, (c) the collection of revenue for commercial vehicles accessing the airport, (d) the dwell time for personal and commercial vehicles at the airport pickup and dropoff locations, and (e) rules covering solicitation by commercial vehicle operators. Rental car operations, along with permitting requirements, are also commonly covered in these sections of the rules and regulations. Airport Operations personnel oversee the movement of vehicles in these areas, often enforcing the solicitation and operation of commercial vehicles, reporting abandoned vehicles or vehicles that exceed their dwell time, and ensuring commercial vehicles have the proper permits. Landside regulations may also address the operations of "skycaps,"[10] including their appearance, demeanor, tipping policies, and so on.

5. **Airside regulations:** These regulations relate to the (a) use and movement of aircraft on the airfield, such as where aircraft may be started and where run-up operations may be conducted, (b) rules regarding the takeoff, landing, taxiing, and positioning of aircraft, (c) aircraft repair and washing requirements, or restrictions, and (d) in some cases, helicopter operational requirements. Aircraft fueling, defueling, and deicing regulations are also commonly addressed in this section. Airport Operations personnel are frequently charged with ensuring that aircraft operators follow these rules. Recall that the FAA air traffic control tower (where it exists) governs the operation of aircraft on the movement area; however, the airport operator governs the operations of aircraft in the non-movement area and has overall responsibility for the safe operation of the entire facility, including the runways and taxiways.

6. **Environmental management:** Airports are required to adhere to environmental laws, and many airports have added an **environmental management system** to identify and prioritize environmental concerns. Airports can cause significant environmental issues through the use of deicing fluid, occasional fuel spills, hazardous waste generation and use (primarily by air carriers), wetland issues, solid waste generation (particularly from construction projects), migratory birds, sewage, ozone-depleting compounds, pavement deicers, lubricants, solvents, wash fluids, and noise. Airport operational personnel are often charged with overseeing environmental issues, such as fuel spills and cleanup, and ensuring that tenants comply with minimum standards concerning environmental responsibilities.

7. **Operation and control of Concourse Gates:** At commercial service airports, aeronautical use agreements commonly include preferential use options for gates. Airport Operations personnel

---

[10]A skycap is a porter or baggage handler.

are often charged with managing the preferential use of these gates or providing oversight to ensure their proper use by the proper tenants at the proper times.

8. **Noise abatement and runway procedures:** Through approved, noise-abatement studies and various FAA Orders, airports frequently implement noise-abatement procedures. Airport Operations (Ops) personnel often oversee these procedures, such as preferential runway use, maximum performance climb out, curfews, and others. When a violation is observed, operations personnel report the N-number to the airport operator to assess required penalties or other type of follow-up.

Some airports have "unauthorized flight instructors" or "unauthorized maintenance providers" who do not meet the requirements of the airport's minimum standards, yet attempt to provide flight training or aircraft maintenance services on the property. Airport Operations personnel are frequently charged with attempting to locate and interdict such activities, reporting the individual to either airport management or law enforcement, as appropriate.

Minimum standards also relate to the business Operating Standards for aeronautical businesses on the airport. Airport Operations personnel ensure that businesses are meeting these required standards as set forth by the airport operator. Examples of minimum airport business Operating Standards are shown in Figure 3.2.

Airport stakeholders who do not follow minimum standards—either policies or regulations—as specified by the airport operator may be cited, issued a violation, or prosecuted via legal action. Depending on the violation, when Airport Operations personnel identify a violation of the minimum standards, they may either take immediate, authorized action to remedy the violation and follow up with airport management, or report the incident to airport management for further evaluation and potential action.

- *Hours of operation.*
- *Facility maintenance and appearance.*
- *Appearance and conduct of personnel.*
- *Fueling: ensuring Fixed Base Operators are providing fuel on a timely basis to all tenants and that corporate operators with their own fuel farms are not providing fuel to other tenants.*
- *Compliance with environmental regulations.*
- *Removal of aircraft that are disabled on the runway or in the movement area.*
- *Ensuring only those who are authorized to operate a commercial business on the airport are doing so.*
- *Ensure that tenants are operating their facilities in a safe manner.*

FIGURE 3.2 Minimum airport business standards.

Minimum airport business Operating Standards are numerous and vary greatly among airports. This list represents a small sample of those types of standards.

AIRPORT STAKEHOLDERS

Many private businesses, including airlines, FBOs, specialized aviation service operators, concessionaires, vendors, and other operators not conducting commerce, rely on the airport for their livelihood (refer to Figure 2.3). All of these stakeholders rely on the airport to facilitate their business or functional interests. These tenants may also include the military, corporations with aircraft that need storage, maintenance and fuel companies at a Base of operations, aircraft manufacturers, and recreational pilots needing hangar or tie-down space. Federal agencies, including **U.S. Customs and Border Protection (CBP)**, **U.S. Immigration and Customs Enforcement (ICE)**, **U.S. Transportation Security Administration (TSA)**, and FAA **Air Traffic Control (ATC)**, and related FAA **navigational aids (NAVAIDS)**, have requirements that must be carried out on airports. Surrounding the airport are businesses that rely on the airport, such as the hotel, rental car, and restaurant industries, along with residents who, while they rely on air transportation from time to time, are not always pleased with the noise from the aircraft operating at the airport or other related environmental factors generated from Airport Operations.

AIR CARRIERS

Air carriers, both passenger and cargo airlines, are the most significant stakeholder contributing to the viability of a commercial service airport. Air carriers understand and use this dynamic as leverage when negotiating aeronautical use agreements, which are essentially operating agreements with the airport sponsor. Not only do air carriers comprise a significant amount of the direct revenue to the airport in the form of landing fees, renting space for ticket counters, baggage claim areas, and administrative areas, and fuel flowage fees, a successful air carrier will also bring in significant residual revenue for the airport, such as concessionaires and other businesses.

Air carriers negotiate aeronautical use agreements with the airport sponsor that provide a guaranteed revenue stream for the airport operator for a period of time, notwithstanding unplanned bankruptcies, and allow the air carrier operating rights at the airport. Air carriers who invest a significant amount of capital and resources in the airport are often given **signatory status.** Signatory status may provide the air carrier certain approval rights as related to decision making and managing the airport. Most significantly, signatory status, as articulated through majority-in-interest clauses in **airport use agreements**, provides airlines some modicum of control over airport **capital improvement projects (CIPs)**, which can have a direct effect on airport operational concerns.

Airport use agreements can affect Airport Operations personnel in two ways: (a) many user agreements require certain air carrier performance standards, such as a percentage of gate usage, which is often monitored by Airport Operations personnel, and (b) airline staff of signatory status carriers may sometimes feel that because they have more control over certain elements of airport management, such as the CIP process, that control also extends to influencing the way the airport is managed in other ways. While rarely talked or written about, Airport Operations personnel are often well aware that this inferred influence sometimes turns into political capital and occasionally results in some favoritism that is outside the user agreement. This situation is considered part of the political realities of operating an airport.

Air carriers attract or bring passengers to the airport. These travelers require parking and arrive either by commercial or private means, such as public transportation, private automobile, and rental cars. Parking and Ground Transportation access fees, such as fees paid by limousine companies, airport shuttles, taxis, and other services, represent a significant revenue stream for airport operators. Without air carrier service, these revenue streams diminish, as most GA airports, which is what an airport becomes after losing its air carrier service, do not have a significant customer base that can be charged for parking or landside access. In some cases, GA airports have low levels of air carrier service, below 2,500 enplanements per year, or small charter operations, which operate similarly to an air carrier operation, and may therefore have lease and use agreements with the airport. In these cases, Airport Operations personnel must be designated at the GA airport to oversee operations, enforce penalties and compliance, and, in some cases, collect fees just as commercial Airport Operations personnnel are required to do.

The air carrier also relies significantly on Airport Operations personnel to maintain a safe, secure, and efficient, airport-operating environment. When an air carrier aircraft is experiencing a problem or emergency, the air carrier usually depends on Airport Operations to help solve the problem. When it is snowing, air carriers and Airport Operations and maintenance personnel typically work side-by-side (literally, in some cases, for example, in the snow command center) to coordinate the removal of snow and the opening and closing of runways to allow flight operations in between snow removal operations. If an air carrier aircraft is experiencing a security incident, Airport Operations will coordinate incident response between police, fire, emergency medical services, and other agencies. Part of this coordination is dedicated to continuing flight operations during the incident (if possible) or, if flight operations must be stopped, to handle the incident and reopen the airport as soon as possible.

FIXED BASE OPERATORS AND GENERAL AVIATION AIRPORTS

The FBO is most closely associated with providing aircraft and passenger services to the private flying community. At some commercial service airports, the FBO may also provide fueling services to the air carrier. At most GA airports, the FBO is the equivalent to the air carrier as the most significant tenant on the field. While an FBO may be associated with large, corporate jets or turboprop types of aircraft, they also provide services for smaller aircraft, such as tie-down, hangar storage (short- and long-term), and minor maintenance services. While the FBO may not be granted signatory rights similar to an air carrier, many airport executives understand that FBOs are typically responsible for a good percentage of the income for the airport through land lease, fuel sales, aircraft rentals, and flight training. FBOs are also important to the local economy through job stimulus and private business air travel.

FBOs provide private terminal operations for private and charter aircraft. They also can provide fuel, maintenance, Ground Transportation, weather and flight planning services, Internet, pilot lounges, and restaurant or food services. Occasionally, FBOs will also provide the airport sponsor office space since not all GA airports have a separate terminal building. Many FBOs also rent training or meeting room space. Some FBOs at smaller GA airports provide airport management services, such as runway inspections, Unicom[11] services, and response to incidents. In these cases, the FBO is often a contractor to the airport sponsor on a term basis.

---

[11]At uncontrolled fields, or at a controlled field when the air traffic control tower is not operational, FBO personnel may provide wind and weather advisories, along with other related aeronautical information to pilots.

Because of the nature of the FBO's clientele, FBOs commonly allow limousines and private vehicles onto their ramp space to pick up and drop off passengers directly from the airplane. It is typically the responsibility of FBO personnel to ensure that these vehicles do not move from the leasehold area and that they obey airfield-driving regulations related to the movement of vehicles and aircraft on the airfield. GA Airport Operations personnel frequently provide enforcement and oversight, watching for vehicles that may depart from the leasehold area and enter the movement area or other airside locations.

Airport Operations and FBO personnel frequently work together to remove snow and handle disabled aircraft on the movement area. Coordination of very important persons (VIPs)[12] is another function that requires airport and FBO personnel to work together. The business/private aircraft industry is inherently private, and, in some cases, media, paparazzi, or others may be interested in the movements of certain individuals using the private aircraft system. GA operational personnel, as well as commercial service Airport Operations, work with airlines and private aircraft operators to restrict access by these groups to VIP passengers.

Aircraft charter operations at GA airports are frequently owned and operated by flight schools or FBOs. GA aircraft charter services provide many services, including sightseeing and executive travel, in all sizes and types of aircraft. Certain charter operators are even required to adhere to TSA security programs, such as the **TSA 12-5 Security Program**[13] or the **Private Charter Standard Security Program (PCSSP)**,[14] which implies that TSA personnel or authorized aircraft operator personnel may be conducting screening within the charter or FBO areas. Airport Operations (GA or commercial airport) are not responsible for ensuring that aircraft operators are adhering to TSA-regulated security programs. However, the charter operator may need assistance from Airport Operations in the performance of certain TSA- or security-related functions, such as deployment of equipment, shuttling personnel, or providing law enforcement support and incident management.

SPECIALIZED AVIATION SERVICE OPERATORS

Specialized Aviation Service Operators (SASOs) are on-field entities that focus on providing specific aviation-related services. Some of these services may also be offered by FBOs, but generally, SASO organizations target specific clientele. Examples include flight training, **aviation maintenance operations (AMOs)**, aircraft charter and rental, avionics maintenance, propeller shops, and helicopter operations. While SASO businesses may not provide the significant revenue stream typically associated with air carriers or FBOs, they are often critical to the revenue of an airport, particularly at GA airports, and provide necessary services for stakeholders to the airport.

Airport Operations personnel often oversee compliance with the airport's minimum standards and rules and regulations related to the operations of FBOs or SASOs. Airport Operations personnel

---

[12]When designated by the FAA, this type of operation is referred to as a "very important person movement" or VIP movement.

[13]TSA security program applied to aircraft weighing more than 12,500 pounds and engaged in various flight operations, such as scheduled, cargo, or chartered flight Ops.

[14]Additional TSA security requirements for aircraft operators using aircraft with a maximum takeoff weight (MTOW) of greater than 100,309.3 pounds or with a seating configuration of 61 or more.

may provide immediate, short-term intervention when they see a violation of the minimum standards and frequently follow that up with the appropriate entity within the airport management structure for potential further actions. In this capacity, airport Ops personnel are the enforcers.

Airport Operations personnel may also rely on FBOs and SASOs to assist with airport incidents or issues, or even to support the airport during special events, such as VIP movements, airshows, and public open houses. Airport Operations personnel should keep in mind that while FBOs and SASOs are required to follow minimum standards, rules, and regulations, they are also customers of the airport and provide a vital revenue stream. Alternatively, violations of safety- and security-related minimum standards, rules, and regulations are rarely tolerated, regardless of the economic importance of the FBO or SASO to the airport. Other minimum business standards or "lesser" rules and regulations, as interpreted by operational personnel or airport management, may not be as strictly enforced as a result of the nature of the economic relationship between the airport and FBO or SASO organizations.

CONCESSIONAIRES

Although rare at the GA airport, concessionaires are essential to most commercial service airports. For a GA airport, concessions range from a vending machine to a full-service restaurant, which, in many cases, is part of an FBO. At commercial service airports, concessions usually represent a significant revenue stream in addition to providing needed services and products for the traveling public, employees, and meeters and greeters to the airport. While not regulated under the FAA's compliance guidance, concessionaires have contracts with the airport or with a master lessee, who subsequently has a lease with the airport operator, through which certain business, health, and customer service standards must be maintained. Also, Airport Operations personnel are commonly charged with managing security responsibilities as applied to concessionaires. Security responsibilities as related to concessions primarily focus on ensuring that items prohibited in Sterile Areas of the airport that concessions are allowed to have and use, such as knives and box cutters, are not left in public view or accessible by the public.

VENDORS

Vendors provide a variety of services to the airport, including stocking the shelves of the concessionaires. Vendor deliveries to the Sterile or Secured Areas of the airport are required by TSA to be inspected. Even though these deliveries are typically the responsibility of the Airport Security department, Airport Operations personnel may assume a small role in oversight or inspection of these processes to ensure they are being carried out in accordance with the requirements of the **Airport Security Program (ASP)** of the airport.

CONTRACTORS

Contractors are typically associated with construction projects on airports. Contractors also provide continuing services such as information technology (IT) support, routine maintenance, and tenant utilities. Some construction projects may last a short period of time, such as a few weeks or months, while others last for several years. The use of contractors on an airfield is an operational necessity but creates safety and security concerns, as contractor personnel are not always used to working in the airport environment. Construction processes at airports can affect through alteration perimeter fencing, access points, and walls within buildings that may separate public and Security Areas, which creates security and safety concerns. Airport management is charged with operational safety during construction on airports and usually delegates the day-to-day safety and security oversight of construction projects to Airport Operations.

PRIVATE AND CORPORATE AIRCRAFT TENANTS

Airports host an extensive variety of aircraft. Small aircraft owners typically lease hangar space, known as T-hangars, box hangars, or port-a-port depending on make and model, from either the airport operator through a lease agreement or through an FBO, sometimes referred to as **commercial hangar operators**. In some cases, private developers build hangars on airport property leased directly from the airport operator. In this way, airport operators manage their hangars similar to the way apartment managers lease and maintain apartments.

Some corporate tenants have large operations, with sizeable hangars and leased property, and large support structures such as maintenance facilities, office and meeting room space, and their own fuel farm. Under the grant assurances, airports are required to allow airport operators to self-fuel, provided the tenant meets the minimum standards for self-fueling. These standards generally include that the fuel only be used for the tenant and cannot be pumped, shared, or sold into other aircraft for which the tenant does not have an ownership interest, and that the tenant must use their own personnel (on payroll) to do the fueling operations, rather than hiring a third party. Abuses of the self-fueling policy occasionally occur, with airport tenants fueling their friends and other aircraft, either at cost or for a profit. Airport operational personnel are typically in an enforcement capacity, monitoring fueling operations to ensure that corporate operators are only fueling their own aircraft using their own personnel. Large corporate operators may also have automobile garages for VIPs, and limousines and private vehicles are often seen on their leasehold space as they pick up or drop off passengers.

A unique type of aircraft operation is known as "fractional ownership," or **fractionals**. Fractionals operate similar to charter operations, except that the passengers in some capacity represent an ownership interest in the aircraft. Therefore, fractional aircraft operations are not treated as air charters from a regulatory perspective. However, from an operational perspective, fractionals may resemble more traditional aircraft charter operations, with many aircraft on ramp areas, passenger traffic in lobby areas, and access to parking lots. Fractional operators usually have a lease agreement with the airport or with an FBO who is subleasing the necessary ramp, office, and hangar space. Fractionals must also adhere to any relevant minimum standards and rules and regulations, which are enforced by Airport Operations.

MILITARY

Some public-use airports are colocated with military facilities. These may be small operations, such as the U.S. Coast Guard Air Station at San Francisco International Airport, or a significant military presence, such as Northwest Florida Regional Airport, which is located at Eglin Air Force Base. Eglin is considered a **joint-use airport**, meaning it is owned by the Department of

Defense, at which the military accommodates civilian sponsors desiring to use the airport (FAA, n.d.a). A **shared-use airport** means a U.S. government-owned airport (i.e., military) that is colocated with an airport specified under Part 139.1(a) and at which portions of the movement areas and safety areas are shared by both parties (FAA, n.d.b). A good example of a shared-use airport is Colorado Springs Regional Airport in Colorado Springs, CO. The south and west sides of the airfield are a public-use, Part 139, commercial service airport, while the north side of the airport is Peterson Air Force Base, operational home to the 21st Space Wing, which provides missile warning and space control to the North American Aerospace Defense Command. Both entities, the commercial and GA aircraft and the military aircraft, make shared use of the runway and taxiway system.

Operations at a joint- or shared-use airport can create beneficial and, in some cases, challenging dynamics to operating the public-use portion of the facility. For example, airports such as Colorado Springs or Northwest Florida Regional can take advantage of the military's aircraft rescue and firefighting units and personnel to meet their **Part 139 Aircraft Rescue and Firefighting (ARFF)** requirements. Oftentimes, the military standard for aircraft rescue and firefighting exceeds the FAA's Part 139 standard. However, the presence of the military may also make the airport a more likely target for terrorist attack. Colorado Springs, Peterson Air Force Base is a strategic and vital component to national defense and would be a priority target for attack. Therefore, Operational Security at joint- or shared-use airports can be extremely complex to operationally plan and manage.

Other operational challenges at a joint- or shared-use airport include managing capacity and airspace issues, as well as serving national priorities. For example, commercial service or GA aircraft might be delayed to give priority handling to a U.S. Coast Guard helicopter on a rescue mission.

Airport Operations personnel must clearly understand their role at a joint- or shared-use airport. At some joint-use airports, the military is responsible for airfield inspections, as well as many of the other roles that are required under Part 139, and does not allow civilian personnel, including airport Ops, police, fire, and airport management personnel, into military controlled areas, such as runways and taxiways, without prior permission. While at a shared-use airport, Airport Operations personnel may be responsible for all Part 139 functions, with the exception of ARFF response. Each joint- and shared-use airport has unique procedures and agreements defining which entities are responsible for various operational functions.

GOVERNMENT AVIATION FUNCTIONS

Besides the military, U.S., state, and local governments operate a large number of aircraft, such as weather research aircraft (e.g., National Oceanic and Atmospheric Administration), law enforcement aircraft (Drug Enforcement Agency [DEA], Federal Bureau of Investigation [FBI], state and local fixed-wing and rotary-wing aircraft), search and rescue aircraft, and firefighting aircraft, either directly or through a contract. These operations may necessitate operational changes to the airport, particularly in the case of firefighting aircraft when there is a high volume of aerial fire tankers operating on the ramp.

Government agencies do have leases with the airport operator, and Airport Operations personnel must clearly understand the requirements within the lease for access to airport facilities and resources. Based on the nature of some government operations, occasional changes to the operation of the airport, such as priority handling for certain government-owned aircraft, may occur.

AIRCRAFT MANUFACTURERS

Some airports also have businesses that specialize in various aspects of aircraft manufacturing on their field. Aircraft manufacturers are often seen as a significant revenue source to the airport and represent jobs and economic stimulus to the community. Aircraft manufacturers occasionally conduct flight-testing at the airports with significant amounts of aircraft or aircraft component manufacturing are sometimes called "Industrial" airports. Although the FAA does not yet have a distinct category within the NPIAS for an Industrial Airport, the term is used by AAAE and some in the airport industry, to more accurately describe certain airports with dominant aircraft manufacturer tenants. Some aircraft manufacturers do not lease airport property, but either lease or own property adjacent to the airport and have an access agreement with airport management to use the landing facilities. Commonly called a **through-the-fence agreement**, airport Ops personnel may be required to monitor or facilitate access for any entity that holds through-the-fence privileges. A few airports also have aviation maintenance schools located adjacent to or on airport property, and may have occasion to access the airport to move an aircraft between the airfield and their school's maintenance facility.

TRANSPORTATION SECURITY ADMINISTRATION

TSA personnel are stationed at approximately 450 commercial service airports throughout the United States. In addition to the screeners, known as **Transportation Security Officers (TSOs)**, the TSA has security inspectors who ensure that the airport, aircraft operators, and air cargo operators are following their required security programs. Various other personnel, including bomb appraisal officers, behavior detection officers, Federal Security Directors, and Assistant Federal Security Directors, along with supervisory and management personnel overseeing the various security functions, are assigned.

On a daily basis, Airport Operations personnel have very little contact with the screener workforce. TSA personnel carry out screening functions both at passenger checkpoints and in checked baggage screening areas. TSA agents advise airport management and operational personnel of any significant issue arising at screening checkpoints. Typically, prohibited items are discovered at passenger screening checkpoints on a daily basis, and each case usually requires law enforcement response. Typically these issues are handled quickly and without significant disruption to passenger movement.

However, if a potential **improvised explosive device (IED)** or highly suspicious item is discovered, the airport operator must implement its incident management procedure as specified in the airport's ASP. TSA personnel may decide to evacuate the checkpoint or the checked bag screening resolution area. At the same time, local airport police, K-9 units, and bomb disposal personnel arrive at critical areas. Airport Operations personnel must now manage the shutdown of a screening checkpoint and make decisions about how best to handle the flow of passengers, while also preparing for the arrival of the FBI and other agencies that are part of the incident management action team.

The general public is most familiar with TSA TSOs conducting screening at the security checkpoints. In contrast, TSA **security inspectors** are lesser-known and typically do not wear a uniform of any type with the possible exception of a jacket with the words "TSA Inspector" inscribed across the back of the jacket. TSA security inspectors are an integral part of the aviation security system.

Inspectors can be found virtually anywhere within the airport environment—in the air operations, terminal, or landside areas—inspecting the airport and air carrier security procedures to ensure compliance with federal regulations. They have the authority to conduct tests of the security system and they often engage Airport Operations personnel in discussion about how certain security practices are being carried out. If an inspector finds a violation of the ASP, the inspector may issue a fine to the airport. Some of these findings range in the tens to hundreds of thousands of dollars.

By nature, Airport Operations personnel possess a higher knowledge of activities on the airfield and should therefore be trained and current in the requirements of the ASP. Ops personnel are often the primary enforcers of the ASP. They not only save the airport hundreds of thousands of dollars in fines, more importantly, they may prevent criminal or terrorist acts against the airport or the airlines. From a practical perspective, the airport Ops personnel initiate the Incident Command and response to security incidents and should therefore be thoroughly trained in security protocols, regulations, and best practices.

FEDERAL AVIATION ADMINISTRATION AND CONTROL TOWERS

A common misconception is that every airport has a control tower and that FAA personnel staff every airport with a control tower. Control towers are located at high-volume airports where safety is enhanced and aircraft separation is provided by an **air traffic control tower (ATCT)**. The FAA operates most ATCTs, but some airports with lower traffic volumes have contract towers, staffed by contract controllers rather than FAA personnel. Airports with even lower traffic volumes may operate using a **Unicom or Common Traffic Advisory Frequency (CTAF)**, which is a common radio frequency for pilots to seek or issue advisories regarding air traffic and airport conditions. The type of air traffic control provided at an airport is essential to processes that Airport Operations personnel use to manage the airport operating environment.

Personnel in the tower typically include at least two positions: "tower" and "ground." Tower controllers are responsible for air and vehicle traffic on the runway, as well as air traffic in the air traffic control pattern and within the immediate vicinity of the airport. Tower controllers may handle air traffic out to a distance of 10 miles or more, depending upon the coverage of other air traffic control facilities, such as Terminal Radar Approach Control Facilities (TRACON) or Air Route Traffic Control Centers (ARTCC). Ground controllers are responsible for the movement of aircraft, other vehicles, and personnel on taxiways in the AMA.

At airports with a control tower, Airport Operations and FAA controllers must work closely to ensure the safe and efficient flow of air traffic. While airport management controls the operation of the entire facility, the FAA air traffic controller is responsible for approving movement on the runway and taxiway system. When Airport Operations personnel must conduct inspections of the runway and taxiway, they must integrate with aircraft operations, receiving permission and instructions from the air traffic control ground controller. If there is an aircraft emergency, the response of police, fire, and other rescue units, along with Airport Operations and sometimes airport-maintenance and airline maintenance vehicles and personnel, must all be coordinated with the ATCT and ground controller.

At large-hub airports, multiple tower and ground controllers handle different sectors of the airfield. Some towers may have a **clearance delivery** function to provide flight clearance information to pilots entering the air traffic control system. Clearance delivery may also coordinate aircraft pushback and engine starts, but "ramp control" personnel may also handle this function at some airports. **Ramp controllers** may be Airport Operations personnel or airline operations personnel who coordinate movement of aircraft in the non-movement area.

In addition to air traffic control personnel, other FAA personnel at an airport include facilities maintenance, who are responsible for maintenance of the airport's NAVAIDS and approach lighting system; **Airport District Office (ADO)** inspectors, who oversee the airport's compliance with Part 139; and **Flight Standards District Office (FSDO)** personnel. FSDO inspectors possess specialized credentials and are authorized to conduct what are known as "line checks" or "ramp checks" on pilots and aircraft. These checks are conducted to ensure the pilot is operating the aircraft lawfully and safely. **Ramp checks** are not popular with pilots, and Airport Operations personnel may be called to assist with resolving disputes between the FSDO inspector and the pilot, or, in some extreme cases, an FAA inspector may find cause to ground an aircraft or a member of its flight crew, which may impact the flow of passenger and aircraft operations.

OTHER GOVERNMENT AGENCIES AT THE AIRPORT

A variety of other government agencies routinely operate at airports, and many others operate periodically. The CBP and the ICE agencies operate at airports with international traffic. Even small GA airports have occasional flights requiring customs services. If there are significant levels of international activities, a customs officer may be stationed at the airport, otherwise a CBP agent from a nearby area is requested to meet an incoming international flight.

International flights are an important source of revenue for an airport operator. International passengers stay longer in the community and tend to spend more money. Aircraft used for international traffic are considerably larger and heavier than aircraft used for domestic traffic. This results in higher landing fees, which are usually weight-based, and aircraft having to purchase more fuel at the airport, thereby increasing fuel flowage fees. International operations are also important to the community-at-large and are often a primary target for community and airport marketing efforts. Keeping international air carriers pleased with the services and access provided by the airport is critical to retaining international service.

Airport Operations personnel are frequently charged with assisting in customs operations, which may include, to the extent possible, ensuring efficient passenger flow, solving problems with respect to access between the international facility and domestic connecting flights, and providing general oversight of the customs and immigration activity. Airport Managers rely on Airport Operations personnel to solve problems such that international operations continue smoothly. A variety of other operations occur in the airport that require the Airport Operations personnel to work with other government agencies, including:

1. Working with U.S. Secret Service personnel to coordinate the arrival and departure of Air Force One. These operations often require significant levels of coordination with federal, state, and local law enforcement personnel, and personnel representing the President of the United States and the White House. When Air Force One is operating at the airport or within a certain area around the airport, all other aircraft traffic operations cease until the Secret Service determines that normal operations can resume. FAA-issued **Temporary Flight Restrictions (TFRs)** may also be in place during this time at the airport and in areas surrounding the airport.

2. Working with U.S. Department of State security personnel to coordinate movement of domestic and foreign diplomats through the airport.
3. Working with state and local law enforcement personnel to move local VIPs, such as politicians or high-profile celebrities, through the airport. While some in the public may disagree that these individuals should receive special handling because of their social status, Airport Managers understand that these persons might attract extraordinary amounts of attention, which disrupts passenger flow or, in some cases, increases security risks to the general public. Therefore, enhancing the movement of VIPs through the airport is in the airport's best interest. This task typically involves TSA personnel coordinating with Airport Operations personnel to meet the escorted VIP at a location other than the screening checkpoint. Often the VIP will meet Ops personnel at an airfield security gate or public parking area. The individual (or group) is then transported directly to the aircraft. TSA personnel will meet the Ops personnel and their escorted party to conduct the screening process. Prisoner escorts can also be conducted in this manner if the law enforcement office does not want to bring the prisoner through the screening checkpoint.
4. Ops personnel may be tasked with escorting personnel from other government agencies, such as the U.S. Environmental Protection Agency (EPA), U.S. Fish and Wildlife Service (USFWS) personnel, U.S. Department of Agriculture (USDA) personnel, and the FAA, to check on related issues on the airfield. While these personnel may be given an Airport Identification Badge, they are not typically granted driving privileges on the airfield for safety purposes.[15]

   In addition to government personnel requiring access to the airfield, numerous other nongovernmental agencies, such as contractors, vendors, or emergency-ambulance personnel, may require temporary access. The purposes and variety of entities that may require periodic access to the airfield are highly varied. Regardless, Ops is responsible for handling these demands. Airport Operations should also note when certain personnel require more than infrequent access and make recommendations to airport management that these individuals or companies go through the airport badging process, airport vehicle permitting process, and take the associated driver training if needed. Ops should also confirm that third-party vehicles and equipment used by these personnel and companies meet minimum standards on insurance requirements.

CORE FUNCTIONS OF AIRPORT OPERATIONS

Essentially, Airport Operations ensures that the airport continues to function, with Airport Operations personnel solving foreseeable problems, such as snow and other weather-related events, airfield construction, presidential movement, and ensuring rapid response to unforeseeable events, including aircraft emergencies. Regardless of the size of the airport, the core functions operations are relatively similar from one airport to the next.

---

[15]Driving on the airfield is a hazardous activity; the privilege of such should only be granted to individuals who have been trained and have a need to access the Air Operations Area on a regular basis.

AIRPORT INSPECTION

Airports operating under Part 139 are required to have a self-inspection program, whereby certain areas of the Air Operations Area are inspected. These areas include pavement, safety areas, NAVAIDS, airfield lighting, and other areas monitored on a continuous basis for movement of personnel and vehicles on the airfield, wildlife hazards, and other risks. Airports not adhering to Part 139 may still conduct inspections as part of best practices and to help ensure the airport meets the grant assurance requirement #19 (maintenance and operations) for maintaining the airport in a safe and serviceable condition. Inspector personnel must be trained how to conduct the inspection, including how to report deficiencies. Inspections constitute a core function of Airport Operations.

Operations personnel may also conduct terminal inspections and landside-area inspections. While not regulated, terminal and landside inspections ensure that the airport is running smoothly overall and that any hazards, issues, or problems are identified and addressed immediately. At small airports, the airfield inspector may also be responsible for inspecting terminal and landside operations, whereas at large-hub airports, these functions are typically divided into individual areas of responsibility. Since airports are highly complex systems, they must have a well-organized, coordinated, and efficient inspection system to operate effectively.

AIRPORT COMMUNICATIONS

Operations and Communications Centers

A well-organized and efficient communication (comm) and coordination system is also necessary to operate an airport effectively. The central hub of an airport is often called the communications center (or comm center), security operations center, dispatch, Airport Operations or command center, along with other variations (refer to Figure 3.3). The term **comm center** is typically used when referring to the location where communications and monitoring equipment is housed and where communications center–related personnel operate. In this text, the term **Airport Operations Center**, or Ops center, refers to the general area where Airport Operations personnel conduct business. The Ops center usually includes the comm center, emergency dispatch, the **security operations center (SOC)**, the **maintenance control center (MCC)**, and the **Emergency Operations Center (EOC)**, also known as the **incident command center (ICC)**. Usually, comm center personnel have the expertise to quickly implement and support the EOC, powering up the required equipment, establishing access controls for the room, and patching in communications systems.

Communications Center

The hub of airport Ops is the comm center. Its core functions include weather monitoring and communicating with airfield, terminal, and landside operations personnel to support the airport Ops functions. Comm center personnel have access to and are commonly trained on the use of weather and communication reporting systems, the use of radio dispatch panels, basic telephony and office software systems, and on how to issue FAA NOTAMs. Ops personnel are often the key coordinators of airport functions, particularly during emergency or irregular operations, and they primarily serve internal stakeholders, including airport management and other operational and maintenance personnel, air carriers requesting information, and tenant issues. Some communications centers also serve public address operations functions (i.e., the white paging telephone). Communications constitute a primary core function of Airport Operations.

FIGURE 3.3

Example of an Airport Communications Center.

Courtesy of Denver International Airport.

Security Operations Center

Security technology, alarm doors, closed circuit television (CCTV), and radio dispatch of security officers or Airport Operations personnel are commonly housed in the airport communications center. Personnel monitor the airport **Access Control and Alarm Monitoring System (ACAMS)**, which monitors doors accessing Security Areas of the airport. SOC personnel also monitor fire-alarmed doors, which are tied into the ACAMS. When a door alarm occurs, SOC personnel may be able to obtain a camera feed with the particular door associated with the alarm. However, not all security doors at all airports are covered by CCTV, as this is not presently required by TSA. ACAMS will usually give an indication to the SOC operator about the nature of the alarm and may suggest a level of response. Door alarms often sound when:

1. An aviation employee with a valid identification badge attempts to access the door to which the employee is not authorized access. Many times the employee who attempted to access the door will figure out he or she does not have access and go to another door, resulting in the alarm being cleared and no further response being necessary.
2. An unauthorized individual attempts to access a door or successfully accesses a door to a Security Area. This situation results in a door-forced type of alarm to which a security, Ops, or law enforcement officer is dispatched to further investigate the cause. It is common for this alarm to result in the escort of the unauthorized individual back out of the Security Area and into the public area. These alarms tend to happen with individuals who desire to smoke or have made a mistake in attempting to access another part of the airport. In extreme cases, this can be considered a security breach if the individual cannot be immediately found.

The airport may be required to close for a short period of time while the individual is located and the incident investigated.

3. An authorized individual leaves the door open after properly accessing the Security Area. This situation may occur when wind or other weather elements keep the door from shutting properly or when air carrier personnel are boarding the flight, and the door stays open too long. Enforcement action might be taken against the individual that last accessed the door. Sometimes this action is conducted at the discretion of SOC staff, or the case may be referred to the **Airport Security Coordinator (ASC)** for resolution.

4. Personnel in the SOC might also be responsible for monitoring perimeter intrusions, including any installed **perimeter intrusion detection systems (PIDS)**. When an intrusion is detected, a combination of law enforcement, security, and Airport Operations personnel usually respond. Law enforcement personnel take responsibility for apprehending the intruder; security personnel take responsibility for securing the breached area; and operations personnel may have to shut down runways or the airport to ensure the safety of flight operations until the incident is resolved.

Police, Fire, and Emergency Medical Dispatch

Calls for service from police, firefighting, and emergency medical personnel are handled by dispatchers. Dispatch personnel prioritize incoming calls, assess the appropriate responder and level of response, and determine which calls have a more urgent need for response and dispatch personnel. They may also coordinate other responders from neighboring agencies and provide essential information to response personnel about the nature of the incident or individuals involved.

Many states require that dispatchers be certified through an approved certificate program. As a result of this requirement, dispatchers may be different staff from other communications center personnel. Some airports have dispatchers that only handle police, fire, and emergency medical service (EMS) calls, while other, nondispatch certified personnel handle other calls from security and Airport Operations personnel. Some airports have cross-trained their communications center personnel to handle all functions, including emergency dispatch. In some cases, the police dispatch personnel will also dispatch security officer personnel.[16]

At some airports, dispatch is handled by an offsite, emergency call center that handles dispatch functions for a regional area that includes the airport. Large-hub airports typically have their own police, fire, and emergency medical service dispatch centers onsite. This configuration allows better coordination between responding parties on the airfield, but may cause some issues between on- and offsite responders (i.e., mutual aid response). Whether to have on- or offsite dispatching is a consideration for each airport operator and its unique situation.

NOTIFICATIONS

Airports with an Airport Emergency Plan are required to have a notification process for certain incidents, such as an airplane crash or power outage of the airfield lighting system. However, many airports have notification lists for a variety of airport events, such as severe weather in the forecast, or other

---

[16]Security officers are typically unarmed and nonsworn.

incidents and emergencies. A common function of Airport Operations is to act as the initiator of the notification function. This system can be as elementary as a phone call list to other response agencies and personnel, or advanced electronic notification software that allows for critical communications to go out through SMS (short message service), text, email, telephone, or other systems. Certain systems are highly complex and use GPS (Global Positioning System) to allow comm center personnel to see the locations of recipients of the notifications. This location information may assist personnel in coordinating their response to the incident. Operations personnel ensure updates to the notification lists, ensure individuals on the list are in receipt of their notifications, and handle questions and inquiries from notified personnel, while continuously providing additional guidance and information as available.

WEATHER MONITORING AND REPORTING

Weather can significantly affect the operation of an airport. Snowstorms, blizzards, thunderstorms, lightning, tornadoes, hurricanes, and any other severe weather can result in small reductions of airport capacity to widespread shutdowns of the airport and airspace around the region and may even cause damage to the airport. Poor weather conditions can affect flight and ground operations, strand passengers in the terminal building for days, threaten the safety of personnel on the airfield, or prevent access to the airport as a consequence of the shutdown of the surrounding access routes to the airport. Therefore, airports must have highly accurate weather monitoring and comm reporting capabilities.

Airports may have access to local **Doppler radar** feeds, satellite weather reporting data and **Automated Weather Observing Systems (AWOSs),**[17] **Low-Level Windshear Alert Systems (LLWASs),**[18] and **Automated Surface Observing Systems (ASOSs)** (Figure 3.4), which are on-airport, weather-reporting facilities. Depending on the model, AWOS can report:

1. Barometric pressure, necessary for proper aircraft altimeter settings.
2. Wind speed, wind direction, wind gusts, variable wind direction, temperature, dew point, and density altitude.
3. Visibility and precipitation. More complex models identify the type of precipitation (rain, drizzle, freezing rain, snow) and the rate at which the precipitation is accumulating.
4. Ceilometer, which provides cloud height, cloud density, and sky condition.
5. The most capable AWOSs provide lightning strike data and a freezing rain sensor to detect the presence of icing conditions. Icing has been responsible for several Aircraft Accidents throughout aviation's history.

Airport operators often subscribe to specialized, commercial, weather-reporting services and may have direct access to personnel at the **National Weather Service (NWS)**. With the integration

---

[17]Automated Weather Observing System (AWOS) units are operated and controlled by the FAA. These systems are among the oldest automated weather stations and predate the Automated Surface Observing System (ASOS). They generally report at 20-minute intervals and do not report special observations for rapidly changing weather conditions (such as ASOS). National Oceanic and Atmospheric Administration. (n.d.). *Automated Weather Observing System (AWOS)*. Retrieved from: http://ncdc.noaa.gov/data-access/land-based-station-data/land-based-datasets/automated-weather-observing-system-awos (for information regarding ASOS, see http://ncdc.noaa.gov/data-access/land-based-station-data/land-based-datasets/automated-surface-observing-system-asos)

[18]LLWAS provides wind shear and microburst alerts to controllers and pilots operating in the airport area.

FIGURE 3.4

Automated Weather Observation Station.

Source: National Oceanic and Atmospheric Administration.

of **Next Generation Air Transportation System (NextGen)**, the FAA's term for the overall upgrade to the national air traffic control and National Airspace System, airports will have access to **System Wide Integration Management (SWIM)**. According to the FAA:

> SWIM is a FAA advanced technology program designed to facilitate an increased common situational awareness, and a greater sharing of Air Traffic Management (ATM) system information. As one of the five transformational NextGen programs, SWIM is the infrastructure that allows members of the aviation community to access the information needed to facilitate an innovative and efficiently run National Airspace System (NAS). With SWIM at the heart of the NAS, users will have real-time access to the information they need when they need it.[19]

SWIM solves an existing problem by integrating a variety of data systems, including weather (including graphical depictions), communication radar information, traffic flow management systems, and software that analyzes en route flight plan changes, arrival and departure procedures, microburst information, NOTAMs, storm cells, wind shear, and terminal area winds aloft. The FAA website includes information about how to access SWIM products. SWIM is presently available to the airlines, airports, research and development industries, including academic institutions, and other industries, such as aerospace manufacturers and operators.

---

[19]FAA. (n.d.). System Wide Information Management: SWIM questions and answers. Retrieved from: http://www.faa .gov/nextgen/programs/swim/qanda/

SWIM's complexity is beyond the scope of this text, but includes benefits for allowing aviation stakeholders to communicate with each other—the FAA cites an example where airline operations, air traffic managers and controllers, Federal Air Marshals, and the military have shared information in real time via SWIM. In this way, SWIM has benefits for aviation safety, security, capacity, traffic flow, and operations.

AIRPORT MAINTENANCE AND SYSTEM MONITORING

Airport maintenance and system monitoring includes heating, ventilation, air conditioning, electricity, water supply and wastewater management, and, at certain airports, train transit systems. Larger airports may have a separate **Maintenance Control Center (MCC)** where these monitoring functions are carried out. MCC personnel dispatch electricians, plumbers, and others to fix problems when they arise.

Maintenance and communicating the needs and status of maintenance are absolutely critical to an airport's operation. However, *maintenance* is a specialized field, often requiring certifications and special training (electrician, diesel mechanic, etc.). Therefore, it is common for a small airport with minimal staff to first implement a maintenance division or department, and then task maintenance personnel with Ops-related functions. As the airport grows in capacity and size, an Ops department is usually then established, and maintenance is then rolled into the domain of operations.

SUMMARY

All public-use airports that receive federal funds are required to adhere to **grant assurances**. Commercial service airports must adhere to Title 14 CFR Part 139, which means meeting certain safety requirements for the operation of the airfield. All public-use airports, including GA airports, must also meet high standards of safety, as articulated through the *Airport Compliance Manual*. The airport operator enforces safety on the airfield through the use of **minimum standards**, rules, and regulations. Airport Operations personnel are typically charged with enforcing rules and regulations, notifying law enforcement when appropriate, and enforcing certain requirements of the airport's minimum standards or individual, tenant-lease requirements.

The list of companies and individuals that operate routinely on an airfield is long and is reliant upon Airport Operations personnel to keep the airport operating in a safe and serviceable manner by solving problems as they arise and maximizing efficiencies of passenger, baggage, and cargo. The operations personnel are critical to the airport revenue function. When passenger throughput slows down, or when flight operations slow down, the reduced capacity has a direct financial impact on the airport revenue stream. Oftentimes, Airport Operations personnel do not have the ability to solve the problem directly but must work through others to solve problems.

The core functions of Airport Operations are **communication**, **notification**, and **operational coordination** of the airport's assets, equipment, and personnel to ensure the safe, secure, and efficient movement of passengers, cargo, and aircraft. This role includes conducting airport inspections, to comply with Title 14 CFR Part 139, and also to identify hazards and issues in the terminal and landside areas, as well as monitoring systems and resolving problems, such as maintenance issues, communications, and response.

Reflections on the Airport Communications Center

by Meredith Champlin
Airport Operations Representative, Denver International Airport

A colleague of mine, Erik Conerty of Denver International Airport, once remarked to me that the Airport Communications Center [Comm] is the heartbeat of the airport. It is the epicenter through which all information regarding operations in, on, and around the airport is vetted. Maintaining the safety and security of an airport is the most integral purpose of a Comm Center. The center functions 24 hours every day as support to airport management in standard and nonstandard operations, as well as emergency events. Those who staff the Comm Center are responsible for surveillance, dispatching appropriate emergency response personnel to real-time events, and connecting different agencies and airport affiliates to the appropriate parties. Logging and recording events that take place are also important aspects of the Comm Center operation. In the day-to-day commotion of a busy airport environment, in which thousands of employees are working every day and millions of passengers are traveling through every year, the Airport Communications Center is fast paced, with assorted, and challenging operations.

The Comm Center is composed of four major stations with their own designated responsibilities: (a) the Comm Station, (b) the Security Station, (c) the Emergency Dispatcher or Aviation Emergency Dispatch (AED) Station, and (d) the Supervisor Station. The person operating the Comm Station has a wide range of responsibilities. He or she is the main point of contact for Airport Operations and therefore is in the main position to disseminate and relay information to different agencies airport-wide. Standard operations include monitoring and recording weather, issuing NOTAMs (notices to airmen), relaying pertinent information to airfield and Terminal Operations Managers, advising airport maintenance of repair and preventative maintenance issues, monitoring fire systems within the airport, and dispatching fire department structural units and ARFF (Aircraft Rescue and Firefighting) to emergency events such as fires, fuel spills, serious medical calls, and aircraft alerts. During emergency events the Comm Station is responsible for notifying and dispatching appropriate parties and acting as support to Airport Operations management, who in the event of significant emergencies default to the Incident Command System (ICS). In these situations the Emergency Operations Center (EOC) is activated and a Comm Center representative responds to assist as a liaison between the EOC and the Comm Center, and as a situation unit and document unit leader.

The most significant emergency event at an airport is an "aircraft alert," which is an aircraft, either on the ground or airborne, that is known or suspected to have an operational defect, and an aircraft-related emergency is possible, imminent, or has occurred. Aircraft alerts are typically activated by the FAA Tower. The Tower reports on which runway the aircraft will land, the type of aircraft and call sign/airline, the issue the aircraft is having (initially reported by the pilot who requests an emergency landing or priority landing), the number of Souls on Board, the amount of Fuel on Board, and the estimated time of arrival. The Comm Station is responsible for notifying all the proper responding agencies to standby

(Continued)

(Continued)

(or in ARFF situations, to respond near the runway where the aircraft will be landing) in case there is an accident or incident.

The Security Station is responsible for ensuring that the integrity of Airport Security is not compromised. Responsibilities include camera surveillance, monitoring the access control system for the airport doors and gates, issuing Violation Notices to airport employees who violate security regulations, and communicating with and dispatching contract security guards to different events. Apart from the surveillance cameras and security software programs, security guards are the "eyes and ears" for the Security Station; they respond to any alarm or event requested by the Security Station operator, and report any event(s) taking place that require further action or additional personnel. Operators on the Security Station are also required to cross-reference, validate, and in some cases retrieve and cancel employee Security Identification Display Area (SIDA) badges.

The AED Station is responsible for monitoring and dispatching police and paramedics. Airport jurisdiction 911 calls are routed to the AED Station in the Comm Center, and operators are responsible for dispatching the appropriate emergency response personnel and notifying the other Comm Center stations, which then initiate designated notifications and checklists. Larger airports can be equated to small cities, and the different types of emergencies that take place in cities will happen at the airport. These emergencies can vary from medical events that need paramedic response, vehicle accidents, domestic disputes, and airport or aircraft disturbances, to passengers attempting to travel with weapons or drugs. AEDs can also receive reports from other districts or agencies to be on the lookout for certain individuals (reasons vary from wanted criminals, to individuals in need of mental health treatment, to lost children). AEDs can also receive reports from flight crews advising of unruly passengers, medical problems on board, and incoming flight diverts for any number of reasons.

The Comm Center Supervisor Station monitors the other three stations and is a liaison between the Comm Center and airport management, and agencies such as the police, FBI, TSA, National Weather Service, the Airport Security Coordinator (ASC), and the Public Information Officer (PIO). The on-duty Comm Center Supervisor must ensure all appropriate information is disseminated correctly and that the Communications, Security, and AED operators are all on task and performing their functions correctly. The Comm Center Supervisor can also act as a relief or backup support to any station operator who needs a break or has become inundated with simultaneous events and emergencies.

In addition to aircraft alerts, each station operator is trained to respond to severe weather events that could be potential safety hazards for employees and the traveling public (tornadoes, severe thunderstorms, snow storms, etc.), suspicious items or bomb threats, aircraft hijackings, security breaches, HAZMAT[20] spills, infrastructure and landside damage/accidents, and police matter events, just to name a few. All Comm Center stations respond to these emergencies in different ways and have specific checklists to follow in response to

(Continued)

---

[20]HAZMAT, hazardous materials (or Dangerous Goods). See International Air Transportation Association (IATA)'s guide to HAZMAT regulations at http://www.iata.org/whatwedo/cargo/dgr/Pages/index.aspx

(Continued)

potential events. A Comm Center employee must have a team-player mentality and have exceptional communication skills. Operators at each station are expected and trained to act as support structures to one another. It is common that Comm Center personnel are qualified to operate multiple if not all stations and are able to pick up the slack for their partners during busy periods. Being that emergencies are not planned, they can occur at the most inconvenient times and often simultaneously. It is not uncommon for different new emergencies to occur as a result of an already existing emergency taking place, adding to the complexity of a situation. For this reason, Comm Center personnel must be ready to act at a moment's notice and be dexterous at prioritizing and juggling multiple events. The ability to possess situational awareness, being able to anticipate what actions need to be taken next, and taking proactive measures are intrinsic aspects to functioning in the Comm Center.

The Airport Communications Center is a challenging, bustling environment dealing with situations ranging from standard operating procedures to matters requiring actions that can mean the difference between life and death. Operating in the Comm Center can be compared to flying an airplane—repetitively monitoring the cockpit instrumentation, completing routine procedures, and staying calm and relying on training and checklists when something goes wrong. In the nonstop effort to keep an airport running and operating as smoothly as possible, the Communications Center plays an important and essential role, always keeping the safety of the airport's employees and the traveling public at heart.

REFERENCES

Federal Aviation Administration (FAA). (n.d.a). Joint Civilian/Military (Joint-Use) Airports. Retrieved December 21, 2015, from: < http://www.faa.gov/airports/aip/military_airport_program/joint_use_airports/ > .

Federal Aviation Administration (FAA). (n.d.b). Definitions. Retrieved December 21, 2015, from: < http://www.faa.gov/airports/airport_safety/part139_cert/definitions/#shared > .

Federal Aviation Administration (FAA). (2009). *Lifetime of airport real property or useful life of equipment under Surplus Property Act of 1944. Order 5190.6b.* Washington, DC: Federal Aviation Administration. Retrieved from: http://www.faa.gov/airports/resources/publications/orders/compliance_5190_6/media/5190_6b_chap3.pdf.

Prock, G. (2010). *Notice to Airmen (NOTAM): Procedures update: Issuing a NOTAM today digital NOTAM tomorrow.* Retrieved from https://www.faa.gov/about/office_org/headquarters_offices/arc/programs/pacific_aviation_directors_workshop/2010/media/0415_10am_prock.pdf.

SAFETY MANAGEMENT SYSTEMS & AIRPORT OPERATIONS: PART I

4

Aircraft Rescue and Firefighting (ARFF) at Denver International Airport's runway 16R/34L, which is a 16,000-foot-long, 200-foot-wide concrete runway.

Courtesy Denver International Airport, CO [date unknown].

Fueling operation at Denver International Airport, CO.

Image by Shahn Sederberg, courtesy Colorado Division of Aeronautics, 2012.

SAFETY MANAGEMENT SYSTEMS

The core function of Airport Operations has been, and remains, to operate the airport in a safe, secure, and efficient manner. A key component contributing to this success has been the evolution of Airport Operations in conceptualizing and implementing safety-related policies and practices. Over time, these efforts have become essential to formalizing a highly defined **Safety Management System (SMS)**. As will be explored in this chapter, an SMS is made up of a proactive, systematic, and prescriptive set of guidelines, policies, and practices for managing safety at a particular airport, airline, or general aviation (GA)–related operation. The Federal Aviation Administration (FAA) defines SMS as a "formal, top-down business-like approach to managing safety risk. It includes systematic procedures, practices, and policies for the management of safety (including safety risk management, safety policy, safety assurance, and safety promotion)" (FAA, 2007).

MOTIVATIONS FOR AVIATION SAFETY

The need for enhanced safety methods, such as SMS, has been motivated primarily by economic losses to national societies and commerce resulting from incidents and accidents. From these losses to both life and infrastructure, policies and laws were created to mandate methods for reducing risk in aviation. However, the Airport Operations Manager must be cognizant of the need for safety to be grounded in ethical and societal values and not solely based on economic loss. To be proactive, and to create a "safety culture," the astute aviation professional recognizes that the need for continuous enhanced safety is propagated not only from economic concerns, but also from an ethical need to contribute to the safety and well-being of global society.

Aviation in itself is not inherently dangerous. But to an even greater degree than the sea, it is terribly unforgiving of any carelessness, incapacity or neglect.

FIGURE 4.1 Any human endeavor carries some risk.

Even though flying remains one of the safest forms of transportation, proactive safety management relies on the assumption that flight will always be subject to hazards and human error.

Aviation is considered one of the safest forms of transportation. According to the National Safety Council, the odds of an individual dying in a traffic accident over his or her lifetime are 1 in 212 compared to 1 in 8,012 for flying or space-related fatalities (2010). Nonetheless, accidents still occur, and in most of these cases, the root cause of the accident is a safety-related failure that most likely could have been prevented (Figure 4.1). No longer is it acceptable for Airport Managers to employ a reactive safety policy, essentially waiting until an accident occurs to determine what new procedure should be implemented to avoid recurrence.

Proactive systems for managing aviation safety are now a global concern. In 2005, the **International Civil Aviation Organization (ICAO)** required SMS to be developed and implemented by member states to manage safety risks in air operations, maintenance, air traffic control, flight training, aircraft manufacturing, and Airport Operations (FAA, 2014a). In response, U.S. airlines are now required to have formal SMS programs in place by 2018 (Safety Management Systems, 14 CFR § 119.8, 2015). The FAA is now evaluating and encouraging U.S. Part 139 airports to develop and implement SMS for operational concerns. As part of this effort, the FAA issued Advisory Circular 150/5200-37, *Introduction to Safety Management Systems (SMS) for Airport Operators*, to serve as recommended guidelines for implementing SMS in Airport Operations (FAA, 2007). In early 2015, the FAA was still in the rulemaking stage for implementing or mandating SMS at Part 139 airports. Finalization of the rulemaking process to establish SMS as mandatory for Part 139 airports is anticipated by the spring of 2016.

AIRPORT SAFETY AND SAFETY MANAGEMENT SYSTEMS

When SMS was first introduced in the United States, many professionals in Airport Operations perceived that Part 139 had already been established as equivalent to an SMS. Others in aviation considered SMS only to apply to special projects, such as airport construction. Therefore, SMS has been traditionally implemented in U.S. Airport Operations on an ad hoc basis. However, SMS is more than an airfield safety program established by the FAA for commercial service airports. With aviation's current, relatively low rate of accidents, it is difficult to continue making safety improvements without a proactive approach to managing safety that concentrates on the control of processes and makes safety a fully integrated part of the business operation. Consequently, SMS is being mandated or otherwise adopted in many areas of commercial aviation and GA settings within the United States and throughout the world.

SMS is becoming a global, industry standard in aviation safety. Commercial airlines, corporate operators, helicopter operators, and other stakeholders in aviation have implemented SMS in their operations. Similar forms of SMS are used in the medical and occupational health industries. SMS-type programs are used in other fields such as security and environmental management.

Featuring a formal, top-down, business-like approach to managing safety, an SMS is built on four fundamental principles identified by the **Airport Cooperative Research Program (ACRP)** (Ludwig, Andrews, Jester-ten Veen, Laqui, & MITRE, 2007). These principles are:

1. Management commitment to safety
2. Proactive identification of hazards
3. Actions taken to manage risks
4. Evaluation of safety actions

THE EVOLUTION OF SAFETY AND SAFETY MANAGEMENT SYSTEMS IN THE UNITED STATES

SMS is focused on implementing a holistic approach to safety decision making throughout the organization. In the United States, the FAA's adoption of SMS is part of the FAA's continuous effort to improve safety throughout the domain of aviation—commercial and GA. Early aviation pioneers operated aircraft prior to government safety regulations and relied more on practical experience to guide them (FAA, 2014b). Over time, regulations were implemented mostly as a result of accidents. For many decades subsequent to the advent of human flight, the traditional approach to preventing accidents was reactive in response to lessons learned from prior accidents. New safety policies and regulations were born from what was discovered from accidents as they occurred, rather than a proactive approach identifying existing risk factors that could contribute to accidents, and addressing those risks prior to a resulting incident or accident. As accidents occurred, investigators focused on probable causes, which they often determined to be unsafe acts by personnel; then blame was usually attached and punishment meted out for failure to perform safely. This process identifies under what conditions an incident occurred, including what occurred, who was involved, and when the incident took place. The process often left out the "why and how" of contributing factors leading up to the accident that could have been identified prior to the accident; such "why and how" could have been used to prevent future accidents (International Civil Aviation Organization, 2013).

Improvements in technology, such as structural design and aircraft performance, navigational aids, and weather reporting and communication systems, have contributed tremendously to gains in aviation safety. With these gains came the realization that accidents were attributed less to failures in technology, and more to human error. A prime example is low performance by crew in coordination and communication amongst flight deck personnel. By the 1980s, the industry began to focus more on the human aspect of safety with programs such as **cockpit resource management (CRM)** and human factors engineering in aviation. The new millennium is witnessing a shift in focus to enhanced safety performance by all stakeholders in an organization. That focus in the aviation industry is being built with SMS as a primary construct. A tragic example of a lack of organizational performance as related to safety is the explosion of the Space Shuttle *Challenger* in 1986, as described in the following case description.

CASE STUDY

Space Shuttle *Challenger* & Organizational Safety

In her book *The Challenger Launch Decision: Risky Technology, Culture and Deviance at NASA*, Diane Vaughan posits that the *Challenger* explosion was the result of several factors, each pointing to the **safety culture** of the organization, rather than the actions of a particular individual (1996, p. 204). Vaughan uses the term *normalization of deviance* to describe a situation when a deviation from the standard occurs, no incident happens as a result, and therefore the deviation becomes the new standard (p. 78).

An example of the normalization of deviation can be found in the traditional "California stop," which is widely interpreted to mean a rolling stop at a stop sign, without the vehicle coming to a complete stop. A driver may stop the first time at a particular stop sign, notice that there are no hazards, and proceed normally. The second time, the driver might not come to a complete stop, still notice no hazards, and continue on her way. The third time the driver again does not come to a complete stop and continues on her way without incident. Eventually, rolling through the stop sign becomes the normal behavior. This intentional error, also referred to as *practical drift*, increases the possibility of an accident (or a ticket for failing to stop at a stop sign). Vaughan pointed out a five-step process that resulted in the tragedy:

1. Rationalizing 'signals' or evidence of potential danger (O-ring failures in testing) as indications equating to near normal operating performance;
2. Official act acknowledging the escalated risk (Thiokol notifying NASA of the issue) was tempered and delayed in the technical brief so as to appear the warning to be of only minor concern;
3. Review of the risk (by NASA) lead to rationalized and false confidence;
4. Official act indicating the normalization of deviance (rationalizing/accepting the risk) was reached after one engineer was censured for directly indicating the severity of the risk;
5. Decision to launch the Shuttle resulting in its destruction immediately after launch (p. 78).

In NASA's case and according to a U.S. Presidential Commission, Morton Thiokol, the contractor who manufactured the failed O-rings that would eventually doom the shuttle, did not accept the implication of its tests early in the program that the design had a serious and unanticipated flaw (Vaughan, 1996, p. 90). NASA further did not accept the judgment of its own engineers that the design was unacceptable. Eventually, the workgroup involved in launching *Challenger* normalized the statistical deviation of booster technology (p. 91).

In November 2005, the ICAO amended Annex 14, Volume I (Airport Design and Operations) to require member states to have certificated international airports establish an SMS (2013, p. 1.11). The goal of this requirement is to utilize SMS as a means to identify, examine, and evaluate safety in the decision-making process surrounding aviation operations. It allows an organization to adapt safety-related strategies and tactics to elements of operational change, such as increasing operational complexities and limited resources or funds. An SMS also promotes the continuous improvement of safety through specific methods and processes that attempt to identify existing hazards and predict potential ones. Since ICAO's 2005 amendment, SMS has generated wide support, as it delivers definable safety and financial benefits. For example, airport operators adopting SMS may see a reduction in lawsuits, worker's compensation claims, and damage to equipment, while recognizing an increase in revenue and perceived societal value, or goodwill, of their airport to the public.

In 2010, the **Notice of Proposed Rulemaking (NPRM)**[1] for SMS for Part 121 air carrier operators was introduced, with the final rule published on January 8, 2015 (Office of the Federal Register, 2011). The rule requires operators to develop and implement a formal SMS. The FAA also provides guidance for the voluntary implementation of SMS for non–Part 121 operators, including maintenance, repair, and overhaul (MRO) facilities and training organizations.

In February 2007, the FAA issued Advisory Circular (AC) 150/5200-37: *Introduction to Safety Management Systems*. The AC was issued prior to the rulemaking for SMS for airports, which was introduced in 2008, but as of this writing, final rulemaking has not been published. Although it was expected in January 2015, the final rulemaking will not likely be published until 2016. However, several airport operators have already created and implemented SMS at their airports, based on the guidance in the FAA AC, and some were part of FAA SMS test programs.

BENEFITS OF SAFETY MANAGEMENT SYSTEMS

SMS allows an organization to identify potential hazards and to assess areas of risk and other weaknesses before problems arise. With an SMS, airport operators manage risk by creating a specific response and action appropriate to each problem. Additionally, operators can continually monitor and mitigate risks. Trends suggest that SMS will become the prime safety program for commercial service airports in the United States as a result of the many benefits recognized by airport operators who have adopted SMS into their organizational safety programs. These benefits include:

1. The proactive prevention of accidents and incidents;
2. An organizational culture committed to safety because of a systemwide, operational ethic rather than economic motivation;
3. Access to data and information necessary to impel policy makers to fund safety-related projects and to prioritize funding requests;
4. Sustainable standard operating procedures (SOPs);
5. Enhanced management of airport emergencies through more effective risk identification and mitigation; and
6. Increased compliance with safety rules by workers.

(See also the ACRP summation in Figure 4.2.)

---

[1]Notice of Proposed Rulemaking (NPRM) is an official document announcing and explaining an agency's plan to address a problem or accomplish a goal. All proposed rules must be published in the *Federal Register* to notify the public and to give the public an opportunity to submit comments. The proposed rule and the public comments received on it form the basis of the final rule. See https://www.federalregister.gov/uploads/2011/01/the_rulemaking_process.pdf

1. Reduction of costs of accidents, directly and indirectly: fewer fines and repairs costs and reduced insurance premiums.
2. Improved employee morale and productivity by promoting communication between management and staff and throughout the organization.
3. The establishment of a marketable safety record of consistently safe operations that can be used to attract new business and new investment into the airport.
4. A logical prioritization of safety needs through the emphasis of risk mitigation actions, providing the biggest impact on safety and to the airport bottom line.
5. Compliance with legal responsibilities for safety. While SMS is directly related to establishing safety programs for the airfield, additional benefits are derived from implementing SMS throughout the entire airport operation and in all areas.
6. More efficient maintenance scheduling and resource utilization through the reporting of hazards and proactive scheduling of maintenance tasks.
7. Avoidance of incident investigation costs and operational disruptions through improved communication and risk mitigation, which will prevent many accidents from occurring.
8. Continuous improvement of operational processes by the incorporation of lessons learned.

FIGURE 4.2

ACRP summation on SMS.

Source: Airport Cooperative Research Program (ACRP) Report 1 Safety Management Systems for Airports Volume 1: Overview identified several additional benefits of implementing SMS.

Despite the many advantages of SMS, airport operators have been reluctant to implement the program, many of them fearing that they will spend money on a program that is not yet federally approved, only to have the final rule change significantly from the proposed rule. However, regulations should never have to precede effective safety practices.

Some airport operators hesitate to implement SMS at their airports until the federal government issues its final rulemaking on airport-related SMS processes and requirements. Nevertheless, once implemented, any safety program can help establish one of the key principles of SMS, which is the **culture of safety**. Tim O'Krongley, assistant director of Airport Operations at the San Antonio International Airport, contends that if airport-related SMS federal rulemaking changes significantly from the current NPRM, the fact that San Antonio has already implemented SMS will make it easier to adapt to the changes rather than to start from scratch—primarily because the culture of safety has already been imbued in the organization.

THE FOUR PILLARS OF SAFETY MANAGEMENT SYSTEMS

SMS extend responsibility for safe operations throughout all levels and segments of an organization. This effort increases the number of stakeholders looking for safety issues and, therefore, reduces the chance of an undetected hazard. The prime safety hazard throughout all of aviation has been, and remains, **human error**, or human factors. Human error directly affects organizational performance in safety management. Therefore, a prime focus of SMS is to address human error.

One approach to mitigating human error was proposed by James Reason and is now well established as **Reason's Swiss Cheese Model** (Figure 4.3) (Reason, 2000). Reason describes four layers of human error, with each influencing the next. Working backward from the adverse event, the first level depicts the unsafe act that ultimately led to the mishap. In Reason's model, the diagram represents a generic organization with four segments, such as facilities, operations, safety, and management. Reason's original model included the following four elements: (a) organizational factors, (b) unsafe supervision, (c) preconditions for unsafe acts, and (d) unsafe acts.

A properly designed SMS should have a customized set of safety "layers"—policies, procedures, regulations, training, and other strategies, designed to create a culture of safety within an organization. Each of these layers has inherent risks, or holes (see Figure 4.3), symbolizing the potential for a safety hazard to lead to an incident or accident. However, when the layers are unified through SMS, a hazard is much less likely to penetrate all levels without being identified and mitigated (FAA, 2007, pp. 2–3). For example, Figure 4.4 demonstrates how a threat to safety is able to permeate the layers of policy and procedures, yet some aspect of training blocked the threat from moving through the SMS and causing or contributing to an accident or incident.

Annex 6 to the ICAO Chicago Convention requires member states to call for its commercial service airport operators to implement an SMS that includes the following safety principles: (a) hazard identification, (b) remedial actions used to maintain an acceptable level of safety, (c) continuous monitoring, (d) assessment of the safety level achieved, and (e) continuous improvement to the overall level of safety. An SMS is also dependent on the safety qualities inherent to the following efforts: (a) management's commitment to safety, (b) proactive identification of hazards, (c) actions taken to mitigate risk, and (d) evaluation of safety actions. These four elements are critical to the success of a sustainable SMS program in any organization.

The aforementioned principles and qualities form the philosophical foundation of **ICAO's Four Pillars of SMS**. The topology (pillars) establishes the cornerstones needed to develop, implement, and sustain a proactive SMS program (see Figure 4.5).

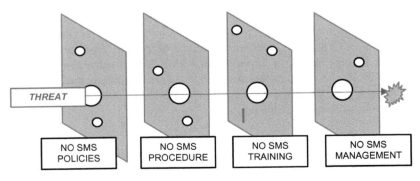

FIGURE 4.3 Reason's Swiss Cheese Model.

Successive layers of conditions in a reactive safety system, breeched by various weaknesses, thereby allowing hazards (e.g., human error, technology failure, environmental factors) to serve as a contributing factor to an accident or incident. Reason's model is a primary construct in the development of a properly designed SMS.

PILLAR I: SAFETY POLICIES

Essential to the success of any SMS program is communication of all SMS policies throughout the organization. Safety policies must be stated and transmitted in ways that clearly reflect management's long-term commitment to safety. The policies must also explain how safety management principles will integrate with and be implemented into the existing organizational structure. Safety

THREAT
SMS POLICIES
SMS PROCEDURE
SMS TRAINING
SMS MANAGEMENT

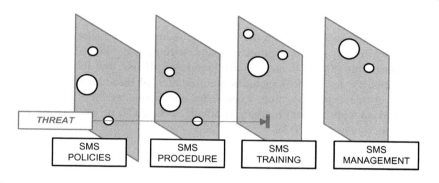

FIGURE 4.4

Examples of successive layers of safety in a proactive SMS, with a threat affecting policy and procedures, but subsequently blocked by proper safety training, as derived from Reason's Swiss Cheese Model.

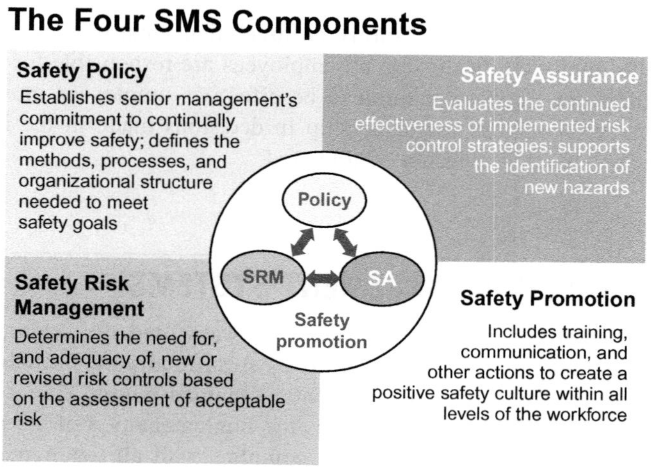

The Four SMS Components
Safety Policy
Establishes senior management's commitment to continually improve safety; defines the methods, processes, and organizational structure needed to meet safety goals
Safety Assurance
Evaluates the continued effectiveness of implemented risk control strategies; supports the identification of new hazards
Policy
SRM
SA
Safety promotion
Safety Risk Management
Determines the need for, and adequacy of, new or revised risk controls based on the assessment of acceptable risk
Safety Promotion
Includes training, communication, and other actions to create a positive safety culture within all levels of the workforce

FIGURE 4.5 The four pillars of SMS as defined by the FAA.

Safety promotion is integrated into all aspects of policy, safety risk management (SRM), and safety assurance (SA).

Source: FAA, 2014a.

policies are contained in written documentation (electronic and paper) from senior management that includes a top-level commitment to the SMS. The documents must also clearly indicate an assurance that executives will: (a) monitor safety performance, (b) encourage employees to report safety issues without fear of reprisal, (c) establish clear standards of acceptable behavior related to safety, and (d) provide resources necessary for long-term sustainability of the SMS (Ludwig et al., 2007, pp. 5−6).

PILLAR II: SAFETY RISK MANAGEMENT

Perhaps most commonly associated with the insurance industry, risk management is an established process with a long history of application in many settings and industries. The prime value of **safety risk management** (SRM) is not the elimination of all risk, but the reduction of risk to an acceptable or predictable level. SRM includes identification of hazards, assessing the risk of each hazard, including, to the extent possible, its severity and frequency, and applying risk mitigation processes, followed up with incident tracking (Ludwig et al., 2007, p. 10). These aspects should be integrated in a properly designed SMS.

PILLAR III: SAFETY ASSURANCE

SMS **safety assurance** (SA) functions include internal audits, external audits, and corrective actions. SA also includes providing feedback on the performance of the organization and, therefore, is inclusive of measuring effectiveness of risk mitigation strategies implemented.

PILLAR IV: SAFETY PROMOTION

Safety promotion focuses on creating a **"safety culture"** that greatly enhances the success of any SMS program. Safety promotion means that all employees are responsible for safety as a key value of the business culture. For safety promotion to be effective, employees must trust that they will have senior management's support and leadership in decisions made in the interest of safety and that intentional breaches of safety will not be tolerated.

IMPLEMENTING SAFETY MANAGEMENT SYSTEMS

An SMS may be designed and implemented in many ways, and the astute airport operator will spend time planning and adapting an SMS plan to its specific airport. Initially, all Part 139 operators will use, as a baseline, the safety requirements contained within Title 14 CFR Part 139 as a first step to developing an SMS. Part 139 requires the implementation of an **Airport Certification Manual (ACM)** that documents how the airport complies with all requirements of Part 139. The ACM also includes a wildlife hazard management plan, snow removal plan (if appropriate), **Airport Emergency Plan (AEP)**, signs and markings plan, and pavement management plan. All of these documents should be used as a baseline for developing an SMS. The ACRP Report 1 offers three strategies for implementing an SMS subsequent to a thorough analysis of the ACM (Ludwig et al., 2007, p. 24):

1. **Evolutionary Style SMS:** SMS principles are integrated and implemented over a period of several years, with safety as a cultural value becoming slowly ingrained in employees' attitudes and actions. This method may take the longest time period for adoption of SMS than all options presented by the ACRP, but may lead to the most viable environment for managing change and sustaining a safety culture.
2. **Phased Methodology SMS:** Specific dates and milestones are established for adoption of an SMS, using the time between phases to assess and address any issues before moving on to the next phase in the plan. This method is built on characteristics of project management, with feedback and outcomes assessment being potential advantages. This strategy requires the most resources and efforts to properly manage.
3. **Fast Track Adoption SMS:** This method implements SMS more quickly than the above strategies. However, while this approach may bring the airport quickly into compliance with SMS, it may not result in fundamental changes in safety practices and attitudes. In other words, employees may not have the time to develop the safety culture that is a critical component of SMS.

The types of strategies and tactics eventually selected for implementing an SMS will largely depend on the structure and culture of the airport. Regardless of the airport, operational managers can anticipate that the process of implementing an SMS will be highly iterative and subject to change. Since an SMS requires extensive planning and dynamic implementation, some airports elect to hire safety managers or consultants with SMS expertise. Some larger airports hire external consultants to assist internal staff charged with developing and implementing an SMS. The ACRP Report 1 identifies several best practices and recommendations for implementing SMS at airports:

1. Recommendation—Do not wait until legislation has been finalized for required Part 139 SMS. Instead, start the SMS implementation process now as a proactive way to meet eventual regulatory requirements. This proposition is challenging, as final rulemaking may differ vastly from initial rulemaking. Thus, some airport operators hesitate to allocate resources, time, and funding to establish an SMS until the final rule has been issued. Nevertheless, after rulemaking is finalized, a period of normalizing will occur, as FAA personnel who approve SMS programs exchange their own best practices and determine what is "compliant" versus what is "noncompliant." SMS, however, have already been implemented throughout much of the world and in a variety of settings and industries. Therefore, it is doubtful that the four pillars of SMS and their underlying principles will change significantly. Implementing an SMS prior to rulemaking is also a highly recommended strategy for establishing a safety culture that will be more receptive to potential changes the FAA could make to initial and subsequent SMS-related rulings.
2. Airport operators are encouraged to use the programs, such as the self-inspection program, that are already in place and can be used in an SMS framework. Risk management is well established; thus, the fundamentals of identifying hazards, determining their consequences and frequency, and identifying mitigation strategies are largely unchanged. By using programs, such as the airport self-inspection program, that are already in place and that emulate SMS principles, airport personnel are encouraged to associate the "new" principles of SMS with ones they already understand.

3. Documentation is essential to demonstrating that an airport has met its due diligence in meeting SMS requirements. An SMS is designed to reduce risk and liability from hazards, incidents, and accidents in all day-to-day operations. Detailed documentation and recordkeeping is needed to demonstrate that the airport has acted responsibly in identifying and mitigating risk, and also continuously utilizes a proactive, systematic program to identify hazards, audit existing safety programs, and instill a safety culture throughout the organization. Documentation also creates a historical record for each generation of personnel to analyze and improve.

4. Development and implementation of an SMS should be accomplished in properly scheduled timeframes. While the fast-track approach is one method of implementing an SMS, it is not an effective or sustainable strategy. Unfortunately, many airport operators may not be able to stay ahead of eventual SMS regulation and requirements prior to final rulemaking. Therefore, some airports may be "under pressure" to implement a compliant SMS program once rulemaking is finalized. As a result, many airports may need to revisit their SMS programs, as management and line personnel identify the weaknesses of the hastily formulated SMS program.

5. Establish and maintain a good working relationship with airport stakeholders and the FAA. Programs are easier to implement and experience less resistance when all parties are involved early in the process. This strategy enables airport stakeholders, such as an air carrier (who has already implemented an SMS) or a regulator, to better understand the challenges of implementing an SMS at the airport.

A challenge to implementing an SMS includes determining who is legally liable and accountable for ensuring the SMS program is implemented and sustained. The SMS introduces the concept of the **Accountable Executive (AE)**, an individual named in the SMS program and essentially responsible for the success of the SMS. Additional challenges include: (a) finding a knowledgeable safety manager, (b) determining the best method to collect data used in risk assessments, (c) determining how to interpret the data, (d) developing a nonpunitive reporting system, and (e) integrating the SMS with other domains, such as the air carrier and the FAA's air traffic control tower (Ludwig et al., 2007, p. 26).

Procedures for establishing an SMS can be divided into four basic elements: (a) establishing a safety policy and assigning safety responsibilities, (b) performing a gap analysis, (c) developing a strategy to implement SMS, and (d) developing the individual elements of SMS (Ludwig et al., 2007, p. 29).

SAFETY POLICY

The principles or guiding actions set forth in the development of an SMS are essential to the overall success of the program's implementation and endurance. A plan for SMS adoption and delivery should include at least the following policy statements:

1. Safety Policy
2. Safety Objectives
3. SMS Organization
4. Safety Accountability
5. Safety Committee
6. Documentation

SAFETY POLICY STATEMENT

The safety policy articulates an organization's vision, mission, and goals for maintaining a safe airport environment. The policy statement declares management's commitment to implement SMS by making the monitoring of safety performance as important as the monitoring of financial performance. The policy statement must encourage employees to report safety issues without fear of reprisals; establish standards for acceptable behaviors; and commit management to providing resources, including money, personnel, and materials, to address safety issues. Key indications of management's commitment to supporting values stated in safety policies is the adequacy of resources and the support of line personnel when making safety-related decisions that affect the operation or revenue stream of the airport.

Organizations may declare they have a safety culture by issuing policies touting "safety first" as a moniker for managing an effective SMS. However, it takes much more long-term planning and effort to instill a safety culture that accurately reflects the intended objectives within those policies. Likewise, it is easy to issue safety polices that make claim to supporting nonpunitive safety systems—that is, safety policies that ensure that stakeholders will not be held in jeopardy or otherwise punished for taking corrective actions that sustain safety above all other priorities. Stakeholders need to see evidence that management will stand by its core value of implementing nonpunitive SMS. At some time, an Airport Operations Manager might need to determine that, from a safety perspective, temporarily closing the airport, perhaps during bad weather, is the best option. After the weather alert has passed, it may come to light that the shutdown was not necessary. If the airport duty manager is punished or reprimanded for making the decision, then it is likely that line personnel will not value the policy statement as the true intent and culture of the airport's SMS.

An Airport Manager may have to defend to the airport sponsor an incorrect or flawed safety-related decision by a member of the manager's staff. In these cases, Airport Directors likely receive more support for the safety program and from other line personnel, but may risk their jobs with unhappy airport sponsors. Despite the benefits to issuing SMS safety-related policies, airport operators should understand that the actual implementation of an SMS program will not be without challenges. However, effective SMS safety policies, along with stakeholder buy-in, including buy-in by the the airport sponsor, will greatly enhance the effectiveness of the Airport Director and line staff to effectively manage a strong safety culture at the airport.

SAFETY OBJECTIVES

Clearly stated safety objectives articulate desired end points to specific activities or processes. The objectives may take a long time to achieve and usually require complex or multiphased solutions. Long-term, safety-related objectives should include a set of intermediate goals that can be measured—usually by combining quantitative and qualitative metrics as a strategy for reducing bias in the interpretation of data analysis. These goals give individuals in the organization measurable targets to work toward (Ayres et al., 2009, p. 10). They provide direction and guidance for safety management activities and are used as a basis for performance measurement.

An example of a safety-related objective is to reduce runway incursions by 25% over the next 12 months. A measurable goal related to this objective may be the requirement that all maintenance personnel attend movement area driver training every six months (rather than every year, which is currently required by the FAA). The installation of enhanced taxiway markings or signs might be another goal to support the overall objective. Organizational objectives should be supported by departmental and divisional safety objectives in order for every operational group within the airport to contribute to the overall organization's stated safety objectives (Ayres et al., 2009, p. 11).

SAFETY MANAGEMENT SYSTEMS ORGANIZATION

The objective for appointing and organizing key aviation safety personnel is to establish a team of professionals who support the development, implementation, and monitoring of safety issues throughout the organization. This team further operates and enhances the SMS once it is in place (Ayres et al., 2009, p. 11). The SMS organization helps to ensure the continuity of the implementation of safety programs and processes throughout the organization (p. 11). The team also coordinates and promotes special programs, supports line management, and collects and analyzes feedback related to all operations and safety-related matters. The SMS organization essentially serves as a "Strike Team" with the mission of ensuring that the SMS is integrated and used throughout the airport environment (p. 11).

The **SMS Manager** (or SMS Safety Coordinator) is designated to oversee the entire SMS program. This individual should have: (a) experience in the operational areas in which the SMS will be implemented; (b) a comprehensive understanding of the SMS; and, most importantly, (c) access to top management when needed to discuss safety issues within and across divisional lines of operation (Ayres et al., 2009, p. 11). The SMS Manager should not have other roles or responsibilities (although at smaller airports, this arrangement may not be possible). In some cases an individual on the SMS team is designated the "SMS Champion" and serves as the prime mentor for the mission of the SMS group and its interaction with all areas of operational concern throughout the airport. In this capacity, the SMS Champion supports the SMS Manager in building organizational support for the SMS program. Of note, *SMS Manager* and *SMS Safety Coordinator* are more desirable titles than the traditional title of *Safety Manager* because the term *safety manager* often creates the perception that airport safety is a single person or department's responsibility rather than the responsibility of everyone at the airport.

The SMS group (or at least the SMS Manager) should be included on the airport organizational chart, along with functional reporting lines of communication to other departments. The group should have access to senior management and, in order to avoid conflicts of interest, should not report to other functional departments. Some airports may be inclined to make the director of operations also the SMS Manager, but this arrangement is not recommended, nor is it recommended for the SMS Manager to report directly to the Director of Operations (Ayres et al., 2009, p. 12). The Director of Operation's duty to operate the airport in a safe and efficient manner may be compromised if asked to control the safety mechanisms that are in place to prevent an incident or accident.

SAFETY ACCOUNTABILITY

Safety accountability refers to the roles, responsibilities, and authorities of those individuals who manage, perform, and verify that a particular operation should be identified and included in the SMS documentation (Ayres et al., 2009, p. 12). This section of SMS introduces the position of the **AE**:

> The Accountable Executive is the person ultimately responsible for the safety of "personnel, business processes, and activities of the airport organization" (p. 12).

The AE should have the full authority for human and financial resource issues and the responsibility to management for all areas of the SMS and, as such, be responsible for all safety issues and all airport activities. In many airport organizations the only person with this level of authority is the airport executive (i.e., Airport Director). Regardless of the ability to have a designated AE, it is expected that the Airport Director will advocate for decisions and processes that will support the SMS program. These factors may include hiring (or firing) certain personnel that either contribute to or detract from the safety processes and culture, and spending financial resources on safety equipment, training, and materials, for example.

Safety is a line responsibility in most organizations, and each department should have an individual assigned to advocating safety. Frequently, only line personnel directly experience or understand safety issues related to their activities or line-related operations. These individuals are immersed in processes that may be "safe" during normal operations, but become unsafe during periods of adversity, such as bad weather or if the operational process is accelerated beyond acceptable scheduling.

SAFETY COMMITTEES

The **Safety Committee** is appointed by the AE to provide a setting to discuss the performance and health of the SMS. Essentially, the Safety Committee serves as a form of quality assurance for the airport's SMS program. The Committee provides recommendations concerning safety issues, policy decisions, and expert advice to mitigate specific problems (Ayres et al., 2009, p. 13). At smaller airports, a standing Safety Committee may not be necessary but may instead be established on an ad hoc basis to address certain problems. The Safety Committee should meet regularly to discuss issues, define outcomes, and establish objectives and timelines for actions.

The Safety Committee is chaired by the safety manager, and it may include tenants, air carriers, and other airport stakeholders, if appropriate and beneficial. If the Safety Committee lacks the expertise to address particular issues, additional personnel may be assigned to the committee on a permanent or temporary basis.

DOCUMENTATION

Airport policies and procedures are communicated through multiple forms of documentation. Documentation includes all written materials necessary to conduct business. Written materials also develop a "corporate memory" and help airports meet legal requirements to maintain effective safety programs (Ayres et al., 2009, p. 14). To control documents, airports should have clear standards on how to track a document throughout its lifecycle, from creation, through modification, and to eventual archive or destruction. As applied to SMS, the ability to store, search, and analyze (e.g., data warehousing, data mining, analytics and statistical process control) documented legacy data and information is critical for detecting trends in airport safety. Another important aspect related to managing documentation is keeping the airport aligned with regulatory and best practice changes. The FAA, Transportation Security Administration (TSA), and other agencies routinely send out safety-related updates to rules, ACs, and other processes. Keeping track of all these changes and modifying safety procedures as needed to comply with these notifications can be overwhelming. SMS Managers can keep track of changes by subscribing to FAA email feeds, but the changes or advisories are not always straightforward and, therefore, take considerable time and resources to address. In some cases, such as with the TSA, the SMS Manager may not have the required access authority to needed information, such as Sensitive Security Information (SSI),[2] and may therefore not even know when the regulations change.[3] At large airports, department or line divisions should keep track of regulatory changes and requirements to comply with federal, state, and local laws and rules affecting safety. When a change affects airport safety, the department or division head is responsible for notifying the SMS Manager. Subsequent meetings and discussions may be scheduled to determine the impact to safety of the new procedure.

Certificated airports are required to comply with at Part 139 and Part 1542 (Airport Security). Airports that are not certificated, but which receive federal funds, are affected by grant assurances, which require the recipient to comply certain practices (i.e., pavement maintenance, safe and serviceable operations) and remain aware of advisories as related to safety. The documentation component of SMS requires that airports identify the applicable federal, state, and municipal regulatory requirements for the airport, track changes and revisions, and ensure information is distributed to those who need it (Ayres et al., 2009, p. 14). Proper documentation helps ensure that procedures are followed. If the airport is sued or otherwise involved in legal or regulatory issues, the documentation can help "tell the story" about what was supposed to happen with regard to meeting safety objectives and goals.

SAFETY MANAGEMENT SYSTEMS INFORMATION CONTROL

Information control in SMS helps to ensure that information is accessible, timely, and up-to-date with existing regulations. The control system further ensures that outdated documents or procedures are archived. An SMS information control system should also contain policies and procedures, such as how to conduct hazard analyses, investigations of incidents and accidents, and safety performance measurement processes (Ayres et al., 2009, p. 15). Documents should be well-structured, cross-referenced, and reviewed periodically for changes. This process may be difficult at times, particularly at large airports where a variety of processes have been developed, often by different entities, including external and internal stakeholders, each with their own particular needs or standards as applied to document formatting, structure, and content.

It is imperative that SMS management at the airport publish standards for formulating documents used by entities engaged in sustaining compliance with regulatory and advisory requirements. The standards must be strict enough to enable the information control function but not so

---

[2]The U.S. TSA defines SSI as information obtained or developed that, if released publicly, would be detrimental to transportation security. See http://www.tsa.gov/stakeholders/sensitive-security-information-ssi

[3]It is recommended that the SMS Manager have the required clearance to access "need-to-know" SSI information.

stringent as to inhibit the actual transmittal of the information in an effective and efficient manner. Numerous software programs are available to help with document control. A traditional method is to have new pages (updates or revisions) in a document distributed to the individuals possessing copies of the document and have them replace the affected content in their own copy (electronic or hardcopy). Software programs can make these updates automatically, but the individual must still be notified that a change has been made.

Certain documents, such as records or documents that are required to be kept by regulation, such as the **ACM**, will be reviewed and analyzed during an incident or accident. These records and documents become part of the legal process, oftentimes to determine liability. The **International Standards Organization (ISO)**[4] defines a record as information created, received, and maintained as evidence. Regardless of the size of the Airport Operation, airports must maintain records for legal purposes but also to analyze activities and look for trends in safety (Ayres et al., 2009, p. 16).

PROACTIVE SAFETY MANAGEMENT SYSTEMS COORDINATION OF EMERGENCY PLANNING AND RESPONSE SAFETY MANAGEMENT SYSTEMS

Every active airport can expect to experience an emergency or incident. An emergency is loosely defined as any situation that warrants a response to save lives or to protect property or the environment, and to do so with the goal of eventually restoring normal operations at the airport. It is well-known that airports are not fully equipped to handle all types of emergencies and must rely on off-airport responders for assistance—a fact that makes the planning and coordination of emergency response with outside stakeholders a necessity for the SMS Manager.

Certificated airports are required to have an **AEP** that describes how that airport will respond during an incident or accident and includes off-airport response. Noncertificated airports should also have an AEP or community response plan to aircraft incidents and accidents.

An effective SMS emergency preparedness and response program can reduce the impact of an aircraft accident (i.e., save lives, property, and the environment), reduce liability and insurance premiums, and reduce negative public relations after the accident or incident. The public expects government entities to be prepared for emergencies and other types of disasters. While noncertificated airports may not have the SMS capability of a certificated airport, plenty of guidance, resource materials, and training are available from the **Federal Emergency Management Agency (FEMA)** on how to develop an SMS emergency response program. Off-airport personnel, such as city, county, or emergency management professionals (consultants or services), can also help in the development of such a program.

At a certificated airport, the SMS program may be incorporated as an appendix to the ACM. It should be considered a living document that can and should be changed to accommodate fluctuations in operational procedures and activities. Figure 4.6 demonstrates processes for managing change and related documentation workflow in SMS requiring coordination by many stakeholders.

---

[4]ISO 9000 provides a foundation of policies and processes for quality management. See http://www.iso.org/iso/iso_9000 for further information.

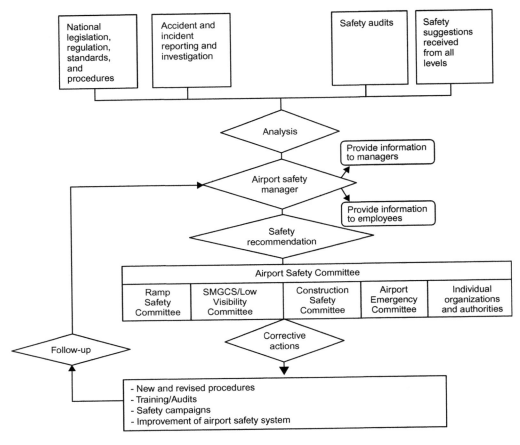

FIGURE 4.6

Example of managing change, documentation flow, and coordination within an SMS.

Source: FAA, 2007.

CASE STUDY

Comair Flight 5191

As part of a proactive approach to coordinate and manage an SMS, airport personnel should scan for and be aware of incidents and accidents that take place at other airports or in similar situations. These occurrences should be routinely studied for coordinating proactive safety improvements at the airport. As an example, when Comair Flight 5191 crashed during takeoff from the Lexington, Kentucky airport in 2006, killing all 47 passengers and two of the three crew members, several lessons were learned from the accident. In this case, one of the contributing factors to the accident was identified as confusing runway configurations and markings. Other airport operators, particularly those with similar runway configurations, used this accident to make safety improvements at their own facility.

The flight departed from the wrong runway, and while the NTSB (National Transportation Safety Board) determined that pilot error was likely the cause of the accident, Comair took responsibility for the crash, alleging that confusing

(Continued)

(Continued)

airfield signs and markings contributed to the accident (Pitsch, 2006). According to Pitsch, this case makes several allegations highlighting flawed airport safety operations as factors in the accident, including:

1. Airport employees failed to make sure that "runways and taxiways were at all times in a safe and unobstructed condition" and complied with government regulations.
2. Airport employees gave inaccurate information to the federal government about the airport layout, which was passed on to pilots.
3. Airport lighting, signage, and markers "were not as required by the ordinary standards of care or by law and/or regulation and were missing or confusing."
4. Construction barriers blocked the view and access to the proper runway (NTSB, 2006).

Lexington, KY is a certificated airport under Part 139 and has an FAA-approved ACM. The Lexington ACM explained safety requirements of the airport operator at the time of the Comair Flight 5191 accident. Operations personnel at Lexington were charged (as with most Part 139 airports) with ensuring that safety requirements are fulfilled through airfield inspections, issuance of applicable Notices to Airmen (NOTAM), and, of specific relevance to this case, ensuring that construction barriers or related operations do not interfere with flight safety.

Subsequent to an accident as was experienced by Flight 5191, proactive SMS Managers should form a team to conduct a case analysis to learn from the event and seek possible strategies for avoiding similar risks at their airport. Questions, listed as examples below, should be openly asked and vetted by many stakeholders to the SMS program conducting the inquiry for lessons learned.

1. Was there evidence to suggest that the airfield layout was confusing to other operators prior to the accident, and, if so, how were those concerns reported? If reported, to whom, and was the report followed up with analysis and action?
2. The NOTAM process can be lengthy in terms of pilots requiring needed flight information. A delay in publishing a NOTAM may be as long as 20 minutes from the time the NOTAM is issued until the time it is approved and posted for public view by the FAA. Did the airport operator, the local FAA office, or the air traffic controllers identify the average amount of time for a NOTAM to appear? Was this issue a problem in the past, and, if so, who identified the problem, and what was done about it?
3. Were there previous reports that the airfield signs, marking, and lighting were confusing, and, if so, to whom were they reported, and what were the follow-up items? Airport inspection checklists would demonstrate when the signs, markings, and lights were last inspected and their overall condition. Were reports analyzed to determine if there were progressive issues at the time of the accident?
4. Were work orders submitted for maintenance items? The airport also had, as part of its ACM, an approved sign-marking-lighting plan. While the airport planning department would likely be directly responsible for any confusing **signs, markings, and lighting (S-M-L)** configurations, the Airport Operations personnel would be responsible for ensuring the S-M-L were within the FAA standards and should report any confusing signs or areas where visibility is blocked.
5. Airport operators are also responsible for airport safety during construction. While we can assume that the construction project had an FAA-approved safety plan, when was the last time the construction area was inspected by operations personnel? Were previous deficiencies noted (e.g., construction equipment blocking navigational aids or obstructing the airport's S-M-L, were construction personnel in unauthorized areas and creating a hazard to Airport Operations)?

The above concerns represent issues falling under the purview of Airport Operations. Another lesson to be realized from this example is that it is one thing to draw up safety plans in a meeting room but quite another when the plan must be implemented. Actual implementation always reveals many variables that may have been unaccounted for, such as personnel not understanding the plan, replacement personnel being used onsite when primary personnel are not available, and construction activities taking place during unusual times due to delays or weather.

Ultimately, in the case of Flight 5191, the airport was not held liable for the accident, and in a subsequent case hearing, the Kentucky Supreme Court found that the airport could not be sued because of sovereign immunity. The NTSB did recommend enhanced taxiway centerlines for use at Lexington. However, the NTSB did not assign fault to the airport in this case. The prime lesson for other airport operators to employ from this case is that by implementing a proactive SMS that seeks best practices and lessons learned, it is possible that the airport can reduce its liability and improve overall safety.

The Comair flight should be a good lesson to Airport Operations professionals that all elements of the airfield are critical to flight operations. While the NTSB did not hold the airport responsible for the crash in any way, the organization, while acknowledging the airport was in compliance with the federal regulations for airport S-M-L, did note in its report that better airport signs and markings may have prevented the crash. This emphasizes a key point in SMS planning and response—regulatory compliance does not always equate to, or ensure, optimal safety.

Some airport operators may come to the conclusion that since the airport was not held liable, the airport did all it reasonably was expected to do to prevent the accident. However, an optimal SMS safety policy will take all of these elements into account and develop additional processes and action plans, with timelines and prioritized funding, to reduce the possibility of further incidents or accidents of this nature.

SAFETY RISK MANAGEMENT

Introduced earlier as a key pillar of SMS, **SRM** consists of: (a) identifying hazards in the workplace or on the airfield or for a particular operation or activity, such as construction, (b) identifying the frequency of the hazard turning into an incident, (c) identifying the consequence of the hazard, (d) prioritizing the hazards, and then (e) applying mitigation and preparedness strategies. Some risks can be eliminated through processes or physical changes to a structure. Other risks, such as Aircraft Accidents, cannot completely be avoided. Nevertheless, a risk assessment can help identify methods the airport can employ for more effective and efficient response to such events. SRM is focused on proactively identifying hazards and taking actions to either reduce the resulting negative consequences or significantly reduce the risk of occurrence.

THE SAFETY RISK MANAGEMENT PROCESS

The ICAO defines a **risk** as "the likelihood of injury to personnel, damage to equipment or structures, loss of material, or reduction of ability to perform a prescribed function, measured in terms of probability and severity." The FAA's definition of a risk is "the composite of predicted severity and likelihood of the potential effect of a hazard in the worst credible system state" (Stolzer & Halford, 2008).

A **hazard** is defined by ICAO as a "condition, object, or activity with the potential of causing injuries to personnel, damage to equipment or structures, loss of material, or reduction of ability to perform a prescribed function." The FAA's definition of a hazard is "any existing or potential condition that can lead to injury, illness, or death to people; damage to or loss of a system, equipment, or property; or damage to the environment." A hazard is a condition that is a "prerequisite to an accident or incident" (Stolzer & Halford, 2008).

The SRM is a fundamental, decision-making pillar of the SMS. It comes from "old school" insurance industry risk assessment, so the concepts of SRM are neither unique nor new, but in the context of an SMS, they fulfill a critical role. The SRM is a five-step process:

1. Describe the system or activity.
2. Identify the hazard(s) along the activity path.

3. Determine the risk.
4. Assess and analyze the risk.
5. Treat and monitor the risk.

Describe the System or Activity

Usually, an SMS Manager will build an ontology for defining and categorizing operational systems by first looking at broad-based, or macro-level, delineations, such as "Airport Operations" or "landside operations." However, for effective identification of systems and cataloging of associated potential risks, these top-level categories must be scaled into subsystems. The major system or activity must be refined in definition such that a finite number of hazards can be identified and potentially mitigated. For example, some hazards will be associated with a location or activity, while others may be associated with the geographical location of the airport, such as the potential for natural disasters or technological disasters (e.g., a nuclear power facility in the proximity of the airport). Security issues can be addressed separately through a Security Management System (SeMS).

Once macro-scaled ontologies are defined, then a taxonomy of subsystem categories is clustered around each associated ontology. For example, airside may be a defined ontological boundary, with physical subcategories such as "Runway 29 left" or "A concourse" listed as systems for further SRM review. Other subsystems may be organizational in nature, such as the "fleet maintenance department," or activity-based such as "construction on Taxiway Alpha." Once the boundaries (categories) for risk identification are determined, brainstorming sessions with various levels of appropriate personnel should result in a thorough list of existing or potential risks (Ludwig et al., 2007, p. 18).

All of the systems delineated for safety risk analysis should include the function, general physical characteristics and resources, and associated operational concerns. Models are typically used to characterize the system. The *ACRP Report 1 SMS for Airports Volume 2 Guidebook* uses the 5M Model as it takes into account the interrelationships and integration of equipment, people, environment, and procedures of the system being examined. The 5M Model has five components:

1. **Mission:** This is the activity or the reason for conducting the activity, such as aircraft marshaling, aircraft fueling, and airport self-inspections.
2. **Man:** This is the human element of the system, provided that the system requires human interaction. Examples include airport construction activity, aircraft rescue and firefighting, and vehicle inspections at security checkpoints.
3. **Machine:** This is the equipment or material element of the system. Examples include vehicles used to conduct self-inspection, airline tugs and maintenance equipment, communications center equipment, or hazardous materials.
4. **Management:** This element includes the organization, policies, procedures, rules, and regulations involved in operating and maintaining the system. Examples include construction activity that will have oversight by engineers, contractors, and inspectors; escorting vehicles or personnel in the Air Operations Area; or procedures related to emergency response.
5. **Media:** This is the environment in which the system will be operated, maintained, or installed. It can include operational environment, which is the conditions involving such factors as

volume of traffic and workload, and ambient conditions, such as temperature, humidity, visible light, and visibility requirements. Examples of media include winter operations or ramp operations with high, ambient, noise levels.

Other looping models are also used in this process. The FAA Industry Training Standard (FITS) three-step model—perceive, process, perform—focuses on the redesign of GA training but can also be used in SMS hazard assessment. Traditional GA training focuses on getting students to pass the FAA's practical test standards, whereas FITS focuses on expertly managed, real-world challenges, also known as scenario-based training (FAA, 2013b). The advantage of the FITS model is that it integrates risk management, decision making, situational awareness, and resource management into every operation (Stolzer & Halford, 2011). Another common model is the OODA (Observation, Orientation, Decision, and Action) loop, which is a four-step, conflict resolution process developed by U.S. Air Force Colonel John Boyd and has been applied in continuous improvement processes. An additional model is referred to commonly as the "5-Step Process Model" and consists of the following elements based in operational risk management:

1. System analysis and design
2. Hazard identification
3. Risk analysis
4. Risk assessment
5. Risk control

Identify the Hazards

FAA AC 150/5200-37 defines a hazard as "any existing or potential condition that can lead to injury, illness, or death to people; damage to or loss of a system, equipment, or property; or damage to the environment" (Ayres et al., 2009, p. 18). Identifying hazards allows airport operators to take action to mitigate, eliminate, or prepare responses to incidents and accidents that could occur as a result. Hazard analysis also helps the airport operator to determine why certain hazards may exist and which ones may be systemic—the result of training (or lack thereof), budgeting, faulty procedures, lack of planning, promoting unqualified individuals, or other organizational factors (p. 68).

Some hazards may not manifest until certain conditions exist, such as sliding on snow or ice on paved areas. Certain hazards may increase in severity or frequency under different operational conditions. Driving on the airfield has inherent risks, but the risks increase during emergency operations when operators are driving response vehicles faster. Hazards should also not be confused with consequences or outcomes. A runway incursion is a hazard—the act of driving onto the runway during flight operations and without authorization from the control tower (i.e., the mode of Man above) is a hazard. Inadequate airfield signs and markings are a hazard (i.e., the mode of Machine above). Inadequate training for vehicle operators on the airfield (i.e., the mode of Management above) is a hazard. Each, or a combination of these hazards, may contribute to the outcome—a runway incursion.

A variety of methods and analytics can be used to identify hazards. These methods include: (a) metric-based quantitative and qualitative studies, (b) workshops, (c) brainstorming sessions, and (d) the Delphi method, plus many others, including checklists, audit forms, records analysis, trends, and scenario analysis. Using a variety of methods rather than relying on one single method is best. Qualitative methods should be combined with quantitative methods to reduce and balance bias inherent to both methods. Hazard identification should include a combination of analysis, both reactive (accident investigation, trend analysis, occurrence reporting) and proactive (self-inspections, checklists, SMS assessment, interviews, and Delphi groups). It is not possible to identify every conceivable hazard, but public agencies are expected to conduct due diligence in identifying reasonably foreseeable hazards (Ayres et al., 2009, p. 67). The following example provides insight on this concern:

An organization decides to conduct a post aircraft crash survival skills exercise at night. The exercise would be conducted in a farmer's field, away from city lights. To receive approval for the exercise, the group must first answer several questions related to risk assessment: Has someone inspected the field during daylight hours for obvious hazards? Have any known hazards been removed, if practical, or marked so they can be seen at night? Will there be someone on standby with medical training to assist anyone needing minor treatment? Is there a plan for transporting someone to a nearby medical facility if someone gets seriously injured? Will a safety supervisor be on scene to oversee the operation, and does that person have the authority to stop or suspend the exercise if the safety supervisor sees a hazardous condition? Do the participants have the ability to make a safety call if they see a hazardous condition, without repercussion? Are there any other hazards that have come up as part of the inspection of the area, or as part of any brainstorming sessions, or lessons learned from previous experiences that must be considered? These are the same types of questions an attorney will ask if something does go wrong!

For an airport context, *ACRP Report 1 SMS for Airports Volume 2: Guidebook* uses an airport construction project as an example. Not only must the hazards be identified of how construction at airports will affect the safety of the facility (e.g., vehicles and personnel operating on the airfield who do not have familiarity with the airport environment, construction debris, movement area, and navigational aid shutdowns), but the Airport Operations can also create safety issues for the construction crews. Issues such as jet blast and aircraft excursions from the movement area, and into the "undershoot or overshoot," or safety areas, can pose risks to construction or other operational concerns. Factors to consider in a hazard analysis commonly include:

1. Personnel (passengers, employees, vendors) accessing the workplace.
2. Hazards that arise from various activities, such as baggage handling or maintenance activities, including lifting, carrying, transporting heavy objects, and pinch-points.
3. Hazards that arise from using equipment or supervising the use of equipment (fire apparatus, deicing operations, vehicles).
4. Hazards arising from operational practices such as snow removal.
5. Hazards that arise from weather such as visibility, temperature, sun exposure, wind.
6. Regulatory processes and procedures, such as runway inspections, and the hazards that could arise from such operations, or hazards that are required to be addressed, such as those listed in the AEP AC 150/5200-31C.
7. Warning and alert systems to detect or notify airport personnel of a system or mechanical failure.
8. Any organizational factors such as policies or training, and budget and allocation of resources for safety purposes (Ayres et al., 2009, pp. 67–68).

Determine Risk

Determining risk is a matter of asking the question: "What could go wrong?" In "Practical Risk Management," Lewis writes: "practical risk management is about realizing that tragic mishaps also lay in our future, unless the multiple hazards that combine to create risk are identified and controlled. The risk management process is the engine that drives a generative safety management system" (Stolzer & Halford, 2011). Lewis promotes the use of the U.S. Navy's risk management model, which includes the following steps:

1. Identify hazards
2. Assess the hazards
3. Make risk decisions
4. Implement controls
5. Supervise and watch for change

In the above model from Lewis, a hazard is defined as a condition with the potential to cause personal injury, death, or property damage. Hazards may result from poor system design, unprofessional or unsafe work practices, inadequate training, a lack of preparation, or, as in the case of military aviation, a highly demanding and threatening environment. In some cases, the conditions may remain hidden until acted upon by external influences or a change to the environment (Stolzer & Halford, 2011).

A critical component for identifying hazards is the ability of individuals to report hazards or situations without fear of reprisal; otherwise, the hazard may continue to go unaddressed. Such a reporting system is found in the SA section of an SMS. The National Aeronautics and Space Administration (NASA) has long had a popular and well-known hazard reporting system known as the **Aviation Safety Reporting System (ASRS)** (NASA, 2015). Pilots who experience an emergency or hazard may file an ASRS report. ASRS receives, processes, and analyzes voluntarily submitted incident reports from pilots, air traffic controllers, dispatchers, cabin crew, maintenance technicians, and other stakeholders. Reports submitted to ASRS may describe both unsafe occurrences and hazardous situations. Information is gathered from these reports and disseminated to stakeholders. ASRS's primary goal is to enhance the quality of human performance in the National Airspace System (NASA, 2015). The ASRS program is voluntary, confidential, and nonpunitive.

Filing an ASRS report may protect an airman from certificate action if the violation is not deliberate and does not involve a criminal offense, among other qualifiers. The reporting system allows researchers to study numerous hazards and make recommendations to improve aviation safety. ASRS services include an **ASRS Alert Message** describing a hazardous situation that might compromise safe flight and is distributed immediately to the pilot community. This is reflective of the U.S. Navy's approach in that if there is a safety hazard identified, the reporting party is expected to take immediate action to mitigate the hazard if possible, then make a report as soon as possible so that further action can be taken if appropriate and feasible.

NASA issues less-urgent safety information through the **For Your Information** notices. These notices are supplemented by periodic safety teleconferences and safety communication programs, such as **CALLBACK**. ASRS's monthly safety newsletter, published since 1979 in a popular "lessons learned" format, presents ASRS report excerpts that are significant, educational, and timely. **ASRS Directline** is a similar past ASRS publication; back issues are available online. NASA, the FAA, and other government agencies have also published myriad safety-related assessments on topics such as weather, deicing, Traffic Collision Avoidance Systems, runway transgressions, and human factors, including communications, memory, confusion, pressure, and judgment.

All of the aforementioned documents can be used to identify and assess existing or potential threats to safety. In addition to these publications, programs such as the **Aviation Safety Action Program**[5] and **Air Traffic Safety Action Program**[6] conduct premishap interviews to predict what could happen (Stolzer & Halford, 2011).

Confidential reporting and nonpunitive elements are considered to be key to the success of safety information sharing systems (Forrest, 2006). According to NASA and many other global safety reporting systems, confidential reporting has several benefits, including:

1. Stakeholders are more willing to share their knowledge if their identities will remain protected and there are no disciplinary or legal consequences.
2. Confidential reporting systems have the capability to more adequately address the question about why a particular system or component failed or why a human erred.

Hazards may be identified by individuals, safety councils, audit teams, and stakeholders. There is value to identifying hazards by those performing the functions being assessed and those identified by outside observers. Individuals who perform certain jobs on a routine basis sometimes become accustomed to situations that may present hazards; however, as a result of the normalization of deviation, the hazard has become less identifiable. In these cases, external observers are more inclined to identify risks or hazards.

ACRP Report 001b has (Ayres et al., 2009) an extensive list of known hazards common to airports. This database includes: (a) the hazard category, (b) main components (characteristics or aspects) of the hazard, and (c) potential consequences of the hazard. While examples of all known hazards are too numerous to list, an example is presented below to demonstrate that hazard risk assessment is typically more complex than what might be initially anticipated. Hazard risk assessment is highly iterative and often results in changes to operational procedures and policies.

EXAMPLE HAZARD: WINTER SERVICES PROCEDURES

1. Main components: Procedures, equipment, training, materials, poor operation conditions, timing, monitoring of surface conditions, reporting of surface conditions
2. Potential consequences:
   a. Lack of or incorrect deicing procedures may diminish the aircraft's ability to fly;
   b. Improper snow removal or anti-icing may lead to reduced braking capability on the runway with risk of overruns and veer-offs;
   c. Asymmetric drag during operations may cause veer-offs;
   d. Poor braking performance causing collisions in movement and non-movement areas;
   e. Lack of sufficient materials;

(Continued)

---

[5]Federal Aviation Administration. (2013). *Aviation safety action program.* Retrieved from: https://www.faa.gov/about/initiatives/asap/
[6]CSSI, Inc. (2015). *Air traffic safety action program.* Retrieved from: https://www.atsapsafety.com/home.seam

(Continued)

   f. Equipment coordination disruption;
   g. Delay to employ safety measures;
   h. Low runway friction;
   i. Pilot unawareness of surface conditions.

Using the above example, SMS Managers must determine what measures are within their control. The SMS Manager or airport operator cannot address hazards outside of their control, although the airport operator or AE may be able to notify the air carrier of a risk that has been identified. Once the risks have been identified, the next step is to assess and analyze the risk.

Assess and Analyze the Risk

Assessing risk begins by asking two primary questions: (a) What potential harm does the hazard present (or what are the consequences)? and (b) How likely is the risk to occur (the probability)? The answers to these questions determine which risks to address first.

The process of estimating a risk includes determining the severity of the threat, in terms of potential impact to operations, personnel, equipment, or activity. "What if" analyses are effective tools in estimating risks. To avoid underestimating risk, severity should be based on the worst credible scenario. The *probability* of a specific hazard can be determined if directly related historical information is available. In other cases, estimating the likelihood of a risk might require the examination of accidents, incidents, or situations similar to the one being assessed. From that effort, an *inference* is made assessing the potential for risk of the issue being examined. Industry accident and incident data, such as from the FAA, NTSB, and NASA, may also provide quality data related to the likelihood of a hazard causing an accident or incident (Ayres et al., 2009, p. 76).

Classifying Risks

Creating a **risk matrix** is a common method of prioritizing risks, with the most important risk being the one with the greatest potential impact on airport activities. A realistic risk assessment should include analysis by a team of experts who are most familiar with the hazards being examined. Other expertise can come from regulations, industry best practices and statistics, manufacturers, training organizations, and safety consultants (Ayres et al., 2009, p. 76).

Risk matrices must be easy to use and simple to understand and must not require an extensive knowledge of quantitative risk analysis. If a risk matrix causes the reviewer to get "caught up in the numbers," then the risk matrix is unlikely to be used with any effectiveness or understood by the personnel charged with mitigating the risks. A risk matrix should also limit the levels of severity and likelihood to the smallest number possible. Too many distinctions cause the matrix to lose its overall meaning. Most individuals understand the difference between a likelihood of "frequent, probable, and remote." However, some users of the information may experience confusion if additional categories like "extremely remote" or "extremely improbable" are included. In these cases, stakeholders usually ask for clarification between improbable and extremely improbable. Even when likelihood and severity is expressed as a probability, larger distinctions should be made. Few individuals can reconcile the difference between an 85% chance of a risk occurring as compared to

Criteria	Risk Severity Classification				
	No Safety Effect **A**	Minor **B**	Major **C**	Hazardous **D**	Catastrophic **E**
Effect on aircraft operations	No effect on safety	Slight reduction in safety margin or functional capabilities	Significant reduction in safety margin or functional capability	Large reduction in safety margin or functional capabilities	Hull loss
Effect on people	Inconvenience	Physical discomfort	Physical distress possibly including injuries	Serious or fatal injury to small number of people	Multiple fatalities
Effect on airport reputation	Slight to moderate impact	Loss of community reputation	Loss of state reputation	Loss of national reputation	Loss of international reputation
Financial loss	Slight damage is less than $10,000	Noticeable damage between $10,000 and $100,000	Large damage between $100,000 and $1,000,000	Major damage between $1,000,000 and $10,000,000	Severe damage exceeds $10,000,000

FIGURE 4.7

Risk severity classification.

a 95% chance. In contrast, individuals more commonly differentiate between percentage benchmarks such as a 25%, 50%, or 75% chance of risk.

As the previous example demonstrates, classifying risks can be a subjective endeavor. Whereas one individual may assign a consequence as minor, another, given the same set of criteria may assess a consequence as major, as both individuals have a different perspective on the value or meaning of minor versus major. ACRP Report 1b (Ayres et al., 2009) recommends more descriptive forms of distinction, for example: *physical discomfort to people* in lieu of *minor consequence*, and *physical distress, possibly including injuries requiring immediate medical attention*, in lieu of *major consequence*. Depending on the individual reviewing the information, these descriptors can leave little doubt as to their meaning or are subject to wide interpretation. The risk severity chart in Figure 4.7 is from ACRP Report 1b.

PRIORITIZE, TREAT, AND MONITOR RISKS

Following the identification and assessment of risk, airport operators develop policies, strategies, and tactics to mitigate the identified risk. Mitigating risk includes reducing the likelihood or the severity of the risk. Strategies for reducing likelihood include raising awareness of the risk; establishing **SOPs** to suspend operations under certain hazardous conditions; establishing safe operating parameters; and increasing supervision of the activity. Strategies for reducing severity include improving emergency response; training; conducting exercises; improving infrastructure, such as Runway Safety Areas; and installing Engineered Material Arresting Systems (Ayres et al., 2009, p. 80).

Risks can often be mitigated in one of two ways: engineering solutions or human solutions. A maxim in Airport Operations is that "if it can't be fixed with an engineering solution, then it must be fixed with an operational or human solution." However, risk mitigation strategies that rely on human performance usually vary in reliability (Ayres et al., 2009, p. 81). Other methods of reducing or mitigating risk include risk avoidance, risk transfer, risk assumption, or risk control.

By using risk avoidance strategies, airport operators strive to prevent moderate and severe risk from occurring through an operational, procedural, or system modification (e.g., by closing a runway near a construction area). Risk may be shared or transferred from one party to another, for instance, when an airport operator issues a NOTAM. The NOTAM may be to identify a hazard, such as a construction crane. Once the operator notifies all of the pilots using the airport of the risk, the in-flight risk is transferred to the pilots. However, the issuance of a NOTAM, as in this case, does not absolve the airport from other issues of liability, such as maintaining obstruction barricades or obstruction clearance lighting.

Risk assumption assumes that the risk is classified at an acceptable level and no further intervention is possible or necessary. *Risk control* includes implementing additional policies, procedures, and engineering solutions to reduce the risk. Mitigation actions are not always a "one-and-done" type of solution. Some risks require numerous strategies, some engineering, some substitution with alternative methods or technologies, some procedural, and some human. Some strategies include implementations over *immediate*, *short*, *medium*, and *long* terms.

EXAMPLE OF SAFETY RISK MANAGEMENT

Jefferson County Airport,[7] a busy GA airport in central Colorado, was experiencing a high level of runway incursions and **vehicle/pedestrian deviations (VPDs)**. The airport was in jeopardy of losing its federal funding for failing to uphold Grant Assurance #19, maintaining the airport in a safe and serviceable condition.

Airport personnel analyzed the numerous incursions and VPDs and determined that the incidents did not share a common cause. There were certainly "hot spots" where more incursions occurred than others, but, all incursions were not at the same location on the airport. The results of the analysis showed that there were problems throughout the airfield, but that one of the most serious problems was an airport culture that, over time, had become tolerant of the safety violations.

With the airport's Grant Assurance funding at risk, the airport staff developed a risk management strategy that incorporated several elements, which were categorized into immediate, short-, medium-, and long-term phases. An immediate action was to close the airport's crosswind runway, which was in use less than 5% of the time per year, and could be reopened without undue delay if needed. Another immediate solution was a "press leak" that the airport would now begin the process of writing an ordinance to fine individuals who committed VPDs or incursions. While the process of drafting an ordinance could take years, the press leak resulted in articles in GA publications about the topic and rumors throughout the airport that a fine system was already in place. The culture shift was underway.

Short-term solutions involved procedural changes to airport access privileges and requiring certain vehicles to use designated Vehicle Service Roads rather than taxiways to access part of the airport. Another short-term solution was to reassign operations personnel to conduct more airport patrols. This solution could only be temporary, as it was not sustainable over the long term because of costs and other job duties of personnel. Medium-term solutions involved a driver-training program for all airport personnel. Long-term solutions involved installation of a wildlife fence

(Continued)

[7]Now known as Rocky Mountain Metropolitan Airport.

(Continued)

surrounding the entire airport, and vehicle access control gates with card reader systems to restrict airfield access to only those who had completed the driver-training program. The result: Within days, the number of VPDs and runway incursions began to drop and continued to drop in the months and years following.

SUMMARY

Flying remains one of the safest forms of transportation. Throughout the history of aviation, government agencies, aircraft and airport operators, and aircraft manufacturers have sought to improve safety. However, many of the safety improvements in the industry have only come after an accident, often only with those resulting in the loss of lives. Improvements in technology, such as weather reporting, continue to reduce the risks to aviation.

An SMS is a methodology designed to identify risks and hazards associated with flying, and to apply mitigation strategies. The benefit of implementing an SMS includes the reduction of costs from accidents and incidents, improved morale and employee productivity, and a logical prioritization of safety needs.

The four pillars of SMS are **safety policy**, **SRM**, **SA**, and **safety promotion**. The first two areas, policy and risk management, were addressed in this chapter. Policy establishes management's commitment to safety. SRM is used to identify hazards and assign severity and likelihood to apply mitigation and prevention strategies. The SA process acts as the quality control system for SMS, ensuring that the mitigation measures are effective. The safety promotion phase is focused on establishing a culture of safety within the airport.

The SRM process includes monitoring to ensure that corrective actions are having their desired effect; establishing a reporting system for safely violations or newly identified hazards; ensuring that internal safety investigations take place to determine the causes of accidents and incidents; improving SOPs; and assessing the impact of safety-related changes.

San Antonio Airport System Jumps into the World of Safety Management Systems—Experiences and Lessons Learned—What We Did, Why We Did It, How We Did It, and How It Is Turning Out Today

by Tim O'Krongley, A.A.E., IAP
Assistant Aviation Director

Between 2007 and 2009 the FAA conducted a series of three pilot studies focusing on various aspects of SMS. The first SMS pilot study required the participating airports to develop their SMS Manual and Implementation Plan. Twenty-six airports participated in the first study program. The second SMS pilot study focused on gathering information on scalability and how smaller airports might implement SMS and was limited to smaller airports. The third SMS pilot study was a Part 139 SMS Implementation Study and was limited to airports that participated in the first or second studies. Since San Antonio International Airport had

(Continued)

(Continued)

participated in the first pilot program and is a medium-hub airport, we participated in the first and third FAA SMS pilot studies.

So *WHY* did the San Antonio Airport System decide to participate in the pilot programs? I had become familiar with the concept of SMS through several different Airports Council International (ACI) training programs focused on international aviation regulations. After conducting our own research, reading International Civil Aviation Organization (ICAO) documents and information from the FAA on the subject, we decided to pursue participation in the initial pilot program. On a personal level, being a pilot and having a background in Airport Operations, I understood and could appreciate the concept of a proactive approach to safety versus the traditional reactive approach. I presented the concepts of SMS to the other members of the Airport's Executive management team to gain consensus; we applied for the first pilot program. The first pilot program was extremely beneficial to our Airport System, because our staff was able to gain a detailed understanding of the benefits that a properly developed SMS program could bring to our airports. It also allowed us to fully understand the challenges that would be associated with designing, implementing, and regulating such a program. In addition to highlighting the benefits and challenges, the pilot program also delineated the firm commitment that would be required by the executive management team, both in *support* and *action* to make the program a success.

We were not eligible to participate in the second pilot program, since it focused on small-hub airports. When the third pilot program was announced, the Airport System eagerly volunteered and was accepted into the study. By the conclusion of the first pilot study we realized the benefits that could be obtained by our Airport System if we elected to proceed in implementing SMS ahead of rulemaking. That is why the third pilot program was enticing. We felt so strongly that the benefits we could gain in increased safety, customer service levels, and risk mitigation efficiencies would outweigh any possible downsides to having to come back later and change the program once rulemaking was finalized. Additionally, we decided to implement SMS across the entire airport. We elected not to concentrate our SMS program solely on the airside or, more specifically, on the movement area.

So why would we do this ahead of rulemaking? The benefits of a top-driven and proactive safety system were clearly evident to us as we finished the pilot programs. Through our research we found that the concept of SMS has been in place in the military and other industries for long periods of time with proven benefits. As a result of the pilot programs and independent research we conducted, our Airport System elected to implement an SMS campus-wide. We understood this would be a large and daunting undertaking, especially ahead of rulemaking. We ran the risk of implementing a program that could have to be drastically changed once rulemaking was finalized. On the other hand, not having the constraint of formal rulemaking and federal requirements allowed us to be creative in designing our program, which presented some unique challenges. First and foremost, developing a culture that ensures an SMS will not only survive but thrive, requires several key items to be addressed early in the process.

(Continued)

(Continued)

1. It must be embraced and championed by the highest management level at the airport.
2. Employee acceptance and participation is a "must" in addition to gain genuine buy-in into the new safety culture.
3. Significant challenges are present if implementation is limited to certain parts of the airport staff. We believed that if the SMS were only applied to a portion of the airport we would not be able to achieve the required *culture* and employee buy-in at all levels. How could we ask a portion of our employees to be proactive, engaged, and participating in this new safety culture while other (i.e., landside operations) employees are not participating in the program?
4. I believe an SMS is scalable in both staffing and implementation, but requires a thoughtful and well-executed plan that is based on the proper culture being implemented in the first place.

So what did we do? We started off by conducting a gap analysis. The purpose of the gap analysis was to examine our current policies and procedures and identify deficiencies in the draft rulemaking language.

Second, we conducted a series of workshops. We invited tenants, employees, and stakeholders. The goal of the workshops was to gather data, inform tenants and key stakeholders, and solicit input. We conducted interviews and focus groups with such companies as AT&T, USAA, and Valero in the United States Air Force—all who operate their own level of SMS. One surprising result for us was that some of our tenants had already been using an SMS for several years. We realized our implementation could happen at a much faster rate by having these partners work with us. We developed a draft review committee for the SMS manual and internal working groups. The internal working groups were key in establishing the basis for the program. This grassroots approach and buy-in also provided the groundwork to change the culture.

Corporate culture is usually defined as the values and behaviors adopted by employees of a company. How corporate culture is developed varies from company to company. It can be established in a formal method with written statements such as adherence to a mission statement, or informal methods such as by merely being understood. There are two overarching principles of SMS related to culture development: First, the employees must adopt an attitude of being proactive rather than reactive. Second, the program must be wholeheartedly supported by the top level of the organization in both words as well as actions. These two principles are the foundation for creating an SMS safety culture. We adopted these principles in creating our SMS program. However, we quickly realized that using these two principles could also be used as building blocks when discussing other areas and behaviors within the organization. The most similar example is adopting these two principles to your security program. We adopted the principles of the Security Management Systems (SeMS). Just like in SMS, the underlying principles of SeMS are being proactive and supported by the top level of management on everything related to security. While this seems like common sense for safety and security, the two basic principles can also be applied to other areas within your

(Continued)

(Continued)

organization. If you develop a culture that clearly directs employees' focus on being proactive and that is supported by executive management, then the corporate culture will reflect this attitude in all aspects of the organization; for example, customer service and fiscal responsibility would benefit from the same type of culture.

So what were some of the big takeaways we discovered during this process?

1. The gap analysis is a good learning tool that forces you to look for areas of improvement with regard to the regulation.
2. Other industries have been using SMS for a number years, and we have the opportunity to learn and seek their advice.
3. SMS quite simply just a different approach to risk, being proactive has benefits
4. Implementing an SMS is not a quick process.
5. We viewed creating the culture as one of our more challenging tasks, and that the program would not succeed without executive leadership and support.
6. We realize that in order for the program to be successful (specifically in dealing with safety assurance) we need to establish mechanisms by which the report system could be measured and a way to identify that we were meeting safety requirements. We did this with internal audits, external audits and self-inspections.
7. You must seek input through nonpunitive reporting systems; therefore we created a confidential safety reporting process.
8. We believe SMS is scalable. We realigned current positions to create a safety division. We relocated positions from one area into the safety division and reclassified current positions with new titles and job descriptions specific to safety and SMS.

Our first-year goals were simple:

1. Hire an SMS Manager.
2. Develop an SMS policy statement.
3. Develop a safety policy. A safety policy is the employer's written commitment to the employee to make the workplace a safe place to work. It is the backbone of your company's safety program. One of the first things that is looked at during a safety audit is whether your safety policy is signed by the existing owners, managers, or executive.
4. Begin writing the SMS manual and create the committees as outlined in the SMS plan.
5. Complete the initial SMS training for all aviation department employees.

After we hired our SMS Manager, the next step was to develop an SMS policy statement. We had three main points in our statement:

1. The safety policy for the San Antonio Airport System identifies its commitment to aviation safety:
   - The San Antonio Aviation Department commits to its employees and airport users to provide a safe environment, while supporting a safety program intended to reduce incidents to the lowest possible level. The Aviation Department is committed to providing and maintaining an environment conducive to the safety and health of its

(Continued)

(Continued)

employees, users, and the public. The Aviation Department has primary responsibility for establishing an SMS; however, safety is a shared responsibility of all employees in the workplace. It is everyone's responsibility to support and actively participate in the SMS and incident prevention programs.

2. The Aviation Department is committed to providing and maintaining an environment conducive to the safety and health of its employees, users, and the public.
3. The Aviation Department has primary responsibility for establishing an SMS; however, safety is a shared responsibility of all employees in the workplace. It is everyone's responsibility is to support and actively participate in the SMS and incident prevention programs.

The next step was to develop a five-year plan. Our five-year plan included the following:

1. Develop practices in SOPs;
2. Develop safety promotion activities and programs;
3. Conduct our first internal and external audits;
4. Develop training programs for staff and tenants;
5. Develop annual safety goals; and
6. Finalize the nonpunitive reporting system.

So how are we doing today? Our SMS program has been a tremendous success based on a number of factors. We have written our SMS manual, trained our employees, implemented an internal audit system, and have implemented the program. We regularly participate in national and international forums related to SMS and include staff members participating on ACI APEX teams conducting SMS reviews. The FAA has sent several airports seeking information about SMS to us. We've hosted many different airports that would like to see how we have structured and implemented our SMS program. We have seen both fiscal benefits from implementing the plan as well as a culture shift that has resulted in safety reports from both internal and external sources. These reports are critical to safe operations and feel without the SMS program we would have never obtained the information especially from external stakeholders. Entities are willing to report information knowing that our program takes safety seriously and investigates all reports thoroughly. Today we enjoy the benefits of our SMS program and look forward to final rulemaking.

REFERENCES

Ayres, M., Jr., Shirzai, H., Cardosos, S., Brown, J., Speir, R., Selezneva, O., & ... McCall, E. (2009). *Safety management systems for airports (Vol. 2): Guidebook.* Washington, DC: Transportation Research Board.

Federal Aviation Administration (FAA). (2007). *Introduction to safety management systems (SMS) for airport operators.* Washington, DC: Federal Aviation Administration, (Advisory Circular 150/5200-37).

Federal Aviation Administration (FAA). (2013b). *FAA—Industry Training Standards (FITS).* Retrieved from: https://www.faa.gov/training_testing/training/fits/more/.

Federal Aviation Administration (FAA). (2014a). *Safety management system—components.* Retrieved from: https://www.faa.gov/about/initiatives/sms/explained/components/.

Federal Aviation Administration (FAA). (2014b). *Safety management system—evolution of safety management.* Retrieved from: https://www.faa.gov/about/initiatives/sms/explained/basis/#evolution.

Forrest, J. S. (2006). *Information policies & practices of knowledge management (KM) as related to the development of the global aviation information network (GAIN)—an applied case study & taxonomy development*. Dissertation Abstracts International. (UMI No. 3226963).

Ludwig, D., Andrews, C., Jester-ten Even, N. R., Laqui, C., & MITRE. (2007). *Safety management systems for airports* (Vol. 1). Washington, DC: Transportation Research Board.

National Aeronautics and Space Administration (NASA). (2015). *Aviation safety reporting system*. Retrieved from: http://asrs.arc.nasa.gov/.

National Safety Council. (2010). *Lifetime odds of death for selected causes, United States, 2010*. http://www.nsc.org/learn/safety-knowledge/Pages/injury-facts-odds-of-dying.aspx.

National Transportation Safety Board (NTSB). (2006). *Attempted takeoff from wrong runway Comair Flight 5191 Bombardier CL-600-2B19, N431CA. Lexington, Kentucky*. Retrieved from: http://www.ntsb.gov/investigations/AccidentReports/Reports/AAR0705.pdf.

Office of the Federal Register. (2011). *A guide to the rulemaking process*. Retrieved from: https://www.federalregister.gov/uploads/2011/01/the_rulemaking_process.pdf.

Pitsch, M. (2006). "Comair suing FAA, Lexington airport." *The Louisville (KY) Courier-Journal*. Retrieved from: http://archives.californiaaviation.org/airport/msg38649.html.

Reason, J. (2000, March 18). *Human error: Models and management*. Retrieved July 23, 2015, from: http://www.ncbi.nlm.nih.gov/pmc/articles/PMC1117770/.

Safety Management Systems, 14 CFR § 119.8 (2015).

Stolzer, A., & Halford, C. (2011). *Practical risk management. Implementing safety management systems in aviation* (Vol. 1). Farnham, Surrey: Ashgate.

Stolzer, A., & Halford, C. (2008). *Safety management systems in aviation* (Vol. 1). Aldershot, Hampshire: Ashgate.

Vaughan, D. (1996). *The Challenger launch decision: Risky technology, culture, and deviance at NASA*. Chicago, IL: University of Chicago Press.

FURTHER READING

Federal Aviation Administration (FAA). (2013a). *Aviation safety action program*. Retrieved from: https://www.faa.gov/about/initiatives/asap/.

Federal Aviation Administration (FAA). (2014c). *Safety management—international collaboration*. Retrieved from: https://www.faa.gov/about/initiatives/sms/international/.

Ferguson, M., & Nelson, S. (2014). *Aviation safety: A balanced industry approach*. Clifton Park, NY: Cengage.

International Civil Aviation Organization. (2013a). *Aerodrome standards* (6th ed.). Montreal, Quebec: ICAO.

International Civil Aviation Organization. (2013b). *Safety management manual (SMM)*. Montreal, Quebec: ICAO.

Lewis, K. (2011). Practical risk management. In A. J. Stolzer, C. D. Halford, & J. J. Goglia (Eds.), *Implementing safety management systems in aviation* (Vol. 1, pp. 351–352). Farnham, Surrey, England: Ashgate.

Transportation Security Administration. (2012). *Sensitive security information (SSI)*. Retrieved from: http://www.tsa.gov/stakeholders/sensitive-security-information-ssi.

Wood, R. (2003). *Aviation safety programs: A management handbook* (3rd ed.) Englewood, CO: Jeppesen Sanderson.

SAFETY MANAGEMENT SYSTEMS: PART II

United Airlines Regional Jet on final approach for runway 15 at the Aspen—Pitkin County Regional Airport (KASE) in Aspen, CO.

Image by Shahn Sederberg, courtesy Colorado Division of Aeronautics, 2013.

Approach lighting system as commercial airliner makes final approach and touchdown at Denver International Airport, 2012.

Image by Shahn Sederberg, courtesy Colorado Division of Aeronautics, 2014.

Airport Operations vehicle at the Aspen–Pitkin County Regional Airport (KASE), 2014.

Image by Shahn Sederberg, courtesy Colorado Division of Aeronautics, 2014.

Safety assurance (SA) is the third pillar of Safety Management Systems (SMS) and is the quality control process, to ensure that the hazard and risk mitigation strategies are effective. SA is characterized by an internal nonpunitive reporting system, external audits, and corrective actions.

SA is an oversight process. In part, SA is provided through some of the elements of safety risk management (SRM), including occurrence reporting and investigation of accidents and incidents. However, SA programs require participants to actively seek out potential hazards based on the available data. SA builds on SRM through the collection and assessment of data to monitor compliance, assess the performance of safety measures, and identify safety trends. SA processes and programs can lead to the discovery of previously unidentified existing hazards and/or risk controls that are outdated or no longer effective (FAA, 2014c). SA provides the means to determine whether the equipment, operations, and procedures meet or exceed acceptable safety levels.

SAFETY ASSURANCE

SA is one of the least understood elements of SMS. Essentially, SA is the process of identifying metrics that indicate whether or not an organization is achieving its safety performance objectives and goals. For example, many construction sites use a performance metric indicating the number of days between each workplace-related injury—the premise being that the longer the construction site goes without a workplace-related incident, the safer the site is. Within an airport structure, a common safety indicator might be the number of runway incursions or Vehicle Pedestrian Deviations.

Identifying a single, safety performance metric rarely describes the state of safety within an organization. For example, frequent runway incursions may indicate one of several underlying problems: perhaps the operators are using unsafe operating practices on the airfield, airfield personnel lack training, or the training program has an error; perhaps the problem is related to an access control issue that is allowing unauthorized individuals who are causing the incursions onto the field. Regardless, effective SA seeks to identify all contributing factors for poor safety performance in a particular operational area, whether the fault is a single incidence or a series of linked, contributing factors.

SA also seeks to discover indications that may be predictive of a potential hazard or risk. SA includes internal and external data analysis reporting and auditing. These processes often help Airport Managers to diagnose trends or underlying issues that may reveal a latent hazard or risk.

According to the FAA, "Safety Assurance is a set of processes that monitor the organization's performance in meeting its current safety standards and objectives as well as contribute to continuous safety improvement." SA is a quality-control system used to ensure that risk mitigation strategies and tactics are having their intended effect (Transportation Research Board of the National Academies, 2012, p. 35). SA and SRM are different in that the purpose of SA is to identify and evaluate deficiencies and improve the performance of the system, whereas SRM assesses individual hazards and associated risks.

ELEMENTS OF SAFETY ASSURANCE

SA is used to evaluate the continued effectiveness of risk control strategies and tactics by identifying new hazards or risks. SA applies controls and ensures organizational compliance with SMS requirements (FAA, 2014b). SMS is iterative in process and continuous in feedback as each new hazard is identified or as operational procedures change. For example, for an event such as airport construction, SA will demand that this new risk be continuously evaluated, mitigated, and monitored (FAA, 2014b).

The history of aviation is replete with examples of SA being applied after a major accident or incident. In these cases, investigations were conducted, the hazards or contributing factors were identified, and mitigation measures were applied to reduce the probability of a recurrence of the same hazard or risk. In contrast, a guiding principle of modern SA is to (a) preemptively ensure that hazards are identified and assessed for predictability, (b) select the appropriate methods or processes for mitigating or controlling the hazards identified or predicted, and (c) assign responsibility for implementing and evaluating the strategies and tactics employed for controlling the existing or predicted risk or hazard (Stolzer & Halford, 2008). In this way, SA is focused on measuring the effectiveness of controls for mitigating or eliminating risks or hazards.

SA is sustained through safety oversight and internal and external auditing. These essential components of SA require continuous safety evaluations through employee feedback, data analysis, and SA system assessment (FAA, 2014b). To be effective, the SA system assessment need be neither extensive nor complex (Airport Safety & Operations Division, 2007). An SMS evaluation of SA should include:

1. Safety performance indicators and targets.
2. Monitoring of adherence to safety policies.
3. Allocation of resources for safety oversight.
4. Solicitation of input utilizing nonpunitive, safety reporting systems.
5. A systematic review of feedback from self-inspections, assessments, reports, safety risk analysis, and safety audits.
6. The communication of findings to staff and the implementation of agreed-upon mitigation strategies.
7. The promotion of a systems approach to safety throughout the overall operation of the airport.

A systematic approach addresses significant safety hazards and the potential risks associated with each of those hazards. Safety oversight, performance monitoring, and a continuous improvement process provide feedback necessary to assess the effectiveness of the SMS program. Safety audits demonstrate how well the airport is meeting its safety objectives.

Internal audits are performed by each department within an organization to ensure personnel are following proper procedures and that the organization is achieving its safety objectives (Ludwig, Andrews, Jester-ten Veen, & Laqui, 2007, p. 10). Operations personnel are usually considered the prime technical experts in their assigned job duties or task functions. Therefore, an SMS SA **internal audit** focuses the immediate responsibility for the safety of the job or task on the person who has operational control over those functions (Stolzer & Halford, 2008). Internal audits should be performed on a regular basis and may be conducted via employee surveys and formal or informal inspections (Ludwig et al., 2007, p. 10).

External audits are conducted by personnel or agencies peripheral to the organization or unit being examined. In the aviation industry, regulatory agencies typically perform external audits. However, the airport operator and SMS Manager should retain other outside agencies, such as firms with expertise in auditing safety programs, to also conduct outside audits. When a regulatory agency conducts an audit, fines or other penalties levied against the airport operator may result. Additionally, regulatory agencies do not regulate all of the operations of an airport and will, therefore, ignore auditing areas not under their regulatory authority.

Regular management review of SA and audit results is one of the most important parts of any sustainable SA program. If an audit or a management review finds a discrepancy, **corrective actions** should be taken to ensure that the hazard or risk is mitigated or resolved (Ludwig et al., p. 11).

Since SA programs at most U.S. airport operators are still in the early stages of implementation, SMS Managers may benefit from examining existing SA programs in the airlines and other related industries. One example of an airline-related, SA process is the **Flight Operations Quality Assurance (FOQA)** program. FOQA data is collected through aircraft data recorders and placed into a data warehouse for analysis by the airline and federal agencies. Flight operations are analyzed by software that identifies trends and looks for areas exceeding established tolerances (Stolzer & Halford, 2008). FOQA data can reduce or eliminate specific safety risks, as well as minimize deviations from regulations. The FAA uses FOQA to analyze national airline safety trends in order to support recommendations to Congress that may mitigate existing or potential associated risks. FOQA can identify operational situations involving increased risk, which allows the airline operator to take corrective action before that risk results in an incident or accident (FAA, 2013).

Another example of an external airline SA process is the **Air Transportation Oversight System (ATOS)**. ATOS is the FAA's primary tool for overseeing the safety of the nation's airlines. The fundamental principle of ATOS is that air carriers must have properly designed systems to eliminate or reduce risks before they result in accidents or incidents (FAA, 2014a). ATOS asks FAA inspectors to look at the air carrier as a whole, as well as how systems-of-systems interact to assure safety, rather than simply inspecting for compliance with rules (FAA, 2014a). The FAA's ATOS **Air Carrier Assessment Tool (ACAT)** examines risk indicators to look for conditions that may be creating hazards in the air carrier's systems, which allows the inspector to prioritize oversight activities in the external SA audit process.

The **Aviation Safety Action Program (ASAP)** is used by line personnel to voluntarily report potential safety hazards to SMS authorities and management. The program is nonpunitive and ensures that reporting parties will not be penalized for reporting inadvertent errors (Stolzer & Halford, 2008). The purpose of ASAP is to obtain reports of safety-related concerns or events in order to identify the associated root cause.

TRUST MANAGEMENT & THE SAFETY CULTURE

Trust management is a key aspect of SA and necessary for building a *safety culture*. Trust management is grounded in ethics—it is greatly dependent on mutual respect of and by all stakeholders within an organization, regardless of position or authority. It requires open and honest communications in a nonpunitive environment for sharing safety-related information across organizational boundaries. It requires managers to be visible, approachable, and proactive in issuing feedback, advisories, and training to employees as related to all safety issues.

Once the root cause or other contributing factors are identified from ASAP data and information, corrective actions and ways to evaluate those corrective actions can be developed to address the contributing factors to the risks or hazards. ASAP is dependent on and enhances **trust management**, an essential component of a sustainable *safety culture* (see "Trust Management & the Safety Culture").

Title 14 CFR Part 139 is considered by many in the industry to be a form of an SMS. Inherent to the issuance of a Part 139 certification, the FAA conducts a hazard analysis and dictates a set of mitigation strategies, performance standards, and inspection requirements for commercial service airports. However, Part 139 only applies to certain areas of the airport, including the commercial service-use runways and associated taxiways. Certain other measures in 139, such as wildlife controls, affect the entire airport but only to the extent that wildlife could impact commercial-flight operations. An airport developing an SMS program should add SA elements to its preexisting Part 139 self-inspection process by including all nonregulated portions of the airfield, such as ramp areas, non-movement areas, fuel farms, and baggage makeup areas. While the FAA has previously stated it does not intend to require airports to extend SMS to landside and terminal areas, an airport may voluntarily (and should) do so.

SAFETY ASSURANCE OVERSIGHT AND MEASUREMENT

As described above, trust management and SA are mutually related. To enhance safety through trust management, it is vital for management to establish and publish an SA oversight and outcomes measurement process. SA oversight programs should include the following activities:

1. Conducting internal assessments of operational processes at regularly scheduled intervals;
2. Using checklists when conducting safety evaluations;
3. Assessing when contractor and tenant activities may affect the safety of the airport's operation;
4. Using an outside entity to evaluate processes;
5. Documenting results and corrective actions;
6. Documenting positive observations;
7. Categorizing findings of investigations and audits, as well as prioritizing corrective actions; and
8. Sharing the results with personnel (Joint Helicopter Safety Implementation Team of the International Helicopter Safety Team, 2007).

According to the International Civil Aviation Organization (ICAO) *Safety Management Manual*, adequate safety management requires feedback on safety performance (ICAO, 2013). Numerous parties are interested in improving the safety process. However, perspectives on how to categorize or evaluate safety (i.e., deciding what is safe, and what is not) vary among an organization's stakeholders. For example, staff generally desire a safe, sustainable, work environment, whereas supervisory personnel tend to be more concerned with allocating resources and assets to meet safety goals and regulations, while keeping the production goals of the operation in mind. Passengers are concerned with their own safety and their desire to arrive at their destination—on time and injury free. Upper management may be concerned with protecting the corporate image, while shareholders are interested in protecting their investment (ICAO, 2013).

Deciding whether a process or operation is "safe enough" depends on how stakeholders view or value safety. Senior management is often guilty of setting "**zero accidents**" as a goal (see "The Myth of 'Zero Accidents'");[1] however, as long as aviation involves risk, accidents will happen.

---

[1]In 1995, Secretary of Transportation Federico Pena and FAA Administrator David Hinson committed to a safety goal of zero accidents for the aviation community. Consistent with this zero-accident goal, the FAA initiated Challenge 2000, a comprehensive review of the agency's safety oversight capabilities: http://www.gpo.gov/fdsys/pkg/FR-1995-11-02/html/95-27229.htm. Also note the primary motivation for the Global Aviation Information Network was to seek a zero-accident goal (Forrest, 2006).

THE MYTH OF "ZERO ACCIDENTS"

The concept of creating plans and processes for seeking an operational safety goal of zero accidents has been sought by many cultures, organizations, and industries. While perhaps noble in intent, no human system or artifact has been designed yet that is not subject to some level of risk. A caution to SMS Managers and airport authorities should be made in this regard. Fixation on trying to achieve a zero-accident rate on any element of Airport Operations can actually cause safety to regress across the airport environment. This can happen by allocating a disproportional amount of time and resources to address a specific safety concern for achieving 0% risk. An SMS program should seek to balance and dedicate resources to help ensure safety to those elements posing the greatest risks at the airport, rather than focus on a safety related goal that is not sustainable in the long run.

A more realistic goal would be to concentrate on mitigating risks and identifying hazards throughout the organization and in all processes. Regulatory requirements are another unreliable measure of organizational safety, as they typically describe minimum "safe" operating parameters, but not necessarily the best or most effective. This fact is evident in the drafting of the **Airport Certification Manual (ACM)** for commercial service airports.

The ACM is a document written by airport staff that explains how the airport will comply with Title 14 CFR Part 139. This practice effectively has the airport operator creating its own regulations, which are reviewed and approved by the FAA. Once approved, the ACM becomes the "regulations" for that airport and can be held to regulatory enforcement practices. Within the industry, regulated parties (i.e., airport operators) are often advised to write their procedures, such as the ACM, to comply with the regulatory minimum, but to attempt to exceed the minimum safety standards in practice. Writing to a higher regulatory standard may put the airport in the position of assigning itself unrealistic or unsustainable regulations. Additionally, once something is a "regulation," it is exposed to the subjective interpretation of a government inspector, who may or may not completely understand the nature of the operation or the intent of the regulation. A similar situation exists in the aviation security side of the house. Airport operators draft their own **Airport Security Programs (ASPs)**, explaining how their airport will comply with the requirements of Title 49 CFR Part 1542 (Airport Security), which are then reviewed and approved by the Transportation Security Administration (TSA). Anything written in the ASP becomes a regulation for the airport operator and subject to regulatory enforcement (e.g., fines) if the airport cannot sustain the requirements of the ASP. While some argue that a safety-conscious organization should hold itself to a higher standard and be willing to write regulations to match, far too many regulators readily misinterpret the requirements in a way that puts the airport in the position of constantly arguing over fines rather than focusing on safe operating practices.

While statistical measures, such as number of days since the last workplace-related injury, or thousands of hours flown without an accident, may be useful to assess whether safety is getting better or worse, they must be viewed in context. For example, a small airline operating throughout Alaska would likely have a higher accident rate than an airline flying the same type of aircraft throughout the Midwest part of the United States. While pilots in Alaska are exceptional when it comes to recognizing weather patterns and flying in bad weather, the terrain and dynamic weather create more risks to flying than the American Great Plains. Additionally, while an organization may go without an accident or incident for a long period of time, that may not accurately reflect a safe organization—there may be latent conditions that are revealed over a course of time, such as the normalization of deviation that was one of the causes of the Space Shuttle *Challenger* explosion.

SAFETY REPORTING AT AIRPORTS

Numerous government regulations already require airport operators to report when safety-related incidents or issues occur. Many of these requirements can be adopted as performance measures, but since the failure to report each one may result in a compliance violation, it may be best to identify the factors that lead up to each of these failures. These contributing factors can then be tracked as part of the SA program.

In ACRP (Airport Cooperative Research Program) Synthesis Report 58, researchers discovered that airports commonly use three types of data in collecting and reporting issues. Internal airport use included airport safety data, accidents, incidents, health and safety, near misses on the airfield, and terminal and landside mishaps. State, regional, or multiairport reporting systems where the information is shared throughout the system is another method to track safety data and trends. External airport safety data reporting, such as through the FAA, National Transportation Safety Board (NTSB), and other government agencies, was used to gather information on means and methods of reporting data, along with analysis of follow-up practices and procedures (Transportation Research Board of the National Academies, 2012, p. 1).

Airports certificated under Part 139 are required to collect several safety-related data elements to maintain safe operations. The most prolific is the daily checklist. Part 139 requires the airport operator to conduct a safety self-inspection at least once prior to the beginning of commercial-flight operations that day and at least once prior to the beginning of commercial-flight operations at night. These checklists identify required elements of compliance under Part 139 and include areas such as pavement condition, the condition of the safety areas, signs, marking, lighting, and numerous other factors. In addition to any accidents or incidents, airport operators are also required to report wildlife strikes through the FAA's Wildlife Strike Database.

Inspection records are required to be kept for 12 consecutive calendar months, and every airfield inspector must be trained how to inspect the airfield annually. Training records for these personnel are kept on file for 24 months, along with the curriculums used for their initial and recertification training programs. On an annual basis, the **FAA Airport Certification Safety Inspector (ACSI)** conducts an audit to ensure compliance with Part 139.

Airport operators are also required to keep the FAA up-to-date about the conditions of the airfield. Short-term conditions are expressed through the NOTAM (Notices to Airmen) process. Permanent changes must be filed with the FAA using FAA Form 5010−1, otherwise known as the **Airport Data Record**. The Airport Data Record contains information on the airport's operation, numbers of enplanements, flight operations and type, and services provided by the airport, such as the provision of certain types of aviation fuel and oxidant (thermal stability/mixture of fuel). Also included in the Airport Data Record is information relating to the runways, including their strength, width, and length; whether they are asphalt or concrete; and whether they are grooved. Along with any permanent NOTAM, the approach and airfield lighting systems are also included on the data record. Whenever a change is made to the airport's infrastructure, it must be reported using a Form 7460 Notice of Proposed Construction or Alteration, and the appropriate updates must be made to the Airport Data Record during the update period.

Obstructions to airspace must also be reported to the FAA. Short-term obstructions typically include construction cranes that have been erected overnight without prior notification to the FAA. Obstructions created as a result of airfield construction, or permanent obstructions as a result of on-airport or off-airport construction, are reported to the FAA under Title 14 CFR Part 157, which requires notice, submitted on Form 7460-1 Notice of Proposed Construction or Alteration. For on-airfield construction, once the construction has been completed, the airport operator files a Form 7460-2 Notice of Actual Construction or Alteration.

The U.S. **Occupational Safety and Health Administration (OSHA)** requires the reporting of accidents involving personnel. However, state and local government workers are excluded from federal coverage. The Occupational Safety and Health Act of 1970 encourages states to operate their own safety- and health-related programs. OSHA language requires each state plan to include "coverage of public employees of the State" and to be "at least as effective as Federal OSHA's protection of private sector employees" (Transportation Research Board of the National Academies, 2012, p. 5).

Title 49 CFR Part 830 requires aircraft operators to report accidents or incidents to the **NTSB**. While Part 830 does not specify that airport operators have such a reporting requirement under Part 139.325 Airport Emergency Plan, airport operators must plan for Aircraft Accidents and incidents, along with other emergencies articulated under 139, and report such accidents to the NTSB.

In addition to the reports airport operators are required to make, numerous voluntary programs provide incident or hazard tracking. This voluntary safety data reporting can come from airport tenant or user groups and include accident or incident information, safety concerns, hazardous conditions on the airport, or hazardous behaviors by airport operators or tenants. Some airports implement the FAA's Runway Safety Action Team and also have developed Runway Safety Action Plans, which engage airport stakeholders in helping to reduce runway incursions and Vehicle Pedestrian Deviations. These teams typically create data about airfield safety that can be analyzed so that risks can be identified and mitigated and to track the success (or lack thereof) of safety initiatives.

Airports looking for more data sources to track should also include airport police and airport fire personnel. Because of the legal reporting requirements, along with the record of dispatching police, fire, and emergency medical personnel, there is typically an accurate record of incidents that have required emergency response and the means and methods of reporting data, along with analysis of follow-up practices and procedures (Transportation Research Board of the National Academies, 2012, p. 17). For example, the number of fires, slips-and-falls in the terminal building, or automobile accidents could provide indicators of an overall safe environment.

Tracking police response, the issuance of citations or tickets, and arrests and the types of arrest made, along with tracking criminal reports, such as theft, can provide airport operators information about the status of criminal activity on the airport. This data can indicate compliance with general rules and regulations, often related to motor vehicle violations means and methods of reporting data, along with analysis of follow-up practices and procedures. These violations can be tracked either on the Air Operations Area (AOA) or landside. Additionally, many large, commercial service airports employ unarmed security officers who must enforce the airport's rules and regulations through some type of Violation Notice process. By assessing the type and numbers of Violation Notices issued, the airport operator can better determine overall compliance with the rules and regulations.

Airport tenants can also be engaged to provide safety-related data such as foreign object debris on the airfield, or activities such as smoking near fueling operations means and methods of reporting data, along with analysis of follow-up practices and procedures (Transportation Research Board of the National Academies, 2012, p. 19). Passengers, pilots, and even third-party vendors and construction contractors can provide safety-related information to airport management. Pilots may see unsafe activities while observing ramp operations from the passenger departure lounge. Pilots can report foreign object debris, wildlife strikes, and weather-related issues, such as airfield surface conditions. Airfield construction managers and individuals overseeing the construction safety plan can also provide data on safety-related violations or concerns at the worksite (p. 20).

While many sources report safety issues, the airport operator must analyze and interpret all of the data and take action, when appropriate. Any action that is causing an imminent danger to personnel or flight operations should be immediately addressed. Unfortunately, many hazards are not readily identifiable. In many cases, individuals might notice an activity they believed to be hazardous, but do not see another way to perform the function and make sure the job still gets done. A method of reporting these types of concerns and ensuring they are properly addressed is essential.

Staff at some airports share their concerns on a daily basis as part of daily shift meetings. Verbal reports are often considered the most efficient means, particularly for a short-term or immediate-fix type of problem (Transportation Research Board of the National Academies, 2012, p. 26). Although the problem may have been reported verbally, a written record should still be created for tracking purposes. Daily, weekly, and monthly operations and maintenance staff meetings are the most common form for staff to report safety issues and for management to communicate resolutions or seek additional input (p. 26).

PROTECTING THE IDENTITY OF THE REPORTING PARTY

ACRP Report 58 Safety Reporting Systems at Airports cites a report by the Flight Safety Foundation "that estimated nearly 98% of the aviation safety related information obtained under the voluntary disclosure programs would no longer be available if participants were subject to prosecution and penalties" (Transportation Research Board of the National Academies, 2012, p. 35). For any safety program to work, individuals who report safety issues must experience a comfortable level of anonymity.

SAFETY ASSURANCE AT THE ORGANIZATIONAL LEVEL

At the international level, the **ICAO Universal Safety Oversight Audit Programme** monitors safety performance of Contracting States.[2] Each country is then responsible for safety oversight, often through the establishment of regulations that are enforced by inspectors from each national agency. Regardless of the national agencies involved, the organizational level of any airport must determine the best methods for establishing and maintaining an effective, safety oversight program. The following methods are suggested:

1. Frontline supervisors maintain vigilance by monitoring daily activities
2. Regular inspections of daily activities

---

[2]ICAO refers to countries as Contracting States, meaning that a particular country is a signatory to the 1944 Convention on International Civil Aviation (Chicago Convention).

3. Surveys from employees on how they view safety
4. Systematic review and follow-up of identified safety issues
5. Data collection related to day-to-day performance (i.e., airport self-inspection records)
6. Conduct safety studies
7. Follow a regular audit program, internally and externally
8. Communicate the results of safety programs, hazards, etc., to all affected personnel

Inspections can be as simple as a "walk-around" by safety inspectors or supervisory personnel to assess all areas of the organization. Talking to workers and supervisors, as well as witnessing how the work is actually carried out, in a non-structured way, can provide valuable safety insights (Stolzer & Halford, 2008). Employee surveys can also provide management with an understanding of hazards and risks inherent in the environment. Surveys provide the perceptions and opinions of operational personnel, teamwork issues, problem areas, current areas of dissent or confusion, and an overall assessment of the *safety culture*. An anonymous survey can reveal information that would not normally be revealed in a direct interview.

SAFETY AUDITS

Safety audits are a core management activity. Audits provide a means for assessing how well the airport is meeting its safety objectives, along with feedback to managers about the safety performance of the organization. The ACRP *Guidebook* defines internal audits as "an internal inspection or assessment of the activities, systems, and processes used by the organization related to the safety and the SMS."[3]

Considering that the history of implementation of SMS at many airports is still in the development stages, it may be useful to look at similar safety audit programs. The air carrier industry uses a variety of safety audit processes. The **Line Operations Safety Audit (LOSA)** is one such audit program that has seen excellent safety results for the airline industry.

Line Operations Safety Audit versus Transportation Security Administration

In a LOSA, highly trained observers ride in the jump seat of an air carrier aircraft to collect safety-related data on flight crew performance, operational factors, and environmental conditions (environmental conditions refer to factors such as inside aircraft status-flight-deck conditions, crew status, passenger issues, etc.) (Stolzer & Halford, 2008). The program relies on confidential data collection and an assurance that action will not be taken against pilots who are observed committing errors. In general, the airline industry holds that LOSA offers the following benefits (Stolzer & Halford, 2008):

1. Identification of threats in the airline operating environment
2. Degree-of-transference training assessment
3. Assurance of quality and usability of procedures
4. Identification of human/machine interface problems
5. Identification of pilot shortcuts and workarounds (critical to identifying the normalization of deviation)

---

[3]http://onlinepubs.trb.org/onlinepubs/acrp/acrp_syn_037.pdf

6. Assessment of safety margins

7. Establishment of a baseline for organizational change

8. Determination of a rationale for the allocation of resources

One of the most significant challenges in any reporting system is confidentiality and fear of retribution. Individuals must be protected, legally, from retribution by management or by coworkers when they report a safety violation. For any safety reporting system to be effective, sources and information contained in certain reporting systems must always be kept confidential. While this anonymity is important to protect the identity of individuals making safety reports, it is also critical to have a system in which a company may "self-report" a violation it becomes aware of—not for the purposes of protecting it from legal blowback or regulatory citation, but so that safety issues can be addressed.

One such program used by the airline industry is the **Voluntary Disclosure Reporting Program (VDRP)**. Under the VDRP, if a company becomes aware that a potential violation of the regulations has or might have occurred, it should immediately notify its FAA office, disclosing that information along with corrective actions (Stolzer & Halford, 2008). The FAA then reviews the facts of the situation to determine whether the incident occurred from careless or reckless disregard for safety on the company's part, which is rarely the case (Stolzer & Halford, 2008). The FAA can then accept the report and agree not to pursue fines or certificate action against the airline, provided the company follows up with a "comprehensive fix" addressing the underlying causes of the event (Stolzer & Halford, 2008).

In the airport industry, the TSA has a similar program known as "voluntary disclosure." Airport and air carrier security entities that have regulated security programs under the TSA can voluntarily disclose when they are aware of the potential violation of the security regulations. Provided that the regulatory violation was not intentional, that it was corrected immediately, and that an action plan has been put into place to prevent or reduce the likelihood of further such instances, the TSA will agree not to fine or take certificate action against the airport or air carrier. Unfortunately, because of the nature of these TSA reports, which are classified as Sensitive Security Information (SSI), they are not available to the public or to other airport operators.

Some in the academic world have tried to create a security reporting system, similar to VDRP, but the TSA does not have a method to disseminate the information to other airports and air carriers. The TSA can track incidents and do some trend analysis through the **Performance and Results Information System (PARIS)**, which is used to track and report security breaches, along with the **Transportation Security Operations Center (TSOC)** (Department of Homeland Security, Office of Inspector General, 2012, p. 3). Unfortunately, the TSA does not have a centralized mechanism in place to consolidate the information about all security breaches and, therefore, has a limited ability to monitor trends or make general improvements to security (p. 8). TSA employees do not always properly report, track, and analyze all security breaches, nor do they always document their own actions to correct security breach vulnerabilities (p. 8).

Another challenge with the TSA in supporting security information sharing is that the TSA's responsibility for standard Airport Operation and line-security concerns cease when they became employees of TSA. They are no longer involved in the day-to-day challenges and issues of line security personnel, such as Airport Security Coordinators, police officers, and security personnel. This detachment of involvement in Airport Operations and security decreases the volume and effectiveness of the information that TSA agents are able to report. This aspect, coupled with not having the means to share SSI security data or information, or even conduct and share analysis of the data or information, leaves many SMS Managers and airport operators lacking in best practices or understanding of current issues as related to Airport Security.

Safety (or security) information sharing systems must have a feedback process to remain sustainable and to build trust in all stakeholders in the system. As part of any SA program, the anonymity of the reporting parties must be maintained for the program to be effective; however, the hazards and risks that are identified cannot be kept a secret, nor can the measures that are put into place to mitigate the hazard or risk. In some cases, it may be riskier to implement a particular type of solution that can only be identified by others familiar with the operation. In other words, SA does not exist in a vacuum. If an issue is reported to management, management should collaborate with all stakeholders to determine the appropriate corrective action. The risk or hazard must be shared in order to gain the benefit of the perspective of several parties throughout the chain of command so that the best corrective actions can be identified.

International Civil Aviation Organization Safety Audit Recommendations

The key issues in performing safety audits include *surveillance and compliance, areas and degree of risk, and competence and safety management* (ICAO, 2013). Although the ICAO safety audit guidance is for Contracting States (i.e., countries) and their regulatory agencies, some lessons learned can be taken and applied to airport SMS programs.

1. **Surveillance and Compliance:** Airport operators should ensure that the regulatory requirements and standard operating procedures are complied with. Inspections, observation, and reporting systems can provide insights into whether regulations are being violated and to what degree.
2. **Areas and Degree of Risk:** A safety audit should ensure the organization's SMS is based on sound principles and procedures. The airport must have a system in place to periodically review procedures to ensure all safety standards are continuously met.[4]
3. **Competence and Safety Mangement:** Staff must be adequately trained to ensure the SMS functions as intended. This does not necessarily mean the safety manager must be trained to a high level of competence in all of the airport systems. However, highly competent individuals with the level of expertise necessary to evaluate the performance of a procedure and determine whether it is within standards should be identified within the organization.

In its *Safety Management Manual*, ICAO includes a self-audit checklist for an organization to assess the completeness and effectiveness of the organization's safety processes. The checklist includes categories such as *management structure, corporate stability, financial stability, management selection and training, workforce, and relationships with regulatory authorities.*

The safety audit is a core activity of the SMS. Audits ensure the structure of the SMS is sound and has the appropriate levels of staffing. Audits ensure the organization is complying with procedures, regulations, and standard operating procedures (SOPs). They ensure that personnel have a satisfactory level of competence in training to maintain their levels of performance and that

---

[4]http://www.icao.int/safety/SafetyManagement/Documents/Doc.9859.3rd%20Edition.alltext.en.pdf

equipment is performing adequately for the level of safety desired (ICAO, 2013, pp. 2–17). Audits can also identify whether effective systems for promoting safety and monitoring safety performance are in place and whether the organization is able to handle foreseeable emergencies (ICAO, 2013).

Safety audits should be conducted regularly and include a detailed review of the safety performance and practices of each work unit that is assigned safety responsibilities. The audit team must also assess whether the procedures that are in use are appropriate to the specific risk or hazard being addressed, and they must also measure the ability of those processes to mitigate potential negative consequences resulting from the safety issue (ICAO, 2013).

Checklists are frequently used to identify the items to be reviewed during an audit to help ensure all intended areas for examination are covered. Audits should never be punitive in nature. The objective is to gain knowledge about the state of safety within the airport operational system. Auditors should produce a written report describing their findings and recommendations, which are then presented to the appropriate workgroup. The auditor should also provide positive feedback, identify deficiencies (avoiding negative criticism if possible), and develop a plan of action to resolve the deficiencies (ICAO, 2013). Follow-up audits should be conducted to ensure that any prescribed corrective actions were taken.

This audit process is similar to what the FAA does on an annual basis to certify commercial service airports under Part 139. The FAA inspector conducts an annual inspection of all Part 139 checklisted items to ensure compliance with regulations. If deficiencies are identified, the airport operator is counseled and expected to produce a plan of action to correct the deficiencies. The FAA may make spot inspections throughout the year, particularly for corrective action items with deadlines of less than a year, to ensure that action is being taken. Deficiencies repeated the following year may bring enforcement penalties or put the airport's Airport Improvement Plan (AIP) funding in jeopardy due to failure to comply with the grant assurances.

At their core, safety audits are about identifying the right things to be done, checking to ensure that they are being accomplished, and, if not, taking corrective actions or finding alternative solutions to the ineffective procedure or process.

SAFETY ASSURANCE—LESSONS LEARNED

ACRP Synthesis 37 Lessons Learned from **Airport SMS Pilot Studies** (completed in 2012) assessed the results of several airport pilot studies. Unfortunately, because of the short duration of the SMS implementation study, many participating airports were unable to conduct audits within the 13-month study timeframe. In many of the pilot studies, airports implemented SMS only for the airside areas. Several indicated they were planning to or had expanded beyond the movement area. Only a few airports surveyed were planning to expand SMS into other areas of the airport. Although the FAA does not yet require airports to implement SMS outside of the airside operational areas, that is, to land and terminal areas, an airport may do so voluntarily.

One airport, however, did expand its SMS program into the baggage makeup areas, to address safety concerns such as speeding by tug drivers, foreign object debris, and ground service provider, staff, and tenant baggage carts and tug operations (Transportation Research Board of the National Academies, 2012). However, the majority of the results of the study focused on airside operations.

Many of the airports involved in the study had yet to identify performance measures for their SA processes. Several were still in the process of identifying performance measures, and some were acquiring software or database systems in order to capture and correlate the data. However, these airports replied that they were using a formal SMS SA system, which included three primary categories: accidents, incidents, and wildlife (Transportation Research Board of the National Academies, 2012).

ACRP Synthesis 37 also documented that conducting an SA program audit in the first year can be challenging for any airport (Transportation Research Board of the National Academies, 2012). The report further suggested that a program evaluation where incremental milestones have been achieved may be more beneficial to management in assessing SMS policy objectives and goals (Transportation Research Board of the National Academies, 2012). Data collection is also an issue, but several software programs are available commercially off-the-shelf for use in SA audit data collection and related analytics.[5]

According to ACRP Legal Research Digest 19, *Legal Issues Related to Developing Safety Management Systems and Safety Risk Management at U.S. Airports*, the FAA has stated it will synchronize its SMS efforts both internally and externally (Bannard & Foley & Lardner LLP, 2013). The FAA is committed to an integrated approach to SMS including common definitions, an understanding of risk, consistent methods for analyzing and assessing safety risks, risk management techniques, SA procedures, and a common approach to defining acceptable levels of risk (Bannard & Foley & Lardner LLP, 2013).

SA is one of the more difficult elements of SMS. As SMS is in development at U.S. airports, it is clear that corrective actions should not be taken too quickly after risk management programs and mitigation strategies have been put into place—to do so will inhibit adoption of SMS and degrade trust management. While the effects of SMS and SA strategies might be apparent rapidly after implementation, it will take a period of time in most cases to determine appropriate outcomes assessment and evaluation through SA auditing.

Another challenge to the SA process is that for every mitigated risk or hazard, certain performance indicators must be measured. These performance indicators may not be fully identified until risks have been identified and appropriate mitigating measures have been applied. Some time to track the activity for proper analyses is also necessary. Even when certain performance measures, such as the number of runway incursions, can be used, there may be underlying performance measures that are contributing to the hazard, which cannot be identified until some period of time has passed.

From an organizational and industry perspective, SMS for airport operational safety is still in its infancy. Common performance measures have not been identified, thus no common themes in SA auditing can be uniformly applied to all Part 139 airports in the United States. With time, these performance measures should be identified, and certain commonalities should appear. Furthermore, establishing SA is not just a local activity, but one that needs to actively engage regulators, such as the FAA and other federal, state, and local regulatory agencies. Nonpunitive reporting programs must be established at all levels so that lessons learned can be shared throughout the industry and from one airport to another.

---

[5]For examples, see: http://www.asms-pro.com/or https://cmo-software.com/solutions/other/aviation-sms-safety-management -system/ or http://www.etq.com/airsafety/ plus many others.

THE CULTURE OF SAFETY

A *safety culture* can be defined as an organizational commitment to safety throughout all levels of the organization. Safety cultures can be difficult to describe and quantify but when one is established, it is perceptible and obvious (Ayres et al., 2009). The safety promotion pillar of SMS involves the establishment of a safety culture. Dan McCune, Curt Lewis, and Don Arendt, writing in *Implementing Safety Management Systems*, state: a safety culture is "most difficult to foster" (Stolzer & Halford, 2011, p. 184). While experts agree that a safety culture is a fundamental element to the prevention of accidents and incidents, an effective safety culture must include promotional activities that instill and reinforce that culture. The authors further claim that one of the most significant challenges to implementing and sustaining an effective aviation safety culture is the constant battle between protection (safety) and productivity.

Unfortunately, justifying the implementation of safety measures as a way to increase productivity or financial gain is not often easy. It can be difficult to show top management how many accidents have been prevented by having a strong safety culture (Stolzer & Halford, 2011). However, when an accident or incident does occur, typically it uncovers a problem within the organization's safety culture. The TSA has a similar challenge with many of its security programs. Some programs have been criticized for failing to catch a terrorist; however, it is difficult to measure the effectiveness of a strategy that is designed to deter criminal and terrorist activities.

Safety culture alone is not a pillar of SMS, but it contributes strongly to the SMS pillar of safety promotion. Safety promotion typically includes training and education, safety communication, and continuous improvement. Whether these promotional elements are effective is reliant on the culture of safety (or lack thereof) that has been established at the workplace. This culture either rewards safe behavior or rewards hazardous behavior. All of the posters, safety training, and SA programs obtainable will not contribute to a safe operating environment if the culture within an airport tolerates risky behavior.

TRADITIONAL MODELS OF SAFETY

For decades, many accident investigations have focused on technological failures, bad weather, and human errors as root causes (Ayres et al., 2009, p. 91). However, investigators eventually concluded that there could be other triggers to risk, such as communication breakdowns, decision-making conflicts, and a lack of effective coordination, which could also contribute to accidents and incidents (Ayres et al., 2009, p. 92). For these reasons, airlines began to focus on concepts such as cockpit resource management, and later on crew resource management (CRM), to encourage aircrews to communicate effectively with each other and to make decisions while respecting the opinions of other flight crew members.

James Reason (see the discussion of Reason's Swiss Cheese Model in "The Four Pillars of Safety Management Systems" in Chapter 4) outlined that a safety culture has five characteristics: its membership is (a) informed of safety-related issues, (b) encouraged by and values the act of reporting risks, (c) motivated to learn about safety-related issues, (d) supported by a just culture, and (e) a part of a flexible culture, willing to adapt to change (Reason, 1990). In an informed culture, workers understand the inherent dangers in their work, and they also understand how their work impacts the safety of others; in a reporting culture, employees are encouraged to report safety concerns without fear of punishment or ridicule, and action is actually taken based on the feedback provided; a learning culture is characterized by a questioning attitude aimed at continuous improvement, with employees continually asking the question, "How can we do this better?" (Ayres et al., 2009, p. 92). A flexible culture is comprised of members at all levels willing and able to adopt change necessary for increased safety. A just culture recognizes most errors are unintentional with management attempting to understand and correct the conditions of the work that made the error likely—that is, they learn from feedback and mistakes.

A prime characteristic of a strong safety culture is retaining employees who are proactive in questioning procedures they know to be outdated or making recommendations of new procedures that are safer and more effective. In this way, employees view safety as their responsibility and not only management's responsibility. They understand the nature of their work in terms of safety concerns and inherent associated risks, as well as the organization's stated objectives and goals for SA and continued improved safety.

THE ELEMENTS OF SAFETY PROMOTION

Promoting and enhancing a safety culture includes training, personnel competencies, communication, and awareness. A good safety culture is one in which senior management places a strong emphasis on safety, is willing to accept criticism, and is willing to invest in changing how things are done (Stolzer & Halford, 2011). Additional management measures include promoting realistic and flexible safety rules and ensuring personnel are well trained.

In an effective safety promotion system, the safety manager is responsible for providing current information and training all staff on safety issues. Training programs should include curricula that address any regulatory requirements, validation that measures whether the training was effective, and training that includes human factors and organizational factors. Safety managers should conduct an initial training for all personnel, which addresses safety, in general, in the workplace. Recurrent training should also be required. New employees should be indoctrinated into the SMS process with the highest-level official communicating safety goals and procedures to all employees. However, personnel can be suspicious of the motives of senior management; therefore, it is imperative that safety goals and procedures are also communicated by mid-level management and supervisory and line personnel. Newly hired personnel who can see that safety is a way of doing business will be more open to adopting appropriate safety practices and will become ambassadors of the safety management program. However, if only top management communicates the safety goals, and these goals are not reinforced by supervisory or line personnel, new-hire personnel quickly see that the policies are not supported throughout all levels of the organization.

An example of safety promotion can be observed in the U.S. Coast Guard aviation program. Coast Guard aviators routinely fly in hazardous conditions. While there is an old saying in the Coast Guard that *you have to go out but you don't have to come back*, meaning that you can never turn down a mission, Coast Guard aviation today has fully embraced a safety culture, while continuing to carry out its mission.

Professor Patrick Hudson offers a model with increasing levels of criteria for evaluating the strength of a safety culture (Hudson, 2011). The lowest level in the model is referred to as pathological and is characterized by an attitude similar to *"we don't care as long as we don't get caught."* This attitude is dangerous in any role or profession, but especially in aviation. In some organizations, safety procedures are not encouraged, and hazardous behaviors are encouraged and unofficially rewarded (Torres, 2011). While no manager would be likely to go on record bragging about their organization having a pathological safety culture, such cultures do exist in aviation settings. In pathological organizations, employees openly relate examples of taking unnecessary risks—often bragging of their ability to do so.

At the next level in Hudson's (2011) model, the organization's safety culture is reactive, characterized by an attitude similar to *"safety is important; we do it every time there is an accident."* The aviation industry was, unfortunately, stuck in the reactive mode for many years, reacting to hazards only after the damage was done. Some organizations continue to be reactive because of their size or lack of financial capability to provide adequate levels of safety assurances. In some businesses, financial concerns, or the drive for higher levels of production, may create a reactive safety environment with management waiting until something has gone wrong before addressing the risk.

A **calculative** culture is characterized by an attitude similar to *"we have a system in place to manage all hazards"* (Hudson, 2011). Even though this culture is a significant step up from a reactive one, it puts organizations in an area between reactive and being proactive. While the organization may be forward-thinking in managing existing hazards, it has not yet made a commitment to identify future hazards or hazards that result as processes, technologies, and programs evolve. A calculative culture also provides a false sense of safety—anticipating all possible hazards is unlikely!

In a **proactive** culture, management and staff actively seek out hazards and underlying elements that contribute to hazards and incidents. Managers use safety audits, volunteer reporting systems, and surveys to shift the organizational mindset to one of being proactive rather than reactive (Hudson, 2011). The challenge of a proactive management culture is maintenance. Frequently, after an incident or accident, an organization will take numerous proactive measures, launch safety campaigns, and place a significant focus on identifying risks and hazards, only to have the programs fall to the wayside as time moves farther away from the triggering incident.

A **generative** safety culture is the ultimate goal. A generative safety culture is one that is characterized similar to *"Safety is how we do business."* In a generative safety culture, management uses analytics, especially forecasting tools and modeling techniques, to identify vulnerabilities before they develop into hazards (Hudson, 2011).

CASE STUDY: AVIATION SAFETY IN THE U.S. COAST GUARD

The motto of the U.S. Coast Guard (USCG) is *Semper Paratus*, meaning, "Always Ready." The USCG supports the most advanced integration of aviation Search and Rescue, law enforcement, counterdrug, and maritime fisheries enforcement in the world. After 9/11, the USCG took on additional responsibilities in national counterterrorism. USCG aircraft must be ready to launch within 30 minutes of an alert in all types of weather conditions. To support the demands and high risks that USCG personnel must endure, the branch has a robust safety program with each air station having a dedicated safety department (or division), flight safety officer, and ground safety officer.

The flight safety officer acts as the commanding officer's representative and advisor on all aviation-safety-related matters, reports to the commanding officer on a monthly basis regarding the unit's safety posture, distributes aviation safety literature, and manages a safety incentive program. The flight safety officer further coordinates aviation safety training, manages safety surveys, ensures the completion of mishap reports, and distributes the results of corrective actions.

Using the qualities of safety culture as defined by Reason (1990), the USCG can be characterized as an informed safety culture. For example, the USCG issues directives that are high risk, yet realistic, in terms of the unit's ability to ensure safety of personnel. The USCG communicates and makes certain that all personnel understand all known risks inherent to each operation. It also communicates how safety measures will be applied to keep risks within acceptable limits. Issues such as measures for decreasing fatalities and injuries, as well as the loss of property, are specifically discussed and trained for all personnel for each specific mission. Ultimately, these efforts preserve safety and mission readiness in high-risk environments (Torres, 2011).

As part of being an informed safety culture, the USCG also directs personnel to exercise professional judgment, particularly in the absence of clear guidance or immediate supervision. Coast Guard aviators frequently make decisions at far distances at sea without immediate communication. Even when a Coast Guard aviator can communicate with a command authority, the pilot-in-command is typically provided with safety-related, decision-making authority during the mission, especially at the scene of the emergency or threat.

USCG personnel actively look out for each other's safety, as well as learn about safety from each other. Personnel at all levels are cultured to adopt a proactive way of identifying safety hazards and then following up with appropriate corrective action. The USCG supports letting safety control the situation, as opposed to letting conditions of the incident or threat control safety.

SIGNIFICANT INFLUENCERS AND THE SHARING OF SAFETY INFORMATION WITHIN A SAFETY CULTURE

In many work environments there are "Significant Influencers"—these are peers who may not hold or be charged with formal power, but who have influence or informal power over various stakeholders in the organization. Significant Influencers are usually senior in tenure and are sought by others for advice or guidance. Significant Influencers are critical in providing guidance to junior employees as to how to behave within a culture. When a new individual is hired into the workplace they will observe what behavior is rewarded or punished by observing the actions of the Significant Influencers.

When a Significant Influencer takes a risk, such as reporting their own error or other safety concern, and they are neither punished nor do they experience negative consequences in the work culture—others will see the act of safety reporting as a cultural norm. If, however, a Significant Influencer making these reports is punished or exposed as a source of concern by management, then existing employees will hesitate from sharing safety-related concerns and Significant Influencers will mentor junior employees or peers not to relay safety concerns (or other important information) to management or other stakeholders. At this point, the effort and viability of the work placed into developing an SMS becomes greatly diminished. The ability to sustain SMS in a culture of safety and trust depends on the integrity of the organization's management to demonstrate commitment to the objectives and goals of a safety culture and within it the nonpunitive sharing of safety information.

The Coast Guard fosters a reporting culture, in which all individuals are prepared to report their errors and near misses through clearly defined guidelines (Torres, 2011). Nevertheless, motivating individuals to voluntarily report safety-related errors or threats remains the most difficult challenge in the USCG's informed safety culture. Kent Hollinger (2013) promotes the concept of having a few "reporting pioneers" (p. 199) to be examples to the rest of the organization. These individuals, or "Significant Influencers" (see "Significant Influencers and the Sharing of Safety Information Within a Safety Culture"), can be those with an established reputation for mentorship or with formal or informal power to influence members in the organization to adopt desired cultural values. In addition to utilizing reporting pioneers, the USCG issues formal recognition for excellence in reporting errors and safety issues that can contribute to developing a safety reporting culture. If the identification of legitimate risks or issues is rewarded on a consistent basis, personnel may soon see that as the higher objective over operational productivity.

As a critical component to supporting an informed safety culture, the USCG fosters a just culture, creating an atmosphere of trust in which stakeholders are encouraged and rewarded for providing safety-related information. To sustain these values, the USCG recognizes that certain elements of investigative reporting and analysis may contain information that should only be used for safety purposes and only reviewed by personnel involved with accident investigation and incident prevention. The primary objective in these cases is to keep the identities of those reporting or that have been involved with safety-related issues confidential. Unless laws have been broken or circumstances were caused by deliberate action or negligence, then protecting the identities of those involved is critical for creating an informed safety culture at the USCG.

Another value of the USCG's informed safety culture is to acknowledge that human safety has priority over potential risk to aircraft or other infrastructure. In this case, personnel understand that it is an acceptable norm to make decisions that may jeopardize equipment in seeking a successful mission, yet still protect human life and well-being as the first priority.

The USCG also advocates for a learning culture. In a learning culture, organizations are willing to identify the lessons learned from accidents and incidents, report safety issues, and make changes when the reform is needed (see "Implementing Lessons Learned"). These changes establish new policies and operational procedures that become adopted as standards for higher levels of safety. As part of an informed learning culture, standards are implicit to ensuring safety and continuity of flight operations. For example, during Hurricane Katrina, USCG personnel and operational units were mustered from all over the United States to work together in response to the storm. Because of high levels of standardization in operational requirements and safety, it did not matter whether, for example, winch operators, rescue swimmers, or pilots had worked together previously—they could still execute the mission safely and effectively through their training in standards and safety. While it might seem that standardization would reduce personnel's flexibility to make safety-related decisions, the opposite is true. Standardization is a basic method of routine and repetitive processes. Once individuals are trained in and comply with standard procedures, they can use that experience and skill set as a foundation to make safer ephemeral and adaptive decisions. The USCG also understands the importance of being able to rapidly modify standards in order to safely embrace new or unexpected risks or hazards. In this regard, an informed learning culture remains flexible to meet these challenges. The Coast Guard's ability to do so, however, is based in a strong culture of training and operational standards.

IMPLEMENTING LESSONS LEARNED

All too often, lessons learned are soon forgotten or fail to see implementation after efforts in training have been facilitated. In some cases, training is viewed by management as a way to demonstrate due diligence in SMS without follow-up implementation of the lessons learned. A learning culture within an SMS must take the time and make the expenditure to effect procedural change as the result of training and new knowledge to improve safety.

The ability of an individual and organization to multitask and maintain situational awareness is also codependent on remaining flexible while employing SOPs (see "Target-Fixation and Impulsivity in the Safety Culture"). USCG remains safe and flexible in high-stress, multitasking environments by remaining proactive in its status as an informed safety culture. Torres (2011) outlines the following characteristics as key to the USCG's informed safety culture:

1. Communicating and training personnel in organizational safety objectives;
2. Employing effective safety processes and ensuring an adequate presence of resources;
3. Requiring standardized collaboration processes for operational safety effectiveness;
4. Advocating flexibility in operational procedures that place safety first;
5. Fostering a systemwide culture of trust, especially in regard to voluntarily sharing or reporting safety data or information; and
6. Sustaining a safety culture as a prime directive for the mission of the USCG.

TARGET-FIXATION AND IMPULSIVITY IN THE SAFETY CULTURE

In high-stress/high-risk work environments, employees often become fixated on "getting the job done." This motivation can be intrinsically or extrinsically derived depending on the organizational structure and level of authority of the individual under pressure to perform. The drive to focus on a single objective or goal can lead to a loss of situational awareness and can degrade the ability to sustain a safe environment. The military refers to this phenomenon as **target-fixation**. For example, in both the military and civilian flight environments, a pilot can become so fixated on completing the mission that the pilot fails to continue flying the aircraft safely.

In the civil aviation world, the colloquialisms of "get-there-itis" and "get-down-itis" have similar ramifications to target-fixation. For example, pilots may sometimes make poor decisions or follow improper operating procedures when motivated to "get the airplane on the ground," as a result of feeling pressure from factors such as bad weather or emergency situations. The Aircraft Owners and Pilots Association (AOPA) refers to this hazardous attitude as **impulsivity**. Impulsivity can be experienced by Airport Operations personnel performing in similar high-stress situations as pilots—poor weather, airport emergencies, tight deadlines, etc.

Operations personnel experience hazardous impulsivity, particularly when the airport or runway is closed for snow removal or for a foreign object debris (FOD) check. In these cases, the Airport Operations inspector knows that accomplishing their job quickly is critical to meeting airline scheduling. The inspector may experience pressure from air traffic control (ATC), airlines, and private aircraft operators asking them to expedite the runway inspection. In a safety culture, personnel must feel comfortable reporting issues related to target-fixation and impulsivity. These mutually related hazardous motivations are critical concerns to safety in high-stress and high-risk environments. Target-fixation or impulsivity must be reported to top management by all affected operations personnel without fear of reprisal or punishment.

STRONG SAFETY CULTURES

A culture is a set of shared values held by the employees and the organization, in general (Ayres et al., 2009, p. 95). Changing the culture means changing the values, which may not be easy, particularly when the existing set of values has been entrenched for a long time. Changing values is a process that is achieved by changing practices (Ayres et al., 2009, p. 95). Although safety posters and newsletters are tools of the safety promotion process, safety promotion also includes a demonstrable and visible change in management's attitude and leadership, with a focus on altering how work gets accomplished (Ayres et al., 2009, p. 95).

In an effective safety assessment, management will likely discover that elements of strong and weak cultural values affect safety in their organization. Management should strive to strengthen the weak areas and identify why the areas that are strong are working that way, as this may provide clues on how to improve the overall safety culture.

Signs of a strong safety culture include employees who will report an unsafe situation and believe it is their responsibility to do so. Employees should truly believe that management's policies and words are reflected in their actions and that upper management takes an active role in safety promotion by conducting themselves in a manner they wish their employees to emulate (Ayres et al., 2009, p. 93). In a strong safety culture, errors are understood as unintentional; however, willful violations should not be tolerated by either upper management or fellow workers (Ayres et al., 2009, p. 93). Weak safety cultures feature employees who believe safety is someone else's responsibility, typically their supervisor and senior managers delegating safety functions to lower-level employees.

Boston Logan International Airport is a strong leader in promoting a safety culture. After 9/11, management at Boston/Logan adopted a philosophy of "Never Again." In this case, "Never Again" refers to the goal that their airport will never again be used as the launch site of a terrorist attack against the United States. Boston/Logan was not liable, or even indirectly responsible, for the aircraft that departed and were used in the attacks of 9/11. Nevertheless, its management decided to ensure that no future attacks would be conducted in the same way from Boston/Logan. During this effort, one of the key strategies managers adopted is known as the "8:30 AM Safety and Security Meeting" (see "The Daily Security and Safety Meeting"). Every morning, top managers from the airport, airlines, federal agencies, Massport Police, and other key stakeholders meet at 8:30 AM to discuss safety and security issues. This meeting provides an opportunity for the highest-level decision makers at the airport to discuss numerous issues focused on safety management. Police, Fire Chiefs, senior airport operational managers, airline officials, TSA, and FBI (Federal Bureau of Investigation) usually attend these meetings. Boston/Logan demonstrates strong levels of safety promotion by requiring senior leadership to attend each of these meetings.

THE DAILY SECURITY AND SAFETY MEETING

Airport operators must ensure that senior management and stakeholders (e.g., police, fire, TSA) critical to the airport operating environment attend routine safety and security meetings. Knowledge sharing and problem solving are essential objectives of these meetings. Over time, top management must be sure that these meetings do not degrade in importance and become attended by junior personnel or assistants assigned only as "note takers."

A strong safety culture and related safety promotional efforts might also include the presence of government officials and regulators at safety meetings. The challenge in having government regulators participate in safety promotional efforts is that their task and responsibility in regulatory enforcement can cause conflicts of interest, as well as act as a barrier to sharing aviation safety information. For example, regulatory personnel may provide suggestions about regulatory best practices, but often stop short of telling an airport operator specifically how to comply with regulations. While this stance may be perceived as unhelpful, it is reflective of regulatory agencies' attempt to allow airport operators to determine how best to comply with the regulations while still serving the mission of the airport. A safety regulator, or compliance inspector, who is willing to help the airport achieve higher levels of safety, can be an invaluable asset for an airport. Regulators are experts at the application of the regulation and, most importantly, can provide guidance on what is acceptable in terms of alternative safety procedures that still meet regulatory concerns.

WEAK SAFETY CULTURES

The safety health of an airport is an indication of the airport's ability to mitigate hazards and respond to threats or unexpected conditions (ICAO, 2013, p. 10-3). In terms of safety, the minimum standard for an airport to be considered healthy is to meet the minimum acceptable levels of regulatory compliance. However at this minimum level, a compliance violation or serious hazard can be tenuous to the airport's ability to sustain a safety level that will protect the well-being of individuals and infrastructure. Therefore, managers should measure the safety health of an organization to determine how far above the minimum standard of compliance the organization is operating (ICAO, 2013, p. 10-3).

Organizations engage in best practices, implement SMS, stay current with the latest research in safety management principles and airport operating practices, and have a robust training program for all of their staff (not only upper management) to improve their safety health. An organization can use statistical safety performance indicators, such as number of runway incursions or airfield accidents, to determine the health of the organization from a safety perspective. However, because incidents and serious accidents are relatively rare in aviation, these statistics might not provide a full assessment. Less-than-desirable SMS rely only on common metrics, regardless of their validity or reliability. Other performance indicators should be developed for a healthy safety culture, for example, the number of hours individuals are trained to operate on the airfield, currency of retraining, test scores, and the results of comprehensive audits.

Key to the safety health of the airport is management's support and leadership for leveraging all airport personnel's knowledge and skills in SMS and airport safety operations. For example, commercial service airports must provide initial training and recertification training for their Part 139 airfield inspectors. Many airports meet this obligation by using a computer-based training system or by bringing in a trainer to retrain their entire staff on an annual basis. Both of these methods are effective strategies for increasing the knowledge-base of employees and maintaining compliance. In contrast, some Airport Managers will send one of their staff to a training course, requiring them to gather as much of the training material as possible from the course, including instructor's materials, if possible, then return to the airport and use that experience and materials to train all other stakeholders. This type of training is frequently ineffective since training is a skill and not everyone is an effective trainer; the information becomes second-hand when it passes from the student on to colleagues at the airport. An airport with potentially stronger safety health at least cycles all employees through the required training as provided by the expert source.

Another way that safety training can degrade is by sending individuals to a required training course, but booking their return flights so that they have to leave the training early. This situation causes the individuals being trained to place pressure on the training facilitators to rush the program delivery. This practice is, unfortunately, widespread. Companies or individuals providing the training know that if they do not meet the demands of the client, they will go elsewhere to receive the training. Many trainers feel it is better to "do their best" within the time allowed.

Management can also subvert effective safety promotion by cutting corners in the acquisition of necessary equipment and materials. While it might be a nice public relations announcement to say that the airport has acquired firefighting gear for its operations staff (who, let us assume, are already trained as Aircraft Rescue and Firefighters), if that gear is torn and no longer meets the required standards for such material, then management has not truly supported its own safety policies.

SMS Managers should realize that it could take up to 10 years to change a culture (Hollinger, 2013, p. 193). If top management does not remain cognizant of this possibility, then evaluation of SMS and its related safety culture may be falsely interpreted. To compensate for this weakness, management may revert to evaluating an SMS program solely on intuition or perception. The intuitive method is simply believing or assuming that the airport has a strong or weak safety culture, but lacks any valid or reliable data. The prime challenge to relying solely on intuition is that perceptions and opinions as to the state of safety and corresponding viable strategies for addressing those impressions will vary. Additionally, if an incident or accident occurs, the airport may be asked to demonstrate, from a legal perspective that it has been assessing its safety programs through a documented, valid, and reliable process (see "Internal Safety Surveys"). In this regard, intuition alone adds significantly to many levels of risk, ranging from regulatory issues to probability of occurrence.

INTERNAL SAFETY SURVEYS

Internal safety-related surveys are useful tools for measuring the attitude and perceptions of employees toward safety issues (Ayres et al., 2009, pp. 94–95). As one of many examples, the Likert Scale response survey, shown here, is favored by many SMS Managers:

1. Strongly disagree
2. Disagree
3. Neither agree nor disagree
4. Agree
5. Strongly agree

The Likert Scale can be modified to help refine precision of information gained by each response. For example, one might eliminate option #3, requiring the respondent to choose between agreeing and disagreeing. An additional category, "#6. Not applicable," could be added for use in those cases where the question does not relate to the individual's job function, experience, or knowledge.

Airport Managers may also conduct an **external audit**, considered the most objective and accurate way to evaluate the strength of an organization's safety culture. External auditors typically are not closely connected to the employees and, therefore, are less likely to show favoritism or to be influenced one way or the other. However, in certain cases auditors and consultants are retained and are given an expected outcome by management. This practice unduly influences the process and taints the audit. This is another example in which leadership must allow a clean audit to take place, accepting the findings of the auditors and working to improve the gaps, rather than trying to influence the auditors.

BUILDING A SAFETY CULTURE

A healthy safety culture should be measurable in all areas of the airport, especially starting with top management's approach to developing a safety culture. Safety initiatives that are not backed by management typically fail. A safety culture is based on how seriously the organization views safety. Without strong safety leadership, airports usually develop a default style of safety culture using their own values. Seldom is this "safety by default" strategy desirable or even safe (Ferguson & Nelson, 2014, p. 101). The default safety culture is not deliberate, intentional, or proactive and is most likely event-driven and reactionary (Ferguson & Nelson, 2014, p. 101). An effective safety culture requires management's firm, consistent, and unwavering support (Ferguson & Nelson, 2014, p. 101). These values must be communicated to line personnel and consistently supported through safety-conscious decision making and positive vocal support of safety. Positive affirmation of employees who demonstrate good safety behaviors and decision making can help foster trust between employees and their leadership and encourage others to demonstrate proper safety characteristics and values (Ferguson & Nelson, 2014, p. 102). Another behavior that can contribute to safety is the practice of **Management by Walking Around**. Line personnel who do not see their managers or supervisors routinely walking about the work area and engaging the employees in conversation to talk about issues and challenges in an attempt to better understand their perspectives come to feel that management is disassociated and does not understand what is happening in the operational environment (Ayres et al., 2009, p. 98).

Managers must have written proclamations of safety via, for example, email or memos posted, and be active in the process of creating safety policies and procedures. Formal incentive programs, such as Safety Employee of the Month or Safety Team of the Month, can provide recognition for employees or teams for their ideas and contributions to safety within the organization. Competitions can also be organized for safety posters or to solve safety issues (Ayres et al., 2009, p. 98).

Management must also actively engage and believe in nonpunitive safety reporting. Once someone is punished for reporting a safety concern, long-term trust will be severely damaged. However, the implementation of a nonpunitive safety information sharing system does not preclude administrative or legal action against an individual that through negligence or by intent violates a safety policy or law. Other tools that enhance safety promotion include:

1. **Safety newsletters:** These publications discuss safety issues, feature reports on industry-related activities and lessons learned, and serve as a platform to recognize individuals and teams that have won safety awards. Industry white papers on safety, ACRP Report summaries, and other related information can also be included. While the newsletter can be produced electronically, consideration should be given to disseminating it in both written form and in an easy to read HTML format.
2. **Safety briefings:** Individuals such as the SMS Manager or accountable executive can be assigned to peruse airport and industry-related publications and summarize these sources as related to airport safety, challenges, solutions, and lessons learned. Another effective safety promotion practice is to engage, encourage, and, at the very least, recognize the airport's staff who take the initiative to research and publish their own safety-related publications.
3. **Safety posters:** Posters or placards are used to remind employees of hazards and precautions or to foster ideas and safety-related values. They are often considered a passive training method

and therefore should be frequently changed or they become part of the environment and eventually ignored. Safety posters can be disseminated electronically, as well. For example, when an employee or other stakeholder logs into their computer, a safety message that must be cleared before they can proceed can pop up. In some cases, the popup might be a safety question that must be answered correctly before the individual is allowed to log on. The safety question should be relatively easy, not requiring research but rather reflection as related to safety.

4. **Safety seminars:** Seminars bring people together from various areas of the industry, including experts on safety or operations, to discuss best practices and exchange ideas. The airport operator should endeavor to be a significant part of these seminars. Universities with aviation programs occasionally host safety seminars for industry and the public. Additionally, trade organizations frequently host safety-related meetings or meetings related to various elements of Airport Operations. The airport authority should support these programs by sending members of the SMS staff, Operations, and senior management.

5. **Safety stand-downs:** The U.S. military uses a practice referred to as a **safety stand-down**. During safety stand-downs, units halt their operations and spend a day (usually) focusing on relevant safety topics. The stand-down is performed at least annually. If there are repeat problems within an operational area, command may issue a stand-down focused on only those safety problem areas. A safety stand-down does not imply that all normal operations cease. In the USCG, readiness is maintained in case an emergency occurs during a stand-down, but all other activities, such as flight training, recurrence flights, maintenance, maintenance checks, and other activities, cease. While a commercial service airport cannot reasonably "stand-down," alternatives can be implemented. Personnel can be paid overtime to come in on what would otherwise be their day off for a day of safety briefings and activities, while minimal staffing requirements continue to be met. Certainly, if a large-scale incident takes place, the stand-down can be cancelled (and the airport will have plenty of staff to deal with the incident that particular day).

6. **Training:** Top management should support safety-related training and recurrent safety training efforts. All personnel should be given initial general workplace safety training along with job-specific training. It is important that the attitude of the training cadre reflect the safety values of the organization. Newly hired personnel often place credibility with senior individuals assigned to train them, and if those individuals do not exemplify the safety values desired by the organization, then it will be difficult for the new employee to adopt those desired safety values later on in their tenure. Safety promotion should also place emphasis on "training-the-trainers," so that they can effectively transfer knowledge on to others in the organization. It is also important to remember that training is a perishable skill. Periodic retraining in certain areas should be part of any robust SMS training program.

7. **Industry news:** The FAA, NTSB, and airline and airport trade organizations, such as American Association of Airport Executives (AAAE), International Air Transport Association (IATA), Airlines for America (A4A), National Air Transportation Association (NATA), National Business Aviation Association (NBAA), AOPA, and others, frequently publish safety bulletins and host training and webinars on current safety-related issues. The SMS Manager, or a designated individual within each operational workgroup, should be assigned to monitor these bulletins and other activities, disseminating and sharing the guidance throughout the organization.

The safety promotion process also relates to the SA process in terms of measurable results. As previously stated, because of the low number of actual accidents and incidents in aviation, it might not be effective to mark the organizational safety status based on the number of incidents or accidents. However, the organization can set measurable activities using the aforementioned list. The organization can set goals such as:

1. Publishing at least four safety-related newsletters per year;
2. Sending staff to at least three industry safety-related conferences per year;
3. Conducting at least six presentations by staff on safety-related issues (the expectation being that the individuals who attended the safety conferences would all create a presentation, while others in the workplace who were unable to attend the safety conferences can do their own research and present their findings);
4. Hosting or attending at least one safety seminar per year;
5. Ensuring all personnel have completed initial and recurrent training; and
6. Ensuring that on a bimonthly basis, the Safety Bulletin Board is refreshed with new information.

SAFETY TRAINING AND THE U.S. MILITARY

The U.S. military places great emphasis on safety training. The military also spends significant time and money on training its trainers so that they can effectively transfer their knowledge to others. Oftentimes, there is no civilian equivalent to the level of training that a military service member receives, except for perhaps some of the most demanding jobs (e.g., physician, pilot, lawyer, nuclear engineer, astronaut). An important lesson learned can be taken from the military: extensive and repetitive training is critical to high levels of safety.

Routine and rigorous safety training is a force-multiplier when each Operations personnel trained receives new knowledge and skills. Therefore, it is advantageous to the airport's safety culture to cross-train operational personnel in areas that exceed Part 139 requirements. For example, since Airport Operations agents interact with all areas of the airport, it would increase overall safety if they were also trained in skills such as first aid and first-responder actions and provided with knowledge in the basic enforcement policies of the ASP, Incident Command, snow removal, and customer service areas. At a joint-use or shared-military use airport, training on military safety and emergency response may also enhance overall safety at the airport (see "Safety Training and the U.S. Military").

SUMMARY

An effective safety program fundamentally requires top management's written commitment to safety, supported with adequate funding, resources, and ongoing training. Risks must be identified that are inherent to factors associated with operating an airport, including normal flow of aircraft and passengers, airfield construction, emergency or irregular operations, and severe weather events. Risks are evaluated and assigned a level of severity in terms of consequences, and potential frequencies are identified. The most severe and frequent risks are given high priority for mitigation and preparedness. Once mitigation actions are implemented, they are monitored through audits and employee reporting, and, when necessary, corrective actions are taken. For an operation to be safety-focused, a *culture of safety* must be inculcated into the workforce. Changing cultures takes time and requires both the strong support of management and key individuals, or *significant influencers*, supporting the values that reflect a safe organization.

Reflections on SMS Implementation

by Stephen Thompson
Manager of Airport Safety, Denver International Airport, Denver, CO (DEN)[6]

Airports around the world have operated with impressive and improving safety records for many decades. Countless lessons have been learned; countless improvements have been made to enhance safety over the years. The industry is at a point, however, where we do not need a significant event to investigate in order to identify the next improvement to safety. Instead, airport operators are leveraging expertise and past experience to proactively address hazards and manage risk. This evolution is best facilitated though the implementation of an SMS.

The resources required to develop and manage a successful SMS at an airport are greatly influenced by the airport's size, scope, and many operational factors. A wide range exists in terms of the number of commercial operations, number of airport employees, and number of tenant organizations. An important characteristic of the SMS is that the concept is scalable. SMS provides a platform and structure that can be adopted to fit this wide range of airports that exist within our National Airspace System.

An initial consideration in implementing an SMS involves understanding how elements of the current airport safety and operational programs can be leveraged to support an airport-wide safety program. Adopting the SMS platform then becomes a less daunting task and instead an effort to pair existing programs with new SMS initiatives to develop a program that fits the airport environment. A gap analysis can be employed, which allows the operator to determine where its program stands and where it needs to go. Following the construct that SMS provides, the safety program will than take shape as gaps are identified and opportunities are exposed. The four pillars or components of SMS provide the roadmap for developing a successful program and provide criteria for evaluating gaps or opportunities to be addressed. The SMS structure also allows for greater interoperability and communications between stakeholders across the airport who are likely using the same SMS construct.

A key foundational piece that underscores a program of any size exists in its safety policies. Publishing an overarching safety policy provides basic direction for airport employees and tenants alike. A comprehensive policy demonstrates the commitment of senior leadership and should emphasize the importance of working across organizational boundaries to produce a truly airport-wide safety effort. When this policy portrays both the overall safety focus of the airport operator and the specific objectives that the program will pursue, a clear path has been chartered. Additional operational safety policies and procedures then provide detailed guidance around topics from PPE (Personal Protective Equipment) to vehicle

(Continued)

---

[6]Denver International Airport (DEN) is also commonly referred to as DIA or listed by ICAO as KDEN.

(Continued)

operations to construction site activities. This documentation becomes the backbone of the program.

Communicating this policy and direction across all areas of the airport is critical to a successful implementation effort. It is through safety promotion that all stakeholders are provided with key information, including policies and directives put in place by the airport operator. Effective promotion ensures support from senior leadership is linked with boots on the ground efforts of frontline employees. Safety committee meetings with frontline employees and "summits" with mid- to upper-level management provide great environments for open communications. Recurring safety committee meetings provide opportunities for airport stakeholders to share ideas and safety successes and should be considered a key arena for pursuing the promotion of the safety program. Consistent messaging through this and a variety of mediums demonstrates the airport operator's commitment to safety and the expectations put forth by leaders at all levels.

Safety promotion also involves efforts to rally support for the SMS and equip personnel with the tools and training necessary to play their role in sustaining a strong safety culture. A robust Safety Recognition Program can be used to highlight employees who go "above and beyond" in their efforts to support safety. When team members see their peers being recognized for contributing to making the airport environment safer, they become mobilized to do their part. Public recognition goes a long way in garnering support for the SMS. Highlighting best practices of tenant organizations, such as electronic safety bulletin boards, newsletters, and other methods of communication, will also assist in promotion efforts while recognizing successes of tenants.

The SRM component is where the rubber meets the road in the airport's SMS. The airport operator no longer just waits around for an incident to occur, anxious to run out and investigate causes and contributing factors. While this function is still an integral capability of the program, through risk assessment processes the airport also proactively manages risk. We can anticipate many hazards based on past occurrences, inputs from subject matter experts, and our employees' experience. Our operations managers do this every day when they conduct Part 139 inspections and canvass the airport property for potential hazards. Operations and maintenance personnel constantly mitigate hazards and prevent incidents from occurring. Whether they are collecting FOD, dispersing wildlife, or identifying ineffective pavement markings, these professionals are key to the airport's management of risk.

Through a more formal risk assessment process, airport personnel analyze construction projects, significant events, and operational changes that may introduce new hazards to the airfield. A five-step risk assessment process is used to guide a group of subject matter experts through the exercise of identifying hazards, analyzing risk, and developing mitigation strategies. This documented process helps to insure that risk is managed at an acceptable level, in advance of a construction project, event, or operational change. By including personnel from tenant organizations across the airport, a unified effort to identify

(Continued)

(Continued)

all types of hazards and generate the most effective mitigation strategies is possible. It is not just the safety staff or operations personnel that contribute to this process. First responders, airline employees, and support staff can all contribute the necessary knowledge to manage risks proactively. It is also important that the group understand that not all anticipated risks will be eliminated, but by managing risk to an acceptable level, potential incidents and accidents can be minimized.

Ensuring that the airport operator's efforts and programs are having a positive impact on safety completes the loop within an SMS. Through SA, the program's effectiveness can be measured. Tracking and trending employee injuries, hazard mitigation implementation, and vehicle incidents all provide measures for senior leadership to evaluate and direct (sometimes redirect) the safety program. The expenditure of resources and time will be justified when measurements validate the success of a program.

SA is also pursued through an effective method of enforcing safety rules and policies that exist at the airport. A progressive discipline program can be used to create accountability for following rules such as the wearing of reflective garments in the Airport Operations Area or containing smoking activities to designated areas. A point system in which point values are assigned to various infractions provides a means of tracking individual noncompliance (Figure 5.1). If an individual accrues a designated sum of points, this results in increased disciplinary measures. This type of accountability program helps to ensure that employees understand the importance of safety policies and rules and holds each person accountable for their actions. The progressive nature also creates an environment where rather than a one strike and you're out mentality, employees can be retrained and reeducated before a pattern of noncompliance develops.

Each component of the airport's SMS provides tools and techniques that are critical to the development of a successful safety program. Those tools and techniques, however, are only as strong and effective as the employees charged with their use. The airport's safety culture creates an umbrella under which each of the SMS components can thrive. Just as support from senior leadership is crucial to success, so is commitment on the front line. Every employee plays a pivotal role in ensuring a safe working environment exists at the airport, every day. Without their commitment, safety policies fall on deaf ears and risk management falls short of expectations.

By fostering a culture of trust, commitment, and shared values, the airport operator can leverage the human resources present in every organization operating at the airport. When each employee feels a sense of responsibility for the safe movement of aircraft and passengers, and for the safety of their peers, the SMS comes to life with a powerful force. The airport staff is in an ideal position to achieve synergy among the various employee groups, to set the example and standard, and to both reward outstanding safety efforts and enforce compliance for those who fall short. The SMS provides a playbook for a successful team effort.

(Continued)

(Continued)

Denver Municipal Airport System Rules and Regulations
Source: Official business Web site of Denver International Airport (business.flydenver.com)

PART 35 – Infraction Accountability Program and Appeals Process

35.01   Basis

All Denver International Airport ("DEN") employees including those employed by the City and County of Denver, contractors, vendors, and tenants are expected to comply with Airport Rules and Regulations, Company policies and directives, and standard safety practices. Each DEN badge holder will be held accountable for contributing to a safe work environment. In an effort to encourage participation in creating this safe environment and identifying necessary retraining and education efforts, an infraction point system will be used to document incidents that violate rules and expose airport employees and/or resources to unnecessary risk. Points will be assessed to an individual according to the allocation chart in Appendix A.

35.02   Administration

a. Personnel designated by the Senior Vice President of Airport Operations, will issue Infraction Notices to individuals for failure to adhere to Airport Rules and Regulations. Infraction Notices will be recorded electronically through an application on the issuer's handheld device or entered via a computer workstation. The individual's badge number, nature of infraction and other necessary information will be collected and entered into an electronic Infraction Notice form. The captured information will be transmitted and stored within the Infraction Accountability Database.

b. Designated program administration personnel will review the database and generate a letter to be sent to the employee's company in addition to a copy of the Infraction Notice. The letter will be sent to the Authorized Signatory on file with the DEN Security department. This letter will describe the nature of the infraction and points assessed. Further reeducation and/or disciplinary action will be left to the discretion of the employing company and individual's supervisor. If an individual accrues 12 or more points in a 12 month consecutive period, the individual will be subject to a hearing conducted by designated personnel. The hearing will be conducted to determine action to be taken. This may include temporary removal of driving privileges, retraining, or suspension of the badge. At the hearing, the badge holder will be given the opportunity to present facts and arguments as to why the Infraction Notice(s) was not properly issued, and the Hearing Officer shall consider the facts in support of the Infraction Notice(s). The Hearing Officer shall then decide whether the accumulated points justify action against the employee's badge. Appeal procedures can be found in section 35.05 below.

35.03   Scope and Procedures

a. This program applies to all Denver International Airport (DEN) employees in possession of a DEN Airport Identification Badge. Employees include those people employed by the City and County of Denver along with all contractors, vendors, and tenants. This program is not intended to replace existing methods of enforcement, such as those programs utilized by the Denver Police Department and DEN Airport Security.

Part 35: Infraction Accountability Program and Appeals Process
Effective Date: April 2015

FIGURE 5.1

Part 35—Infraction Accountability Program and Appeals Process.
Source: Denver International Airport. (2015). Infraction Accountability Program and Appeals Process. Retrieved from: http://www.flydenver.com/sites/default/files/rules/35_operations_infraction.pdf.

(Continued)

(Continued)

Denver Municipal Airport System Rules and Regulations
Source: Official business Web site of Denver International Airport (business.flydenver.com)

b. Points will be assessed for each offense listed on the Infraction Notice. Points are cumulative and will become part of the recipient's record for as long as they are badged at the airport. Points will be tracked against an individual, not against separate badges in instances where an individual may have multiple badges.

35.04   Responsibilities

a. The employing company and/or supervisor will be expected to assist in training their employees regarding rules and regulations, address any infraction(s) and determine corrective action.

b. The DEN Operations Division will be responsible for maintaining the Infraction database, distributing Infraction Notices to authorized signatories of affected companies, and creating reports as requested by management.

c. The DEN Operations Division will conduct hearings when an individual has accumulated 12 or more points in a 12 month period. A pre-hearing letter will be sent via email and/or U.S. Mail informing the Authorized Signatory or Senior Company Manager that a Hearing must be scheduled with Airport Operations or designee within ten (10) business days of the date of the letter, and that a management representative or Authorized Signatory of the company/department must attend with the employee. If the prescribed time frame is not met, the individual who received the violation may have his or her Airport ID badge suspended until a hearing takes place. If following the hearing, the Assistant Director of Operations or designee determines that the violation is valid, this will be communicated in writing to the Authorized Signatory of the company/department, indicating that a violation was believed to have been committed by the individual and the consequences for such violations. Such decision (except a decision to withdraw a Violation Infraction Notice) may be appealed as detailed within this Rule 35.

35.05   Operations Infraction Accountability Program Appeals Process

a. Following the employee hearing, the individual may request an appeal with the Senior Director of Airport Operations or Manager of Airport Safety ("Appeals Officer"), and will be required to coordinate this through their supervisor. An appeal must be filed within ten (10) business days from issuance of the hearing decision. If the prescribed time frame is not met, the hearing decision becomes final. The Appeals Hearing shall be conducted as expeditiously as possible. In all matters, the petitioner shall have the burden of proof to show by a preponderance of the evidence the correctness of his or her position. The Appeals Officer shall thereafter make a final written determination as to the action being appealed.

b. Airport Operations, serving on behalf of the City and County of Denver ("CCD") reserves the right to deny, revoke or limit the scope of an individual's Airport issued ID badge, endorsements or privileges based upon reasonable grounds and giving due consideration to the nature of the offense.

Part 35: Infraction Accountability Program and Appeals Process
Effective Date: April 2015

FIGURE 5.1

(Continued)

(Continued)

Denver Municipal Airport System Rules and Regulations
Source: Official business Web site of Denver International Airport (business.flydenver.com)

c. A request for reconsideration of the determination may be made if filed in writing with the Senior Vice President of Airport Operations within fifteen (15) calendar days of the date of determination, or the final determination of the Appeals Officer may be reviewed under Rule 106(a)(4) of the Colorado Rules of Civil Procedure. If a request for reconsideration is made, the Senior Vice President of Airport Operations shall review the record, and issue a written order concerning the reconsideration. The reconsideration determination shall be considered a final order on behalf of the Manager of Aviation upon the date the reconsideration determination is issued. The reconsideration determination shall be the final order and may be reviewed under Rule 106(a)(4) of the Colorado Rules of Civil Procedure.

d. An employee requesting an Airport ID badge must resolve all pending or valid violations before being allowed to proceed in the badging process. If the employee no longer works for the company listed on the Violation Infraction Notice, and is attempting to be employed by a different company, a management representative from the "new" company must attend the Violation Infraction Notice Hearing with the employee.

Part 35: Infraction Accountability Program and Appeals Process
Effective Date: April 2015

FIGURE 5.1

(Continued)

(Continued)

Denver Municipal Airport System Rules and Regulations
Source: Official business Web site of Denver International Airport (business.flydenver.com)

Appendix A

Infraction Point Allocation Chart

Movement Area Surface Deviation / Incursion	12	130.06-1,2
Non-Movement Area Deviation / Pedestrian, Vehicle	6	40.14-1, 40.15
Failure to yield to Aircraft or Emergency Response Vehicle	6	130.03-3, 4
Operating a vehicle in an area or manner not authorized	4	130.03, 130.04-1, 130.05-1
Failure to provide proper vehicle escort	4	130.08-3
Unsafe Operation of Vehicle	4	130.10-1, 2, 3, 130.17
Unsafe Fueling Operation	4	150.01-24
Unsafe or Unauthorized Operation of Electric Carts	4	40.09-11, 12, 14, 15
Unsafe Operation of Baggage cart train	3	130.12-1,2
Parking Violation	3	80.01-80.10
Failure to display Airport Vehicle Permit	2	20.14
Failure to provide required Operator Documents	2	20.04-1,2,3,4
Smoking outside of designated areas	4	30.13-1,2, 40.23-1,2
Environmental infraction	4	40.02-4, 5, 180.03, 180.04
Failure to wear required Personal Protective Equipment	3	30.15-1, 2, 40.22-1, 2
Vandalism	3	40.04, 40.06
FOD Hazard, Littering, Feeding of wildlife	3	40.02-1, 40.03
General Conduct	3	20.09
Warning for any of the above infractions	0	

Part 35: Infraction Accountability Program and Appeals Process
Effective Date: April 2015

FIGURE 5.1

REFERENCES

Airport Safety & Operations Division. (2007). *Introduction to safety management systems (SMS) for airport operators*. Washington, DC: Federal Aviation Administration (Advisory Circular 150/5200-37).

Ayres, M., Shirazi, H., Cardoso, S., Brown, J., Speir, R., Selezneva, O., & . . . Puzin, T. (2009). *Safety management systems for airports*. Washington, DC: Transportation Research Board (ACRP Report 1, Vol 2).

Bannard, D. Y., Foley & Lardner LLP. (2013). *Legal issues related to developing safety management systems and safety risk management at U.S. airports*. Legal Research Digest, 19. Retrieved from: http://onlinepubs.trb.org/onlinepubs/acrp/acrp_lrd_019.pdf.

Department of Homeland Security, Office of Inspector General. (2012). *Transportation Security Administration's efforts to identify and track security breaches at our nation's airports (redacted)*. Retrieved from: https://www.oig.dhs.gov/assets/Mgmt/2012/OIG_12-80_May12.pdf.

Federal Aviation Administration (FAA). (2013). *Flight operational quality assurance (FOQA)*. Retrieved from: https://www.faa.gov/about/initiatives/atos/air_carrier/foqa/.

Federal Aviation Administration (FAA). (2014a). *Air transportation oversight system (ATOS)*. Retrieved from: http://www.faa.gov/about/initiatives/atos/.

Federal Aviation Administration (FAA). (2014b). *Safety management system—components*. Retrieved from: https://www.faa.gov/about/initiatives/sms/explained/components/#srm.

Federal Aviation Administration (FAA). (2014c). *SMS safety management system manual*. Version 4.0. Retrieved from: https://www.faa.gov/air_traffic/publications/media/faa_ato_SMS_manual_v4_20140901.pdf.

Ferguson, M., & Nelson, S. (2014). *Aviation safety: A balanced industry approach*. Independence, KY: Cengage.

Forrest, J. S. (2006). *Information policies & practices of knowledge management (KM) as related to the development of the global aviation information network (GAIN)—an applied case study & taxonomy development*. Dissertation Abstracts International. (UMI No. 3226963).

Hudson, P. T. W. (2011). In A. Stolzer, & C. Halford (Eds.), *Implementing safety management systems in aviation*. Aldershot, Hampshire: Ashgate.

Hollinger, K. (2013). *Safety management systems for aviation practitioners: Real-world lessons*. Reston, VA: American Institute of Aeronautics and Astronautics.

International Civil Aviation Organization (ICAO). (2013). *Safety management manual (SMM)* (3rd ed.). Montreal, Quebec.

Joint Helicopter Safety Implementation Team of the International Helicopter Safety Team. (2007). *Safety management system toolkit*. Paper presented at The International Helicopter Safety Symposium 2007, Montreal, Quebec.

Ludwig, D. A., Andrews, C. R., Jester-ten Veen, N. R., & Laqui, C. (2007). *Safety management systems for airports*. Washington, DC: Transportation Research Board.

Reason, J. (1990). The contribution of latent human failures to the breakdown of complex systems. *Philosophical Transactions of the Royal Society of London. Series B, Biological Sciences*, *327*(1241), 475−484. Available from: http://dx.doi.org/10.1098/rstb.1990.0090.

Stolzer, A., & Halford, C. (2008). *Safety management systems in aviation*. Aldershot, Hampshire, UK: Ashgate.

Stolzer, A., & Halford, C. (2011). *Implementing safety management systems in aviation*. Aldershot, Hampshire: Ashgate.

Torres, R. H. (2011). In A. Stolzer, & C. Halford (Eds.), *Implementing safety management systems in aviation*. Aldershot, Hampshire: Ashgate.

Transportation Research Board of the National Academies. (2012). *Lessons learned from airport safety management systems pilot studies*. Washington, DC: Federal Aviation Administration.

FURTHER READING

Wood, R. (2003). *Aviation safety programs: A management handbook* (3rd ed.). Snohomish, Washington: Jeppesen Sanderson.

AIRSIDE OPERATIONS: SAFETY SELF-INSPECTIONS

Airside Operations self-inspection vehicle in the movement area at Centennial Airport (CO).

Image by Shahn Sederberg, courtesy Colorado Division of Aeronautics, 2013.

U.S. Department of Agriculture Wildlife Biologist Kendra Cross monitoring wildlife activity at Denver International Airport (CO) (used with permission of K. Cross).

Image by Shahn Sederberg, courtesy Colorado Division of Aeronautics, 2009.

Airport Operations personnel are usually charged by top management with ensuring compliance with applicable federal, state, local, and airport-specific safety regulations. At large, commercial service airports, Airport Operations personnel typically oversee and enforce safety regulations. Overlapping with this effort are additional personnel, such as police officers and unarmed security officers contracted specifically to enforce security regulations. As the airport size lessens (medium-hub, small-hub, non-hub, and then general aviation [GA]; Figure 6.1), typically fewer law enforcement or security personnel are required on the airfield. Regardless of the size of the airport or organizational structure, the Airport Manager is ultimately responsible for airport safety.

While GA airports are not required to adhere to Part 139, many GA airport operators attempt to achieve Part 139 standards as best practice in their safety management program or Safety Management Systems (SMS). Airports that sustain Part 139 safety standards, whether commercial service or GA, provide a strong benefit to their tenants in that some corporate operators receive a reduction in insurance costs for locating at an airport meeting Part 139 standards. Even without the motivation of reduced insurance costs, many tenants are attracted to GA airports that voluntarily enforce Part 139 safety policies and procedures.

In addition to Part 139, grant assurances (specifically #19—Operations and Maintenance) require the airport operator to keep the airport in a safe and serviceable condition for aeronautical

Airport Classifications		Hub Type: Percentage of Annual Passenger Boardings	Common Name
Commercial Service: Publicly owned airports that have *at least 2,500* passenger boardings each calendar year and receive scheduled passenger service §47102(7)	**Primary:** Have *more than 10,000* passenger boardings each year §47102(11)	**Large:** 1% or more	**Large Hub**
		Medium: At least 0.25%, but less than 1%	**Medium Hub**
		Small: At least 0.05%, but less than 0.25%	**Small Hub**
		Nonhub: More than 10,000, but less than 0.05%	**Nonhub Primary**
	Nonprimary	**Nonhub:** At least 2,500 and no more than than 10,000	**Nonprimary Commercial Service**
Nonprimary (Except Commercial Service)		Not Applicable	**Reliever** §47102(18)

FIGURE 6.1

Airport hub size by activity and annual passenger boarding.

Source: FAA, 2014.

operations, airport tenants, and other stakeholders. This is especially true for airside operations at an airport. Within the airport's environment, *airside*-designated sections include all secured passenger movement, cargo, and aircraft operational areas. Airside areas at commercial service airports are heavily regulated and strictly monitored for compliance with safety regulations, policies, and procedures. The primary step to ensuring these operational values and standards is to support routine, self-inspection audits for airside safety concerns. The **Airport Operations Manager (AOM)** has primary responsibility for managing airside and other Part 139 self-inspections.

Safety self-inspections are required under Part 139, and the exact steps are defined in the Airport Certification Manual (ACM). Within Part 139, the Federal Aviation Administration (FAA) characterizes self-inspections in the following way:

> While some hazardous airport conditions develop virtually instantaneously, others are gradual. It is important that the airport operator have an airport safety self-inspection program that monitors specific airport conditions in order to identify unsatisfactory conditions for prompt corrective actions. A number of airport operators have some form of a safety self-inspection program. The programs vary in scope and effectiveness from verbal instructions and unscheduled and unrecorded inspections to very comprehensive inspection programs with multiple daily schedules and widely distributed responsibilities (FAA, 2004, p. 2).

THE AIRPORT MANAGER AND AIRSIDE OPERATIONS

Airports that have a formal operations department usually designate an employee to be responsible for the overall operation of the airport. At smaller airports, this charge may be combined with other responsibilities, such as assigned to an individual in the maintenance department, or perhaps even the Airport Manager. Titles for this position vary greatly, including the following examples: (a) AOM, (b) AOM on duty, (c) airport duty officer, (d) airport agent, (e) airport safety manager, (f) airport safety officer, and (g) operations officer. In this text, **AOM** is the most common title used to refer to this position.

A large-hub airport may have several AOMs "on duty," plus various assistant AOMs. Each manager is assigned to specific functions such as airside and landside operations, terminal operations, ramp control, emergency management, or communications center manager or supervisor on duty. In some cases, the AOM is also a qualified, airport safety self-inspector. At other airports, Operations (Ops) personnel are designated the job title of **Part 139 Inspector.** In these cases, the AOM oversees the general operation of the airport, while the Part 139 Inspector carries out the Part 139 self-inspection requirements. Individuals designated as Part 139 self-inspection personnel must be aware of and follow extensive FAA requirements. At a basic level, Part 139 self-inspection personnel must meet these (and many other) requirements:

1. Inspectors should know the location and types of airport facilities and airport rules and regulations and, at Part 139 airports, be familiar with the FAA-approved Airport Certification Manual.
   (a) Airport familiarization, including airport signs, marking, and lighting;
   (b) Airport Emergency Plan (if the airport has one);
   (c) Notice to Airmen (NOTAM) notification procedures;
   (d) Procedures for pedestrians and ground vehicles in movement areas and safety areas;
   (e) Airport inspection procedures and techniques; and
   (f) Discrepancy reporting procedures (FAA, 2004).

AOMs usually rotate shifts but may be called back to the airport to conduct or participate in various urgent activities, such as snow removal operations or major emergencies. AOMs frequently have a significant amount of experience in the Ops community, as well as excellent communication skills and the ability to adapt to quality decision making. AOMs are an extension of the Airport Manager and the airport sponsor and must reflect the values of those roles, while clearly understanding the mission of the airport. The AOM is often called on to resolve disputes between airport stakeholders, including air carriers, tenants, and construction contractors. AOMs monitor the weather and mobilize the snow removal plan when appropriate. They also resolve security issues, respond to and act as the Incident Commander for airport-related emergencies, and generally act as the airport's chief ambassador to all stakeholders. Though not required under Part 139, AOMs commonly make decisions related to security issues and often act as the Incident Commander, or operations group leader, for security incidents.

A top priority in airport safety is self-inspection as applied to airside operations. In airside safety management, it is critical that the AOM and Part 139 Inspectors (if designated) thoroughly understand (a) the requirements of Part 139, (b) regulations for various flight operations, (c) the Airport Operating Certificate (AOC) and ACM, and how these elements relate to self-inspection requirements. The following sections address each of these concerns as related to airside operations.

REGULATORY REVIEW OF TITLE 14 CFR PART 139 AND AIRSIDE OPERATIONS

Title 14 CFR Part 139 Certification of Airports was created in 1970 as part of the Airport and Airway Development Act. Part 139 ensures that commercial service airports meet certain standards for airfield safety and maintenance and that plans are in place to handle irregular operations, including snow removal, natural disasters, and emergencies.

Part 139 applies to commercial service airports with air carrier operations or to airports that provide service to air carrier operations. Commercial service airports, as defined under the FAA's **National Plan of Integrated Airport Systems (NPIAS)**, are airports that have 2,500 or more annual passenger enplanements. Initially, Part 139 applied to airports that served scheduled or unscheduled passenger air carrier operations in an aircraft with a seating capacity of more than 30 passengers (Wells & Young, 2011, p. 143). However, in 2004 the FAA expanded Part 139 to include airports serving scheduled, air carrier[1] aircraft with a seating capacity of 10 or more passengers. Also in 2004, the FAA classified airports into four different classes depending on the type of air carrier operation and the size of the aircraft (Figure 6.2). Part 139 does not apply to Alaskan airports that do not serve air carrier aircraft with more than 30 seats, or when not serving air carrier aircraft with more than 30 seats.

Airports exist to serve private aircraft operations, Part 139 certificated operations, and other commercial operations not requiring Part 139 oversight. Even many private operations are considered to be business-oriented, and many regulatory delineations determine whether an operation is private (or recreational), private for business, or a commercial operation. For example, an individual may own a plane for private recreational use, but also use it in the course of business. This operation is not considered commercial and is used incidental to the purpose of the business (i.e., not a flight service provider). If a business aircraft owner decides to hire a professional pilot, then that employment does not automatically cause the operation to be considered a commercial flight operation as defined by the FAA. In this case, the flights are being conducted for business purposes, with the owner paying the pilot to fly

Type of Air Carrier Operation	Class I	Class II	Class III	Class IV
Scheduled Large Air Carrier Aircraft (30+ seats)	X			
Unscheduled Large Air Carrier Aircraft (30+ seats)	X	X		X
Scheduled Small Air Carrier Aircraft (10–30 seats)	X	X	X	

FIGURE 6.2

Air carrier operations at each Part 139 airport class.

Source: FAA, 2015a.

[1]An air carrier operation is defined as a takeoff or landing of an aircraft operating under Title 14 CFR Part 121: Operating Requirements: Domestic, Flag and Supplemental Operations, most commonly known as the scheduled passenger airlines.

as an employee or contract personnel to the owner's company or organization. If the aircraft owner allows an associate to use the plane for a business use, but does not charge the associate beyond reasonable expenses to cover fuel and maintenance costs, it is still not considered "commercial air service." However, once the aircraft owner (or lessee) begins charging individuals for transportation services, or charging for the use of the aircraft, the owner must reference Title 14 CFR Part 119 *Certification: Air Carriers and Commercial Operators*, to determine which regulations they must follow.

Other types of flight operation that can be confusing to an airport operator are **fractionals**. Fractional flight operations are not considered a traditional commercial air-service operation. They are addressed under Title 14 Part 91, Subpart K. Fractional operations are similar to timeshares, with numerous owners each buying a share of interest in an aircraft or a fleet of aircraft. Fractionals operate in the gray area between private and commercial flying operations, but an airport does not have to meet the Part 139 certification in order for fractional operators to conduct business on the airport, as it would for a Part 121 operator to conduct business.

REGULATORY REVIEW OF FLIGHT AND RELATED AIRSIDE OPERATIONS

It is important to understand the various regulations that govern flight operations in order to understand whether the airport must comply with Part 139 or when a new or existing commercial operation would force the airport to consider whether compliance with 139 would be necessary. GA airports commonly have businesses that provide various levels of air charter and air taxi services operating under **Title 14 CFR Part 135—Commuter and On Demand Operations** (FAA, 2015a). However, in some instances, a charter company may seek to or begin offering air service in a manner consistent with a Part 121 operator. This operation would normally require the airport to become Part 139 certificated; however, no entity can force a GA airport to become certificated under Part 139. This situation can create conflict between the aircraft operator, community, airport sponsor, and the FAA. As related, Title 14 CFR Part 121.590(f) includes the following definition:

> Special Statutory Requirement to Operate to or From a Part 139 Airport. Each air carrier that provides—in an aircraft designed for more than 9 passenger seats—regularly scheduled charter air transportation for which the public is provided in advance a schedule containing the departure location, departure time, and arrival location of the flight must operate to and from an airport certificated under part 139 of this chapter in accordance with 49 U.S.C. 41104(b). That statutory provision contains stand-alone requirements for such air carriers and special exceptions for operations in Alaska and outside the United States. Certain operations by air carriers that conduct public charter operations under 14 CFR Part 380 are covered by the statutory requirements to operate to and from Part 139 airports. (14 Aeronautics and Space, 2004)

Furthermore, 49 U.S.C. 41114, specifically prohibits an air carrier, including an indirect air carrier, from operating in an aircraft designed for more than nine seats, out of an airport that does not have an AOC issued under Part 139.

Title 14 CFR Part 91, *General Operating and Flight Rules*, sets out the "rules of the road" for aircraft operations conducted within U.S. airspace. A Part 91 operation is considered a private flight operation, as opposed to a commercial-flight service operation. All aircraft follow Part 91 as it pertains to the rules of flight; however § 91.1 Applicability, section (c) notes: "this part applies to each person on board an aircraft being operated under this part, unless otherwise specified," meaning that if the operation is conducted under a different regulation, such as Part 121 or Part 135, other rules also apply. When the National Transportation Safety Board (NTSB) investigates an accident, it notes the type of operation the aircraft was conducting at the time of the accident. For example, a crash of a scheduled airliner would be noted as a Part 121 operation. If the aircraft were not being operated for commercial purposes, however, the NTSB report would reference that the aircraft was conducting a Part 91 operation, meaning a private-flight operation.

An **air carrier** is a person or entity that undertakes directly by lease, or other arrangement, to engage in commercial air transportation. The FAA has stated that air carriers include "an individual, firm, partnership, corporation, company, association, joint-stock association, governmental entity, and a trustee, receiver, assignee, or similar representative of such entities" (Certification of Airports, 2004).

An **air carrier aircraft** is an aircraft operated by an air carrier and is categorized, as determined by the aircraft type certificate issued by a competent civil aviation authority, as either a **large air carrier** aircraft if designed for at least 31 passenger seats or **small air carrier** aircraft, if designed for more than nine passenger seats but less than 31 passenger seats (Certification of Airports, 2004).

A **scheduled operation** is defined as any common-carriage, passenger-carrying operation for compensation or hire conducted by an air carrier for which the air carrier or its representatives offer in advance the departure location, departure time, and arrival location. It does not include any operation that is conducted as a supplemental operation under 14 CFR Part 121 or public charter operations under 14 CFR Part 380. The term "regularly scheduled operation" (used in various areas of the regulations) also means **scheduled operation**.

Under 49 U.S.C. 41104, a regularly scheduled operation does not include an operation for which the departure time, departure location, and arrival location are specifically negotiated with the customer or the customer's representative. Part 121 Supplemental Operations are usually a for-hire operation that does not fall under the normal operations of the 121 carrier and are generally considered to be unscheduled operations. This type of operation, for example, would include a passenger charter of an airliner by a sports team. 14 CFR Part 380 operations are typically considered in effect when a travel organization, such as a vacation club, rents or charters an airliner normally operated under Part 121. Both are typically considered to be unscheduled operations, but that does not mean that the aircraft does not leave at a scheduled time.

An **unscheduled operation** is defined as any common-carriage, passenger-carrying operation for compensation or hire, using aircraft designed for at least 31 passenger seats, conducted by an air carrier for which the departure time, departure location, and arrival location are specifically negotiated with the customer or the customer's representative. This includes any passenger-carrying supplemental operation conducted under 14 CFR Part 121 and any passenger-carrying public charter operation conducted under 14 CFR Part 380 (Title 14, CFR 121 [2004]). Therefore, *unscheduled* means an operation that does not meet the Part 121 requirements of offering in advance the departure location, departure time, and arrival location, and holding itself out to be a scheduled operation.

Title 14 CFR Part 135—*Operating Requirements: Commuter and On Demand Operations and Rules Governing Persons on Board Such Aircraft* addresses what is typically referred to as "air taxi" or "air charter." Part 135 operations are common on GA airports, and the airport is not required to have a Part 139 AOC in order for Part 135 operations to be conducted.

Motor Vehicle Operation	Flight Operation	Federal Aviation Regulations
Privately owned / leased vehicle.	Privately owned / leased aircraft.	Title 14 CFR Part 91
Taxi cab / limousine service.	Aircraft charter / air taxi operation (unscheduled).	Title 14 CFR Part 135
Scheduled public bus.	Scheduled passenger air service operation.	Title 14 CFR Part 121
Chartering a public bus for personal or business use.	Chartering a public or private air taxi or charter operation (unscheduled).	Public Charter, Title 14 CFR Part 380, or Private Charter, Part 121 Supplemental.

FIGURE 6.3

FAA regulations and flight operations as compared to similar activities in motor vehicle operations.

Airport operators can find additional information on the requirements for air carriers under Title 14 CFR Part 119—*Certification: Air Carriers and Commercial Operators*. Essentially, Part 119 explains the basic requirements for a commercial aeronautical activity. Based on the characteristics of the particular flight operation, Part 119 references additional regulations, such as Part 121 or Part 380 or Part 135, which an air carrier may have to comply with. To use a very simple analogy, comparing flight operations to motor vehicle operations, reference Figure 6.3.

PART 139—AIRPORT OPERATING CERTIFICATE AND AIRPORT CERTIFICATION MANUAL

Part 139 Subpart A—*General* is the first section that addresses a variety of administrative requirements for an airport to become certificated. For an airport to be in compliance with Part 139, it must demonstrate that it has fulfilled the requirements of a list of administrative, operational, and planning procedures and processes. An airport determined in compliance with these requirements may be issued an FAA **AOC**. The certificate, commonly referred to as a Part 139 Certificate, represents that the airport has an approved **ACM**. Part 139 commercial service airports are categorized into four classes. It is important to know the type of aircraft operations that are being conducted from the airport, in order to determine whether the airport operator must be in compliance with Part 139, and of which class within that body of regulations.

Classes of airports are distinguished by the type of air carrier operation, whether flights are scheduled or unscheduled, and the size of the aircraft accommodated. Classes I, II, and III airports must demonstrate compliance with 29 listed elements in Part 139. Class IV airports are exempt from certain requirements.

1. **Class I Airport**—An airport certificated to serve scheduled operations of large air carrier aircraft that also serves unscheduled passenger operations of large air carrier aircraft and/or scheduled operations of small air carrier aircraft. The majority of the approximate 450 commercial service airports in the United States are Class I.

2. **Class II Airport**—An airport certificated to serve scheduled operations of small air carrier aircraft and the unscheduled passenger operations of large air carrier aircraft. A Class II airport may not serve scheduled, large air carrier aircraft.
3. **Class III Airport**—An airport certificated to serve scheduled operations of small air carrier aircraft. A Class III airport may not serve scheduled or unscheduled, large air carrier aircraft.
4. **Class IV Airport**—An airport certificated to serve unscheduled, passenger operations of large air carrier aircraft. A Class IV airport may not serve scheduled, large or small air carrier aircraft (FAA, 2015c).

Part 139 applies to an estimated 450, commercial service airports of all sizes and characteristics within the United States. The FAA recognizes that each airport is different in operational requirements and therefore permits the airport authority to describe and justify varying strategies for complying with Part 139 requirements when applying for an AOC. Rationale for these processes are documented within the ACM. The ACM is drafted by the airport operator and describes for the FAA how the airport complies with Part 139. The document is then reviewed and signed by the FAA, making it a legal document and, in effect, creating regulations for that particular airport. If an airport fails to comply with the requirements of its own ACM, it is considered as failing to comply with Part 139. In other words, if an airport fails to comply with an element of its ACM, it cannot make the argument that the language used in its own ACM is not the same as the language in Part 139, and, therefore, it cannot be enforced.

Part 139 certification is not required if an airport's use by Part 121 operators is designated as an alternate destination when planning for route and weather considerations. U.S. government-owned airports or heliports are also exempt from Part 139 certification. Also, airports in Alaska that serve only small, scheduled, air carrier operations are not required to adhere to the requirements of Part 139. Airports operated by the U.S. government, including military airfields, designated either as shared or joint use, must only adhere to Part 139 for those areas where commercial air carrier operations are conducted. The military areas of the airfield are not required to adhere to Part 139, but the military does adhere to different airfield safety and maintenance standards.

Frequently, at joint- or shared-use airports, the military provides self-inspection services, aircraft rescue, and firefighting, or other Part 139—related services. Airport executives at a joint- or shared-use airport should be familiar with the U.S. Department of Defense's (DOD) Unified Facilities Criteria (UFC) Airfield and Heliport Planning and Design, Air Force Instruction 13-204 Airfield Operations Procedures and Programs, and Air Force Pamphlet 32-004 Aircraft Fire Protection for Exercises and Contingency Response Operations. These documents, along with other various DOD publications, provide insight on the inspection standards for joint- or shared-use airports.

It is acceptable for the U.S. government, in the form of military operations on a joint- or shared-use airfield, to help the civilian portion of the airfield meet the requirements of Part 139. However, airport executives must ensure that military standards do in fact meet or exceed the civilian Part 139 standards and that a letter of agreement or memorandum of understanding that commits the military to providing the necessary services to maintain Part 139 standards is in place. Additionally, there must also be an understanding that if the military assets or personnel involved in meeting Part 139 ever fall below required standards an immediate notification by the military must be made to the civilian airport operator. This is an unfortunate occasional occurrence as base closures and restructuring are now a more ubiquitous part of military base management. Also, in certain cases, the military may deploy and take with it some of the assets that were being used to maintain the Part 139 standard at its civilian counterpart.

It is very important for the civilian airport operator to work closely with the military airport operator to understand who will be in charge during an emergency. Military personnel are typically familiar with the Federal Emergency Management Agency's (FEMA) **National Incident Management System (NIMS)** (2014); however, they may not have the experience using NIMS with civilian entities. Airport executives should allocate time in tabletop, orientation, and functional exercises, along with the occasional all-scale safety exercises that involve military personnel. Military elements traditionally take over as Incident Command and are responsible for the full response to an emergency involving their aircraft. Simulated exercises help airport executives understand how a military accident might affect the civilian operations of the airport.

Part 139 is subdivided into three sections, with the first focusing on administrative elements, including the drafting and upkeep of the ACM, general recordkeeping required by Part 139, and training requirements. The second section focuses on maintenance issues such as requirements for pavement, airfield signs, markings, and lighting. The third section focuses on specific plans, such as the Airport Emergency Plan, Wildlife Hazard Management Plan, Snow and Ice Control Plan, and, when necessary, Construction Safety Plans. While all of these plans are traditionally separate documents, they are included as part of the ACM for FAA approval purposes.

Subpart A of Part 139 focuses on the applicability of the regulation, along with a list of definitions. Subpart A also notes that certificate holders (i.e., airport sponsors with an approved AOC) can reference FAA Advisory Circulars (ACs) for methods and procedures for compliance that are acceptable to the FAA. It is also best practice for GA operators to reference the ACs for best practices.

Airports applying for an AOC for the first time must be properly and adequately equipped and able to provide a safe operating environment. Typically, the issuance of an AOC is not subject to the **National Environmental Policy Act (NEPA)** as NEPA is considered an exclusion to the AOC. However, if the issuance of an AOC is likely to be environmentally controversial, such as involving social impacts or substantial division or disruption of an established community, an environmental assessment may be required under Paragraph 606, Extraordinary Circumstances, in the FAA Order 5050.4, *National Environmental Policy Act* (FAA, 2006).

An airport's AOC also outlines specific requirements for reporting of unusual aircraft operations. For example, Part 139 operators (and noncertificated airports, as well) must notify the FAA of intended operations by unscheduled carriers for special circumstances, such as aerial firefighting, air carriers accompanying Air Force One, and public-use charters.

ADMINISTRATIVE REQUIREMENTS AND AIRSIDE OPERATIONS

Part 139 Subpart B—*Certification* addresses a variety of administrative requirements related to the regulation and certification process. In general, this section prohibits an airport from operating under Part 139 without an approved AOC or while in violation of the currently held certificate or approved ACM. This section also includes the application for an initial certificate for an airport to become Part 139 certificated. In this process, it grants the FAA inspection authority to make unannounced inspections or tests to determine compliance with Part 139. These examinations and tests are conducted by the FAA's **Airport Certification Safety Inspectors (ACSIs)** based out of the appropriate FAA **Airport District Office (ADO)**. The formal requirements for the issuance and the duration of the certificate are also addressed in this section. The Part 139 AOC is valid until the certificate holder (airport sponsor) surrenders it or the FAA revokes the certificate. Certificates may be revoked for failing to comply with Part 139; however, in most cases, ACSIs will attempt to work with the airport operator to get them into compliance before threatening to revoke the certificate. ACSIs often switch to issuing fines to the airport operator in an attempt to get the airport to comply with the regulations. It would be a serious action for the FAA to actually revoke a Part 139 certificate, as it would effectively shut down air carrier operations at that airport.

Subpart B addresses **exemptions** to Part 139. The FAA takes Part 139 seriously and, therefore, does not approve exemptions without considerable vetting. An exemption essentially allows an airport to not comply with a particular component of Part 139. It is common, however, for the FAA to exempt certain airport operators from the Aircraft Rescue and Firefighting (ARFF) requirements under Part 139. Some nonhub airports that enplane less than 0.25% of the total number of enplaned passengers of all commercial service airports in the United States have received exemptions from the ARFF requirements. Exemptions are based on the grounds that the ARFF requirement would be unreasonably costly, burdensome, or impractical. Certain nonhub airports may not have the financial wherewithal to support full-time or part-time ARFF personnel and equipment (FAA, 2014).

A **deviation** from requirements in Part 139 may occur anytime an emergency condition requires immediate action for the protection of life or property. In these cases, the airport may deviate from any requirement of Part 139 or the ACM to the extent needed to address the emergency. Any airport that deviates from the requirements of Part 139 must, within 14 days after the emergency, notify the FAA Regional Airport Division Manager of the nature, extent, and duration of the deviation (and in writing if requested by the FAA). Part 139.113 *Deviations* notes that this statement must be in writing if requested by the FAA. Whether the FAA requests notification in writing or not, it is best practice to still provide written notification. Documenting the notification creates a public record of the action and may help protect the airport sponsor from liability.

Deviations contrast with exemptions in that they are reserved for emergencies. The deviation option does not apply to a situation that results from poor safety management. For example, if the airport allocated fire equipment offsite for repairs during air carrier operations, in a way that inadvertently places the airport below its ARFF required ability to respond to an emergency, then this action is not a deviation but rather poor planning and may result in an FAA fine.

If an airport were to exercise a legitimate deviation, top management should also issue a NOTAM (Notice to Airmen) and may even notify air carriers directly such that all stakeholders are completely informed about the status of ARFF at the airport.

Per **FAA Order 5280.5C**, *Airport Certification Program Handbook*, the FAA retains the authority to inspect any element of Part 139 at an airport to determine compliance. The authority includes unannounced inspections and tests, auditing records, and testing personnel for competency and qualifications for assigned duties.

The Airport Certification Manual and Airside Operations

The ACM explains how a particular airport operator complies with the requirements of Part 139. Any airport that is required to have an AOC under Part 139 is required to have an ACM that is approved by the FAA. Every page of the ACM is signed and dated by the FAA-designated authority from the FAA ADO. The ACM must be kept current at all times with at least one complete copy provided to the FAA and one copy available for inspection by the FAA at the airport. **FAA AC 150/5210-22** provides methods and procedures for developing the ACM in a manner acceptable to the FAA. Additional guidance may also be found in the *Airport Certification Program Handbook*. While FAA Orders are technically memorandums to FAA personnel, they often provide airport operators insights on how the FAA enforces compliance and what inspectors look for during inspections and audits.

The ACM explains who specifically is responsible for carrying out each required function within Part 139 and how they are to be implemented. The ACM also specifies when various functions must be conducted, such as airport self-inspections, snow removal activities, and response to emergencies (FAA, 2004, p. 7).

The ACM must contain operating procedures, equipment descriptions, assignments of responsibility to personnel, and any other information needed to comply with Part 139. It must also address any **limitations** imposed by the FAA. A limitation usually relates to an unusual operational characteristic at an airport, such as a need to restrict air carrier operations from using certain areas of the airport. In some airports, only one runway may be certificated under Part 139, while an adjacent runway may only be for GA usage. Not all airports can afford to maintain all available runways and taxiways to the Part 139 standard.

The ACM should be written in an understandable manner, clearly describing what must be accomplished to meet Part 139 requirements. The ACM should also include the identities and roles of individuals responsible for carrying out required tasks as specified in the ACM, such as the role of the AOM in conducting the self-inspection process. The document should be constructed in such a manner that new employees can readily grasp the content and requirements of the ACM. The ACM is not a job description, nor is it intended to provide complete instructions for all operational procedures on the airport; however, at a minimum, it should provide instructions for the critical tasks necessary to comply with Part 139 (FAA, 2004, p. 6).

The ACM should include a revision log to track changes and a method to update individuals who have been issued copies of the ACM when new information is distributed. The ACM should not include information that is not directly related to the requirements of Part 139. Charts, maps, graphics, or tables that complement the required information must also be included in the ACM. The ACM is typically comprised of several individual documents, such as the Snow and Ice Control Plan, Airport Emergency Plan, and Wildlife Hazard Management Plan, that collectively are considered the entire ACM.

The first component of the ACM lists numerous requirements related to airport safety and maintenance standards. In the second component, Part 139 airports must include an Airport Emergency Plan. This plan is often a separate document from the ACM, but is considered to be a component of the ACM, and must be approved by the FAA. The Snow and Ice Control Plan, Wildlife Hazard Management Plan, and Airport Sign and Marking Plan are also considered to be part of the ACM. One plan that is not part of the ACM is the **Irregular Operations Plan**, which explains how airports should handle aircraft that have essentially been stranded on the ramp. This is commonly referred to as the "tarmac rule" and resulted in airports being required to develop **Model Contingency Plans to Deal with Lengthy Onboard Ground Delays** and submit the plans to the U.S. Department of Transportation (DOT). Airport Cooperative Research Program (ACRP) Report 65: *Guidebook for Airport Irregular Operations (IROPS) Contingency Planning* provides airport operators with guidance in the development of these plans and in their implementation.

Fundamentally, the ACM must reflect actual conditions, operations, and procedures that are in effect at the airport. When an FAA ACSI assesses an airport ACM, that individual should find that the operations taking place on the airfield are the same as described in the ACM to the extent that is reasonably possible.

The ACM should be written to meet regulatory standards, but not generally to exceed it. Airport operators are encouraged to exceed the minimum industry standards, but managers also understand that any requirement contained in the ACM becomes a regulation enforceable by the FAA. In this case, standards exceeding what is required by Part 139 should be established as part of the airport's safety culture, but not included in the official ACM. This strategy reduces risk associated with FAA regulatory enforcements and allows the Airport Manager greater flexibility in managing safety and operations.

As described above, airports usually draft a separate operating policy or contingency plan that is above the regulatory standard, but not formally contained in the ACM. For example, Pensacola International Airport in Florida has a **Destructive Weather Plan (DWP)** that is separate from the FAA-approved Airport Emergency Plan (AEP) of the ACM. Hurricanes and tornadoes are still adequately addressed in the airport's AEP, but the additional DWP allows the airport operator greater flexibility in preparing for, responding to, and recovering from weather events, since action can immediately be taken and without FAA approval.

Pensacola's DWP addresses many of the proactive measures the airport would take in advance of a storm, along with terminal and airfield shut-downs, and recovery operations, such as damage assessments and the reopening of the airfield. The AEP addresses the overall functions that must occur during a weather incident (e.g., law enforcement, fire and rescue, crowd control) and the specific actions expected of each agency involved in the plan.

In addition to the regulatory requirements of Part 139, airport operators must also be aware of **CertAlerts**. The FAA issues CertAlerts periodically to FAA inspectors and staff as a rapid method of providing additional guidance and information regarding Part 139 airport certification and related issues. **CertAlerts** are typically categorized as Advisory, Cautionary, or Non-Directive in content (Wells & Young, 2011). The FAA also uses **Program Guidance Letters (PGLs)** to revise guidance about the administration of the *Airport Improvement Program Handbook*.

Considered a "living document," the ACM is routinely updated. Maintenance of the ACM is critical to maintaining compliance with Part 139. The FAA recommends that the ACM be divided into smaller sections assigned to a specific staff member who conducts a periodic review and update of that section. Individuals are chosen on their ability to serve as subject matter experts on their applicable sections of the ACM.

Airport operators can subscribe to email updates from the FAA concerning regulations or ACs. The task of reviewing these updates should be spread across multiple qualified staff members, as the frequency and quantity of these updates may be extensive. The FAA also recommends that sections of the ACM be reviewed on a staggered schedule, so that smaller areas can be focused on over the course of time, rather than trying to schedule a single extensive update.

The ACM must be kept up-to-date at all times. To change the ACM, the airport operator must notify the FAA through an amendment, 30 days in advance of the proposed change. The FAA may also initiate an amendment to an airport ACM provided it gives notice in not less than seven business days. In response, the airport operator may submit written information or arguments as related to the proposed amendment. The FAA then makes a decision about the amendment and notifies the airport operator within 30 days with the decision to move forward with, make changes to, or rescind the amendment. Airports that disagree with an FAA amendment may appeal to the **FAA Associate Administrator for Airports** but must still comply with the conditions of the amendment during the appeal process. The FAA may also issue emergency amendments, which may go into effect immediately and be issued without stay. In this case, the FAA should explain the reasons for the emergency amendment, as well as the lack of a deadline, if appropriate.

Required ACM Elements for Airside Operations

For Classes I, II, and III airports, the ACM must include:

1. Lines of succession for airport operational responsibilities;
2. Any exemption issued to the airport by the FAA;
3. A grid map to identify locations and terrain features around the airport (offsite emergency responders often do not understand how to read airfield signs and markings or the Airport Layout Plan, but a grid map provides enhanced information to determine various locations and features on the incident site);
4. The location of obstructions that are required to be lighted or marked within the airport's area of authority;
5. A description of each movement area and safety area available for air carrier use;
6. During construction activity, procedures for the avoidance of interruption or failure of airport utilities, including power and navigational aids (NAVAIDs) that support air carrier operations;
7. A description of the system used for record retention;
8. A description of personnel training;
9. Procedures for maintaining paved areas;
10. Procedures for maintaining safety areas;
11. A sign-marking-lighting plan;
12. A snow and ice control plan, if required
13. Descriptions of the facilities, equipment, personnel, and procedures for meeting the ARFF requirements and any exemptions to these standards, if applicable;
14. Description and procedures for maintaining the traffic in wind direction indicators;
15. An AEP;
16. Procedures for conducting the self-inspection program;
17. Procedures for controlling pedestrian and ground vehicles in movement areas and safety areas;
18. Procedures for the removal of obstructions, or the marking and lighting of obstructions, as required;
19. Procedures for protecting NAVAIDs;
20. Procedures for protecting the public from hazardous aircraft operations, including jet and propeller blast;
21. Procedures for controlling wildlife;
22. Procedures for airport condition reporting (i.e., NOTAMs[2]);
23. Procedures for identifying, marking, and lighting construction and other unserviceable areas; and
24. Any other item the FAA finds necessary to ensure safety and air transportation.

---

[2]Common industry acronyms for Notice to Airman in plural form are stated as NOTAMS or NOTAMs.

Class IV airports are required to adhere to all of the above listed elements *except*:

1. During construction activity, procedures for the avoidance of interruption or failure of airport utilities, including power and NAVAIDs that support air carrier operations;
2. Procedures for controlling pedestrian and ground vehicles in movement areas and safety areas;
3. Procedures for protecting NAVAIDs;
4. Procedures for protecting the public from hazardous aircraft operations, including jet and propeller blast;
5. Procedures for controlling wildlife; and
6. Procedures for identifying, marking, and lighting construction and other unserviceable areas.

Recordkeeping for Airside Operations

Subparts A, B, and C of Part 139 focus primarily on administrative requirements. Subpart D contains the operational requirements an airport must meet to obtain and retain an AOC. Subpart D also includes some administrative requirements, such as recordkeeping, personnel, and training requirements. The FAA requires airports to maintain records that relate to Part 139 compliance (e.g., self-inspection records, aircraft and incident records, and airport condition reports) for 12 "consecutive calendar months" (CCM). The FAA uses CCM to imply that the period referenced ends at the end of the last calendar month. For example, if a record was created on the 14th of May and was required to be kept for 12 CCM, the record would be kept until the 31st of May, the following year. Part 139 requires records for training in areas such as airport self-inspection, emergency service, movement area, and general safety to be kept for a period of 24 CCM. One inconsistency in the recordkeeping requirements is with fueling-personnel training. Training records for fueling personnel are required to be kept for 12 CCM.

The FAA specifies the minimum period of time to retain various airport records and training records. However, many cities and counties have different record retention schedules as related to local and state airport-operating requirements. Usually, records to be retained for the FAA minimum requirement of the ACM should be kept for 12 or 24 months past the CCM, or as appropriately determined by the airport sponsor, particularly in the case of aircraft incident or accident records. Keeping records of aircraft incidents or accidents for at least 3 years after the event is important, as lawsuits and investigations may extend many years past the date of an incident or accident.

Self-Inspection Personnel for Airside Operations

A critical component of airport safety is the training of personnel to operate in the **Air Operations Area (AOA)**. The FAA requires any individual who is charged with the responsibility of inspecting the AOA for Part 139 compliance to be trained every 12 CCM. For the AOA, airport self-inspectors must, at a minimum, be trained in:

1. Airport familiarization, including the airport signs-marking-lighting systems;
2. The AEP;
3. Procedures for operating in the movement area;
4. Procedures for communicating with the air traffic control tower or, if a tower is not available or in operation at the time, the use of the Common Traffic Advisory Frequency;

5. Procedures for reporting unsafe airport conditions through the Notice to Airmen process;

6. Any duties specified under the ACM;

7. The airport requirements for ARFF;

8. The handling and storage of hazardous substances and materials;

9. The self-inspection program;

10. Pedestrian and ground vehicle operations;

11. Wildlife hazard management procedures and, if applicable, the Wildlife Management Hazard Program (WMHP); and

12. The relevant FAA ACs applicable to the airport.

Airfield inspectors fulfill a critical role on the airfield, as they must ensure that takeoff and landing surfaces, along with the surrounding airspace, are maintained as a safe environment for all aircraft operations. When an inspector spots a discrepancy that cannot be immediately fixed, the inspector must make the appropriate notifications to the air traffic control tower (if one exists at the airport), disseminate NOTAMs, as appropriate, and issue work orders to ensure that the safety-related problems are resolved as soon as possible. In some cases, the discrepancy may be so severe that an immediate shutdown of the affected runway, taxiway, or other movement area may be necessary, until the situation can be corrected.

FAA ACSIs evaluate the quality of each of the airport's employee self-inspectors. When an FAA inspector conducts an annual inspection, the inspector does not expect to find zero discrepancies, as maintaining the entire airfield to the regulatory standard is nearly impossible. Discrepancies are expected and are considered part of "the noise of the system." Rainstorms creating ruts in the safety area or ponding on airport services, pavement damage that occurs during rapid and extreme temperature variations, airfield signs damaged by weather, and issues caused by wildlife or human error are examples of such discrepancies. While all of these examples are noted and addressed by the ACSI, the focus during an evaluation is to reexamine previous discrepancies that were not immediately corrected or discrepancies that were followed up with work orders but perhaps had still not been addressed for weeks or even months after the first notice of the discrepancy. When discrepancies exist, FAA inspectors immediately discuss with the airport operator what plans should be initiated to fix the discrepancy.

The FAA does not mandate the number of self-inspection qualified personnel an airport must have. Instead the FAA requires that an airport must have *sufficient and qualified personnel* to perform the inspection process. Airport management should ensure that there are enough trained inspection personnel to carry out the duties of the ACM and that they are qualified with the requisite skills, knowledge, and abilities to perform the job (Prather, 2011, p. 12). Self-inspectors must operate on an active airfield, which can be a demanding and sometimes hazardous environment. Therefore, in addition to understanding the requirements of the ACM and the self-inspection standards, self-inspectors must be comfortable with driving in movement areas around aircraft that are taking off, landing, and taxiing, and be comfortable enough to communicate with FAA air traffic controllers via two-way radio.[3]

---

[3]Talking on an air traffic control frequency can be an intimidating process for some people. Air traffic controllers and pilots are accustomed to rapid, verbal communication and unique dialog, which can be quite challenging to become proficient at.

Designated self-inspectors must also be properly equipped to carry out the functions of their job. At a minimum they should have a properly marked and lighted vehicle, with a beacon for operations at night or during inclement weather, and a VHF (very high frequency) two-way radio to talk to the air traffic control tower and pilots in the airspace. Inspectors typically have an additional radio operating on another frequency in order to talk to Airport Operations, maintenance, police, or fire personnel. Inspectors should have a checklist covering the required inspection items, copies of (or online access to) existing construction safety plans, and a sketch of the airport.

Although not required, a flashlight, camera, first-aid kit, and spray paint should also be part of an inspector's standard equipment when in the AOA. Cameras are useful to photograph compliance issues such as poor pavement or damaged signs. Spray paint can also be used to note particular locations where maintenance is required. Airport Operations personnel, particularly inspection personnel, are frequently the first to arrive at aircraft accident and incident locations. Therefore, a first-aid kit, blanket, and safety vest should also be part of the standard equipment. Safety vests identify individuals who may have to exit their vehicle while in the AOA. A specially marked command vest also helps to identify the lead Airport Operations person during an emergency. Additional equipment may include liquid spill and hazmat kits, measuring wheels, and smart tablets with self-inspection software.

Some airport operators also provide self-inspection personnel with training in first aid, firefighting, and first responder best practices. At some airports, inspectors carry firearms with live ammunition or pyrotechnics for wildlife mitigation (dispersion or elimination). A shovel, bucket, trash bags, and gloves are also useful items for cleaning up expired wildlife. Binoculars, safety glasses or goggles, and earplugs are also recommended supplies the examiner should have nearby when inspecting the AOA (Prather, 2011, p. 21).

Airport Operations inspector personnel also benefit from training in Incident Command through the NIMS. Training in ICS/100, ICS/200, and ICS/700 comprise the basic requirements to be NIMS-qualified. If inspectors find themselves in the role of Incident Commanders, they should also complete ICS/300 and ICS/400, and it may be beneficial to equip their vehicle with Incident Command tools such as whiteboards and additional radios.

Best Practices: Airside Self-Inspection Training

ACRP Synthesis Report 27 *Airport Self-Inspection Practices* assessed best practices for Airport Safety Self-Inspections for compliance with Part 139. The report found that variations exist among airports in methods and training programs used to train self-inspection personnel (Prather, 2011, p. 2). Prather noted several methods airports use to ensure personnel are trained, including in-house training, computer-based training (CBT) and online training programs, and training conferences. For initial training, most airports utilize on-the-job training (OJT) and self-study methods. Recurrent training at most airports relies on OJT and interactive (CBT, multimedia, etc.) methods (Prather, 2011, p. 3). A concern for using legacy OJT or CBT systems is that without routine updating of content, errors or expired information found in the system has the potential to be taught as valid information. Therefore, as with all areas of SMS, training programs must be audited and updated on a fairly recent and regular basis.

More effective methods of training should include a standardized curriculum for new-hire personnel proctored by qualified trainers. This phase of training would be followed by OJT. OJT programs should require new personnel to accompany a variety of senior personnel (if possible) on daily self-inspections to gain first-hand knowledge of how to properly conduct an inspection (Prather, 2011, p. 15). Even for individuals who have had extensive experience in Airport Operations and self-inspection for Part 139 requirements at other airports, a standardized training curriculum and properly supervised OJT will help new personnel understand characteristics unique to the airport.

Airports are encouraged to develop interactive training programs using airport-specific photos and video, case studies, and active discussions with senior inspection personnel and trainers (Prather, 2011, pp. 15—16). Training should be student-centered, focusing on what the students should know and be able to apply at their airport (Prather, 2011, p. 15). Training programs at some airports may last for several weeks or even several months before an inspector is allowed to conduct self-inspection processes without supervision. Prather (2011) determined, at most U.S. airports, Airport Operations personnel were responsible for inspector training. Much smaller fractions used CBT, a designated training manager, or the Airport Manager.

FAA inspectors seek to examine the training curriculum and instructional materials used in meeting Part 139 training requirements. The FAA places emphasis on reviewing the self-inspector training program and the movement area training program. FAA Part 139 Inspectors normally do not approve informal types of training, such as informal discussions or serendipitous mentoring sessions.[4] FAA inspectors look for well-organized and implemented training programs that ensure that all Part 139 self-inspection items have been properly addressed.

The U.S. military uses a Personnel Qualification System (PQS) in many areas of training. PQS requires individuals to demonstrate specific skills and application of knowledge in required areas before performing the activity on their own. The self-inspection process is a viable application for this type of training.

Top management should ensure that self-inspectors are qualified in the knowledge and requirements of each item under Part 139. Training programs should be periodically audited, kept up-to-date with industry best practices, and aligned with regulatory and airfield operational changes. Recurrent training can be accomplished effectively through the use of a CBT or web-based systems that are routinely updated with current information and practices. Inspection personnel should periodically attend in-classroom facilitated training or industry seminars and conferences, to exchange best practices and identify areas that need correction or improvement.

THE FEDERAL AVIATION ADMINISTRATION'S AIRSIDE INSPECTION PROCESS

Once a year, an FAA Airport Certification Safety Inspector (ACSI) inspects the airport to ensure it is in compliance with the regulatory requirements of Part 139 and any amendments. The review process includes several steps. While ideally an airport constantly strives to be in compliance with

---

[4]Informal or *coffee-talk* meetings are encouraged in other contexts, such as in discussions between personnel of how they would respond in an emergency if it happened *right now* while they are sitting at coffee (or lunch, or dinner), to build relationships with other stakeholders, or to discuss issues and answer questions between staff members. However, these informal meetings are not considered an adequate level of training comprehensiveness to meet the self-inspection or movement area training requirements.

Part 139, the reality is that airport operators often prepare months in advance for an FAA inspection. The FAA inspection includes:

1. **The Preinspection Review:** The Airport Certification Safety Inspector reviews the airport's ACM and any other internal records related to the airport, such as the results of previous inspections and corrective actions the airport was requested to complete.
2. **In-Brief:** FAA and airport personnel discuss schedules for the inspection and interview various airport personnel. Airport management personnel usually attempt to connect the inspector with their best personnel, as it is common for FAA inspectors to question employees on the specific issues as related to safety and Part 139 requirements.
3. **Administrative Inspection of Airport Records:** The Airport Certification Safety Inspector reviews records that the airport is required to maintain including airfield inspection records, personnel training records, training curricula, the Airport Data Record (Airport Master Record-5010 Form[5]), and NOTAMs.
4. **Movement Area Inspection:** Pavement, signs, airfield markings, airfield lighting, and safety areas architecture compliance and overall condition, and the approach slope of each runway checked for obstructions. FAA inspectors also observe ground vehicle operations and pedestrian movement on the ramp. To ensure that rules are followed, they also check for the presence of wildlife and assess the effectiveness of wildlife management techniques. They check the traffic and wind direction indicators for overall condition and inspect airfield fencing and jet blast deflectors (Wells & Young, 2011).
5. **ARFF Inspection:** Inspectors conduct a timed-response drill to ensure that the required fire apparatus can be positioned in the appropriate location to meet regulatory standards. They review records for personnel training, the annual live fire drill, and training in basic emergency medical care. Inspectors also inspect required equipment and protective clothing for overall operation, condition, and availability (Wells & Young, 2011).
6. **Fueling Facilities Inspection:** The fuel farm and mobile fueling apparatus are inspected, records are checked for quarterly inspections of the fuel facility, and certifications are inspected from each tenant fueling agent to ensure that adequate fire safety training has been conducted (Wells & Young, 2011).
7. **Night Inspection:** If the airport conducts air carrier operations at night or the airport has an instrument approach, inspectors should conduct an inspection of lights, reflection of airfield markings, and airport beacon, wind cone, and obstruction lighting.
8. **Postinspection Briefing:** FAA personnel meet with airport personnel to discuss findings, issue any Letter of Correction noting any violations or discrepancies, if they are found, and come to agreement on reasonable dates for correcting violations. Inspectors often also give additional safety recommendations during this meeting (Wells & Young, 2011).

After the FAA Part 139 inspection is complete, it is not uncommon for the ACSI to conduct unannounced drop-in inspections throughout the year. Often these inspections are to check on the status of violations or discrepancies that were noted during the last annual inspection and ensure that corrective actions were met within the agreed-upon deadlines.

---

[5]See https://www.faa.gov/forms/index.cfm/go/document.information/documentID/185474

THE SAFETY SELF-INSPECTION PROGRAM

Once the FAA has approved the airport's AOC, the airport operator must continue to conduct self-inspections to ensure it meets the requirements of Part 139. The airport operator is responsible for meeting the regulatory requirements on a continuous basis, responding to incidents and accidents, managing irregular Airport Operations (snow removal, meteorological events, wildlife), and reporting any safety issue that may affect air carrier operations. While the FAA ensures that the airport initially meets Part 139 requirements, as well as provides an annual inspection to ensure that the requirements are maintained, the day-to-day safety functions of an airport are the responsibility of the local, airport-management personnel.

Airfield conditions can change instantaneously. A safe landing surface for one aircraft may become fouled by foreign object debris, or wildlife, for the next aircraft. Part 139.327 requires airport operators to inspect the airport daily, unless otherwise specified in the ACM, and to conduct special inspections when unusual conditions, such as construction activities or weather, may affect air carrier operations and immediately after an aircraft accident or incident. Inspection personnel do not necessarily have to be part of the Airport Operations department. Depending on the size of the airport, airport inspection personnel may be part of the maintenance staff, the Airport Manager, or even ARFF personnel. In any case, inspection personnel must meet the training requirements for airport inspectors under Part 139. The self-inspection program includes four different types of inspections:

1. The *regularly scheduled inspection*, sometimes referred to as the "daily inspection," which is conducted at least once prior to the beginning of air carrier operations and at least once prior to the beginning of night air carrier operations;
2. The *continuous surveillance inspection*, which is conducted at any time by an individual who is designated and trained as an airport inspector in the AOA;
3. The *periodic condition inspection*, which is conducted at regular intervals to look for discrepancies that may not be noticed on a daily basis;
4. The *special inspection*, which occurs anytime there is an unusual event or condition, such as a meteorological event, spotting of wildlife on the movement area, or a report of debris on operating surfaces (i.e., foreign object debris [FOD]).

An inspection checklist assists the airport inspector in conducting the inspection, minimizing complacency, and providing a historical record of each self-inspection (Prather, 2011, p. 21). An inspection checklist sample is provided in Appendix B, but the essential areas are:

1. Pavement areas;
2. Safety areas;
3. Markings;
4. Signs;
5. Lighting;
6. NAVAIDs;
7. Obstructions;
8. Fueling operations;
9. Snow and ice;
10. Construction;

11. ARFF;
12. Public protection; and
13. Wildlife hazards.

Many airports still use paper-based, self-inspection, checklist systems; however, the airport industry is converting to electronic-based checklists, networked into central database systems. Transitioning to a computer- or Internet-based self-inspection information system provides numerous benefits, including enhanced use of the GPS (Global Positioning System), rapid reporting of discrepancies with automatic entry into a work-order system, and rapid reporting of discrepancies and issuance of NOTAMs. These information and data management systems also provide redundant architecture for backup, archiving, conducting analytics, and the dissemination of relevant data and information to appropriate operational personnel.

Prior to conducting a self-inspection, inspectors must review previous inspection checklists and current NOTAMs and should also check weather reports including the **Automated Terminal Information System (ATIS)** (if available) for the most current airfield conditions prior to conducting the inspection. Many inspection personnel follow a standardized pattern or "flow" around the airfield, using checklist and other documentation to help confirm that all required elements of the inspection have been examined.

However, when inspecting the AOA for unexpected safety hazards, it is sometimes a good strategy to vary the flow of processes during the self-inspection. Routine and standardized flows may give the same inspector lower situational awareness leading to the inability to detect risks or unexpected issues (see "Airside Routine Self-Inspections and Situational Awareness").

AIRSIDE ROUTINE SELF-INSPECTIONS AND SITUATIONAL AWARENESS

By following the same inspection pattern or flow every day, inspectors may miss required elements to the inspection or new and unexpected risks to safety—even when using a checklist. This is a result of the self-inspection process becoming routine and thereby causing a lower state of situational awareness. By varying the flow, the examiner is able to view each inspection area from a slightly different perspective. For example, if a runway is always inspected from north to south, certain signs, markings, and even FOD may be hidden from view. A warning: Using varying inspection patterns may result in an airport inspector missing certain areas because of a lack of standardization. **Consequently, it might be beneficial for the airport operator to establish two or three standardized patterns for each self-inspection that maximize coverage and ensures all areas are visible throughout the day.**

The FAA recommends that runway inspections be conducted in the opposite direction of landing traffic. In contrast, many airports prefer that inspection personnel drive with the direction of landing traffic so as not to slow down flight operations. If the airport inspectors are conducting the inspection prior to the beginning of daily air carrier operations, then there should not be too much landing traffic other than cargo and GA aircraft. Additionally, Airport Managers should understand the difference between conducting the regularly scheduled self-inspections and unscheduled special inspections, such as to remove FOD or wildlife. If possible, scheduled self-inspections should be conducted moving toward landing aircraft such that the inspector has a better chance of seeing aircraft on approach. For special inspections, it is common for the field inspector to drive with the direction of landing traffic in order to enter and exit the runway quickly.

At smaller airports, an individual on shift usually conducts all self-inspections. At large-hub airports, teams of inspectors may be used. Teams may use one vehicle or be distributed in several vehicles in order to accomplish the various self-inspections or cover areas of the airfield. It is preferable to have a team in one vehicle, as the driver may then focus on driving while passengers can focus on required self-inspection items (Prather, 2011, p. 32). This strategy also helps to reduce runway incursions and vehicle accidents. Because conducting the regular self-inspection can be tedious, particularly at large airports, some airports assign individuals varying elements of Part 139 to examine, such as markings or lighting in one self-inspection and pavement and safety areas in the next self-inspection.

In some cases, airport operators may bring a tenant along on the self-inspection in order to provide a different perspective and to let the tenant become more involved in the airport safety process (Prather, 2011, p. 34). However, some airports may have liability issues in taking third-party representatives on self-inspections.

The Airside Regularly Scheduled Self-Inspection

Title 14 CFR Part 139 and AC 150-5200.18C *Airport Safety Self-Inspection* provides specific guidance for Airport Operations safety self-evaluations. Highlights from this advisory include:

1. **Pavement Areas:** Airport pavement is a vital component of the Airport Safety Self-Inspection. Inspectors verify that pavement lips, the area between full-strength operating areas and accompanying shoulders or safety areas, allow water to drain and that the lip height does not exceed 3 inches. Larger pavement lips may cause directional control issues or damage landing gear. Inspectors look for cracks and holes in the pavement wide enough to cause directional control problems for an aircraft. The overall condition of the pavement is checked noting any significant cracks, bumps, vegetation, or FOD that could damage an aircraft. Vegetation growing through pavement cracks is a serious issue as it allows more water to drain into the subbase, accelerating the formation of potholes and contributing to increased cracking.

2. **Safety Areas:** Runways and taxiways include safety areas. Safety areas include the runway and taxiway surface, extend outward from the runway centerline to either side of the runway or taxiway, and extend past the ends of the paved areas. The dimensions of the safety areas vary and are determined by airport design standards. As an example, the safety area for a runway with a precision instrument approach is 250 feet either side of centerline, and 1,000 feet off the approach and departure ends of the runway. The safety area is similar to a shoulder of an interstate, allowing an aircraft to use the area in unusual or emergency situations. Aircraft using safe areas may incur damage to the aircraft structure, although these areas are designed to minimize that prospect. Inspectors check the safety area to ensure that only objects that are "fixed by function" (meaning they are required to be there, such as airfield signs and lights) and "frangible" (meaning they could easily be knocked over causing minimal damage to the aircraft) are in safety areas. The inspector will also check for service variations that could cause damage to aircraft operating in safety areas.

3. **Signs, Marking, and Lighting:** Inspectors check to ensure airport markings are the correct color and are not deteriorating or becoming obscured from environmental issues (e.g., weather, aircraft exhaust, rubber marks from aircraft tires). Airfield signs are checked to ensure they are easy to read and properly illuminated at night, not obscured by

vegetation, dirt, or snow, and have no missing sign panels. Airfield lighting is inspected, typically at night, to ensure that lights are operable, the right color configuration, and are not damaged or misaligned. Markings should also be checked to ensure they are reflective at night.

4. **NAVAIDs:** Airport NAVAIDs are typically owned by the FAA. However, airport operators are responsible for self-inspecting NAVAIDs and reporting problems immediately to the FAA (or appropriate NAVAID owner). Examples of NAVAIDs that require routine inspection include the segmented circle, wind cone, runway surface lights, visual glide slope indicators (PAPI or VASI), and the approach lighting system. In some cases, proper operation of these lighting systems cannot be completely determined by ground-inspection personnel and require confirmation from pilots. For example, a pilot may report a NAVAID out-of-service, at which point the airport operator can issue a NOTAM and also notify the appropriate NAVAID owner. Generally, self-inspectors also ensure that NAVAIDs are clear of vegetation and can be seen from the air (to the extent that can be determined).

5. **Obstructions:** Inspectors visually check any construction underway on the airport that could affect aircraft operations and any construction cranes within the vicinity of the airport. If a new obstruction is discovered, the airport operator must determine if it is properly marked and lighted and that it has been reported to the FAA using Form 7460. Usually, contracted airport construction personnel will not file the appropriate FAA paperwork, so airport operators must ensure that the paperwork is filed and that a NOTAM is issued immediately warning pilots of the obstruction. Self-inspectors should also report any required obstruction lights that are non-functioning.

6. **Fueling Operations:** The daily inspection of airport fueling operations is conducted primarily to comply with fire-safety codes. Fueling inspections include assessing overall security, fire protection, and general housekeeping. Self-inspectors must also check that fueling operators adhere to local fire codes, proper aircraft servicing during fueling, and that no one is smoking during fueling operations.

7. **Snow and Ice:** Inspectors must be familiar with the airport *Snow and Ice Control Plan* (SICP). SICP operations typically require continuous inspections with updates through the NOTAM system regarding airfield conditions. As part of the regularly scheduled SICP self-inspection, inspectors must determine if any NAVAIDs, lights, or signs are obscured or damaged by snow or snow removal operation; that existing snowbanks do not exceed proper clearance for aircraft wingtips, engines, and propellers; and that pavement conditions are appropriate for aircraft operations.

8. **Construction:** Inspectors should be familiar with any airport construction and related safety plans currently taking place on the airfield. Inspectors should determine if stockpiled material is properly stored and protected from wind and jet blast, or *prop wash*. Construction equipment adjacent to movement areas should be properly marked and lighted and barricades properly installed defining construction and hazardous areas. Inspectors especially need to watch for FOD, a significant problem during airfield construction. They must report and monitor dangerous conditions created by construction activity, such as damage to signs, lights, and markings or NAVAIDs. Often during construction the airfield will be modified in and around the construction area, which may cause confusing signs and markings. Inspectors should watch for such situations and issue NOTAMs as appropriate.

9. **ARFF:** Inspecting ARFF includes checking for the status and availability of required fire apparatus, deployment of required ARFF personnel, and ensuring that alarm and emergency notification systems are operable. Inspectors must also check for construction or maintenance activity along ARFF response routes that could affect an emergency response. If any required ARFF vehicle is not available or operative, the airport should immediately issue a NOTAM.

10. **Public Protection:** These self-inspections should confirm that gates, fencing, and locks are in place to prevent the inadvertent entry to movement areas by unauthorized individuals and vehicles. The public must be kept away from any chance of exposure to jet blast. While Part 139 does not address security issues directly, airports that are regulated by the Transportation Security Administration (TSA) have additional requirements for reporting and responding to unauthorized personnel and vehicles within the AOA or other Security Area.

11. **Wildlife Hazard Management:** Airport inspectors should be familiar with the existing *Wildlife Hazard Management Plan* (WHMP) and inspect for wildlife in accordance with the plan. Whether or not a WHMP is available, inspectors should watch for large flocks of birds on or adjacent to the airport, mammals that present a hazard to aircraft operations observed on the airport or near movement areas, or any other wildlife that could create a hazard. Even small wildlife that may not present a hazard to aircraft can attract larger forms of wildlife, which could present a hazard to aircraft operations. Wildlife, deceased or alive, involved in an aircraft strike should be reported to the FAA using the Form 5200-7 Bird/Other Wildlife Strike Report. Inspectors should also check fencing and gates for wildlife accessibility.

In addition to the aforementioned self-inspection items, each airport's ACM may include additional inspection items for that airport and the compliance standards related to each inspection item.

Continuous Surveillance in Airside Self-Inspections

Regularly scheduled self-inspections include all elements in approved checklists, plus any additional required elements listed in the ACM. The requirement for "continuous surveillance" self-inspection is required for all Part 139 inspection requirements. However, ACRP Synthesis Report 27, *Airport Self-Inspection Practices* notes that focus in continuous surveillance is directed to the following areas as a priority:

1. **Ground Vehicle Operations:** Inspectors must ensure that vehicle operators are operating in a safe manner, within airport rules and regulations; following proper procedure for access to and from the movement areas; and reporting any ground-vehicle incidents or accidents.

2. **Airport Construction Activities:** Inspectors must ensure that construction personnel adhere to authorized routes to and from the construction site and watch for debris and equipment parked near flight operations or NAVAIDs. These inspections should also focus on detection of confusing construction signs, markings, or lighting that could mislead pilots (or vehicle operators).

3. **Fueling Operations:** Inspectors must ensure that fueling operations are conducted within the National Fire Protection Association's (NFPA) established standards and related airport rules and regulations. Inspectors should also focus on correct, aircraft-servicing procedures during fuel operations, such as the requirement that fuel trucks not park within 10 feet of another fuel

truck or within 50 feet of any buildings;[6] fueling personnel are not smoking; and proper, fire-extinguishing agents are in place. Fail-safe controls should be available and not blocked. Indications of leaks or spills, debris, or other material that could cause a fire should be immediately addressed during the self-inspection.

4. **Snow and Ice:** Inspectors must ensure that snow removal operations begin at appropriate times, subject to weather conditions, and report on the condition of the airfield through the NOTAM process.

5. **Public Protection:** Inspectors must ensure that airfield fencing and jet- and propeller-blast deflectors are in good condition and appropriately placed or secured.

6. **Wildlife Hazard Management:** Inspectors must ensure wildlife does not cause a hazard to air carrier operations and pick up deceased wildlife on a runway, taxiway, or safety area.

7. **FOD:** Inspectors must ensure that FOD that has accumulated on the airfield is removed (Prather, 2011, p. 21).

SMS and Airport Operations advocate that safety is everyone's responsibility. However, the airport operator is primarily responsible for ensuring that the airport is constantly surveyed, maintaining Part 139 requirements, and reporting when areas are noncompliant. The continuous self-inspection process helps the airport operator fulfill this responsibility, especially in airside operations.

Periodic Condition Inspection

Periodic condition inspections may include items contained within the standard, scheduled self-evaluation, but add additional special tasks, such as aircraft-landing-gear rubber and tire-marking removal. An airport inspector may note during a regularly scheduled self-inspection that tire marks or rubber buildup is increasing in the touchdown zone of the runway. As a result, a periodic inspection will be conducted to measure the amount of buildup and determine if removal is needed.

Some periodic inspection items are conducted annually, while some are conducted every 3 or 6 months. The frequency of inspection is often determined by using a pavement management system, safety management system, or similar program that specifies the time frame for inspections that vary with operating conditions.

Paved areas are so critical to flight safety that they are inspected regularly (self-inspection), periodically, and continuously. A continuous inspection is done at frequent intervals or whenever daily opportunities occur throughout each day. During the regularly scheduled self-inspection, an airport inspector looks to see that (a) pavement lips do not to exceed plus or minus three inches in vertical height separation, (b) pavement provides good draining with no ponding, and (c) no cracks, ruts, or holes would result in the loss of directional control for an aircraft.

During the periodic inspection, pavement is inspected at defined intervals by using a rating system that predicts long-term pavement-maintenance issues. The airport operator is also required to periodically assess airfield markings, signs, and lighting for their overall condition to determine whether maintenance is necessary. While these items may pass the daily inspection, a periodic inspection can help determine when signs or lights need to be completely replaced or when markings need to be repainted or cleaned.

---

[6]Some buildings are fire-rated and constructed to allow for fuel truck parking inside or immediately adjacent to the building.

ARFF services are also part of the daily and periodic condition inspection. The daily inspection focuses on the readiness capabilities of ARFF equipment and personnel, while the periodic inspection focuses on replacement or maintenance of equipment and firefighting materials.

The periodic inspection for obstructions focuses on items that are not noticed on a daily basis, such as tree growth on hills or mountains that surround the airport, and that may penetrate the FAA-designated **imaginary surfaces** of an airport. Imaginary surfaces are a set of airspace standards that help ensure airspace around the airport is free of obstructions. These standards allow for normal aircraft navigation. They also require any obstruction to be properly marked on aeronautical charts, and if necessary and practicable, marked and physically lighted for enhanced visibility. NAVAID inspection is also conducted periodically to ensure proper alignment of NAVAIDs owned and controlled by the airport operator within imaginary surfaces (Figure 6.4).

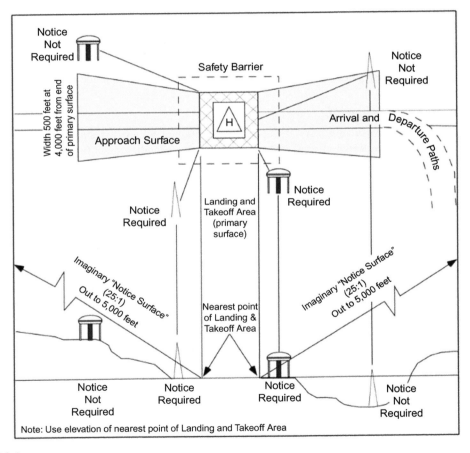

FIGURE 6.4

Depiction of imaginary surfaces as applied to an example heliport (rotor aircraft operations) and obstruction notification requirements.

Source: U.S. DOT FAA, Procedures for Handling Airspace Matters, 2014.

The **fuel farm** (fuel storage areas) must be periodically inspected by fire personnel from an **Authority Having Jurisdiction (AHJ)**, which for most airports is the State Fire Marshall. The complete details and standards for the quarterly fuel farm inspection are fully addressed in Part 139, AC 150/5200_18C, and NFPA 407 *Standard for Aircraft Fuel Servicing*. Periodic inspections of fuel farms include many items that are part of the regularly scheduled inspection or the continuous inspection, but also include:

1. Ensuring fuel storage areas have adequate fencing and security to prevent unauthorized access;
2. "No smoking signs" in and on fueling vehicles and at the fuel farm are clearly visible;
3. Equipment malfunctions or maintenance issues that could cause a fire, including piping, and checking for fuel leaks;
4. Adequate numbers of serviceable fire extinguishers that meet the discharge requirements;
5. Explosion-proof equipment, switches, and wiring that are adequately protected from an ignition source;
6. Serviceable bonding wires and proper dead-man controls;
7. Flammability decals on mobile fuelers;
8. Emergency-cutoff switches and controls are visible and not blocked;
9. Electrical equipment, switches, wiring, and light covers (tail lights, in-cab lights) are properly covered to prevent them from being an ignition source.

Special Inspections

Special inspections are conducted after receiving a complaint or report of an issue from an airport operator, air carrier, air traffic control, or other entity, or are triggered by an unusual condition or event (such as an aircraft has a hard landing or reports unusual sensations on pavement areas, or after an unusual weather event). Special inspections are most commonly conducted to retrieve FOD or deceased wildlife. Airport inspectors can also conduct a special inspection to reopen a movement area after construction, or after an accident or incident to ensure all debris have been properly removed. Meteorological events such as thunderstorms trigger special inspections to check for ponding and edge damming, storm sewer blockage, inlet covers are in place, and erosion that may affect flight or operational safety. Special inspections are also conducted during and after snow and ice operations to determine the condition of the runways and taxiways. Inspectors check to ensure that airfield signs, markings, and lights are visible and that plowed snow does not create a hazard to aircraft navigation. Damaged signs or lights or obscured markings should either be immediately repaired, if possible, or reported through a work order system. A NOTAM should be subsequently issued that identifies the damaged component. Inspectors should also watch for piled snow that blocks NAVAID radiofrequency signals.

Construction activity also requires special inspections to ensure that (a) construction areas are barricaded and properly lighted, (b) construction personnel are parking within assigned areas, and (c) stockpiled material is outside of any safety areas and does not block airfield signs. Inspectors should also check construction sites to ensure adherence to the construction safety plan and also check to ensure security requirements are in compliance.

Some airports are equipped with a **Surface Movement Guidance and Control System (SMGCS)**. SMGCS is a series of lights and markings around the airfield that assist pilots during low-visibility operations. SMGCS is controlled by the air traffic control tower. SMGCS inspections include Stop Bar Lights, Runway Guard Lights, Clearance Bar Lights, Taxiway Centerline Lights, and Taxiway Edge Lights along with a variety of other markings.[7] Airports go into "SMGCS operations" when the horizontal ground visibility is less than 1,200 feet **Runway Visual Range (RVR)**. Some airports have additional SMGCS equipment, enabling the airport to continue operations when RVR is less than 600 RVR. SMGCS lighting systems that are not electronically monitored should be inspected every 2 to 4 hours for operations below 1,200 RVR to 600 RVR. For operations below 600 RVR, inspections should take place every other hour.

Airport Condition Reporting

Airport operators have a responsibility to notify users of the airport of unsafe conditions or any condition on the airport that is not in compliance with the ACM or Part 139. Part of this responsibility is to report the discrepancy to Airport Maintenance or other staff who are responsible for fixing specified discrepancies. When FAA inspectors audit airport records, they do not expect to find a perfect airport, but they do desire to see that when a discrepancy on the airfield has been identified, a NOTAM has been issued to notify airport users and a work order has been submitted or a plan generated to fix the discrepancy (Prather, 2011, p. 35). Part 139 requires airports to "ensure rapid and reliable dissemination of information between the certificate holder's personnel and air carriers." This may also require the airport to close or restrict certain areas until discrepancies or unsafe conditions can be resolved.

SUMMARY

The fundamental premise of Title 14 CFR Part 139 is that it is in the best interest of all stakeholders to establish and maintain a safe environment for aircraft operations. The FAA establishes regulations, as well as guidance on the intent of the regulations, and makes suggestions on how to demonstrate compliance through use of FAA ACs. Furthermore, FAA Orders, which are available to airport operators, describe for FAA personnel how to enforce the provisions of Part 139.

An airport enplaning more than 2,500 passengers per year, and which hosts commercial service operations, is required to possess a Part 139 AOC. Issuance of an AOC is dependent upon the airport operator passing an FAA inspection, demonstrating that the airport meets numerous safety standards, and demonstrating that required safety programs, such as an AEP, SICP, and WHMP, are in place, if required.

Once the AOC is issued, the FAA essentially delegates compliance functions to the airport operator through the safety self-inspection process, comprised of four types of inspections: **regular** (or daily) self-inspection, whereby airport personnel use a checklist to inspect the required elements of Part 139; **special inspections**, conducted when there are unusual conditions, such as weather or after a report of FOD on the airfield; **periodic** inspections, for elements on the inspection checklist that vary over a period of time; and **continuous** inspections, conducted throughout each day, as scheduling and opportunity permits.

---

[7]SMGCS lighting and marking standards are addressed in Chapter 7.

Electronic Inspections

"From Clipboard to the Keyboard"

by Alex Gertsen, C.M.
Certified Member (CM), American Association of Airport Executives

When 14 CFR Part 139 came into existence in 1970, mainframe computers would easily fill an entire room, and punch cards and magnetic tapes coiled on large open reels were state-of-the-art methods for input and data storage. A clipboard and a pen were the primary tools Part 139 Inspectors used to document their self-inspections. Reams of paper forms, archived in three-ring binders, would fill many shelves in the Airport Operations office, patiently awaiting the arrival of the FAA inspector every 12 calendar months, before being archived into boxes or disposed. Work orders in paper form would flow from one in-box to another as a way to communicate what needed to be fixed and to track the discrepancies between Airport Operations and Maintenance Departments. Even if a fix only required a few minutes on the airfield and the necessary parts were in stock, the lifecycle of a discrepancy, from identification to closure, could take days, simply due to the constraints and inefficiencies of the paper process and the human element required to transfer and manage the paper workflow.

Fast forward 45 years to 2015—Computers dubbed "smartphones" are more powerful than the mainframes of the 1970s and are now miniature enough to fit in our pockets. Not only do these devices have bright high-resolution screens and the ability to store gigabytes of data, they are also armed with a camera, GPS receiver, wireless connectivity, and capabilities to make voice and video calls. These gadgets, loaded with applicable software applications (Apps), reference materials, and FAA ACs, along with connectivity to real-time weather, NOTAMs, aircraft tracking, and other valuable information, can turn any ordinary AOM specialist into an airfield version of James Bond (Figure 6.5).

Given the technology currently available, why is it that most Airport Operations departments in the modern day still rely on a clipboard, a pen, and paper rather than a virtual keyboard on their smartphone or tablet to manage their Part 139 program? Why aren't GPS coordinates derived from the device's built-in receiver used for position information of discrepancies? Why don't airports use georeferencing, the process of assigning spatial coordinates to data (i.e., organizing data according to location), to overlay these latitude and longitude points for issues identified on the airfield on high resolution maps instead of using wordy references to locations of discrepancies based on distances from intersections and the AOM's own creative descriptions? Why don't the AOMs unleash the power of the camera built into the device to document discrepancies and to improve communication of issues identified on the airfield? After all, the old cliché "a picture is worth a thousand words" could not be more applicable in the safety-conscious world of airside operations. Why don't the shelves filled with binders and rooms filled with archives get replaced by easily searchable, paperless, georeferenced, cloud-based systems accessible from anywhere on the airfield or from anywhere in the world?

(Continued)

(Continued)

   Answers to these questions vary from airport to airport. However, the challenges that hinder the transition from "clipboard to keyboard" can generally be attributed to limited budgets, lack of computer proficiency on the part of staff, concerns for data loss and for a consistent and reliable system that is accessible 24/7, and the inability to perceive the benefits of the electronic systems—after all, the proven paper method has worked for more than four decades.

   Presently, there are a number of systems, from multiple vendors, available to airports to bring their Part 139 program into the digital age, with the possibility to completely eliminate paper. All of these electronic solutions provide the ability to record and track airfield discrepancies and maintain Part 139 compliance required by the FAA. Systems can be hosted internally on a server located inside the airport firewall or externally in the cloud. Most solutions can be scaled up to accommodate busy large hubs or scaled down to even GA airports that adhere to industry best safety practices following the Part 139 guidance.

   All of the systems provide electronic forms to enter textual information, document discrepancies and incidents with the capability to attach photographs and related documents, generate work orders, and run reports, as well as to assist with tracking the status of open items and analyzing trends. Typically, the basic systems do not include even a static map and thus do not take advantage of the georeferencing capabilities available in other solutions.

FIGURE 6.5

Airport Operations maintenance specialist on a prescribed Part 139 self-inspection.

Image courtesy of Alex Gertsen.

(Continued)

(Continued)

The top-tier products have differentiated themselves by providing a moving map and, for some products, an integrated Runway Incursion Warning System (RIWS) specifically designed for airfield vehicles and compliant with the FAA AC 150/5210-25. The maps in these applications are typically capable of depicting airfield assets (i.e., lights, markings, airfield signs, pavement slabs, etc.), stored in a Geographic Information System (GIS) database, allowing the inspector to simply touch the asset closest to their depicted GPS position to obtain information on it or to note a fault and generate a work order. These systems leverage the power of GIS to allow for quick entry of discrepancies using the key airfield assets depicted on the map and capabilities for geospatial analysis of the data leading to better decision making. These tools enable an airport operator to illustrate clusters of issues on the map, to analyze and visualize trends, and to quickly identify areas where activities happen more frequently or are related to fixed assets on the airfield. For example, geospatial analysis can reveal areas where non-isolated pavement issues are occurring, densely clustered points representing concentrations of wildlife being spotted at one location could be an indicator of a hole in the fence or a new attractant in that area, and seeing locations where frequent replacement of light bulbs occurs can identify a bad fixture or an issue with a circuit. Some of the systems have basic work order management functions built in, while others also have the capability to integrate with existing Computerized Maintenance Management Systems (CMMS).

Simple "homegrown" electronic solutions can be developed internally by Airport Operations staff at airports that do not have a budget to procure a dedicated, commercial system. This method follows a process similar to completing a paper form, but doing it electronically allows an airport to quickly and cost effectively move away from the clipboard and the three-ring binders. Using Microsoft Office products, AOMs can replicate the layout of existing paper forms and logs by creating electronic form templates in Word or Excel. These templates can then be filled on a computer or smartphone or tablet in the field and stored on a shared network drive with a unique identifier such as the date of the inspection and the shift number or time of day. Daily inspection document files can be organized into folders by the calendar month, making it easier to be presented to the FAA inspector for the annual records review without being printed. It is important that regardless of the solution the airport selects, appropriate procedures for data security and backup are made to protect these records, which are required for Part 139 compliance.

While transitioning to an electronic solution, it is suggested that airports remain in close coordination with their FAA inspectors and obtain early buy-in from them to make the changes. Airports will also need to consider the necessary ACM modifications to reflect new forms, reports, the electronic workflow process, and other changes that may take place as the result of the transition. When going electronic, most airports will simply mimic their paper workflow process with electronic forms and reports to make the transition as simple and seamless as possible. However, some airports may choose to take advantage of this transition to evaluate their processes and procedures on how self-inspections are conducted and

(Continued)

(Continued)

work orders are processed to make improvements to streamline and simplify these processes to gain additional efficiencies.

Despite the industry being slow to adopt electronic Part 139 inspection and reporting systems, a number of factors, such as FAA requirements for airport GIS, electronic Airport Layout Plans (eALPs), and SMS for airports, are serving as catalysts for the new paradigm and are creating a strong foundation for acceptance of Part 139 solutions. Initiatives to reduce runway incursions and to provide better situational awareness for airfield vehicle operators have already opened new funding mechanisms for procuring systems with moving map displays that can serve as a footing for Part 139 solutions. Currently self-inspection forms vary greatly from airport to airport. Deployment of electronic Part 139 solutions enables reporting across all FAA-certificated airports to be in the same standardized format and is likely to be another driver for airports to make the transition and for the FAA to encourage and to possibly even mandate electronic solutions in the future.

In addition to the ease of Part 139 compliance and recordkeeping, there are many benefits to an airport from adopting an electronic solution. These modern computer systems improve efficiency and accuracy of inspections, provide a means for inspectors and vehicle operators to navigate the airfield more safely with runway incursion warnings and increased situational awareness, reduce turnaround time to address deficiencies, improve interdepartmental information exchange, increase data monitoring and safety awareness across all levels of management, and provide the ability for geospatial trend analysis.

The next generation of AOM specialist is likely to embrace the electronic means for managing Part 139 compliance, building on the accomplishments of its predecessors in the 1970s and taking the safety practices and procedures outlined in 14 CFR 139 to the next level.

Airport Operations Management

by Jim Payne
Director of Operations & Planning, BHM

Airport Operations is a unique entity. Most divisions of organizations are fairly defined in their purpose. If you speak with any company and ask what their Finance department does, you will get a very similar answer no matter which company you ask; a company has to balance accounting sheets, pay bills, receive income and perform other various financial tasks. Odds are, unless the business is small enough that it doesn't warrant distinct departments, those functions will fall under Finance in every organization. The same can be said of Human Resources, Administration and so on. However, if you speak to several airports and ask which tasks their Operations department accomplishes, you will likely get several different answers. There are, in fact, a few broad topics which can be broadly lumped into the "standard" Operations definition: Compliance with FAR Part 139, compliance with TSAR

(Continued)

(Continued)

Part 1542, general operation of the airport, and public safety. However, each airport assigns these differently. Some airports have separate security departments to handle the TSA compliance; some airports have separate public safety departments to handle the security, law enforcement and firefighting responsibilities; some airports assign maintenance as a part of operations while others place maintenance in a stand-alone department and so on. Similarly, the tasks that normally accompany these broad functions can vary widely in responsibility. These unique differentiations mean two things: 1. An Airport Operations Manager will have a lifelong adventure of trying to explain to others what he or she does for a living; 2. An Airport Operations Manager must be flexible and adaptable.

The first step of understanding Airport Operations is to try and define it. As mentioned above, this can vary, but the fundamental purpose is the same. Operations is responsible for ensuring that the airport operates (not surprisingly) and functions smoothly throughout the day. Finance departments pay the bills, Human Resource departments handle the personnel, Administration departments take care of the business end, but Operations handles the airport part: Making sure that passengers are able to get from one destination to the next safely, securely, efficiently, and (hopefully) with a pleasant experience. The simplest definition of Airport Operations is "Safety, Security and Regulation compliance."

Once we have an understanding of the fundamental definition of Airport Operations, we can begin to develop an idea of what is required to manage such a function. As is probably apparent by now, managing an Operations department requires one to wear many hats. Each of the broad functions has numerous tasks which must be handled. For example, complying with FAR Part 139 requires adherence to a vast library of regulations. While Part 139 is in itself only 30 pages, each line item requires the Operations Manager to reference a separate document, typically an FAA Advisory Circular, for details of compliance. 139.311 Marking, Signs and Lighting encompasses less than 2 pages of text. However, to comply with that section, the Operations Manager must turn to other supporting documentation including Advisory Circular (AC) 150/5340-1, Standards for Airport Markings, AC 150/5345-44, Specifications for Runway and Taxiway Signs, AC 150/5340-18, Standards for Airport Sign Systems, AC 150/5340-30, Design and Installation Details for Airport Visual Aids, AC 150/5300-13, Airport Design and many more. Each of these documents contains specific and exacting details. For example, AC 150/5340-1 is 136 pages of details on appearance, location and sizing of markings. Every one of those markings you see on an airport must be an exact specification including location color and size to the inch. Each of the other broad categories involved in Airport Operations involves a similar effort. The TSA, or security side is nearly as complex with its share of detailed regulations, as you are certainly becoming familiar with as you read this text. The third aspect, regulation compliance, is broad and can involve everything from state and local laws which could mirror or assist the existing TSA and FAA rules to fire codes, health department rules, zoning, ADA accessibility and numerous other aspects. The field is certainly one of intense documentation.

(Continued)

(Continued)

   As should be evident from the quick snapshot of Operations above, effectively managing this gargantuan division is akin to a massive juggling act. Not only must the Operations Manager have a healthy base of knowledge tucked securely in his mind for quick recall in a sudden situation, he must also have a firm grasp on where each of the pertinent regulations exists so as to know where to look when a situation arises. A simple question of how to handle a situation could require looking in many places. An issue about a repair to a taxiway safety area could require a look at the Airport Certification Manual, Part 139, AC 150/5300-13, AC 150/5370-2, local ordinances, internal contracting and procurement procedures, etc. Knowing where to find each relevant regulation is vital. Prioritizing tasks and needs is particularly important in the Airport Operations field. As is evident, many of the functions involved immediately and directly impact the safety of the users of the airport and must be treated with urgency. However, there are numerous other issues tugging at Operations Management as well. The Operations Manager must also ensure that passengers are able to find, traverse and effectively utilize the facility. Often, multiple issues present themselves at the same time and the manager must find appropriate resolutions to each quickly. At the same time the aforementioned safety area repair needs to be addressed, a security system may have failed, a medical emergency could be occurring in the terminal and a vehicle accident might have blocked access to the terminal. Effective Operations Management requires one who is able to prioritize, assess, determine action, delegate and act quickly and in a manner suitable to continue the safe operation of the field while accepting the intense responsibility that the safety of every airframe, passenger and flight crew using the airport, millions of people each year in many cases, rests securely on his or her shoulders.

REFERENCES

Certification of Airports, 14 CFR Part 139 (2004).
Federal Aviation Administration (FAA). (2004). *Advisory Circular 150/5200-18C: Airport safety self-inspection.* Retrieved from: https://www.faa.gov/regulations_policies/advisory_circulars/index.cfm/go/document.information/documentID/23179.
Federal Aviation Administration (FAA). (2006). *5050.4B National Environmental Policy Act (NEPA) implementing instructions for airport actions.* Retrieved from: https://www.faa.gov/regulations_policies/orders_notices/index.cfm/go/document.information/documentID/14836.
Federal Aviation Administration (FAA). (2015a). *Air transportation division: 135 air carrier operations branch.* Retrieved from: https://www.faa.gov/about/office_org/headquarters_offices/avs/offices/afs/afs200/branches/afs250/.
Federal Aviation Administration (FAA). (2015c). *Part 139 Airport certification: definitions.* Retrieved from: https://www.faa.gov/airports/airport_safety/part139_cert/definitions/.
Federal Aviation Administration (FAA). (2014). *Airport categories: airports.* Retrieved from: http://www.faagov/airports/planning_capacity/passenger_allcargo_stats/categories/.
Federal Emergency Management Agency (FEMA). (2014). National incident management system. Retrieved from: https://www.fema.gov/national-incident-management-system.

Prather, C. D. (2011). *Airport self-inspection practices* (27th ed., Synthesis) (United States, Transportation Research Board, Airport Cooperative Research Program). Washington, DC: National Academy of Sciences.
Wells, A. T., & Young, S. B. (2011). *Airport planning and management*. New York, NY: McGraw-Hill.

FURTHER READING

Federal Aviation Administration (FAA). (2003). *Form 5010-1 Airport master record (existing public use airports).* Retrieved from: https://www.faa.gov/forms/index.cfm/go/document.information/documentID/185474.
Federal Aviation Administration (FAA). (2015b). *Part 139 Airport certification: airports.* Retrieved from: http://www.faa.gov/airports/airport_safety/part139_cert/?p1 = classes.

APPENDIX A **EXAMPLE OPERATIONS TRAINING RECORD**

Employee Name _____

IET Training			
Item/Program	**Date Completed**	**Emp. Initials**	**Supervisor**
SIDA			
Non-movement Driver			
Movement Driver			
Basic Security Awareness			
Physical Vehicle Inspections			
Text Materials			
Item/Program	**Date Completed**	**Emp. Initials**	**Supervisor**
FAR Part 139			
Self-Inspection			
Airfield Signs			
Airfield Markings			
Airfield Lighting			
NOTAMs			
1542			
Security Directives			
BHM ACM			
BHM ASP			
BHM AEP			
Procedure Memos			
Field Training			
Airfield Familiarization			
Radio Usage			
Escort Procedures			
AMA Procedures/Communications			
Movement Driving—Day			

Operations Training Record

Employee Name _____

Field Training (cont.)			
Item/Program	**Date Completed**	**Emp. Initials**	**Supervisor**
Movement Driving—Night			
Runway Inspections			
Airfield Self-Inspection			
Perimeter Inspection			
SIDA Inspection			
Gate Vehicle Inspection			
SIDA Citations			
Safety Violations			
Operations Center Training			
Item/Program	**Date Completed**	**Emp. Initials**	**Supervisor**
Weather Computer			
Bird Cannon System			
Pyrotechnics			
Fire System			
Camera System			
PA System			
Gate Intercom			
Crash Line			
Key Checkout			
Checkpoint Alarms			
Evolve System			
Radio System			
Phone Procedures			
Medical Dispatch			
Badging System			
Fingerprinting System			

Operations Training Record

Employee Name _____

Supervisory Duties			
Item/Program	Date Completed	Emp. Initials	Supervisor
Time System			
Attendance Policy			
Daily Paperwork			
Incident Reports			
Schedule			
Evaluations			
Reprimands			
Emergency Response			
Vehicle Use			

APPENDIX B **AIRPORT SAFETY SELF-INSPECTION CHECKLIST**

CHECKLIST 1

AIRPORT SAFETY SELF-INSPECTION CHECKLIST

DATE: _____   DAY: _____   √ Satisfactory

Day Inspector/Time: _____ Night Inspector/Time: _____   X Unsatisfactory

FACILITIES	CONDITIONS	D	N	REMARKS	RESOLVED BY (Date/Initials)
Pavement Areas	Pavement lips over 3"				
	Hole – 5" diam. 3" deep				
	Cracks/spalling/heaves				
	FOD: gravel/debris/sand				
	Rubber deposits				
	Ponding/edge dams				
Safety Areas	Ruts/humps/erosion				
	Drainage/construction				
	Support equipment/aircraft				
	Frangible bases				
	Unauthorized objects				
Markings	Clearly visible/standard				
	Runway markings				
	Taxiway markings				
	Holding position markings				
	Glass beads				
Signs	Standard/meet Sign Plan				
	Obscured/operable				
	Damaged/retroreflective				

FACILITIES	CONDITIONS	D	N	REMARKS	RESOLVED BY (Date/Initials)
Lighting	Obscured/dirty/operable				
	Damaged/missing				
	Faulty aim/adjustment				
	Runway lighting				
	Taxiway lighting				
	Pilot control lighting				
Navigational Aids	Rotating beacon operable				
	Wind indicators				
	RENLs/VGSI systems				
Obstructions	Obstruction lights operable				
	Cranes/trees				
Fueling Operations	Fencing/gates/signs				
	Fuel marking/labeling				
	Fire extinguishers				
	Frayed wires				
	Fuel leaks/vegetation				
Snow & Ice	Surface conditions				
	Snowbank clearances				
	Lights & signs obscured				
	NAVAIDs				
	Fire access				

FACILITIES	CONDITIONS	D	N	REMARKS	RESOLVED BY (Date/Initials)
Construction	Barricades/lights				
	Equipment parking				
	Material stockpiles				
	Confusing signs/markings				
Aircraft Rescue and Firefighting	Equipment/crew availability				
	Communications/alarms				
	Response routes affected				
Public Protection	Fencing/gates/signs				
	Jet blast problems				
Wildlife Hazards	Wildlife present/location				
	Complying with WHMP				
	Dead birds				

Comments/Remarks _____

_____

_____

_____

_____

_____

_____

_____

_____

_____

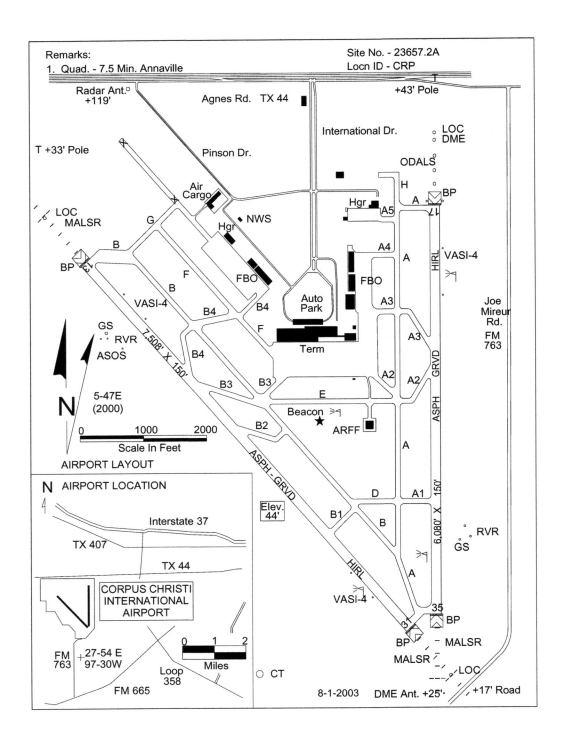

CHECKLIST 2

CONTINUOUS SURVEILLANCE CHECKLIST

		√ Satisfactory	
DATE: _____	DAY: _____	X Unsatisfactory	
TIME: _____	INSPECTOR: _____		

FACILITIES	CONDITIONS	√	REMARKS/ACTIONS TAKEN
Ground Vehicles	Rules/Procedures Followed		
Fueling Operations	Fire/Explosion Hazards		
	Signing/No smoking		
Snow & Ice	Surface Conditions		
Construction	Safety Plan		
	Runway Incursions		
	Runway & Taxiway Use		
	FOD		
Public Protection	Unauthorized Persons		
	Unauthorized Vehicles		
	Gates Clear		
Wildlife Hazards	Birds/Animals		
Miscellaneous	Pedestrians in Movement Areas		
	Passenger Load/Unload		
	Debris in Movement Area		

Additional Remarks

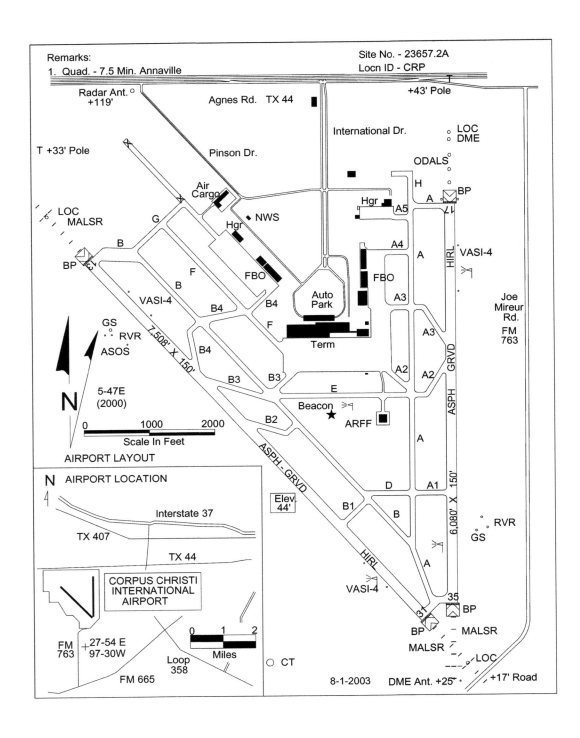

CHECKLIST 3

PERIODIC CONDITION INSPECTION CHECKLIST

√ Satisfactory

DATE: _____   DAY: _____   X Unsatisfactory

TIME: _____   INSPECTOR: _____

FACILITIES	CONDITIONS	√	REMARKS/ACTIONS TAKEN
Pavement Areas	Rubber Deposits		
	Polishing		
Markings and Signs	Visible		
	Standards		
Fueling Operations	Physical Facilities		
	Mobile Fuelers		
	Fire Extinguishers		
	Fuel Marking/Labeling		
	Frayed Wiring		
Navigational Aids	RENLs/VGSI Aiming		
Lighting	Power Generator Check		
	Circuit Resistance Test		
	Aim/Adjustment		
Obstructions	Surveyed Trees/Structures		
	Overhead Power Lines		
Aircraft Rescue and Firefighting	Response Times		
	Live Fire Drills		
	Training		

Additional Remarks

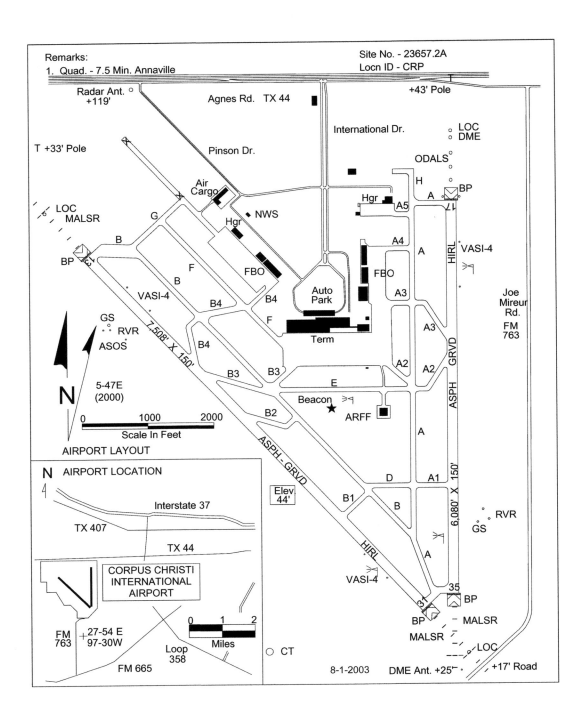

CHECKLIST 4

SPECIAL INSPECTION CHECKLIST

			√ Satisfactory
DATE: _____ DAY: _____			X Unsatisfactory
TIME: _____ INSPECTOR: _____			

FACILITIES	CONDITIONS	√	REMARKS/ACTIONS TAKEN
Pavement Areas	Ponding/Edge Dams		
Markings and Signs	Visible after Rain		
	Standards after Construction		
Safety Areas	Drainage		
	Reopening Runways		
	Reopening Taxiways		
Snow & Ice	Surface Conditions		
	Snowbank Clearance		
	Lights & Signs Obscured		
	FOD		
	Braking Action/MU Reports		
Construction	Barricades		
	Construction Lights		
	Equipment Parking		
SMGCS	SMGCS Lighting		

Additional Remarks

Airfield Map on Reverse Side

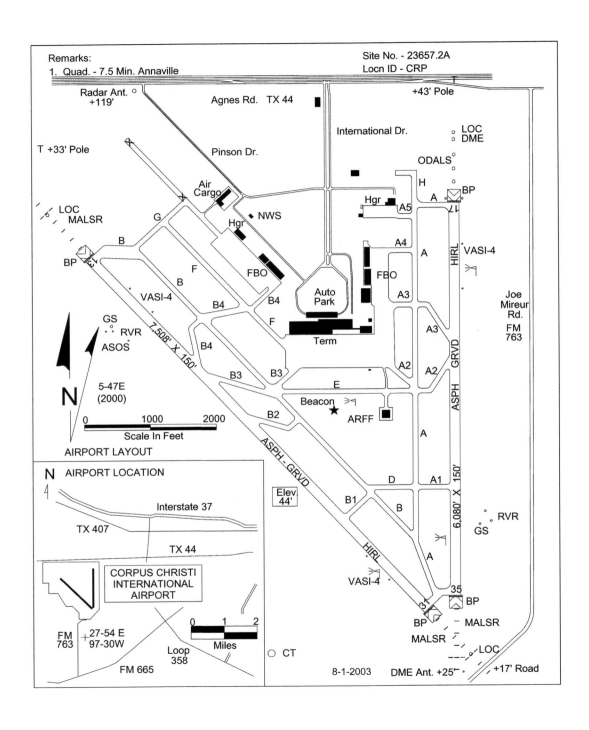

CHECKLIST 5A

QUARTERLY INSPECTION – MOBILE FUELERS

Inspector: _____ Fueling Agent: _____ Date: _____

S – Satisfactory U – Unsatisfactory R – Remark Below	Jet A Fuelers			100LL Fuelers			Other Fueler		
	S	U	R	S	U	R	S	U	R
No Smoking sign in cab									
Flammability Signs/Haz MAT Placards all sides									
Bonding Cables and Clips functional									
Deadman Control for all nozzles									
2 Fire Extinguishers – Proper type/Inspected									
Emergency Shutoffs operable and marked									
No Fuel Leaks – Hoses/Gaskets/Valves									
Vehicle Exhaust System – Shielded/Leak free									
No evidence of Smoking – No ashtray in cab									
Vehicle Parking – 10' apart/50' from buildings									
Explosion proof electrical/Light lens intact									
Ignition Sources (Clothing, Shoes, Matches)									
							No of Mobile Fuelers		
Proper Fueling Procedures Observed							Jet A _____		
Fueling Personnel Meet Training Requirements							100LL _____		
Fueling Personnel Training Records maintained							Other _____		

Remarks:_____
_____
_____
_____
_____
_____
_____
_____
_____
_____
_____
_____
_____
_____
_____
_____

CHECKLIST 5B

QUARTERLY INSPECTION — FUEL STORAGE AREAS

Inspector: _____   Fueling Agent: _____   Date: _____

S – Satisfactory U – Unsatisfactory R – Remark Below	Jet A Section			100LL Section			Other _____		
	S	U	R	S	U	R	S	U	R
Fencing/Locks/Signs									
Piping protected from vehicles									
No Smoking signs posted									
Deadman Controls for loading stations									
2 Fire Extinguishers – Inspected/Accessible									
Boldly Marked Emergency Cutoffs – Location									
No Fuel Leaks									
Bonding wire/clips at loading stations/operable									
Piping/Pumps bonded and grounded									
No vegetation or materials to spread fire									
No evidence of Smoking									
Hoses in good condition									
Explosion Proof Electrical Equipment									

Remarks:_____

_____

_____

_____

_____

_____

_____

_____

_____

_____

_____

APPENDIX C SUGGESTED TOOLS, EDUCATION, AND TRAINING FOR AIRPORT OPERATIONS PERSONNEL

Airport Operations personnel have a wide variety of backgrounds, including previous careers as airline, military, or corporate pilots, and in the past 20 years, many without significant work experience but who possess **undergraduate degrees in aviation and airport management disciplines**. Although these various backgrounds are beneficial, they result in varying levels of training and exposure to certain operations (Ops) principles, which can lead to an unbalanced workforce.

Following Hurricane Katrina, U.S. Coast Guard personnel noted that they were able to seamlessly merge and mix units from Coast Guard stations throughout the country, because of standardized training models (i.e., everyone is trained to a certain standard and can therefore work better to *plug-and-play* with other operational units). What follows is a suggested model for standardizing the training and tools that are used throughout the Airport Operations domain.

TRAINING STANDARDS

Tier One (basic level), at a minimum, an operations agent/manager/officer should have:

1. Initial and annual training in **all** areas addressed in **Part 139.303 (Training)**, i.e., Airport Certification Manual (ACM), movement area driver training, radio communications, etc. A training checklist is included in Appendix B courtesy of the Birmingham/Shuttlesworth International Airport;
2. **Security Identification Display Area (SIDA)** training if at a commercial service airport, required under Title 49 CFR Part 1542.213. If at a general aviation airport, then basic security awareness training as addressed in Transportation Security Administration's (TSA) *General Aviation Airport Security Guidance* document, most recent edition, and in the Aircraft Owners and Pilots Association Airport Watch program.
3. **National Incident Management System (NIMS)** (FEMA [Federal Emergency Management Agency] Incident Command System ICS-100: *Introduction to the Incident Command System*; ICS-200: *Single Resources and Initial Action Incidents*; and IS-700: *National Incident Management System, An Introduction*, minimum; and IS-800: *National Response Framework, An Introduction*, suggested);
4. **First Aid** and **cardiopulmonary resuscitation (CPR)**;
5. **Wildlife** mitigation techniques appropriate to the airport's Wildlife Hazard Management Program.

Tier Two (intermediate level), at a minimum, an operations agent/manager/officer should have:

1. All elements included in Tier One;
2. **FEMA Incident Command System ICS-300**: *Intermediate ICS for Expanding Incidents* and ICS-400: *Advanced ICS for Command and General Staff*;
3. **Basic Airport Operations and Safety School** (or equivalent to American Association of Airport Executives' [AAAE] program);
4. **Physical vehicle inspection**;
5. **Security for Airport Operations Personnel**/or Airport Security Program training and/or Airport Security Coordinator training;

6. **Trauma kit** usage (individual first aid kit);
7. **ARFF (Aircraft Rescue and Firefighting)** training under Part 139.319 (i) (i.e., 40-hour school);
8. **Terminal and Landside** operations course (or ACI [Airports Council International] equivalent).

Tier Three (advanced level), at a minimum, an operations agent/manager/officer should have:

1. All elements included in Tiers One and Two;
2. FEMA IS-701: *NIMS Multiagency Coordination System (MACS)*, IS-702: *NIMS Publication Information Systems*, IS-703: *NIMS Resource Management*, G-191: *Incident Command System/Emergency Operations Center Interface*, and G-775: *Emergency Operations Center (EOC) Management and Operations*;
3. Airport Certified Employee—**Operations** (AAAE program or equivalent);
4. Airport Certified Employee—**Security** (AAAE program or equivalent);
5. **Advanced** Airport Safety and Operations Specialist School (AAAE program or equivalent);
6. Basic Medical Care as described in Part 139.319 (4), or **First Responder/**Emergency Medical responder certification (standards set forth by the National Highway Traffic Safety Administration [NHTSB]).

As part of continuing professional development and training, operations personnel should serve on various operations, safety, and emergency management—related committees in trade organizations so as to stay informed about industry issues and concerns. Additional training may include All-Hazards Specific Courses through FEMA, ARFF Airport Master Firefighter or Airport Fire Officer, AAAE Certified Member or Accredited Airport Executive (A.A.E.) designations and trainings, including airport emergency management, Airport Certified Employee (ACE)-Trusted Agent, ACI Executive Leadership Programme, and other ACI courses and designations. Other training and seminars that may be useful to airport Ops personnel include topics on Safety Management Systems (SMS), Security Management Systems (SeMS), environmental management, customer service, airport business operations, helicopter operations, and medical crew assistance.

VEHICLE AND EQUIPMENT FOR OPERATIONS PERSONNEL

The type of vehicle and equipment issued to airport Ops personnel relates to the job duties assigned. Most airport Ops vehicles are either sport utility vehicles or mid- to large-size pickup trucks. The vehicle should have the appropriate signage identifying the agency (airport/city/county) and the entity (i.e., Airport Operations), crossbar lights on the top (yellow, or a combination of yellow and red, depending on local requirements), and a siren, as well as a spotlight, a bumper guard capable of pushing other vehicles, vehicle-mounted very high frequency (VHF) (i.e., aircraft) and local radios capable of contacting the communiucations center and an external speaker to broadcast the radio, or loudspeaker function.

Equipment and Materials:

1. Handheld radios (VHF and local frequencies)—on person
2. Cell phone with camera—on person
3. Business cards and/or airport office contact information—on person

4. Hearing protection—on person
5. Self-inspection checklist
6. Shovel
7. Leather work gloves
8. Eye protection
9. Rain coat
10. Liquid spill kit
11. Plastic bags (wildlife remnant cleanup)
12. Latex gloves
13. Box cutter/Leatherman
14. Fire extinguisher
15. Phone chargers
16. Airfield grid map
17. Space blanket(s)
18. Flares and landside portable hazard signs
19. Barricade/police tape
20. Reflective vest (with Incident Command appropriate titles)
21. Flashlights

For many of these items, a *Go Bag* should be prepared that can be passed from one Ops agent to another at shift change. A vehicle and Go Bag inspection should be conducted at the beginning of each shift. Depending on the medical qualifications of the operations person, a larger tactical medical pack or kit may be appropriate.

(Special thanks to Jessica Birnbaum and Dan Sprinkle at Denver International Airport, and to Jim Payne at the Birmingham/Shuttlesworth International Airport, for assisting in the preparation of this appendix.)

AIRPORT MAINTENANCE STANDARDS & AIR TRAFFIC CONTROL & AIR OPERATIONS

Airport movement area information sign, Denver International Airport, CO.

Image by Shahn Sederberg, courtesy Colorado Division of Aeronautics, 2012.

Taxiway light next to taxiway directional advisory sign, Centennial Airport, CO.
Image by Shahn Sederberg, courtesy Colorado Division of Aeronautics, 2007.

The inspection items listed in the safety self-inspection are essential safety elements to the overall operation of the airport. The first part of this chapter, "Airport Maintenance Standards," focuses on the core elements of the **maintenance and safety standards** required by Title 14 CFR Part 139, including pavement types, design standards, pavement deterioration, airfield signs, marking and lighting, approach light systems, navigational aids, safety areas, runways, and taxiways. These operational concerns and topics are critical to supporting the safety, traffic control, and air operations on and in the vicinity of the airport. The second part of this chapter, "Air Traffic Control and Air Operations," provides the operations practitioner with an introduction to air traffic control and air operations. All members of an airport's operations and emergency response divisions should firmly understand flight operations, common navigational procedures, and air traffic control.

AIRPORT MAINTENANCE STANDARDS

AIRFIELD MAINTENANCE REQUIREMENTS

In Chapter 6, we examined Part 139 airside self-inspection items essential to the safe and effective operation of the airport. In conjunction with Part 139 self-inspections, airports must also comply with required daily and periodic Part 139 maintenance requirements. Maintenance requirements apply to the same areas of the airport environment that are self-inspected. For example, maintenance includes service to runway and taxiway pavement, airfield signs, marking and lighting, navigational aids, safety areas, air traffic control infrastructure, and construction activity. Part 139 sets forth acceptable standards for maintaining each of these areas, and airport inspectors must ensure the standards are met on a daily or periodic basis.

Maintaining pavement throughout the airfield and Air Operations Area (AOA) is the most important and time-consuming maintenance task for Airport Operations personnel. Safe and functional pavement is the airport's *life-blood*, sustaining the flow of passengers and aircraft within the airport environment. Entire conferences and sessions in airport industry seminars are dedicated to airport pavement, its design, construction, inspection, and preventative maintenance. The airport runway has been called the most expensive piece of pavement in the city and is a top priority for every Airport Manager.

AIR OPERATIONS AREA

The AOA is generally composed of paved surfaces consisting of runways, taxiways, taxi-lanes,[1] aircraft parking areas,[2] and the apron.[3] Title 49 CFR Part 1540.5 defines the AOA in relation to Airport Security as:

> ... a portion of an airport, specified in the Airport Security program, in which security measures specified in this part are carried out. This area includes aircraft movement areas, aircraft parking areas, loading ramps, and safety areas, for use by aircraft regulated under 49 CFR part 1544 or 1546, and any adjacent areas (such as general aviation areas) that are not separated by adequate security systems, measures, or procedures. This area does not include the secured area. ("Terms Used in This Subchapter," 49 C.F.R. § 1540.5, 2009)

Although the term **AOA** commonly refers to security measures that must be carried out under Part 1542 (Airport Security), the term also refers to key elements of the **airfield**. The airfield is generally composed of runways, taxiways, taxi-lanes, and aircraft parking areas (including the tarmac, ramp, or apron). Also included as part of the airfield are, for example, passenger concourses, airside portions of the terminal building, airline maintenance facilities, Aircraft Rescue and Firefighting stations, Airport Maintenance facilities, snow removal equipment storage areas, fuel farms, electrical vaults, airfield lighting, components of the approach lighting system, and other navigational aids. Facilities for Fixed Base Operators (FBOs), corporate-based tenants, flight schools, and other aviation businesses also have buildings that bisect the airfield's landside (public areas) from airside (Restricted Areas). A variety of other structures and facilities may also exist on

---

[1]A taxiway designed for low speed and precise taxiing. A taxi-lane is a taxiway that is usually in the non-movement area, as opposed to taxiways, which are in the movement area and subject to the requirements of Part 139. A taxi-lane provides access from the apron to the taxiways.

[2]Also referred to as tarmac or aircraft tie-down areas.

[3]Also known as the ramp.

the airfield, including the air traffic control tower (ATCT), the airport rotating beacon, and Automated Surface Observing Systems (ASOSs), which are weather stations.

Commercial service airports must designate at least one runway for use by commercial aircraft. The designated runway, and associated taxiways, must meet the Federal Aviation Administration's (FAA) Design Standards under Advisory Circular (AC) 150/5300-13A *Airport Design* (2013a). A runway is defined as a rectangular surface on an airport prepared or suitable for the landing or take-off of aircraft. A taxiway is a defined path, established for the taxiing of aircraft from one area of an airport to another.

The apron (ramp) surface area is an aircraft parking location. A **terminal apron** is adjacent to the passenger terminal, where passengers board and deplane from an aircraft, and typically accommodates multiple activities, such as fueling, maintenance, catering, loading/unloading baggage and cargo, aircraft servicing, boarding bridge maneuvering, passenger boarding/deplaning, and aircraft docking/pushback (FAA, 2013a). A **remote apron** is an area where aircraft are secured or serviced for an extended period (FAA, 2013a, p. 165). Remote aprons are also used at some large-hub, commercial service airports for passenger loading and unloading directly from a conveyance, such as a passenger bus. Used in this manner, a remote apron increases the airport's capacity without requiring the infrastructure of an additional terminal building. A **hangar apron** is positioned outside of a hangar and is used to allow aircraft to move into and out of a hangar.

PAVEMENT

As previously noted, pavement is a top priority for an Airport Manager. An airport with a poorly maintained runway is exposed to greater liability from potential damage to aircraft and increased incidents and accidents. Air carriers expect pavement to be of adequate strength, level, dry, and well-maintained. Sponsor assurances require airports to address preventative maintenance for project applications involving airfield pavements (FAA, n.d.a) and ensure that for any pavement replacement or reconstruction, the airport must assure the FAA that it has implemented an effective pavement maintenance management program. Furthermore, the FAA states, "the goal of any maintenance program is to provide a safe and operable pavement system at the least feasible cost" (FAA, n.d.a). Therefore, in addition to the daily pavement inspection conducted by airport personnel, airports should have a comprehensive **Airfield Pavement Management System (APMS)** to ensure that issues are addressed as soon as possible and that there is a long-term strategic plan for the ongoing maintenance and replacement of paved surfaces.

Timely maintenance renews the condition of airport pavements and prolongs their life. According to the FAA, every $1 spent for preventative maintenance early in the life of the pavement is equivalent to $4 to $5 in repairs spent later in the life of the pavement. The goal of an APMS is to maintain the pavement in excellent condition with the least amount of expenditure and to determine the optimum frequency to effectively use funds for maintenance.

Pavement Type and Structure

Although virtually any surface can be considered a landing area, aircraft operators expect that airports in the contiguous United States be paved. Airport runways and taxiways are constructed of two types of pavement, **flexible** (asphalt) or **rigid** (concrete) materials. Grass, dirt, and gravel are also considered flexible surfaces for landing purposes, but these types of surfaces for air carrier aircraft are usually only found in Alaska or other remote areas in the United States. Most large, commercial service airports have concrete runways and taxiways in order to handle heavier commercial service aircraft. Smaller airports, particularly general aviation airports, have asphalt runways, and even where they may have a concrete runway, the taxiways are still typically asphalt. Asphalt is laid without expansion joints. It is generally less expensive and faster to install than concrete, but requires higher maintenance. Asphalt is primarily a petroleum-based product and therefore more susceptible to oxidation and the reaction of fuel or oil spills (Price & Forrest, 2014).

Concrete is more rigid and poured into distinctive slabs with seams or joints to allow for expansion and contraction. Concrete resists weathering and oil and fuel spillage and typically has twice the service life of asphalt.

Airport pavement is exposed to weather all year long and can experience expansion and thawing from varying temperature swings. On a daily basis, it can be exposed to rain, snow, wind, and aircraft thrust and exhaust. Depending on where an airport is located, pavements may also be constructed on less-than-stable soils, such as swelling clay, or they may be located in an area that experiences earthquakes. Paved areas must also provide a smooth, skid-resistant, and safe riding surface (Prather, 2014a, p. 3). Runways, in particular, must be strong enough to support the loads imposed by aircraft, and they must be able to withstand adverse weather conditions, as well as the abrasive, pounding, and sudden load that impacts the pavement when an aircraft lands (FAA, 2009, p. 1). Runway pavement must also be designed to handle repetitive flight operations in a variety of meteorological conditions.

A typical, flexible, payment structure begins with subgrade, the soil immediately below and supporting the pavement surface. The surface is layered with a subbase if necessary to provide frost protection; then a base layer and hot-mix asphalt surface are applied. A typical, rigid, pavement structure consists of subgrade frost protection, and a subbase course, which may or may not be stabilized (Figure 7.1).

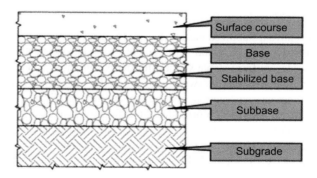

FIGURE 7.1

General categories of layers (courses) to airport runway pavement.

Source: Scott, J. A. (2003). Design guide supplement portland cement concrete: Airport pavements. Retrieved from: http://www.faa.gov/airports/northwest_mountain/engineering/design_resources/media/des-pcc.pdf.

FIGURE 7.2

Example of a concrete (ridged) runway surface depicting expansion joints.

Source: Retrieved from: https://www.flickr.com/photos/44073224@N04/15812825923/in/photolist-q6jSeH-b6kEM2-moC4PT-fDWf7X-
9qLPRi-474NcF-9qU3am-9qU1hL-9qTR2Q-9qQDxn-9qLYTz-rgVUib-9qU2EJ-9qTMHy-q8ARs-ryuEsP-4WTjJC-5BVNu1-48rXim-
7yu6zm-9qTYgh-9qTHXo-9qLYx6-9qPT6u-9qPS3u-9qPPbN-qANRVV-2NCh2p-jHWN14-9qTMuh-dSk6f3-rgUNjE-9qQZua-9qQDRH-
9qTxZG-9qPRFq-eusjpe-bVRDtz-9qQP9B-9qPVWj-euvqFs-6V7pQN-j5rjfH-8dEYR2-9qQAmK-c9KYnh-9qQZ4i-oFfzmU-5kS85E-5Bviwq.

1. **Subgrade:** As with asphalt, the subgrade is the soil that provides the foundation for the rest of the pavement structure.
2. **Subbase:** The subbase layer is used where severe frost occurs and is the same material as used in the asphalt subbase.
3. **Stabilized Base:** New, rigid pavements designed to accommodate aircraft weighing more than 100,000 pounds must have a stabilized base (FAA, 2007, p. 5). The base typically consists of a layer of crushed or uncrushed aggregate bound with a stabilizer, such as portland cement or asphalt cement.
4. **Base:** The base provides uniform stable support for the pavement slab. The base also controls frost, provides subsurface drainage, controls swelling of subgrade soils, provides a stable construction platform for rigid pavement construction, and prevents pumping[4] (FAA, 2007, p. 5).
5. **Surface Course:** The pavement slab provides aircraft structural support and a skid-resistant surface and prevents the infiltration of surface water into the subbase (FAA, 2007, p. 5). A common type of runway concrete pavement construction is referred to as the **portland cement concrete pavement (PCCP)**[5] method (Figure 7.2).

---

[4]Pumping is the ejection of water and underlying material through the joints or cracks in a pavement. As the water is ejected, it carries particles of gravel, sand, clay, or silt with it, resulting in a progressive loss of pavement support that can lead to cracking (FAA, 2007, p. 14).

[5]See http://www.faa.gov/airports/northwest_mountain/engineering/design_resources/media/des-pcc.pdf

> ## PORTLAND CEMENT CONCRETE PAVEMENT
>
> PCCP is one of the most common pavement types used on airports.... The jointing and construction of PCCP causes the design to be more complicated than an asphalt pavement section. PCCP is a common method for unsupported pavement surfaces at airports, but is also viable for runways with varying subbase courses as well.

Asphalt pavement courses typically include these four courses:

1. **Subgrade:** The subgrade is the soil that forms the foundation of the pavement section. Subgrade soils receive less stress than the surface, base, and subbase courses. The combined thickness of subbase, base, and surface courses must be great enough to reduce the stresses occurring in the subgrade so as not to cause excessive distortion or displacement of the subgrade soil layer (FAA, 2007, p. 4). The condition of the soil that comprises the subgrade, such as lower density or higher water content, can affect the stability of the subgrade.

2. **Subbase:** The subbase is used in areas where frost is severe or the subgrade soil is weak. The subbase course is similar to the base course, but material requirements are not as strict because the subbase is subjected to lower load stresses. The subbase consists of stabilized or properly compacted granular material (FAA, 2007, p 4).

3. **Base:** The base course consists of a variety of different materials, either treated or untreated. An untreated base consists of crushed or uncrushed aggregates, while the treated base consists of crushed or uncrushed aggregates mixed with a stabilizer, such as cement or bitumen (FAA, 2007, p.1). The base course is the principal structural component of flexible pavement, serving to distribute the wheel load to the pavement foundation, the subbase, or the subgrade (FAA, 2007, p. 4). Base is composed of hard, durable aggregates, which are either stabilized or granular. Stabilized bases typically consist of crushed or uncrushed aggregate bound with a stabilizer, such as portland cement concrete (PCC) or asphalt cement. Granular bases typically consist of crushed or uncrushed aggregate constructed on a prepared subgrade (FAA, 2007, p. 4).

4. **Bituminous Surface:**[6] A hot-mix asphalt (HMA), which prevents the penetration of surface water into the base course, provides a smooth, well-bonded, and skid-resistant surface without causing undue stress on aircraft tires and resists the stress of aircraft loads (FAA, 2007, p. 4) (Figure 7.3).

For references that describe airport pavement concerns in detail, please consult AC 150/5320-6—*Airport Pavement Design and Evaluation*[7] and AC 150/5370-10—*Standards for Specifying Construction of Airports.*[8]

---

[6]The bituminous surface, or wearing course, is made up of a mixture of various selected aggregates bound together with asphalt cement or other bituminous binders (FAA, 2007, p. 4). Bitumen is a black, viscous mixture of hydrocarbons obtained naturally or as a residue from petroleum distillation.

[7]See http://www.faa.gov/airports/resources/advisory_circulars/index.cfm/go/document.current/documentNumber/150_5320-6

[8]See http://www.faa.gov/airports/resources/advisory_circulars/index.cfm/go/document.current/documentnumber/150_5370-10

FIGURE 7.3

Example of a smooth asphalt runway surface.

Source: https://www.flickr.com/photos/oddsock/3031053687/in/photolist-5BQWEk-oBhsr-4aVvGK-pyNQ8W-q6jSeH-q8ARs-ryuEsP-
b6kEM2-moC4PT-4WTjJC-fDWf7X-5BVNu1-9qLPRi-474NcF-9qU3am-9qU1hL-9qTR2Q-9qQDxn-9qLYTz-rgVUib-9qU2EJ-9qTMHy-
48rXim-bVRDtz-7yu6zm-9qTYgh-9qQP9B-9qTHXo-9qLYx6-9qPVWj-9qPT6u-9qPS3u-9qPPbN-qANRVV-2NCh2p-jHWN14-9qTMuh-
rgUNjE-dSk6f3-9qQZua-9qQDRH-9qTxZG-9qPRFq-euvqFs-6V7pQN-eusjpe-j5rjfH-8dEYR2-9qQAmK-9qLQ6c.

Pavement Deterioration

Once any type of pavement is installed, it is subject to erosion and other forms of deterioration. During pavement installation and immediately after completion, a priority is to examine the pavement (and various courses as applied) for early detection and repair of defects. Failure to perform initial inspections and subsequent routine maintenance can result in severely distressed runway surface areas requiring extensive and costly repairs. Pavement requires continual routine maintenance, rehabilitation, and upgrades. **Rigid pavement** (concrete and low flexibility) can last longer than 30 years compared to 5 to 15 years for **flexible pavement** (asphalt). Ultimately, the longevity of pavement is highly dependent on an APMS that focuses on preventative maintenance. Maintenance includes any regular or recurring work necessary to sustaining airport pavement in a good condition. Examples of these processes include routine cleaning, crack sealing, patching, seal coatings, pavement edge grading, and restoring pavement markings. Airport pavement is traditionally engineered for a minimum of a 20-year structural life, provided that the airport operator performs regular and routine maintenance (FAA, 2007).

As part of the daily self-inspection, airport inspectors may find pieces of pavement breaking away from the surface or edges and can typically identify the type of crack, distortion, or other form of pavement distress causing the deterioration. During the periodic self-inspections, airport personnel, typically maintenance personnel, conduct a close inspection of all airport pavements to determine the type of cracking and causes. This information is then added to the airport's pavement maintenance management system. At large, commercial service airports, there is so much pavement that traditional requirements for periodic inspections are conducted on a continual basis focusing on sections of the airfield during the course of a year.

Structural loads and weather affect airport pavement. Water is particularly destructive to pavement. Water leaks through the surface course and eventually into the base, subbase, and subgrade courses, creating pockets of air mixed with water, which lubricates and erodes the soils and various subbases. In rigid pavements, when water is trapped beneath the surface, an aircraft load can cause "pumping" (essentially, the movement of water by compression and expansion), which accelerates the erosion of the subsurface courses, creating voids, or pockets of air. These air pockets are further weakened by continual structural loads from aircraft and usually result in the formation of potholes or surface collapse. Therefore, pavement, particularly runways, must be constructed to allow water to drain off the paved areas and not pool beneath the surface course or surrounding runway foundation.

Airport pavement should be constructed so that water from rain, melting snow, and ice drains off to the edges of the paved surface. Some water will always penetrate the pavement, so subsurface drainage is provided by a permeable layer of aggregate or stabilized layers of longitudinal pipes for collecting water and redirecting it away from the pavement base layers and foundation. As part of the airport inspection process, during the daily self-inspection, but particularly during special inspections after rainstorms or snow melting, drainage inspection should be conducted to ensure that water is being properly drained and not ponding along the edges of the paved surface. Other signs of drainage issues include soil buildup at the pavement edges, clogged or silted inlet grades, broken or deformed pipes, and discoloration of pavement at joints or cracks. Ponding can also be a wildlife attractant and therefore adds additional risks to operations (FAA, 2007, p. 7).

The most effective means of preserving airport runways, taxiways, and other paved areas is through the implementation of a comprehensive maintenance program. Airport Improvement Program (AIP) grant language also requires that airports develop and maintain an effective airport pavement maintenance-management program. In AC 150-53890-C, the FAA discussed the use of a Pavement Management Program (PMP), usually referred to as an APMS by Airport Operations. An APMS (or PMP) provides one method of establishing an effective repair system by creating systematic procedures for scheduling maintenance and rehabilitation. An APMS evaluates the present condition of the pavement and can be used to forecast future conditions. By projecting the rate of deterioration, an APMS can assist planning for maintenance that occurs at optimal periods. Maintenance that occurs too early results in the airport operator spending money before necessary and not benefiting from the full life span of the pavement. Maintenance that occurs too late results in greatly increased maintenance pavement deterioration, meaning that it will cost incrementally more money the longer the airport waits to repair the pavement. The primary metric of an APMS is the **Pavement Condition Index (PCI)** rating or index system. The PCI is a rating of the surface condition of the pavement and provides an indication of the functional capability of the surface course. By conducting periodic PCI determinations, changes can be detected in performance levels and as can when optimal rehabilitation will be necessary.

Airport pavement needs to withstand varying structural loads, resist weathering and other environmental detriments (such as alternating freeze—thaw, solar radiation), and at the same time provide sufficient friction characteristics for various aircraft and vehicle operations. Pavement friction varies over time and is affected primarily by frequency and type of aircraft traffic. Skid resistance deteriorates as a consequence of mechanical wear (i.e., a polishing action) from aircraft tires on the paved surface and the accumulation of expended rubber on the pavement. Rubber deposits occur mostly at the touchdown areas of runways causing aircraft to lose directional control and reducing braking effectiveness. Additionally, rubber buildup can completely cover the pavement surface and runway markings, causing an increased risk to operations. Contaminants, such as fuel and oil spillage, water, snow, ice, and slush, also reduce friction (FAA, 2007, p. 8).

Pavement deterioration, or distress, occurs in a variety of ways and is affected by whether the pavement surface is flexible or rigid. For example, cracking in flexible pavement is caused by deflection of the surface over an unstable foundation, shrinkage, expansion, and contraction that occur with temperature fluctuations and age. Cracking includes longitudinal and transverse cracks, block cracking, reflection cracking, alligator or fatigue cracking, and slippage cracking. Disintegration of pavement compositions is caused by climate, insufficient compaction of the runway surface, insufficient asphalt binder, loss of adhesion between the asphalt coating in the aggregate, or overheating the asphalt mix. Raveling (loose asphalt debris), asphalt stripping, jet blast erosion, and patching also cause disintegration of flexible pavement. Asphalt distortion is often caused by settlement of the foundation, insufficient compaction of the pavement course, a lack of stability in the asphalt mix, swelling soils or frost in the subgrade, and a poor bond between the surface and underlying layer of the pavement (FAA, 2007). Flexible pavement distortion includes rutting, corrugation, shoving, depressions, and swelling. Loss of skid resistance is caused by too much asphalt in the bituminous mix paint and buildup to contaminants such as rubber or poor aggregate that is subject to wear (FAA, 2007).

Examples of Cracking in Flexible Pavements

1. **Longitudinal and transverse cracks:** A longitudinal crack runs parallel to the runway, while a transverse crack runs perpendicular. These cracks are typically not related to load bearing, but usually result from shrinkage or contraction of the HMA and oxidation and hardening of the asphalt over time. Variations in temperature cause contractions of the asphalt. As the asphalt hardens, it reduces its ability to flex with the temperature and various operational loads, which subsequently causes cracks. Longitudinal cracks are considered to be more hazardous to aircraft operations as they are more likely to affect the directional control of an airplane.
2. **Block cracking:** Block cracking also is not typically related to load bearing, as these are interconnected cracks dividing the pavement into rectangular pieces. Typically, these are caused by daily temperature variations and are an indication that the asphalt is beginning to harden.
3. **Reflection cracking:** Expansion and contraction caused by temperature, moisture, and traffic load cause either vertical or horizontal movement in the pavement beneath an overlay, referred to as reflection cracking. The cracks in the HMA overlay reflect the crack pattern or joint pattern in the underlying pavement (FAA, 2007, p. 9). Essentially, periodic maintenance may have resulted in an overlay of fresh asphalt over previously cracked asphalt. Reflection cracking occurs as a result of the old asphalt moving beneath the new asphalt.
4. **Alligator or fatigue cracking:** This type of cracking occurs as a result of repeated traffic loading beginning at the bottom of the HMA surface where pavement stress and strain are the

highest under an aircraft wheel load (FAA, 2007, p. 9). The cracks move to the surface, and after repeated aircraft landings, they connect and form a pattern resembling an alligator skin.

5. **Slippage cracks:** Slippage cracks occur when an aircraft brakes or turns on pavement, causing the pavement surface to slide in the direction of force resulting from the vehicle or aircraft operation. These cracks are crescent or half-moon shape and can occur when pavement is at relatively high temperatures and aircraft loads are also comparatively high.

Examples of Disintegration in Flexible Pavements

1. **Raveling:** This form of disintegration is caused by the dislodging of aggregate particles on the surface course, indicating the asphalt is beginning to age and harden. The pavement takes on a rough appearance and may produce chunks of asphalt creating foreign object debris.
2. **Weathering:** Weathering occurs as the asphalt and fine aggregate erodes away from the pavement surface. This process is primarily caused by climate and other environmental factors. Weathering is usually accompanied by a fading of the asphalt color.
3. **Potholes:** Potholes occur when portions of the underlying pavement material have broken away, leaving a hole or depression. Most potholes are a result of deterioration or fatigue of the pavement surface course caused by underlying structural failures. As cracks develop, they begin to interlock and eventually work themselves loose up through the surface course.
4. **Asphalt stripping:** When moisture penetrates the HMA, it can lead to stripping of the bitumen from the aggregate particles. Water vapor pressures within the mixture, which eventually scrub the binder from the aggregate, can also cause stripping, causing the runway to lose sustainable flexibility.
5. **Jet blast erosion:** Jet blast can leave a darkened area on paved surfaces where the bituminous binder has been burned or carbonized by the hot exhaust. This erosion accelerates other forms of pavement failure that may be present.
6. **Patching:** Patching is defined as an area where the original pavement has been removed and replaced by filler. A patch will deteriorate at a higher rate than the original pavement and can contribute to bumpiness and foreign object debris (FOD).

Examples of Distortion in Flexible Pavements

1. **Rutting:** Ruts occur from repeated aircraft loads consolidating in the same surface areas, which creates a surface depression along the wheel path. Ponding water is an early indication that a rut is forming.
2. **Corrugation:** Corrugation is caused by a lack of stability in the pavement mix or a poor bond between material layers. Corrugation has the appearance of patterned ripples across the surface.
3. **Depressions:** Depressions often result from bearing heavier traffic loads than the pavement was designed for, settlement of the underlying pavement layer, or poor construction methods. Depressions are low areas on the pavement, typically only noticeable after rain when ponding occurs.
4. **Swelling:** Swelling is typically caused by frost surrounding dissimilar material types in the subgrade or by swelling soils, such as clay soils. Swelling produces an awkward vault in the pavement surface and can occur quickly or build up over the course of time.

Examples of Loss of Skid Resistance in Flexible Pavements

1. **Polished aggregate:** Occurs by repeated aircraft traffic causing the aggregate to lose its coarseness and thus reduces skid resistance.
2. **Contaminants:** Rubber or other materials can reduce the skid resistance and increase the likelihood of hydroplaning.
3. **Bleeding:** Characterized by a film of bituminous material on the page surface that resembles a shiny, glasslike surface and can become sticky. Bleeding is caused by excessive amounts of asphalt binder in the mix or low, air-void content. It may also result when an excessive tack coat is applied prior to the HMA surface.
4. **Fuel/Oil Spillage:** The older oil on a HMA surface softens the asphalt. Minor spills usually heal without repair, but major spills may have a significant impact and contribute to deterioration of the pavement (FAA, 2007).

Rigid pavement cracking is similar to flexible pavement cracking and occurs from stresses in the pavement caused by expansion and contraction. High aircraft loads and improper installation of the pavement may also contribute to cracking. Rigid pavement cracking includes longitudinal, transverse, and diagonal cracks, corner breaks, durability cracking, shrinkage cracking, and shattered slab, or intersecting, cracks. **Joint seal damage** is particular to rigid pavement and occurs when soil or rocks accumulate in the joints, which allows water to infiltrate the base and contributes to pumping. **Disintegration** is the breaking up of pavement into small, loose pieces and occurs by improper curing and finishing of the concrete, improper mixing of the concrete, or using unsuitable aggregate. **Distortion** is the movement of pavement from its original position. It results from settlement of the foundation, expansive or frost-susceptible soils, or loss of fines[9] because of improperly designed subdrains. **Loss of skid resistance** occurs on rigid pavement for the same reasons it occurs on flexible pavement, which is essentially the buildup of rubber or the wearing down of the surface coat through use and weathering (FAA, 2007).

Examples of Cracking in Rigid Pavements

1. **Longitudinal, transverse, and diagonal cracks:** Combinations of crack types can result from repeated usage of and shrinkage in rigid pavement. Shrinkage occurs when pavement dries and contributes to frictional and wheel load pavement stress. In rigid pavement, these types of cracks divide the slab into multiple pieces.
2. **Corner breaks:** Corner breaks can result from repeated loads, combined with a loss of support due to dynamic pumping or loss of load transfer at the joints. Curling (warping) stresses also cause corner breaks when thermal gradients in the concrete slab are relatively great and vary seasonally.
3. **Durability "D" cracking:** D cracking is caused by freeze–thaw expansion of the large aggregate within the PCC slab, a consequence of using expansive aggregates. D cracking may eventually lead to disintegration of the concrete.
4. **Shrinkage cracking:** Shrinking cracks are hairline cracks formed during setting of the PCC and usually do not extend through the entire depth of the slab. Common causes are construction

---

[9]Fines are a waste byproduct of asphalt mixing and are typically recycled as part of the filler portion of a HMA mixture. Fines can be crushed stone, sand, or gravel.

issues and improper curing techniques. These cracks can typically be sealed and are not considered a significant issue unless left untreated.

5. **Shattered slab/intersecting cracks:** Shattering occurs when a slab breaks into four or more pieces—primarily caused by overloading or an inadequate foundation (FAA, 2007).

Examples of Disintegration in Rigid Pavements

1. **Scaling, map cracking, and crazing:** These combinations are caused by the disintegration and loss of the surface coat. Surfaces that are weakened by improper curing or freeze–thaw cycles lead to scaling. Map cracking, or crazing, features a series of hairline cracks that extend only through the upper surface.

2. **Alkali–silica reaction (ASR):** ASR is associated with map cracking and is caused by an expansive reaction between the alkaline contained in the cement paste and elements within the aggregate. The reactive materials form a gel that attracts and absorbs water. Once the gel has absorbed enough water, the substance becomes an alkali silica gel and then escapes to surrounding cracks. The water–gel mix also causes expansion and damages the concrete. Typical indications of ASR on pavement often occur in a map pattern *(Isle of Man Cracking)* that is white, brown, gray, or another color present at the surface (Alkali–Aggregate Reaction, 2008). This particular type of disintegration created millions of dollars in damage at airports throughout the U.S. Midwest, where alkali levels in the soils are typically higher than in other areas of the United States. ASR can be controlled, to some extent, by avoiding aggregates such as limestone, sandstone, and river rock. Using a low-alkali cement or a low water-to-cement ratio can also help reduce ASR. In severe circumstances, the pavement can fracture the aggregates, which results in cracking, pop-outs, and spalling (Alkali–Aggregate Reaction, 2008).

3. **Joint spalling:** Joint spalling often results from excessive stresses at the joint or crack by the infiltration of incompressible materials or weak concrete. Joint spalling is the breakdown of the slab edge within 2 feet of the joint but does not extend through the slab vertically but intersects the joint at an angle.

4. **Corner spalling:** Corner spalling is the raveling or breakdown of the slab within 2 feet of the corner. The causes are the same as for joint spalling but may appear sooner because of the increased exposure of the geometric area of the corner to environmental conditions.

5. **Blowups:** Blowups usually occur as a result of the infiltration of incompressible materials or by the closure of a joint caused by expansion resulting from ASR. When the expansive pressure cannot be relieved, buckling or shattering occurs and pushes the pavement upward. The blowup can occur within minutes, but the buildup of pressures occurs over a period of time, which may provide an airport safety inspector the opportunity to observe early indications of a potential blowup forming.

6. **Pop-outs:** Pop-outs are small pieces of pavement that break loose from the concrete surface. Caused by expansive aggregates, ASR, and the freeze–thaw reaction, pop outs usually range from 1 to 4 inches in diameter. Clay balls in the concrete mix can also cause pop-outs.

7. **Patching:** Patching is an area where the original pavement has been removed and replaced by filler. Small patches are defined as an area less than 5 feet; large patches and utility pavement cuts are defined as an area of greater than 5 feet or, in the case of a utility cut, a patch that has replaced the original pavement because of the placement of underground utilities (FAA, 2007).

Examples of Distortion in Rigid Pavements

1. **Pumping:** The ejection of water and underlined material through joints or cracks in pavement can be caused by hydrodynamic pumping. Evidence of pumping includes surface staining and base or subgrade materials on the pavement near joints or cracks.
2. **Settlement or faulting:** Settlement or faulting can occur when there is a difference in elevations of surface areas at a joint or cracks and can be caused by frost heave or swelling soils.
3. **Shoving:** Shoving is a localized bulging of the pavement surface caused by a lack of stability in the mix, movements at interlayer, or lateral stress produced by portland concrete cement pavement during expansion (FAA, 2007).

Examples of Loss of Skid Resistance in Rigid Pavements

1. **Polished aggregates:** Polished aggregates occur when surface concrete aggregate materials become smoothed under friction from traffic loads.
2. **Contaminants:** Contaminants such as tire-rubber deposits, oil spills, and water can reduce surface friction on rigid surfaces. Engineered cuts in the concrete, or "runway grooving," can reduce the likelihood of skidding or hydroplaning caused by contaminants (FAA, 2007).

Proper pavement maintenance requires crack and joint sealing material, power saws, jackhammers, and a variety of other tools and materials. Specific maintenance techniques can be found in FAA AC 150/5380−6C.

RUNWAY SAFETY AREAS

FAA AC 150/5300-13A Airport Design defines the **Runway Safety Area (RSA)** as surface areas surrounding the runway that reduce risk of damage to aircraft in the event of an undershoot, overshoot, or excursion from the runway while taxiing, landing, or during takeoff. A **Taxiway/Taxi-lane Safety Area** is a defined surface alongside the taxiway designed to reduce risk to aircraft deviating from the taxiway.

RUNWAY DESIGN AND OPERATIONS

Runway design criteria is determined by the following parameters:

1. Aircraft Approach Category (AAC)
2. Airplane Design Group (ADG)
3. Taxiway Design Group (TDG)

The AAC and ADG, along with FAA-specified, approach-visibility minimums, are combined to establish the **Runway Design Code (RDC)**. The RDC provides planners and operational personnel information necessary to determine design standards that apply to a specific runway. The first component of the RDC, depicted by a letter, is the **AAC**, which relates to the aircraft approach or runway threshold crossing speed (commonly referred to as "Vref"). Vref as related to the aircraft performance requirements of the Part 139 runway (see Design Aircraft in Figure 7.4) is a key driver to determining needed runway width, runway-to-taxiway separation, runway-to-fixed object distances,

AAC	V_{REF}/ Approach Speed
A	Approach speed less than 91 knots
B	Approach speed 91 knots or more but less than 121 knots
C	Approach speed 121 knots or more but less than 141 knots
D	Approach speed 141 knots or more but less than 166 knots
E	Approach speed 166 knots or more

FIGURE 7.4

Runway Design Aircraft Vref and approach category.

Source: Airport design advisory circular, AC No: 150/5300-13A.

and the locations of other required runway operating areas.[10] The landing and takeoff distance of the Design Aircraft also relates to the runway length, although this is not expressed in the RDC.

RUNWAY DESIGN AIRCRAFT

A Part 139 designated runway is constructed to accommodate the maximum performance requirements of the aircraft using the runway for Part 139 operations. For planning and operational considerations, these performance constraints are collectively referred to as the "Design Aircraft." The Design Aircraft can be representative of a single aircraft or a composite of different aircraft representing the most demanding characteristics of each plane. The Design Aircraft is a key driver to the geometric and load-bearing requirements of the runway (plus many other factors as related to airport planning and design). Aircraft operations that exceed the maximum limitations of the Design Aircraft could result in an unsafe operation, reduced safety margins, or reduced operational capacity. The Design Aircraft is also specified in the Airport Master Plan and is used in future runway construction planning and design efforts.

The second component of the RDC (depicted by a Roman numeral) is the **Aircraft Design Group**, which is derived from aircraft wingspan or tail height, whichever is most restrictive (FAA, 2013a). Wingspan and tail heights are used to help designate the design of taxiways and apron or **Object-Free Areas**,[11] the aircraft parking configuration, aircraft hangar locations, taxiway-to-taxiway separation, and runway-to-taxiway separation.

The third component of the RDC relates visibility minimums expressed by **Runway Visual Range (RVR)** (required horizontal ground visibility ranges for landing, expressed in feet; e.g., 1,200, 1,600, 2,400, 4,000, and 5,000 feet and as measured by a transmissometer[12] on the airfield). RVR also affects the required design and size of the **Runway Protection Zone (RPZ)** and the aircraft approach slope. The RPZ is a trapezoidal area "... 'off the end of the runway end that serves to enhance the protection of people and property on the ground' in the event an aircraft lands or crashes beyond the runway end."[13]

---

[10]For example, the Runway Safety Area (RSA), Runway Object-Free Area (ROFA), and the Runway Protection Zone (RPZ). See FAA AC 150/5300-13A at http://www.faa.gov/documentLibrary/media/Advisory_Circular/draft_150_5300_13a.pdf

[11]Areas designated to have specified three-dimensional clearance from obstructions or other structures permitting Design Aircraft operations.

[12]A transmissometer is a ground-based visibility detection system that usually uses a sensed laser beam to detect the degradation of visibility over specific distances.

[13]See FAA *Airport Division—Runway Protection Zones*. Retrieved from: http://portal.hud.gov/hudportal/documents/huddoc?id = airportdivision.pdf

Other runway design considerations include general safety concerns, effects on the environment, visibility categories for various aircraft-instrument approaches supported at the airport,[14] the location of the ATCT, the availability of land zoned for expansion, cost to acquire land for expansion, potential security threats and required security measures, and location of existing facilities. In addition to these factors, local meteorological conditions, the surrounding topography, and the volume of air traffic expected at the airport all affect the design, location, and orientation of the airport's runway system.

TAXIWAY DESIGN

Taxiways are also designed to accommodate the Design Aircraft. Primary aircraft characteristics that affect **TDG** metrics include the **flight deck to main gear distance** (distance in feet of flight deck to main gear) and the **main gear separation width**, also in feet. The TDG determines the taxiway width, the fillet[15] design, the apron areas, and aircraft parking layout.

RUNWAY LOCATION, ORIENTATION, AND MOVEMENT AREAS

Three of the most important considerations for runway design are (a) runway location, (b) orientation, and (c) alignment with prevailing, seasonal winds, featuring runway orientations that favor parallel to average, annual, prevailing winds in the airport's geographic area of operations. Pilots always try to takeoff and land into the wind. Wind data analysis for runway orientation considers the wind speed and direction (velocity) using historical and forecasted metrological data. Taking off into the wind shortens the aircraft takeoff distance, while landing into the wind allows aircraft to use less of the runway and achieve a slower touchdown speed. Therefore, runway location and orientation are vital to airport safety, airspace efficiency, and economic and environmental impacts (FAA, 2013a).

Ideally, runway orientation(s) should accommodate 95% of the annual aircraft operations at the airport. If an airport with a single runway provides less than 95% of annual service, then a **"crosswind runway"** is recommended (FAA, 2013a, p. 43). The RDC is also partially determined by the ability of the Design Aircraft (one or more) to handle a given crosswind. RDCs of A-I and B-I (small aircraft) have an allowable crosswind component of 10.5 knots, whereas RDCs E-I through E-VI have an allowable crosswind component of 20 knots. Some larger aircraft also have tailwind components allowing them to takeoff and operate with low tailwind speeds. Most aircraft are capable of a takeoff or landing with a very limited tailwind; however, the pilot must take into account an additional distance for takeoff roll or landing rollout.[16] Failure to do so could result in the

---

[14]For example, visual approach, nonprecision approach, approach procedure with vertical guidance, and precision approach. See http://www.faa.gov/regulations_policies/handbooks_manuals/aviation/instrument_procedures_handbook/media/Chapter_4.pdf

[15]Fillets are areas of pavement that are in addition to the standard width of a taxiway, providing additional room to turn the aircraft and still maintain the **Taxiway Edge Safety Margins (TESMs)**. The TESM is the distance between the outer edge of the landing gear of an airplane with its nose gear on the taxiway centerline and the edge of the taxiway pavement.

[16]Tailwind operations: taking off with a prevailing wind velocity that is moving in the direction of the takeoff (from behind the aircraft) is considered a potentially hazardous operation. Tailwind takeoffs can lead to loss of control of the aircraft, reduced climb angles, and greatly increased takeoff distances. Pilots consult their FAA-approved aircraft **Pilot Operating Handbook (POH)** for guidance on tailwind takeoffs specific to the aircraft they are flying.

aircraft running off the runway before it has the opportunity to achieve its takeoff speed or the ability to stop on the remaining paved surface of the runway.

Other factors to consider when planning and designing the layout of a runway system include:

1. Locations of nearby bird sanctuaries, landfills, and other features that attract wildlife.
2. Layout of airport landside interfaces or transportation networks (such as roads located outside secured areas, light rail access).
3. Location of existing navigational aids.
4. Location of control tower (if present).

MOVEMENT AREAS

Runways and taxiways comprise the movement area of the airfield. The non-movement area includes the aircraft apron areas (for aircraft parking) and taxi-lanes that connect the apron to the taxiway system. Other elements in the airfield also include the terminal building, concourses, Aircraft Rescue and Firefighting facilities, snow removal equipment storage and maintenance facilities, aircraft fuel farms, ground vehicle maintenance and fueling areas, air cargo facilities, private tenant leaseholds, fixed base operations, specialized aviation service operators providing a variety of aeronautical services (flight training, charter, aircraft maintenance), and concessionaire buildings.

FAA or FAA-designated control towers issue clearance to access and use taxiways and runways designated for Part 139 operations by aircraft and ground vehicles. However, the airport authority has jurisdiction to open or close a taxiway or runway. Those areas that are under the operational control of the FAA are designated as a movement area. Movement areas are defined by the FAA as:

> The runways, taxiways, and other areas of an airport that are used for taxiing or hover taxiing, air taxiing, takeoff, and landing of aircraft including helicopters and tilt-rotors, exclusive of loading aprons and aircraft parking areas.

Location of the movement areas for each airport is negotiated through a letter of agreement between the airport authority and the FAA. Airport operators typically draft rules and regulations that include the procedures and authority for access to movement areas.

Under Part 139, airport operators are also required to have a movement area driver training program, and each individual that operates a ground vehicle in the movement area must receive initial driver training and recurrent training every 12 consecutive calendar months. Driver training is not required for personnel and vehicles that operate in non-movement areas. However, many large- and medium-hub airports, and even smaller airports, require driver training for personnel operating on **Vehicle Service Roads (VSRs)**, aircraft ramps, taxi lanes, and other non-movement areas.

Airports without a tower or controlling agency, or uncontrolled airports, do not have a designated movement area. At an uncontrolled airport, pilots use either a **Common Traffic Advisory Frequency (CTAF)**, or **Unicom**, to self-announce (radio broadcast) their positions on the runway, in the air traffic pattern, or while operating in the vicinity of the airport. For vehicle operations on the runway or taxiway, airport authorities typically designate entities authorized to access these areas. It is recommended at any uncontrolled airport that any vehicle or pedestrian operating on the runway give way to all aircraft traffic and self-announce their position on the airfield and their intent to access or depart the runway via the CTAF or Unicom.

RUNWAY AND TAXIWAY ELEMENTS

To enhance the safety of flight and taxiing operations, safety areas and zones have been created around runways and taxiways. Some of these areas are tangible, such as the safety area, which is an area of level ground surrounding a runway or taxiway, while others are created by imaginary lines (boundaries) bordering the runway (and sometimes the taxiway). The imaginary lines provide operations personnel information about what activities and materials are in and around the runway or taxiway.

Runway blast pads are paved areas that provide protection from erosion caused by aircraft engine blast and are located at the end of a runway. They are marked with yellow chevrons indicating that the area is not intended for aircraft operations. Some blast pads also serve as a **stopway**, which is an area beyond the takeoff runway, centered on the extended runway centerline, and designated by the airport authority for use in decelerating an aircraft during an aborted takeoff (FAA, 2012, p. 77).

Safety areas are formed by imaginary, rectangular boxes around both runways and taxiways. A safety area is a defined surface surrounding the runway prepared or suitable for reducing the risk of damage to airplanes in the event of undershooting, overshooting, or excursion from the runway (FAA, 2015). In the early days of aviation, aircraft took off and landed from unimproved airfields. Eventually, takeoff and landing paths were established and became known as "landing strips," which described the graded areas upon which the runway was constructed, along with adjacent areas available for aircraft overruns. These areas are now called **RSAs** (Figure 7.5). A safety area is a rectangular box surrounding the runway and is based on the RDC. Safety areas are centered on the runway centerline and can extend up to 1,000 feet from the approach and departure ends of the runway and to a width of up to 250 feet, either side of the centerline. Taxiways also have safety areas, which are smaller in dimension than an RSA because of the lower speeds at which aircraft operate while taxiing versus taking off or landing. Per FAA AC 150-5300-13A *Airport Design* (FAA, 2013a), current safety area standards require safety areas to be:

1. Cleared and graded and have no potentially hazardous ruts, humps, depressions, or other surface variations;
2. Drained by grading or storm sewers to prevent water accumulation;

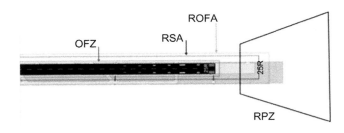

FIGURE 7.5

Examples of runway Obstacle Free Zone (OFZ), Runway Safety Area (RSA), Runway Object-Free Area (ROFA) and Runway Protection Zone (RPZ).

Source: Courtesy of Jeffrey Price.

3. Capable, under dry conditions, of supporting snow removal equipment, Aircraft Rescue and Firefighting (ARFF) equipment, and the occasional passage of aircraft;

4. Free of objects, except for objects that need to be located in the RSA because of their function. The commonly used term fixed-by-function refers to objects required to be located within the RSA. Airfield signs, lights, and some navigational aids fall into this category. Objects that are in the RSA that exceed 3 inches in height above grade must be mounted at the lowest possible height and with a frangible (i.e., breakaway) point no higher than 3 inches above grade. Frangible mounts allow for the object to more easily break away if struck by an aircraft, thereby minimizing damage to the aircraft.

RSA dimensions are different for each runway and based on a variety of factors, including the Design Aircraft, environmental issues, and features that surround the airport, such as preexisting railroad tracks, swamps, rivers, or other areas that would be too costly or difficult to relocate.[17] RSA dimensions are based on 90% of overruns being contained within the RSA (FAA, 2012, p. 39). In some cases, airports are not able to meet the required safety area standards, in which case **Engineered Material Arresting System (EMAS)**[18] materials may be substituted. EMAS materials are compressible blocks of lightweight, crushable, cellular cement designed to safely stop airplanes that overshoot runways, or a foamed silica bed, which is made from recycled glass and is contained within a high-strength plastic mesh system anchored to the pavement at the end of the runway.[19]

Two other imaginary surfaces to protect aircraft operations surround airport runways. The **Obstacle Free Zone (OFZ)** is a defined volume of airspace centered on the runway centerline and extending 200 feet beyond each end of the runway. The width of a runway OFZ varies based on the approach visibility minimums or the approach speed of the aircraft designed to use the runway, or the type of aircraft (small versus large).[20] The runway OFZ extends to a height of 150 feet above the runway surface. There are additional inner approach OFZs, inner transitional OFZs, and RPZs, with various dimensions that also provide protection for aircraft during flight operations. The dimensions vary based on a variety of factors, including the type of aircraft and the type of approach (i.e., visual, precision) that the runway is designed to accommodate.

During aircraft operations, nothing may be in the OFZ except as fixed-by-function (meaning essential) and frangible. However, certain objects and operations are acceptable within the RPZ, including farming, irrigation channels, airport service roads, underground facilities, and unstaffed navigational aids. In some cases, buildings and major thoroughfares run through the RPZ. At Los Angeles International Airport, Sepulveda Boulevard (a major thoroughfare) runs through some of the RPZ along with several hotels and other businesses. The reason for this configuration is that the concept of the RPZ was established after developments had been established around airport runways. As part of the Airport Design guidance from the FAA, future RPZs should not include any other use other than what is authorized, and airport operators should strive whenever possible to reduce or eliminate unsuitable land use within existing RPZs. Note that taxiways do not have OFZs.

---

[17]RSAs are measured from the centerline and may include shoulders, island areas, blast pads, and stopways.

[18]See AC No. 150/5220-9A at http://www.skybrary.aero/bookshelf/books/2978.pdf

[19]As an example of EMAS effectiveness, during the first 8 months of 2015, EMAS safely stopped nine aircraft overruns with a total of 243 passengers and crew on board within the United States.

[20]Large aircraft means aircraft of more than 12,500 pounds, maximum certificated takeoff weight. See 14 CFR 1.1 for additional requirements to this definition, at http://www.ecfr.gov/cgi-bin/text-idx?rgn = div8&node = 14:1.0.1.1.1.0.1.1

Another imaginary protection line that surrounds runways and taxiways is the **Object-Free Areas (OFAs)**, known as a **ROFA (Runway Object-Free Area)** when surrounding a runway or a **TOFA (Taxiway Object-Free Area)** when surrounding a taxiway. The OFA must be clear of objects that are not fixed-by-function and frangible; however, it is acceptable for aircraft that are taxiing or in a hold position waiting for takeoff (or having just landed and exiting the runway) to be in the ROFA. The dimensions of the OFA depend on the **ADG**, that is, the approach speed and wingspan of the critical aircraft.

The OFAs, RSA, RPZ, and OFZ are relevant to Airport Operations personnel who must often make decisions about whether maintenance operations, such as fixing airfield lights, signs, or mowing operations, or construction activities can take place around the runway or taxiway, during flight operations. All four areas are depicted on the **Airport Layout Plan (ALP)**,[21] such that Airport Operations personnel can refer to the ALP to determine what operations can take place in specific areas. Construction may not occur within the RSA while the runway is open for aircraft operations, but airport operators can restrict aircraft operations to smaller aircraft, thus effectively reducing the size of the RSA for the duration of the restriction. For the purposes of air traffic control, the RSA is considered a non-movement area for aircraft and vehicles. Vehicles, mowing equipment, or any other large equipment may not penetrate the OFZ during flight operations. According to FAA CertAlert No. 03-07 *Personnel and Equipment in the Runway Safety Area, 11/23/2003*, mowing equipment and other large equipment (not including hand tools or small equipment that will not cause damage to an aircraft in case of a collision) is not considered acceptable objects in the safety area during air carrier aircraft operations except:

1. Access by vehicular, mowing, and other equipment is limited to areas more than 200 feet from the runway centerline or the current RSA.
2. Personnel may enter the RSA if necessary to drop off light or small equipment, and a vehicle may be brought into the area between air carrier operations, provided it is then removed from the RSA immediately.

UNPAVED AREAS

Not all commercial service runways are paved. Certain runways, mostly located in Alaska, consist of gravel, grass, compacted snow, or other nonpavement surfaces. The FAA requires that unpaved areas do not have a slope from the edge of the full-strength surface downward greater than 2:1 to the existing terrain and that unpaved, full-strength surfaces have adequate crown or grade to assure sufficient drainage. Additionally, full-strength surfaces must be compacted and stable in order to prevent rutting, loosening, or buildup of surface material, which could impair directional control of aircraft, as well as water drainage. As with pavement, full-strength, unpaved surfaces should not have holes or depressions exceeding 3 inches in depth and should be free of debris and foreign objects.

[21]The ALP is a scaled drawing (and a set of drawings collectively referred to as the ALP), in either traditional or electronic form, of current and future airport facilities that provides a graphic representation of the existing and long-term development plan for the airport and demonstrates the preservation and continuity of safety, utility, and efficiency of the airport to the satisfaction of the FAA.

AIRFIELD SIGNS, MARKINGS, AND LIGHTING

Properly designed airport signs, markings, and lighting can contribute greatly to the overall safety of flight operations and the efficiency of the airport. Pilots use a variety of signs, airfield markings, and lighting configurations for a variety of safety-related reasons, including:

1. Identifying their location on the airfield and how to get to their desired location.
2. Enhancing visibility of the movement area during takeoff, landing, and taxiing operations.
3. Providing relevant information to pilots, air traffic controllers, and vehicle operators on the airfield.

Airfield signs, markings, and lighting have different meanings and different symbols than signs, markings, and lighting on city streets and highways. Understanding airfield signs, markings, and lighting is critical to the safety of the airfield, particularly for personnel who drive on the movement area. The FAA requires any individual who drives on the movement area to receive training every year. The training must include instruction on how to read airfield signs, markings, and lighting (configuration, patterns, colors, etc.). Runway incursions often occur because an individual fails to understand a particular sign, marking, or lighting system.

A challenge in designing and placing airfield signs, markings, and lighting is that while all of these elements are standardized, each airport is different. Even at airports with similar runway and taxiway configurations, the number of signs, or markings, or different lighting systems may vary to provide the pilot with needed guidance. Airports regulated under Part 139 are required to have a signs-and-markings plan as part of the Airport Certification Manual.

SIGNS

FAA AC 150/5340-18L *Standards for Airport Sign Systems* provides guidance for the siting and installation of signs on airport runways and taxiways. Nine different types of signs are used on an airport:

1. **Mandatory instruction signs** (Figure 7.6) feature white lettering on a red background and indicate taxiway/runway intersections, runway/runway intersections, Instrument Landing System (ILS) critical areas, precision OFZ boundaries, runway approach areas, CAT II/III operations areas, military landing zones, and no-entry areas. These are among the most important signs on an airfield, as they typically protect a runway, the approach to a runway, or the clear zone needed for the airport precision instrument approach system to properly function. Pilots are often taught a mnemonic device, *red and white, runway in sight*, to identify the mandatory instruction sign.
2. **Location signs** tell the pilot or vehicle operator the taxiway or runway upon which they are located. Location signs have a yellow lettering with a black background (Figure 7.7). The memory mnemonic is: *black square, you're there.*
3. **Direction signs** (Figure 7.8) indicate the direction of taxiways, leading to an intersection, and are also used to indicate a taxiway exit from a runway. They have black lettering on a yellow background and always feature an arrow.

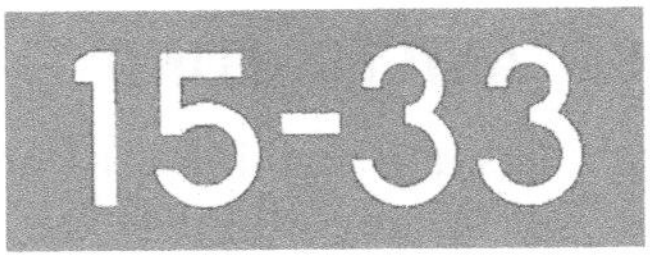

15-33

FIGURE 7.6

Runway location sign.

Source: FAA, 2013b.

FIGURE 7.7

Holding position sign.

Source: FAA, 2013b.

FIGURE 7.8

Direction sign.

Source: FAA, 2013b.

4. **Boundary signs** (Figure 7.9) are used to identify the boundary of the RSA, OFZs, or ILS critical area. These signs have black lettering on yellow backgrounds.
5. **Taxiway ending marker** (Figure 7.10) signs indicate a taxiway does not continue beyond an intersection.
6. **Destination signs** (Figure 7.11). Like a direction sign, a destination sign has black lettering on a yellow background and always contains an arrow. These signs indicate the general direction to a remote location, such as to a military area of the airport, or an FBO, cargo area, terminal, or other area.

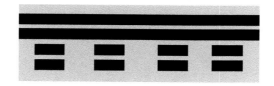

FIGURE 7.9

Boundary sign for RSA/OFZ and runway approach area.

Source: FAA, 2013b.

FIGURE 7.10

Taxiway ending marker.

Source: FAA, 2013b.

FIGURE 7.11

Inbound destination sign.

Source: FAA, 2013b.

BGR - VORTAC
114.8 (CH 95) 153/333
DME 3.8 NM

FIGURE 7.12

Direction sign.

Source: FAA, 2013b.

7. **Information signs** (Figure 7.12) are installed on the airside of an airport and provide information other than mandatory holding positions, taxiway guidance, and remaining runway distance. An information sign has a black inscription on a yellow background.
8. **Vehicle roadway signs** (Figure 7.13) are located on the airfield and are intended solely for vehicle operators.

FIGURE 7.13

Vehicle roadway sign.

Source: FAA, 2013b.

FIGURE 7.14

Runway distance remaining sign.

Source: FAA, 2013b.

9. **Runway distance remaining signs** (Figure 7.14) are used for providing distance remaining information to pilots during takeoff and landing operations. The sign has a white numeral inscription on a black background. The number indicates the distance in thousands of feet of remaining runway (Figure 7.15).

Airport signs should readily identify routes toward desired destinations, be easy-to-read from the perspective of flight crews and Ops personnel, and clearly indicate mandatory holding positions. In some cases, signs cannot be installed due to wide paved areas, in which case they may be painted on the pavement. FAA AC 150/5340-1 *Standards for Airport Markings* provides additional guidance for adding painted signs onto pavement. Signs are typically installed on the left side of the paved area, except where there is a right side turnoff. In these cases, signs may be placed on both sides of the runway or taxiway (Figure 7.16).

EXAMPLE	TYPE OF SIGN	PURPOSE	LOCATION/CONVENTION
4 - 22	Mandatory: Hold position for taxiway/ runway intersection.	Denotes entrance to runway from a taxiway.	Located L side of taxiway within 10 feet of hold position markings.
22 - 4	Mandatory: Holding position for runway /runway intersection.	Denotes intersecting runway.	Located L side of rwy prior to intersection, & R side if rwy more than 150' wide, used as taxiway, or has "land & hold short" Ops.
4 - APCH	Mandatory: Holding position for runway approach area.	Denotes area to be protected for aircraft approaching or departing a runway.	Located on taxiways crossing thru runway approach areas where an aircraft would enter an RSA or apch/departure airspace.
ILS	Mandatory: Holding position for ILS critical area/precision Obstacle Free Zone.	Denotes entrance to area to be protected for an ILS signal or approach airspace.	Located on twys where the twys enter the NAVAID critical area or where aircraft on taxiway would violate ILS apch airspace (including POFZ).
⊖	Mandatory: No entry.	Denotes aircraft entry is prohibited.	Located on paved areas that aircraft should not enter.
B	Taxiway Location.	Identifies taxiway on which the aircraft is located.	Located along taxiway by itself, as part of an array of taxiway direction signs, or combined with a runway/taxiway hold sign.
22	Runway Location.	Identifies the runway on which the aircraft is located.	Normally located where the proximity of two rwys to one another could cause confusion.
= = =	Runway Safety Area / OFZ and Runway Approach Area Boundary.	Identifies exit boundary for an RSA / OFZ or rwy approach.	Located on taxiways on back side of certain runway/ taxiway holding position signs or runway approach area signs.
⊓⊓⊓⊓	ILS Critical Area/POFZ Boundary.	Identifies ILS critical area exit boundary.	Located on taxiways on back side of ILS critical area signs.
J →	Direction: Taxiway.	Defines designation/direction of intersecting taxiway(s).	Located on L side, prior to intersection, with an array L to R in clockwise manner.
↖ L	Runway Exit.	Defines designation/direction of exit taxiways from the rwy.	Located on same side of runway as exit, prior to exit.
22 ↑	Outbound Destination.	Defines directions to take-off runway(s).	Located on taxi routes to runway(s). Never collocated or combined with other signs.
FBO ↘	Inbound Destination.	Defines directions to airport destinations for arriving aircraft.	Located on taxi routes to airport destinations. Never collocated or combined with other types of signs.
NOISE ABATEMENT PROCEDURES IN EFFECT 2300 - 0500	Information.	Provides procedural or other specialized information.	Located along taxi routes or aircraft parking/Staging Areas. May not be lighted.
/////////	Taxiway Ending Marker.	Indicates taxiway does not continue beyond intersection.	Installed at taxiway end or far side of intersection, if visual cues are inadequate.
7	Distance Remaining.	Distance remaining info for take-off/landing.	Located along the sides of runways at 1000' increments.

FIGURE 7.15

FAA guide to airport signs.

Source: http://www.faa.gov/airports/runway_safety/news/publications/media/QuickReferenceGuideProof8.pdf.

AIRFIELD LIGHTING

The two primary components of airfield lighting are **airport lighting** and the **approach lighting system (ALS)** (Figure 7.17). Airport lighting consists of runway and taxiway lights and other lights on the ramp and in aircraft operations areas. These lights are typically controlled and maintained by the airport operator but must adhere to FAA standards. The ALS consists of sequenced flashers, approach lighting, and crossbar lighting and is almost always controlled and maintained by the FAA. The runway threshold lights are the demarcation line between the airport lighting system and the ALS. At some airports, the runway threshold lights are the responsibility of the FAA, whereas at other airports they are the responsibility of the airport operator. The responsible entity for the threshold lights can be articulated in an agreement between the FAA and the airport operator. Additional airport lighting may include obstruction lights and the airport beacon. Some airports use a low-visibility program known as the **Surface Movement Guidance and Control System (SMCGS)**, which features several additional lights and markings (Figure 7.18).

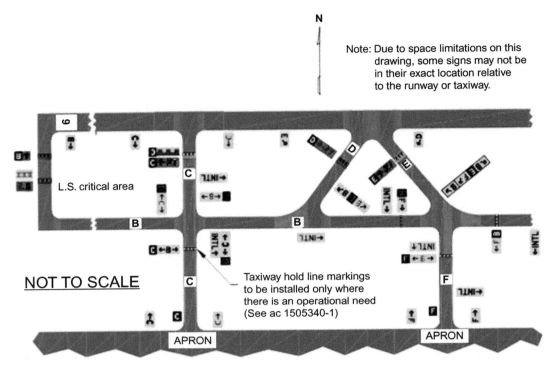

N

Note: Due to space limitations on this drawing, some signs may not be in their exact location relative to the runway or taxiway.

L.S. critical area

NOT TO SCALE

Taxiway hold line markings to be installed only where there is an operational need (See ac 1505340-1)

APRON

APRON

FIGURE 7.16

Example of airport sign configuration.

Source: FAA. (2010). AC 150/5340-18F, Standards for Airport Sign Systems. Washington, DC: U.S. Department of Transportation, Federal Aviation Administration.

MARKINGS

Airfield markings provide pilots and vehicle operators with important information about their location on the airport, enhance visibility of the runway for pilots, and provide pilots with information about the length of a runway, as well as how much runway remains for landing or takeoff (Figure 7.19). Overall, runway markings are white and taxiway markings are yellow. VSRs also have white markings but are highly distinguishable from the white markings on a runway. FAA AC 150/5340-1L *Standards for Airport Markings* provides specific guidance on the location, color, size, and other characteristics of airport markings. Proper design and placement for airport markings must include:

1. Ensuring that markings that denote a feature, particularly of a runway or taxiway, do not conflict with markings from a nearby taxiway or runway.
2. The possible addition of silica sand on the marking immediately after painting, to increase the coefficient of friction (such that the aircraft's breaking and directional control is not impeded if a wheel touches the marking), or incorporate glass beads into the paint.
3. The use of striated (grooved or ridged) markings in areas subject to frost and heaving.

FIGURE 7.17

MALSR (Medium Intensity Approach Lighting System with Runway Alignment Indicator Lights).

Source: https://www.faa.gov/about/office_org/headquarters_offices/ato/service_units/techops/navservices/lsg/malsr/.

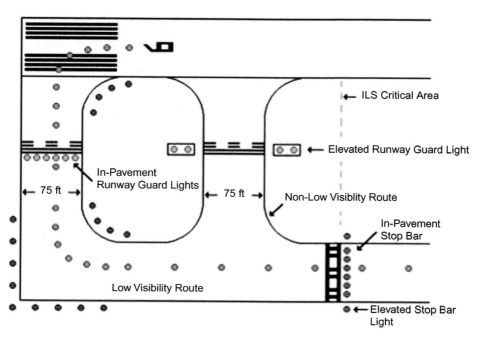

FIGURE 7.18

Sample lighting configuration for operations below 600 ft. RVR.

Source: Surface Movement Guidance and Control System Advisory Circular, AC No: 120-57A.

FIGURE 7.19

Surface painted holding position sign for taxiway widths equal to or less than 35 feet.

Source: FAA, 2013b.

4. The use of temporary markings, which may be difficult to remove once they are no longer necessary.
5. The removal of markings that are no longer needed; painting over markings is ineffective because it actually preserves the old marking and creates confusion for pilots. Markings must typically be removed through water blasting, shot blasting, or chemical removal.

Additionally, the condition of the pavement affects the marking requirements. Light-colored pavement may reduce the visibility of the marking, in which case, the FAA requires the use of black borders on concrete or light-colored pavements. Glass beads are also normally required to be applied with airport markings to enhance the visibility of the markings, particularly at night.

AIR TRAFFIC CONTROL AND AIR OPERATIONS

The maintenance and safety standards required by Title 14 CFR Part 139, described in "Airport Maintenance Standards" above, are essential to supporting flight safety and operations. Air traffic control is highly integrated into this complex system of regulations and procedures, and its ability to enable air operations is highly dependent on Airport Maintenance and related safety protocols.

As noted in "Airport Maintenance Standards" above, marking requirements for a runway are predicated on the types of approach and landing procedures for which the runway is certificated. The FAA defines a variety of approach procedures and classifications. General characteristics of the more common types of approaches defined by the FAA are:

1. A runway that does not support aircraft in minimal meteorological conditions is restricted to visual approaches and must report meteorological conditions of (a) a ceiling of at least 1,000 feet (cloud base height, above the airport surface area or reporting station) *and* (b) at least 3 miles of horizontal flight or ground visibility.[22] These meteorological conditions are classified

---

[22]For private pilots, these requirements can be reduced to 1 mile flight and ground visibility (during day operations only) and clear of clouds in uncontrolled airspace. Required meteorological flight restrictions, operational requirements, and pilot certifications are much more complex than what is discussed in this section. For a summary of these requirements, see: http://flighttraining.aopa.org/students/solo/topics/SA02_Airspace_for_Everyone.pdf

as **Visual Meteorological Conditions (VMC)**. In a visual approach, the pilot can see well enough to maintain visual contact of the runway and the plane. FAA-certified private, recreational, or sport pilots are restricted to visual approaches. If a pilot desires to use navigational aids to fly in weather that is less than VMC, known as Instrument Meteorological Conditions (IMC), the pilot must earn an Instrument Rating from the FAA. An Instrument Rating allows a pilot[23] to fly a nonprecision or Category I or II precision instrument approach (explained below).

2. During a **nonprecision approach**, the pilot uses a navigational aid that provides lateral positioning information to the pilot. In this case, the pilot uses the navigational aid to get into the proximity of the airport and descends to a published minimum descent altitude (commonly referred to as "MDA"). The pilot continues to fly at that altitude while looking for the runway environment. If the pilot cannot see the runway environment after a predetermined period of time or by a certain point over the ground, the pilot must execute a missed approach.[24] In a missed approach, a pilot climbs to a higher altitude while turning the aircraft away from the airport. The pilot then contacts air traffic control for vectors back to the initial approach fix to attempt another landing or the pilot proceeds to an alternative destination.

3. During a **precision approach**, the pilot uses a navigational aid, typically an **ILS**, which provides both lateral and vertical positioning information. There are three types of ILS approaches, each with different decision heights,[25] commonly referred to as "DH," and visibility requirements. These approaches are labeled precision approach Category I, precision approach Category II, and precision approach Category III. A "Cat III" precision instrument approach is also referred to as auto-land. While any pilot with an Instrument Rating can conduct a Cat I or Cat II instrument approach (provided the airport has the proper equipment), only certain pilots with special training and approval can fly Cat III approaches. For a Cat III approach, the aircraft must also be equipped with special technology (that essentially allows the plane to fly itself), and the airport must be equipped with a Cat III ILS system.

4. A **contact approach** is part of an established instrument approach and is issued where the pilot has at least 1 mile visibility, is clear of clouds, and is cleared by air traffic control (ATC) to use visual references to land. A contact approach is requested by the pilot, and is not issued by ATC.

Operations personnel can use the following generalized characterizations to reference various types of common approaches: **Visual approaches** are used when VMC exist. An instrument approach is either precision or nonprecision. **Precision instrument approaches** use horizontal and vertical guidance and routes established by the FAA. **Nonprecision approaches** use horizontal guidance only. A third type of approach is the **contact approach**, which is the result of an instrument approach, where the pilot has at least 1 mile visibility and is cleared by ATC to use visual references to land.

---

[23]Recreational and sport pilots are not allowed to fly in IMC or seek an FAA Instrument Rating.

[24]At a designated missed approach point, the pilot must determine that the pilot has the runway environment in sight and can proceed from that point to safely land the aircraft, or the pilot must abandon the approach and declare a missed approach. Depending on circumstances, the pilot may return to attempt the approach again or fly to an alternative airport.

[25]DH is the "missed approach" point on an ILS approach, which is a height in altitude at which a pilot must have the runway environment in visual sight, or execute a go-around, or declare a missed approach.

The type of runway approach (visual, nonprecision, or precision) determines the runway marking scheme, with visual runways having the least amount of markings and Cat III instrument approach runways having the most.

TYPES OF RUNWAY MARKINGS
RUNWAY LANDING DESIGNATOR MARKING

Runways are identified by a number, such as 35, 9, or 17. These numbers refer to the end of the runway being used for takeoffs, landings, or other operations. The numbering refers to directions as aligned to the magnetic compass (as opposed to longitudinal true north). This numbering system corresponds to the magnetic compass in aircraft, which is the minimal requirement for directional guidance in most U.S. aircraft. For a single-digit runway, the number is not preceded by a zero. The zero is also dropped from two-digit markings; for example, for a runway that is pointed 360 degrees magnetic north to 180 degrees magnetic south, the zeros would be eliminated and only 36 would be painted on the approach end of the runway with flight operations heading north, and 18 would be painted on the approach end of the runway with flight operations heading south. A runway that is aligned east to west (90 degrees and 270 degrees) would be marked as 9 for operations heading east and 27 for operations heading west. In the case of parallel runways, each runway is identified by a number and a letter, e.g., 35R or 35L, to distinguish between runways 35 Right and 35 Left. Runway numbers are painted white.

RUNWAY CENTERLINE MARKING

The runway centerline marking is a dashed white line that identifies the physical center of the runway width and provides alignment to pilots during takeoff and landing (FAA, 2013b).

RUNWAY THRESHOLD MARKING

The runway threshold marking is a white line perpendicular to the direction of the runway that identifies the beginning point of the runway, that is, the beginning of usable pavement. However, any pilot attempting to land exactly on the runway threshold marking would not provide themselves the proper margin of safety in the case of an undershoot. The number of runway threshold stripes do relate to standard widths of a runway (Figure 7.20).

RUNWAY AIMING POINT MARKING

The aiming point marking is a visual reference used to help pilots judge the point of touchdown. Aiming point markings feature two white rectangular markings, placed 1,000 feet from the runway threshold.

Standard runway widths	Number of symmetrical stripes
60 feet (18.3 m)	4
75 feet (22.9 m)	6
100 feet (30.5 m)	8
150 feet (45.7 m)	12
200 feet (61 m)	16

FIGURE 7.20

Runway widths and required number of threshold symmetrical stripes.

Source: FAA. (2010). AC 150/5340-1K, Standards for Airport Markings. Washington, DC: U.S. Department of Transportation, Federal Aviation Administration.

RUNWAY TOUCHDOWN ZONE MARKING

The touchdown zone marking identifies the touchdown zone in 500-foot increments on a precision instrument approach runway, except at the 1,000 foot mark where it is superimposed by the aiming point. Touchdown zone markings help the pilot judge the distance traveled beyond the runway threshold. The marking begins 500 feet from the runway threshold, is white in color, and has two sets of three parallel stripes on either side of the runway centerline. At the 1,500-foot and 2,000-foot marks, there are two sets of two stripes per side, and at the 2,500-foot and 3,000-foot marks, there is one stripe per side. On short runways, touchdown zones are marked on both ends. Any marking within 900 feet of the midpoint of the runway is not painted; thus, in some cases, a precision instrument runway may not have all of the touchdown zone markings.

RUNWAY EDGE MARKING

Runway edge markings provide enhanced visual contrast between the runway edge and the surrounding terrain, runway shoulder, or islands between runways, taxiways, and other movement areas. Runway edge markings are white in color and required for runways supporting precision instrument approach procedures. In some cases, runway shoulder markings may be used to supplement runway side stripes and identify areas not to be used by aircraft, except in an emergency. Runway shoulder markings are yellow and are diagonal to the runway heading (Figure 7.21).

RUNWAY DISPLACED THRESHOLD MARKING

In some cases, the runway threshold might not be at the beginning of the paved surface. Runway thresholds are displaced for a variety of reasons, including obstruction clearance for aircraft on approach, as part of a noise abatement mitigation measure to raise the approach path for landing aircraft, or for temporary reasons, such as airfield construction or maintenance. Displaced threshold markings (Figure 7.22) are white arrows leading up to the runway threshold marking, with a series of white arrowheads just prior to the runway threshold marking. Displaced thresholds shorten the

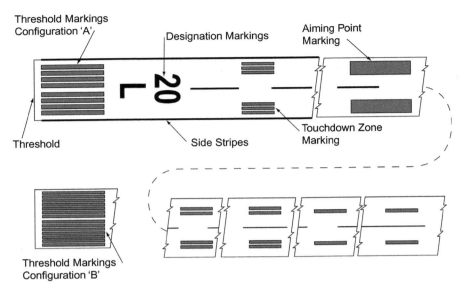

FIGURE 7.21

Precision instrument runway markings.

Source: http://tfmlearning.faa.gov/Publications/atpubs/AIM/Chap2/aim0203.html.

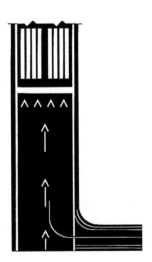

FIGURE 7.22

Displaced threshold marking.

Source: http://tfmlearning.faa.gov/Publications/atpubs/AIM/Chap2/aim0203.html.

distance available for landing, but they can provide a longer takeoff distance than the published runway length. Displaced thresholds can be used for takeoff or as a rollout area when landing from the opposite end.

RUNWAY DEMARCATION BAR MARKING

The runway demarcation bar marking is yellow and delineates the beginning of the displaced threshold, separating the displaced threshold from a blast pad, stopway, or taxiway. In some cases, a taxiway may precede a displaced threshold. In this case, the taxiway markings are yellow up until the demarcation bar, with yellow arrowheads just prior to the demarcation bar.

CHEVRON MARKINGS FOR BLAST PADS, STOPWAYS, AND ENGINEERED MATERIAL ARRESTING SYSTEMS

Yellow chevrons are used to show pavement areas aligned with the runway that are unusable for landing, takeoff, or taxiing.

RUNWAY SHOULDER MARKING

Runway shoulder markings (Figure 7.23) are yellow and are optional, but are used to further delineate a paved runway that pilots may mistake for usable runway. It is used only in conjunction with the white runway edge marking. The stripes start at the runway midpoint and are slanted at an angle of 45 degrees to the runway centerline.

TYPES OF TAXIWAY MARKINGS

All taxiways should have a centerline marking and a runway holding position (hold-short position[26]) marking whenever a taxiway intersects a runway. Taxiways that intersect the runway must also have a surface-painted runway, holding-position sign and enhanced taxiway centerline markings. Because inadvertently entering the runway during flight operations could result in catastrophe, the airport operator must be sure to include all appropriate visual aids that reduce the chance of an inadvertent runway incursion.

HOLDING POSITION MARKINGS

Holding position markings are among the most important markings on the airfield, as they protect either the runway or a critical area for a precision ILS. Holding position markings, often referred to as runway boundary markings or "the hold/short" bar, are a pair of large, solid, parallel, yellow lines,[27] adjacent to a pair of large, dashed, yellow lines. The solid lines are always on the side

---

[26]Hold-short runway marking positions require ATC clearance at controlled airports for taxi or vehicle movement beyond and on to an active runway.
[27]All taxiway markings are yellow.

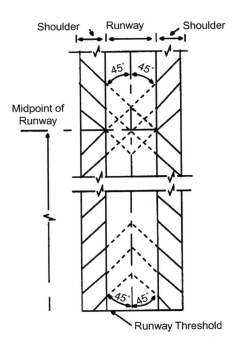

FIGURE 7.23

Runway shoulder markings.

Source: http://tfmlearning.faa.gov/Publications/atpubs/AIM/Chap2/aim0203.html.

furthest from the runway. A pilot or vehicle operator cannot cross the solid lines without the permission of ATC. However, if a pilot or vehicle operator approaches from the dashed lines, they are to proceed across the marking, then immediately stop and contact ATC for further directions (or proceed to follow previously issued ATC instructions). The specific locations of the runway boundary markings vary depending on several factors, such as whether there is a crosswind runway, intersecting runway, ILS critical area, or location of taxiways. As a rule-of-thumb, Airport Operations personnel hold that runway boundary marking is typically colocated with the outer boundary of the RSA. In certain cases, a runway boundary marking may be located on a runway. This condition is common as a **Land-and-Hold-Short Operation (LAHSO)**, in which case a landing aircraft comes to a complete stop (holds short) before the marked LAHSO on the active runway to allow traffic on an intersecting runway to conduct operations. A holding position marking for an ILS critical area is yellow, ladder-shaped, and painted perpendicular to the direction of travel. It is usually colocated with an airfield ILS critical area sign and is established to reduce the chance of interference with radio signal transmissions of the ILS system (Figure 7.24).

TAXIWAY CENTERLINE MARKING

The taxiway centerline (Figure 7.25) provides continual visual guidance to pilots, which ideally will place the aircraft's nose gear slightly to the left or right of the centerline for enhanced slow

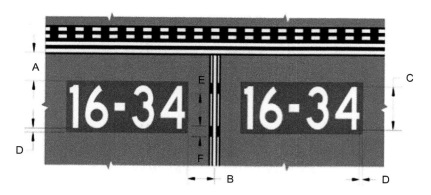

FIGURE 7.24

Runway widths and holding position marking.

Source: FAA. (2010). AC 150/5340-1K, Standards for Airport Markings. Washington, DC: U.S. Department of Transportation, Federal Aviation Administration.

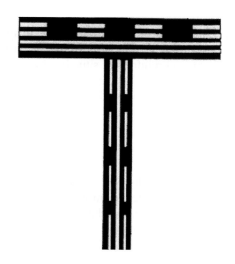

FIGURE 7.25

Taxiway centerline marking.

Source: http://tfmlearning.faa.gov/Publications/atpubs/AIM/Chap2/aim0203.html.

speed taxi visual reference.[28] For taxiways that intersect a runway, the taxiway centerline is stopped either at the runway edge or the outer edge of the runway edge marking. Taxiway centerline (lead-on and lead-off) lines continue onto the runway in certain situations, such as displaced thresholds, low-visibility taxi operations (associated with the SMCGS plan), or for taxiways that intersect the runway at other locations other than the end of the runway. In no case will taxiway centerline

---

[28]Some pilots will taxi slightly right or left of centerline for better visibility.

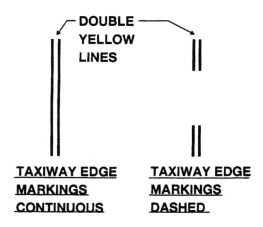

FIGURE 7.26

Taxiway edge marking.

Source: http://tfmlearning.faa.gov/Publications/atpubs/AIM/Chap2/aim0203.html.

markings be painted over the runway markings. **Enhanced taxiway centerline** markings provide additional visual cues to alert pilots of an upcoming runway boundary marking, ideally minimizing the potential for a runway incursion and reinforcing situational awareness prior to entering the runway (FAA, 2013b). Enhanced taxiway centerline markings consist of two parallel lines of yellow dashes on either side of a standard taxiway centerline. Additional standards apply when taxiway centerlines are either converging, intersecting, or serving two runway holding position markings.[29]

TAXIWAY EDGE MARKING

Taxiway edge markings (Figure 7.26) are double, parallel, continuous, yellow markings, located along a taxi route to alert pilots where the demarcation line exists between the taxiway and unusable adjacent pavement or areas. In certain cases, when the edge of a taxiway borders usable pavement, such as a ramp area, the taxiway edge marking is a double, dashed, yellow marking.

SURFACE-PAINTED HOLDING-POSITION SIGNS (MARKING)

The surface-painted holding-position sign provides additional visual cues that alert pilots and vehicle operators of the location of an upcoming holding position. The location is determined by the width of the taxiway entrance and the number of taxiway centerlines intersecting the same holding position marking (FAA, 2013b).[30]

---

[29]See AC 150/5340-IL for more details.

[30]It is critically important to note that there are numerous requirements for the variety of configurations and circumstances within each of these markings. Airport operators should always verify the specific requirements for their airfield configuration by consulting the proper advisory circulars.

SURFACE-PAINTED TAXIWAY DIRECTION SIGNS (MARKING)

Surface-painted taxiway direction signs (Figure 7.27) are the same color configuration as taxiway directional signs (black lettering against a yellow background with an arrow) and are used to provide additional directional guidance at taxiway intersections. This marking is required where it is not possible to use a taxiway direction sign, but can also be used in conjunction with a taxiway direction sign to assist pilots and vehicle operators with improved ground navigation.

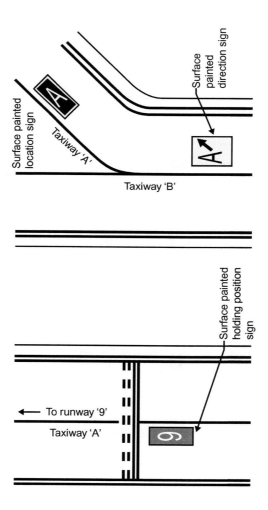

FIGURE 7.27

Surface-painted direction sign.

Source: http://tfmlearning.faa.gov/Publications/atpubs/AIM/Chap2/aim0203.html.

SURFACE-PAINTED TAXIWAY LOCATION SIGNS (MARKING)

Surface-painted taxiway location signs (Figure 7.28) are identical to and supplement taxiway location signs (yellow lettering on a black background). They are required when deemed necessary by the FAA or where they may assist pilots and vehicle operators with enhanced ground navigation.

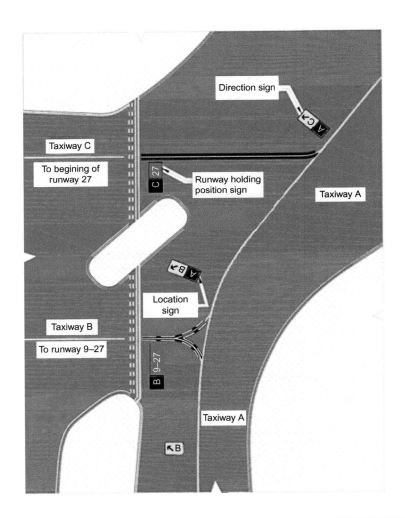

FIGURE 7.28

Surface-painted signs.

Source: FAA. (2010). AC 150/5340-1K, Standards for Airport Markings. Washington, DC: U.S. Department of Transportation, Federal Aviation Administration.

SURFACE-PAINTED GATE-DESTINATION SIGNS (MARKING)

Surface-painted destination signs (Figure 7.29) have a solid yellow background with a black inscription and are used to assist pilots in locating their assigned terminal gate, especially during low-visibility operations.

SURFACE-PAINTED APRON-ENTRANCE POINT SIGNS (MARKING)

The surface-painted apron-entrance point sign (Figure 7.30) is a bright entrance point sign (yellow background with black lettering) and assists pilots in other vehicles in locating their position along the edges of large, continuous aprons serving the terminal gates (FAA, 2013b). These designations are sometimes referred to as the beginning of the "ramp spot."[31]

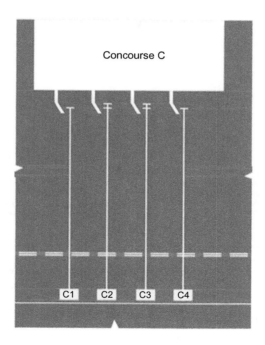

FIGURE 7.29

Surface-painted gate-destination sign.

Source: FAA. (2010). AC 150/5340-1K, Standards for Airport Markings. Washington, DC: U.S. Department of Transportation, Federal Aviation Administration.

---

[31]Aircraft parking area.

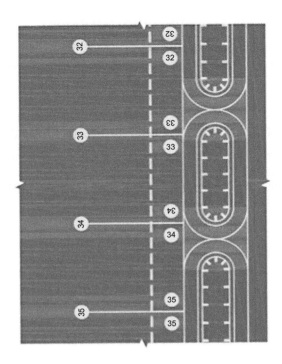

Note:
Centerline at apron entrance point locations may be marked with a radius marking rather than with a "T" configuration as shown.

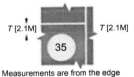

Measurements are from the edge of centerline to edge of sign

FIGURE 7.30

Surface-painted apron-entrance point sign.

Source: FAA. (2010). AC 150/5340-1K, Standards for Airport Markings. Washington, DC: U.S. Department of Transportation, Federal Aviation Administration.

TAXIWAY SHOULDER MARKINGS

Taxiway shoulder markings (Figure 7.31) are painted using perpendicular lines drawn from the taxiway edge lines (with the centerline as a reference). Taxiway shoulders are occasionally paved to prevent ground erosion attributed to aircraft exhaust or water runoff; however, pilots may confuse this pavement with usable taxiway, which is why it is delineated with shoulder markings.

GEOGRAPHIC POSITION MARKING

The geographic position marking (GPM) (Figure 7.32) is a pink circle with black lettering, sometimes referred to as the "pink spot." It is used during low-visibility operations for pilots to confirm with ATC that they are holding at a designated GPM location in the movement area.

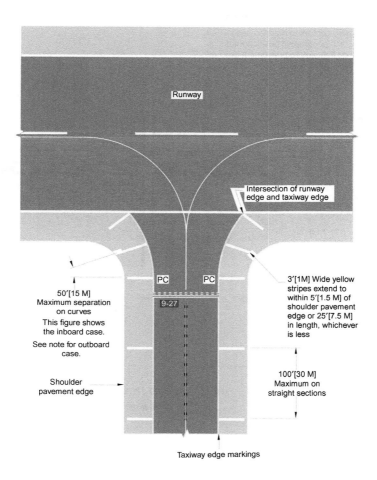

FIGURE 7.31

Taxiway shoulder markings.

Source: FAA. (2010). AC 150/5340-1K, Standards for Airport Markings. Washington, DC: U.S. Department of Transportation, Federal Aviation Administration.

RAMP CONTROL MARKINGS

Ramp control markings have black lettering on a yellow background and are used by the ramp control tower, or FAA ATCT, to assist in the movement of vehicles between the paved areas, the non-movement areas, and the movement areas. From a regulatory perspective, they are an optional marking, but from an operational perspective, at large airports, ramp control markings are essential for the smooth flow of aircraft parking and pushback operations.

NON-MOVEMENT AREA BOUNDARY MARKINGS

The non-movement area boundary marking (Figure 7.33) is yellow in color and consists of two parallel yellow lines, one solid and one dashed. The solid line is located on the non-movement side,

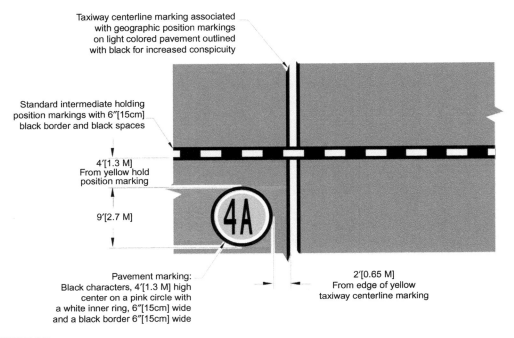

Taxiway centerline marking associated with geographic position markings on light colored pavement outlined with black for increased conspicuity

Standard intermediate holding position markings with 6"[15cm] black border and black spaces

4'[1.3 M] From yellow hold position marking

9'[2.7 M]

Pavement marking: Black characters, 4'[1.3 M] high center on a pink circle with a white inner ring, 6"[15cm] wide and a black border 6"[15cm] wide

4A

2'[0.65 M] From edge of yellow taxiway centerline marking

FIGURE 7.32

Geographic position markings.

Source: FAA. (2010). AC 150/5340-1K, Standards for Airport Markings. Washington, DC: U.S. Department of Transportation, Federal Aviation Administration.

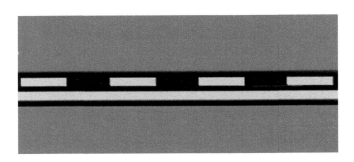

FIGURE 7.33

Non-movement area boundary markings.

Source: FAA. (2010). AC 150/5340-1K, Standards for Airport Markings. Washington, DC: U.S. Department of Transportation, Federal Aviation Administration.

and the dashed line is located on the movement area side. The marking is used to delineate the movement areas under control by the ATCT, or for airports without a tower, to help delineate aircraft traffic routes and parking limitations, and also areas where vehicle operators must exercise additional caution.

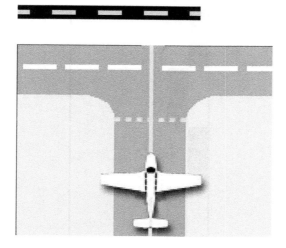

FIGURE 7.34

Intermediate holding position marking.

Source: FAA. (2010). AC 150/5340-1K, Standards for Airport Markings. Washington, DC: U.S.
Department of Transportation, Federal Aviation Administration.

INTERMEDIATE HOLDING POSITION MARKING FOR TAXIWAY/TAXIWAY INTERSECTIONS

An intermediate holding position marking (Figure 7.34) for taxiways is a single yellow dashed line, extending the width of the taxiway. It is commonly used at airports with congested intersections and, in some cases, to delineate a holding pad for aircraft deicing.

OTHER SURFACE MARKINGS

A variety of other markings are used on airfields, including (a) vehicle roadways or VSRs, (b) very-high-frequency omnidirectional range (VOR) receiver checkpoints, (c) temporarily closed runways and taxiways, (d) arresting gear,[32] (e) hazardous construction areas, (f) aircraft deicing facilities, and (g) helipads.

VEHICLE SERVICE ROAD MARKINGS

VSR markings on airfields are similar to markings on surface streets. Markings are white and consist of side stripes with a white, dashed centerline. Markings used for aircraft traffic, including

---

[32]"Aircraft arresting systems serve primarily to save lives by preventing aircraft from overrunning runways in cases where the pilot is unable to stop the aircraft during landing or aborted takeoff operations. They also serve to save aircraft and prevent major damage." See AC No 150/5220-9A at http://www.skybrary.aero/bookshelf/books/2978.pdf

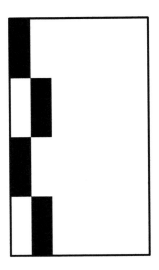

FIGURE 7.35

Roadway edge stripes, white, zipper style.

Source: http://tfmlearning.faa.gov/Publications/atpubs/AIM/Chap2/aim0203.html.

runway boundary markings, direction sign/markings, and the like, should never be used in areas exclusively designated for surface vehicle traffic. To the extent possible, the U.S. Department of Transportation's *Manual on Uniform Traffic Control Devices*[33] should be used for guidance in vehicle markings on the airfield. This is not to say that vehicle operators do not adhere to airfield markings, such as the runway boundary marking, but only that aircraft markings should not be used only on airport service roads as it is confusing to pilots and increases operational risk. Vehicle roadway markings side stripes are either solid white lines, or zippered lines, with a dashed line in the middle. Zippered lines are occasionally used for the side strips, when the airport operator determines the roadway edge needs enhanced delineation, such as during low-visibility operations (Figure 7.35). Some airport operators have bordered their road markings with red lines, to increase visibility. Any roadway that crosses a taxi route must have a solid stop line (bar) (FAA, 2013b).

VERY-HIGH-FREQUENCY OMNIDIRECTIONAL RANGE RECEIVER CHECKPOINT MARKING

VOR receiver checkpoints are designated surface areas that pilots use to determine required accuracies of onboard VOR navigational receivers. The surface checkpoint areas are marked with a yellow arrow aligned toward the appropriate VOR facility. The interior of the circle is painted black, and the outside may be bordered with a black band (Figure 7.36).

---

[33]See http://mutcd.fhwa.dot.gov/

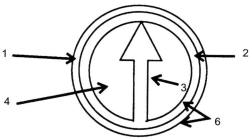

1. WHITE
2. YELLOW
3. YELLOW ARROW ALIGNED TOWARD THE FACILITY
4. INTERIOR OF CIRCLE BLACK (CONCRETE SURFACE ONLY)
5. CIRCLE MAY BE BORDERED ON INSIDE AND OUTSIDE WITH
6. BLACK BAND IF NECESSARY FOR CONTRAST

FIGURE 7.36

Ground receiver checkpoint marking.

Source: http://tfmlearning.faa.gov/Publications/atpubs/AIM/Chap2/aim0203.html.

MARKING AND LIGHTING OF PERMANENTLY CLOSED RUNWAYS AND TAXIWAYS

Permanently closed runways and taxiways are indicated by a solid yellow "X" painted at both ends of the runway (Figure 7.37).

TEMPORARILY CLOSED RUNWAYS AND TAXIWAYS

There are two options for a temporarily closed runway: the installation of a raised lighted "X" on each end of the runway or the use of removable material, such as plywood, snow fencing, or other fabric to create a yellow "X" on either end of the runway. Materials used should be anchored to the ground so as not to create a FOD hazard or be susceptible to movement by the wind.

RUNWAY AND TAXIWAY LIGHTING

There are numerous configurations for runway lighting, but overall, runway edge lights and runway centerline lights on visual approach runways are white; taxiway edge lights are blue; and taxiway centerline lights are green. Lead-in/lead-off centerline lighting, which features alternating yellow and green lights, is an exception. The lighting configuration for a precision instrument approach runway is white edge and centerline lights for the majority of the runway. At the 2,000-feet-of-runway-remaining point, the edge lights change to yellow for the remainder of the runway. At 3,000 feet of runway remaining, the centerline lights switch from white to alternating red and white, for a distance of 2,000 feet, at which point the lights switch to all red for the last 1,000 feet. Runway and taxiway edge light fixtures can be between 14 inches and 30 inches in height. Taller fixtures are used at airports that receive significant amounts of snowfall (Figure 7.38).

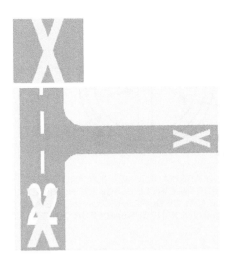

FIGURE 7.37

Closed runway marking.

Source: https://www.faa.gov/mobile/index.cfm?event = Runway.card&cardNum = 13.

FIGURE 7.38

Runway lighting in Atlanta.

Source: https://commons.wikimedia.org/wiki/File:ATL_TWY_B_-_RWY_Crossing_(13534655025).jpg#file.

Under AC 150/5340-30, *Design and Installation Details for Airport Visual Aids*, the FAA addresses five categories of lighting: (a) runway and taxiway edge lights, (b) runway centerline and touchdown zone lights, (c) taxiway lighting systems, (d) land and hold-short lighting systems, and (e) airfield miscellaneous aid (such as the airport beacon). AC 150/5340-30 also addresses fixtures and mounting, general equipment and material, power distributions and control systems for airfield lighting, and variations in placing airfield lighting onto airport pavement either rigid or flexible.

Airfield lighting uses one of four types of lamps: incandescent, tungsten-halogen, fluorescent, or light emitting diode (LED). LED lights produce brighter light, have longer lamp life, and consume less energy, but do not emit significant amounts of heat. The disadvantage is that LED lights do not generate enough heat to melt snow or ice that accumulates on the land. Therefore, LED lights that are used in climates characterized by snow may require supplemental heater coils, thereby reducing the energy savings associated with LEDs.

RUNWAY CENTERLINE LIGHTING

Runway centerline lighting is required for runways with a CAT II or CAT III ILS approach and for CAT I runways when visibility is below 2,400 feet RVR. Centerline lights are installed in the pavement and are sometimes bidirectional based on the type of approach for each direction of the runway. They are located at 50-foot intervals along the runway centerline marking. **Touchdown Zone Lights** enhance the location of the touchdown zone markings and consist of two rows of transverse light bars on either side of the runway centerline.

RUNWAY EDGE LIGHTING SYSTEMS

Runway Edge Lighting Systems define the edge of the runway and are low, medium, or high intensity. Runway edge lights are spaced from 2 to 10 feet from the edge of the full strength pavement and are spaced no greater than 200 feet apart.[34]

Taxiway Edge Lighting Systems define the edge of the taxiway and are of medium intensity. The intensity of runway lighting is dependent upon the type of approach for which the runway is certificated. **Low-intensity** runway lights are used on Visual Flight Rule (VFR) runways. **Medium-intensity** runway lighting is used on airports with visual runways or nonprecision instrument runways. **High-intensity** runway lighting is used on runways with precision ILSs. Medium-intensity taxiway lighting is used on taxiways and aprons where runway lighting systems have been installed (FAA, 2012).

THRESHOLD OR RUNWAY END LIGHTS

Threshold or Runway End Lights (Figure 7.39) emit a green light outward from the approach end of the runway to mark the beginning of usable pavement, and emit a red light toward the runway to mark the end of the runway surface. Runways with displaced thresholds, runways with taxiways at the end, and runways with a blast pad have slightly different lighting configurations.

---

[34]Certain exceptions are allowed for various situations, such as in the case of intersecting runways.

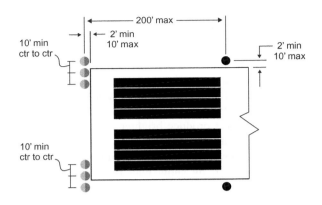

FIGURE 7.39

Visual runway end/threshold light.

Source: FAA, 2011.

TAXIWAY EDGE LIGHTS

Taxiway Edge Lights are blue in color. In some cases, blue edge reflectors can be used instead of lights. Airports may also be able to install a combination of edge lights and reflectors (in between the lights) to enhance taxiway lighting systems installed on short taxiway sections, curves, and intersections (FAA, 2012). Reflectors are also permitted in lieu of edge lights where a centerline light system is installed (FAA, 2012). Taxiway centerline lights are green and, like the yellow taxiway centerline marking, provide guidance between the runway and ramp areas.

Land and hold-short lights are used to indicate the holding position on certain runways that are approved for LAHSO. Plan and hold-short lights are a row of pulsing white lights installed across the runway, in the pavement at the runway boundary marking.

SURFACE MOVEMENT GUIDANCE AND CONTROL SYSTEM LIGHTING

To reduce the likelihood of runway incursions, many airports install additional lighting aids, such as **Runway Guard Lights (RGLs)**, **Stop Bars**, and **Clearance Bars**. Additionally, these aids are components of the Surface Movement Guidance and Control System (SMGCS), which is used at some airports that experience a significant number of days of low visibility.

RGLs are commonly called "wigwags." RGLs can be elevated on a sign or placed in-pavement and provide a visual indication to pilots and vehicle operators that they are approaching a runway. Elevated RGLs consist of a pair of yellow lights, mounted side-by-side, and alternately flashing left and right. In-pavement RGLs consist of a row of unidirectional lights. Stop bar lighting is a row of red in-pavement lights, or elevated red lights on each side of the taxiway, that provide a visual reference to a pilot or vehicle operator that they are approaching a runway. Clearance Bars consist of a row of three in-pavement lights and indicate a low-visibility hold point.

APPROACH LIGHT SYSTEMS

ALS provide pilots with the means to transition from instrument flight to visual flight in preparation for landing. ALS are a configuration of signal lights starting at the landing threshold and extending into the approach area for a distance of 2,400 feet to 3,000 feet for precision instrument runways and 1,400 feet to 1,500 feet for nonprecision instrument runways. The approach light system is typically controlled and maintained by the FAA, not the airport operator. There are also **economy approach aids**, which are relatively low-cost visual aids for airports that provide landing guidance to pilots. It is helpful for airport operators to understand the basic nomenclature of the more common ALSs:[35]

1. **Medium-Intensity Approach Lighting System (MALS).** MALS is an economy type system for nonprecision approaches.
2. **Medium-Intensity Approach Lighting System with Sequenced Flashers (MALSF).** MALSF are equipped with three sequenced flashers at locations where it is difficult to identify the approach area.
3. **Medium-Intensity Approach Lighting System with Runway Alignment Indicator Lights (MALSR).** MALSR is an economy type system used as the FAA standard for Category I precision runways.
4. **Simplified Short Approach Lighting System with Runway Alignment Indicator Lights (SSALR).** SSALR is another economical (but older) approach light system used when Category I conditions exist on Category II designated runways with a dual mode ALS (ALSF-2/SSALR).
5. **Omnidirectional Approach Lighting System (ODALS).** ODALS is a configuration of seven omnidirectional sequenced flashing lights located in the runway approach area. The ODALS provides circling, offset, and straight-in visual guidance for nonprecision approach runways.
6. **Runway End Identifier Lights (REILs).** REILs identify the end of a runway. REILs are two synchronized flashing lights, unidirectional or omnidirectional, on each side of the runway landing threshold. The unidirectional flashing lights face the approach area. The strobe effect of the lights makes the REILs effective for runway identification where other lighting surrounds the airport or runway area, or the runway lacks contrast with surrounding terrain.
7. **Lead-In Lighting System (LDIN).** LDIN provides visual guidance along a curved or straight approach path where problems exist with hazardous terrain, obstructions, or noise abatement procedures. An LDIN is one or more series of flashing lights installed along the approach path at or near ground level.
8. **Visual Approach Slope Indicators (VASIs).** VASI (Figure 7.40) is a system of lights adjacent to the runway, arranged to provide visual descent guidance information to the pilot during the approach to the runway. The lights are visible from 3 to 5 miles during the day and up to 20 miles or more at night and provide safe obstruction clearance of plus or minus 10 degrees of the extended runway centerline and out to 4 nautical miles from the runway threshold. The basic principle of the VASI is a color differentiation between red and white.

---

[35]A variety of approach light systems at airports are beyond the scope of this book, but more information may be found in FAA Order JO 6850.2B Visual Guidance Lighting Systems.

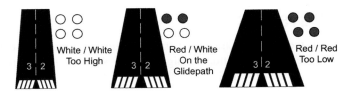

FIGURE 7.40

VASI lights.

Source: http://tfmlearning.faa.gov/Publications/atpubs/AIM/Chap2/aim0201.html.

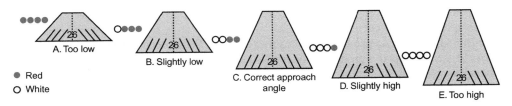

FIGURE 7.41

PAPI.

Source: FAA. (2014). AC 150/5340-26C, Maintenance of Airport Visual Aid Facilities Washington, DC: U.S. Department of Transportation, Federal Aviation Administration.

Each light unit projects a beam of light having a white segment in the upper part of the beam and red segment in the lower part of the beam. A pilot seeing white over white is above the desired glide slope; a pilot seeing white over red is on the proper glide slope; and a pilot seeing red over red is below the safe glideslope path.

9. **Precision Approach Path Indicator (PAPI).** PAPIs (Figure 7.41) are slowly replacing the older VASI technology. PAPIs provides visual approach slope information and are visible from 5 miles out during the day and up to 20 miles at night. The visual glide path of the PAPI typically provides safe obstruction clearance plus or minus 10 degrees of the extended runway centerline and to 4 statute miles from the runway threshold. The PAPI is a single horizontal bar with four lights and operates on the same theory as the VASI (except the visual display is lateral, not staggered). A pilot who is too high on the glide slope will see a row of four white lights. Descending slightly the light configuration changes to three white and one red, which indicates to the pilot that the aircraft is slightly above the desired glide path to the runway. If the pilot sees two white lights next to two red lights, that is the indication that the aircraft is on the proper glide path. An indication of three red lights and one white light indicates that the aircraft is slightly below the safe glide path, and an indication of four red lights indicates the aircraft is lower than the safe glide path.

10. **Pulsating Visual Approach Slope Indicators (PVASIs).** PVASI normally consists of a single light unit projecting a two-color visual approach path into the final approach area of the runway on which the indicator is installed. PVASI is installed at some heliports.

11. **High Intensity Approach Light Sequenced Flasher-2 (ALSF-2).** ALSF-2 is used for Category II and Category III runways. The ALSF-2 consists of a bar of white lights with five equally spaced lights, which start 100 feet from the runway threshold and continue out at 500-foot intervals to 2,400 feet from the threshold. **Light bars** are installed perpendicular to the extended runway centerline and aimed away from the runway threshold. The **centerline light bar**, located 1,000 feet from the threshold, is supplemented with eight additional white lights on either side forming a light bar of 100 feet, containing 21 lights. This bar is the 1,000-foot distance marker, known as the **crossbar**, with another crossbar 500 feet from the threshold. **Side row bars** are light bars with three red filtered lights each, on either side of the centerline bars within the inner 900 feet of the approach light system. The **threshold bar** is the row of green filtered lights on 5-foot centers located within 10 feet of the runway threshold and extending across the runway threshold and outward a distance of approximately 45 feet from the runway edge on either side of the runway. All lights are aimed into the approach to the runway and slightly away from the runway threshold, to avoid blinding the pilot on final approach.

- **Sequenced Flashers for ALSF-2:** When sequenced flashers are installed within the approach light system, the centerline white light is changed from steady-burning to a bluish-white strobe light. The lights flash in sequence toward the runway threshold at a rate of twice per second and appear as a ball of light traveling toward the runway threshold. The sequenced flashers are installed 1,000 feet from the threshold and extend out to the end of the system approach light system. **Runway Alignment Indicator Lights (RAILs)**, are a series of five lights that extend past the 1,000-foot mark of the approach lights.

ADDITIONAL AIRPORT LIGHTS

The **airport rotating beacon** provides pilots the location of the airport at night and during periods of low visibility. Rotating beacons are similar to a lighthouse used in the maritime community and project a beam of light in two directions, 180 degrees apart. The light pattern distinguishes the airport type. For civilian land airports, the beacon alternates between white and green. The beacon is operated from dusk till dawn and sometimes during the day. When the visibility is less than 3 statute miles, or the cloud ceiling is less than 1,000 feet (indicating less than VMC), the beacon may also be activated; however, airports are not required to do so. Military airport beacons flash white twice rapidly, then one green. Heliports, water airports, and hospital and emergency services heliports have different patterns and colors.

Wind cones provide the wind direction and, to some extent, wind velocity near the surface of the airport. At airports with a control tower, wind information may be delivered from the ATCT or from an FBO using a CTAF or Unicom frequency. When none of these services are available, then a wind cone (or "wind sock"), tetrahedron, or wind tee may be used. A tetrahedron only provides wind direction, not speed. Wind tees and tetrahedrons swing freely and align themselves with the wind direction, but they may also be manually set to align with runways that have a fixed landing/takeoff direction. A primary wind cone is needed at any airport without a 24-hour ATCT. The use of a wind cone is required for Part 139 airports, regardless of whether the ATCT is full-time or

FIGURE 7.42

Wind sock.

Source: https://commons.wikimedia.org/wiki/File:Anemoscopi.JPG.

part-time, and if the air carrier operations are conducted at night, the wind cone must be lighted. Supplemental wind cones may also be needed at the runway ends, if visibility to the primary wind sock (Figure 7.42) is blocked on approach ends of runways or if the airport typically has greatly varying surface wind patterns.[36]

Obstruction lights are used to identify obstructions in and around the airport that represent a hazard to aircraft operations. FAA AC 70/7460-1, *Obstruction Lighting and Marking*, contains guidance on the type of obstruction lights to be used, as well as the placement and number of lights required to properly light the obstruction.

---

[36]Wind socks can be found at the midpoint of runways and/or at the ends of runways at locations where topography creates varying surface turbulence or wind shear. At uncontrolled airports, this added configuration aids the pilot in determining the best runway to use for takeoffs and landings.

SURFACE MOVEMENT GUIDANCE AND CONTROL SYSTEMS

Airports prone to frequent, low-visibility conditions may install an SMCGS to enhance visibility and improve safety for taxiing aircraft. An SMGCS includes a series of in-pavement and elevated lights, as well as airfield markings and signs. SMGCS lighting systems are controlled by the ATCT. Air traffic controllers can turn on and off taxiway centerline lighting to provide paths for taxiing aircraft. Taxiways also may be marked with the GPMs to aid in the location of taxiing aircraft.

SMGCS have two levels of operations. The first level is initiated when conditions are at or below 1,200 feet RVR. SMCGS is greatly enhanced when combined with **Airport Surface Detection Radar-X (ASDE-X)**. ASDE-X is a surface guidance radar that enables air traffic controllers to identify the locations of vehicles and aircraft that are equipped with transponders, operating in the movement area. The next level of SMCGS occurs at 600 feet RVR, where additional airfield lighting is necessary to conduct operations.

Stop bar lights are required at intersections to taxiways and active runways when operations during periods of RVR of 600 feet or less. When ATC issues a clearance for a pilot to enter the runway they activate a timer which causes red stop bar lights to extinguish and green lead-on lights to illuminate indicating to the pilot it is safe to proceed. Once the aircraft has passed the lighted stop bar, the lead-on lights behind it extinguish and a set of lights in front of the plane then illuminate, which continues to guide the aircraft onto the runway. This protects the runway against the inadvertent entry by a trailing aircraft or vehicle. The aircraft then activates another sensor farther away from the stop bar lights, which extinguishes the remaining lead-on lights.

AIRCRAFT NAVIGATIONAL AIDS

Pilots rely on a variety of navigational aids for both in-flight navigation and to make airport approaches and departures. In the early days of flight across the country, pilots relied on ground reference points, such as water towers or road intersections, to navigate. Early navigational aids consisted of yellow arrows that were paved and pointed to the next arrow. At night, bonfires were sometimes lit to mark the path for early air-mail pilots. As aviation advanced, towers with beacons were constructed, similar to lighthouses, and pilots would navigate visually from one tower to the next.

For air transportation to be effective, pilots must navigate from one point to another. For air transportation to be reliable, pilots must navigate from one point to another, repeatedly. Navigation is composed of four elements: (a) current position, (b) bearing or direction of flight, (c) distance from current location to destination, and (d) estimated time en route. Early aviators commonly relied on a technique in aerial navigation known as pilotage. Pilotage is navigating by using outside visual references or landmarks, such as water towers, roads, and towns. The early air-mail pilots were restricted to mostly visual flight operations (in semi-decent weather) and used a combination of visual references, a compass, and a watch to navigate. Early pilots also adapted the maritime navigation method of dead reckoning, by using time-speed-and-distance calculations to derive position information. Pilots are still taught and expected to demonstrate pilotage and dead reckoning.

Navigational aids are rated on four basic requirements: **integrity**, **accuracy**, **availability**, and **reliability**. **Integrity** refers to the ability of the system to monitor its own operational status and notify a user if it should not be used for navigation. **Accuracy** refers to the ability of the system to show the true position of the aircraft at any time. Accuracy can be influenced by obstructions or electromagnetic signals such as radio waves. **Availability** is the ability to provide the service whenever it is needed by the user. It is based on a percentage of time that the signal is expected to be received and usable. **Reliability** refers to the continuous reception of the signal (similar to cell phone coverage).

Navigational aids can be used for cross-country navigation or as part of an instrument approach. Navigational aids are also used by pilots to fly **Standard Departures (SDs)** or **Standard Terminal Arrival Routes (STARs)**. SDs and STARs are established to reduce the burden of repeating the same ATC clearance instructions and to enhance the flow of arriving and departing aircraft. SDs and STARs are instructional maps for pilots that depict air routes, navigational aids, and expected performance requirements.

An instrument approach into an airport is established under guidelines known as **Terminal Procedures (TERPs)**. TERPs[37] can expand the capacity of an airport. Without a nonprecision or precision instrument approach, an airport that has runways only usable under VMC is effectively closed for business when the weather is below operational minimums. Airport operators can request that a TERP be developed for their airport to allow for use of the runways during inclement weather. A downside of a TERP is that it also mandates flight paths that may have a negative noise impact on individuals or communities that live under the newly established approach or departure pattern (Prather, 2014b, p. 24).

AERONAUTICAL CHARTS

In addition to radio-navigational aids, pilots use aeronautical charts, or maps, throughout most of the world's airspace system. In the United States, pilots commonly use aeronautical charts, including the VFR Sectional Chart, the Low-Altitude En Route Chart, and the High-Altitude En Route Chart.

CHARTS

Sectional Chart

Sectional Charts (Figure 7.43) can be used by all pilots, but these charts are most commonly referenced by pilots of slow- to medium-speed aircraft when conducting cross-country navigation under VMC operations and typically below 18,000 feet mean sea-level (MSL) (see Figures 7.41 and 7.42).[38] Sectional Charts contain topographic information and other data pertinent to pilots such as: airports, obstructions, navigational facilities, airways, airspace, and radio frequencies. A significant feature of the Sectional Chart is the extensive obstruction and terrain information that is included.

---

[37]Content published in FAA-approved instrument approach procedures is established by the Flight Procedure Standards Branch—Terminal Instrument Procedures (TERPS) of the FAA.

[38]Mean sea-level (MSL) is a height measured from and above the average global oceanic surface as a datum for adjusting for various altimetry requirements when flying at or above 18,000 feet MSL.

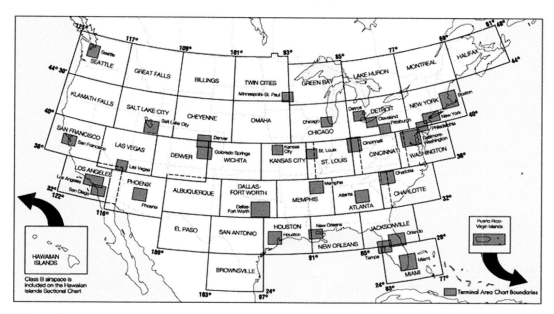

FIGURE 7.43

Sectional Chart—index of coverage also depicting availability of larger scale Class B inserts.

Source: FAA. http://www.faa.gov/air_traffic/flight_info/aeronav/productcatalog/vfrcharts/sectional/.

Because Sectional Charts are used under VMC, pilots must be able to see and avoid obstructions and identify significant landmarks as a reference for navigation. When a new building or tower is erected that affects the safety of flight, that structure is often noted on a Sectional Chart (Figure 7.44). To make corrections or modifications to the charts, airport operators should contact the local FAA Flight Standards District Office and the FAA Airport District Office (ADO).

Instrument Flight Rules Low-Altitude En Route Charts and High-Altitude Jet Route Charts

For IMC, either instrument flight rules (IFR) Low-Altitude En Route Chart (for flights below 18,000 feet MSL; see Figure 7.43) or High-Altitude En Route Chart (above 18,000 feet MSL) are used. IFR charts have significantly less terrain or obstruction features noted. The charts denote "highway" routes through the sky. These routes are identified as Victor Airways below 18,000 feet MSL or as Jet Routes above 18,000 feet MSL and shown usually from one navigational point to another. These routes guarantee clearance of obstructions, provided pilots maintain a specified minimum altitude (Figure 7.45).

NONDIRECTIONAL BEACONS

As flying became more sophisticated, radio frequency antennas were constructed, which broadcasted a signal that could be detected by pilots using special equipment. A **nondirectional beacon**

FIGURE 7.44

Example of cartographic information depicted on a Sectional Chart (small sample taken from Salt Lake City Sectional).

Source: FAA. http://www.faa.gov/air_traffic/flight_info/aeronav/productcatalog/vfrcharts/sectional/.

(NDB) is a large antenna that broadcasts along AM radio frequencies[39] and operates effectively in mountainous terrain. NDBs are used today throughout the United States as a low-cost navigation aid, particularly in the Rocky Mountains and Alaska. The NDB signal is omnidirectional and can be received by an aircraft equipped with an **Automatic Direction Finder (ADF)**. When a particular NDB's frequency is tuned in to the ADF, a needle on the ADF instrument points in the direction of the NDB antenna (known as a "bearing"). NDBs allow pilots to fly more accurately using position fixes and even to "home-in" on a particular location. Many NDBs are no longer owned by the U.S. government and may be the responsibility of an airport authority or a state aeronautics division. NDBs are used to navigate cross-country or to conduct nonprecision instrument approaches, but NDBs can be affected by weather, lightning, rain, and interference from other radio stations.

When a pilot flies a nonprecision approach, the pilot has horizontal information only (essentially, the pilot knows whether the navigational aid or the runway threshold is right or left of the present course). Pilots on a nonprecision approach fly to a published **Final Approach Fix (FAF)** or a **MDA** and maintain an altitude (usually between 600 and 800 feet above ground level [AGL])[40] while visually scanning for the runway environment (depending on visual conditions). If the pilot cannot find the runway environment, the pilot executes a missed approach (explained below). If the pilot identifies the runway environment, the pilot can transition to a visual approach and land. In some cases, a navigational aid is set up for a circling approach, which means that the pilot descends to a specified altitude and, if the runway environment is in sight, enters the ATC

---

[39]In some cases, pilots use AM radio stations as homing devices, provided they generally know where the radio station is broadcasting from.
[40]Altitude above ground level (AGL), expressed in feet.

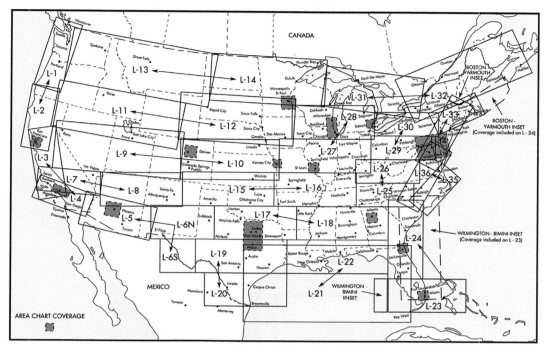

FIGURE 7.45

Coverage areas for low-altitude IFR En Route Charts.

Source: FAA. http://www.faa.gov/air_traffic/flight_info/aeronav/digital_products/aero_guide/.

pattern and lands on the runway in use, which is sometimes in the opposite direction of the nonprecision approach path. From the perspective of an Airport Operations Manager, a distinction is made in the Aeronautical Information Manual (AIM)[41] between a *go-around* and a missed approach. The term *go-around* is used when an air traffic controller instructs a pilot to execute a missed approach. A *missed approach* is a maneuver conducted by a pilot when an instrument approach cannot be completed.

VERY-HIGH-FREQUENCY OMNIDIRECTIONAL RANGE

A VOR transmits a very-high-frequency (VHF)[42] radio signal in a finite number of compass headings. VORs are located throughout the country and, up until the advent of global positioning systems (GPSs), was the primary navigational aid for pilots. As the VOR transmitting station broadcasts a signal, an instrument in the flight deck, also known as a "VOR receiver," can be tuned to receive the signal. The needle in the VOR receiver can be adjusted to align with a specific

---

[41]See http://www.faa.gov/air_traffic/publications/media/aim_basic_4-03-14.pdf

[42]VHF electromagnetic radio waves: 30 MHz to 300 MHz.

FIGURE 7.46

Example FAA VORTAC ground station.

Source: FAA. https://www.faasafety.gov/gslac/ALC/course_content.aspx?cID=43&sID=257&preview=true.

compass heading, allowing the pilot to home-in on a particular VOR station or to triangulate their position using multiple VORs. The military version of the VOR is known as **Tactical Air Navigation (TACAN)**.[43] TACAN operates on ultra-high frequencies (UHFs) and when colocated with a VOR is known as a **VORTAC** (Figure 7.46).

Most VORs are owned and operated by the FAA, but a few are owned and maintained by the local airport or a local government. VORs are based on line-of-sight (VOR station to receiving aircraft) and are affected by terrain. VORs can be used for long-range navigation, and some are used for local approaches to an airport; these are known as **Terminal VORs** and have a range of 25 nautical miles. Terminal VORs can be located on or near airport property and require a 750-foot to 1,000-foot protected clear radius around the facility. Typically, VORs are fenced off, even within the airfield, to prevent ground vehicle operators from inadvertently driving too close and disrupting

---

[43]UHF electromagnetic radio waves: 300 MHz and 3 GHz.

the signal. Airport Operations personnel should include the VOR in their daily and continuous inspections to ensure the safety and the security of the facility, especially watching for any obstructions, such as blown debris, or individuals trespassing within the 1,000-foot boundary.

Distance Measuring Equipment (DME) provides distance information from a selected VOR station or instrument approach localizer antenna. VORs and localizer antennas can provide bearing information only. The implementation of DME into VORs, localizers, and GPS approaches can reduce the need for various other navigational ground devices (e.g., marker beacons as used in ILS; see "The Instrument Landing System" below).

THE INSTRUMENT LANDING SYSTEM

The ILS is a precision instrument approach used at airports throughout the United States. The system provides both horizontal and vertical guidance to the pilot. An ILS consists of a localizer antenna that sits at the opposite end of the approach runway and projects a radiofrequency beam down the approach path. A VOR receiver in the flight deck can pick up the signal and indicate whether the pilot is left or right of the runway centerline. The second component of the ILS is the glide slope transmitter. The glide slope antenna sits adjacent to the approach end of the runway and projects a radiofrequency signal outward from the runway upward along the specified approach angle. Instrumentation in the flight deck (the same device used for the localizer) tells the pilot whether the aircraft is too high or too low on the glide slope. Marker beacons have traditionally been used on ILS approaches but are being replaced by DME. Where still available, marker beacons consist of an outer marker some 4 to 7 nautical miles from the runway, a middle marker located one-half to three-quarters of a mile from the runway threshold, and, in some rare cases, an inner marker located at the runway threshold. Another critical component of the ILS is the approach light system, previously discussed.

An ILS guides the pilot down to an FAA-predetermined **DH** (see Figure 7.47). Upon reaching the DH, the pilot either has the runway environment in sight, to the extent that the pilot can transition to a visual approach landing,[44] or if the pilot does not have the runway environment in sight, the pilot will execute a missed approach. During a missed approach, the pilot climbs to a published altitude and on a published heading, upward and away from the airport. The pilot then notifies ATC, which can provide vectors to either attempt another landing or to an alternate airport. Missed approach procedures[45] are published on the ILS "approach plate," which is a textual and graphic description describing flight procedures for executing a specific approach to a specific airport. Up until recently, pilots carried books of paper approach plates as needed for their flight operations. Many pilots and air carriers are now adopting the **Electronic Flight Bag (EFB)** to replace traditional hardcopy approach plates, along with other needed flight information. EFBs are electronic, computer-based tablets that integrate into other aircraft systems for enhanced information visualization and retrieval.

---

[44]Ground-based VASI or PAPI systems provide visual cues to help the pilot(s) make a decision at the DH to either land or declare a missed approach.

[45]Approach plates and other related forms of flight navigational information are published by the FAA through the U.S. National Aeronautical Charting Office (NACO). Content published in FAA-approved instrument approach procedures (IAPs) is established through the Flight Procedure Standards Branch—Terminal Instrument Procedures (TERPS) of the FAA. IAPs have expiration dates and can be updated at any time. A new procedure is then published.

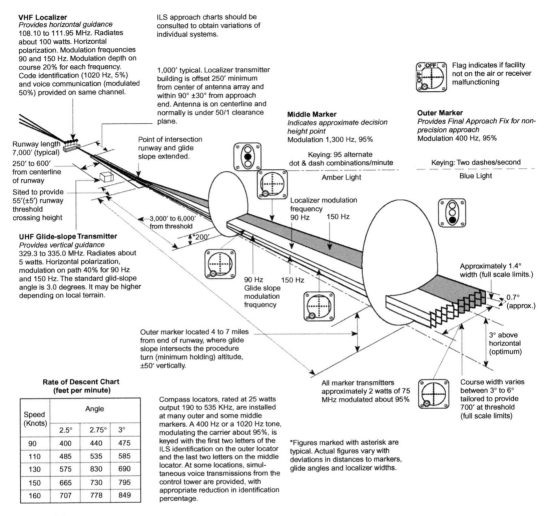

VHF Localizer
Provides horizontal guidance
108.10 to 111.95 MHz. Radiates
about 100 watts. Horizontal
polarization. Modulation frequencies
90 and 150 Hz. Modulation depth on
course 20% for each frequency.
Code identification (1020 Hz, 5%)
and voice communication (modulated
50%) provided on same channel.

ILS approach charts should be
consulted to obtain variations of
individual systems.

1,000′ typical. Localizer transmitter
building is offset 250′ minimum
from center of antenna array and
within 90° ±30° from approach
end. Antenna is on centerline and
normally is under 50/1 clearance
plane.

Flag indicates if facility
not on the air or receiver
malfunctioning

Middle Marker
*Indicates approximate decision
height point*
Modulation 1,300 Hz, 95%

Keying: 95 alternate
dot & dash combinations/minute

Amber Light

Outer Marker
*Provides Final Approach Fix for non-
precision approach*
Modulation 400 Hz, 95%

Keying: Two dashes/second

Blue Light

Runway length
7,000′ (typical)

250′ to 600′
from centerline
of runway

Sited to provide
55′(±5′) runway
threshold
crossing height

Point of intersection
runway and glide
slope extended.

3,000′ to 6,000′
from threshold

*200′

Localizer modulation
frequency
90 Hz   150 Hz

UHF Glide-slope Transmitter
Provides vertical guidance
329.3 to 335.0 MHz. Radiates about
5 watts. Horizontal polarization,
modulation on path 40% for 90 Hz
and 150 Hz. The standard glid-slope
angle is 3.0 degrees. It may be higher
depending on local terrain.

90 Hz   150 Hz
Glide slope
modulation
frequency

Approximately 1.4°
width (full scale limits.)

0.7°
(approx.)

3° above
horizontal
(optimum)

Outer marker located 4 to 7 miles
from end of runway, where glide
slope intersects the procedure
turn (minimum holding) altitude,
±50′ vertically.

All marker transmitters
approximately 2 watts of 75
MHz modulated about 95%

Course width varies
between 3° to 6°
tailored to provide
700′ at threshold
(full scale limits)

Rate of Descent Chart
(feet per minute)

Speed (Knots)	Angle		
	2.5°	2.75°	3°
90	400	440	475
110	485	535	585
130	575	830	690
150	665	730	795
160	707	778	849

Compass locators, rated at 25 watts
output 190 to 535 KHz, are installed
at many outer and some middle
markers. A 400 Hz or a 1020 Hz tone,
modulating the carrier about 95%, is
keyed with the first two letters of the
ILS identification on the outer locator
and the last two letters on the middle
locator. At some locations, simultaneous voice transmissions from the
control tower are provided, with
appropriate reduction in identification
percentage.

*Figures marked with asterisk are
typical. Actual figures vary with
deviations in distances to markers,
glide angles and localizer widths.

FIGURE 7.47

Components of a standard FAA ILS.

Source: FAA. http://tfmlearning.fly.faa.gov/publications/atpubs/aim/Chap1/aim0101.html.

ILS systems are subdivided into three levels of approaches identified on the approach plates as CAT I, CAT II, and CAT III. Each of these classifications is directly related to the specified DH and visibility requirements stated and depicted in the approach procedure. CAT III, which requires special instrumentation in the flight deck and on the airport, is the most accurate of the three systems. CAT III also has a subcategory (C) that provides for aircraft auto-land, allowing the aircraft to land itself using an autopilot function that, in some advanced airliners, will even apply the brakes. Pilots, in this case, must receive special training to properly monitor the auto-land system, and they must take manual control if the auto-land function is not working.

As previously described, another component of the ILS is the RVR measuring equipment. Rain, smoke, haze, and fog can affect the visibility on the airfield. Various weather conditions refract the infrared light, which is beamed between two points in the RVR system. The unit processes the degree the infrared beam is affected by particulates and transmits the RVR to a control center for reporting. RVRs are often colocated with an Automated Weather Observing System (AWOS) or ASOS can be located independently near the runway areas.

From an Airport Operations perspective, it is important to prevent vehicles and aircraft from stopping or operating in front of the ILS glide slope antenna while the ILS is in use. ATC normally controls this through the use of holding instructions and airfield signs and markings (the "ladder" marking), but in some cases, such as during airfield mowing operations or construction activities, personnel may inadvertently operate or leave equipment or stockpiled material in front of the glide slope antenna.

GLOBAL POSITIONING SYSTEMS

The GPS is a satellite-based navigation system, which is in the process of replacing the land-based navigation systems (VORs and NDBs). The GPS is actually a constellation of 27 satellites (Figure 7.48) in lower Earth orbit (24 satellites are in operation with three backup satellites in place, referred to as the "expandable 24").[46] Each satellite completes a rotation around the earth every day and at any point in time anywhere on earth, at least four satellites are "visible" to GPS

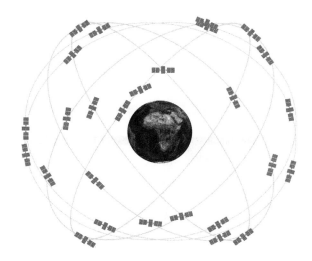

FIGURE 7.48

"Expandable 24" GPS system.

Source: From GPS.Gov NOAA [National Oceanic and Atmospheric Administration].

[46]See http://www.gps.gov/systems/gps/space/

navigational equipment. A minimum of four satellites is necessary—three for trilateration (triangulating a position by drawing lines of bearing from three known points) and a fourth for determining time. The GPS receiver in the aircraft and the GPS satellite constellation interrogate radio waves, which travel at the speed of light. The receiver in the aircraft can determine how far the signal has traveled by timing how long it took the signal to arrive. This calculation is also used to determine location and to estimate times of arrival.

Previously, many GPS satellites were designed to deny the hostile use of GPS positioning data, through a process known as selective availability (SA), and although this is no longer true, many GPS receivers are designed to assume it is still active. SA added intentional time varying errors of up to 100 meters to navigational signals in order to deny an enemy the use of GPS receivers for precision weapons guidance. SA has been turned off since the year 2000, and the military has developed other systems to deny the use of GPS to hostile forces in a specific area of crisis, rather than systemwide.

GPS is used routinely for navigation throughout the world, but in order to improve accuracy, integrity, and availability of GPS, the FAA developed the **Wide Area Augmentation System (WAAS)**. WAAS stations are positioned at 24 locations throughout the United States and can improve GPS signals at numerous airport runways and within a certain radius (approximately 23 nautical miles) of the WAAS installation. WAAS improves approaches at airports with CAT I ILS without additional expense (Prather, 2011, p. 33). The FAA is also developing **Ground-Based Augmentation Systems (GBASs)** (Figure 7.49) to augment GPS signals and provide

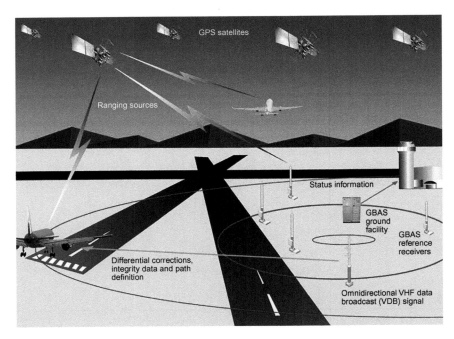

FIGURE 7.49

Ground-Based Augmentation System.

Source: FAA. http://www.faa.gov/about/office_org/headquarters_offices/ato/service_units/techops/navservices/gnss/laas/.

enhanced guidance equivalent to CAT II or CAT III ILS approach minimums. A GBAS is a ground-based transmitter and functions the same as the WAAS. From an Airport Operations perspective, airport personnel should know the location of any GBASs and should include the station as part of a daily and, if practical, continuous inspection for safety and security purposes.

AUTOMATED FLIGHT SERVICE STATIONS

Flight Service Stations (FSSs) are part of the Air Traffic Organization of the FAA. FSSs are air traffic facilities that provide pilot briefings, process flight plans, and provide in-flight radio communications, Search and Rescue (SAR) services, and assistance to lost aircraft and aircraft in emergency situations. FSSs also relay ATC clearances; process Notices to Airmen (NOTAMs); broadcast aviation, meteorological, and aeronautical information; and notify Customs and Border Protection of trans-border flights (Flight Service Operations, 2015). Many of these functions are now handled online through the **Automated Flight Services Stations (AFSS)** contract, which is awarded to a private company. The AFSS enables pilots to file and close flight plans online, receive text or email messages and satellite alerts regarding dangerous conditions, and activate SAR capabilities. AFSS also provides preflight and in-flight meteorological and aeronautical briefings, NOTAMs, and weather forecasting for the destination.

Many pilots presently use the Direct User Access Terminal (DUAT) system as an online form of flight service information. The DUAT service is an FAA computerized system allowing pilots to directly access FAA weather data and flight planning systems. The service is paid for by aviation taxes and is free to individuals with pilot certificates.

AIRPORT-BASED WEATHER OBSERVATION STATIONS

Hundreds of **ASOSs** and **AWOSs** have been installed at airports and other sites nationwide to provide current and reliable weather information to pilots, the AFSS, and other aviation users. AWOS and ASOS use an array of sophisticated electronic sensors to carefully measure meteorological conditions. ASOS and AWOS are 24-hour, real-time, weather data collection and display systems that transmit computer-generated voice reports about conditions at the location of the ASOS. The reports can also be accessed by telephone. The automated systems continuously monitor the weather and update their observations every minute (Rossier, 1998).

AWOS stations are part of the daily inspection items on an airport. While the airport operator would not likely know if the weather station were correctly reporting the observed weather, the airport operator could inspect for wildlife; debris; damage caused by weather, wind, or blown objects; and the overall integrity of the structure.

Various levels of AWOSs and ASOSs exist. A basic AWOS measures barometric pressure and altimeter setting, whereas an AWOS IV Z/R (the maximum) measures barometric pressure and altimeter setting, visibility, sky condition, cloud height, precipitation, including rain, snow, drizzle, and freezing rain, thunderstorms (via lighting detector), and runway surface condition. An ASOS typically reports all the elements that an AWOS reports, but an ASOS also reports temperature, dew point, present weather, and sea-level pressure.

AIRSPACE AND AIR TRAFFIC CONTROL

Although airspace and ATC considerations are not inspection items under Part 139, they help Airport Operations personnel understand how these elements affect what they do at the field level.

AIRSPACE

During the early days of aviation, all airspace was considered uncontrolled, and pilots generally assumed that if they remained clear of clouds and had at least one mile visibility, they would be able to see other airplanes and terrain in time to avoid a collision. These conditions supported the beginning of the "see-and-avoid" pilot technique and formed the basis for VORs (Landsberg, 2014). Pilots soon recognized that their vision was reduced at night; thus, higher weather minimums, along with minimum cloud clearances, were created for night flying.

The invention of flight instruments enabling flight through clouds or in conditions with limited visibility led to the creation of ATC and controlled airspace. The government established a system of airways, each 8 nautical miles wide with the base altitude of 1,200 feet AGL, designating the airspace within as controlled (Landsberg, 2014). The airway system was defined by a network of radio beacons, many of which were located on airports, or in the vicinity of the airport. These airways are now known as "Victor" Airways.

For flight in conditions with limited visibility or distances from clouds, pilots were eventually required to earn an FAA Instrument Rating (for flight in IFR) as part of their legal certification to fly in these conditions. Pilots now have to be qualified (FAA documentation and appropriate medical certification), current ("recency of experience"), and equipped for instrument flights. For IFR operations, pilots file instrument flight plans and coordinate their positions with ATC. Even in good weather, pilots can still fly an instrument flight plan, but are responsible for seeing and avoiding other aircraft.

Controlled airspace does not imply that all flight within that airspace is controlled by ATC. Rather, controlled airspace means that IFR services are available to qualified pilots who choose to use them. VFR pilots may still fly freely in controlled airspace provided they abide by the rules for flying weather conditions, such as cloud clearance and visibility limitations, and other related regulations that require various forms of communication and equipment.

With the invention of land-based, radio-navigation aids, instrument approaches became possible, which expanded the capacity of the airport and improved the utility of airplanes. "Close calls" (i.e., near misses) between aircraft flying on instrument flight plans and aircraft flying using VFRs led to the creation of transition areas. Transition areas surround airports with instrument approaches and provide IFR pilots with airspace and ATC service that ensure separation from VFR traffic during arrival and departures.

Today, a variety of airspace classifications exist throughout the United States, primarily to provide safety in flight operations. Airspace in the United States is divided into four categories: controlled, uncontrolled, special use, and other.

Controlled airspace is regulated by the FAA and includes (see Figure 7.50):

1. Class A
2. Class B

3. Class C
4. Class D
5. Class E

Uncontrolled airspace consists of (see Figure 7.50):

1. Class G

Special Use Airspace is controlled by the U.S. military and includes:

1. Restricted Areas
2. Prohibited Areas
3. Military Operations Areas (MOAs)
4. Military Training Routes (MTRs)
5. Warning Areas
6. Alert Areas
7. Controlled Firing Areas
8. National Security Areas
9. Air Defense Identification Zones (ADIZs)

Other airspace classifications include:

1. Local Airport Advisory (LAA)
2. Temporary Flight Restrictions (TFRs)
3. Parachute Jump Aircraft Operations
4. Published VFR routes
5. Terminal Radar Service Areas (TRSAs)

Controlled Airspace

Class A airspace is intended for high-speed, en route air travel. Pilots flying in Class A airspace must be instrument rated, have filed an IFR flight plan, and must be in contact with ATC. Class A airspace begins at 18,000 MSL and extends up to and includes flight level (FL) 600 (60,000 feet— at or above 18,000 MSL are referred to as FLs). Class A airspace includes airspace overlying the United States out to a distance of 12 nautical miles from the U.S. coastline. Class A airspace is sometimes called *en route* airspace and is controlled by FAA Air Route Traffic Control Centers (ARTCCs) (Figure 7.50).

Class B airspace is intended for large airports with significant levels of air traffic. It typically encompasses approximately 30 nautical miles around major airports (large hubs) in the United States. The significant number of aircraft and their size and speed capabilities requires additional space for ATC to safely transition aircraft through the Class B airspace and to airports within or underneath Class B airspace. Much of the traffic in Class B airspace is on an IFR flight plan, but VFR traffic is allowed with the permission of ATC.[47] Class B airspace extends from the surface up to 10,000 feet MSL. Aircraft within Class B airspace are limited to a top speed of 250

---

[47]VFR pilots contact the appropriate Class B traffic control service prior to entering Class B airspace and request a clearance to operate in the Class B airspace. Other regulatory requirements also determine the ability for a pilot to enter Class B airspace, including aircraft equipment, pilot qualifications, and weather conditions.

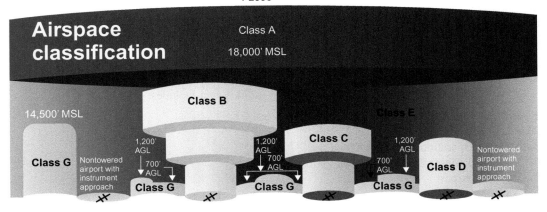

FIGURE 7.50

FAA classification of controlled and uncontrolled airspace.

Source: FAA. https://www.faasafety.gov/gslac/ALC/course_content.aspx?cID=42&sID=505&preview=true.

knots,[48] but below Class B airspace the maximum speed limit is 200 knots. The specific configuration is tailored to the location of the airport, the surrounding airports, and airspace classifications, but Class B airspace is often described as an "upside down wedding cake." Student pilots are not authorized to operate within Class B airspace unless they have received documented instruction by an FAA-certified flight instructor for operations in the specific Class B airspace for solo flight. Other commercial service and general aviation airports are often within or underneath Class B airspace, within Class C or Class D airspace, or uncontrolled. The majority of flight operations in Class B airspace are controlled by a **Terminal Radar Approach Control Facility (TRACON)**. The TRACON controls traffic within the Class B airspace and handles traffic as it approaches and departs Class B airspace. TRACON is also referred to as "Approach Control or Departure Control," depending on whether the aircraft is arriving or departing (see Figure 7.50).

Class C airspace services airports with less activity than Class B airspace airports. Class C airspace typically has an inner circle radius of 5 nautical miles (surface to and including 4,000 AGL), with an outer circle that extends to 10 nautical miles, beginning at 1,200 feet AGL and extending up to 4,000 feet AGL (depicted on charts as MSL). Class C airspace is usually served by an operational ATCT, with radar approach control. Pilots can determine the exact dimensions of a Class C airspace by referencing the proper aeronautical chart or airport facility directory (AFD).[49] Aircraft must establish two-way radio communications with ATC prior to entering the airspace, and the maximum speed limit is 200 knots (see Figure 7.50).

Class D airspace surrounds airports that are less busy than Class C airspace airports but still meet the level of operations necessary to have an ATCT. Class D airspace extends out to a radius of 4 to 5 miles from the airport and from the surface to 2,500 feet AGL (depicted on charts as MSL). The

---

[48]All civil aircraft operating under 10,000 feet MSL in the United States are restricted to a speed limit of 250 knots.
[49]See https://www.faa.gov/air_traffic/flight_info/aeronav/digital_products/dafd/

specific configuration of this airspace may be modified to accommodate instrument approach procedures. Aircraft must establish two-way radio communications to enter Class D airspace, but radar vectoring is not available. The maximum speed limit is 200 knots, which begins below 2,500 feet AGL within 4 nautical miles of the Class D airspace airport (see Figure 7.50).

Class E airspace includes all airspace that is not otherwise classified as A, B, C, or D and is considered *controlled* airspace. The term *controlled* can be very confusing in this context as the presumption is any aircraft in Class C airspace is under ATC. However, in this case, the term *controlled* relates to the designation of federal airways that are used for instrument flight, and specifically relates to the visibility requirements for pilots and the minimum distance from clouds. Controlled, in this context, means that IFR services are available, and pilots on IFR flight plans are provided with traffic information. Pilots operating under VFR may also operate in Class E airspace, but must be aware that the airspace does have federal airways extending throughout and must see and avoid IFR and VFR traffic. For this reason, Class E airspace visibility limits are higher than in uncontrolled airspace. The higher visibility limits and cloud clearances are so that a VFR pilot may be able to see and avoid a pilot on an instrument flight plan. VFR-only pilots should not be in Class E airspace during IMC (see Figure 7.50).

Uncontrolled Airspace

Class G airspace includes all airspace that is not otherwise designated as A, B, C, D, or E. There is no Class F airspace in the United States. Class G airspace extends from the surface to the base of the overlying Class B airspace or up to 14,000 feet MSL. ATC has no authority or responsibility to control air traffic in this area. Many ultralight operations take place in Class G airspace as ultralights can be denied access in Class B, Class C, and Class D airspace because of incompatibility problems with other aircraft (see Figure 7.50).

Special Use Airspace

Airspace designated for certain activities, such as military operations, or prohibited from entry by certain civil aircraft is considered Special Use Airspace. Special Use Airspace is depicted on instrument charts and, where required, includes the effective altitude, time, and weather conditions of operations and the controlling agency.

Prohibited Areas contain airspace in which aircraft flight is prohibited, typically for reasons of national security, such as over Camp David.

Restricted Areas denote airspace that may be used for hazards that are visible to aircraft, such as aerial gunnery, guided missiles, or artillery firing. Aircraft on an instrument flight plan may be authorized to transit the airspace, but pilots operating an aircraft under VFR should ensure that the Restricted Area is not active prior to entering the airspace.

Warning Areas delimit airspace over international waters and extend from 3 miles beyond the shore. The FAA has no authority over these areas; warning areas are advisory in nature and alert pilots they may be entering areas of hazardous activity.

MOAs separate high-speed military traffic from general aviation and commercial aviation traffic. Military operations, such as air combat training, formation flying, and aerial refueling, may take place within a MOA. Pilots may request traffic advisories from the controlling agency prior to entry into a MOA.

MTRs are one-way high-speed routes for military traffic flying below 10,000 MSL. Pilots are not restricted from flying through MTRs, but are encouraged to keep alert for military operations. There have been several instances of military aircraft colliding with civilian light aircraft along MTRs.

Alert Areas are airspace in which an unusual activity is taking place. Alert areas are used to advise pilots of potential conflicts, but these areas have no special rules. Examples of alert areas are around Pensacola, Florida. Naval Air Station Pensacola and Naval Air Station Milton Field are the primary areas where Naval Aviators are trained, so civilian pilots are notified (by way of the alert area being noted on aeronautical charts) of high volumes of fixed- and rotor-wing traffic.

Control Firing Areas (CFAs) contain activities that could be hazardous to nonparticipating aircraft, but the activities are immediately suspended when spotter aircraft, radar, or a ground lookout indicates that an aircraft may be approaching. These areas are not depicted on aeronautical charts.

National Security Areas consist of airspace of defined vertical and lateral dimensions established at locations where increased security and safety of ground facilities is necessary.

ADIZs exist around the borders of the United States and over Washington, DC. All aircraft entering domestic U.S. airspace from points outside must provide identification prior to entry. The ADIZ facilitates early aircraft identification of all aircraft in the vicinity of the United States and international airspace boundaries.

A **Flight Restriction Zone (FRZ)** exists over the Capitol, White House, and surrounding areas. Only aircraft on IFR flight plans that have been approved, such as commercial service or certain general aviation operations, are allowed within the flight restriction zone.

Other Airspace Classifications

Airport Advisory Areas exist at airports without a control tower but that have an on-field FAA FSS in operation. Within this area, the FSS provides advisory service to arriving and departing aircraft. The **LAA** is typically a weather reporting voice broadcasting service provided by facilities that do not have an ATCT or when the tower is closed.

Parachute Jump Areas are published locations where parachute activities occur. Pilots should remain clear of these areas, but when not possible to remain clear, should attempt to monitor the frequency of the aircraft carrying the skydivers.

TFR areas are imposed to preclude aircraft from entering the area in which an incident occurred, such as a natural disaster, and can also be used to protect the airspace over the president of the United States or over significant events such as a Super Bowl, the Olympics, or a National Aeronautics and Space Administration (NASA) rocket launch.

Published VFR Routes are for transitioning around, under, or through complex airspace such as through the airspace over Los Angeles, California. These are known as **VFR corridors** or transition routes and are found on the VFR sectional area chart.

TRSAs are areas where participating pilots can receive additional radar services (if available) and typically overlay Class D airspace.

THE AIR TRAFFIC CONTROL TOWER AND RELATED SERVICES

ATCTs provide a safe, orderly, and expeditious flow of traffic on and in the vicinity of an airport. In the early days of aviation there were so few aircraft that pilots could watch out for other aircraft operating in the airspace and around the airport. However, as air traffic increased, particularly at major airports, the need for some sort of control become apparent. ATCTs were developed for and are partially responsible for sequencing and separating aircraft arriving and departing the airport. The FAA describes the responsibilities of an ATCT as:

> . . . work in the glassed-in towers you see at airports. They manage traffic from the airport to a radius of 3 to 30 miles out. They give pilots taxiing and take off instructions, air traffic clearance, and advice based on their own observations and experience. They provide separation between landing and departing aircraft, transfer control of aircraft to the en route center controllers when the aircraft leave their airspace, and receive control of aircraft on flights coming into their airspace. (FAA, n.d.b)

When operating an aircraft within airport movement areas and airspace controlled by an ATCT, a clearance authorization is required from the tower prior to conducting those operations.[50] A ground controller (located in the tower) has the responsibility of managing all aircraft and vehicular activity on the airport's taxiways. Anytime a vehicle moves from a noncontrolled area to a controlled area, it is entering the movement area and must have clearance from the ground controller unless an agreement exists with the ATCT stating different procedures. Tower control (or "local controller"[51]) is responsible for handling arriving and departing aircraft on the active runways and within the assigned airport airspace (Figure 7.51).

Automated Terminal Information Service (ATIS) is a recorded message from the ATCT that continuously transmits airport information on a separate, assigned frequency or over the voice feature of an airport's AWOS. ATIS information is updated hourly, or more frequently if conditions warrant, and is identified by a phonetic letter code. It includes the following information: (a) airport identifier, (b) UTC (Coordinated Universal Time), (c) wind direction and speed, (d) visibility, (e) cloud ceiling, (f) temperature and dew point, (g) altimeter setting, (h) instrument approaches and runways in use, (i) NOTAMs applicable to landing, (j) weather advisories, (k) braking action reports, (l) wind shear reports, (m) construction activity, and (n) other information of importance to the pilot and other airport users. ATIS eliminates repetitive announcements of basic information made to pilots when they first contact the control tower.

With the advent of GBAS and related ground-based surveillance radar, air traffic controllers are better able to "see," identify, and separate aircraft. Eventually, two types of radar facilities would be established: TRACON (previously discussed) and the ARTCC (ARTCC is usually referred to as "*Name* Center;" e.g., "Denver Center"; Figure 7.52). ARTCCs have long-range radars (approximately 100 to 250 nm) and control vast areas of airspace throughout the United States. There are 19 ARTCCs throughout the United States, including Alaska and Hawaii. The boundaries of ARTCC are defined and resemble large puzzle pieces over the United States. Within each "piece," the airspace is further divided up, and controllers are given responsibility for each section. As a pilot flies across the country, the pilot moves from one parcel of airspace to another, each time changing frequencies to talk to a different controller, who sometimes provides altitude and heading changes.

---

[50]When operating an aircraft or a ground vehicle at an airport without an ATCT, operators are required to call out their positions on a Unicom frequency or CTAF whenever they are on the runways or taxiways or in the traffic pattern.
[51]At larger airports, local controllers are assigned responsibility for specific movement areas and runways.

FIGURE 7.51

Inside the "cab" portion of an ATCT at Reno-Tahoe International Airport (RNO).

Image courtesy of Alex Gertsen, C.M.

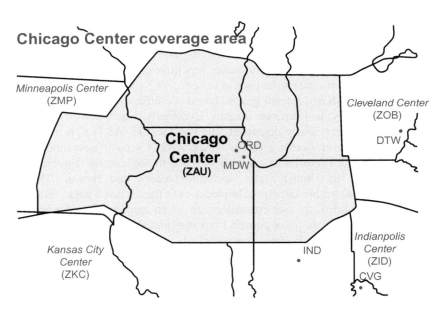

FIGURE 7.52

Example of an ARTCC: Chicago Center, with surrounding ARTCCs.

Source: FAA. http://www.faa.gov/about/office_org/headquarters_offices/ato/service_units/
air_traffic_services/artcc/chicago/information/media/chicago_artcc_coverage_map.pdf.

Class C airspace was established to better handle instrument approaches and to provide radar coverage for the area surrounding the airport, instead of visual reference and situational awareness. Additional airspace was also developed to separate IFR from VFR traffic. Class B airspace was developed for the busiest airspace, located over the busiest airports. Class B airspace provides a way for ATC to guarantee separation of air traffic by expanding larger than Class C airspace, which allows controllers to sequence traffic farther away from the airport. The airspace definitions have been previously discussed, but the key invention that made the control of airspace possible is radar.

RADAR

Radar is the primary tool used to control and separate aircraft in-flight. Radar, which stands for radio detection and ranging, consists of four components: (1) transmitter, (2) antenna, (3) receiver, and (4) display. The transmitter sends out the radiofrequency signal. When the signal intercepts an object such as an aircraft, it is reflected back to the receiver whereupon a time-speed-distance calculation determines the relative location of the aircraft. Airplanes with transponders can also send back altitude information and a unique transponder code when interrogated by the radar antenna. Unfortunately, without a transponder, it is difficult to distinguish one aircraft from another aircraft—or from a flock of birds or ground clutter. The use of a transponder is required to operate about FL 180 (Class A airspace), as well as in Class B and Class C airspaces.

An aircraft with a transponder will "squawk" a discrete code, which is generally assigned by ATC. In the case of a VFR flight not in Class A, B, C, or D airspace, the pilot can squawk 1200, which is the general code for a VFR operation. Not all aircraft in the United States are required to have a transponder or to use it, unless in certain types of airspace. Airplanes equipped with Mode C will also broadcast the altitude of the plane. Mode S enhanced transponders provide aircraft speed, rate of climb (or descent), magnetic heading, ground speed, and indicated airspeed, along with traffic advisories.

Primary surveillance radar uses a continually rotating antenna, transmitting electromagnetic waves that reflect back to the antenna whenever the signal hits an object, such as an aircraft. The radar calculates the aircraft's time-speed-distance based on the difference between the time of the transmission and the return. This data is used to calculate the direction of the aircraft in relation to the antenna. Primary radar systems are susceptible to atmospheric conditions and do not provide information on aircraft altitude. Secondary radar uses an additional radar antenna attached to the primary radar to transmit and receive aircraft data, including altitude, identification (squawk code), and emergency conditions. Pilots may also use the following squawk codes to indicate three specific emergency situations:

1. 7700 for any type of emergency;
2. 7600 for radio failures or other communication issues; and
3. 7500 for a hijacking or other intrusions or acts causing the pilots to not have total control of the aircraft.

The five primary types of radar in use by civil air traffic controllers and one specific to the military are: **Air Route Surveillance Radar (ARSR), Airport Surveillance Radar (ASR), Airport**

Surface Detection Equipment (ASDE-3 or ASDE-X[52]**)**, and **Precision Runway Monitoring (PRM)**. The military also uses **Precision Approach Radar (PAR)**, which may also be installed at joint- or shared-use airports, but is mostly used by military pilots.[53] These systems are supplemented with the **Automated Radar Terminal System (ARTS)** that assists in the prediction of flight paths and determines potential conflicts with other aircraft.

ASDE-3 is a ground surveillance radar that provides information to air traffic controllers about the location of vehicles (with transponders) and aircraft on the airfield. ASDE is used during nighttime and when there is poor visibility to prevent runway incursions. Rather than receiving information from a single radar source (ASDE-3), ASDE-X receives information on ground activity from multiple sources, including the radar feed, ARTS, and Multilateration (MLAT) sensors. ASDE-X has an improved ability to track targets and generates fewer false signals. Combined with ASDE is a conflict alert system known as **Airport Movement Area Safety System (AMASS)**, which activates and alerts pilots that a runway is active or a potential conflict with another aircraft exists.

PRM is a high-update radar coupled with a high resolution ATC display that allows more accurate tracking of inbound aircraft, so much so that aircraft in IMC can fly closer than 4,300 feet (but not less than 3,000 feet) onto two parallel runways. PRM enables controllers to monitor two or more aircraft on simultaneous approaches to two or more parallel runways during poor visibility. A nontransgression zone separates the approaches, and a monitoring controller will intervene if either aircraft begins to stray into the nontransgression zone. ILS/PRM approaches facilitate greater airport capacity in IFR conditions when visibility is greatly reduced.

A PAR is a radar used by the U.S. military and provides both lateral and vertical guidance. PAR approaches also involve verbal guidance from air traffic controllers who provide that information directly to the pilot.

Until the 21st Century of Aviation Act was passed in 2003, the ATC and navigational aids used by pilots remained a land-based system. Victor Airways and Jet Routes were determined by VOR or other ground-based navigational aids, which were not always the most efficient routes of flight. With the growth of global air travel and the design of more efficient, maneuverable, and faster aircraft, the current ATC system is being stressed to its maximum capacity. These concerns, plus the advent of new flight technologies, such as those being implemented with the integration of Unmanned Aerial Systems (UAS) and commercial space operations, are causing greater demands for improved ATC methods and technologies.

NEXTGEN

NextGen is the comprehensive update of the nation's entire ATC system. It includes numerous new technologies and systems designed to enhance the safety of flight and increase its efficiency and security. The most significant component is the transition from a land-based navigation system to a

---

[52]The recently released ASDE-X is an alternate system to ASDE-3, allowing improved situational awareness for aircraft and vehicles operating in the movement area, as well as flights in the vicinity of the airport.
[53]In some joint civil and military airports, a PAR may be issued to civilian pilots on request and at the discretion of the U.S. military controller.

satellite-based system integrated with flight and land navigational technologies. Radar can take up to 30 seconds to provide a return to a controller on a fast-moving aircraft. By the time the radar return has reached the controller, an aircraft traveling at 500 mph groundspeed has already traveled just over 4 miles. Satellites provide real-time information to pilots and controllers, allowing controllers to guide and track aircraft more safely and efficiently.

NextGen will allow more aircraft to fly closer together on more direct routes. New electronic data provides pilots with access to real-time weather and better information about the locations of other aircraft and the ground. Thus, pilots are able to make better decisions, ultimately reducing major diversions around severe weather and reducing ground delays and fuel costs.

Many NextGen elements will have varying effects on pilots, aircraft operators, and Airport Operations personnel. NextGen is designed for overall enhancement of a safer air transportation system with greater efficiencies.

A primary development in the NextGen system of technology is the **Performance-Based Navigation (PBN)** system. PBN is a new system of "road maps" for pilots to follow—a PBN route is a pathway defined with specific headings, altitudes, and climb/descent rates, plus other requirements. PBN routes will eventually replace many of the existing routes pilots use to enter and exit airspace and airport areas. PBN navigation requires pilots to have certain equipment in the flight deck to perform the required maneuvers to descend or depart the airspace addressed in the procedure, hence the name "Performance-Based Navigation." PBN is comprised of Area Navigation (RNAV) and Required Navigation Performance (RNP), which are elements that must be approved and onboard the flight deck to use PBN. PBN improves access to airports in reduced visibility with an approach that can curve to the runway, enabling more accurate, flexible, and predictable flight paths.

PBN and other new satellite-based flight navigation systems are already changing the traditional flight paths—and, citizens who live underneath these new routes have taken notice! As a result of the changing flight patterns, airports are already experiencing noise complaints from communities that have not previously had noise abatement issues.

Communication in ATC is still very much based on voice, two-way radio technology. Some aircraft and aircraft-to-ground stations have adopted a short text-message system known as **Aircraft Communications Addressing and Reporting System (ACARS)**. Voice communications are less efficient and often result in multiple read-backs and errors. In new NextGen communications technology, **Data Communications** ("Data Comm") will enable air traffic controllers to transmit critical route information to pilots via digital text, replacing most two-way radio transmissions with aircraft that have NextGen equipment on the flight deck. Data Comm will speed up departure queues and enable controllers to provide reroute information to airplane flight decks during a flight, thus saving time, reducing fuel costs, and streamlining air traffic flow across the National Airspace System (NAS) (Price & Forrest, 2014). Formerly called the **Aeronautical Data Link System (ADLS)**, Data Comm will replace or supplement routine voice communications with digital messages (i.e., text messaging). Data Comm could also provide aircraft data directly to emergency response vehicles in the event of declared emergencies (Prather, 2014b, p. 37).

System Wide Information Management (SWIM) is a platform that shares up-to-date and identical information among pilots, air traffic controllers, airline dispatchers, the military, government agencies, and other users of the NAS. SWIM also processes information from different information and data systems, such as airport operational status, weather information, flight data, status of Special Use Airspace, and airspace system restrictions (Price & Forrest, 2014).

Airport enhancements related to NextGen include **Geographic Information System (GIS)** integration, to provide detailed geospatial data about obstructions at airports, and transponder technology for surface vehicles operating in the movement area, to take better advantage of **Automatic Dependent Surveillance-Broadcast (ADS-B)**.

ADS-B is the component of NextGen that will eventually replace the use of radar in the air traffic system. Different from radar, ADS-B uses conventional **Global Navigation Satellite System (GNSS)**[54] technology and a broadcast communications link as its fundamental components. The ADS-B–capable aircraft uses a GNSS receiver to derive its precise position and then combines that position with additional aircraft information such as speed, heading, altitude, and flight number. This information is then simultaneously broadcast to other ADS-B–capable aircraft and to ADS-B ground or satellite communications transceivers, which then relay the aircraft's position and additional information to ATC centers in real-time. ADS-B is based on the assumption that all aircraft in the United States will be equipped with a GPS receiver and transmitter. ADS-B features the following qualities:

1. Automatic—always on and requires no operator intervention.
2. Dependent—depends on accurate GNSS signals for position data.
3. Surveillance—provides "radar-like" surveillance services.
4. Broadcast—continuously broadcasts aircraft position and other data to aircraft and ground stations equipped to receive ADS-B.

ADS-B technology derives its precision from a combination of GNSS positional data and any number of aircraft flight parameters, such as speed, heading, altitude, and flight number. This information is simultaneously broadcast to other ADS-B–capable aircraft, as well as to ADS-B ground or satellite communications transceivers, which relay the aircraft's position and additional information to ATC centers in real-time (Price & Forrest, 2014). The assumption is that as radar is slowly replaced by ADS-B, vehicles operating in the movement area will also be equipped with ADS-B technology in order to broadcast their positions to ATC.

BLENDED AIRSPACE

As part of NextGen, Blended Airspace is a new system of radar service technology currently being developed and tested in the State of Colorado. This project is known as the Colorado Surveillance Project (CSP) and is jointly managed by the FAA and the Colorado Department of Transportation (CDOT). Blended Airspace enables an integrated and seamless control of air traffic by offering radar services at nontowered and remote locations. In the Blended Airspace configuration, **MLAT** or **Wide Area Multilateration (WAM)** sensors are used to interrogate with an aircraft's transponder and relay that information on to an ATC radar controller that is located at a distance where traditional radar coverage is not available (Figure 7.53). MLAT sensors are distributed at nontowered airports and other remote areas to enhance operational radar services to aircraft. MLAT combined with ADS-B equipment will provide for continuous radar coverage of participating aircraft from published route segments to the surface of the airport. Blended Airspace is expected to affect operations personnel at many airports by increasing traffic to remotely located airfields and requiring new technologies to be located and maintained at the accommodating airport for Blended Airspace.

---

[54]As of 2015, the U.S. GPS and Russian GLONASS satellite system along with the developing EU/ESA Galileo and Chinese BeiDou satellite constellations comprise the evolving GNSS global positioning service.

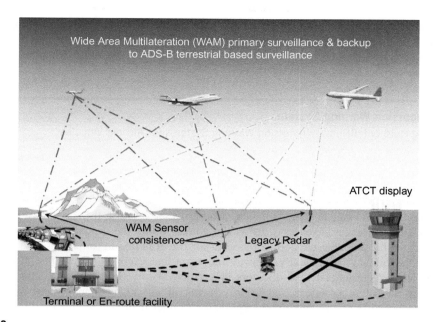

FIGURE 7.53

NextGen Blended Airspace depicting radar services to an aircraft beyond legacy radar services.

Source: CDOT. https://www.codot.gov/news/documents/WAMimage.jpg.

SUMMARY

Part 139 Certification of Airports includes several airfield maintenance and safety standards intended to provide a safe and efficient operating environment for aircraft operators. The airfield consists of runways, taxiways, aprons, terminal buildings, and other facilities necessary to provide for aviation activities. Although "airfield" is not a defined term, it is generally considered to be everything inside the airport perimeter fence (where one exists).

Aircraft reach high speeds on takeoff and landing and are not able to safely and quickly evade traffic or other objects on the runway. Therefore, runways are protected by a variety of methods, including the establishment of safety areas, OFAs, OFZs, and RPZs. The safety area is one of the most important elements and a required inspection item under Part 139. The safety area consists of a flat area to either side of the runway and off the approach and departure ends of the runway in the case of an aircraft departing the paved surface.

For nearly every airport in the United States, the condition of pavement is the airport's most important asset. The FAA requires that pavement be inspected to meet certain conditions and that pavement be constructed using specific procedures. Airport signs, markings, and lighting provide both pilots and vehicle operators information on how to safely navigate the airport and must also be maintained within certain standards.

Navigational aids provide pilots guidance information for en route flight and on approach to the airport. The condition of navigational aids must be inspected by airport personnel to ensure they are performing in the required manner. The inability of a navigational aid to function can affect the capacity of the airport and the safety of flight.

Runway Incursion Warning System

Approaching Hold Line! Runway Incursion Warning Systems for Airfield Vehicles

by Alex Gertsen, C.M.
Certified Member (CM), American Association of Airport Executives

Over the 110-plus years since powered flight has been a reality, continuous advances in safety have made aviation the safest means of travel. Despite this fact, it is not unusual to encounter a "white knuckle flier," someone who grips the armrest of their seat as the aircraft becomes airborne and relaxes as soon as the wheels touch the ground. Yet at the present time, statistically the most dangerous phase of air travel is taxiing on the ground and while being on the runway. Historically, runway incursion and excursion accidents have contributed to some of the largest fatal disasters in aviation history (Figure 7.54). Thus, thanks to great leaps in safety practices and improvements in air traffic management and aircraft safety, we should see more "white knuckle taxiers" rather than "white knuckle fliers."

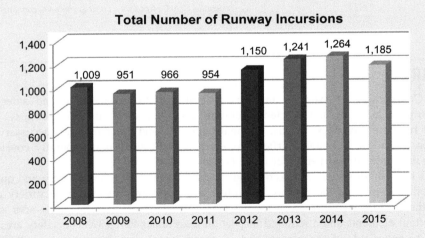

FIGURE 7.54

Frequency of U.S. runway incursions by year.

Source: Courtesy Alex Gertsen.

(Continued)

(Continued)

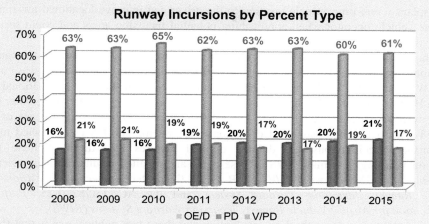

FIGURE 7.55

Operational error deviation (OE/D), pedestrian deviation (PD), and vehicle–pilot deviation (V/PD) incursions by yearly relative percentages.

Source: Courtesy Alex Gertsen.

A significant amount of responsibility for preventing runway incursions rests on the shoulders of Airport Operations staff and other vehicle operators who drive on the airfield. When they err, the resulting incursion would be classified as a Vehicle Pedestrian Deviation (VPD). This type of incursion accounts for approximately 20% of all incursions annually, as recorded by the FAA. Reviewing the statistics over the past 3 years, there are nearly 1,200 runway incursions recorded annually, with roughly 200 being attributed to VPDs. While the total numbers of incursions fluctuate slightly from year to year, it is interesting to observe that the relative percentages of the types of incursions, including VPDs, hold steady (Figure 7.55).

Navigating the airfield in a vehicle can be a challenge, and a loss of situational awareness could lead to a runway incursion and, in an extreme case, a major accident should a vehicle collide with an aircraft. An operator's situational awareness can be hindered by many factors such as reduced visibility, nighttime when the airfield turns into a "sea of lights," inclement weather, winter operations when white snow can obscure pavement markings, and distractions such as time pressure to complete airfield inspection related tasks, phone calls and radio transmissions, and use of electronic devices. Fatigue, complacency, and other human factors can also contribute to the increased risk of runway incursions.

The FAA recognizes the challenge of driving on the airfield and continuously assesses ways to reduce runway and other airport operational incursions. A recent area of interest has been on the use of GPS moving-map technology to reduce VPDs. A moving-map device

(Continued)

(Continued)

that displays a real-time vehicle position to the driver can improve locational awareness and alert the vehicle operator when approaching potential incursion areas and could serve as an effective runway incursion mitigation tool.

In the 2010–2011 timeframe, the FAA conducted research and evaluation of a stand-alone incursion warning system designed for airfield vehicle operators. The research was conducted at the William J. Hughes Technical Center, located at the Atlantic City International Airport in Egg Harbor Township, NJ. Two existing systems, one preconfigured and the other customizable, were used for the evaluation. The FAA initiative resulted in the release of recommended criteria for the design and operation of a system. The FAA established minimum performance specifications and defined optimal features for Airport Vehicle Runway Incursion Warning Systems (RIWS). These items and detailed results from the research are captured in the FAA report DOT/FAA/AR-11/26, titled *Development of an Airport Ground Vehicle Runway Incursion Warning System*, and the AC 150/5210-25, *Performance Specification for Airport Vehicle Runway Incursion Warning Systems (RIWS)*.

The key takeaway from the FAA evaluation and these two publications is that the warning distance must vary with speed. The FAA recommends that the RIWS trigger a proximity warning to alert the vehicle operator 60 feet in advance of approaching a boundary when traveling 10 miles per hour or less and that the warning distance increase 6 feet for every 1 mile per hour increase in speed. The FAA also recommends that a 30-foot warning buffer be established in advance of the key alert areas such as holding position markings, RSA boundaries, ILS critical area markings, and movement/non-movement area lines that could cause a surface incident. As an example, a vehicle traveling 30 miles per hour should receive an RIWS alert 210 feet in advance of approaching a runway hold line.

The RIWS device is intended to supplement, not replace, required airport familiarity, situational awareness, and ATC instructions. The FAA recommends that the RIWS devices provide both visual and audible alerts to allow the operator to discern key items with a quick glance at the screen as well as to hear alerts and encouraging the majority of the operator's attention to looking outside the vehicle and not on the moving-map display. RIWS devices can benefit the operator of any airfield vehicle—from the traditional Airport Operations truck or SUV, to the winter operations fleet, to mowers and other maintenance equipment.

Moving-map displays and incursion warning systems are already prevalent on the flight decks of modern, technologically advanced aircraft and have proved to be effective runway incursion mitigation tools. Research has shown that having technology that can alert the pilot directly, rather than the traditional method of the air traffic controller alerting the pilot via a radio transmission, reduces delay and saves the pilot valuable time to react. Recent developments in vehicle RIWSs can greatly assist airfield vehicle operators to maintain situational awareness and to overcome numerous challenges associated with driving on an airfield, especially during nighttime, low-visibility, and inclement weather conditions. Embracing this technology can help make driving on the airfield safer, greatly reduce the number of VPDs, and cause the fatality statistics associated with runway incursions to become part of the past.

(Continued)

(Continued)

Note: See FAA report DOT/FAA/AR-11/26 at: http://www.airtech.tc.faa.gov/safety/downloads/Development%20of%20an%20Airport%20Ground%20Vehicle%20Runway%20Incursion%20Warning%20System%2011-26.pdf

Part 139 Compliance

by Jim Payne
Director of Operations & Planning, BHM

"Commercial Service" airports exist primarily to serve passengers desiring to fly from point A to point B on an air carrier after purchasing a ticket. In order to allow scheduled air carrier service and serve those passengers, an airport must be certificated according to 14 CFR Part 139. This means that while it is often a daunting task, Part 139 compliance is the life blood of a commercial service airport. This vital aspect of airport management seems to be frequently overlooked in the classroom study programs leading into aviation management. This is unfortunate since without this compliance, an airport will not serve passengers and thus will not serve its purpose. A person intending to pursue a career in aviation management would be well served to spend considerable time focusing on Part 139 and the associated requirements.

To understand Part 139 and the associated requirements, the first step is to understand applicability. Even within the aviation industry, there is a divide on the regulations regarding an airport and its operation. These are typically built around whether the airport allows scheduled passenger service. It is best to use the words "scheduled air carrier" rather than, "commercial" when referring to 139 and the associated issues as "commercial" has a different definition for the FAA. Any airport can allow commercial traffic; i.e. pilots operating an aircraft for financial gain. However, to allow for air carrier use, i.e. scheduled operations of aircraft configured for more than 9 passengers or unscheduled operations of aircraft configured to carry at least 31 passengers, an airport must adhere to Part 139. Once an airport has complied with this regulation to the satisfaction of the FAA, the airport is issued an operating certificate and is then a certificated, or "Part 139" airport.

The intent of Part 139 is to ensure the safety of all airports allowing air carriers to serve passengers. Individuals boarding a general aviation aircraft understand the risks associated with that activity and accept those risks when choosing to fly. However, most passengers boarding air carrier aircraft assume that they will be safely conveyed from point A to point B. The regulations set by the FAA are intended to create as much safety as possible around the activity of flying, and to create consistency in what pilots and operators can expect from one airport to the next. To that end, Part 139 specifies many physical aspects of the airport such as the paved areas, unpaved areas, safety areas, signs, markings and lighting, wind

(Continued)

(Continued)

indicators and fuel storage. Part 139 also specifies support and procedural items such as Aircraft Rescue and Firefighting, snow and ice control, control of vehicles and pedestrians, training and recordkeeping. These specifications help to ensure safety of the airport.

Complying with the different aspects of Part 139 can be overwhelming. As with many regulations affecting the aviation industry, Part 139 sets the basics and leads one to other documents for the details. Though some aspects of the regulation set forth virtually the entire rule (mainly ARFF requirements of 139.15, .317 and .319), in most cases, 139 simply provides a quick outline of what the airport must do. For example, section 139.323-Traffic and Wind Direction Indicators states:

> In a manner authorized by the Administrator, each certificate holder must provide and maintain the following on its airport:
>
> a. A wind cone that visually provides surface wind direction information to pilots. For each runway available for air carrier use, a supplemental wind cone must be installed at the end of the runway or at least at one point visible to the pilot while on final approach and prior to takeoff. If the airport is open for air carrier operations at night, the wind direction indicators, including the required supplemental indicators, must be lighted.
>
> b. For airports serving any air carrier operation when there is no control tower operating, a segmented circle, a landing strip indicator and a traffic pattern indicator must be installed around a wind cone for each runway with a right-hand traffic pattern.
>
> c. FAA Advisory Circulars contain methods and procedures for the installation, lighting, and maintenance of traffic and wind indicators that are acceptable to the Administrator.

The opening line and the final item are the key to this section, and indeed most of Part 139. These items allow the FAA to direct the user to Advisory Circulars for specific guidance. The fact that a certificated airport accepts federal funding and accepts the requirements of the certificate change the ACs from advisory in nature to regulatory and thus binding upon the certificated airport. To find the regulations required to comply with the specific section noted above, one would refer to Advisory Circulars 150/5345-27, 150/5340-5, 150/5340-30 and 150/5300-13. Together, these documents represent hundreds of pages of data, with over a dozen pages dedicated solely to wind and traffic indicators. Combing through these vast libraries of specifications requires a great deal of time and dedication.

Ultimately, complying with Part 139 is about ensuring safety of the airfield. As defined in the regulation itself, airport operators are expected to take on this task themselves and self-inspect for compliance. Though they can inspect at any time without notice, the FAA typically only inspects an airport for compliance with Part 139 annually. This inspection captures a snapshot of the airport and of how well it is fulfilling the requirements of the regulation. Daily compliance and self-auditing to ensure said compliance falls on the airport operator. Thus, this is a major function for a certificated airport and one which requires a great deal of time and attention. However, performing this monumental task well ensures the safety of the millions of passengers using the national aviation system and keeping airports funded and operating.

REFERENCES

Alkali–Aggregate Reaction. (2008, July 1). Retrieved June 26, 2015, from: http://www.pavementinteractive. org/article/alkali-aggregate-reaction/.

Federal Aviation Administration (FAA). (n.d.a). *Airport obligations: Pavement maintenance*. Retrieved June 8, 2015, from: http://www.faa.gov/airports/central/airport_compliance/pavement_maintenance/.

Federal Aviation Administration (FAA). (n.d.b). Roles and Responsibilities of Air Traffic Control Facilities. Retrieved December 10, 2015, from: https://www.faa.gov/jobs/career_fields/aviation_careers/atc_roles/

Federal Aviation Administration (FAA). (2007). AC 150/5380-6, *Guidelines and procedures for maintenance of airport pavements*. Washington, DC: U.S. Department of Transportation, Federal Aviation Administration.

Federal Aviation Administration (FAA). (2009). AC 150/5320-6E, *Airport pavement design and evaluation*. Washington, DC: U.S. Department of Transportation, Federal Aviation Administration.

Federal Aviation Administration (FAA). (2011). Airfield Standards: A quick reference. Washington, DC: U.S. Department of Transportation, Federal Aviation Administration.

Federal Aviation Administration (FAA). (2012). AC 150/5340-30G, *Design and installation details for airport visual aids*. Washington, DC: U.S. Department of Transportation, Federal Aviation Administration.

Federal Aviation Administration (FAA). (2013a). A/C 150/5300-13A, *Airport design*. Washington, DC: U.S. Department of Transportation, Federal Aviation Administration.

Federal Aviation Administration (FAA). (2013b). AC 150/5340-1L, *Standards for airport markings*. Washington, DC: U.S. Department of Transportation, Federal Aviation Administration.

Federal Aviation Administration (FAA). (2015). *"Runway and taxiway safety areas FAQ."* (n.d.): n. pag. *Runway and taxiway safety areas*. FAA Southern Region, 10 Feb. 2015. Retrieved July 8, 2015, https:// www.faa.gov/airports/southern/airport_safety/runway_safety/media/rsa-tsa-faq.pdf.

Flight Service Operations. (2015, January 21). Retrieved July 22, 2015, from: http://www.faa.gov/about/office_org/headquarters_offices/ato/service_units/systemops/fs/.

Landsberg, B. (2014). Airspace for everyone. *AOPA Safety Advisor*, (1). Available from: http://dx.doi.org/10.1007/978-3-642-41714-6_11217.

Prather, C. D. (2011). *Airport self-inspection practices* (27th ed., Synthesis) (Transportation Research Board, Airport Cooperative Research Program). Washington, DC: National Academy of Sciences.

Prather, C. D. (2014a). *Airport certified employee-operations* (2nd ed.). Alexandria, VA: American Association of Airport Executives.

Prather, C. D. (2014b). *ACE-operations* (2nd ed., (2014). Print. Mod 3). Alexandria, VA: AAAE.

Price, J. C., & Forrest, J. S. (2014). *Certified member body of knowledge* (5th ed., Ser. 3). Alexandria, VA: American Association of Airport Executives.

Rossier, R. (1998, October). *Automatic weather*. Retrieved July 22, 2015, from: http://flighttraining.aopa.org/magazine/1998/October/199810_Features_Automatic_Weather.html.

FURTHER READING

Certification of Airports. (2004). 14 CFR Part 139.

Federal Aviation Administration (FAA). (2004). A/C 150/5210-22, *Airport certification manual*. Washington, DC: U.S. Department of Transportation, Federal Aviation Administration.

Whitlock, F., & Barnhart, T. L. (2007). *Capt. Jepp and the Little Black Book: How Barnstormer and Aviation Pioneer Elrey B. Jeppesen Made the Skies Safer for Everyone* [Kindle version]. Superior, WI: Savage.

AIRPORT SAFETY PROGRAMS

Runway lighting clearing system and snow plow, Aspen-Pitkin County Airport, CO.

Image by Shahn Sederberg, courtesy Colorado Division of Aeronautics, 2013.

Runway friction test vehicle and friction wheel, Aspen-Pitkin County Airport, CO.

Image by Shahn Sederberg, courtesy Colorado Division of Aeronautics, 2014.

Runway snow plow operations.

Courtesy Wichita Airport Authority (date unknown).

Title 14 Part 139 requires several safety- and operations-related programs that commercial service airports must maintain in order to be compliant with federal regulations. The programs are related to wildlife hazard management, snow and ice control, Aircraft Rescue and Firefighting response, pedestrian and ground vehicle operations, management of hazardous substances, and materials and construction safety. Performance measures, or standards, are in place within each of these programs, and each standard requires a written program in order to demonstrate compliance.

The Wildlife Hazard Management Plan (WHMP), the Snow and Ice Control Plan (SICP), and the Airport Emergency Plan (AEP) (each addressed in subsequent paragraphs), are typically physically separated documents from the Airport Certification Manual (ACM). The pedestrian- and ground-vehicle operations, Hazardous Material (HAZMAT), and Aircraft Rescue and Firefighting (ARFF) procedures are usually included in the body of the ACM whether physically separated or incorporated in the body of the ACM, the aforementioned plans are all considered part of the approved ACM from and FAA and airport sponsor perspective.

AIRPORT CONDITION REPORTING—NOTICES TO AIRMEN

In addition to the Airport Maintenance and safety standards (discussed in Chapter 7) and the airport safety program, one of the most critical components of Part 139 is the reporting of safety hazards and conditions of noncompliance to Part 121 air carriers. The main way to report such information is the Notices to Airmen (NOTAM) process, but other methods may be approved. One notable exception is during snow removal operations. Often the NOTAM process takes extra time between issuance of the NOTAM and its availability to the air carriers. During snow removal operations, airport operators commonly activate a snow control center and include an individual designated as a "snow boss." The snow boss (other names are used depending on the airport) commonly has the role of communicating airfield information directly to the air carriers through the use of a common, "ringdown phone,"[1] which air-carrier-operations personnel can access directly whenever there is an update. NOTAMs are still issued to reach the general aviation (GA) community, for general liability purposes, and to meet the regulatory requirement to notify air carriers via the NOTAM process, to ensure that information is disseminated throughout proper airport channels but may lag behind actual field conditions.

Items related to the movement areas, safety areas, aircraft-loading ramps and aprons required to be reported under Part 139 include:

1. Airport construction activities;
2. Surface irregularities or objects;
3. Snow, ice, slush or water and piled or drifting snow;
4. Airfield lighting malfunctions, holding position signs, or Instrument Landing System (ILS) critical area signs;
5. Wildlife hazards;
6. Status of ARFF equipment, personnel, and materials, if below the Part 139—required ARFF Index; and

---

[1]A ringdown phone automatically connects to other designated phones on the same line by lifting the handset. No dialing is needed to make the call.

7. Any other condition that could affect the safety operation of air carriers or called for by the ACM.

Federal Aviation Administration (FAA) Advisory Circular (AC) 150/5200-28, *Notices to Airmen (NOTAMs) for Airport Operators*, provides guidance to airport operators on the NOTAM process (FAA, 2008b, p. 6). From a practical perspective, NOTAMs are issued through a computer terminal, known as the ENII system or the Digital AIM/NOTAM Manager. Users must have email and a password in order to sign in and must be approved to issue NOTAMs. NOTAMs are typically issued by Airport Operations, but only certain individuals within the operations department have the authority to issue a NOTAM. Although another individual, such as someone in the communications center, may do the actual data entry, the NOTAM must contain the initials of the approved individual issuing the notice.

Previously, NOTAMs were issued either by direct telephone call with a Flight Service Station, a fax, or a phone call to the air traffic control tower. Computer technology allowed NOTAMs to be delivered electronically; however, the FAA would still review each NOTAM before allowing it into the National Airspace System. This process was time-consuming and often resulted in a delay of up to 20 minutes between the time a NOTAM was entered into the computer at the airport and finally approved and sent out to airmen. A list of authorized personnel must be on file with the Flight Service Station listed in the airport facility directory. NOTAMs can be issued immediately upon discovering an unsafe or a noncompliant condition, or they can be issued up to 3 days in advance for certain upcoming activities, such as planned runway closures because of construction.

NOTAMs must contain the following information in the order listed here:

1. Automatic Data Processing (ADP) code. This is always an exclamation point (!).
2. Three-letter identifier code for the accountability location (typically the airport's three-letter identifier) and a three-letter identifier code for the affected location.
3. One of 12 keywords, such as AD for Aerodrome, AIRSPACE for hazards relating to Special Use Airspace, RWY (runway), or TWY (taxiway); a complete list is in AC 150/5200-28D.
4. If appropriate, the Surface Identification, such as RWY 12/30, or a facility component such as APRON PARKING APRON ADJ TWY B, which means the affected area is the Apron, specifically the parking apron adjacent to taxiway B.
5. The year, month, day, and time for the beginning and end of the condition or the effective time (if known). NOTAMs are only issued in Coordinated Universal Time (UTC) time.
6. Keywords that describe the condition or situation, such as CLSD (closed), WEF (With Effect From), UFN (Until Further Notice).

This is an example NOTAM: **!ATL ATL APRON NORTH TWY L3 APRON CLSD 1505041300-1505041700**. It means: The Atlanta/Hartsfield Airport issues a Notice to Airmen regarding its own airport, notifying users that the North Taxiway L3 Apron is Closed effective 1300 May 4th 2015 until May 4th 1700 hours.

Whenever possible, NOTAMs must use official contractions and abbreviations, which can be found in FAA Order 7930.2 *Notices to Airmen*. NOTAMs must always state the abnormal condition, not the normal condition, and should be clear and concise. The only exception is when previously published information is being updated; for instance, issuing a NOTAM indicating that a previously closed runway is now open is acceptable.

TYPES OF NOTICES TO AIRMEN

The U.S. NOTAM Office (USNOF) is the authority ensuring NOTAM formats. NOTAM types include:

1. **NOTAM D:** Information that requires wide dissemination and pertains to navigational aids (NAVAIDs), civil, public-use airports listed in the Airport Facility Directories (AFDs), facilities, services, and procedures related to the National Airspace System. Airport operators issue D NOTAMs. The term *D NOTAMs* comes from a point in time when there were "L," or Local, NOTAMs, and "D," or Distant, NOTAMs. This terminology was confusing, so the term *Local NOTAM* was eliminated in favor of *D NOTAM*.
2. **Flight Data Center (FDC) NOTAMs:** FDS NOTAMs are normally used to disseminate safety of flight information relating to regulatory material, as well as all Instrument Flight Procedures, and are issued through the USNOF. FDC NOTAMs typically address changes to standard instrument approach procedures, instrument departure procedures, and special instrument flight operations.
3. **FDC: Air Defense Emergency NOTAMs:** Air Defense Emergency NOTAMs are issued as an FDC NOTAM, such as the NOTAM issued on 9/11, which effectively shut down the U.S. airspace system.
4. **FDC: Center Area NOTAMs:** Center Area NOTAMs are issued on airway changes, Temporary Flight Restrictions (TFRs), and [approved] laser light[2] activity that fall within an ARTCCs [Air Route Traffic Control Centers][3] airspace. FDC NOTAMs are also used to notify users of NAVAIDs and weather reporting stations that are out of service, public airports that are closed, and changes to runway identifiers.
5. **FDC: International NOTAMs:** International NOTAMs typically relate to outages of Omega (ONS) and GPS navigational systems and certain Special Use Airspace and warning areas.
6. **Military NOTAMs:** Military NOTAMs are used to notify users about outages of military NAVAIDs (U.S. Air Force, Army, Marines, Navy, and Coast Guard) that are part of the National Airspace System.
7. **Pointer NOTAMs:** Pointer NOTAMs are issued by the FSS (Flight Service Station)[4] to highlight or point out another NOTAM, such as an FDC or PJE (parachute jumping/skydiving) NOTAM. This type of NOTAM assists users in cross-referencing important information that may not be found under an airport or NAVAID identifier.

Digital Notices to Airmen

As part of NextGen, several upgrades are occurring in the NOTAM community. The **Federal NOTAM System (FNS) Concept of Operations (ConOps)** describes the modernization of the NOTAM system. Under the ConOps, the NOTAM process has been reengineered to support improved NOTAM origination, management, and distribution, with the NOTAM originator able to

---

[2]Some amusement parks use lasers nightly as part of a show, and other times lasers can be approved for outdoor concerts and other activities. The FAA must preapprove the use of the large lasers used in these types of activities.

[3]Position and hold (now Line Up and Wait) is an air traffic control (ATC) phrase that instructs a pilot to enter the active runway, line up the pilot's aircraft with the centerline, and then hold in position until given clearance to take off.

[4]Unicom is Universal Communication and is used for air-to-ground communication between pilot and FBO at an uncontrolled airport. CTAF is used for air-to-air communication between pilots at an uncontrolled airfield.

generate and submit the NOTAM using a web-based standard template (FAA, 2014b). FNS includes an eNOTAM II (ENII) application that improves the process for FAA Flight Services to review, approve, and coordinate analog NOTAMs. Electronic NOTAMs, referred to as **eNOTAMs**, allow NOTAMs to be transmitted to all air traffic management systems simultaneously and rapidly. NOTAM originators can use the ENII while preparing for transitioning to issuing digital NOTAMs. Some facilities have already made the move to the **NOTAM Manager**, a web interface similar to ENII but an upgraded version. The goal is that all NOTAM originators, including airports, will be part of the digital NOTAM system.

RUNWAY INCURSION PREVENTION

> Probably the most hazardous situation on any airport is a runway incursion, or the unauthorized or accidental entry of a vehicle, aircraft, or pedestrian onto the runway during flight operations. The potential for a catastrophic result dramatically increases as the number of persons, vehicles, and aircraft on the airport environment conduct operations closer to the runway.
>
> **Jim Payne, CM, ACE, Director of Operations & Planning, Birmingham Airport**

CASE STUDY

Tenerife Los Rodeo Airport

The deadliest accident in the history of aviation occurred in 1977, on the runway of the Los Rodeos Airport (now Tenerife North Airport) located on the island of Tenerife. While nearly 3,000 were killed on 9/11, the Tenerife event remains the deadliest incident to occur owing to a flaw in safety, not a terrorist or criminal attack; however, terrorism played a role in the tragedy. Both of the 747s were chartered, one a Pan Am flight out of New York by way of Los Angeles and the other a KLM flight out of Amsterdam to the Canary Islands, where passengers were supposed board cruise ships. Neither aircraft was supposed to board at Tenerife, however, a bomb planted by Canary Island separatists had recently exploded in an airport flower shop at the Las Palmas Airport, causing the diversion of several flights to other airports, including both 747's.

The collision of the two 747s resulted in the deaths of 583 of the 644 passengers on board both aircraft. Both aircraft were already on the ground at Tenerife and had been cleared to depart. However, several other diverted aircraft were also at the airport, blocking the sole taxiway. Aircraft were forced to use the active runway to taxi to the end of the runway, whereupon they would make a 180-degree turn and take off in the opposite direction. This process is known as a "back taxi." The KLM flight was leading the way down the runway with Pan Am following. Pan Am was supposed to make a turn off onto one of the taxiway connectors to allow the KLM flight to take off at the appropriate time, but the low visibility caused the Pan Am pilots to miss the turn. The few moments longer that Pan Am stayed on the runway in order to make the next taxiway connector would prove deadly.

The KLM flight taxied to the end of the runway and made its U-turn; however, because of garbled communications and low visibility, the KLM pilots thought they had received clearance to take off, not seeing or realizing that Pan Am was still on the runway. The KLM pilots realized at the last second that they were on a collision course and attempted to climb over the Pan Am flight, at the same time the Pan Am pilots realized what was happening and attempted to drive the aircraft into the grass. The undercarriage of the KLM flight struck the top of the Pan Am flight, setting off a series of explosions. All 248 passengers and crew aboard the KLM flight were killed, while 61 occupants of the Pan Am flight survived, including the 5 crew members in the cockpit.

Throughout the history of aviation, numerous aircraft collisions with other aircraft, vehicles, and personnel have occurred during takeoff and landing. The FAA has put a tremendous amount of effort into the prevention of runway incursions, a significant focus of Title 14 CFR Part 139.329.

RUNWAY INCURSIONS AND SURFACE INCIDENTS

The FAA defines a **runway incursion** as *"any occurrence at an aerodrome involving the incorrect presence of an aircraft, vehicle or person on the protected area of the surface designated for the landing and takeoff of aircraft"* (FAA, n.d.). The FAA defines a **surface incident** as *"the unauthorized or unapproved movement within the designated movement area, or an occurrence in that same area associated with the operation of an aircraft that affects or could affect the safety of flight"* (FAA, n.d.). To clarify, whenever an unauthorized vehicle, aircraft, or individual is on the movement area or in the wrong part of the movement area, the incident can be classified as a surface incident. A runway incursion is a surface incident that specifically involves the unauthorized presence of an aircraft, vehicle, or person on the runway (as opposed to the taxiway). For example, a vehicle operator inadvertently driving into the movement area and onto an active taxiway would be considered a surface incident, specifically of the Vehicle Pedestrian Deviation type. If a vehicle operator enters the runway or goes beyond the hold line without permission, this would be a surface incident and a runway incursion. The FAA divides runway incursions into five categories:

1. **Category A** is a serious incident in which a collision is narrowly avoided. In a Category A runway incursion, typically either an aircraft operator or the vehicle operator, must take evasive action to avoid a collision. An example could be a vehicle entering the active runway while an aircraft is landing, and either the vehicle operator or pilot must take evasive action to avoid a collision.
2. **Category B** is an incident in which separation decreases and there is a significant potential for collision, which may result in a time-critical, corrective/evasive response to avoid a collision. Often, the difference between a Category A and Category B runway incursion is the severity of the type of evasive action, along with the proximity of the aircraft to either the vehicle or the individual. Continuing with the previous example, a Category B incursion could be the aircraft or vehicle still takes evasive action but the separation was farther than in the case of Category A.
3. **Category C** is an incident characterized by ample time and/or distance to avoid a collision. An example in this case may be the vehicle entering the runway, but the aircraft is still a half mile or so away and the vehicle exits the runway long before the aircraft arrives.
4. **Category D** is an incident that meets the definition of a runway incursion, such as incorrect presence of a single vehicle/person/aircraft on the protected area of a surface designated for the landing and takeoff of aircraft but with no immediate safety consequences. An example in this case is a vehicle or pedestrian entering the runway without permission, with no aircraft on takeoff or landing, and the vehicle exiting the runway without incident.
5. A fifth type of runway incursion is an accident, which is an incursion resulting in a collision.

The severity of a runway incursion is based on several factors including the available reaction time, evasive or corrective action necessary to avoid the collision, environmental conditions, speed of the aircraft and/or vehicle, and proximity of the aircraft and or vehicle (Figure 8.1).

Runway incursions and surface incidents are also distinguished by who was potentially at fault. An *operational incident* is when an air traffic controller causes a situation that results in less than the required minimum separation between two or more aircraft or between an aircraft and obstacles, such as vehicles, equipment, and personnel on the runway, or clearing an aircraft to take off or land on a closed runway. Air traffic controllers unofficially refer to this as a *deal*. A *pilot deviation*

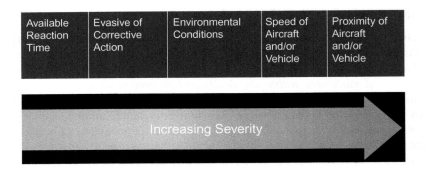

FIGURE 8.1

Primary factors leading to increased runway incursion severity.

Courtesy FAA from http://www.faa.gov/airports/runway_safety/news/runway_incursions/.

is when a pilot takes an action that violates the Federal Aviation Regulation, such as crossing the roadway without a clearance. A *Vehicle Pedestrian Deviation* (VPD) is when a pedestrian or vehicle enters any portion of the movement area (runways or taxiways) without authorization from air traffic control.

In 2014, the number of runway incursions totaled 1,264. Of those, 18% were VPDs, 20% were operational incidents, and the remaining 60% were pilot deviations. Although Part 139.329 specifically addresses the actions of vehicles and pedestrians on the movement area, airport operators should also support FAA and trade association safety programs that focus on pilot operating procedures while on the airport. A quick review of the runway incursion and surface incident totals recorded since 2011 indicates that VPDs have steadily increased. The FAA recommends the following methods to reduce VPDs (Oetzell, 2014):

1. Require initial and recurrent driver training;
2. Distribute to tenants newsletters, flyers, emails, and posters that focus on VPD awareness and prevention;
3. During special events, such as airshows, or airfield construction, ensure all personnel understand the limits of their movement on the airfield;
4. Inform and reinforce with airport tenants that unescorted visitors to the airport represent a significant opportunity for a VPD or runway incursion;
5. Consider enacting consequences for noncompliance with airport rules and regulations related to driving on the airfield that could include fines, revocation or suspension of driving privileges, or suspension of escort privileges, particularly in cases involving repeat offenders or egregious events; and,
6. Ensure all personnel involved with construction activities are familiar with the established ingress/egress routes and construction haul roads.

Part 139.329 calls for airport operators to limit access to the movement and safety areas to only those who are necessary for the operation of the airport and further to establish and implement procedures for access to an operation in the movement and safety areas by pedestrians and ground vehicles. The regulation separates the different responsibilities for airports with or without a control tower, including required training for all individuals that operate in the movement area on an annual basis.

The short length of the regulation can be deceptive compared to the importance placed on the concept. A significant amount of the FAA's resources and focus is on the prevention of runway incursions. FAA AC 150/5210-20 *Ground Vehicle Operations on Airports* (FAA, 2002) provides guidance to airport operators in developing an airfield driver training program and programs for the safe movement of ground vehicles and pedestrians on the airside of the airport. Although the FAA does not presently require that vehicle operators who only operate in the non-movement area receive any sort of driver training, it is considered a best practice to have such a program in place.

According to the FAA, every year, accidents and incidents involving aircraft, pedestrians, and ground vehicles occur at airports, leading to property damage, injury, and death. Many of the events result from inadequate security measures, a failure to maintain airfield signs, markings, and lighting, and inadequate vehicle operator training (FAA, 2002). Pursuant to the FAA Modernization and Reform Act of 2012 (Pub. L. No. 112-95, Section 314(a)), the FAA developed *The Strategic Runway Safety Plan* (FAA, 2012). The extensive report outlines numerous strategies to reduce runway incursions on airports, including efforts by the FAA to use voluntary, self-reporting systems for Air Traffic Operations (ATO) personnel; conducting initial and periodic safety reviews at airports where departures on the wrong runway are of greatest concern; implementing enhanced taxiway centerline markings at all Part 139–certificated airports; and reviewing airport vehicle operator training (FAA, 2012, p. 2). Numerous other strategies are outlined, including accelerating the deployment of Airport Surface Detection Equipment (ASDE-X) and runway status lighting systems at the busiest airports and adoption of standardized air-traffic controller runway clearance phraseology (replacing the previous "position and hold"[3] to the international standard of "line up and wait").

In a report titled the ***National Runway Safety Plan, 2009–2011***, the FAA outlined several measures to reduce runway incursions. First was establishing Runway Safety Performance metrics (FAA, 2009c). These metrics include the frequency, severity, and type of runway incursion. Classifying runway incursions allows the FAA and the airport operator to provide targeted solutions to reduce incursions. The second measure included providing numerous recommendations that applied more specifically to pilot operations; however, there were a few notable programs mentioned related to Airport Operations. **Runway Safety Action Teams** conduct meetings at airports that experience frequent or severe runway incursion incidents. The teams meet to identify and address existing and potential runway safety problems and to identify corrective actions to further improve runway safety (FAA, 2009c). The teams also identify "hot spots" on airports. The International Civil Aviation Organization (ICAO) defines a "hot spot" as a location on the movement area with a history or potential risk of collision or runway incursion and where heightened attention by pilots/drivers is necessary. Hot spot brochures were developed and distributed to 50 airports. These hot spots are also now notated on aeronautical charts.

Limit Access to the Movement Area

Part 139.329(a) requires airport operators to limit access to the movement area to only the pedestrians and vehicles that are necessary for Airport Operations and maintenance. Reducing the number of vehicles and pedestrians in the movement area lessens the opportunity for a vehicle or pedestrian to interfere with the movement of an aircraft. Airport operators are ultimately responsible for the safety of the movement area and should establish strict policies on which individuals may operate in the movement area and when. Some airport operators require personnel to contact a duty manager to receive permission to enter the movement area, before asking for permission from air traffic control. Others assume that once the individual has completed the movement area driver-training program, the individual may access the movement area as needed to perform routine job duties. If the individual is found to be accessing the movement area outside of job parameters, disciplinary action may be warranted. During certain airfield conditions, such as emergency situations, periods of low visibility, and snow removal operations, airport operators may further limit the vehicles and personnel who are allowed to enter the movement area.

Airfield driver-training programs are required under Part 139 for all individuals who operate in the movement area. However, airport operators may determine whether an individual needs to operate a vehicle in the movement area with enough frequency that the individual should be trained or determine that the individual's activities in the movement area are infrequent and that it is therefore safer to provide an escort to the worksite. Airport firefighters, Airport Operations personnel, and airfield maintenance personnel, by necessity, should be authorized to operate vehicles in the movement area. Some airport personnel, particularly FAA maintenance personnel, only frequent the airport a few times a year and should be escorted to their work locations. FAA Tech Services personnel are responsible for maintaining many of the airport's NAVAIDs and the approach lighting system. While these personnel are familiar with operating on airport movement areas, each airport is different, and the infrequency with which they operate at a particular airport may result in a dangerous level of unfamiliarity. The airport operator must make the judgment call. Some FAA Tech Services personnel work frequently at the airport and should be provided driver training as constantly escorting them throughout the movement area is impractical.

Whether airport police should be provided routine access to the movement area and receive movement area driver training is a topic of debate in the industry. Some airport operators argue that police should have access to all areas of the airport, including runways and taxiways, at any time. Others counter that police officers do not normally patrol runways and taxiways and only need to access the movement area during an emergency. If an emergency occurs, Airport Operations or Air Traffic Control Tower personnel can immediately close the impacted sections of the airport to flight operations, in which case airport police are free to proceed to the incident site. A common compromise is to provide airfield driver training to all police officers but not require them to patrol the runways and taxiways as part of their normal patrol pattern. This reduces the number of unnecessary vehicles in the movement area yet still provides them the baseline information necessary for talking to the tower in responding to staging locations if necessary.

With some exceptions, airport tenants, contractors, and vendors should not receive movement area driver training, nor be allowed access to the movement area, unless under escort. At certain small airports, crossing taxiways may be the only viable method for tenants, such as Fixed Base Operators (FBOs) or air carrier personnel, to move from one location of the airport to another. In this case, it would make sense to provide the FBO with movement area driver training. Otherwise, tenants, vendors, and contractors have little reason to operate in the movement area.

Additionally, inadvertent access to the movement area (and non-movement area) also poses a danger to aircraft operations. Airports should use fencing, gates, natural barriers such as land berms and culverts, and other methods to prevent the inadvertent access to the airfield by unauthorized personnel. There have also been incidents where an individual intentionally accessed the movement area by jumping the airport perimeter fence. Procedures should be in place with the airport operator and Air Traffic Control (ATC) to immediately cease flight operations upon becoming aware of such an intrusion and police notified to interdict the intruder. Personnel who routinely operate in the movement area should also always be aware of unauthorized personnel or vehicles, or unusual activity taking place in the movement area.

AIRFIELD DRIVER TRAINING

Part 139 airports are required to provide driver training to individuals operating in the movement area on an initial and annual basis (every 12 consecutive calendar months). Many Part 139 airports also require non-movement area driver training. Although not presently required by the FAA, doing so is considered a best practice. GA airports should follow the Part 139 airports in this regard, under the auspices of Grant Assurance #19—Operations and Maintenance, which requires the airport operator to operate the facility in a safe condition.

Another distinction between movement area and non-movement area driver training is that in most cases, movement area driver training requires the trainee to accompany an instructor into the movement area and practice scenarios moving from one point to another on the airfield. It is often impractical at large airports to ask trainees to demonstrate their driving ability, so "driving tours" with an airfield driver trainer and a vanload of trainees are more commonly used. If individuals have a surface incident or runway incursion, then a demonstration of their driving ability may be required before they are granted access to the movement area in the future.

Non-movement area driver training usually consists of computer- or classroom-based instruction rather than a practical demonstration. Some tenants are also given the authority to conduct non-movement area driver training for their employees. They should have a robust training program to ensure that their personnel are not involved in a surface incident or runway incursion.

Airfield driver training must also take into account emergency operations and irregular operations, such as airfield construction activities, snow removal activities, VIP (very important person) arrivals and departures, and low-visibility operations. Irregular operations may also include film-making activities, aircraft static displays (i.e., airport open house), airshows, and other unique situations that arise from time to time. Vehicle and pedestrian activities during irregular operations should be carefully reviewed to ensure the safety of the movement area and flight operations.

Any policy on who may access the movement area and when must also include the minimum vehicle equipment requirements. At a minimum:

1. Vehicles should be clearly marked/flagged for high daytime visibility and lighted for night operations.
2. **Aircraft always have the right-of-way** over vehicles in the movement and non-movement area, even over emergency response vehicles, except when ATC has specifically instructed an aircraft to hold or give way to vehicles. Common sense must also prevail—if ATC clears a vehicle to enter a runway while an aircraft is on takeoff or landing, then the vehicle operator should have received training on these types of situations (when someone else is making a mistake and causing a safety situation to occur) and take the appropriate action.
3. Vehicles operators should have a two-way radio to communicate with the ATC tower (ATCT) and a radio or other approved means of communications with Airport Operations.

4. At airports without an operating control tower, vehicles and FBO personnel accessing the taxiways and runways should broadcast their intentions over the ATC frequency in use at the airport for the benefit of airport operators but should refrain from using the VHF (very high frequency) aircraft frequency for discussions between other vehicle operators.

5. Many airports also establish minimum insurance requirements for vehicles accessing the movement area and minimum vehicle condition standards.

Overall, general best practices for operating vehicles in the movement and safety areas include:

1. Vehicle operators should use designated Vehicle Service Roads (VSRs) at all times, when able, rather than crossing a runway or taxiway. Additionally, normal road signs should be used on VSRs whenever possible, to reduce confusion that may be caused by using airfield markings and signage.

2. Any vehicle operated by a driver who has not received movement area driver training should be escorted by an approved driver while operating on the airfield. This is also true of vehicles that intend to operate only in the non-movement area. Vehicle operators who are unfamiliar with airport markings may easily end up driving on a runway if left to drive solo in the air operations area.

3. Construction areas should have adequate signage or barricades to prevent inadvertent entry into the safety area or movement area.

4. When operating loud equipment, such as mowing vehicles, operators should use noise-cancelling headsets tuned into the tower frequency. Additionally, Airport Maintenance and operations vehicles should have an external speaker for times when personnel are outside their vehicle in the movement or safety areas, so that they can monitor ATC communications.

5. Operators should focus on maintaining **situational awareness (SA)**. SA is a term often used in the pilot community that generally means to be paying attention to and aware of one's surroundings. Texting, cell phone use, vague communications, running behind schedule, or being overtasked contribute to a loss of SA, which can result in a runway incursion. Bad weather, low visibility, fatigue, and stress may also reduce SA. Drivers should never text while driving in the movement area (or anywhere else), while the vehicle is in motion, or use the cell phone for nonessential situations. Drivers should be trained to continually scan the area that may be in or converging with the path of the vehicle and to take the appropriate action early on to avoid a conflict.

6. Before entering any runway, check for aircraft that may be on approach, takeoff, or landing, and ensure that the ATC clearance to enter the runway was for that particular vehicle operator.

Upon establishing a policy and a driver-training program, airport operators should focus on continual training of personnel operating in the movement area and enforcement of rules and regulations related to access to the movement area. The basics of managing a vehicle access control program include an identification system, which can often be combined with the airport badging system for an airport that is required to have identification badges under Title 49 CFR Part 1542 (Airport Security). Additionally, airport operators should require vehicle driver permits that are nontransferable to other vehicles, and airport law enforcement and operations and security personnel should conduct periodic checks to ensure individuals on the airfield have the appropriate authorization. Commercial service airports commonly have a badging system; however, it is less common for GA airports to require identification badges to enter the airfield. Certain high-use GA airports have installed fences and gates and have implemented an identification badge process; however, in most cases, the requirements for a badge at a GA airport do not extend to the level of requirements to receive an Airport Identification Badge at a commercial service airport, as GA airports are typically not regulated by the Transportation Security Administration (TSA). FAA AC 150/5210-20 (FAA, 2002) contains a complete curriculum to develop an airfield driver-training program.

SNOW REMOVAL OPERATIONS AND RUNWAY INCURSIONS

Many runway incursions and surface incidents take place during periods of low visibility and inclement weather, specifically snow and ice control operations. In 2008, *Airport Cooperative Research Program (ACRP) Synthesis 12: Preventing Vehicle—Aircraft Incidents During Winter Operations and Periods of Low Visibility* was published, documenting best practices as applied to these concerns (Quilty, 2008). Quilty identified several elements that contribute to surface incidents and runway incursions, along with mitigating and preventative measures, and identified seven specific categories:

1. Communication
2. Environment
3. Human Performance
4. Situational Awareness
5. Pressure to Keep the Runway Open
6. Vehicle and Equipment Resources
7. Operational Factors

Quilty also identified an extensive list of technological developments designed to reduce surface incidents and runway incursions.

Communication

Poor communication is often cited as a primary factor that increases the risk of a collision. The vehicle operators' failure to switch frequencies, operating on the wrong frequency, radio congestion, or background noise contribute to communication issues (Quilty, 2008, p. 12). Talking on the tower frequency can be intimidating for the uninitiated. Air traffic controllers and pilots talk very fast and tend to fall into a rhythm that can sound completely foreign for a first-time-in-VHF radio user. The process at an airport with the control tower when a vehicle driver desires to talk to the ATCT is to first ensure one is on the correct frequency. Then listen for a few moments to determine if a pilot or other vehicle operator and a controller are already having an exchange. When there is a break in communication, depress the talk button on the radio and say who you are calling, identify who you are, and wait for a response from ground or tower control. Upon acknowledgment from either ground or tower, as appropriate, respond with your identity, where you are located, and your request or intentions. Then wait for a response. After the response, repeat back any transmission that involves holding short at a hold line, and preferably read back enough of the instructions so that the ground or tower operator understands that you understand and will comply with the instructions.

This exchange is slightly different for pilots who are used to calling the tower or ground control, identifying themselves, and including their location and request in one transmission. At an airport without a control tower, come up on Unicom or the Common Traffic Advisory Frequency stating the airport name, identifying your vehicle and position and your intentions, and then restating the airport name. There are often several airports using the same frequency on **Unicom** or **Common Traffic Advisory Frequency (CTAF)**,[4] so it is a good idea to repeat the airport's name at the beginning and the end of the transmission.

From a training perspective, it might be beneficial for vehicle operators to spend a few minutes monitoring the tower frequency from time to time in order to get used to the tempo and vocabulary used by ATC and pilots. A significant distraction in a vehicle operating in the movement area can be the very radio frequencies the vehicle operator is required to monitor. Some drivers, particularly lead vehicles in a snowplow team, must monitor two or three different frequencies, so from a technological standpoint, having the capability to tune in different frequencies to different speakers within the vehicle cab is helpful (Quilty, 2008, p. 17). To combat driver fatigue, a few operators indicated they use AM/FM music radios to help keep them awake. Driver fatigue is a major issue that is better managed through means that address the root cause and do not contribute to driver distraction (Quilty, 2008, p. 17). Additionally, the use of personal musical devices often involves earplugs or headphones, and research indicates that many drivers would rather pay attention to the vehicle noises to listen for anomalies or issues (Quilty, 2008, p. 17). Proper radio communication procedures, monitoring, and transmitting on the proper frequencies in minimizing unnecessary radio calls can improve communications and reduce errors in communication on the airfield.

Environment

Environmental factors that are typically encountered during winter operations and may result in a surface incident include changing weather conditions; gusting winds and blowing snow; whiteout conditions; night operations; poor traction resulting from ice, snow, glycol, or runway deicing chemicals on the airfield; and congestion of vehicles and aircraft (Quilty, 2008, p. 13). Quilty noted that poor visibility was the most often cited factor related to environmental conditions and the potential for an accident (Quilty, 2008, p. 13). Although weather and visibility conditions contribute to navigational difficulties for vehicle operators, bright lights on the runways and taxiways, amplified and refracted during wet conditions, and the increased speed of vehicles also contribute to collision hazards. Airport operators may wish to establish an RVR (Runway Visual Range), below which vehicle operations on the airfield are ceased, or flight operations are ceased, while vehicles continue to clear snow and ice (Quilty, 2008, p. 22).

Human Performance

Fatigue was the second most often cited factor affecting the possible risk of a collision during winter operations, and not just fatigue of vehicle operators but also of air traffic controllers and pilots. Sleep deprivation, sensory overload, radio chatter, repetition of activity, physiological needs, and the expectation to keep the airport open all contribute to reduced human performance while operating on the airfield (Quilty, 2008, p. 13). Snow removal operations at an airport occur in a fast-paced, high-stress environment, with the push to get snow cleared and the runway open and available for flight operations. Snow removal crews typically work 12 hours on and 12 hours off for several days at a time and may not have the opportunity to go home in the meantime, either because of severe weather conditions in the community or their need to be quickly back on shift. Some airports may make accommodations in local hotels for snowplow operators to stay during their 12 hours off, while other personnel may not be so fortunate and may need to find a comfortable location in someone's office. Some airports have developed snooze rooms for crews to rest in between shifts. The nature of snow removal operations also contributes to fatigue, particularly at night. Forward visibility from the vehicle can be severely limited, with falling snow, blowing snow, or snow being cast from another snowplow creating a vertigo effect for the driver. Fatigue is basically an individual's inability to maintain sufficient alertness for the job (Quilty, 2008, p. 23). Acute fatigue is short-term and is the result of a strenuous exercise or intense mental concentration, which can occur during winter storm operations (Quilty, 2008, p. 23). Chronic fatigue is a continued state of tiredness and decreased alertness and is directly related to the physiological need for sleep. Chronic fatigue is more severe and can take longer to recover from than acute fatigue (Quilty, 2008, p. 23). Fatigue is effectively reduced with sleep and by meeting other needs of the physiology, including adequate sleep or rest facilities, nutritional foods and beverages, and ergonomic considerations in the design of the vehicle cab (Quilty, 2008, p. 26). Limiting duty time and providing frequent breaks can also reduce fatigue, as can rotating assignments between plows, blowers, sweepers, and other assignments that require the use of different motor skills and different mental processes (Quilty, 2008, p. 26). The use of stimulants such as caffeine is effective in the short term, but vehicle operators should also be taught some basic stretching exercises and the foods and drinks that will provide them longer-term endurance (Quilty, 2008, p. 27).

Situational Awareness

As previously discussed, SA refers to the ability of an individual to pay attention to and be aware of the individual's surroundings. While other elements are commonly cited as a factor for a surface incident or runway incursion, Quilty identified that a common element in many Vehicle Pedestrian Deviations is that the individual lost SA or never had it to begin with (Quilty, 2008, p. 13). Unfortunately, in the pilot community, accidents are commonly the result of a loss of SA. Pilots become overwhelmed by the events of the situation and do not notice the accident chain beginning to form before it is too late. Similarly, many automobile accidents are the result of a loss of SA, many times caused by distracted drivers. On an airfield, a loss of SA can happen to vehicle operators, pilots, or air traffic controllers. Vehicle operators can increase SA by reviewing the airport surface conditions before beginning snow removal operations and even before accessing the airfield (Quilty, 2008, p. 30). This mental pre-preparation can effectively "prime the pump," preparing the operator to enter the airfield environment. Limiting conversations while on the runway, particularly with others who may be in the vehicle, being aware of the airport surface condition, and verifying radio transmissions from the tower increase SA. If the radio fails or the driver loses SA, moving a safe distance off the runway before stopping is better than stopping on a potentially active runway. Airports should develop emergency procedures for vehicle operators unable to communicate via radio. The typical lost communications process is to turn your vehicle toward the tower, flash your lights, stand by, and wait for light gun signals from the tower, but this can be impractical during snow operations. Additionally, the light gun signal technique was developed before the advent of cell phones, so there were few alternatives for a vehicle driver with lost communications to do, other than park the vehicle and flash the headlights at the tower until someone noticed.

Time Pressures

Individuals conducting snow removal operations are often under intense pressure by ATC, air carriers, and their own supervisory personnel to complete the snow removal operation as quickly as possible in order to keep aircraft moving. This pressure, previously discussed in the safety management sections of this text, can cause individuals to make poor decisions that can result in a collision. *ACRP Synthesis 12* identified several sources of pressure, including the pressure by airline tenants to remove snow from their operational areas, aircraft delays or canceled flights, airport management's decision to keep the airport open when other airports are closed, pressure by ATC to not close a runway and then to reopen it as quickly as possible, and the impact of airport closures on the financial status of the airport (Quilty, 2008, p. 32). Methods management may use to reduce time pressure include setting realistic expectations about the time it takes to remove snow and the complexities of snow removal operations; providing sufficient resources in terms of personnel, materials, and equipment; providing better direction and prioritization of tasks; recognizing that not everything can be priority one; and finally realizing that sometimes Mother Nature wins that round (Quilty, 2008, p. 34). Sometimes the airport must occasionally shut down in order to allow snow removal personnel to catch up with the storm.

Personnel, Vehicles, and Equipment Resources

Not having enough vehicles, equipment, or personnel may contribute to collision hazards. Also the speed of vehicles on the airfield, airfield signage and lighting, and vehicle design elements are also factors cited in collision hazards (Quilty, 2008, p. 13). In December 2006, at Denver International Airport, a snowstorm overwhelmed the airport's ability to maintain an open status. While most people understand that any airport, no matter how much personnel, materials, and resources it may have available, cannot defeat every possible storm, Denver's criticism came in their inability to quickly reopen the airport days after the snow stopped falling. In an after-action analysis produced by Critical Path, the consultant determined that the airport did not have enough equipment to handle 4 inches of snowfall on the ramp, that the airport did not have adequate space to use as a snow dump and should purchase snow melters, and that the airport should purchase high-speed, multifunction, snow removal equipment that combines plowing, sweeping, and snow blowing (at a low level) in one unit (Associated Press [AP], 2007). While Denver experiences routine snowstorms and the occasional blizzard throughout the winter season, typically within a day or so the sun melts the majority of stockpiled snow and allows snow crews to catch up. The storm of 2006 demonstrated that sun melt is not always an effective plan. Denver International Airport (DEN) purchased numerous pieces of multifunction equipment and snow melters and revised its entire snow removal operations plan in order to better accommodate future storms (AP, 2007). Other factors that contribute to reducing collision hazards related to equipment include effective windshield wiper and defrosting systems on the vehicle and procedural measures so that plow drivers do not follow too closely behind the vehicle in front, which can ice their windshield up to the point at which wipers and defrost measures are ineffective (Quilty, 2008, p. 36).

Operational Factors

Related to *Synthesis Report 12*, operational factors include a variety of other elements, including non-routine vehicle and aircraft traffic patterns causing congestion, changes in the airfield configuration as a result of wind changes or snow blocking areas of the movement area, and new or inexperienced employees or contractors operating on the airfield (Quilty, 2008, p. 13). Airport operators commonly employ contractors or temporary help during winter snow operations. Operational factors include a variety of other challenges that increase the chance of collision hazards on an airfield during snow removal. Airport tenants are often required to plow snow from their own leasehold areas, which puts contractors on the airfield and increases the potential for a surface incident or runway incursion. However, most airport operators also use contract personnel or temporary personnel for snow removal operations. While many of the contractors are restricted to landside snow removal activities, airport operators commonly certify airport administrative personnel and allow them to draw overtime during winter operations, in effect leaving the cubicle to come outside and plow snow. While these individuals may have high levels of familiarity and experience on the airfield, they typically do not have recent experience because they are only used a portion of the time each year. Some common practices overall to reduce runway collision hazards include putting one person in charge of all snow removal operations and using the Incident Command span of control rule so that no one individual is supervising more than five to seven individuals at any given time. Additional measures include closing a runway during snow removal operations using full-scale driving simulators that can both train drivers how to operate on the airfield and can also present situational challenges, and developing methods or procedures to ensure that vehicles are clear of a runway prior to reopening (Quilty, 2008, pp. 42–43).

Technologies to Reduce Runway Incidents During Snow Removal Operations

In addition to airfield driving simulators, a variety of technologies are being implemented to reduce collision hazards on the airfield. These technologies include the use of ASDE-X; the Airport Movement Area Safety System; Automatic Dependent Surveillance-Broadcast (ADS-B); Runway Status Lights; Global Positioning System (GPS) vehicle tracking with a computer monitor located in the operations office; the control tower and other vehicles that can track vehicles on the airport; and driver-enhanced vision systems similar to a heads-up display or night vision goggles, which may enhance visibility during darkness and poor visibility. Runway Guard Lights, enhanced runway lead-on lights, and enhanced taxiway surface markings are technologies and solutions that are already being implemented.

SNOW AND ICE CONTROL PLAN

Snow and ice can cause hazardous conditions on an airfield. Snow reduces friction, braking action, and directional control of both aircraft and vehicles and can impede aircraft acceleration for take-off. Accumulations of snow on an aircraft increase the weight of the airplane and may disrupt the aerodynamic flow of air over the wings, which can have disastrous results. The crash of an Air Florida flight into the Potomac River as it departed Washington National Airport (now known as Washington/Reagan National) in 1982 and the crash of a Continental Airlines flight out of Stapleton International Airport in Denver, Colorado, in 1987, were both attributed two snow and ice accumulating on the aircraft surface. Both aircraft waited too long after deicing operations to take off, and their control surfaces started to refreeze.

Snow also can significantly reduce airfield capacity, causing airlines to cancel flights and Airport Operations to significantly slow down, or, in some cases, to stop entirely. Part 139.313 requires every Part 139–certificated airport to have an **SICP**. The plan must address procedures for the prompt removal or control of snow, ice, and slush on the movement areas and the positioning of snow away from movement areas so as to be clear of propellers, engine pods, rotors, and wingtips, using approved materials. The plan must also provide for the timely commencement of snow and ice control operations and the prompt notification to all air carriers of the condition of the runways and taxiways in use. Passengers and air carriers have an expectation that airports that experience snow should be able to handle routine snowstorms and keep aircraft moving as much as possible. FAA AC 150/5200-30C *Airport Winter Safety and Operations* (FAA, 2008a) addresses best practices and techniques for developing an SICP, snow and ice control and removal techniques, and runway surface assessment and reporting.

Although the airport operator is ultimately responsible for overseeing snow removal operations, the individuals performing the function may work for a variety of entities. Small airports may rely on the snow removal resources of their sponsor in the case of a city- or county-operated airport. In this regard, the airport may simply be rolled into a component of the city or county's overall snow removal program. This situation is not desirable for an air carrier airport and may not be approved by the FAA if the airport cannot meet the requirement for the timely commencement of snow removal operations. It is preferable for airports to have their own snow removal equipment so that the airport operator can retain control of the equipment and the equipment and materials are specific to Airport Operations, as opposed to normal road snowplows.

The FAA provides airport operators with optimal snow removal clearance times to guide them in determining the amount of snow removal equipment that is optimal for their airport. Additionally, snow removal personnel may be Airport Operations or maintenance personnel; contracted personnel; airport tenants such as airlines and FBOs; or city, county, or state snow removal equipment operators. The FAA provides significant guidance on snow removal at airports. In addition to the AC, the FAA also publishes Program Guidance Letters (PGLs) and CertAlerts to clarify certain areas of the SICP, along with an SICP template.

THE SNOW AND ICE CONTROL COMMITTEE

All airports that are subject to icy conditions or annual snowfall of 6 inches or more should have a Snow and Ice Control Committee (SICC). The SICC focuses on preseason planning, improving runway safety and communications during a snow event, addressing the needs of airport users, and critiquing snow removal performance from the previous season (FAA, 2008a). The size of the committee varies based on the airport and its individual characteristics but should generally include Airport Operations and maintenance staff, airline flight operations and FBO personnel, ATC personnel, and any other key stakeholders, such as the U.S. military at a joint- or shared-use airport. The FAA's template on the SICP includes a significant list of topics to be discussed in the committee, including designating airfield priorities in snow removal, reviewing the status of procurement contracts for snow removal and deicing materials, training issues, staffing requirements, and equipment inventory. The committee should also address air carrier or FBO deicing, anti-icing, and snow removal operations. The offseason is when the committee meets most frequently, when equipment is repaired, materials are acquired, and most training of snow removal operators is conducted. Timelines should also be established for the readiness of equipment and materials at least 30 to 60 days prior to the beginning of the expected snow season.

In addition to SICC meetings during the offseason, after each snow event, airport management should host a meeting and invite the FAA, airlines, and FBOs to evaluate the snow events and the response. An action meeting should also be held at the end of snow season, prior to the more formal SICC meetings in the summer.

The FAA strongly recommends that the SICP contain specific safety procedures to reduce and prevent surface incident/runway incursions during snow removal operations (FAA, 2008a).

SNOW AND ICE REMOVAL CRITERIA

The SICP should address the following elements (FAA, 2008a):

1. Who or what entity is responsible for weather forecasting and what equipment is present or needed.
2. **Chain of command** to determine the responsible parties to monitor the airfield, inspect the airfield, and establish a Snow Alert Callout.
3. The triggers for initiating snow removal operation such as a certain level of precipitation (e.g., depth in inches of slush, wet snow, dry snow, or ice or freezing rain).
4. Personnel responsible for snow removal operations at the airport inspection, NOTAM issuance and command.
5. The operation of the **Snow Control Center (SCC)**. Depending on the size of the airport, the SCC, sometimes referred to as a "snow desk," might be in a small operations office, or the command vehicle of the lead operations agent in charge of snow removal, or an Incident Command center at the airport. The SCC manages snow-clearing operations; is the primary source of field condition reporting (braking action, snow accumulations); advises the ATCT, air carriers, and other tenants of runway closures and openings; and issues NOTAMs (FAA, 2008a). Some large-hub airports will assign a "snow boss" whose only responsibility is to provide real-time updates to the airlines during snow removal operations. SCCs may also contain weather reporting and monitoring equipment or be integrated with the airport's communications center or operations center.
6. **Airfield clearing priorities:** Priority 1 areas are the most critical portions of the movement area and supporting facilities, including primary runways, turnoffs, associated taxiways, terminal and cargo ramps, ARFF stations, and designated response roads for ARFF equipment to respond to the runway, and any associated NAVAIDs. Priority 2 areas are of less importance than Priority 1 and typically include the crosswind or secondary runways. Priority 3 areas are typically not essential to flight operations or use on a daily basis. Some airports will only establish Priority 1 or Priority 2 areas, whereas others may go beyond and establish Priority 3, 4, and 5 areas, with the last designator usually focused on landside operations. For a large, outdoor, medium-hub airport, however, they will typically have separate equipment to clear landside operations, conducted simultaneously with airfield snow removal operations. While it is a regulatory function to ensure the removal of snow from, for example, movement areas, it is a practical consideration that passengers must be able to access the airport landside in order for the airport to continue functioning during snow events.
7. **Airfield clearance times:** The FAA publishes airfield clearance times and goals, but these goals are not required to be met (FAA, 2008a, p. 3). Each airport should use the FAA's **clearance times for commercial service airports** (Figures 8.2 and 8.3) as a baseline to establish their own clearance objectives. The FAA says that airports should have sufficient equipment to clear within a reasonable time 1 inch of snow weighing up to 25 lb/ft^3. The term *reasonable time* is based on the airport's type and number of annual operations.

Annual Airplane Operations (includes cargo operations)	Clearance Time[1] (hour)
40,000 or more	½
10,000 – but less than 40,000	1
6,000 – but less than 10,000	1½
Less than 6,000	2
General: Commercial Service Airport means a public-use airport that the U.S. Secretary of Transportation determines has at least 2,500 passenger boardings each year and that receives scheduled passenger airplane service [reference Title 49 United States Code, Section 47102(7)]. Footnote 1: These airports should have sufficient equipment to clear 1 inch (2.54 cm) of falling snow weighing up to 25 lb/ft³ (400 kg/m³) from Priority 1 areas within the recommended clearance times.	

FIGURE 8.2

Clearance times for commercial service airports.

Source: FAA (2008a). AC 150/5200-30C, Airport winter safety and operations. Retrieved from http://www.faa.gov/regulations_policies/ advisory_circulars/index.cfm/go/document.information/documentNumber/150_5200-30C.

Annual Airplane Operations (includes cargo operations)	Clearance Time[1] (hour)
40,000 or more	2
10,000 – but less than 40,000	3
6,000 – but less than 10,000	4
Less than 6,000	6
General: Although not specifically defined, Non-Commercial Service Airports are airports that are not classified as Commercial Service Airports [see Table 1-1, general note]. Footnote 1: These airports may wish to have sufficient equipment to clear 1 inch (2.54 cm) of falling snow weighing up to 25 lb/ft³ (400 kg/m³) from Priority 1 areas within the recommended clearance times.	

FIGURE 8.3

Clearance times for non−commercial service airports.

Source: FAA (2008a). AC 150/5200-30C, Airport winter safety and operations. Retrieved from http://www.faa.gov/regulations_policies/ advisory_circulars/index.cfm/go/document.information/documentNumber/150_5200-30C.

8. **Snow equipment list:** The list of available snow removal equipment should be listed by year, make, and model. As part of FEMA's *resource typing* process used for emergency management, the airport operator may also wish to include performance measures, when appropriate, such as the amount of snow a rotary plow (snow blower) can displace over a period of time.

9. **Storage of snow removal equipment:** The FAA recommends that, whenever possible, snow removal equipment be stored in a heated building in order to prolong its useful life (FAA, 2008a). Repair facilities should be onsite and able to perform maintenance during snow events (functioning like a pit stop). Equipment should be inspected after each use to determine whether additional maintenance is necessary before the next snow event.

10. Definitions: The FAA uses specific definitions to describe snow. By distinguishing among the various types of snow, the FAA can better inform airport operators about how to remove it. For example, using a "broom," snow removal vehicle can be highly ineffective on wet snow, when a blade plow is better suited. The specific definitions are in AC 150/5200-30C (FAA, 2008a) but essentially are as follows:

    a. Contaminant: Any substance on a runway, including snow, ice, standing water, or deicing chemical.

    b. Dry Snow: Snow that has insufficient water to cause cohesion, and in a NOTAM, describes a surface that is neither wet nor contaminated

    c. Wet Snow: Snow that has enough water to bind the snow mass together but no excess water. Water will not squeeze out of wet snow. Wet is a term used on a NOTAM to describe a surface that is neither dry nor contaminated but has visible dampness, moisture, and/or water less than 1/8 inch in depth. The word THIN is used in a NOTAM for reporting snow depths less than 1/8 inch.

    d. Slush: Snow with a high water content. Water will freely drain from slush.

    e. Compacted Snow: Snow that has been compressed into a solid mass that will resist further compression.

    f. Patchy Conditions: This term denotes when there are areas of bare pavement showing through snow and/or ice covered pavements. Snow (in some form), and in a NOTAM is used to describe a condition where patchy snow or ice covers 25% or less of the cleared/treated surface.

    g. Approved Chemicals: A chemical, either solid or liquid, that meets a generic SAE (Society of Automotive Engineers) or MIL (U.S. military) standards specification and is approved for use on the airfield.[5] It is very important to remember that sand and standard road deicing or anti-icing materials are typically not approved for use on the airfield. The use of such materials can result in damage to aircraft, particularly landing gear.

    h. Primary Runway: A runway used under the existing atmospheric and storm event conditions where most of the takeoff and landing operations take place.

    i. Secondary Runway: A runway that supports a primary runway. Takeoff and landing operations on such a runway are generally less frequent than on a primary runway.

    As part of the annual meeting of the SICC, airport operators should review the SICP and make any updates or modifications as necessary. The FAA may have to approve the changes as the SICP is part of the ACM. Additionally, responsibility must be placed on airport operators to mitigate the negative impacts of snow clearing operations on storm water run-off at the airport. Deicing and anti-icing chemicals are among the most significant sources of hazardous waste produced at an airport, second only to construction materials and activities (during times of airfield construction). Melted snow, whether melted by the sun or melted by a mechanical melting device, produces water runoff that can contaminate the storm water system.

SNOW CLEARING OPERATIONS AND ICE PREVENTION

The goal of snow removal is to remove snow as expeditiously as possible in a "no worse than wet" condition (FAA, 2008a, p. 7). Snow removal operations must be conducted in a manner so as to

---

[5] See SAE Standards at http://www.sae.org/standards/.

prevent runway incursions or interference with aircraft operations. Period surface friction can be improved by plowing snow or ice and by the application of sand, anti-icing, or deicing chemicals. Postclearing operations must ensure airfield signs and markings are visible to pilots (FAA, 2008a).

Taking a recommendation from the emergency management community, when the SICP has been developed, airport operators should conduct scenario-based exercises or games to determine the effectiveness of the plan. Software simulations, or tabletop and discussion-based exercises[6] can be used. Game scenarios may include removing a critical piece of equipment or challenging the team to develop the plan with the elimination of a key material, such as a runway deicer or airfield sand. Games in which teams of airport personnel compete for the best solution build teamwork, inspire creativity, and identify unique solutions to problems. Too often airport operators make the mistake of assuming that snowstorms and other events will always occur when all personnel are readily available, when all equipment is operating at 100% efficiency, and all materials are fully stocked.

Snow Clearing Principles

Although winter conditions are capricious and inconsistent, some basic guidelines apply to all airports and should be followed as closely as possible (FAA, 2008a). The top priority is that the airport operator should notify airport users promptly about the condition of the airfield, specifically the runway and taxiway surface, using a NOTAM and other expedient methods.

Runway and taxiway clearing objectives should focus on keeping the entire runway clear of snow accumulations or ice build-up. If the entire runway cannot be cleared, snow removal teams should focus on clearing the minimum width required by the aircraft type (generally 100 feet) for transport category aircraft. Because of the different types of snow, often as a result of the varying water content present in snow throughout the season, different types of strategies should be used to address different types of snow conditions. Broom operations are generally best to remove dry snow. However, wet snow cannot be removed as effectively with a broom; wet snow will readily compact when run over by airplane tires and must be removed by the blade of the displacement plow. Residual snow left over after the displacement plow operation may be able to be removed through grooming or high-speed air blowers (placed at the end of a multifunction equipment truck).

When the snow first begins to fall, airport operators typically use sweepers or brooms, which are also effective when snow begins to melt or ice begins to separate from the pavement. Once snow has accumulated to a depth that cannot be effectively handled by sweepers or brooms, displacement plows and rotary plows, or snowblowers, should take over primary snow removal operations. Sweepers and brooms can continue to clear off residual snow (FAA, 2008a).

Displacement plows typically form an echelon or wedge formation and push snow to a single windrow at the edge of the runway that can be cast over the runway lights by a rotary snowplow (FAA, 2008a). In-pavement surface-condition sensors can greatly assist snow control operations personnel in determining both the form of the contaminant on the runway (snow, ice, etc.), and determine the freezing point at the pavement level. Depending on the duration of the snowfall or

---

[6]The Homeland Security Exercise and Evaluation Program (HSEEP) provides guidance for the construction of exercises to test the readiness of agencies in responding to an emergency. In some cases, airport operators treat snow removal operations as an "incident" and manage the event using Federal Emergency Management Agency's (FEMA) Incident Command System (ICS) model.

the local climatic conditions, snow can be cast into the grassy areas of the airfield for solar melting, or it can be cast from the rotary plow into a carrier truck and hauled to an approved snow dump location. A third alternative is to haul the snow to an industrial snow melter that can melt thousands of gallons of snow in a short period of time and disposing of it into the storm-water system. Although expensive, snowmelt tours reduce the need for large, paved, snow dump locations, the capacity of which, depending on the level of snowfall throughout the year, may be exceeded.

Ramp and terminal snow removal clearing objectives should take into consideration that thin layers of ice on ramps and airplane parking positions can create safety hazards. Pilots may also apply increased engine thrust to break away or maneuver on snow. This excessive engine thrust may cause objects to blow across the ramp areas, which can damage other aircraft, rent equipment, or personnel. Also, stockpiled snow should not obscure taxiway signs or terminal visual aids nor should it interfere with aircraft operations or NAVAIDs (FAA, 2008a).

Snow Removal Equipment

FAA AC 150/522-20A *Airport Snow and Ice Control Equipment* (FAA, 2014a) describes the various types and capabilities of common airport snow removal equipment and considerations in selecting the right piece(s) of equipment. As we have seen with other areas in Airport Operations, the type and quantity of equipment depend on the level and nature of aircraft operations. It may be impractical for a small GA airport to have multifunction equipment, whereas a large, air carrier airport would certainly be expected to have such equipment. AC 150/522-20A provides calculation methods necessary to determine the amount of snow removal equipment an airport should have to meet the desired clearance standards, based on the amount of Priority 1 paved areas on the airport. Airport operators can then make effective decisions about how much snow removal equipment they need and whether they should reduce or alter their Priority 1 paved areas to fit into their budget and overall capabilities.

Seven apparatuses used to remove snow and ice are:

1. Displacement Plow
2. Rotary Plow (Snowblower)
3. Material Spreader
4. Broom (Sweeper)
5. Carrier Vehicle
6. Multifunction Equipment (a combination of displacement plow, broom, and air blast)
7. Melter

Other equipment often used in snow removal includes friction-testing devices or special friction-testing vehicles, operations or maintenance command vehicles, and landside, snow removal operations vehicles.

Displacement plows consist of a cutting edge to sheer snow from the pavement and a moldboard to lift and cast the snow to the side of the clear path (Figure 8.4). Cutting edges may ride in contact with the pavement or be held a small distance above it using shoes or castor wheels. A variety of snowplow sizes exist, with the smallest having a cutting edge of approximately 6 to 10 feet, all the way up to extralarge with cutting edge length greater than 22 feet. Plow blades are normally mounted on the front of a carrier vehicle but can also be mounted on the side or underneath the vehicle. A variety of plow blades exist: the basic is the one-way, fixed-angle snowplow, which is

FIGURE 8.4

Airport Operations displacement snowplows.

Courtesy Jeffrey Price.

primarily used in large, open-area plow operations that require a high volume and vehicle speed. Fixed blades are either left- or right-cutting angles (FAA, 2014a), and the reversible snowplow has mechanical linkages that allow the blade to move to a left- or right-cutting angle.

Rollover snowplows are used for large, open-area plowing operations with either a right- or left-cutting angle. The design of the blade reduces snow spillage by confining, and *ramp dozers* are primarily used in confined areas that require wide swath plowing but may also be used to transport and dump snow spreading it through a tapered floorboard design. Plows can also be fitted with *extension* or *leveling wings* mounted to either side of the carrier vehicle to increase the swath of the snowplow (FAA, 2014a).

Rotary plows, or snowblowers, are used to cast heavy concentrations of snow away from runways and taxiways (Figure 8.5). The snowblower and its capability to move snow (expressed in tons per hour), as well as the distance it can cast snow, dictate the speed and capability of the rest of the snowplow operation. Although displacement plows can move the snow off the paved surface, the plow blades leave a windrow beside the paved surface. The windrow, which is essentially a long snowbank, is a hazard to aircraft operations and should be removed before allowing aircraft to use the pavement. Therefore, the ability of the snowblower to quickly knock down this windrow is the determining factor in the overall speed of the snow removal process. The snowblower dictates the number of displacement plows, which, in turn, dictates the number of brooms, friction-testing

FIGURE 8.5

Snowblower, John F. Kennedy Airport, New York.

Courtesy Jeffrey Price.

equipment, carrier trucks, etc. By adding a snowblower, the airport can increase its snow removal speed, but all other factors must be taken into consideration (e.g., Does the additional blower increase the speed of a particular team without adding displacement trucks?).

Airports use two types of snowblowers: single-stage and two-stage. A single-stage plow uses one rotating device to both disaggregate and cast the snow, whereas a two-stage plow separates the snow gathering from the casting function. Snowblowers are rated by their ability to discharge a certain volume of snow and the distance the blower can cast the snow. As noted, snowblower capacities are measured in tons per hour. However, the casting distance is also important, particularly for airports that do not cast snow into a carrier vehicle but instead cast it into the grassy areas of the airfield for solar melting. High-speed snowblowers should be capable of removing the volume of snow from the Priority 1 paved area with a predetermined casting distance to comply with runway and taxiway snow bank clearance criteria in AC 150/5200-30 (FAA, 2014a, p. 8).

Material spreaders provide a continuous, unrestricted, accurately metered flow of sand and solid or liquid deicers/anti-icers to a paved surface, over a predetermined spread area (FAA, 2014a). Dry material spreaders use hopper-type spreaders for dispersion of sand or solid de-icers/anti-icers and can include a liquid reservoir for prewetting sand with de-icer/anti-icer chemicals.

Liquid-material spreaders may be self-contained or mounted on a carrier vehicle and apply chemical via a spray applicator system.

Runway brooms are used for the high-speed sweeping and cleaning of snow, slush, ice, and debris by using a rotating cartridge of brushes with bristles (Figure 8.6). These cartridges may be mounted on the front of a carrier vehicle, the underbody, or on a trailer arrangement towed by a carrier vehicle. Some brooms are complemented with an air blast system located behind the brush assembly to clear debris and residual snow from around runway lights. Small swath sweepers have a width of not more than 12 feet, while a large swath sweeper has a width greater than 12 feet (FAA, 2014a).

Carrier vehicles are self-propelled vehicles that haul snow, slush, ice, and other debris from the pavement during winter operations. There are a variety of carrier vehicles, including those that also include a plow blade or are custom designed to receive snow from a snowblower, which is then hauled to a dump site or a melting location.

Multitasking equipment (MTE), or multifunction equipment (MFE), provides the ability to plow snow with a front-end blade, sweep snow residue with a center-mounted broom, and then air

FIGURE 8.6

Runway broom at Denver International Airport, Colorado.

Courtesy Jeffrey Price.

blast the residue to push snow beyond the airfield lights. Multifunction trucks can cut down snow removal times by as much as 50% as compared to single-function trucks.

Melters are industrial-level technology that melts snow, ice, and slush and deposits it into a drainage system. As snow is deposited into the melter, it is deposited onto a melting pan, constructed above a hot water bath containing heat-exchanger tubes. As snow is dumped onto the melting pan, warm water is sprayed over the snow. The water then travels through filters to catch debris and back into the water copper to be reheated. As the water level rises, it is discharged under the melter into a storm drain, catch basin, or into a hose to divert to a secondary location. Melting snow can reduce costs that are associated with labor and equipment by reducing the overall number of carrier vehicle drivers and dump sites and eliminating the snow rather than accumulating it in a finite number of dump locations.

With advances in technology, snow removal manufacturers continue to develop new and innovative methods of removing snow. Some of these include a convergent rotary plow designed like an inverse displacement plow blade, which can act as both displacement and rotary plow in one unit, combined with a broom cartridge and air blast system. To address the challenges of plowed snow around airfield lights, some companies are constructing runway light sweepers attachments. The attachment is a pair of vertically mounted, high-speed, rotating bristles next to a rotary or displacement plow. As the plow operator drives next to the runway or taxiway lights, the attached light sweeper cartridge brushes snow from around the lights. Some of these new attachments are side mounted, but in one case, the brooms were mounted underneath a displacement plow vehicle, fitted with a blade that separates as it approaches a runway or taxiway light. GPS technology can also assist plow operators in identifying the locations of runway and taxiway signs and lights, particularly those on secondary priority areas that have been covered by snowfall.

During the offseason, some snow removal equipment can have other uses, such as removing foreign object debris (FOD) from the paved areas or hauling maintenance and construction materials around the airport. Since much of the airport snow removal equipment is acquired with the assistance of federal funding, the FAA had interpreted that use of snow removal equipment for any activity other than removing snow and ice from airfield pavements and airport roads was not allowable. However, the FAA has since reversed its position (for nonprimary airports) and in the *Airport Improvement Program Handbook* (FAA Order 5100.38D, 9/30/14, p. M-4) notes that MTE equipment may be used for secondary activities if it does not significantly degrade the useful life of the equipment, it will not be used off the airport, it will only be used by airport employees, and it will generally be used for activities on Airport Improvement Program (AIP)-eligible surfaces.

Surface Assessment and Reporting

A critical role of Airport Operations is to notify aircraft operators about the conditions of the paved surfaces. Conducting assessments and reporting the surface condition of a runway can be particularly challenging because of the methods used in conducting the assessment, and various interpretations made about the reported information. Pilots typically use pilot braking action reports as the source of braking action information, but those reports can vary significantly based on the experience of the pilot, the type of aircraft conducting the operation, and the actual condition of the pavement at the time the report was made versus the condition of the pavement several minutes later (FAA, 2008a).

The goal in runway reporting is to provide pilots with the best information available. In past years, it was common practice for airports to conduct friction tests and report the braking action as either good, fair, poor, or nil. This practice has since been abandoned and was replaced for a period of time by transmitting μ (stated as **mu** values derived as the coefficient of friction calculations under varying conditions[7]) through the NOTAM process. It was generally considered that a mu reading of more than 0.40[8] was considered "good" braking action[9] (a rating of 1.0 is the top of the scale, with a rating of 0 the equivalent of no braking action). Airport operators can still report the mu readings, but must not use them as the sole indicator of runway slipperiness, and the numerical value has no particular significance other than to provide trend information on changing roadway conditions when associated with previous or subsequent runway friction measurements (FAA, 2008a).

Part 139 requires airport operators to promptly notify air carriers using the airport when any portion of the movement area, normally available to them, is less than satisfactorily cleared for safe operation by their aircraft. It is critical that field condition reports be accurate and timely, specifically noting the type and depth of the contaminant (i.e., snow, slush, or ice) as these elements have the potential for a significant impact on the performance capabilities of aircraft during takeoff and landing. A runway condition report must indicate the type of contamination, as well as when the cleared runway width is less than the full runway width. New runway condition reports should be issued any time the runway surface condition changes because of weather, the application of chemicals or sand, or plowing or sweeping operations. Aircraft operations should not be allowed to continue until after a condition report has been issued (FAA, 2008a). Runway friction surveys can be conducted using FAA-approved friction-measuring equipment, but airport operators must not correlate friction readings (mu numbers) to good/medium (formerly known as fair)/poor or nil runway surface conditions. Good, medium, etc., are examples of pilot braking action terminology.

FAA Part 139 CertAlert No. 11-13, issued 2/15/2011, notes that airport operators must cancel any mu ratings on NOTAMs when the condition NOTAM moves outside the parameters for taking a friction assessment. These parameters are:

1. Conditions acceptable to use decelerometers or continuous friction-measuring equipment to conduct runway friction surveys on frozen contaminated surfaces. The data obtained from such runway friction surveys are only considered to be reliable when the surface is contaminated under any of the following conditions:
   (a) Ice or wet ice. *Wet ice* is a term used to denote ice surfaces that are covered with a thin film of moisture caused by melting. The liquid water film deposit is of minimal depth of 0.04 inch (1 mm) or less, insufficient to cause hydroplaning.
   (b) Compacted snow at any depth.
   (c) Dry snow 1 inch or less.
   (d) Wet snow or slush ⅛ inch or less.

---

[7]For example, μ_{max} = maximum friction coefficient. See http://www.iata.org/iata/RERR-toolkit/assets/Content/Contributing%20Reports/ICAO_Circular_on_Rwy_Surface_Condition_Assessment_Measurement_and_Reporting.pdf
[8]Or, often stated on a scale of 0 to 100, with mu 40 equal to mu 0.4 (i.e., percentage metric reporting).
[9]The FAA is in the process of adopting ICAO terminology to express runway friction measurements. ICAO uses "good," "good to medium," "medium," "medium to poor," and "poor."

2. It is not acceptable to use decelerometers or continuous friction-measuring equipment to assess any contaminants outside of these parameters.[10]

Also, NOTAMs are not to be issued when all mus are above the value of 0.4. However, if any of the three mu values (runways are broken down into three zones for NOTAM reporting purposes: first-third, center-third, and third-third) are below 0.4, and the remaining mu values are above 0.4, then all three mu values are to be reported.

There are a variety of friction-measuring devices including the **decelerometers** (electronic and mechanical) and **Continuous Friction-Measuring Equipment (CFME)**. CFME is preferred for use at airports with significant levels of aircraft operation, in which runway closure time must be minimized. CFME provides a continuous, graphic record of the pavement surface friction characteristics, averaging each one-third zone of the runway length. Decelerometers are a lower cost method to measure friction but take longer to conduct. Electronic decelerometers are preferable to mechanical; electronic decelerometers eliminate potential human error by automatically computing and recording the protection averages for each one-third zone of the runway and providing a printed record of the friction survey data (FAA, 2008a, p. 40). Mechanical decelerometers are recommended primarily as a backup to an electronic decelerometer, as they do not provide automatic friction averages or a printed copy of the data. Measurements from mechanical decelerometers may have to be transmitted via radio to the SCC, increasing the potential for a reporting error because of radio transmission and interpretation of the received information.

Snow Removal Considerations

The 2014−2015 snow season for the Boston, Massachusetts, area was significant in terms of annual snowfall and lower than average temperatures, which inhibited the airport from clearing snow in a manner that had previously worked. This situation forced Airport Operations to develop new strategies and considerations in handling snow events. In a presentation at the 2015 American Association of Airport Executives (AAAE) Annual Conference and Exposition, Vincent Cardillo, A.A.E., ACE, Deputy Director of Aviation Operations, Massachusetts Port Authority, presented on lessons learned during the season. In summary, the key points (Cardillo, 2015) are (with author annotations):

1. Work closely with the airlines to determine if they are "pulling down" their schedule, which indicates they are ceasing operations, and check with other airport tenants to determine their intention for flight operations (Cardillo, 2015). This may impact the priorities and timeliness of your snow removal operations.

2. Annual training for snow removal should not just include driver training for snowplow operators but also training in issuance of NOTAMs, communications, and notifications (Cardillo, 2015). Everbridge is a popular mass notification program for airports, but not all airports have automated notification processes and must still call individual agencies and personnel by phone. These phone numbers are best verified during the summer months. The media in public alert and notification processes should also be verified. Also, review the SICP for long-term considerations, such as equipment that needs to be replaced or different standard operating procedures that need to be trained.

---

[10]See https://www.faa.gov/airports/airport_safety/certalerts/media/cert1103.pdf.

3. Determine the plan to continue snow removal operations after the airport is shut down; have an airport shutdown plan along with an airport reopening plan; that is: What conditions and capabilities do you need to achieve to reopen the airport?
4. Considers human factors such as fatigue and how long a snowplow operator can continue to safely plow snow.
5. Have contingency plans that address alternatives of equipment, personnel, or materials.
6. Improve or upgrade weather reporting and forecasting systems (Cardillo, 2015).

Snow removal operations and snow present significant operational challenges for airport operators. Even airports that only have small amounts of snow for which the SICP calls for the airport to shut down until the snow melts should still have some level of response. Airports that receive significant amounts of snowfall throughout the year should focus a large number of assets on managing snow removal operations to ensure first for the safety of flight and second to sustain the capacity of the airport to as high a level as possible.

WILDLIFE HAZARD CONTROL

The ditching of U.S. Airways Flight 1549 in the Hudson River in 2009 emphasized the significant threat of wildlife to aircraft operations. Wildlife strikes number in the ten thousands, with a direct cost exceeding $200 million annually. However, it was not until Captain Chesley Sullenberger and First Officer Jeffrey Skiles, along with the heroic actions of the cabin crew, passengers, first responders, and small boat operators, saved the lives of everyone on board the U.S. Airways Airbus after striking a flock of Canada geese that many realized the significance of the risks and costs related to threats from wildlife strikes.

Since 1988, wildlife strikes on aircraft have killed more than 255 people and destroyed over 243 aircraft (FAA, 2013). Contributing to the higher number of wildlife strikes are increased air traffic and quieter, turbofan-powered aircraft. Birds comprise 97% of the reported strikes, with the remaining being mammals (2%) and smaller percentages of bats and reptiles. The number of strikes increased 6.1% between 1990 and 2013 (142,603 strikes during that time) but has recently declined for commercial aircraft. However, damaging strikes have not declined for GA aircraft (FAA, 2013). Birds are more likely to be struck during the day, while terrestrial mammals are more likely to be struck during the evening and more likely on landing (versus takeoff). The majority of bird strikes takes place below 500 feet above ground level (AGL).

Since the U.S. Airways incident, the FAA and U.S. Department of Agriculture (USDA) have placed airport wildlife mitigation near the top of their list. Previously, airports were only required to conduct a Wildlife Hazard Assessment (WHA) if there were certain triggering events; however, as of 2014, the FAA reported that 100% of Part 139 airports have completed or are in the processing of completing an assessment or have accepted a federal grant to conduct an assessment. The FAA has also since issued performance metrics to monitor strike reporting trends and GA wildlife mitigation, including the percentage of damaging strikes, strike reporting rates, and tracking of GA airports that conduct assessments. The FAA has made a correlation that when strike reporting has increased, the amount of damaging strikes have declined (FAA, 2013). When Wildlife Hazard Assessments are conducted, an accurate number of wildlife strikes can better inform the wildlife biologist and airport operator about the types of mitigation strategies that are required, which ones are working, and which are ineffective. Efforts to reduce wildlife strikes include:

1. Alternative habitat management strategies to reduce attraction to airports of hazardous wildlife species; there is also an element of biodiversity involved in wildlife management—previously, the overall impact on wildlife from wildlife mitigation measures was deemed less important than the safety of flight operations. While the safety of flight remains a priority, airport operators are now encouraged to take biodiversity into account in their wildlife management mitigation programs.
2. Techniques for restricting access of hazardous wildlife species to attractive features like storm water ponds;
3. Technologies for harassing and deterring hazardous species;
4. Evaluation of avian radar systems for detecting and tracking birds on or near airports; and
5. Aircraft-mounted lighting systems to enhance bird detection and avoidance of aircraft.

WILDLIFE MANAGEMENT REQUIREMENTS OF PART 139 OPERATORS

Part 139.337 requires Airport Managers to show that they have established instructions and procedures for the prevention or removal of factors on the airport that attract, or might attract, wildlife. A wildlife attractant is considered to be any manmade structure, land use practice, or geomorphic feature that might attract or sustain hazardous wildlife within the landing or departure airspace, aircraft movement area, loading ramps, or aircraft parking areas of an airport (Price & Forrest, 2014). Under Part 139.337, the triggering events for a WHA are:

1. An air carrier aircraft experiences multiple bird strikes.
2. An air carrier aircraft experiences substantial damage from striking wildlife.
3. An air carrier aircraft experiences an engine ingestion of wildlife.
4. Wildlife of a large enough size, or in numbers that are capable of causing an accident, are observed to have access to any airport flight pattern or aircraft movement area.

Notice that the first three triggers relate directly to air carrier aircraft, but the fourth is a catchall that can apply to nearly any observation of wildlife in or around airports. As previously noted, although the regulation has not changed, all Part 139 airports have either completed a WHA or are in the process of completing one. However, after the 2009 U.S. Airways incident, the FAA identified 96 airports that had experienced one or more of the above listed events but had not conducted an assessment (FAA, 2010). The FAA argues that all air carrier airports should conduct a WHA and is developing a program to conduct assessments at more than 2,000 GA airports.

The ACM AC 150/5210-22 (FAA, 2004) requires airport operators to include a section on Wildlife Hazard Management and must include one of the following (for Categories I, II, and III airports):

1. A statement of no wildlife activity (unlikely at most airports);
2. A statement that a WHA is being conducted;
3. A brief statement of the no-hazard findings from a recent WHA;
4. A statement indicating that a WHMP is currently being developed; or
5. A statement indicating that the airport has a WHMP, which must be included in the ACM, usually as an appendix.

A WHA may take 1 to 2 years to properly document the seasonal patterns of birds and other wildlife using the airport and surrounding area over an annual cycle. The assessment must be conducted by a qualified wildlife biologist and should include:

1. An analysis of the events or circumstances that prompted the assessment;
2. Identification of the wildlife species observed and their numbers, locations, local movements, and daily and seasonal occurrences;
3. Identification and location of features on and near the airport that attract wildlife;
4. A description of wildlife hazards to air carrier operations; and
5. Recommended actions for reducing identified wildlife hazards to air carriers.

Upon completion of the WHA, the document must be submitted to the FAA administrator for approval; the administrator then determines the need for a WHMP. Once implemented, the WHMP must be reviewed and evaluated annually by the biologist who helped to prepare the plan (if possible) and the airport's Wildlife Hazard Working Group. The review includes summary reporting of annual data, which includes a strike reporting, wildlife observations and control measures, a review of significant wildlife attractions on or near the airport, summary reports of the effectiveness of dispersal and other strategies that are used in wildlife mitigation, and any recommendations to update the existing WHMP.

The **Wildlife Hazard Working Group** (FAA, 2007) is similar in form and function to the SICC. This group should meet at least annually to evaluate the effectiveness of the wildlife hazard plan and to determine if changes are necessary. The group should include the Airport Director, the operations and maintenance department, a wildlife biologist, the planning or engineering department, FAA ATC, and major tenants such as air carriers or FBOs. Some airports have a large, corporate operation, and therefore should be represented on the group. GA airports tend to have tenant associations, and any representative of that association should also be included in the group. Owners of adjacent residential areas, golf courses, parks, or landfills should be invited to be part of the group.

The Wildlife Hazard Management Plan

The goal of an airport's **WHMP** is to minimize the risk to aviation safety, airport structures or equipment, or human health posed by populations of hazardous wildlife on and around the airport. After a WHA, a WHMP is developed with a list of short-, medium-, and long-term measures, along with continuing measures the airport operator is expected to complete or conduct to mitigate wildlife at the airport. The WHMP identifies hazardous wildlife attractants on or near the airport and the appropriate wildlife damage management techniques to minimize the wildlife hazard, while providing priorities for the management measures (FAA, 2007, p. 14).

Effective wildlife control programs include effective techniques against the specific type of wildlife issue, the abilities of airport personnel, and the support of management. Wildlife control is based on two primary approaches:[11] (1) **habitat modification**, including the elimination of food, water, and shelter, and exclusion techniques, such as the use of physical barriers to stop wildlife from gaining access to food, water, and shelter, and (2) **active control** techniques, which include repelling techniques and population management. NOTAMs are also occasionally used as a wildlife

---

[11]Various industry professionals have categorized these as more than one approach, addressing exclusion separately, or separating repelling techniques from population management.

management technique. While airport operators will issue a NOTAM when there is a wildlife hazard observed on or near the airport, some airport wildlife hazard management programs call for a NOTAM, or a notation in the AFD, warning of potential nesting areas, particularly by protected species.

In addition to measures designed to alleviate or eliminate wildlife hazards to air carrier operations, the WHMP must include a list of the individuals with the authority and responsibility for the plan and a list prioritizing the actions identified in the WHA with target dates for their completion. The wildlife biologist must also conduct a training program to those personnel (typically airport Ops or maintenance) who are delegated to carry out the wildlife mitigation tasks.

Habitat Modification Strategies

FAA AC 150/5200-33B, *Hazardous Wildlife Attractants on or Near Airports* (FAA, 2007), addresses land use management strategies to reduce the potential for wildlife strikes on the airport. Typical habitat modification measures include land use changes, more effective storm water management strategies (to reduce ponding), a review of wastewater treatment facilities, the reduction of wetlands, and building design changes to reduce the availability or possibility of nesting animals. The FAA also recommends looking at alternative uses for airport land and adjacent land besides agricultural uses and golf courses; however, these last two measures can be difficult to implement at some airports that rely on the revenue from agricultural operations or golf course operations on airport property.

Off-airport wildlife attractants must also be considered. The FAA recommends a distance of 5 statute miles between the farther edge of the Air Operations Area and any hazardous wildlife attractants, such as a landfill, with particular attention to any attractants near the approach and departure paths of the airport. Wildlife's needs to survive are the same as a human's needs: water, food, and shelter. Wildlife also desire to reproduce and avoid predators. Eliminating sources that meet these needs reduces the possibility of wildlife on or near the airport. Certain wildlife are attracted to certain terrain features (Belant & Ayers, 2014) in order to maximize their potential to meet their needs. Airport operators must strive to provide a safe operating environment but must also balance the needs of the aircraft operation with federal, state, and local laws that may place restrictions on the procedures airport operators can use to mitigate wildlife.

ACRP Synthesis Report 52, *Habitat Management to Deter Wildlife at Airports* (Belant & Martin, 2011), addressed seven categories of habitat mitigation measures:

1. **Airfield turf management:** Reducing the height of grasses on the airfield reduces the cover and concealment that are desired by many animals. Replacing airfield turf grass with artificial turf or asphalt milling virtually eliminates the advantages that wildlife enjoy with real grass, and the use of certain types of vegetations that are not as attractive to wildlife can reduce the likelihood they will nest (Belant & Ayers, 2014, pp. 5–6).
2. **Landscaping:** Electrical poles, antennas, and tall dense trees attract raptors (Belant & Ayers, 2014, p. 12). Airport operators should avoid planting fruit-bearing trees and bushes on the airport and move toward trees with more vertical branch structures, which are less attractive to perching and nesting.
3. **Airport structures: perching, nesting, and denning:** Tall structures are attractive to a variety of bird species as they provide an excellent view of their surroundings for both hunting and to

watch for predators. Reducing the horizontal service area of the structures and replacing them with smooth curved and sloping surfaces with sharp domes or points make it more difficult for birds to perch (Belant & Ayers, 2014, p. 14). Culverts and drains are also used by numerous species, particularly coyotes and raccoons, as dens or nesting, or as an underground pathway to other areas. Covering culverts and drains with cage wire is an effective deterrent.

4. **Alternative energy:** Solar-powered, electricity-producing structures may provide new shelters for wildlife, unless properly maintained.

5. **Agriculture:** Crop fields, grains, wheat, and livestock feedlots may attract a variety of species, such as white-tailed deer and birds, particularly migratory species, such as Canada geese. In some cases, grazing livestock can serve as an alternative method of turf grass management, providing an economic benefit to the airport and reducing habitat for wildlife that prefer tall grasses and thick vegetation, such as rabbits, deer, and rodents. However, it is critical that the livestock remain fenced in an area away from the Air Operations Area (AOA), or they can become a serious hazard to aircraft operations. As previously mentioned, it can be difficult for an airport to eliminate all agriculture on or near the airport, particularly when it is a source of revenue. In some cases, chemicals have been used to seed crOps to keep away birds, but thus far, the chemicals only work against some types of birds (Belant & Ayers, 2014, p. 24).

6. **Other vegetation:** An analysis of the types of wildlife observed on the airport, as well as their mating and eating patterns, can help airport operators to determine the appropriate mitigative measure. Overall, airport operators should watch for dense vegetation, small patches of high-quality habitats close together, and conservation areas such as wetlands, grasslands, or forested areas and woodlots (Belant & Ayers, 2014, pp. 26—28).

7. **Water resources:** Water is an essential resource for all humans and wildlife and is a major attractant even in small quantities (Belant & Ayers, 2014, p. 29). Open water can be a safe zone for birds such as ducks and geese and is sought out for consumption by all wildlife. Airport operators should seek to reduce standing water on the airfield as much as possible. Effective storm water management, the reduction of ponding on the airfield, the use of permeable material such as gravel or asphalt millings for road surfaces, effective slopes, and drainage systems throughout the airport all contribute to reducing water as an attractant.

Active control wildlife management strategies can be controversial because of their effect on birds and mammals on or near the airport. The specific methods of airport wildlife population control are directed at (1) directly increasing mortality of wildlife at the airport, (2) directly reducing reproduction, and (3) indirectly manipulating mortality, reproduction, or both (DeFusco & Unangst, 2013, p. 9). While habitat modification strategies focus on creating a less than inviting environment for wildlife, active control measures focus on eliminating, trapping (and relocating), and dispersing wildlife.

Before using any wildlife population control measure (e.g., taking migratory birds, dispersing roosts, manipulating nests or eggs, live trapping, lethal trapping, applying toxicants, and shooting with live ammunition) as part of an airport wildlife management program, airports must first secure a Migratory Bird Depredation Permit from the U.S. Fish and Wildlife Service (USFWS) to comply with federal law (DeFusco & Unangst, 2013, p. 11). Depredation permits are not required to scare or herd depredating migratory birds, other than threatened and endangered species or Bald or Golden Eagles (DeFusco & Unangst, 2013, p. 11). Certain species of migratory birds do not currently require a depredation permit, but airport operators should check the most current federal, state, and local regulations to determine which species require a permit and which do not. Under certain circumstances, the removal of wildlife from airports using traps, chemicals, egg and nest removal, and live ammunition shooting is necessary.

Active control techniques should be identified in the WHMP. Once a targeted species is identified, the airport operator must use the appropriate wildlife control method (DeFusco & Unangst, 2013). The following active control methods are used at airports:

1. **Repelling techniques:** These include the use of various audio, visual, or chemical repellents to harass and repel problem wildlife (Belant & Martin, 2011, p. 4). Many measures experience a reduction in effectiveness over time, making the use of a combination of repelling techniques, rather than relying on a single technique, more effective. Both auditory and visual techniques may be used.

   a. *Ultrasonic devices* which are not effective in repelling birds, gas-operated exploders (propane cannons) offer some temporary efficacy for birds, biosonics (alarm and distress calls), which also have some efficacy for birds, and pyrotechnics are all auditory techniques (Belant & Martin, 2011, pp. 10—12).

      i. **Pyrotechnics** are among the most common techniques and rely on an explosion or other type of loud noise to deter birds from an area. Some can produce visual stimuli such as a flash of light or burst of smoke. Devices include rifles and shotguns firing live ammunition or blanks and 12-gauge shotguns and flare pistols that shoot exploding or noisy projectiles, including shell crackers, bird bombs, bird whistles, whistle bombs, or racket bombs (Belant & Martin, 2011, p. 12).

   b. *Effigies, lasers, reflecting tape, lights and mirrors, dogs*, and *falconry* are considered *visual techniques.*

      i. **Effigies** and **predator models** (i.e., scarecrows, predator mimicking devices such as a Hawk or owl, or human shaped effigy) have some efficacy depending on the species (Belant & Martin, 2011, p. 14).

      ii. **Lasers** have been effective in some cases in deterring birds, but the effectiveness varies depending on the species and the wavelength, that is, color of the transmitted light (Belant & Martin, 2011, p. 14). Airport operators should also use lasers with extreme caution when operating around aircraft.

      iii. **Reflecting tape, reflectors, flags, lights and mirrors** appear to have limited efficacy but more research is needed (Belant & Martin, 2011, p. 15).

      iv. **Dogs and falconry** have had various levels of efficacy, most notably in Delaware where the use of dogs reduced bird numbers by 99.9% (Belant & Martin, 2011, p. 15). More research is needed on the efficacy of falconry, but in one test at John F. Kennedy Airport, demonstrated that falconry did not provide additional efficacy over a shooting program, but did increase the public acceptance of the wildlife management program at the airport (Belant & Martin, 2011, p. 15).

   c. **Chemicals** are another form of repellent. Certain poisons in sublethal doses may cause disorientation and erratic behavior, often causing the bird to flop around on the ground. This behavior often alarms other birds and causes them to fly away. However, airport operators using this technique may experience some public relations issues.

FIGURE 8.7

Falcon used in wildlife control, JFK Airport, New York.

Courtesy Jeffrey Price.

2. **Prey control:** Certain animals prey on other animals, so reducing the number of prey will reduce the number of predators (Figure 8.7). This strategy is similar to habitat management strategies by eliminating certain plants, but in this case it is the elimination of smaller and abundant organisms, such as insects, earthworms, rodents, fish, and smaller birds (DeFusco & Unangst, 2013, p. 13).
3. **Lethal trapping:** Lethal traps are most often used on small animals. Traps should be checked frequently to minimize scavenger species and for overall public relations purposes. The USFWS and USDA, along with state and local wildlife regulatory agencies, should be consulted to determine the types of traps to be used in a particular situation (DeFusco & Unangst, 2013, pp. 14–15).
4. **Live trapping:** Live traps include simple snares and leg holds, boxes, and barrel-type traps. Live traps must be checked frequently to evaluate their success and minimize the captured animals' distress. State and local regulations may also restrict the use of some types of traps and the ability to relocate trapped animals.
5. **Egg/roost site manipulation:** Certain migratory birds and other hazardous species must not be allowed to nest on airport property (DeFusco & Unangst, 2013, p. 16). Current control techniques include breaking the eggs and removing nest material, and then dispersing the adult birds from the airport. Water spray, water cannons, and sprinkler systems have occasionally been used to prevent roosting or nesting in urban and agricultural areas.
6. **Live ammunition shooting:** The use of firearms on an airport is heavily restricted and should be used only after all other wildlife control methods have failed (DeFusco & Unangst, 2013, p. 19). Shooting birds generally falls into two categories: quietly or loudly. Pigeons can be shot at night with an air rifle, and, if done quietly, will result in little disturbance, allowing the

maximum number to be removed (DeFusco & Unangst, 2013, p. 19). Gulls and geese that do not respond to various repellent methods can be shot with a 12-gauge shotgun, the noise of which also acts as a scaring and dispersal tactic (DeFusco & Unangst, 2013, p. 19). Shooting only one bird may be needed to illustrate the significance of loud, sharp noises on the rest of the flock, making them more likely to respond to noise-making devices, and thus reducing the need to eliminate more birds (DeFusco & Unangst, 2013, p. 19).

7. **Chemical euthanization (pesticides, insecticides, fungicides, rodenticides, fumigants):** Chemicals and poisons can also be used in certain situations and generally fall into one of three categories: acute toxins that kill after the ingestion of a single lethal dose; anticoagulants and decalcifiers, which require the ingestion of several doses over a period of days; and fumigants that suffocate burrowing animals in the ground. Poisons are generally used on small animals, specifically rodents (DeFusco & Unangst, 2013, p. 21).

Airport operators should be aware that many wildlife control techniques cause a significant negative public reaction and should strive to minimize the impact on the wildlife as much as possible, particularly before implementing lethal trapping, live ammunition, or chemical or poison strategies. Also, certain species are protected under the Federal Endangered Species Act of 1973, and other birds or mammals may require a game permit in order to be taken. The Migratory Bird Treaty Act and associated regulations establish procedures for issuing permits to take federally protected species. Federal law protects all migratory birds (almost all native bird species in the United States), including their nests and eggs. A federal depredation permit, issued by the USFWS, must be obtained before any nongame migratory birds may be taken or before any migratory game birds may be taken outside of the normal hunting season or beyond established bag limits (DeFusco & Unangst, 2013). Certain state and local laws may also apply to protect threatened or endangered species.

Wildlife Strike Reporting

On April 24, 2009, the FAA made the bird strike database available to the public. In an analysis of the events, it was revealed that the total number of strikes reported increased by 20% during the period from 1990 to 1994 and increased by 39% during the period from 2004 to 2008 and that the majority of strike reports are filed at Part 139 airports (FAA, 2010). Airport and aircraft operators can report a wildlife strike at the FAA's website, http://wildlife.faa.gov (FAA Form 5200-7 *Bird/Other Wildlife Strike Report*).

Airport operators should report strikes of all birds, bats, and terrestrial mammals weighing more than 2.2 pounds (e.g., rabbits, armadillos, deer, and coyotes should be reported, but not rats, mice, voles, or chipmunks) and all reptiles weighing more than 2.2 pounds.

A strike should be reported when it has been witnessed, or evidence or damage from the strike has been identified on an aircraft, or when bird or other wildlife remains, whether in whole or part, are found within 250 feet of the runway centerline or within 1,000 feet of a runway, unless another reason for the animal's death is identified or suspected. Strikes should also be reported on a taxiway or anywhere else on or off the airport that the reporting party has reason to believe was the result of a strike with an aircraft. A strike should also be reported to the database if the presence of birds or other wildlife on or off the airport had a significant negative effect on a flight, such as an aborted takeoff or an aborted landing, a high-speed emergency stop, or the aircraft left the pavement to avoid collision with wildlife (FAA, 2013).

Species identification is critical for wildlife—aircraft strike-reduction programs. Wildlife remains that cannot be readily identified by airport personnel or a local wildlife biologist should be collected in an approved manner and sent to the Feather Identification Lab at the U.S. Smithsonian Institution, Museum of Natural History, for proper identification.

Wildlife continues to be a challenge for airport and aircraft operators. Wildlife management is not a "one-and-done" strategy but an ongoing effort to mitigate the damaging effects of wildlife on airplanes. The FAA's website lists a variety of resources related to wildlife management, including certification alerts, advisory circulars, and Airport Cooperative Research Program (ACRP) reports.

AIRCRAFT RESCUE AND FIREFIGHTING

An entire field of study is devoted to firefighting, in particular, Aircraft Rescue and Firefighting. Rather than delving into the science of fighting aircraft fires, this text outlines the regulatory requirements under Part 139 for a commercial service airport to meet its ARFF requirements.

ARFF stands for **Aircraft Rescue and Firefighting**. Note that the acronym begins with the word, *aircraft* not *airport*. This means that ARFF requirements are focused on responding to emergencies on or involving aircraft that serve the aircraft, not the airport. The airport must still have structural fire response plans as part of the AEP, but Part 139 does not require minimum personnel, equipment, and materials for structural fires (Price & Forrest, 2014). Survivability in an aircraft crash depends on several factors, the most significant of which is being in a crash that is survivable. Second are the actions of the crew members who are the effective first responders for the initial phases of the incident. Even in a best-case scenario, ARFF personnel are several minutes from the accident scene, which is why airline crew members are trained in evacuation procedures, basic firefighting (using onboard extinguishers), and basic first aid and cardiopulmonary resuscitation (CPR). Once on scene, ARFF personnel move passengers and crew from the aircraft and apply fire-extinguishing agents to mitigate fire and explosion.

The survivability window for passengers and crew caught in a fuselage fire that remains intact after an accident is roughly 3 minutes. It takes only 90 seconds for a fire to burn through a fuselage skin. Once temperatures reach 400 degrees Fahrenheit, the cabin is no longer considered survivable. With rapid response and prompt application of the extinguishing agent, escape and survival from a major aircraft fire are possible.

Many in the airport firefighting community understand that large-scale airplane accidents are a rarity and that, if their airport experiences a large-scale airplane accident, their resources will be quickly overwhelmed. Airport fire departments rely heavily on off-airport responders through mutual aid agreements.

THE AIRCRAFT RESCUE AND FIREFIGHTING INDEX

Part 139.317 identifies the level of emergency capability (i.e., "index"), including the amount of equipment and firefighting agents, and the operational requirements of the Aircraft Rescue and Firefighting response (Price & Forrest, 2014). The determination of equipment and agent needs is based on the airport's firefighting index. The index is calculated on the length of the longest air carrier aircraft that serves the airport with more than five average daily departures (Figure 8.8). If there are fewer than five

Index	Aircraft Length (feet)
A	Less than 90
B	At least 90 but less than 126
C	At least 126 but less than 159
D	At least 159 but less than 200
E	At least 200

FIGURE 8.8

ARFF Index based on aircraft length.

Source: FAA, 2011a.

Aircraft Occupants	Number of Casualties	20% casualties Immediate Care Priority I	30% casualties Delayed Care Priority II	50% casualties Minor Care Priority III
500	375	75	113	187
450	338	68	101	169
400	300	60	90	150
350	263	53	79	131
300	225	45	68	112
250	188	38	56	94
200	150	30	45	75
150	113	23	34	56
100	75	15	23	37
50	38	8	11	19

These figures are based on the assumption that the maximum number of surviving casualties at an aircraft accident occurring on or in the vicinity of the airport is estimated to be about 75% of the aircraft occupants.

FIGURE 8.9

Estimated casualty list.

Source: FAA, 2009b.

average daily departures, the next lower index applies. For Part 139–certificated airports, the minimum index level is Index A. The index also defines the minimum amount of water, foam, dry chemical, or Halon or a Clean Agent extinguishing agent that a certificated airport is required to have. The two criteria of aircraft length and frequency of service are used to calculate the number of ARFF vehicles required. ARFF vehicles are also typically equipped with a Class D heavy metal fire extinguisher in addition to other extinguishing agents. The length determines the fire response, while the seating capacity of the aircraft indicates the level of casualty-handling facilities that may be needed (Figure 8.9).

The amounts and types of extinguishing agents needed are a result of studies that determined the capability of an agent to extinguish or control a fire based on an aircraft's fuel capacity. Extinguishing agents work by *smothering* the fire to prevent oxygen from mixing with hydrocarbons, by *suppressing* the release of fuel vapors, by *separating* the combustible materials, or by *lowering the temperature* through a cooling effect (Price & Forrest, 2014, p. 33) or, in some cases, depending on the agent, a combination of these factors.

Fires are classified as:

1. **Class A**—Fires in ordinary combustible materials, such as wood, cloth, paper, rubber, and many plastics;
2. **Class B**—Fires in flammable liquids, oils, greases, tars, oil-based paints, lacquers, etc., and flammable gases;
3. **Class C**—Fires involving "live" electrical equipment where the use of a nonconducting fire-suppression agent is of prime importance;
4. **Class D**—Fires involving combustible metals and their alloys, such as magnesium, sodium, and potassium.

Many aircraft fires are of the Class B variety because of the presence of hydrocarbon-based fuels on board.

Fire burns because there are four elements present: a heat source, fuel, air (oxygen), and a chemical chain reaction. Under normal circumstances, if any one of the elements is removed or disrupted, the fire goes out (Price & Forrest, 2014). Water, if used on a standard, hydrocarbon fuel, is heavier than most of those liquids and, if applied directly to the fuel surface, will sink to the bottom, having little or no effect on extinguishment or vapor suppression (General Foam Information, n.d.). Therefore, foam is the primary fire-extinguishing agent for all potential hazards or areas where flammable liquids are transported, processed, stored, or used as an energy source, such as in an aircraft fire. Simply applying water to a flammable fluid fire is not recommended. Water is carried on ARFF vehicles to mix with a concentrate to produce an aqueous film-forming foam (Figure 8.10), which is a more effective extinguishing agent. Water is a good substance, however, to apply to structural or grass fires.

Aqueous Film-Forming Foam (AFFF) is the most common extinguishing agent used at airports. AFFF extinguishes hydrocarbon, flammable liquid fires the same way as protein or fluoroprotein foams; however, AFFF has an additional feature—an aqueous film is formed on the surface of the flammable liquid by the foam solution as it drains from the foam blanket. The aqueous film is fluid and floats on the surface of most hydrocarbon fuels, such as Avgas and jet fuel, giving AFFF superior speed in fire control and knockdown when used on a typical hydrocarbon spill fire (General Foam Information, n.d.). AFFF is a concentrate that is mixed in a ratio of 3% to 6%[12] with water (seawater or fresh water) at the time of application. When applied through air-aspirating equipment, it expands from 6 to 10 times its original volume.

Firefighting foam does not interfere in the chemical reaction but instead:

1. Blankets the fuel surface, thus smothering the fire;
2. Separates the flames/ignition source from the fuel surface;
3. Cools the fuel and any adjacent metal surfaces; and
4. Suppresses the release of flammable vapors that can mix with air.

---

[12]For every 100 gallons of foam solution required, 6 gallons of the foam concentrate would have to be included, meaning that 6 gallons of foam is required with 934 gallons of water, to achieve 100 gallons of AFFF. A 3% concentrate is twice as concentrated as 6% and requires less foam concentrate to achieve the equivalent 100 gallons of AFFF.

FIGURE 8.10

ARFF truck, Denver International Airport, CO.

Courtesy Jeffrey Price.

The two basic flammable, or combustible, fuel groups are:

1. Standard hydrocarbon fuels, such as gasoline, diesel, kerosene, and jet fuel. These products do not mix with water but rather float on top of water and, for the most part, do not intermix.
2. Polar solvent or alcohol-type fuels are those that readily mix with water or are miscible (capable of being mixed) in water.

When fighting a flammable liquid fire, the proper fuel group and the fuel group to which the involved flammable liquid belongs must be identified. In certain situations, ARFF crews may use a dry chemical fire extinguisher, particularly in the case of an avionics fire in the cockpit or elsewhere on the aircraft. **Dry chemical** fire extinguishers extinguish the fire primarily by interrupting the **chemical reaction** of the fire triangle. Some examples include **Halon**, also known as a **Clean Agent**.

A *Clean Agent* is an electrically nonconducting, volatile, or gaseous fire-extinguishing agent that does not leave a residue after evaporation. Halon is a liquefied, compressed gas that stops the spread of fire by chemically disrupting combustion. Halon 1211 (a liquid streaming agent) and Halon 1301 (a gaseous flooding agent) leave no residue and are safe for human exposure. Halon is rated for Class B (flammable liquids) and Class C (electrical fires), but it is also effective on Class A (common combustible) fires (Price & Forrest, 2014, p. 34).

Index	Equipment	500 lbs sodium-based dry chemical, halon 1211, or clean agent	450 lbs potassium-based dry chemical and water with a commensurate quantity of AFFF to total 100 gallons for simultaneous dry chem and AFFF application	Minimum gallons of water and the commensurate quantity of AFFF for foam production carried by ALL vehicles combined
A	One vehicle	X or	X	
B	(option 1) One vehicle:	X		1500
	or			
	(option 2) Two vehicles:			1500
	Vehicle 1:	X or	X	
	Vehicle 2:			Water/AFFF
C	(option 1) Three vehicles:			3000
	Vehicle 1:	X or	X	
	Vehicle 2:			Water/AFFF
	Vehicle 3:			Water/AFFF
	or			
	(option 2) Two vehicles:			3000
	Vehicle 1:	X		(Note 1)
	Vehicle 2:			Water/AFFF
D	Three vehicles			4000
	Vehicle 1:	X or	X	
	Vehicle 2:			Water/AFFF
	Vehicle 3:			Water/AFFF
E	Three vehicles			6000
	Vehicle 1:	X or	X	
	Vehicle 2:			Water/AFFF
	Vehicle 3:			Water/AFFF

Note 1: Vehicle 1 must carry at least 1500 gallons of water and the commensurate quantity of AFFF for foam production.

FIGURE 8.11

Basic ARFF Index requirements.

Source: FAA, 2011a.

Many ARFF trucks also include a Class D fire extinguisher, which is a dry powder. Class D fires consist of combustible metals, such as magnesium, potassium, titanium, and zirconium. Water and other common firefighting materials can excite metal fires and make them worse. Using a dry-chemical fire extinguisher on a combustible metal can actually increase the intensity of the fire. Many aircraft wheels are made from either aluminum or magnesium alloys, so there is the possibility of having to fight a fire that requires a Class D extinguisher.

The **National Fire Protection Agency (NFPA)**[13] recommends that metal fires be fought with "dry powder" extinguishing agents. Dry powder agents work by smothering and heat absorption but should not be confused with dry chemicals such as Halon or other related Clean Agents (Price & Forrest, 2014). FAA AC 150/5220-10E, *Guide Specification for Aircraft Rescue and Fire Fighting Vehicles* (FAA, 2011c), provides specific information on determining and meeting the ARFF Index (Figure 8.11) at a commercial service airport.

PERFORMANCE REQUIREMENTS

The primary responsibility of ARFF crew members is to create a path for the evacuation and/or rescue of aircraft passengers and crew members. The secondary responsibility is to extinguish or neutralize the fire

---

[13]See http://www.nfpa.org/.

and explosion or the potential for such. Once a fire is extinguished, primary ARFF responders can switch from evacuation duties to emergency medical functions until additional medical help arrives.

There is wide industry confusion on the next point. The performance requirements for ARFF at certificated airports are as follows: from its assigned post, the first responding piece of ARFF equipment that meets the index must reach the midpoint of the farthest air carrier runway and begin to apply the firefighting agent, within 3 minutes from the time the alarm sounds, with all required onboard personnel in full protective gear. All other vehicles (if required) must reach the same point within 4 minutes. This criterion is set in order to meet certification purposes as set forth and explained in Title 14 CFR Part 139.319(h)(1)(ii). Many in the industry believe that ARFF personnel must arrive at the scene of an actual aircraft incident within 3 to 4 minutes. While that is a worthy objective, there is no guarantee the incident will take place at the midpoint of the farthest runway (it may be closer, farther away, or outside the airport fence). ARFF equipment and personnel must respond to any actual incident as quickly as possible.

ARFF equipment must be available 15 minutes prior to the arrival of the air carrier aircraft and remain for 15 minutes after it departs. If the requirements cannot be met because of equipment repair or breakdown or the unavailability of personnel, a NOTAM is required and air carrier activity is restricted. The regulations permit a temporary reduction in ARFF presence during periods of lower index, air carrier activity, but certain baseline conditions must be met and written into the ACM (Price & Forrest, 2014).

Of note, the FAA does not require airports to meet the guidance established by NFPA 403, *Standard for Aircraft Rescue and Fire-Fighting Services at Airports.* This issue was brought up under Section 311 of H.R. 915 EH, *FAA Reauthorization Act of 2009*, which called for more closely aligning ARFF regulations under Part 139 with ICAO and NFPA 403 standards (Golaszewski, Helledy, Castellano, & David, 2009, p. 1). The airport community was concerned about the cost of meeting these new standards, and thus an ACRP report was commissioned to study the potential impacts on airports aligning to the standards.

NFPA standards are written for airports of all sizes that have all-cargo and GA operations, as well as air carrier passenger operations. Traditionally, the FAA and the NFPA have worked together to adopt common standards for airports whenever possible (Golaszewski et al., 2009). Response standards differ between FAA, NFPA and the International Civil Aviation Organization (ICAO). While the FAA uses the standard of "to the midpoint of the farthest runway," NFPA guidance states "to reach any point on an operational runway," (NFPA 401-10) while the ICAO standard is to the end of the farthest runway. For US airport operators, the FAA standard is the standard that must be met. There are also differences in determining required numbers of staff and minimum numbers of ARFF vehicles (Figure 8.12).

The ACRP report concludes that the increased cost to meet ICAO and NFPA standards would be most pronounced at the smallest airports. Additional personnel, vehicles, and fire stations would have to be added to meet the new standard, along with additional maintenance costs and training costs. The report also analyzed various aircraft accidents and concluded that, even if the NFPA standards were in effect, the survivability of the accidents would not have changed. Eventually, the legislation requiring the FAA to meet the ICAO and NFPA standards would not survive the lawmaking process. However, some airports have individually decided to meet the performance standards of the ICAO and NFPA.

Airport Operations personnel whose duties relate to Aircraft Rescue and Firefighting, as well as management personnel who oversee ARFF compliance with Part 139, should become familiar with the NFPA guidlines and vocabulary, as ARFF personnel sometimes use them in their planning and

FIGURE 8.12

Interior of ARFF truck, Denver International Airport, CO.

Courtesy Jeffrey Price.

response actions. In one example, NFPA uses the term **Authority Having Jurisdiction (AHJ)**, which is an organization, office, or individual responsible for enforcing the requirements of a code or standard, or for approving equipment, materials, an installation, or a procedure, whereas the FAA uses the term *Airport Sponsor* or simply *Airport*.

PERSONNEL REQUIREMENTS

FAA AC 150/5210-17B, *Programs for Training of Aircraft Rescue and Firefighting Personnel* (FAA, 2009a), provides additional guidance for approved training curricula for ARFF personnel. As discussed throughout this text, identifying the individual responsible for a particular mission is highly dependent upon the number of aircraft operations and the size of the airport. With ARFF duties, Airport Managers must also take into consideration the possible presence of a military base colocated with a commercial service airport. Typically, the military operation will also take over ARFF responsibilities, but this is dependent upon the level of the military's operation. For example, airports with an Air National Guard base or Air Force base will have in place Aircraft Rescue and Firefighting equipment, whereas an airport with a small Coast Guard station or other small military facility may have to rely on the commercial service airport's firefighting capabilities. CertAlert No.

12-15, dated 7/13/2012, addresses Joint Use Airport Operators at which the Department of Defense (DOD) provides primary ARFF services.

There is another distinction between large and small airports. Large, commercial service airports typically have their own dedicated firefighting personnel. These personnel may be part of the city or county's fire response and assigned to the airport, or they may be a separate firefighting department altogether, dedicated to the airport. In some cases, a local fire district can provide response services. At smaller commercial service airports and many GA airports, operations and maintenance personnel are often cross-trained as ARFF personnel. There are additional variations such as where Airport Operations or maintenance personnel are cross-trained but are assigned fire suppression only, while a local city, county, or fire district is responsible for rescue and overall support to an aircraft incident. Memoranda of understanding articulate these relationships and responsibilities.

Part 139 regulations require airport ARFF crews to undertake both initial and recurring training. All individuals responsible for initial ARFF response are required to receive training and experience in 11 different subject areas:[14]

1. Airport familiarization;
2. Aircraft familiarization;
3. Rescue and firefighting personnel safety;
4. Emergency communications systems on the airport;
5. Use of fire hoses, nozzles, turrets, and other appliances;
6. Application of all types of extinguishing agents;
7. Emergency aircraft evacuation assistance;
8. Firefighting operations;
9. Adapting and using structural rescue (Figure 8.13);
10. Aircraft cargo hazards; and
11. Familiarization with firefighters' duties under the AEP.

All rescue and firefighting personnel are required to receive initial live-fire training and participate in the same training at least every 12 months. The size of the fire used in the drill must replicate the size of a potential fire created by typical aircraft used at that particular airport (Price & Forrest, 2014). While in the fire community ARFF is a special certification, in the airport community, ARFF personnel are not required to meet the Basic Fire Fighter 1 and 2 standard but only to receive the required 40 hours of ARFF training. However, the FAA does see meeting the NFPA 1003 *Standard for Professional Qualifications for Airport Fire Fighters* as a worthwhile goal (FAA, 2015, p. 7). At least one ARFF personnel on duty during air carrier operations must be trained and current in Basic Medical Care, with at least 40 hours of training covering:

1. Primary patient survey;
2. Triage;
3. CPR;
4. Bleeding;
5. Shock;

---

[14]Within each of these key points is a laundry list of sublevel requirements that go beyond the scope of this text but should be referenced by the AHJ for an airport fire department or function.

FIGURE 8.13

Structural fire unit and truck, Denver International Airport, CO.

Courtesy Jeffrey Price.

6. Injuries to the skull, spine, chest, and extremities;

7. Internal injuries;

8. Moving patients; and

9. Burns.

The training in Basic Medical Care does not mean that emergency medical personnel must also be ARFF-qualified. The Emergency Medical Technician (EMT) or Paramedic level of certification meets the requirements of the training, but this level of certification is not necessary to meet the FAA requirement.

SUPPORTING RESOURCES IN AIRCRAFT RESCUE AND FIREFIGHTING

A variety of resources in ARFF, including the ARFF Working Group (below), are available to the airport operator. The FAA disseminates information in support of ARFF, including all relevant ACs, CertAlerts, safety alerts, and ACRP reports.[15]

---

[15]See http://www.faa.gov/airports/airport_safety/aircraft_rescue_fire_fighting/.

The **ARFF Working Group (ARFFWG)** was organized to create an active network of information sharing among airport fire rescue professionals.[16] ARFFWG develOps and delivers comprehensive education programs on a wide variety of ARFF topics and provides guidance to aviation-related organizations about ARFF-related issues. ARFF news, seminars, and an annual meeting support members of the ARFF community. The AAAE and the ARFFWG, together known as the ARFF Training Alliance, now host the **ARFF Certification Program**. The program includes the Airport Master Firefighter (AMF), the first level of the ARFF Professional Designation Program, which ensures the individual understands the essential responsibilities of managing an airport fire department, and also has a basic understanding of airport administration and management.

HAZARDOUS MATERIAL AND FIRE PREVENTION ON AIRPORTS

Airport management is also required by Part 139 to protect against fire and explosion from the storing, dispensing, and handling of fuel, lubricants, and oxygen on the airport. This requirement is in addition to the numerous environmental laws and regulations with which an airport must comply (Price & Forrest, 2014).

HAZARDOUS MATERIAL

Compliance is accomplished by establishing procedures in the ACM for the safe storage and handling of HAZMAT. Airports must consider a dual definition when dealing with this danger; one definition is applied to material shipped as aircraft cargo, and the other is applied to material in the form of fuels, lubricants, and the like, used for the operation of aircraft (Price & Forrest, 2014). The former falls under the general heading of HAZMAT, while the latter group falls under the general heading of "fuel."

The establishment of fueling safety standards under Part 139 requires airport management to inspect various fueling operations on the airport every 3 months. The FAA has established generally accepted standards and often cites guidelines proposed by NFPA 407 *Standard for Aircraft Fuel Servicing* as being acceptable to comply with the general standards (Price & Forrest, 2014).

In addition to NFPA, other standards exist, such as those of individual air carriers, local fire and building codes, and petroleum and fuel producers. The standards developed should be a result of determining what level of risk each party is willing to accept, competing economic and liability issues, and the level of authority and responsibility for managing the risk (Price & Forrest, 2014).

When inspecting aircraft fueling operations, inspectors should look for common problems concerning compliance with local fire safety codes at fuel storage areas and with mobile fuelers. The inspection should include security, fire protection, general housekeeping, and fuel-dispensing facilities and procedures (Price & Forrest, 2014). Inspectors should ensure that proper electrostatic conductive bonding cable is being used, inspect that "deadman controls" are not circumvented, emergency fuel shutoffs are not blocked, smoking prohibitions are being observed, and that aircraft

---

[16]See www.arffwg.org.

are not being fueled inside hangars. Inspectors should also check for proper parking of mobile fuelers (at least 10 feet apart and 50 feet from buildings) and for fuel leaks or spills in the fuel storage area and around mobile fuelers. Inspectors should determine if the fuel farm is free of flammable materials, including litter and vegetation.

Airport safety self-inspectors should continuously:

1. Determine if the fueling operator is conducting unsafe fueling practices or is in violation of local fire code, such as failure to bond aircraft with the mobile fuelers during fueling operations or fueling personnel smoking while fueling aircraft;
2. Check to ensure that the appropriate signs for the fuel farm are installed and that all gates are locked, except when the facility is occupied by an authorized user; and
3. Check that the facility is lighted at night (Price & Forrest, 2014, p. 37).

The HAZMAT requirements apply only if the airport is the handling agent for hazardous cargo identified by Department of Transportation (DOT) 14 CFR Part 171 *Hazardous Material Regulations*. If the handling agents are the air carriers or the air cargo operators, then the DOT regulations do not apply to the airport. For those cases in which the airport operator is the HAZMAT agent, the ACM must include procedures that cover the regulations.

For emergencies involving HAZMAT, several agencies provide communication "hot lines" to assist responding personnel on how to cope with chemical HAZMAT situations. Despite strict regulations, combustible or hazardous chemicals transported by aircraft can leak or spill, creating immediate emergencies. For those cases in which bodies of water are involved, federal law requires that anyone who releases a reportable quantity of a hazardous substance or a material identified as a marine pollutant, including oil, must immediately notify the National Response Center (NRC), which is staffed by the U.S. Coast Guard.

With any HAZMAT or substance, the community's right-to-know provision under the Superfund Amendments and Reauthorization Act (SARA) requires that airport management have material safety data sheets (MSDSs) available and posted in all workplaces where HAZMAT exists (Price & Forrest, 2014). MSDSs now known as SDS, or simply, Safety Data Sheets are technical bulletins that describe how to use, handle, and dispose of specific chemical hazards. Airports are also required to have a **Spill Prevention and Control and Countermeasures Plan** and **Storm Water Pollution Prevention Plan** to control the accidental release of HAZMAT. Airport Operations personnel should be thoroughly trained in the contents of these plans and the necessary actions to take should a spill occur.

FIRE PREVENTION

Part 139 also places responsibility on airport management to exercise control over tenant fueling practices and requires management to establish standards that address facilities, procedures, and training of fueling personnel. Fuel fires are caused by a number of likely sources. Some examples of fuel fires are ruptured tanks, leaking fuel hoses, leaking tank trucks, and leaking fuel tank farms (Price & Forrest, 2014). Airport Safety Self-Inspection personnel should continuously inspect for potential fire hazards, particularly around fueling operations.

Fires result when a combustible or flammable material is exposed to an ignition or heat source in the presence of oxygen. The traditional fire triangle consists of a combustible material (solid, liquid, or gas), the presence of oxygen, and a heat or ignition source. The fire tetrahedron represents the addition of a fourth component, the chemical chain reaction, to the three already present in the fire triangle. Once a fire has started, the resulting exothermic chain reaction sustains the fire and allows it to continue until some or at least one of the elements of the fire is blocked. Foam can be used to deny the fire the oxygen it needs. Water can be used to lower the temperature of the fuel below the ignition point or to remove or disperse the fuel.

The degree or ease of ignition refers to the flash point of the various materials or substances. The flash point is reached when the vapors released form an ignitable mixture. Although a truck filled with fuel may pose a danger, a partially filled truck poses a greater risk for ignitability because of the mixture of fuel vapors and air within the tank. The availability and amount of combustible material reflect the amount of energy encountered. The more fuel in any one container, the greater the risk and hazard for damage. Avgas (aviation gasoline), however, has more explosive potential than Jet A because of its rapid flame spread rate (Price & Forrest, 2014).

Identifying and preventing ignition sources is where the FAA's major efforts are made to reduce or eliminate fire or explosion risk on airports. Sources of ignition include lightning, open flame, electrical spark, static discharge, chemical reaction, or any heat source that can raise or ignite the fuel-air vapor mixture. Safe handling practices will address each of those possibilities.

The difference between a combustible and a flammable material is the flash point. A material with a flash point at or above 100 degrees Fahrenheit is considered combustible. Flammable material is distinguished by flash points below 100 degrees Fahrenheit and/or a vapor pressure not exceeding 40 psi (pounds per square inch). Jet A fuel is considered a combustible fluid because it has a flash point greater than 100 degrees Fahrenheit. Avgas, with a flash point well below 100 degrees Fahrenheit, is considered a flammable fluid.

OPERATIONAL SAFETY DURING CONSTRUCTION ON AIRPORTS

Construction is a fact of life at most airports. Airports are almost always in a constant state of either constructing something new, rehabbing or maintaining something existing, or replacing something old. However, airfield construction must take place with minimal impact to aircraft operations. The formal regulation is Part 139.341, *Identifying, Marking, and Lighting Construction and Other Unserviceable Areas*. FAA AC 150/5370-2F, *Operational Safety on Airports During Construction* (FAA, 2011b), provides guidance for safety on airports during construction activities. Although an airport construction project can consist of many different entities and personnel, who work for a variety of different contractors, vendors, and even the airport, airport management must ensure the safety of aircraft and Airport Operations during construction. Construction activity poses a significant risk to aircraft operations and makes operational impacts unavoidable. Through careful planning, scheduling, training, and coordination of construction activities, the airport operator can avoid situations that compromise the airport's safety.

Airport capital improvement projects typically originate in the airport planning or engineering department, as personnel apply for funding and design of the project. Airport Operations personnel should be brought into the construction planning process as early as possible, in order to identify potential operational and safety issues. The earlier Operations is brought into the planning, the more money will be saved later by not having to redesign elements of the project or change access requirements or project schedules. Airport Operations personnel must also understand that there will be some aircraft operations that will be affected by the construction and, in consultation with airport users, ARFF, ATC, tenants, and other stakeholders should plan to accommodate changes to normal aircraft operating procedures. In other words, there must be a balance between constructing the project, which has been deemed necessary for the airport, and continuing to operate the airport in a safe manner. Taking the approach of *how can we do this* rather than *this can't be done* will go a long way in ensuring that the goals of the planning and engineering department and the operations department, along with other airport stakeholders, are achieved. Many airports that are implementing Safety Management Systems (SMS) have already begun to apply SMS principles to airport construction projects.

CONSTRUCTION SAFETY PLAN

Preconstruction planning includes the development of a safety plan. The focus of the plan is not just to address the safety and efficiency of flight operations but also to address the safety of construction personnel and others associated with the project from injury caused by collision, jet blast, or other airfield hazards. FAA AC 150/5370-2F, *Operational Safety on Airports During Construction* (FAA, 2011b), addresses the elements of an effective construction safety plan on an airport.

Safety, maintaining aircraft operations, and construction costs are interrelated concepts, as safety must not be compromised, and the airport operator must strike a balance between maintaining aircraft operations and construction costs. This balance depends on the operational needs and resources of the airport and requires early coordination with airport users and the FAA. As the project is designed, construction locations, support activities, and associated costs are identified and assessed, related to their impact on Airport Operations. This planning effort ultimately results in a project **Construction Safety and Phasing Plan (CSPP)** (FAA, 2011b). The CSPP is a five-step process:

1. **Identify the affected areas and the type of project** by determining the geographic areas on the airport affected by the construction project and what the project is (runway extension, runway overlay, taxiway connector, etc.).
2. **Describe the current level of operations** (capacity, arrival and departure rates, the Airport Reference Code and Runway Design Group), as well as the most demanding aircraft, Surface Movement Guidance and Control System (SMGCS) plan (if any), and any ATC services.
3. **Allow for temporary changes to operations** by identifying and prioritizing the airport's most important operations with construction activities planned through phasing, to minimize the impact on flight operations.
4. **Take required measures to revised operations** by determining the necessary safety measures and operational changes that are needed so that aircraft may continue to safely operate, minimize revenue loss, and still ensure the project is completed.
5. **Manage safety risk** by conducting a Safety Risk Assessment that is required by the project; as a matter of best practice, however, one should be conducted regardless of whether it is required.

A CSPP has to be completed for each on-airfield construction project that is funded by AIP or Passenger Facility Charge (PFC) funding, on a certificated airport, and it is the airport operator who is responsible for establishing and enforcing the CSPP (FAA, 2011b). Key elements of an effective CSPP include accurate contact information for all key parties; weekly (or even daily) safety meetings; notification to ARFF, ATC, and stakeholders about construction that may adversely affect flight operations (via NOTAMs); and inspection of the construction areas as part of the daily, continuous, and at the end of each construction day, a special inspection. The special inspection ensures that there are no uncovered or unmarked excavations or trenches, that the safety area standards are still maintained, and that no construction equipment is parked where it can block aircraft movement or affect the accuracy and performance of an NAVAID.

Airport Operations personnel should also monitor the status of and update all NOTAMs when necessary. A construction startup and shutdown checklist should be used by Airport Operations. Construction sites should also be inspected at the beginning of operations as well as the end. Airport Operations agents, or officers, should familiarize themselves with each CSPP at the beginning of their shift and brief their oncoming relief of any changes.

Airport operators must also ensure that the FAA Form 7460-1, *Notice of Proposed Construction or Alteration*, is submitted and an aeronautical study of potential obstructions (cranes, stockpiles, etc.) has been addressed (FAA, 2011b, p. 4). The FAA must be notified if there are changes to the CSPP and must coordinate with other agencies (such as the TSA, CBP [Customs and Border Protection], or EPA [Environmental Protection Agency]) and the state environmental agencies, regarding any other requirements for construction.

Contractors are also required to submit a **Safety Plan Compliance Document (SPCD)** that describes how the contractor will comply with the CSPP. The contractor must:

1. Ensure construction personnel are familiar with safety procedures and regulations and provide a primary **point of contact (POC)** (ideally, 24/7) who can resolve issues;
2. Identify the contractor's employees who are responsible for the SPCD, onsite.
3. Conduct inspections of the work areas to ensure compliance with the CSPP and SPCD;
4. Restrict movement of construction vehicles and personnel to permitted construction areas only, using flagging, barricading, temporary fencing, approved escorts, or other means (FAA, 2011b, p. 4);
5. Ensure contractor employees do not enter the AOA unless authorized; and
6. Ensure submittal of Form 7460-1, *Notice of Proposed Construction or Alteration*, as needed.

If an airport tenant is performing construction, the tenant must develop a CSPP and their contractor a SPCD—both documents must be submitted to the airport prior to construction. Although most tenant construction will not take place in the movement area, construction activities and personnel may inadvertently cross over to the movement or safety areas. Thus, a primary focus of the tenant CSPP and SPCD is the prevention of unauthorized access to the movement and safety areas.

Preconstruction Planning

At the preconstruction planning meeting, Airport Operations personnel should meet with contractors, tenants, and affected parties, long before beginning construction. It may not be practical to have tenants and air carriers in the early meetings with the planning, engineering, and contractor personnel, so the Airport Operations representative must also serve as a liaison to those parties and represent their concerns as best as possible. Key areas of focus during the preconstruction planning meeting is addressing the construction vehicle safety plan, establishing haul routes and gate access procedures, and minimizing the impact on aircraft operations.

Haul roads represent a significant safety hazard. Typically, airfield speed limits are kept to a minimum, so as to increase the available reaction time between potential aircraft-to-vehicle conflicts. Haul roads are for trucks and other construction vehicles to move directly from an access point to the construction site and are characterized by large, fast-moving vehicles. An aircraft inadvertently crossing a haul road could be catastrophic, and even an airport vehicle, such as operations or maintenance, crossing a haul road could result in an accident. Also, haul road locations and routes may change throughout the project. Haul roads should be clearly marked, and personnel operating on the haul roads should adhere to set speed limits.

Another consideration is that construction personnel are not typically used to working on airport construction sites. While it may be the same construction company that was on the airport the previous year, construction personnel are transient in nature, moving from one construction job to the next, as a job becomes available. Even seasoned construction personnel may have challenges, as the airport project is likely to be at a different location on the airport, with different access points and different haul road configurations. When construction personnel work at nonairport sites, they are without the concerns of aircraft movement, interference with NAVAIDs, the dangers of leaving trenches open or unsecured materials, pop inspections by TSA, or attempts to penetrate, inadvertently or intentionally, the construction area. Airport Operations should ensure that all contractors are required to provide their personnel an overview of construction safety and security issues on airports, along with the potential consequences.

Limits should be placed on construction activities, with notification and approval processes in place for changes to the daily construction schedule. Weather, availability of materials, and personnel can all affect construction schedules, and occasionally contractors will want to move to a different location on the airfield to do work, if the area planned for work that day is not available for any of the aforementioned reasons. In such cases, it is essential for construction personnel to notify Airport Operations of any changes to the planned schedule and for the contractors to receive approval before relocating their construction activities. Hours of allowable construction activity should also be established, with the understanding that much construction activity takes place on the evenings and weekends. Airport Operations should prepare an SPCD, detailing how the contractors will comply with the CSPP.

CONSTRUCTION SAFETY AND PHASING PLAN

The following areas should be thoroughly addressed in the plan:

1. Safety Areas and Work Limits
   a. Protection of AOA, movement and non-movement areas activity, runway closure notifications, and reopening procedures
   b. Security (site/access-control security and credentialing)
   c. Airport access (escorts, driving on the AOA)
   d. Protection of airspace (i.e., obstructions)
   e. Protection of runway, taxiway, and safety areas
   f. Protection of NAVAIDs
   g. Construction site safety (parking, Staging Areas, trenches, excavations, stockpiled materials, FOD, debris and dust control, personnel safety, use of barricades, warning signs, hazard markings, artificial lighting for work areas and light discipline, obstruction lighting)
   h. Underground utilities
   i. Wildlife management

2. Special Conditions and Emergencies
   a. Severe weather plan
   b. HAZMAT incident
   c. Medical assistance
   d. Low-visibility operations
   e. Snow removal
   f. Aircraft in distress
   g. Aircraft accident
   h. Security breach
   i. VPD or runway incursion
3. Ground Vehicle Operations
   a. Vehicle activity on the airfield (airport traffic and regulations, vehicle marking and identification)
   b. Aircraft safety (jet blast, aircraft operations—landing and taking off)
4. Marking, Signs, and Lights
   a. Runway, taxiway light configurations for closed/open runways
   b. Signage plan
   c. Runway and taxiway visual aids
   d. Runway Guard Lights
   e. Marking and signs for access roads

Safety Areas and Work Limits

Safety areas and work limits address a variety of topics but are focused on the overall safety of the construction operation and the continued safe operation of aircraft.

Protection of the AOA is of prime importance, particularly the movement area and safety areas, but also the non-movement areas (as they provide access to the movement and safety areas). There should be defined processes for closing and reopening runways, taxiways, and other areas of the AOA, which should include a check for FOD, deceiving signs and markings, and any other hazards to navigation or noncompliance with Part 139. NOTAMs should be issued to identify any area of the airport that is not available for use because of construction.

Security

Construction activities represent a security vulnerability—airport perimeter fencing is often torn down and replaced with snow fencing. Security or construction personnel may be responsible for monitoring areas where the perimeter does not meet the standards called for in the **Airport Security Program (ASP)**. Within the terminal building, construction can tear down walls that previously acted as a barrier between the Sterile Area[17] and the Public Area, and contractors have been known to inadvertently (or intentionally[18]) disable airport door alarms. For individuals

---

[17]The Sterile Area is the part of the airport where individuals and their belonging must first undergo screening as conducted by the aircraft operator, TSA or the airport operator, as appropriate.
[18]Some electricians are familiar enough with access control systems to be able to disable a door or gate access reader. This should be a cause for severe enforcement measures under Title 49 CFR Part 1540, §1540.105(a)(1), *Security Responsibilities of Employees and Other Persons*, which prohibits the tampering or interference with, compromise, modify, attempt to circumvent, or cause a person to tamper or interfere with, compromise, modify, or attempt to circumvent any security system, measure, or procedure.

attempting to illegally access the airfield, construction activities present a good opportunity, as there are numerous individuals on the airfield who are not normally there; consequently, individuals attempting to illegally access the airfield do not stand out as much as they would if they had just jumped the fence. TSA and Airport Security inspectors have also been known to attempt to access a construction site as part of a test of Airport Security measures; often the security personnel used for construction sites are not the same officers that are used for general security enforcement at the airport and are unfamiliar with the rules of access.

Whenever there is an upcoming construction project, Airport Operations personnel should notify the Airport Security Coordinator (ASC), who must then submit an amendment to the TSA for approval. Also, any time there is a changed condition, meaning that any portion of the airport described in the ASP is not currently the way it is described, the ASC must notify the TSA within 6 hours. Failure to do so may result in fines from the TSA, which can range up to $11,000, or, worse, a breach of security.

Security personnel should be trained in the relevant areas of the ASP. Site security and gate security provided by tenant or contractor personnel should be inspected frequently, ensuring that the proper procedures are being followed and that the security officer is in possession of and using a current *stop list*.[19] Security officers should also be trained to identify the proper credentials in use on airport property and for the construction site.

Protection of Airspace: Obstructions

Construction or alterations at the airport that affect navigable airspace, as defined in Part 77, must notify the FAA through FAA Form 7460-1, *Notice of Proposed Construction or Alteration*. This includes construction equipment and proposed parking areas for this equipment (i.e., cranes, graders, other equipment) on airports.

Protection of Runway, Taxiway, and Safety Areas

The plan must include explanations for how the Object-Free Area, Obstacle-Free Zones, approach and departure surfaces (or takeoff and glide angles used by aircraft), and runway and taxiway safety areas will be protected during construction. Since the aforementioned areas are imaginary lines that can only be identified on the Airport Layout Plan, the airport operator should install visible barriers (low-mass barricades, snow fencing, etc.) to prevent the inadvertent access into these areas by construction personnel. Plain language signage should be used instead of airfield marking or sign standards. Construction is prohibited in the Runway Safety Area (RSA) while the runway is in use. Stockpiled materials and equipment are not to be stored in the RSA or the Obstacle-Free Zone (OFZ). Open trenches or excavations not permitted in the RSA during air carrier operations. *Note:* Trenches and excavations are allowable during runway closures but must be adequately filled or covered prior to the runway being reopened. Any covering must meet the standards of the RSA (support an aircraft, snowplow, or ARFF vehicle).

---

[19]A Stop List, is a list of airport identification media (badges) that are no longer in use because the listed employees have left employment at the airport but have not turned in their badges. Each listed badge has been deactivated in the security system but is still visually valid until it reaches its expiration date, at which time it's taken off the Stop List. No holder of an expired Airport Identification Badge should be allowed access to any nonpublic or Security Area of an airport.

Any closing or partial closing of runways, taxiways, and apron areas, closing of ARFF response routes, closing of airport access routes used by airline and airport support (i.e., operations, maintenance) vehicle must be coordinated in advance with all affected parties. A NOTAM should always be issued upon closure. Displaced thresholds may be considered in lieu of full-length runway closures. Procedures for marking and signs of closed or partially closed runways and taxiways are found in AC 150/5370-2F (FAA, 2011b). A lighted X (on a stand) or painted X on the runway is the universally known airfield marking for a closed surface.

Protection of Navigational Aids

A complete inventory of airport NAVAIDs should be conducted in the area of intended construction to identify adverse impacts. FAA Tech Operations personnel should be involved in this assessment, as the FAA operates many NAVAIDs and they are familiar with the operating parameters. Also, ATCT should be consulted to ensure any visibility issues are addressed since construction cranes and other activity sometimes obstruct the view from the tower. If a NAVAID may be affected, the CSPP and SPCD must show an understanding of the "critical area" associated with each NAVAID and describe how it will be protected (FAA, 2011b, p. 13).

The airport operator must provide at least a 45-day notice to the FAA if an airport-owned NAVAID is going to be shut down for more than 24 hours or for more than 4 hours daily on consecutive days. For FAA-owned NAVAIDs, the airport operator must notify the FAA ATO 45 days prior to the event and coordinate with the FAA in advance. Additionally, the airport operator must notify the FAA again, 7 days prior to the actual shutdown.

Construction Site Safety

Construction sites must include parking considerations for contractor vehicles, Staging Areas, trenches, excavations, stockpiled materials, FOD, dust control, personnel safety, use of barricades, warning signs, hazard markings, artificial lighting for work areas, light discipline, and obstruction lighting. Vehicle parking areas for contractor employees must be designated in advance and located in a way to prevent any unauthorized entry of persons or vehicles onto the AOA, while still providing reasonable contractor employee access to the job site (FAA, 2011b).

Contractor employees must park and service all construction vehicles in an area designated by the airport operator outside the Obstacle-Free Zones and never in the safety area of an active runway or taxiway. If it is necessary to leave specialized equipment on a closed taxiway or runway at night, the equipment must be adequately illuminated (pilots have been known to land on closed runways, and even mistakenly on taxiways). Parking areas must not obstruct the clear line of sight by the ATCT to any taxiways or runways under ATC or obstruct any runway visual aids, signs, or navigation aids (FAA, 2011b).

Foreign Object Debris Management

FOD includes waste and loose materials that are capable of causing damage to landing gear, propellers, and jet engines. Contractors must not leave or place FOD on or near active, aircraft-movement areas. Materials capable of creating FOD must be continuously removed during the construction project. Fencing (other than security fencing) may be necessary to contain material that can be carried by wind into areas where aircraft operate. Dust mitigation must also be addressed.

Construction personnel must be familiar with safety procedures and regulations on the airport. A POC is responsible for initiating a response to correct any construction-related activity or issue that may adversely affect the operational safety of the airport, must be designated onsite. Workplace safety rules should be followed at all times. The use of any barricades, artificial lighting, warning signs, and obstruction lighting must be in accordance with the CSPP.

Barricades (weighted or sturdily attached to the surface), including traffic cones, are acceptable methods used to identify and define the limits of construction and hazardous areas on airports. Equipment that poses the least danger to aircraft but is sturdy enough to remain in place when subjected to typical winds, propeller wash, and jet blast should be selected. Barricade spacing must be such that a breach is physically prevented barring a deliberate act. For example, if barricades are intended to exclude vehicles, gaps between barricades must be smaller than the width of the excluded vehicles, generally 4 feet (FAA, 2011b, p. 24). Provision must be made for ARFF access if necessary. If barricades are intended to exclude pedestrians, they must be continuously linked by the use of ropes and securely attached to prevent FOD. Acceptable barricades have low mass and height and are weighted, retroreflective, and frangible (if attached to the ground). Unacceptable barricades in the movement area include railroad ties, cement blocks, tall barrels or metal drums, cement jersey barriers, amber (or yellow) hazard lights, wooden sawhorses, heavy metal A-frames, and concrete-filled buckets.

Barricade lights must be red, either steady burning or flashing, and must meet the luminance requirements of the state highway department. Lights must be mounted on barricades and spaced at no more than 10 feet apart and must be operated between sunset and sunrise and during periods of low visibility or whenever the airport is open for operations. Supplement barricades with signs (e.g., "No Entry," "No Vehicles") should be used as necessary (FAA, 2011b, p. 24). The overriding guidance for the use of barricades and signs should be whether personnel can see and comprehend the barricade and signs and make the correct decision upon encountering them.

Underground Utilities

The CSPP and/or SPCD must include procedures for locating and protecting existing underground utilities, cables, wires, pipelines, and other underground facilities in excavation areas (FAA, 2011b). This requirement may involve coordinating with public utilities and FAA ATO/Technical Operations. Interruptions to utilities that provide water for firefighting, airfield lighting power, or other critical utilities should be avoided if at all possible. If interruptions are necessary, affected parties should be given adequate advance notice.

Penalties

The CSPP should describe specific penalties imposed for noncompliance with airport rules and regulations, including the CSPP, Security Identification Display Area violations, VPDs, and others.

Wildlife Management

The CSPP and SPCD take into account the airport WHMP. Contractors must control and continuously remove waste or loose materials that might attract wildlife and be aware of and avoid construction activities that create wildlife hazards on airports (FAA, 2011b). The following items attract wildlife: trash (food scraps), standing water, tall grass, and seeds. Poorly maintained fences and gates or the replacement of airport fencing with temporary fencing may allow wildlife to access the AOA. Additionally, construction activities may disrupt the current airport ecosystem, resulting in wildlife relocating or becoming attracted to other parts of the AOA.

Special Conditions and Emergencies

Severe Weather Plan

The severe weather plan must identify the conditions upon which construction activities will be stopped because of weather (such as lightning within 5 miles of the airport or snow) or hazardous visibility conditions. Construction activity should cease before the airport reaches 1200 RVR, which is the threshold for implementation of the SMGCS plan. Construction equipment and personnel should be well clear of the AOA prior to the initiation of SMGCS. There should be one individual onsite with a line of communication to the Airport Operations officer or airport communications center who can be notified when hazardous weather is approaching. The construction shutdown plan should be initiated upon direction from Airport Operations. Since this is not a normal "end-of-the-day" shutdown, and hazardous weather can approach quickly, it is particularly important to watch for vehicles being left in runway protected areas or in NAVAID clearance areas.

Hazardous Material Incidents

Fuel or hydraulic leaks from construction vehicles can create HAZMAT incidents. Contractors operating construction vehicles and equipment on the airport must be prepared to expeditiously contain and clean up spills resulting from fuel or hydraulic fluid leaks (FAA, 2011b). Transport and handling of other HAZMAT on an airport also require special procedures that should be outlined in the CSPP. Procedures should also address fuel deliveries, spill recovery procedures, MSDS availability, and other considerations.

Provisions should be made for requesting medical assistance required by workplace-related injuries, including notification to ARFF or emergency medical service (EMS) personnel as appropriate, escort of EMS vehicles to the worksite, and work stoppages.

The CSPP should address contractor procedures to be followed where an inbound aircraft that is in distress may affect construction activities or Airport Operations. Also, if there is an aircraft accident, there should be procedures in place for contractor personnel to be notified of what actions to take (generally, depart the airfield if such departure will not hamper emergency response or, in some cases, at least stop work until the situation is secure).

Contractor personnel must have procedures to report a security breach (and to stop work until the breach is resolved) and must know what actions to take when a security breach occurs on the AOA. Typical procedures include stopping work, stopping vehicles entering and exiting the airport, providing identifying information to airport police or security personnel, and if appropriate, keeping the potential violator in sight. If the breach is witnessed by a contractor, that individual should remain onsite until interviewed and released by police.

Ground Vehicle Operations

All traffic regulations, vehicle markings, and identification must adhere to the CSPP. Drivers should also be trained in avoidance and hazards associated with jet blast, propeller blast, and vehicle airspeed and rules. Procedures should be in place for a VPD or runway incursion, which typically includes a work stoppage and the requirement for the driver to remain onsite, until Airport Operations can respond.

Marking, Signs, and Lights

The CSPP must specify maximum gaps between barricades and the maximum spacing of hazard lighting. It should also identify one individual and at least one alternate who are responsible for maintenance of hazard marking and lighting equipment. The CSPP should include a review of the runway and taxiway light configurations for closed/open runways and the overall signage plan (FAA, 2011b).

SUMMARY

Several safety programs are a core element for an airport to maintain compliance with Title 14 CFR Part 139. These programs include a WHMP, an SICP, an AEP (addressed Chapters 10–12 throughout), a reporting system to notify airport users of hazards to flight or noncompliant condition, and a plan for addressing vehicle and pedestrian movement on the AOA.

The NOTAM system is the approved reporting method for airports to notify users of any condition on the airport that does not comply with Part 139, or is unsafe, or different from what is otherwise published in the AFD. NOTAMs are issued by an individual, typically the Airport Operations Manager or ATCT controller,[20] or by the FAA through the Flight Data Center (FDC).[21]

The prevention of runway incursions is a top priority at every airport. While not specifically calling for a separate "plan," Part 139 does require the airport operator to address vehicles and pedestrians in the movement area. Airport operators implement the plan in their rules and regulations and through the use of airfield driver-training programs. The prevention of runway incursions is also a national priority for the FAA, and penalties for individuals causing an incursion are often severe.

Commercial service airports attempt to remain open during a variety of weather conditions, including snow. SICPs are required for Part 139–certificated airports that experience annual snowfalls. The plan describes how the airport operator will remove snow from the paved surfaces and notify airport users, such as air carriers and GA operators, about the condition of the runways and taxiways.

Until the ditching of U.S. Airways Flight 1549, Part 139–certificated airports were only required to conduct WHAs when certain triggering events occurred. After the aircraft landed in

---

[20]ATC towers can request a written agreement to be in the NOTAM loop for issuance authority.

[21]"Although the airport operator has primary NOTAM origination responsibilities for the movement areas, the ATC facility managing the NOTAM system is responsible for, and has the authority to ensure the compatibility of the format and content of the proposed NOTAM message." From FAA AC No.: 150/5200-28D available at https://www.faa.gov/regulations_policies/advisory_circulars/index.cfm/go/document.information/documentID/73588.

the Hudson River after striking a flock of Canada geese, all commercial service airports have either conducted or are in the process of conducting a WHA. The WHA results in a WHMP that focuses on habitat modification and active control measures to mitigate the effects of wildlife on aircraft operations.

While not specified as an ARFF "plan," Part 139 airports are required to maintain a certain level of emergency response capability. This is known as the ARFF Index and is determined by the longest air carrier aircraft serving the airport five or more times a day. The Index calls for a minimum amount of equipment and firefighting materials that must be available during air carrier operations.

At many airports, HAZMAT consists primarily of aircraft fueling operations, although air carriers do trade in other shippable HAZMAT materials. Part 139 airports are required to have a plan in place to inspect fueling operations and mitigate sources of fire.

Construction on airports is a fact of life at every airport. Part 139 airports that perform construction are required to have a CSPP, which articulates the policies and procedures for safety on the airport during construction activities.

Operational Safety During Airport Construction

by Tim Barth, C.M.[1] and Jim Schell, C.M.[2]
[1] Director of Aviation, Cheyenne Regional Airport
[2] Deputy Director of Aviation, Cheyenne Regional Airport

Aviation safety is the primary consideration at every airport, regardless of the size or nature of the airport: commercial service versus GA versus seaport. In order to achieve a maximum level of safety without impacting Airport Operations to the extent of financial hardship requires the airport operator to develop a systematic approach to identify potential hazards and mitigate or manage them effectively.

Airports are unique when it comes to construction projects. Safety management related to airport construction by far exceeds the complexity of considerations found at other types of construction projects. For example, lane closures for road work only require minimal signage, cones or barricades, maybe a flagger, and, for the most part, traffic moving in only one direction. Airports on the other hand have traffic moving in all directions. And not just vehicles but also aircraft, tugs, emergency equipment, pedestrians, and motorized jet bridges. While a road project often can use a detour, an airport can't. A detour for an airport, using another airport, is a revenue loss for the airport and the airline and an inconvenience for the traveling public. There are many hazards and many hazard mitigation techniques on an airport during construction. For example, unlike highway construction or vertical construction, stockpiled material, equipment, and open excavations are only allowed in certain areas of an airport. An airport is not allowed to have abutting pavement edges in excess of 3 inches. Debris, malfunctioning lights, or wildlife attractants all present serious hazards to aircraft in motion, whether flying or on the ground. There cannot be any construction outside of designated areas on an airport without jeopardizing safety. All cranes, drills, rigging platforms,

(Continued)

(Continued)

and tanks exceeding a certain height must be properly marked and, during nighttime operations, properly lighted.

The FAA, AAAE, ICAO, and U.S. Contractors Association[22] all provide numerous resources for airport safety during construction projects. Many of these resources are combined into one document at most airports, which is known as an SMS Plan. In terms of implementation and oversight, the document is referred to as the CSPP. These plans, while different for each project, essentially look at the five most common elements of a construction project on an airport: (1) defining the affected areas on the airport; (2) identifying the normal operations in the affected area; (3) analyzing the airport's most important operations and accommodating the temporary changes to those operations in order to minimize disruption to aircraft operations, (4) preparing a Construction Safety Plan to manage the safety risk; and (5) communicating, participating, and implementing the plan, with the emphasis on *communicating*.

In its most common form the CSPP has three primary purposes. First, the CSPP establishes the project requirements to ensure and maintain safety during construction. Second, the CSPP provides guidance for the actions of onsite construction, inspection, consulting and airport personnel, and equipment. Last, aviation safety is the primary consideration during airport construction. All activities need to be planned and scheduled in advance to minimize disruption of normal aircraft activities.

In addition to the CSPP, the contractor is required to compose and submit for review to the airport operator an SPCD. Not only do the contractors have "automatic buy-in" in the safety process, it's also a requirement under FAA AC 150/5370-2F (FAA, 2011b). Like the CSPP, the compliance document's key to success is, again, *communication*! This compliance document must be reviewed and understood by all levels of workers on the job in order to minimize risk to the greatest extent possible. In its most basic form, the SPCD is a certified statement from the contractor indicating that the contractor understands and will comply with the safety and operational requirements of the CSPP. Most important, no deviations from the SPCD are allowed unless both authorized by the airport operator and reviewed by the FAA for any re-coordination efforts that are necessary to maintain the integrity of the safety plan.

Nearly everyone has heard the adage that "safety is everyone's responsibility"; that is more true in an airport construction environment than in a civilian construction environment. Therefore, it is necessary to compose a direct, concise, and clearly understood document for both the CSPP and the SPCD.

In August 2014, the FAA updated its "Tips for Operational Safety on Airports During Construction."[23] While that document provides a checklist that basically covers the same five topics mentioned previously and also provides references to the various ACs that pertain to the topic, it does not adequately address the fundamental questions of who, what, where,

(Continued)

---

[22]See The Associated General Contractors of America at: https://www.agc.org/.

[23]See http://www.faa.gov/airports/southern/airport_safety/part139_cert/media/airport-construction-safety-tips.pdf.

(Continued)

when, and how. By keeping with a simple format in regard to safety, an airport can better assure a more thorough understanding of the operational safety parameters when working on an airport. All too often, those in the airport environment are familiar with the numerous acronyms and dialogue which seems common place to those in the industry. For those outside the industry, the acronyms and dialogue can be confusing and easily misunderstood. Therefore, when preparing both documents, the airport operator and the contractor should compose the document in basic and easy to understand language, in which critical elements are clearly spelled out. Why is this important? Quite simply, the airport operator has the overall responsibility for construction activities on an airport.

In order for the CSPP and the SPCD to be truly effective, full participation, cooperation, and support of all parties are necessary to prevent accidents and ensure the health and safety of all personnel and property involved in the project. There are many participants in the CSPP, including, but not limited to, airport tenants (airlines, FBOs, fuelers, hangar owners, ATC, ARFF, caterers, maintenance personnel, etc.), the engineering consultant, the contractor, FAA/State Division of Aeronautics, subcontractors, and sometimes the media.

While the participation list may seem extensive, the number of participants will vary depending on the type, scope, and nature of the airport construction project. However, the more inclusive the participation, the more likely the project has a chance of success. Why is this important? FAA AC 150/5370-2F, *Operational Safety on Airports During Construction*, spells out approximately 20 critical elements of the safety plan that need to be addressed. While not all elements affect every entity on an airport, there is sure to be one element that will affect at least one entity and how that entity goes about its day-to-day business operations. Some of the most basic elements of the CSPP at some point will affect everyone on the airport. For example, emergency contact information, areas affected by construction, basic coordination, contractor access, and notification of construction activities and special conditions normally affect everyone on the airport. Individuals and entities not directly affected by the construction may also be able to provide guidance or information about the project to their customers, or other entities.

Communication is by far the most important element in any safety plan. The theme of a good CSPP and SPCD is communication, communication, and more communication! This is especially important when the airport experiences special or irregular conditions. These usually manifest in the form of preplanned special events, emergency or law enforcement actions, unusual helicopter activity, unusual military activity, or emergencies occurring on the airport.

How the tenants and users of the airport are kept informed of information during a construction project is just as important as the key information itself. There are many acceptable platforms available to airport operators to provide information. Obviously, the first step is to have a preconstruction meeting with those most affected. This meeting is typically arranged by the airport operator in conjunction with the consultant and contractor. It's of paramount importance to include ARFF in all construction planning, updates, and NOTAM notifications.

(Continued)

(Continued)

Moving forward, it's critical that airport operators have weekly construction safety meetings with the affected parties. More important, there should be daily safety briefs for the onsite workers to review the day's activities. Social media via website updates, Twitter, texting, and the like are useful tools in reaching the airport tenants, the traveling public, and the media. Keep updates short and relevant. Issuing NOTAMs 72 hours in advance helps the airlines and GA fleet coordinate their daily operations. Keeping NOTAMs current and updated, along with ensuring physical pavement closures on the airfield match the status of current NOTAMs is essential to any project's success. Last, ensure that all of the contractor's personnel on the project have essential contact information for the airport operator, ARFF, and others and that your staff has the appropriate contact information for the contractor(s) in the field. Reinforcing with the construction crews that "when in doubt, call someone" is always a good practice to ensure open lines of communication and enhance overall safety.

Utilizing the various tools, components, and strategies outlined above should make any project a success. As with daily operations at every airport, there are many moving pieces, requiring them all working together to make the entire system operate safely and efficiently. This is no different during construction projects, in fact even more so. Even with the most experienced and "airport-familiar" construction crews, the dynamic environment that airfields present provides many obstacles to overcome. Each project typically provides a much different set of challenges than the one before it. With the pressures of keeping each project on schedule and on budget, sometimes it can be easy to lose sight of the ultimate goal of safety. Providing the traveling public with a safe airfield from which to operate and at the same time minimizing delays to everyday operations are always the top priorities. Safety is the central theme to every construction project, and timely coordination with all tenants and stakeholders is paramount in ensuring safety is never compromised. Communicating with your stakeholders through all phases of a project will ensure a positive outcome.

Large-Hub Airport Operations

by Dan Sprinkle
Vice President of Operations, Denver International Airport

Commercial Service Airports are complex and dynamic business machines. They can make or break any city and are the backbone of every transportation hub. Many are owned and operated by city municipality governments and in order to attract service, retain competitiveness and compete on a global level, they must operate as streamlined corporations. As a manager, this means coming to work every day seeking creative ways to lead and motivate teams in reducing costs, increasing profits and keeping staff members highly engaged. Similar to other profitable businesses, Commercial Service Airports must compete for limited resources while operating in a highly regulated environment. They are subject to the same industry volatility of other transportation systems while trying to find creative ways to survive.

(Continued)

(Continued)

Airport Operations

The role of Airport Operations can vary from airport to airport. At smaller airports, staffing levels may include anywhere from 3 to 30 people, many of whom are cross-trained in various disciplines. For example, you may have an Airport Operations Specialist who's primary role is to perform regulatory airfield inspections but may also be certified to operate the Aircraft Rescue Firefighting equipment and write Airport Improvement Program Grants. At larger airports, staffing levels may be in the hundreds and many of the airport roles are taken care of by highly specialized personnel. As a whole, the field of Airport Operations is very exciting and rewarding. Many duties within this field include the following: work directly with the traveling public, perform regulatory inspections of the airfield, enforce security protocols throughout the airport environment, perform wildlife mitigation measures, respond to airport emergencies and work directly with airport stakeholders (e.g., FAA, Airlines, TSA, FBI, FAM, Concessions, Police, Fire, Paramedics, etc.). For those who inspire to run small-, medium- or large-hub airports as a career, the field of Airport Operations is a great place to start. You gain the hands-on experience needed to make future decisions that may be complex and impactful.

Snow Removal

Snow removal at Commercial Service Airports requires a few key components in order to operate safely and efficiently. First, you must have a plan. One that every operator, supervisor, manager and stakeholder clearly understands and follows. This requires many hours of building relationships and trust with everyone involved at your airport even before a plan is started. Developing a plan is often the hardest part. You want to write it in such a way that it covers the smallest to the largest scenarios, one that is easily understood and one that is attainable by all. Second, you must communicate your plan to everyone involved. This often begins 24 to 48 hours before the first snow flake falls. Third, follow your plan. This includes everyone involved. Sometimes plans are not followed due to poor snow plan development or poor training, all of which may require adjusting after the storm. Finally, perform a post-storm review to see if your plan worked, needs adjusting or overhauled. Continuous improvement is something that every airport must strive for because it benefits the customers and helps ensure you are remaining competitive. The overarching goal of snow and ice removal at any airport is safety and efficiency. While ensuring runway occupancy times are minimal is important for increasing capacity, the safety of the airfield snow plow drivers, pilots, crew and passengers is paramount and must never be deviated from. This requires airports to hire, train and motivate great people.

The level of equipment and tools needed to operate a snow operation varies from airport to airport, mainly based upon their geographical location. Some airports may be concerned with ice, while others may have ice, snow and other contaminants to manage. Each airport operator uses a different mix of snow removal equipment, chemicals (liquid and/or solid) and methods to ward off mother-nature, all of which are identified and approved by the FAA within the Airport Certification Manual.

(Continued)

(Continued)

Airfield Safety

The FAA provides minimal safety standards required for airports through issuance of Regulations, Advisor Circulars, inspections and other means. Airport operators understand these are just the starting points for running a safe and efficient airport. Additional inspection items and internal best practices and are often put in place by each airport in order to mitigate risk, reduce the likelihood and severity of an incident or accident and ensure those using the airport are protected. You can think of safety within the airport environment as a large blanket. After policies and procedures are developed, airport operators ensure that every portion of their work is covered with the blanket. It is something that can never be ignored, must not be eliminated and can always be adjusted. Unfortunately, some airports choose to implement safety measures only after an accident occurs. The challenge of today's airport operator is to identify risks before they happen and implement safety measures to either eliminate incidents or accidents or at lease reduce the likelihood and severity of them happening. This is where the SMS system comes into play. SMS is not a new concept and is being developed within the FAA's system for airports to follow to help airport operators run a safe operation.

Construction

As our nation's airports continue to age and deteriorate, it is vital for airport operators to plan for and build for the future. This includes performing scheduled maintenance on current infrastructure and expanding/building for future growth. Careful planning must take place when identifying construction projects and requires lots of planning even before the first contractor places foot on your property. Funding sources can come from various sources to include the Airport's Capital Budget (Airport Revenue Bonds), PFC's and FAA AIP Grants, depending on the project. Airports perform pre-construction meetings (SMS process) with the FAA in order to identify hazards and minimize or eliminate their impacts. This may include reviewing contractor's access to the site, review construction safety plans, haul routes, FOD, lighting and marking the site(s), and NOTAMs for pilots to understand the boundaries of the project. Once the project has been approved, contractors are allowed onto the airport property and work under the control of a project manager and quality control specialist. The airport works with the project manager closely to ensure the site is safe and meets the requirements identified in the construction safety plan. One of the biggest concerns for the airport operator is safety. Contractors are not always accustomed to driving on the airport thus training and strong oversight is important. Also, pilots must be aware of the boundaries of each construction site so clear concise NOTAMs are important and marking and lighting the project is mandatory. The FAA provides guidance on how to coordinate and manage construction activity and the airport operator normally adds to those requirements based upon their individual circumstances.

REFERENCES

Associated Press (AP). (2007, January 29). Preliminary report: Denver airport was not prepared for big blizzard. *USA Today*. Retrieved July 23, 2015, from http://usatoday30.usatoday.com/weather/news/2007-01-29-denver-airport-blizzard_x.htm.

Belant, J., & Ayers, C. (2014). *Bird harassment, repellent, and deterrent techniques for use on and near airports*. Washington, DC: Transportation Review Board (TRB), (TRB, ACRP).

Belant, J., & Martin, J. (2011). *Habitat management to deter wildlife at airports*. Washington, DC: Transportation Review Board (TRB), (TRB, ACRP).

Cardillo, V. (2015, June 10). *Winter operations technology and best practices*. Lecture presented at American Association of Airport Executives (AAAE) Annual Conference and Exposition in Philadelphia Convention Center, Philadelphia.

DeFusco, R., & Unangst, E. (2013). *Airport wildlife population management: a synthesis of airport practice*. Washington, DC: Airport Cooperative Research Program (ACRP), (TRB, ACRP).

Federal Aviation Administration (FAA). (2002). AC 150/5210-20, *Ground vehicle operations on airports*. Washington, DC: Federal Aviation Administration (FAA).

Federal Aviation Administration (FAA). (2004). A/C 150/5210-22, Airport certification manual. Washington, DC: U.S. Department of Transportation, Federal Aviation Administration.

Federal Aviation Administration (FAA). (2007). AC 150/5200-33B, *Hazardous wildlife attractants on or near airports*. Washington, DC: U.S. Department of Transportation, Federal Aviation Administration.

Federal Aviation Administration (FAA). (2008a). AC 150/5200-30C, *Airport winter safety and operations*. Washington, DC: U.S. Department of Transportation, Federal Aviation Administration.

Federal Aviation Administration (FAA). (2008b). AC 150/5200-28, Notices to Airmen (NOTAMS) for Airport Operators. Washington DC: Federal Aviation Administration (FAA).

Federal Aviation Administration (FAA). (2009a). AC 150/5210-17B, *Programs for training of aircraft rescue and firefighting personnel*. Washington, DC: U.S. Department of Transportation, Federal Aviation Administration.

Federal Aviation Administration (FAA). (2009b). AC 150/5200-31C, *Airport emergency plan*. Washington, DC: U.S. Department of Transportation, Federal Aviation Administration.

Federal Aviation Administration (FAA) (2009c). *National runway safety plan, 2009−2011*. Washington, DC: Federal Aviation Administration.

Federal Aviation Administration (FAA). (2010, January 14). *Fact sheet−FAA wildlife hazard mitigation program*. Retrieved July 26, 2015, from https://www.faa.gov/news/fact_sheets/news_story.cfm?newsId=11105.

Federal Aviation Administration (FAA) (2011a). *A quick reference: airfield standards* (2nd ed.). Washington, DC: U.S. Department of Transportation, Federal Aviation Administration.

Federal Aviation Administration (FAA). (2011b). AC 150/5370-2F, *Operational safety on airports during construction*. Washington, DC: U.S. Department of Transportation, Federal Aviation Administration.

Federal Aviation Administration (FAA). (2011c). AC 150/5220-10e Guide Specification for Aircraft Rescue and Fire Fighting Vehicles. Washington DC: Federal Aviation Administration (FAA).

Federal Aviation Administration (FAA). (2012, November). *The strategic runway safety plan*. Retrieved July 23, 2015, from http://www.faa.gov/airports/runway_safety/news/congressional_reports/media/The%20Strategic%20Runway%20Safety%20Plan.pdf.

Federal Aviation Administration (FAA). (2013). AC 150/5200-32B, *Reporting wildlife aircraft strikes*. Washington, DC: U.S. Department of Transportation, Federal Aviation Administration.

Federal Aviation Administration (FAA). (2014a). AC 150/5220-30A, *Airport snow and ice control equipment*. Washington, DC: U.S. Department of Transportation, Federal Aviation Administration.

Federal Aviation Administration (FAA). (2014b, September 26). *Federal NOTAM system.* Retrieved July 22, 2015, from https://notams.aim.faa.gov/#Applications.

Federal Aviation Administration (FAA). (2015). AC 150/5210-17C, *Programs for training of aircraft rescue and firefighting personnel.* Washington, DC: U.S. Department of Transportation, Federal Aviation Administration.

General Foam Information. (n.d.). Retrieved July 26, 2015, from http://www.chemguard.com/about-us/documents-library/foam-info/general.htm.

Golaszewski, R., Helledy, G., Castellano, B., & David, R. (2009). *How proposed ARFF standards would impact airports* (ACRP Project 11-02, Task 11) (TRB, ACRP). Washington, DC: Airport Cooperative Research Program (ACRP). Retrieved July 26, 2015, from http://onlinepubs.trb.org/onlinepubs/acrp/acrp_webdoc_007.pdf.

Oetzell, S. (2014, spring). Vanquishing the VPD. *FAA Airports Division Western-Pacific Region Newsletter.* Retrieved 2014, from http://www.faa.gov/airports/western_pacific/newsletter/media/VPD-q1y14.pdf.

Price, J. C., & Forrest, J. S. (2014). *Certified member body of knowledge* (5th ed., Ser. 3). Alexandria, VA: American Association of Airport Executives (AAAE).

Quilty, S. (2008). *Preventing vehicle—aircraft incidents during winter operations and periods of low visibility: a synthesis of airport practice.* Washington, DC: Airport Cooperative Research Program (TRB, ACRP).

LANDSIDE AND TERMINAL OPERATIONS

Inside the main terminal "Great Hall" and exterior of "the Tent" in the main terminal at Denver International Airport, CO.

Image by Shahn Sederberg, courtesy Colorado Division of Aeronautics, 2014.

Passenger parking and rental car agencies, Denver International Airport, CO.

Image by Shahn Sederberg, courtesy Colorado Division of Aeronautics, 2012.

While the U.S. federal government heavily regulates the airside areas of a commercial service airport, the operation of the terminal building and the landside areas of the airport are predominantly controlled by local or state regulations, and to a certain extent, by the Federal Aviation Administration's grant assurances. There is not a Federal Aviation Administration (FAA) equivalent to Part 139 that addresses landside and terminal operations.

Landside typically refers to those areas beginning with passenger pickup and dropoff curb areas of the airport and extending out to the community highway, railway, and other intermodal forms of transportation. The **terminal** is the airport's main passenger structure, beginning at the curb and extending to the screening checkpoint. Additionally, the concourses beyond the screening checkpoint are also considered to be part of terminal operations.

The primary purpose of an airport is the safe and efficient operations of aircraft, but aircraft cannot operate in an efficient manner if passengers cannot access the facility, if cargo cannot get to the aircraft in time, and if the passengers' luggage, flight crews, employees, and others who support the airport and aircraft operations cannot get to their places of business. Additionally, the terminal areas and even landside areas, in some cases, are subject to regulation by the Transportation Security Administration (TSA) through the passenger screening process and the requirement to prevent unauthorized access to the **Sterile and Secured Areas**[1] of the airfield. Certain aviation security regulations also call for the removal of unattended vehicles from curbside and unattended items from the public and Sterile Areas of the airport.

---

[1]Passengers are not authorized to enter airport Secured Areas (airside where passenger aircraft are loaded and unloaded) nor the airport Sterile Areas (passenger and baggage screening and subsequent areas to gates) without being properly screened. All Airport Security Areas are thoroughly addressed in *Practical Aviation Security: Predicting and Preventing Future Threats* (Price & Forrest, 2013).

While not federally regulated, the terminal building and landside areas serve a vital role in the airport revenue structure. These areas include leased space, concession agreements, which provide the airport operator a share of profits, parking garage and lot fees, landside access fees, and other revenue opportunities that finance Airport Operations and capital projects. However, varying philosophies about how airport terminals should be operated exist. The *airport-dominant* philosophy, sometimes called the European model, generally means that the airport operator provides the staff to run terminal services, including apron and ramp management (often through contract personnel) and baggage and passenger handling services (Ashford, Stanton, Moore, Coutu, & Beasley, 2013, p. 221). The *airline-dominant* model generally means that the air carriers provide passenger and baggage handling services. Most major airports work on a mixed-model blending both of these philosophies.

Airport Operations personnel assigned to the terminal or landside areas often assume roles of overseer and observer, responding to incidents that may affect vehicle and passenger flow, the passenger experience, and, in some cases, the airport revenue stream all under the watchful eye of the general public and, to a larger extent, the world. Terminal managers should always be aware that their dealings with the public may be recorded by audio or video and transmitted around the world in seconds via any of the numerous forms of social media.

THE LANDSIDE AND TERMINAL SYSTEM

A fundamental role of the airport passenger terminal is to transition passengers from Ground Transportation to air transportation and then back to Ground Transportation. The terminal is the major interface between the airfield and the rest of the airport, connecting the landside operations to airside operations. The terminal includes facilities for passenger and baggage processing, Airport Maintenance and operational activities, airport and airline administration, and cargo handling (Horonjeff, McKelvey, Sproule, & Young, 2010).

An airport terminal provides for the safe, efficient, and comfortable transfer of passengers and their baggage to and from aircraft and various modes of Ground Transportation. To accomplish these objectives, essential elements such as ticketing, passenger processing, baggage handling, and security inspection are required. Food service, car rental, shops, restrooms, airport management, and other ancillary functions also support these elements. For general aviation (GA) airports, terminal design provides for a common waiting area supported by service counters, food service, restrooms, pilot services, airport or Fixed Base Operator (FBO) management, and other ancillary functions (Price & Forrest, 2014).

The passenger terminal system is comprised of three elements: the access interface (for activities such as landside operations, intermodal transportation, parking, and vehicle circulation, loading, and unloading); the passenger-processing interface (ticketing, baggage claim, security screening, and Federal Inspection Services); and the flight interface (conveyances to and from aircraft loading and unloading areas) (Horonjeff et al., 2010).

AIRPORT OPERATIONS RESPONSIBILITIES IN LANDSIDE AND TERMINAL AREAS

The amount of personnel required to oversee operations in the airport terminal, in concourses, and on landside is directly related to the size of the airport. At a small- or medium-hub airport, the airfield operations manager, who is responsible for the Part 139 airfield inspections, may also have responsibilities in the airport terminals and on landside. At a large-hub airport, airfield inspectors typically focus solely on Part 139 in the overall operation of the airfield, while others fill the role of **Terminal Operation Managers**,[2] who oversee activities in the terminal and on landside. Additional personnel may also be needed to ensure compliance in the landside areas, such as in the commercial Ground Transportation operations, overseeing taxicab and limousine operations.

The Terminal Operation Manager fills many roles, not the least of which is being an ambassador for the airport sponsor, and often times a problem solver, an Incident Commander, a representative of the city, county or airport authority, and any other endless number of roles. Essentially the Terminal Operations Manager does whatever is necessary within the confines of the airport rules and regulations to ensure the continuous throughput of passengers, baggage, and cargo.

An effective Terminal Operations Manager is a good relationship builder. At large, commercial-service airports, limited numbers of terminal operations personnel are available; in these cases, Terminal Operations Managers delegate many tasks to their subordinates. Terminal Operations Managers should have close relationships with the airport police and emergency medical services (EMS), as they will typically respond with police officers or emergency medical personnel to represent the airport from a legal and liability perspective, as well as to handle general logistics, including crowd control and vehicle or traffic management, and to apprise the Airport Operations Manager of the situation. Terminal Operations Managers should also have good relationships with the TSA Transportation Security Manager, the senior representative at a screening checkpoint on a day-to-day basis, as well as the concessionaires, vendors, and contractors that service the terminal and its tenants.

Considering that terminal operations encompass a wide variety of responsibilities that essentially keep the passengers moving and the airport operational, a better way to describe the roles of terminal operations personnel is to list examples of issues that terminal operations personnel face on the job:

1. When an individual falls down in the terminal, terminal operations personnel ensure that emergency medical personnel have been notified and provide contact information for the individual to follow up for insurance and liability purposes.
2. During a severe weather event, such as a tornado or hurricane, terminal operations personnel ensure that individuals are directed to shelter.
3. During a snowstorm that has closed the airport, terminal operations personnel ensure that individuals stranded in the airport are taken care of by working with vendors and caterers to provide food, blankets, and pillows, and to ensure the toilets remain clean and operational to the extent possible.
4. During an active shooter,[3] vehicle bombing, or mass casualty event, terminal operations personnel provide first aid and establish Incident Command, ingress, and egress locations for emergency responders and Staging Areas.

---

[2]Although these job titles may be different from one airport to the next, we use the title Terminal Operations Manager in this text. In some cases, the title Landside Operations Manager is used to differentiate the dynamic at large-hub airports where there are often two or more individuals fulfilling these roles, each assigned to specific areas (i.e., terminal or landside).

[3]After the shooter is down and the scene is relatively safe. Most terminal Operations (Ops) personnel are not armed law enforcement personnel, and their direction during an active shooter is to get away from the shooter, or incident, until the scene is reasonably secure. If a terminal Ops manager, or any airport worker, could not escape from the event, but had to instead hide, the person should be trained in assisting passengers in getting to a rally point or designated location (but after the shooter is down).

5. For international flights, terminal operations personnel ensure that passengers are directed to their proper locations, whether that is to have baggage rechecked to connect to a domestic flight, to the customs or immigration checkpoint, or to the terminal building. Additionally, terminal operations personnel ensure that international passengers have a ready supply of baggage carts. International passengers tend to have a lot of baggage, and it is important for them to have a positive passenger experience.

6. If an elevator, escalator, or moving walkway has shut down, terminal operations personnel notify maintenance to get it back into operation.

7. If a food vendor continues to close early, prior to the time noted in their lease that they are required to stay open, terminal operations personnel notify the airport properties office for follow up and possible enforcement action.

8. If an airline claims it is using a preferred-use gate, but other airlines claim that the airline is not using the terminal at the required frequency, terminal operations personnel may be required to monitor and document the usage of the gate by all airlines to resolve the dispute.

9. If the screening checkpoint line is backing up and causing significant passenger delays, terminal operations personnel work with the TSA on moving staff, calling in more help, and opening more lanes (Figure 9.1). Terminal operations personnel may also work with the airlines to keep them abreast of the situation, so that the airlines can make accommodations if possible.

10. If passengers are stranded after a canceled flight, terminal operations personnel ensure that the airport's irregular operations plan for tarmac delays is implemented.

11. Terminal operations personnel assist with passengers who have functional needs.

FIGURE 9.1

Terminal operations personnel assist passengers waiting in long screening lines.

Source: Jeffrey Price, Denver International Airport, 2015.

12. Assist with VIP (very important person) movement through the terminal. Celebrities, politicians, and other high-profile individuals may need to be escorted to the front of the screening line, or TSA personnel may need to be brought to them at the gate in order to be screened. This is not a privilege afforded to them because of their high-profile status, but is, in fact, an operational benefit to not have the attention these individuals attract slow down the screening lines and passenger flow.
13. Assist with lost-and-found items and people.
14. Oversee the airport's ambassador program.

Applying Part 139 safety principles to the terminal operations positions generates parallels and a list of additional responsibilities. Terminal operations personnel must:

1. Inspect public areas for maintenance issues and safety hazards, such as spills, damaged flooring or carpeting, lights not working, or foreign object debris on the terminal floor that could present a trip hazard.
2. Monitor leasing issues with airport concessions and tenants.
3. Work with TSA on screening-line mitigation.
4. Respond to security situations, such as a door alarm, or assist a security officer on an alarm response.
5. Ensure terminal signs are lighted when necessary, in good condition, and visible.
6. Manage emergency- or security-related incidents in the terminal or landside.
7. Report to airport police, fire, EMS, or other appropriate party any issue requiring response.
8. Act as the on-scene commander for any terminal incident, until properly relieved.
9. Report or assist media who often film from the airport for aviation-related stories.
10. Assist airlines, tenants, and concessionaires with issues, such as customer service, functional needs passengers, disagreements, or other related calls for service.

To be an effective Terminal Operations Manager, an individual should have good customer service skills, attention to detail to notice when small things are not working well, such as when security lines are starting to back up at unusual times of the day, and the ability to make decisions in a timely manner. Overall, a Terminal Operations Manager must remain aware of what a slowdown in the passenger throughput means to the airport operator, tenants, and the airlines.

Trends in concessions include the addition of musical groups in the terminal, local events celebrating cultures and holidays, art programs, landscaping, amusement park–type rides, movie theaters, spas, massages, salons offering pedicures and manicures, peaceful sitting, meditation and reading areas (church and worship areas have long been a part of airport terminals), exercise and yoga rooms (Airports Council International [ACI], 2013) (Figure 9.2). Internet access is essential. While many users prefer free Internet, many airports have found a balance by providing a slower level of Internet service, useful for sending email, for free, while faster Internet, capable of streaming videos, is available for a fee.

TERMINAL DESIGN AND OPERATIONS

The Airport Operations profession often focuses on "passenger throughput modeling." Modeling is extremely useful in operations and aviation management, especially in aiding in the development

Food and Beverage	Services	Sundries and Specialties	Amenities and Services
• Vending machines • Fast food restaurants • Casual dining restaurants • Bars • Ice cream shops • Snack food shops • Coffee shops	• Rental car agency • Post office • Currency exchange • Airline clubs • Banks/ATMs • Shoeshine • Business centers	• Newsstands • Duty free shops • Specialty retail (local goods or national chain, jewelry, leather goods, toys, clothing, regional arts and crafts, sports apparel, etc.) • Bookstores • Electronic stores	• Baggage storage • Charging stations • Medical offices • Pet relief area • Travelers Aid • Welcome area • Designated smoking area • In terminal advertising • Hair salons and barbershops • Game rooms • Luggage carts • Massage services

FIGURE 9.2

Typical airport concessions.

of efficient terminal design. However, this focus is really on terminal design concepts as related to operations, but does not address the day-to-day practical requirements of a commercial service airport to ensure that passengers, baggage, and cargo continue to flow efficiently and effectively. In this and the following sections, the relationships of terminal design and operations to the practical day-to-day concerns of the operations personnel are described.

AIRPORT TYPES

Airports are classified using a variety of methods (e.g., commercial service vs. GA, shared-use (military) vs. civilian, and cargo vs. commercial service, to name a few). Airports can also be classified by the dominant type of passenger traffic: originating-terminating (often called **origination/destination**[4] or **O&D**), **Transfer or Through** airports. At O&D airports, 70% to 90% of passengers begin or end their travel at the airport (Horonjeff et al., 2010, p. 394). The airport classification will help determine the need and type of terminal and landside support operations.

O&D-designed airports must support high levels of originating and arriving passenger traffic, which means extensive ticketing and baggage claim facilities, curb frontage, and vehicle parking. Extensive, landside-operations personnel are required at O&D airports to handle the volume of

---

[4]Origination/Destination is the common term used in the United States.

vehicle traffic. Many O&D airports also serve international air carrier operations and experience long turnaround times for flights, which means more terminal operations personnel are generally required to ensure that the needs of international passengers[5] are met.

Transfer (or connecting) airports experience high levels of total passengers arriving from a different airport and connecting to another flight to depart to another airport without ever leaving the Sterile Area.[6] Typically, airports with more than 50% of the enplaned passengers transferring to another flight are considered transfer airports. Airports where airlines conduct hub operations are frequently transfer airports, but some airports have characteristics of both O&D and transfer traffic. Transfer airports are designed for more efficient movement of passengers from one gate or concourse to another, without having to go through the screening checkpoint again. Transfer airports must also have efficient baggage-handling systems to ensure intraline[7] and interline baggage is moved from flight to flight, with a minimal loss rate. Fewer landside operations personnel and fewer parking spaces are necessary for transfer airports, unless the airport also has high levels of O&D traffic.

Through airports experience a high percentage of originating passengers and a low percentage of originating flights. Many small-hub and non-hub airports are classified as *through* and are characterized by a few flight operations per day, with the majority of passengers not debarking during the stopover. Through airports typically do not have challenges with vehicle congestion and often have enough parking to handle the low level of passenger demand.

THE AIRPORT PASSENGER SUPPLY CHAIN

Passenger throughput can be divided into three areas: the access interface, the passenger-processing functions, and the flight interface.

The access interface begins and ends with the intermodal connections to the community that surround the airport. The access interface includes curb frontage for the loading and unloading of passengers, parking facilities, public transit, taxi and limousine services, pedestrian walkways for crossing roads, including tunnels, bridges, or automated people-moving devices, and service roads and fire lanes that provide access for Airport Maintenance, vendor deliveries, airfreight, and similar support activities (Horonjeff et al., 2010).

The **passenger-processing** system includes airline ticket counters, baggage claim areas, Flight Information Display Screens, concessions, public lobbies, and food preparation areas. The passenger-processing interface also includes areas that passengers typically do not see, such as space for the interlining of baggage, baggage sorting areas (typically located behind the walls of the ticket counter or underneath the terminal building), airport administration offices (access control/badging, human resources, airport administration), maintenance areas, and Federal Inspection. The

---

[5]In general, international passengers stay longer in a community, spend more money when on travel, and have more money to spend when they travel (ACI, 2013).

[6]The Sterile Area is that area beyond the passenger screening checkpoint, extending to the passenger boarding bridges to the aircraft. All individuals in the Sterile Area must undergo a form of screening by either TSA, the aircraft operator or the airport operator.

[7]Intraline is when a bag is transferred from one flight to another on the same air carrier. Interline is when a bag is transferred from one flight on one air carrier to another flight on another air carrier. Many airlines have interline baggage agreements to ensure bags are transferred without the passenger having to pick up their bag at bag claim and recheck it to their next connecting flight.

Security Screening Checkpoint is also within the passenger-processing area of the terminal. Certain nonpublic areas, such as employee daycare facilities for the children of individuals who work at the airport, vendor storage areas, and physical fitness facilities for employees, may also be included (Price & Forrest, 2014, p. 71).

The **flight interface** includes the concourses and connections to other concourses to accommodate transferring passengers, departure lounge areas where passengers wait to board their flights, passenger-boarding devices such as jet bridges or air stairs, airline operational and administrative spaces, and, in some cases, nonpublic areas, such as vendor storage spaces that are used to maintain stock for concessionaires (Price & Forrest, 2014, p. 71).

TERMINAL CONFIGURATIONS

Throughout the history of aviation, terminal buildings have continued to expand, and airport terminals have been designed to accommodate increased passenger demand. The configuration of an airport terminal affects the passenger experience and the way landside and terminal operations are conducted.

Early terminal buildings were simple structures consisting mostly of a square or rectangular building, with a vehicle parking lot on one side, and airside operations on the other. Fencing, when it existed, typically extended out from the terminal building for a short distance along the airside perimeter, but was mostly for the purpose of preventing inadvertent access by passengers and vehicles onto the airfield. The terminal building housed some airline ticketing locations, airport management offices, perhaps a concessionaire or two of some sort, and, often, located atop the building, the FAA control tower. Essentially, the terminal building originally served as protection from weather while passengers awaited their plane. Early terminal designs concentrated all activities into a central location, a design called *centralized*. Centralized designs were basic in layout with aircraft usually parked parallel to the terminal building, in order to reduce the need for a pushback procedure.

As more people started using commercial air transportation, airports needed to increase in size, which was usually done by expanding the original building. The simple terminal building became lengthened into what is known as a **linear terminal concept**. In some cases, where space was limited, a **curvilinear terminal concept** was used, and at larger airports, multiple terminals were created. This design became known as the **unit-terminal airport concept**. The unit-terminal represented a move from the centralized terminal process, where all passenger processing was conducted in one building, to separate buildings, to a **decentralized process**. In a decentralized process, passenger processing is either separated into multiple buildings, or certain processes, such as ticketing and screening, are conducted in one facility, while aircraft loading and unloading are conducted in a separate facility. Decentralized can also mean separating linear terminal buildings (i.e., unit-terminal), connected by landside circulation roads and, in some cases, airside through the use of an Airport **Automated People Mover (APM)**.

As traffic increased, piers or fingers, commonly called **concourses**, were constructed from the main building and extended into the airfield. Aircraft began nose-in or angled-in parking directly toward the concourse, with the aircraft connecting to the concourse by way of a jet bridge. However, larger terminal buildings meant longer passenger walking distances. Airport planners then started constructing concourses in the airfield, connecting them to the terminal building through the use of APMs, further pushing the decentralized passenger-processing concept.

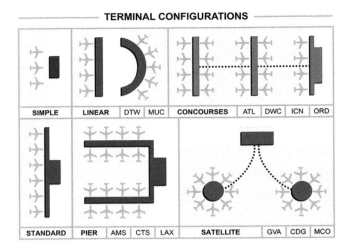

FIGURE 9.3

Terminal configurations and associated example airports.

Source: https://commons.wikimedia.org/wiki/File:Terminal-Configurations.png.

Vehicle congestion also started to become a problem with more and more vehicles arriving at the airport to pick up and drop off passengers. In the days before 9/11, anyone could walk all the way to the boarding gate to greet or see off passengers, so larger facilities had to be constructed to accommodate the increased passenger demand. As the number of passengers increased, so did vehicle congestion at the vehicle dropoff and pickup lanes. To spread out passengers and reduce vehicle, passenger, and even aircraft congestion, terminal planners have used two passenger distribution models, *horizontal* and *vertical*. There are four basic horizontal distribution configurations: (a) linear, (b) pier, (c) satellite, and (d) transporter, along with three vertical design concepts (Figure 9.3).

PASSENGER DISTRIBUTION MODELS

Horizontal distribution models are designed to spread out passengers and air carriers throughout the available space at the airport. The **linear horizontal distribution** model (Figure 9.4) is a simple terminal lengthened to accommodate more aircraft traffic. It can be expanded if space is available and the ends of the building are free of structural impediments (Price & Forrest, 2014). Increasing the terminal length produces longer walking distances between connecting flights or between the gate and terminal. Linear is the fundamental terminal concept, where passengers can park on one side of the building, access the facility and check-in, process through screening, and then board the aircraft on the other side. In some instances, jet bridges connect the building to the aircraft, while in other instances, passengers walk directly onto the ramp and into the plane. This layout is typical of a non-hub airport, such as Eagle County Airport in Colorado. An example of a larger linear terminal is Kansas City International Airport, in Missouri, which has three, large, curvilinear (nearly oval) terminal buildings. Linear concepts feature short walking distances between vehicle

FIGURE 9.4

Los Angeles International Airport is designed around a unit-terminal horizontal passenger distribution model.

Source: Jeffrey Price, Los Angeles International Airport, 2015.

and aircraft parking, but generally work for low-activity, origination-destination airports. However, some airports, such as Dallas/Ft-Worth International Airport, which also features a curvilinear (unit-terminal) design, experience high levels of O&D traffic, plus a significant percentage (60%) of transfer passenger traffic.

Los Angeles International Airport, John F. Kennedy International Airport, and Dallas/Ft. Worth International Airport are all examples of unit-terminal airport concepts. Each airport features multiple terminal buildings, centered on a landside circulation framework. Each separate terminal is a centralized stand-alone facility, with concourses extending from the central facility.

Pier fingers can be constructed onto the ramp area from the main terminal of a simple- or linear-style terminal. The concept allows for continued centralization of passenger processes while retaining airline-operating efficiencies. The piers allow aircraft to park along their length, but the primary disadvantage of a pier layout is longer walking distances for passengers—up to 1,500 feet at some airports. Additionally, the pier concept allows for more use of airside space to construct gates, but by accommodating more aircraft, vehicle curb space may remain the same—this results in increased access congestion, and even longer walking distances, as automobile parking is extended away from the terminal. From a terminal operational perspective, longer walking distances may result in more medical calls as individuals suffer fatigue or injury from carrying heavy bags. This problem occurs particularly at airports at higher altitudes, where many visitors are not accustomed to the thin air.

In the case of multiple piers and depending on the distances between concourses, aircraft congestion can occur with only a few aircraft able to pushback at once. What may have once been enough room for simultaneous pushback operations may become less with larger and larger aircraft using the airport over time. This situation occurred at Denver's previous Stapleton International Airport. Opening in 1929 and evolving into a pier design, the airport's piers were eventually able to accommodate simultaneous pushbacks, until the 1970s. As aircraft size increased, the airport could no longer perform simultaneous pushbacks between Concourse B and Concourse C, which contributed to flight delays.

Long walking distances from pier to pier may result in delayed response to incidents by terminal operations, police, and EMS personnel, unless they have a vehicle to drive from pier to pier. A vehicle may still not guarantee a rapid response due to airfield congestion, and, at some airports, vehicle access is heavily restricted because of safety issues. The use of bicycles, Segways, and golf carts by police, operations, and EMS personnel may increase response time without the additional safety risk incurred by driving on the airfield.

According to Landrum & Brown et al. (2010), pier models work well for moderate to heavy activity at O&D and **hubbing-airports**.[8] Current pier-style airports include LaGuardia Airport in New York and Reagan National Airport in Virginia.

A **satellite design concept** means passenger-processing facilities, such as ticketing, check-in, and baggage claim, are located in one or more terminal buildings, with separate concourses located in the airfield, where aircraft loading and unloading takes place. The facilities are connected by an APM system. Airports use a variety of people-movers, including underground subway systems, aboveground rail systems, or, as at Dulles International Airport, "mobile lounges," which transfer passengers from the main terminal to the concourses across the airfield.[9] In some satellite airports, the terminal is connected directly to the concourse(s) by a long passenger corridor instead of an underground or aboveground conveyance. In this design, gates are only constructed at the end of the corridor, not alongside as in a pier model. Passenger walking distance is reduced through the use of moving walkways.

The satellite model allows passenger check-in, retail, food concessions, baggage claim, and Ground Transportation Services to be clustered around a central location in the terminal. Ground Transportation and parking services can also be clustered near passenger circulation flows as passengers exit the Sterile Area. The satellite model also allows passenger and airside functions to develop independently. With widespread use of common-use facilities, an airline adding flights or gates does not automatically mean that the ticketing and baggage claim areas will have to expand to match. Although allowing each area to develop independently may reduce some capital costs, operational costs may actually increase as a result of the duplication of resources and personnel. Baggage has to be transported a longer distance, and it takes more personnel to cover both the ticketing and boarding areas. According to Landrum & Brown et al. (2010), the satellite configuration works well for heavy-activity airports with a large percentage of O&D traffic and a large percentage of connecting passengers. Denver International Airport, Orlando International Airport, and Atlanta/Hartsfield International Airport are all examples of airports designed as satellite models.

From a terminal operations perspective, people-movers must continue to operate as this is the primary means of transit for passengers between the terminal building and the aircraft boarding gates. Airports plan for a certain number of passengers to be transported per hour through the APM system, but when the system breaks down, significant delays can occur. At Atlanta/Hartsfield, the passenger corridor adjacent to the train system features moving walkways to facilitate the movement of passengers if the train shuts down. However, even with the corridor, passenger transit and connecting times will be significantly increased, and many passengers with functional needs will have difficulty making their flights. With the additional personnel in the corridors, moving

---

[8]Hubbing-airports have a high volume and frequency of transferring or transitioning passengers.
[9]The Dulles mobile lounge is also considered a transporter model, but in many transporter models, passengers are moved from the terminal directly to an aircraft boarding bridge or stairs instead of to a gate holding area.

walkways may experience a higher breakdown rate, and the corridor could likely become jammed with passengers trying to get to their flights.

Denver International Airport does not have a walkway adjacent to its underground transit system, and passengers must rely on a busing operation to get to their flights if the train shuts down. Busing causes security concerns, as passengers must first undergo screening at the terminal and then be bused to the concourse with airport personnel ensuring the integrity of the screening process is maintained, or temporary screening checkpoints can be set up at the concourse ramp areas. In the second option, passengers would have to be bused across the airfield to a concourse door (with elevator access to meet passengers with functional needs), escorted off the bus and through the Secured Area, and then processed through a temporary screening area before being allowed access to the concourse. In either case, passenger throughput will drop into the hundreds per hour, instead of the thousands per hour the transit systems are designed to accommodate. Therefore, it is essential that the trains operate and that any maintenance issue be quickly addressed. Train operation at any satellite airport is a top priority for Terminal Operations Managers.

Contingency plans should be put into effect (and practiced or gamed[10]) on how the airport will continue to transfer passengers if the automated systems are disabled for an extended period of time. Additionally, specific contingency plans should be derived for problems that could occur on any passenger movement system, such as a train, including fire, smoke, or evacuation.

Security and Satellite Airports

Satellite airports also have a unique security risk. In 1995, members of the Aum Shinryko cult placed a chemical weapon, sarin gas, in the Tokyo subway system. The attack killed 12 and hospitalized 1,000. An additional 1,000 citizens, believing to have been sickened, also headed to the hospitals, overwhelming the health care professionals. After the attack, airports with transit systems were directed to study the risk of a similar attack occurring with an airport subway transit system. Prior to 9/11, airports were more susceptible to this type of attack because of the lower screening standards for both passengers and employees. Chemical weapons are most effective when spread by air, and a release of a chemical into either the subway tunnel, or one of the cars, could quickly spread throughout the entire transit system of the airport and into the heating, ventilating, and air conditioning (HVAC) system of the terminals and concourses. First responders would likely mistake the gas for smoke from a fire and also become casualties. Also, it may take a while to distinguish between a chemical agent, such as sarin, or a biological agent such as anthrax. Many biological agents may not immediately present symptoms, or they may present symptoms that resemble those of a chemical attack.

Some airport subway ventilation systems can be "flushed" into the open air, which begets the moral question of whether this is an acceptable alternative: Should the airport operator flush the system in order to save the lives of individuals in the underground transit system, but put the local community at risk by spreading the deadly agent, or keep the system closed, thus condemning those inside but sparing a larger outbreak (particularly if a biological weapon is identified)?

---

[10]With the high volumes of passengers these systems must transport on a daily basis, taking the system out of service for an exercise could be difficult; thus, using games/computer simulations may be a better option to help develop and test contingency plans.

Post 9/11, screening standards for both passengers and employees have reduced the probability of a chemical, biological, or radiological attack on an airport train system taking place, but the possibility remains. The deployment of biochemical sensors and radiological sensors throughout the airport, particularly in the train system, can better inform both first responders and terminal operations personnel about the nature of the threat. In 2010, the Department of Homeland Security Science and Technology Directorate put forth an initiative to develop a cellphone app that could detect chemicals (Homeland Security, 2010).

The **transporter** design concept is a complete separation of passenger facilities (amenities) from passenger-processing facilities (screening and security check). According to Landrum and Brown (2010) *passengers access the aircraft via the mobile lounges that leave from the terminal gates, go directly to the aircraft, and attach to the aircraft to provide weather-protected transit.* In some cases the transporter is a bus, which lets off passengers on the ramp, and **mobile airstairs** are used to move passengers into the airplane.

Originally, the concept did not win wide acceptance in the United States, but it has gained some momentum in recent years, as there are several benefits. First, the use of a transporter or mobile lounge allows an aircraft to be remotely parked anywhere on a ramp area—a building or concourse is not required, simply a *hardstand* where the aircraft can park. Second, the concept allows for excellent aircraft maneuvering and less congestion at the concourse or terminal gates. However, the primary disadvantages are increased passenger processing time, the necessity for earlier close-out of flights, and a costly and labor-intensive operating system compared with other design alternatives.

Many international airports, as well as some in the United States, including Los Angeles International Airport and John F. Kennedy Airport, have adopted the hardstand, or plane-stand, concept. From an operational perspective, a shutdown of the mobile lounge may not have as much impact as the shutdown of a mobile lounge or system, as each conveyance is independent of the other conveyances (different buses, lounges, etc.). As previously mentioned, Dulles International Airport was one of the first airports to adopt a transporter model, with the modification that passengers are delivered to a concourse rather than directly to the airplane. The significant challenge of this model is the number of safety issues related to driving a large conveyance across the aircraft operational areas.

Many airports today represent a mixed-bag of terminal design philosophies and procedures. Seattle-Tacoma is an excellent example of an airport that started with a centralized linear terminal, which grew into a pier design. Then later, as concourses were added and an underground transit system was installed, the airport developed somewhat of a hybrid design, combining the features of centralized, linear design with decentralized pier and satellite operations.

PASSENGER ENPLANEMENTS

In 1975, U.S. airports enplaned over 196 million passengers per year (U.S. Air Carrier Aircraft Departures, Enplaned Revenue Passengers, and Enplaned Revenue Tons, 2015). However, in 1978, the U.S. government passed the Deregulation Act, eliminating economic controls over commercial air traffic. Deregulation impacted airport terminal and landside design and operations in several ways. First, passenger enplanements increased as airfares dropped and new, low-cost airlines entered the market, opening up more travel options. Second, airlines no longer needed the U.S. government's permission to operate on a particular air route—the airlines were now free to negotiate with whichever

(Continued)

> **(Continued)**
>
> airport they desired, to sign lease agreements, and to expand or reduce traffic as they deemed appropriate. By 1980, passenger enplanements increased to over 280 million, an increase of over 84 million in 5 years (U.S. Air Carrier Aircraft Departures, 2015). By 1985, with the effects of deregulation in full swing, passenger traffic exceeded 360 million passengers. Air cargo and aircraft operations also experienced significant growth throughout these years, forcing airports to expand cargo-handling facilities and to add more runways and taxiways. For the period of July 2014 to July 2015, U.S. scheduled and unscheduled domestic passenger enplanements reached approximately 710 million passengers.[11]

In addition to horizontal distribution of passengers, airport planners have also discovered methods to vertically distribute passengers. A **single-level terminal** is common at small-activity airports with all passenger functions taking place on one level. A **two-level terminal** is used at airports with slightly more activity, with ticketing and passenger departure activities on the upper level of the terminal and baggage claim and arrivals on a lower level. This makes for more efficient use of space by doubling up landside operations. Baggage claim is usually on the lower level of any two-level or three-level terminal to minimize the need for the passenger to have to haul bags upstairs. The two-level concept can extend into the concourses, with passenger/aircraft loading operations on the upper level and airline operations, baggage sorting and screening operations, and service areas on lower levels. The **three-level terminal** is often used at international airports and segregates international arriving passengers to the top level to keep them separate from domestic passengers until they are processed through the **Federal Inspection Service (FIS)** areas.

Some large-hub airports have further vertically separated landside traffic. At Denver International Airport, Level 6 is reserved for private vehicles with departing passengers, Level 5 is reserved for commercial vehicles, and Level 4 is reserved for private vehicles meeting arriving passengers. Vehicle traffic can also be distributed horizontally through the use of paved islands separating each lane, with the lanes designated for a certain type of traffic, that is, taxis in one lane and buses in another, hotel shuttle vans and off-airport parking in another, or some other distribution as decided by the airport operator.

PASSENGER-RELATED PROCESSES: CURBSIDE TO GATE

As passengers arrive at the airport from the intermodal connections, such as subway, roadway, light rail, and other transportation systems, they begin the passenger-processing phase (Figure 9.5). The **Ticketing and Check-In** process includes two primary functions: (a) obtaining a boarding pass and (b) checking or dropping off any luggage intended for travel in the cargo hold of the airplane (Cassidy & Navarrete, 2009). Significant changes have occurred to the Ticketing and Check-In Area in the past 15 years, as self-service kiosks have replaced many of the airline ticketing personnel. Today, airline ticket counters will have a few personnel who work directly for the airline to assist with passenger ticketing and check-in issues. The airline will then usually have additional personnel who are contract employees of the airline, whose primary job is to assist the self-service passenger

---

[11]Approximation based on data from the U.S. Bureau of Transportation Statistics, *T-100 Market and Segment* at http://www.rita.dot.gov/bts/acts

FIGURE 9.5

Passenger arrival curb.

Source: Jeffrey Price, Denver International Airport, 2015.

with putting a bag claim tag on their checked luggage, and moving it to the bag belt. A variety of other functions may also be performed during the check-in process, including making reservations, changing seats, upgrading to a different class, such as to first class or business class, and presenting a passport or other documents required for international travel (Cassidy & Navarrete, 2009).

All passengers must check in for their flight, which allows them to acquire a boarding pass. However, by using electronic ticketing and apps on smartphones, most passengers have already checked in prior to their arrival at the terminal. Kiosks at hotels and the ability to check in online and print a boarding pass have also contributed to expedited passenger processing and reduced the space necessary for airline ticket counters. Many airlines also offer an automatic check-in for passengers on return flights.

Airlines have established separate check-in facilities for different classes of passengers and typically will provide separate airline ticketing agents to service first-class and business class passengers (Figure 9.6). Airlines also separate ticketing lines based on domestic versus international flights, as airlines are required to ensure passengers have their passport prior to boarding the aircraft for an international flight (Cassidy & Navarrete, 2009). International passengers also typically have significantly larger amounts of luggage as they tend to stay for longer periods of time on their trips than domestic travelers, so the lines here tend to be longer.

The amount of money a passenger has paid for a flight, coupled with the passenger's frequent flyer status, affects how the individual is processed (Cassidy & Navarrete, 2009). Passengers

FIGURE 9.6

Passenger ticketing.

Source: Jeffrey Price, Denver International Airport, 2015.

purchasing nonrefundable coach seats receive the least priority, whereas passengers purchasing first-class tickets, or who hold frequent flyer status (of varying levels), receive preferred service.

Passengers who have already checked in and do not have to check baggage need not stop at the ticket counter and can proceed directly to the passenger Security Screening Checkpoint. Some passengers check in at curbside with a skycap who also handles their bags. Most skycaps provide check-in services, but they often cannot make ticket changes, upgrades, or provide other services typically provided by the airline-ticketing counter (this varies from one airline to the next). Passengers are expected to provide a tip to the skycap for the convenience of being able to drop the bags right at the curb and not have to take them inside.

Many airlines today charge a fee for checked bags or other services. Some airlines offer an amount of free checked bags, while others charge for both carry-on and checked bags, premium seats with extended legroom, and priority boarding. When airlines charge for checked bags, this practice puts a premium on space for carry-on bags in the aircraft. The "race for space" by airline passengers today relates to their ability to board prior to other passengers to take advantage of the overhead bag space before it is all gone. The majority of passengers traveling today realize that they may be charged for additional services, beyond the provision of an airline ticket, but there are still some passengers, many who have not traveled in a long time, who may be taken by surprise at the extra charges. This situation may create customer service issues for both the airline and the airport operator.

Common Use

Common use makes terminal assets available for multiple airlines and service providers and has fundamentally changed the way airlines conduct business. Common-use areas, including ticket counters, gate areas, jet bridges, parking areas, apron, and airport lounge/club facilities, allow airlines to share assets. Common use represents a move away from exclusive-use airline facilities. Exclusive use means that the airline is assigned exclusive ticket counter, office space, gates, and aircraft parking areas and pays for the space even when it was not being used. The exclusive-use model resulted in inflexibility for both the airline and the airport operator (ACI, 2013). In the common-use model, the airport operator may be responsible for assets such as jet bridges, gate space, and common-use equipment, resulting in more efficient use of space (if one airline is not using it, another can). This model enhances the passenger experience as a result of more efficient use of terminal space and spreading peaks in flight schedules across the airport. In some cases, terminal managers or ramp control managers must manage a preferential-use agreement, allowing for first right of use or first right of refusal to use a specific gate or ticket counter space.

The move toward common use is made possible by more flexible airport use agreements between the airport and airline, as well as by technology that allows multiple software programs to connect to a single **Airport Operational Database (AOD)**. The AOD allows better integration of gate management software, digital (dynamic) signage, and faster updates to screens displaying flight and bag information.

Common use has developed its own vocabulary and includes Common Use Terminal Equipment (CUTE) (or common use technology equipment), Common Use Self-Service (CUSS) kiosks, and Common Use Passenger Processing System (CUPPS). From an operational perspective, the term *common use* encapsulates all of these different terms.

Airports that have embraced common use can also take advantage of remote, landside check-in and baggage dropoff, which reduces congestion at the curbside and the terminal check-in areas of the airport (Figure 9.7). Off-airport bag dropoff facilities and resort operations are common at airports that connect to cruise ship operations or transport sports teams. Some airports have specialty operations due to their proximity to major tourist attractions, such as Walt Disney World. The *Disney Magical Express* is a bus that takes passengers from Orlando International Airport directly to the park of their choice, with park personnel picking up and delivering their luggage right to their hotel room. An off-airport bag check-in facility is located at the hotels in the park, so that departing passengers can check-in their bags at the hotel, where they are sent to the airport, onto their aircraft, and to their final destination.

Security Screening

In between the Ticketing/Check-In process and the passenger Security Screening Checkpoint are concessions and airline and airport administrative areas or, in some cases, nothing except a corridor or line to the checkpoint. Prior to 9/11, the passenger-screening process took a short period of time, lines of any duration were infrequent, and anyone could go through the checkpoint, not only ticketed passengers. Nearly every U.S. commercial service airport was constructed based on this model. Post-9/11 brought a significant change to passenger processing as only ticketed passengers were allowed through the screening checkpoint, along with a few other approved individuals (parents accompanying children to the gate or picking them up, individuals assisting elderly passengers

FIGURE 9.7

Common use kiosks, Ted Stevens/Anchorage International Airport.

Source: Jeffrey Price, Denver International Airport, 2015.

or those with functional needs). This event changed the game for concessionaires at airports. Initially, the lack of "meeters and greeters" coming to the gate area was thought to be a negative for concessionaires in the Sterile Area. However, because of the length of time it now takes to get through a passenger-screening checkpoint, passengers' behavior has changed. Transferring passengers spend hours in the Sterile Area waiting for their connecting flight rather than risk being caught in a long security line, while departing passengers arrive 90 minutes to two hours before their flight to give themselves ample time to get through the line. This shift in practice has affected usage of the public areas at airports, as many passengers now meet and greet by the exit lane from the Sterile Area or at the beginning of the checkpoint queue line. Concessionaires located in the public areas have experienced a drop in business with fewer people waiting for passengers to arrive. Cell phone lots have also reduced the amount of people in the public areas of the airport, with drivers having the ability to wait in a remote location until the person they are picking up calls them.

The **Security Screening Checkpoint (SSC)** is where TSA personnel or the aircraft operator performs the screening function to ensure those entering the Sterile Area (and eventually the airplane) are not in possession of guns, explosive materials, or any prohibited item that could be used as a weapon (Figure 9.8). The terrorist attacks on 9/11 significantly changed the screening process, and the impact on passenger travel extends beyond the process itself. Many passengers lament that before 9/11, air travel was fun and exciting, whereas now it is an annoyance to be suffered for the benefit of getting to their destination more quickly than by other means of transportation.

FIGURE 9.8

Travel Document Checkpoint.

Source: Jeffrey Price, Denver International Airport, 2015.

Unfortunately, the screening process is an area where airport management has little influence; thus, terminal operations personnel have little ability to speed up the process.

Several airport operators have tried to speed up lines by contracting personnel to manage the queue lines, helping passengers figure out which line they are supposed to be in. Small- and medium-hub, commercial service airports may only have a few checkpoints and one or two lines, but large-hub airports have multiple checkpoints and several lines, divided by passenger category. Most passengers enter the screening checkpoint and go through the regular passenger line. Separate waiting lines may also exist for those with a frequent flyers classification, **TSA PreCheck** lines (or **TSA Pre✓**),[12] CLEAR™ registered traveler lines,[13] and airport/airline employee lines. Passengers' classification will determine, to some extent, the level of screening the passenger will undergo and thus the amount of time it takes for the passenger to process through the checkpoint.

Passengers age 18 and over are required to show identification at the **Travel Document Checkpoint (TDC)** in order to board an aircraft. A list of approved identification can be found on the TSA's website, and there are accommodations for individuals who may have lost their ID, and these procedures typically include additional scrutiny by TSA personnel, and secondary screening processes. Once through the TDC, the passenger goes to the divestiture table and begins the process of removing shoes, liquids, laptops, or whatever protocol the TSA requires at the time. The security

---

[12]Transportation Security Administration. (n.d.) *TSA Pre✓*. Retrieved from: https://www.tsa.gov/tsa-precheck
[13]CLEAR. (n.d.) *What is clear?* Retrieved from: https://www.clearme.com/

screening process is ever evolving to respond to various threats and to move passengers more efficiently through the process. Passenger belongings go through an **AT X-ray machine (advanced technology)** where they are inspected by TSA, while passengers go through an **Automated Imaging Technology (AIT)** device, otherwise known as a body imager. An **Automatic Threat Recognition (ATR)** screen identifies any areas of suspicion on the passenger that require additional inspection by TSA personnel, often referred to as the "pat down." Some passengers are chosen for additional screening, referred to as secondary screening, during which they may have their bags emptied and inspected by the TSA. TSA personnel may also swab the individual or their belongings with a small tissue paper to conduct an **Explosive Trace Detection (ETD)** test. The ETD determines if the individual has come into contact with explosive elements.

After clearing the body-imaging device, the passengers pick up their belongings at the recomposure table. Many airports provide additional seating just beyond the checkpoint so passengers can put their shoes, belts, and coats back on.

Passengers who are part of TSA's PreCheck program have already undergone a criminal history record check and had their identities compared to the Terrorist Screening Center database. They are allowed to go through the walk-through metal detector (instead of the body imager) and can keep liquids and laptops in their containers and their shoes on. Some passengers are still selected for random ETD inspections, and K-9 teams often roam through the screening checkpoint looking for explosive elements.

Some passengers are members of a registered traveler program known as **CLEAR**™. CLEAR passengers pay an annual fee for a front-of-the-line privilege, even moving ahead of **PreCheck** passengers. CLEAR was supposed to be the original "trusted traveler" program, but previous TSA administrators never moved forward with developing risk-based screening, which was required under the Aviation and Transportation Security Act of 2001. CLEAR passengers either go through the regular checkpoint process, or through PreCheck if they are accepted members of the program.

The rate at which individuals move through the screening checkpoint is measured in the amount of time it takes an individual to move from the queue line to the recomposure area. The average time is different throughout the country, but passengers typically expect to spend 20 minutes, or slightly more, in the screening process during normal operations. For busy travel days, passengers are advised to get to the airport much earlier than the usual two-hour timeframe, as screening can take 30 to 45 minutes or more during these periods (ACI, 2013).

To the Gate

The **Concourse and Gate Areas** are beyond the screening checkpoints, and they provide passengers access to the aircraft. Airline passengers commonly proceed directly from the screening checkpoint to their gate, even if the flight is not for quite some time. This practice seems to be a basic need for passengers, to ensure themselves they have enough time to get to their gate, before finding concessions, rest rooms, shopping, or other activities (ACI, 2013) (Figure 9.9).

Concourse areas are populated by concessionaires of many varieties, such as restaurants, gift shops, clothing stores, bookstores, and kiosks that sell a variety of items. Concourses also contain restrooms, seating areas for passengers waiting for flights, airline administrative offices, and airline operations centers. Some airports have installed play areas for kids, games, or artwork throughout to keep passengers entertained while waiting for their flight to depart. Artwork, statues, and other items also help passengers find their way throughout the terminal. With the popularity of

FIGURE 9.9

Statues and artwork can help provide passengers waypoint information.

Source: Jeffrey Price, Denver International Airport, 2015.

laptops, smartphones, and tablets, AC/DC outlets are in high demand throughout the concourse. Many airports have accommodated this demand by purchasing lobby seating with additional power outlets or by installing charging stations. With the airlines serving fewer full meals, airport concessions have also stepped up to meet passenger food requirements.

The **FIS** facility is located at international airports with a **Port of Entry** into the United States. Passengers arriving from a foreign country first debark and are routed to the FIS facility where **Immigration and Customs Enforcement (ICE)** personnel check passports and other identifying information. Once cleared by ICE, **Customs and Border Protection (CBP)** agents may inspect a passenger's checked or carry-on baggage prior to being allowed access to the United States. International passengers connecting to a domestic flight may have to recheck their checked bags at a domestic ticket counter. Some airport recheck processes take place while still within the FIS, so the passenger does not have to go to the ticketing area of the airport, and can just proceed to the screening checkpoint.

PASSENGER-RELATED PROCESSES: GATE TO CURBSIDE

Shortly after parking the aircraft, a gate agent will open the aircraft door allowing passengers to debark. The deplaning passengers exit the aircraft at the gate area and enter the concourse. If they are transferring to another flight, they will look for a **Flight Information Display Screen (FIDS)** to determine the gate from which their next flight is departing. If their travel is terminating at the airport, they will look for landmarks to direct them to the baggage claim area. The exit lane from the Sterile Area is the transition point back to the public area of the terminal. The exit lane presents its own set of challenges for terminal managers. One of the most important functions of TSA is preventing access to the Sterile Area by passengers or others who have not undergone the screening process.

Exit Lane

While it is difficult to move through the screening checkpoint without undergoing the process, or at least being spotted attempting to sneak by, it is far easier to enter the Sterile Area, inadvertently or intentionally, through the exit lane. Many airport exit lanes are open spaces without doors or other access controls, and only one or two individuals guard these areas. Entering the Sterile Area without being screened is a **security breach**, which may result in the immediate shutdown of that terminal. If the individual is not quickly spotted, a search of the entire terminal or concourse Sterile Area may have to be conducted prior to the resumption of flight operations. Such a disruption can cost the airlines tens or hundreds of thousands of dollars, as well as disrupt the National Airspace System. In the worst case scenario, the entire concourse must be evacuated of passengers, a search conducted through all the areas where an individual could have hidden, or could have hidden a weapon or explosive, prior to resuming flight operations. All the passengers must then undergo the screening process again, making for long lines, flight delays, flight cancellations, and missed flights.

Presently, the TSA protects exit lanes adjacent to the screening checkpoint. If the exit lane is physically separated from the checkpoint, then the airport operator must protect the exit lane, usually through the operator's own personnel or a contractor.

Terminal operations personnel often play a significant role in managing the evacuation of the concourse and likely the search operation, as well. Passenger dissatisfaction will be extremely high, and additional problems will occur, as restroom facilities back up and concessions run out of food. Passenger stress increases due to the crowded conditions, tempers tend to flare, and there can be an increase in police calls for service to break up fights, as well as calls for medical assistance as passengers experience stress-related medical conditions.

An airport terminal is designed to handle a particular volume of passengers, known as the **Peak Hourly Enplaning and Deplaning Passenger**. The number of restrooms, the lobby and waiting area spaces, the concessions, food stores, and other factors are based on this figure, but when several thousand individuals who have already been through the screening process and are waiting to depart have to reenter the terminal and start the process all over, adding to the passengers that are already in the terminal waiting to start their screening process, the airport capacity for processing passengers is quickly exceeded. An exit lane or Sterile Area breach is a significant disruption to the airport, and it may take hours to re-establish normal operations.

Baggage Claim

Once in baggage claim, passengers look for a **Baggage Information Display Screen (BIDS)** to tell them on which carousel their bags will appear. From the baggage carousel, passengers look for their means to exit the airport, either through private transportation (pickup or parking lot), or commercial transportation, such as taxis or limos. Passengers without checked bags bypass the carousels and proceed directly to the curb to their preferred mode of land transportation (Figure 9.10).

FIGURE 9.10

Ground Transportation information at Denver International Airport.

Source: Jeffrey Price, Denver International Airport, 2015.

NONPUBLIC AREAS

Terminal operations are mostly focused on the public and Sterile Areas of an airport, but many nonpublic areas are located throughout the terminal and concourses. Nonpublic areas include utility corridors, airline and airport administrative offices, storage rooms for vendors and concessionaires, workout facilities for airport personnel, daycare areas for their children, and various offices for other airport workers. Additionally, many airport terminal buildings have a loading dock, which is a nonsecure area, but considered to be nonpublic. Loading dock procedures are often developed to ensure the safety of the operations, considering large trucks with poor visibility from the vehicle cab are inherent to the operation. Some vehicle management may also be necessary to manage the daily influx of deliveries and a limited amount of space.

There is not a safety- or security-related definition of a nonpublic area. These areas are usually defined, and named, in the Airport Security Program or the airport rules and regulations. Sometimes called "Restricted Areas," "Non-Public Access," or "Controlled Areas," terminal operations personnel must include many of these areas within their daily patrol. Some nonpublic areas have doors that access Security Areas and require response when they go into alarm. Airline operations and administrative offices are often within the Sterile Area, but in nonpublic areas of the concourses. Terminal operations personnel should be familiar with these locations in case response should be necessary to resolve an issue or concern, but personnel should be cautious about using these areas as "hangouts," remembering that they are private leaseholds. Individuals with a lease for space at the airport have an ownership interest in the property and have a right to quiet enjoyment of their property. Quiet enjoyment essentially means that the lessor does not have the right to be on its leased property for no good reason. Inspections, response to emergencies, and routine patrol to check for lease violations or other safety or security related issues are acceptable.

Lesser-used utility corridors can become places where criminal or other inappropriate activity takes place and should be patrolled with regularity. Some corridors and stairwells at airports are notorious locations for drug trafficking or prostitution. While it may seem absurd that these activities take place at a facility known for its high security compared to other public areas, such as shopping malls, criminal activity does occur. Some airports have upward of 50,000 badged employees working at the airport, with a transient population of hundreds of thousands of passengers daily. It is an accurate assumption that not all 50,000 employees are law-abiding citizens.

Some nonpublic areas may include Incident Command or Airport Operations Centers and have higher access requirements. Airport administrative facilities often will have a visitor badge process to provide a higher level of security to that location.

AIRLINE OPERATIONS

Usually located in the nonpublic areas of the Sterile Area (i.e., the concourses) are airline operations offices. Airline operations focuses on flight dispatch and flight planning, flight crew briefing, and crew lounge and sleep facilities, as well as other administrative and operational functions associated with ensuring aircraft arrive and depart on time. At large-hub airports, airlines may have significant operations, known as **zone control**.

Zone control is an operations center staffed with Zone Controllers, each one having authority over a certain number of gates at the airport. The Zone Controller is responsible for ensuring the aircraft and crew have everything they need to get the aircraft into and out of their gate, including baggage, passengers, catering, cleaning, personnel, fuel, and maintenance. Zone controllers may go by the title Airport Operations Zone Controller, and it is also not uncommon to see airline ticket, ramp, or gate personnel using the title Airport Operations Agent, or Airport Operations Supervisor. These titles can be confusing when not used in context, as they are the same or similar titles to Airport Operations personnel. Both groups have entirely different job functions, but the same objective, to ensure the safe, secure, and ontime arrival and departure of air traffic. At large-hub airports, dominant airline(s) commonly have ramp control positions, assigning gates and authorizing pushbacks for their aircraft.

At smaller airports, the function of zone control may be handled entirely by a senior operations agent or Station Manager. The Station Manager is the individual directly in charge of airline operations at a particular airport. Small airport Station Managers handle a wide variety of administrative and operational functions, while at large airports, the Station Manager may focus mostly on administrative duties, whereas a *director of operations* focuses on the arrival and departure of aircraft.

The airline operational offices are not necessarily off-limits to Airport Operations personnel. However, the airlines do have leases for the space and do have the right to quiet enjoyment of their property, without undue interference by the lessor, which includes representatives of the lessor. Airport Operations, security, and other related personnel should have legitimate business in the airline operational offices before entering the premises.

Airline operations offices at larger airports may consist of a flight dispatch and flight planning area. Flight dispatchers essentially plan the flight for an airline crew. Planning includes an analysis of the weather at the departure airport, at the arrival airport, along the route of flight, and at a selection of alternate airports should the primary airport become unavailable because of weather or an unexpected condition, such as a runway or airport shutdown owing to safety, security, or natural disaster. Other flight dispatch functions include computing the weight and balance of the aircraft, determining how much cargo it can take on in addition to passenger baggage, determining the distance required for takeoff and landing, and reviewing Notices to Airmen (NOTAMs) relevant to the flight.

Pilots arrive at least one hour prior to the flight and enter the flight planning room to review the material assembled by the flight dispatcher. Pilots may decide to add some fuel for the flight, or they may make other adjustments to the flight plan. Pilots are also required to check for any maintenance squawks, or issues, on the aircraft they are assigned to fly, and they check for any new TSA Security Directives or FAA notices relevant to their operation. There are usually crew rest areas and sleep or *quiet rooms*, with lounge chairs and couches where crews that are between flights may rest. Some airline offices have workout facilities and their own cafeteria, along with various administrative offices.

THE PASSENGER EXPERIENCE

The primary role of terminal operations is to keep people and vehicles moving safely and efficiently. However, also near the top of the list is to ensure that passengers have a pleasant experience at the airport. Providing good customer service is a core goal for an Airport Director. Good customer service is good for business and provides a less-stressful airport experience. Often, the airport is the first thing a passenger experiences of a city she is visiting, and it is often the last thing she sees as she departs. A fun trip to a destination can be ruined by a bad experience at the departing airport. Research shows that happy customers are more likely to spend money at the airport and increase nonaeronautical revenue, and good customer reviews can improve the airport's image and competitive ranking (Horonjeff et al., 2010).

Unfortunately, changes in airline pricing, staffing, and operational models have created significant challenges to the ability of the Airport Manager to provide a positive customer experience to passengers. While self-service kiosks have decreased the time it takes for a passenger to check-in, they have also resulted in fewer airline customer service personnel available to handle problems and questions. Since many airlines have followed suit with new pricing models, along with lower levels of personal service throughout the airport, the negative feelings passengers have with these decisions can, unfortunately, spread to the airport and hurt the airport's ability to provide a positive customer experience. Similarly, the passenger experience can be affected by the presence of uniformed, armed, government personnel such as CBP personnel in the FIS areas of the airport, and the authoritative and intimidating nature of the process. To counter these issues, many airports have hired their own customer service personnel and created information booths throughout the terminal; airports have also hired contractors to help manage queue lines, and they have brought in therapy dogs and play calming music throughout the terminal to help with passenger stress. Terminal operations personnel should always know the location of and have access to blankets, pillows, and temporary beds, or cots, for stranded passengers, in addition to baby formula, diapers, bottled water, and food (ACI, 2013).

CUSTOMER SATISFACTION

Customer satisfaction is the degree to which a product, service, or experience meets a customer's expectations (ACI, 2013). Terminal and landside operations managers, serving as the airport's representatives to the public, are focused on not only the safe, efficient, and secure movement of passengers, but they also attempt to provide a positive customer experience.

AIRPORT FEEDBACK FROM A U.S. VICE PRESIDENT

In a speech related to declining transportation infrastructure in the United States, Vice President Joe Biden remarked that, "If I took you and blindfolded you and took you to LaGuardia Airport in New York, you'd think, 'I must be in some third-world country.'" In response to laughter from the crowd, Biden replied, "I'm not joking!" ("News conference, Vice President Joe Biden," February 6, 2014, Philadelphia, PA. Available at http://www.theverge.com/2014/2/6/5387148/joe-biden-laguardia-airport-third-world-country)

Terminal and landside managers provide essential feedback to airport management on how the airport is meeting its expectations related to its benchmarks, which drive future action plans to improve customer satisfaction. While many airports would like feedback from visitors in order to judge how well they are meeting customer expectations, many customers will not provide feedback, negative or positive, so frequently the evaluation of the customer experience comes from the direct observation by terminal and landside personnel.

A satisfied customer increases "word-of-mouth marketing" and nonaeronautical revenue since the satisfied customer is more inclined to spend money at the airport. It is also important to recognize that a passenger on a flight almost always judges at least two airports each time the passenger flies, the airport of departure and the airport of arrival (ACI, 2013).

Customer-centric customer service takes the customer's perspective in airport design and operations. The overall customer experience is a combination of all the experiences a customer has at an airport. Customer centric puts the customer at the center of the experience by providing effective terminal design, services amenities, and communications that are engineered from the customer's perspective, rather than from the airport operator's perspective. Customer service experience management is focused on satisfying the customer experience throughout the entire service delivery chain (ACI, 2013).

Passenger types typically include business versus leisure travelers, domestic passengers versus international passengers, transfer or connecting passengers, passengers with functional needs, such as disabilities or reduced mobility, unaccompanied minors, or the elderly. Understanding the passenger type can provide a better experience for the passenger by understanding the needs they are attempting to fulfill at the airport. For example, business travelers typically look for Wi-Fi access, power outlets to recharge their electronic devices, airline flight clubs or business centers, and a variety of food options. International passengers usually seek duty-free shops, currency exchange locations, and directions to landside transportation options. Passengers with functional needs look for unobstructed access throughout the terminal, while all passengers appreciate clean restrooms, clean restaurants and facilities, clear wayfinding and signs, and a friendly, respectful, and professional staff throughout the entire airport supply chain (ACI, 2013).

Primary drivers of customer satisfaction include a smooth and predictable journey through the airport supply chain and the ability to meet basic traveler needs, such as food, water, entertainment, an area to rest and relax, and an area to work. Airport operators must also stay up to date on the latest trends; for example, water bottle filling stations have taken the place of conventional drinking fountains.

Word-of-mouth has taken on an entirely new level of significance with the advent of social media. Previously, an unsatisfied (or satisfied) airport visitor had a rather limited audience of close friends and families to influence when sharing a customer experience. However, now Twitter, Facebook, and LinkedIn posts spread both bad news and good news around the globe instantaneously.

The **airport service delivery chain**, as defined by ACI, encompasses all of the organizations and companies doing business at the airport, who are interconnected, codependent, and serving the same airport customer either directly or indirectly (ACI, 2013). This chain is often achieved through collaborative partnerships, maintaining airport customer service standards, active employee engagement, and open lines of communication. Passengers engage with a variety of personnel as they move through the airport system:

1. Airline or airline-contractor ticketing and baggage check-in personnel, or skycaps;
2. Airport customer service representatives;
3. Security screeners;
4. Food, beverage, and retail staff;
5. Airline gate agents;
6. Wheelchair attendants;
7. Parking lot attendants;
8. Custodial staff;
9. Queue managers;
10. Government employees.

ACI's **Airport Service Quality (ASQ) Program**[14] is the leading airport customer satisfaction benchmark program and includes 190 airports in more than 50 countries. The survey allows all airports to identify best practices and measure their own performance as it relates to providing effective customer service.

There is a direct link between customer centric communications and customer satisfaction, as the more information, knowledge, and understanding customers have about their travel experience the better they are prepared for travel and have more realistic expectations (ACI, 2013). Management of customer expectations is a critical component of providing good customer experiences.

Customer service standards are the rules and principles used to guide and monitor service delivery across the supply chain. They should be viewed as the minimal acceptable level of service

---

[14]Airports Council International. *Airport service quality.* Retrieved from: http://www.aci.aero/Airport-Service-Quality/ASQ-Home

only. Standards typically relate to the condition of the facility and its cleanliness, its operational efficiency, employee behavior, appearance, knowledge and skills, wayfinding and signage, ease of access throughout the terminal, and minimal impacts on visitors during airport construction activity. Some airports have placed customer service near the top of their values and have established customer service committees that involve key stakeholders at the airport meeting to discuss customer service issues, challenges, and performance (ACI, 2013).

Another key element of customer satisfaction is providing effective communications about the airport layout and ways to get around, providing timely information about the status of flights, the status of the parking garage or parking lots, and local weather conditions. Prior to the advent of smartphones, passengers had to rely on Flight Information Display Screens, the airport paging system, and other visual references in the terminal for information. Today, customers consistently go online using the Internet or apps to get the same information that used to be provided at the airport. However, not all of the online information is accurate because of delays in updating the information, particularly in regard to the status of flights, and it is important to remember that the entire population does not rely on the Internet or on their smartphone apps. Many infrequent fliers still must rely on the visual information provided in the airport. To the airport operator, this means they must serve both audiences, the Internet-savvy online audience along with the traditional traveler.

Five essential customer touch points influence the passenger experience: physical, subliminal, human, procedural, and communication (Price & Forrest, 2014, p. 78).

1. **Physical** includes the layout and design of the facility itself, its ease of use, even the design of the restrooms (and their odor, or lack thereof), and whether the stall doors swing out (desirable) or swing in (undesirable as it makes it difficult to maneuver oneself with one's luggage within the stall).
2. **Subliminal** relates to the overall atmosphere and "feel" of the airport.
3. **Human touch** points relate to the interactions passengers have with airport, airline, and tenant staff.
4. **Procedural** touch points relate to the processes encountered by the passenger, including the screening checkpoint, ticketing and baggage handling, and lost and found or other airport services.
5. **Communication** touch points relate to airport websites, brochures, and signage (ACI, 2013).

A significant challenge for Airport Directors is that customers will experience many processes and encounter many individuals throughout the airport, over the majority of which the Airport Director has very limited control or influence. This includes airline ticket and gate agents, security screeners, concession staff, parking lot and custodial personnel, and various government and customer service personnel. Airport ambassador programs have been shown to be effective in improving the passenger experience. Airport ambassadors are often volunteers and/or retired persons who are provided with free parking and access to the airport and are there to provide information and assistance to passengers (ACI, 2013).

When customers have a good experience at the airport, this contributes to customer loyalty, positive word-of-mouth marketing, and increased nonaeronautical revenues. People tend to buy more when they are happy. Airport executives should take a leadership role in working with airport stakeholders to manage the customer satisfaction process. This practice enhances safety and security because a more orderly and efficient airport operation contributes to reduce passenger stress, which results in fewer safety issues caused by passengers (ACI, 2013).

Terminal operations personnel must take into account both internal and external customers. External customers include passengers arriving or departing from the airport; visitors such as "meeters-and-greeters"; airport employees who buy goods, food, and beverages from the airport; and other businesses that do business with the airport operator. Internal customers are employees or business departments who receive services from other employees or business departments of the same organization (ACI, 2013).

The passenger experience must also take into consideration passengers with functional needs, such as passengers with disabilities or reduced mobility, families traveling with young children, the elderly, or unaccompanied minors traveling without an adult companion. With these examples, the success of the passenger experience depends on the relationships between the various members of the airport community such as the airline, airline and airport contractors, and others. Accommodations for individuals with functional needs are addressed below.

While it is important to focus on what terminal operations personnel can control about the passenger's overall experience, it is also important to recognize things that may be beyond their control such as (ACI, 2013):

1. The passenger's previous experience with the airport or other airports;
2. The passenger traveling during peak times, such as during the holidays;
3. The passenger's demographic profile, the frequency with which the passenger travels, and his familiarity with the airport;
4. The customer's mobility—passengers without functional needs may be able to navigate through the airport supply chain without issue, but those with needs may find it difficult if the terminal design has not taken them into consideration;
5. The passenger's airline status (frequent flyer) and security status (PreCheck and/or CLEAR member).

The overall goal of terminal operations is to move passengers, minimize passenger stress, increase dwell time in the concessions area, and increase nonaeronautical revenue potential in the terminal. Passengers expect terminals to be well maintained and attractive, with furniture that is in good condition, sufficient lighting, and ample space for passengers to relax and avoid crowding. Effective queue management can sometimes be within the control of the airport operator and contributes to higher levels of customer satisfaction. Overall, customers want a seamless transition throughout the airport service delivery supply chain (ACI, 2013).

Lost and Found

Managing the lost-and-found operations is an important function of the airport operator. With thousands of passengers traveling through an airport on a daily basis, items are bound to be lost, so an effective lost-and-found tracking system could improve customer satisfaction. Also, many tenants and airlines have their own lost-and-found processes, so airport lost-and-found personnel often have to coordinate efforts to locate and return lost items to passengers and others with other agencies. Some airports also offer bag storage lockers in the Sterile Area, which leads to the management of abandoned items, and bag storage locations in the public area. Public area bag storage locations must include the screening of stored items to ensure an improvised explosive device has not been hidden inside. In 1974, a bomb exploded that was stored in a public locker at LaGuardia

Airport, leading to the eventual removal of public storage lockers or facilities at airports, unless the item(s) were first screened.

Terminal Zoning

Some airports have followed a *terminal zoning* concept, creating separate areas for certain experiences, such as child play areas; separate quiet zones for individuals who want to rest; work station zones with access to power outlets and Wi-Fi; comfortable rest zones that offer seating arranged so that people can talk (Birmingham/Shuttlesworth International Airport is an excellent example); and food courts with a variety of options. Other areas include relaxation zones featuring comfortable seating, soft music, natural foliage, or fountains; exhibition zones to showcase local art and culture, and museum areas. Some airport terminals have United Service Organization (USO) areas for military personnel to rest and recreate while on route. Although largely replaced by personal cell phones, some passengers still require pay phones and Internet kiosks. Some airports are also experimenting with avatars, standing-holograms programmed to provide information to the traveling public.

Individuals with Functional Needs

Under the **Americans with Disabilities Act (ADA) of 1990**, individuals with functional needs must be provided the same access rights and privileges as those without functional needs. For example, during a shelter-in-place contingency in response to a tornado warning, individuals with functional needs cannot be told (nor expected) to wait until last to be evacuated simply because of their need.

ADA requires that any public or private entity that provides public accommodations must: (a) ensure that new buildings and facilities are designed and constructed to be free of architectural and communication barriers that restrict access or use by individuals with disabilities; (b) ensure that existing buildings and facilities are altered to be readily accessible by individuals with disabilities to the maximum extent feasible; and (c) furnish auxiliary aids, services, and/or telecommunication devices to afford communication by the disabled. Also, the vocabulary has changed over time from "disabilities" or "disabled person" to an ***individual with functional needs***. The term provides a more accurate description of individuals requiring additional assistance. The general ADA rule (informal) is: *whatever you do or provide for a person without the need for special ADA accommodation, you must do for a person with a functional needs disability.*

Terminal operations personnel must understand that many disabilities are invisible, including brain injuries, mental health, IDD (intellectual/development disabilities), nonobvious medical conditions, and vision, hearing, or learning disabilities. The effect(s) of a disability can vary depending on the person and many circumstances, for example, mood, fatigue, memory, financial status, family, lifestyle, housing, and self-esteem, and can be affected by medications the individual may be taking. What seems like an individual or misbehaving child demonstrating behavioral issues, such as being rude, difficult, obnoxious, lazy, or even violent, may actually be an individual with a functional need. It is important to remember that *things may not always be as they seem* when assessing the needs of the public. Anyone in a public contact position should approach any individual with a functional need, or that is elderly, with the perspective that if you had a son, daughter, mother, father, sister, or brother with a functional need, how would you want them to be treated in your absence?

The U.S. Department of Transportation (DOT) has adopted **ADA Accessibility Guidelines (ADAAG)**[15] as the accessibility standard for all transportation facilities or vehicles acquired by public and private entities using federal funds. State and local government buildings, including airport facilities, are required to comply with ADAAG and the Architectural Barriers Act of 1968, which applies to new construction and alterations of existing airport buildings (Price & Forrest, 2014, p. 89).

With respect to an individual, the term *functional need* means: (a) a physical or mental impairment that substantially limits one or more of the major life activities of an individual, (b) a record of any such impairment, or (c) being regarded as having such impairment (Price & Forrest, 2014, p. 89). If an individual meets any one of the above three tests, the individual is considered to be a person with a disability for purposes of coverage under the ADA.

SAFETY AND SECURITY ROLES OF THE TERMINAL MANAGER

In addition to watching for maintenance hazards, liquid spills, and other safety-related issues, terminal managers may have to coordinate evacuations of the terminal during hazardous weather conditions or shelter-in-place operations, such as during tornadoes or other events requiring immediate shelter. Many shelter-in-place contingencies call for passengers to enter nonpublic and Secured Areas of the airport for the duration of the event. Evacuations can cause significant disruption to Airport Operations, particularly if there are passengers in the Secured Area that must be accounted for prior to restarting flight operations. The Terminal Operations Manager works closely with TSA, airport police, and security personnel to determine if the airport is secure enough to begin operations. Also, under Title 14 CFR Part 139, personnel accessing the ramp areas during an evacuation must also be accounted for, before flight operations can begin.

In extreme circumstances, such as the active shooter incident at Los Angeles International Airport in 2013, the terminal manager often becomes simply another individual attempting to save him- or herself. Unarmed, Airport Operations personnel are taught the **run-hide-fight** strategy during an active shooter event. While some personnel may attempt to save others, or direct others to safety during an attack, this is clearly above and beyond the call of duty. Once the situation is relatively[16] secure, with the known shooter or shooters neutralized by law enforcement personnel, Terminal Operations Managers can, if trained and willing, assist the wounded. It is also the job of a terminal manager to assist in the collection of others that are in hiding and redirect them to a designated Staging Area for processing and debriefing. The return to normal operations is likely to take hours, and managers should have training in Incident Command to understand the various elements involved in recovery from such an event.

---

[15]See United States Access Board. *ADA accessibility guidelines*. Retrieved from: https://www.access-board.gov/guidelines-and-standards/buildings-and-sites/about-the-ada-standards/background/adaag

[16]After a shooting it will be some time before the area is deemed secure, however, passengers, paramedics, and others may still desire to assist the wounded after the time the known shooter(s) is down, but before a declaration by police that the situation is secure. This is sometimes referred to as the "Warm Zone," which is loosely defined as an area of relative security, but not completely secure. A Hot Zone is a completely unsecured situation and a Cold Zone is a completely secure situation or location.

The increase of natural and manmade disasters at airport terminals, including snowstorms, hurricanes, earthquakes, tornadoes, structural fires, power failures, security breaches, bomb threats, and active shooter situations, along with the increase of infectious diseases and their impact on air transportation, has demonstrated the need for a more comprehensive response to protect the traveling public (explored in more detail in subsequent sections of Chapters 10–12).

In addition to the safety of the passengers, terminal managers may also have security-related duties. With the exception of the screening checkpoint, which TSA primarily controls, other security regulations and procedures are primarily enforced by the airport operator, through the use of unarmed security officers, police officers, and Airport Operations personnel. When an access door goes into alarm, TSR Part 1542 requires that if the door accesses the Sterile Area, the Secured Area (the ramp surrounding airline parking locations), or the **Security Identification Display Area (SIDA)**, an airport representative must respond and investigate the cause of the alarm. In some cases, CCTV (closed circuit television) cameras provide some information about the identity of the person that trigged the alarm. Personnel are required to conduct a "sweep" of the area to look for potential intruders. At many airports, security officers or police officers conduct this duty, but Terminal Operations Managers may occasionally either perform this function, or they may be called to assist police or security personnel in mitigating the incident.

Many times an employee with an Airport Identification Badge has caused the alarm through their inadvertent or intentional action, and a **Violation Notice**[17] must be issued. This is similar to receiving a traffic violation and can cause arguments between the recipient and the issuer of the violation. If an employee has violated a significant security rule,[18] such as blocking an access door open that provides unfettered access between the public or Sterile Area to the Secured Area, then their ID badge may be confiscated immediately, with the individual being escorted to the public area. In some rare cases, passengers have pushed through an emergency fire access push bar door and entered the Secured Area. The most common cause are passengers, particularly exiting international flights, looking for a place to smoke, but in some cases, individuals will attempt to breach security by accessing the airfield. This breach is similar to an exit lane breach, and flight operations may have to cease until the individual is found. The Terminal Operations Manager will often be the individual with the authority and responsibility to notify TSA and airport police, as well as to make the determination, along with the Federal Security Director or their designate, about whether to cease flight operations or make a judgment that the breach does not represent a threat (often based on other information, such as CCTV camera feeds, but not all alarmed access doors at all airports have cameras pointing at them).

Other security-related functions of a terminal manager may be observing concessions to ensure personnel are not leaving scissors, knives, or other prohibited items, that they are authorized to have in the course of their duties, accessible by passengers.

---

[17]These go by different names depending on the airport.

[18]Airports develop their own security programs to comply with the regulations under TSR Part 1542, which is approved by TSA. There are some violations that are considered significant, such as loaning the airport ID badge, blocking a door or gate open, or intentionally circumventing the security system. The consequences are also variable, depending on the airport and the severity of the offense. Many offenses require the employee to be retrained in their security responsibilities, but the most severe consequences result in immediate and sometimes permanent revocation of the badge.

Passengers will have medical conditions requiring immediate aid and, in some cases, emergency transport from the airport to a hospital. Terminal Operations Managers may be required to assist in escorting an ambulance or EMS personnel to the airfield and, in some cases, assist in landing a medical evacuation helicopter on the airport ramp. Personnel should be well trained in helicopter operations to ensure the safety of themselves and others on the ramp.

LANDSIDE OPERATIONS

Landside operations encompasses the intermodal connections from the city to the airport and includes the passenger dropoff and pickup locations, the parking lots, and the access roads into or out of the airport. Landside **Ground Transportation**, or **Ground Transportation Operations**, represents a significant source of revenue for the airport operator in terms of **Customer Facility Charges (CFCs)**, which is a fee charged to customers accessing the airport by commercial transportation (taxis, limos, or ride-share), leased space for rental car operations, and parking lot revenue.

At some airports, the landside operations manager is a stand-alone position, or at small airports the landside operations manager may also fulfill the role of the terminal manager and the airside operations manager. Large-hub airports tend to have entire departments devoted to landside operations and may have several landside operations managers on duty at any given time.

Passengers expect a safe and efficient roadway operation that can handle the capacities the airport experiences throughout the year. While many passengers already factor in waiting times at the TSA screening checkpoint, unless they are very familiar with the airport, they may not factor in the amount of time it takes to access the airport from its intermodal connections.

Airport roadways provide access to and from the multiple land uses on an airport including: passenger pickup and dropoff for both commercial and private vehicles, parking garages and surface parking lots, access roads to cargo areas, loading docks, employee parking lots, the GA part of a commercial service airport, U.S. postal facilities, airfield access points, and, when located offsite, rental car facilities. Landside operations also provides a significant revenue stream for the airport. For the purposes of this text, visitors to the airport refers to *meeters and greeters* and well-wishers either dropping off or picking up passengers.

Passenger vehicles can be divided into two categories: private and commercial. Privately owned automobiles and motorcycles transport passengers to the curbside areas, parking facilities, and cell phone lots (LeighFisher et al., 2010). Commercial operations include on demand taxicabs, reserved taxicabs (for airline flight crews on occasion, or passengers with special travel requirements, such as skis, golf clubs, large amounts of luggage, or functional needs), prearranged and on demand limousines, door-to-door or shared ride vans that often transport up to 10 passengers and make multiple stops at area hotels, courtesy vehicles provided by hotel, rental car, and private or airport parking lot surface operators, charter buses, public scheduled buses, and service and delivery vehicles. Some airports further subcategorize operators depending on the nature of the operation and the audience that is served. Rental car operations are also considered commercial operations but are operated by private individuals when accessing the airport and so are addressed differently than other commercial operations. In addition to scheduled bus service, many airports are served by subway or light rail systems.

Ground Transportation rules and regulations are typically found in the airport's rules and regulations. The regulations identify the various commercial operators, outline their operating parameters, procedures for obtaining permits and Automated Vehicle Identification tags, security-related issues, conduct of personnel, motor vehicle requirements, and fee structures.

At many commercial service airports, commercial vehicle operations are charged access fees to conduct business at the airport. Public buses and courtesy vehicles, such as hotel shuttles, are typically exempt, but other courtesy vehicles, such as privately owned parking lot operators, may still be required to pay an access fee. The collection of these fees is typically automatic through an **Automated Vehicle Identification (AVI)** system that uses a radio transceiver mounted to the windshield of a commercial vehicle. Whenever the vehicle passes by a radio antenna connected to the AVI system, the vehicle is charged the fee with invoices typically being sent out monthly.

In recent years, a new type of commercial operation has provided some challenges to the commercial vehicle revenue model. **Ride-sharing** companies, such as Uber and Lyft, are providing competition to taxicab and limousine operators, and initially were accessing airports to pick up and drop off passengers without paying the commercial vehicle access fees. While some airports have already negotiated fees and worked out structures to handle the ride-sharing companies, many others continue to struggle with the issue.

THE AIRPORT ROADWAY LAYOUT

The most significant roadways on the airport are those that allow visitors to access and egress from the terminal building—these are known as **access roadways**. Additional roadways have a variety of other uses including access to other parts of the airport and employee traffic. Large commercial service airport roadways are typically characterized by the vertical distribution of vehicles to various levels, with each level designated for a particular type of operation, such as private vehicle arrivals, private vehicle departures, and commercial vehicle operations. Some airports horizontally separate traffic using islands between the lanes, and at the busiest airports both vertical and horizontal distribution models are used. For airports with double-level curbsides, the upper level is for airline passenger ticketing and check-in, while the lower level is typically at the same grade as the baggage claim facility and is for passenger pickup (LeighFisher et al., 2010).

Curbside roadways are considered to be those roadways where the pickup and dropoff of airline passengers and their baggage occurs, while outer lanes are used for maneuvering or to bypass traffic (LeighFisher et al., 2010). The innermost lanes are where vehicles stop, while passengers either board or egress from the vehicles. Security regulations implemented in 1995 after the bombing of the Alfred P. Murrah building in Oklahoma City, OK, prohibit drivers from leaving their vehicles unattended for any period of time. Not only did this regulatory change increase security and reduce the possibility of a vehicle-borne improvised explosive device, it also served the dual function of keeping traffic moving. Prior to 1995, it was not uncommon to see vehicle operators leave vehicles parked curbside for extended periods of time. Aggressive enforcement by law enforcement or code compliance personnel, and immediate towing of unattended vehicles, is a necessity both from a regulatory perspective and from a vehicle flow perspective.

Circulation roadways serve lower volumes of traffic and typically operate at lower speeds to allow for multiple decision points (LeighFisher et al., 2010). Circulation roadways allow vehicle operators to drop off passengers at curbside and then circulate back toward the parking structures or out to a cell phone lot. Circulation roadways are also used heavily by commercial vehicles that may need to pick up at multiple locations at the airport. At airports with more than one terminal with landside access, circulation roadways provide connections between the terminals.

Service roads link airport access roadways with on airport hotels, employee parking areas, aircraft maintenance facilities, cargo and air freight facilities, post offices, military bases, and the GA areas of the airport. Traffic on service roads may consist of employees and cargo vehicles and often times a higher proportion of trucks, semitrucks, and other heavy vehicles than would normally be experienced on the primary airport access roadways (LeighFisher et al., 2010).

Airfield roads, often called **Vehicle Service Roads (VSRs)**, are located on the aircraft operating area within the perimeter fence of the airfield. They are used for ground-service equipment to service aircraft, baggage carts, Airport Operations and maintenance personnel, police, fire, and emergency medical personnel, airline management and contractor vehicles, and vendor vehicles delivering goods to the various concourses on the airport. Certain ground-service-equipment vehicles are not authorized or licensed to operate on public streets, and in accordance with title 14 CFR Part 139, any vehicle operated on the movement area must be authorized, and the operator must have received driver training.

Airport roadways and operations are unique for a variety of reasons, including a high proportion of motorists that are unfamiliar with the airport and the many lanes and options available. Directional signs often provide more information than those on public roadways, such as long lists of airlines serving various terminals, directions to parking facilities, rental car options, arrivals and departures, and commercial vehicle operations. The fonts, symbols, messages and colors may also differ from those typically used on public roadways (LeighFisher et al., 2010). Information overload is a common problem for airport visitors, and people are easily lost in the Ground Transportation system.

Motorists can also be under more stress when operating around the airport as they try to find the correct place to drop off or pick up passengers, often on a time crunch in an environment that is more complicated than a typical roadway situation. One wrong turn may set off a chain of events that can delay a vacation, business meeting, or other important event (LeighFisher et al., 2010). Also, a high proportion of large vehicles (10% to 20%) operate around the airport in the form of scheduled passenger buses, door-to-door vans, and shuttle vehicles, along with cabdrivers and limousine drivers, many of whom are well experienced (20% to 30%) in navigating the airport landside system and may not always have the patience necessary when driving around those less familiar (LeighFisher et al., 2010, p. 9). All of this adds to the stress of driving to the airport.

Adding even more stress to airport driving are airport roads that incorporate weaving, which is defined as the crossing of two or more traffic streams traveling in the same direction without the aid of a traffic signal or other control device (LeighFisher et al., 2010). Often vehicles may be traveling the same direction, but individuals in the right lane are making lane changes to the left, while individuals in the left lane are making lane changes to the right, which may result in a higher proportion of vehicle accidents. Often, the distance between successive decision points is less than that suggested by the highway design standards, forcing drivers who are already in an unfamiliar situation to make decisions more rapidly than they are accustomed.

Airport landside operations personnel must learn how to best manage the roadway design that is already in place, as they typically do not have input into how the design was originally laid out. Patience with drivers, particularly those who have been involved in a collision, will go a long way toward reducing stress. To a certain extent, visitors coming to the airport may need to be treated similar to traumatized victims of a car accident or plane crash, who are so psychologically over-whelmed that they can only understand basic instructions stated in direct terms. They are unlikely to understand a complex set of directions, and they are more likely to follow instruction when the direction is clear and simple.

Curbside operations can be particularly hazardous locations, as vehicles maneuver into and out of curbside areas, with other vehicles traveling on the bypass lanes, while passengers weave in and out of both moving and stationary vehicles, hauling luggage and possibly trying to handle kids. Extreme caution should be emphasized and low speed limits strictly enforced. It is also important to understand that people typically do not park with the same level of care and precision normally associated with a parking lot. Motorists leave space between successive vehicles to ensure they are not blocked when trying to leave and to allow access to the trunk of their vehicle. They rarely will park their vehicles parallel to the curbside, typically angling in and parking askew, which can fur-ther complicate access for other vehicles. Some motorists who cannot find a position to park may stop in the bypass lane, creating a significant traffic jam in a short period of time.

LANDSIDE OPERATIONS MANAGEMENT

Landside operations personnel typically plan, monitor, and supervise functions and activities for the Ground Transportation areas, typically including the permitting and enforcement process. They may be expected to resolve conflicts between taxicab, ride-share, and limousine operators, resolve customer service issues, make recommendations to management on better methods to manage traf-fic or problems that are being experienced, and make entries into the computerized revenue man-agement system. Other common duties may include crowd control and vehicle queue management, evacuation of vehicles and personnel during severe weather or other emergency events, providing first response with medical assistance and be responsible for notifying appropriate emergency per-sonnel, and establishing Incident Command for larger scale accidents or incidents.

Landside operations personnel may also oversee parking lot operations. Security officer contrac-tors and parking contractors often monitor the day-to-day activities of the parking garage, including ensuring vehicles are not parked beyond the maximum allowable time. Parking lot personnel may also provide information to landside operations personnel to update digital information signs on the airport's primary access roadways to make announcements about which parking garages are full and which still have space. Many airports also provide a courtesy car-start service for visitors who have dead batteries or minor maintenance issues such as a flat tire.

By default, landside operations personnel become de facto ambassadors to the airport and, essentially, act as walking information booths. A command of airport terminal operations, the locations of airline ticket counters, TSA checkpoints, and other essential services visitors and passengers look for upon arrival is essential.

Landside operations personnel may oversee vehicle operations, while traffic management per-sonnel or police officers direct and control traffic operations or may be directly involved in traffic management, depending on the size of the airport. Landside operations personnel must also report any hazardous material spills at or above reportable quantities or those that access the storm water system. Vehicle accidents can result in spilled fuel and oils that can harm the environment.

Vehicle Access

Passengers arrive and depart the airport in a variety of conveyances, including private passenger vehicles, rental cars, taxicabs, limousines, courtesy shuttles, contracted shuttles, charter buses or vehicles, shared-ride vans and buses, ride-share services such as Uber or Lyft, and public transportation, which includes scheduled buses, light rail, and subway access. Some airports can even be accessed via ferry or helicopter.

Private vehicle operations include individuals arriving at the airport and either parking or being dropped off or picked up by an associate, such as a friend or family member. In the United States, the majority of passengers arriving at an airport arrive by private transportation, while at many airports in Europe and Asia, the primary access may be public transportation. U.S. airports have therefore been designed to accommodate the preference of the U.S. flying population by providing dedicated lanes for private vehicles, as well as extensive parking systems (Figure 9.11).

The dwell time for private vehicles at the curbside is normally restricted because of security regulations, but also to reduce congestion. Individuals are not allowed to leave their cars unattended in pickup and dropoff lanes. In the days before the advent of cell phones, "meeters and greeters" would often park in short-term parking and wait inside the terminal building or even at the gate. Post 9/11, with visitors no longer able to wait at the gate, and with the advent of cell phones, drivers wait off site until their passenger has made it to baggage claim, then call to be picked up. This situation initially created congestion problems on airport roadways, with dozens of vehicles

FIGURE 9.11

Landside vehicle operations, Wichita Dwight D. Eisenhower National Airport.

Source: Jeffrey Price, 2015.

parked alongside the access roadways. Most airports have since developed **cell phone lots** where private vehicle operators can wait until called by their rider. Initially, people were not typically allowed to leave their cars while in a cell phone lot, but some airports, such as Denver International Airport (DEN), have created special food courts and parking areas as a nonaeronautical revenue source. DEN's cell lot is located 3 miles from the terminal building and is known as *Final Approach*. It features plenty of parking, an adjacent gas station, five different restaurants, free Wi-Fi, a children's seating and play area with iPads built into tabletops that provide access to games, indoor rest rooms, and Flight Information Display Boards (Cell Phone Waiting Lot | Denver International Airport, n.d.).

Car rental operations include service counters either inside the airport or at a remote facility, parking bays (where vehicles are stored prior to rental), and vehicle maintenance facilities. Some airports have rental car operations in the parking garage, while others have an offsite facility that can only be accessed by a shuttle bus. Offsite facilities are sometimes necessary because of space limitations in the parking garage or adjacent to the airport, and do reduce vehicle congestion in the terminal area, but are less desirable for the business traveler. Business travelers look for quick access to the rental car facility for both pickup and dropoff. This is one area where the desires of the airport operator (reduce congestion and increase non-aeronautical revenue through leasing more land to rental car operators) conflict with the desires of the traveler.

Taxicabs provide essential commercial transportation for many visitors to the airport. However, too many cabs in the curbside area of the airport will create high levels of congestion, so cab stands (sometimes called "hold lots") are established near the terminal building, but far enough away to avoid congestion. Cab drivers remain at the Staging Areas until called up by a cab attendant.

Cabs typically have two types of cab fares: **metered** (known as flag drop or meter drop) and flat-rate (or standard) fare. In a metered-fares cab, the meter showing the amount owed is displayed on the dashboard and viewable by the rider. The cost is based on time and distance, tolls, surcharges for airport access, and special services, such as baggage handling. **Flat-rate fares** are a set rate and are common for popular destinations, such as from any of the Port Authority of New York and New Jersey (PANYNJ) airports to Manhattan, or from the airport to certain "zones," geographical areas around the city.

Cities typically issue a license for an individual to operate a taxicab. Such a license is sometimes called a medallion, or "hack" license (English colloquialism for the "Hackney Carriage" taxi), and only licensed cab drivers are allowed to access the airport to pick up passengers. Many airports and cities require cab drivers to accept credit cards and prohibit them from refusing a trip or a specific destination. Landside operations managers are often on the lookout for unlicensed or unapproved cab operators, sometimes referred to as "bandit taxis."

Standard vehicle markings identify a cab or commercial vehicle along with a specific license plate and usually a permit affixed to the windshield or side window. Taxicab operators often must adhere to airport regulations relating to vehicle maintenance, cleanliness, insurance minimums, ability to provide receipts to customers, dress codes, and behaviors, such as no texting or cell phone calls while driving (ACI, 2013). Taxi companies that are authorized to pick up at the airport are awarded a concessions contract.

Shared-ride services are for-profit vehicles, usually buses or large vans that transport several individuals to a variety of locations. Carriage may be booked in advance through the Internet, phone call or app, or at the airport. The low cost of transport is offset by the time it takes to arrive at the destination. Passengers going to the airport via shared-ride must account for the additional time it takes to make several stops en route to the airport. Many shared-ride companies provide estimates, based on the passenger's airline departure time.

Town car limousine service, or "car service," provides premium transportation services for passengers who desire a luxury vehicle and are willing to pay a premium for high-quality service (ACI, 2013). Drivers usually park in short-term parking and meet the passenger at baggage claim or a predetermined door number. The driver assists the passengers with their luggage and escorts them to the vehicle. Limousine operators typically pay an access fee to the airport operator.

Courtesy vans and buses include rides to local hotels, on- or off-airport parking lots operated by the airport, private parking lot operators, shuttles to car rental facilities and specialty vehicles such as cruise ship operators, Walt Disney World resorts, and the like, and charter buses for sports teams, school, church, or community groups. Access fees are sometimes charged for charter operators, depending on the rules and regulations of the airport.

Public transportation systems, such as buses, light rail, and subways, run on fixed schedules but are lower in cost than other forms of commercial transportation, such as cabs or limos. Airport employees are primary users of public transportation along with a percentage of airline passengers.

Ride-share services such as Uber and Lyft are challenging the traditional roles of commercial vehicle operations. While taxicab, limousine, and other commercial operators are concerned with the impact these operations have on their bottom line, airports seem to be primarily concerned with collecting the revenue associated with access fees and adapting to the wishes of airport users. At the time of this writing, the airport industry is still working out the various revenue collection models for the ride-share operators.

SAFETY AND SECURITY ROLES OF THE LANDSIDE OPERATIONS MANAGER

Safety issues related to landside operations include pedestrians that must share the terminal curbside and the passenger pickup and dropoff lanes with vehicles. Many airports use security personnel or law enforcement personnel to manage traffic at the pickup and dropoff areas. Airports that have an elevated or subterranean tunnel from the parking garage or passenger pickup and dropoff locations to the terminal building will reduce the likelihood of a vehicle/person collision.

Parking lots are unfortunately prime areas for crime to occur, including vehicle theft and robbery of persons using the lot. Frequent security patrols, CCTV, and good lighting can deter some crime. Some airports offer an escort service by security or law enforcement personnel upon request. Other security issues in landside typically relate to heated arguments between landside transportation providers competing for fares. These arguments occasionally turn violent and require police intervention.

Terrorist security issues in landside relate to the potential **vehicle-borne improvised explosive device (VBIED** or "car bomb") detonating curbside. The catastrophic devastation and loss of life that occurred as a result of the truck bombing of the Murrah Federal Building in Oklahoma City, in 1995, along with the previous bombing of the World Trade Center in 1993, resulted in airports conducting vulnerability assessments to determine the risk and consequences of a vehicle bomb at the airport. At the time, the FAA implemented the "300-foot rule" whereby no unattended (i.e., parked) vehicle was allowed within 300 feet of any airport terminal building[19] or FAA control facility including the control tower.

Most major airports have since conducted vulnerability assessments and, in some cases, included blast-resistant building techniques, such as bollards to provide standoff distance, structures reinforced with Rhino Linings, and window glazing to reduce glass shards, in their terminal upgrades. However, the 300-foot rule still exists in Airport Security Programs and may be used when the threat level increases, at which time airports may be forced to drastically reduce parking spaces and even search for and tow vehicles that are within the existing 300-foot zone of the terminal building.

Landside operations personnel, police officers, and others that work in the Ground Transportation areas (curbside), should be trained in identifying the signs of a potential VBIED and what to do when they believe one has been spotted. Also, it is important to note that the "300-foot rule" is a standoff distance that will theoretically prevent the total devastation of a building but is *never* to be considered a safe distance to stand from a truck bomb. The **Bureau of Alcohol, Tobacco, Firearms and Explosives (ATF)** standoff card puts the "safe" distance from a rental truck—size car bomb at 850 feet for building evacuation and 3,750 feet for outdoor evacuation. Landside operations personnel should have available the ATF's safe standoff distance card and have contingencies in place (and practiced or gamed) on the procedure to take if a VBIED is suspected or confirmed.

A truck bomb the size of the one that took down the Murrah building could cause complete destruction of an airport terminal. While some new terminal designs have incorporated window glazing, many have not. Unlike the Murrah building, which was an older brick-and-mortar construction, newer airport terminal designs are comprised of lower-density materials and lots of glass. In 1999, the International Arrivals Hall at the Los Angeles International Airport was the target of a car bomb, but the attempt failed when the bomber was caught by an alert customs agent at the Port Angeles ferry crossing in Washington State. In 2007, the terminal building in Glasgow Airport in Scotland was the target of a somewhat successful vehicle bomb attack, although the explosion did not reach the attackers' desired magnitude.

Landside operations personnel should also be trained in contingencies and incident response to bomb threats, suspected improvised explosive devices, and active shooters. First responder or first-aid and cardiopulmonary resuscitation (CPR) training are recommended. Trauma kits or individual first-aid kits should also be issued to landside operations personnel, with such kits to include, at a minimum, a compression or tactical tourniquet, battle dressing or combat gauze (pushed into the wound to control bleeding), a face shield, and gloves. Larger trauma kits should be available in a vehicle or nearby work or first-aid station. In an active shooter incident, the number of wounded may quickly exceed the ability of on airport EMS personnel available for response. Individuals should always receive training in the use of their medical supplies and resources. Landside Ops personnel should also be trained in Incident Command as they may find themselves the first responder to a vehicle accident or vehicle—pedestrian injury.

---

[19]Notwithstanding paragraph 1 of this chapter: While the federal government heavily regulates the airside areas of a commercial service airport, the operation of the terminal building and the landside areas of the airport are predominantly controlled by local or state regulations and, to a certain extent, by the FAA's grant assurances. There is not an FAA equivalent to Part 139 that addresses landside and terminal operations.

GROUND TRANSPORTATION REVENUE AND CONGESTION MANAGEMENT

Traffic jams are a fact of life at many large-hub airports, and even at smaller airports during peak travel seasons. There are numerous Ground Transportation management strategies, but most must be applied during the design/build phase, rather than the operational phase. Ground Transportation facilities are also significant revenue generators for the airport's nonaeronautical revenue stream, and landside Ops personnel are often in the position of ensuring that revenue is collected, that agreements are enforced, and that individuals who do not pay for access, are not allowed to conduct business at the airport.

Revenue Management

Ground Transportation systems are classified as open, closed, or semiclosed. At most airports, vehicles are permitted to drop off passengers, but only authorized commercial vehicles are permitted to pick up passengers. In an open system, commercial Ground Transportation operators are allowed to pick up passengers at the airport, with the airport deciding how and where the transportation services are offered, the fee charged for the transportation service, and the requirement of a permit prior to operating at the airport, but the airport not restricting the number of transportation service operators as long as the operator complies with the airport's rules and regulations (ACI, 2013).

A closed system regulates the number of transportation service operators permitted to operate at the airport. Operators are required to go through a procurement process "RFP (request for proposal)" and comply with the minimum standards for safety, vehicle maintenance, insurance, and driver training (ACI, 2013). A semiclosed system provides a combination of both open and closed systems, but the number of operators is generally not limited in a semiclosed system.

Operators are either required to have a permit to pick up passengers at the airport or be part of a concession agreement that can provide access to curb space and either exclusive or semiexclusive rights to provide certain types of transportation. **Concession agreements** typically dictate the hours of operation, mandate an adequate supply of vehicles along with maximum waiting times, published fares or surcharges, certain geographic coverage, and destination served, along with vehicle and driver minimum standards. Ground Transportation operators often compete for passengers with other operators so rules and regulations must be established and strictly enforced, which is a primary role of a landside operations manager.

Congestion Management

Most congestion management strategies have already been discussed at various points throughout the chapter, but are provided here for consideration. These typically include separating departure and arrival levels, separating traffic types (private from commercial), effective wayfinding, an airport Ground Transportation center, and a landside operations control center, parking space availability systems, and consolidated rental car facilities (ACI, 2013). Other strategies include:

1. Consolidating commercial and private vehicle waiting locations, including taxi and limousine staging and dispatch areas;
2. Cell phone lots;
3. Free short-term parking;
4. Encouraging the use of public transportation options;

5. Pedestrian crosswalks over or under vehicle lanes;
6. Curbside space allocations;
7. Ground Transportation service counters;
8. Airport service or information desks, staffed with customer service personnel that can provide information to passengers on Ground Transportation options and, in some cases, even book trips.

Chicago O'Hare uses a Ground Transportation center, which is completely separated from the passenger terminal. Commercial vehicles pickup and dropoff passengers at the center, which also includes rest rooms and a comfortable waiting area with concessions, chairs, and tables.

Another option is the establishment of a **landside operations control center**. Similar to the Airport Operations control center, which focuses on activities on the air operations area, a landside traffic center can be used to dispatch traffic officers to handle congestion, open or close overflow parking facilities, change digital advisory signs, notify police or fire in case of an emergency, monitor overall landside traffic operations, and keep the Airport Operations manager advised.

Landside Ops managers cannot control how the airport was designed and often have limited or no say in how access agreements and RFPs are drafted, but they can influence the overall operation through effective relationship management. Ground Transportation relationships are important as visitors and airport officials demand high-quality services and will reject poor or overpriced services, which can also create a negative impression of the airport and the community the airport represents (ACI, 2013). Elected officials and passengers are also becoming increasingly sensitive to the environmental impact of Ground Transportation and want to see Ground Transportation operators doing more to mitigate the effects of carbon emissions (ACI, 2013). Relationships can be managed by establishing both formal and informal business relationships with Ground Transportation providers, understanding the expectations and the needs of the commercial Ground Transportation operator and the desires of the passenger.

AIRPORT PARKING LOT OPERATIONS

Parking lot revenue is often significant at a commercial service airport and can represent the third largest contributor to the revenue stream (behind retail concessions and property leases). The parking experience is also one of the first passenger touch points that can make a lasting impression on the passenger, positive or negative. Landside operations managers should understand that the arriving passenger is primarily concerned about successfully boarding their flight on time and therefore typically is under more stress. They are less tolerant of long waiting times for a shuttle bus, long searches for empty parking spaces, and, for airport employees, long walks to work from the terminal building.

Parking lot personnel are responsible for the safe, courteous, and efficient operation of the parking facility including the collection of parking fees, maintenance of automatic revenue control equipment, patrolling parking lots to prevent vehicle theft or damage, providing information and driving directions to motorists, reporting accidents or unsafe areas, and keeping the facilities clean (ACI, 2013).

Parking operations are generally focused on maintaining the safety and security of the facility and the drivers and visitors, often through the use of closed circuit television, gates and fences, ample lighting, and regular patrols by Airport Security officers and law enforcement officers (ACI, 2013). To reduce damage to vehicles and subsequent liability claims, roadways and parking areas should be kept clean and pavement well-maintained. Vagrants, homesteaders, and loitering should not be allowed in the parking garage. Snow, ice, and rainwater must be allowed to drain from the parking lot, and paved areas in the parking lot must be designed in order to get snow removal equipment through the facility. An airport parking operation characterized by long queue lines, poor lighting, and debris and trash strewn about will reflect negatively on the airport's image.

On average, more than 70% of passengers departing the airport park at the airport (ACI, 2013). At small-hub airports, annual parking lot revenues exceed $10 million, and at large-hub airports, revenues exceed over $100 million (ACI, 2013). The airport operator should strive to manage the parking area as a line of business, with a focus on increasing customer satisfaction and expanding service offerings. This practice can best be accomplished by offering various parking services, such as variable rates for the time spent at the airport and reserved parking options. Many parking lot operations, including duties performed by parking attendants, cashiers, and parking shuttle drivers, are contracted. Parking operations typically require higher specialized skills and expertise and can often be delivered more effectively by a third party and at a lower cost (ACI, 2013).

PARKING OPTIONS AND SERVICES

Most airports offer five types of parking: short-term (hourly), medium-term (daily), long-term or extended (weekly), and valet, or free, parking:

1. **Short-term**, or hourly, parking typically consists of a duration of 3 to 4 hours. Short-term parking helps reduce curbside and roadway congestion and is typically the most expensive of all the parking options with the exception of valet.
2. **Medium-term** parking, often referred to as daily parking, is typically designed for passengers who desire to leave their car for one to 7 days. These rates are typically lower than short-term rates but higher than longer-term parking.
3. **Long-term** parking, also referred to as multiday, economy, or extended-term, can provide parking for a week or more. Most airports restrict long-term or extended parking to a maximum of one month. Long-term parking fees are typically the lowest-cost option, but may have extraordinarily long walking distances or even a long shuttle bus ride from the parking lot to the terminal.
4. **Valet** parking provides customers, with the option of dropping their vehicle off, typically curbside, and picking it up at the same location. Valet personnel park and retrieve the vehicle at a secure parking facility at the airport. Valet parking fees are typically the highest fees of all parking options at an airport.
5. **Free** parking is common at small airports. In some cases, airports that are trying to reduce congestion may offer free parking for a limited time. Free short-term parking, generally for the first 30 minutes, can reduce congestion curbside by allowing visitors more time to say goodbye to departing passengers (ACI, 2013). Since these lots are typically close to the terminal building, visitors who are picking up arriving passengers typically spend less time in the terminal building and less time in the Ground Transportation system.

Airports feature two types of parking options: surface lots or garages. A **single-level** parking lot, or surface lot, is used when the terminal is generally within walking distance of the parking lot. In some cases, surface lots located a considerable distance from the terminal may have a shuttle bus that circulates. Parking fees are usually proportional to the distance to the terminal—the closer you park, the more you pay. Some parking lots provide shaded or covered areas for vehicles, often at increased cost. Some airports have dedicated employee lots, which must also be patrolled, and may have a shuttle bus access depending on their distance to the terminal. Airport employee parking lots may also have shuttle buses that provide access through an airfield perimeter gate and take employees directly to a concourse.

Multilevel parking areas, or parking garages, are generally close to the terminal and connected by passenger-bridge, or stop-light controls through the Ground Transportation lanes. Passengers frequently forget where they park their cars, so a simple system of letters and numbers are used, but some airports try to use more memorable systems, such as letters that represent an animal. **Multiuse parking facilities** accommodate passengers, rental cars, and employees and may be divided by concrete islands and designated vehicle lanes.

During holiday seasons or high travel times, when the number of vehicles parking at the airport exceeds the typical peak passenger volumes for the airport, airports may use **overflow-parking** areas. Temporary parking areas are often established on airport land or adjacent property for a short-term basis.

Some airports offer customers supplementary services for using the airport parking facility, such as baggage check-in, laundry and dry cleaning drop off, groceries, flowers, candy, and gift items, that can be ordered in advance and placed in the vehicle upon the passenger's return (ACI, 2013). Other services include movie rentals, preordered in-flight meals, and vehicle maintenance, such as carwash and detailing, tune-ups, refueling, and oil change.

Many airports now provide electric charging stations for customers who drive electric-powered vehicles and oversized parking spaces for vehicles that require more space (ACI, 2013). A few airports have loyalty programs that provide reduced parking rates, combined with access to VIP (very important person) lounges or expedited passenger processing benefits, such as a CLEAR membership, through the airport (Figure 9.12). Pet care services are offered at some airports so that pets can be brought to the parking lot and given over to an attendant who will board the pet for the duration of the passengers' time away from home.

Other ways to expedite parking are to offer prepaid parking through a smartphone app or to allow frequent airport visitors to purchase an AVI tag, similar to what is used for commercial vehicles. This strategy reduces congestion at the parking lot entrance and exit. Also, many airports have replaced personnel at a parking booth with an automated credit card machine, so that individuals departing the parking garage can have the benefit of a complete self-service payment function. This practice reduces staffing requirements for the parking office and decreases vehicle congestion.

Parking space availability systems provide inbound passengers with advance information and real-time data on the status of the airport parking lots and available spaces. A variety of availability systems are in place, from simple, digital-signage notifications to arriving traffic about the status of the airport parking lots and garages, to complex lighting systems installed throughout a parking garage that provide the number of spaces available per row, as well as their location.

Many airports that experience significant parking challenges include the status of the parking garages and surface lots on their website and on mobile applications. Radio stations also broadcast parking-related information. Frequently updated digital signage also helps passengers to make

FIGURE 9.12

Passengers pass through the CLEAR lane.

Source: Jeffrey Price, 2015.

decisions about where to park, and more complex systems identify how many spaces are available (ACI, 2013). Many airport parking systems now employ license-plate identification systems that allow for better control of parking lot revenue and help to identify stolen vehicles.

More advanced availability systems include a comprehensive lighting system installed in the airport garage. A red light appears over each occupied space, and a green light indicates an unoccupied space. At the beginning of each row, digital signage provides the visitor the number of spaces available in that row. The systems are far more accurate and effective in managing parking lot traffic then by having individuals drive around counting spaces and reporting back to the landside operations center.

Since many passengers have a difficult time remembering where they parked their car, particularly if they have been gone an extended period, some airports feature automated vehicle locators in which the passenger inserts a ticket into a reader located near a major walkway, and the display shows the individual the general location where the car is parked. Some of these systems may also be used to collect payment prior to the individual accessing the individual's car.

SUMMARY

Overall, the terminal or landside manager must continually balance the changing needs of customers and commercial operators, while managing congestion on the airport curbside and roadways, parking areas, and, to the extent possible, intermodal connections, all while attempting to increase nonaeronautical revenues and provide a positive customer experience to the passenger. Landside operations managers must be familiar with any contracts, agreements, rules, and regulations in place to ensure fairness and transparency in the operation of the Ground Transportation function, which also includes providing the exclusive rights as outlined in a specific contract. Landside operations managers must also do their best to ensure that customers are not taken advantage of or intimidated by unauthorized service providers who try to solicit services at the airport.

The *aerotropolis* concept of airport planning may significantly affect the way landside and terminal operations are carried out at an airport, but further research is necessary to determine what impacts (if any) will occur.

Terminal Operations at Charlotte Douglas International Airport (CLT)

by Martha Edge
Terminal Operations Manager at City of Charlotte, Airport Operations Supervisor at City of Charlotte

Charlotte Douglas International Airport (CLT) handles approximately 44 million passengers per year, averaging out to roughly 121,000 passengers per day. CLT's throughput has steadily increased in passenger numbers over the years, creating the need for additional airport resources. In November of 2013, the Terminal Operations department was created in an effort to offer additional resources for passengers, business partners, and the airport. CLT's Terminal Operations team consists of a Terminal Operations Manager, Terminal Operations Supervisor, International Arrivals Assistants, Information Specialists, Pre-Security Customer Service Representatives, and a Lost-and-Found Administrator. In addition to the Terminal Operations team, there are also various contractors that support the daily customer service offering, such as a Visitor Information team, and FIS staffing that assists with Automated Passport Control kiosks and claiming and rechecking of bags for international arrivals.

The Terminal Operations Manager is responsible for overseeing the airport's day-to-day customer service efforts in the ticketing and baggage lobbies, FIS, and Lost-and-Found department. In addition to these areas, when irregular operations occur, the Terminal Operations Manager aids and coordinates overnight amenity efforts, which occasionally include distributing cots and sleeping mats when passengers remain in the Sterile Area overnight.

The Terminal Operations Supervisor is responsible for overseeing the operation of the FIS staff; International Arrivals Assistants and contact staffing that deals with Automated Passport Control kiosks, claiming and rechecking of international bags. When needed the supervisor is also involved in the coordination of overnight amenities for stranded passenger events.

The International Arrivals Assistants are assigned to CLT's FIS area and provide translation and customer service to CLT's arriving international travelers. The International Arrivals Assistants are a key component to the arrival process controlled by the CBP.

(Continued)

(Continued)

One of the many customer service responsibilities in the FIS is to translate for our federal partners, the CBP.

The Information Specialists are assigned to CLT's Airport Services Counter, located on the ticketing/departures level. As a group of six employees, Airport Services handles all walkup passenger traffic and the airport's main switchboard. This experienced group of employees offers a high level of customer service to CLT's visitors, both in person and over the phone. Employees of Airport Services can be heard throughout the airport on the public address system and have been dubbed "the voice of Charlotte Douglas" by airport employees.

The Lost-and-Found Administrator is responsible for CLT's lost-and-found department. Like many other major airports, there are several different lost-and-found areas located in CLT. Airlines, concessionaires, and TSA all have their own lost-and-found departments. CLT's lost and found administrator works with all other lost-and-found departments in the airport while attempting to reconnect customers with their belongings.

In addition to the Terminal Operations team, when irregular operations (IROPs) occur, other divisions within CLT are the key to assuring optimal customer service is experienced by travelers. Airport Operations management, supervisors, and officers also assist with coordinating and distributing overnight amenities to stranded travelers. CLT housekeeping personnel are on hand to aid with the distribution, collection and cleaning of cots and sleeping mats. They are also cognizant of customer needs and have basic comfort items on hand that can be offered as needed (e.g., toothbrushes, mouthwash, diapers, formula, small stuffed animals, airport-branded playing cards, etc.).

Now that I've provided an overview of the Terminal Operations team, here is a concern that I believe airports face as it regards customer interaction. When IROPs are experienced by air carriers, where does the air-carrier customer service effort end and the airport's begin? This is a question I imagine many airports in the United States, and around the world, deal with on a regular basis. Each group involved has its own expectation about who's responsibility "after hours" customer service is, but what happens when the groups involved haven't come together to break down every possible situation and agree on a game plan for the terminal and terminal IROPs? The most common answer is that one group typically ends up handling all the efforts. Wouldn't it be much easier if all the groups came together and addressed every possible scenario and then had a list of duties/responsibilities that would be carried out? (This could be something similar to an emergency checklist found in an airport's Airport Certification Manual [ACM] and Airport Security Program [ASP] manual.) With air travel on the rise again, more focus is required on the passenger terminal, and it's not always the air carriers that should be responsible for travelers.

Another challenge associated with the airport providing customer service is the addition of automation and self-service options for passengers. Many self-service kiosks offer customers options to change flights when IROPs occur and can sometimes replace the face-to-face contact with customer service personnel, which is typically in very high demand during these challenging times for the customer. Air carriers have been known to decrease staffing head counts when automated machines are available, but we know too well that when an IROP occurs, it's the face-to-face contact that really makes a difference to the customer.

(Continued)

(Continued)

I'd like to share an example of a multiple-day IROP CLT experienced in February 2014.

In February 2014, many U.S. airports experienced harsh winter weather. CLT received snow and ice, which caused air carriers to thin their operations, and on one afternoon/evening, cease flight operations altogether. Being the second largest hub to the "New American," and an airport that serves roughly 80% connecting passengers, this meant lots of stranded travelers. As you can imagine area hotels were already full as the weather event spanned about a week, and being that flight operations were impacted because of weather, airlines, per their internal policies, did not cover hotel expenses. In addition to the customer pay issue, many of the main artery roadways were iced over and shuttle busses and taxis were not operational. People had little to no options and were "stuck" at the airport. External resources, such as the Red Cross, were asked to aid in the efforts to accommodate passenger needs. They were able to supplement airport cot and blanket supplies, in an effort to provide as many overnight comforts to the stranded travelers as possible. Some airport concessions remained open around the clock to ensure dining options and convenience items were available as needed. TSA personnel assisted by extending screening hours, which provided passengers the opportunity to pass from the non-Sterile to the Sterile Area outside normal operating hours. The entire week was made up of constant communication with all airport stakeholders, as at this point, we all needed each other to maintain the airport and take good care of the customers. This constant communication was key to our success. Another very important factor was the already established good working relationship amongst the group.

REFERENCES

Airports Council International (ACI). (2013, September 8). *Customer experience management: The airport environment, a complex business.* [Online learning module].

Ashford, N., Stanton, H. P., Moore, C. A., Coutu, P., & Beasley, J. R. (2013). *Airport operations.* New York, NY: McGraw-Hill.

Cassidy, M., & Navarrete, J. (2009). *Airport passenger related processing rates guidebook* (TRB, ACRP). Washington, DC: Airport Cooperative Research Program (ACRP).

Cell Phone Waiting Lot | Denver International Airport. (n.d.). Retrieved August 12, 2015, from: http://www.flydenver.com/parking_transit/parking/cell-phone-waiting-lot.

Homeland Security. (2010). *Cell-all: Super smartphones sniff out suspicious substances.* Retrieved August 12, 2015, from: http://www.dhs.gov/science-and-technology/cell-all-super-smartphones-sniff-out-suspicious-substances.

Horonjeff, R., McKelvey, F., Sproule, W., & Young, S. (2010). *Planning and design of airports* (5th ed., [Kindle]). New York, NY: McGraw-Hill.

Landrum & Brown, Hirsch Associates, Ltd., Kimley-Horn and Associates, Inc., Jacobs Consultancy, the S-A-P Group, TranSecure Inc., Steven Winter Associates Inc., Star Systems, LLC., Presentation & Design, Inc. (2010). *Airport passenger terminal planning and design* (TRB, ACRP). Washington DC: ACRP.

LeighFisher, Dowling Assoc., JD Franz, WILTEC. (2010). *Airport curbside and terminal area roadway operations* (TRB, ACRP). Washington DC: Airport Cooperative Research Program (ACRP).

Price, J. C., & Forrest, J. S. (2013). *Practical aviation security: Predicting & preventing future threats* (2nd ed.). New York, NY: Butterworth-Heinemann.

Price, J. C., & Forrest, J. S. (2014). *Certified member body of knowledge* (5th ed., Ser. 2). Alexandria, VA: American Association of Airport Executives (AAAE).

U.S. Air Carrier Aircraft Departures. *Enplaned revenue passengers, and enplaned revenue tons. (2015).* Bureau of Transportation Statistics. Retrieved July 29, 2015, from: U.S. Air Carrier Aircraft Departures, Enplaned Revenue Passengers, and Enplaned Revenue Tons. http://www.rita.dot.gov/bts/sites/rita.dot.gov. bts/files/publications/national_transportation_statistics/html/table_01_37.html.

AIRPORT EMERGENCY PLANNING, PART I

Aircraft Rescue and Firefighting (ARFF) equipment at the Gunnison-Crested Butte Regional Airport, CO.

Image by Shahn Sederberg, courtesy Colorado Division of Aeronautics, 2005.

ARFF training facility at Denver International Airport, CO.

Image by Shahn Sederberg, courtesy Colorado Division of Aeronautics, 2012.

Statistically, aviation remains the safest mode of transportation; however, with millions of aircraft operations occurring throughout the world every year, some Aircraft Accidents or incidents will happen. Therefore, certificated airports are required to have an **Airport Emergency Plan (AEP)**, the resources to support the implementation of the plan, and personnel who are trained and exercised on the plan.

The number of fatalities attributed to aircraft crashes in 2014 was 1,320[1] worldwide (Yan & Marsh, 2014), compared to 1.24 million fatalities in automobile accidents during the same year (Gresser, 2014). However, when an aircraft crashes, regardless of the size, the crash almost always makes headlines. The way an airport handles an aircraft crash directly impacts the lives that can be saved and also reflects on the credibility, training standards, and overall professionalism of airport management.

Although 9/11 changed the aviation security domain, a series of events, including 9/11, Hurricane Katrina, and several other natural disasters, along with some notable Aircraft Accidents, such as the San Francisco Airport crash of Asiana Airlines Flight 214, changed the aviation emergency management domain. In 2010, the Federal Aviation Administration (FAA) revised its guidance on airport emergency planning to incorporate lessons learned, along with changes brought on by the Department of Homeland Security—specifically the incorporation of the National Incident Management System (NIMS) into all emergency planning functions. The airport industry has also placed greater emphasis on emergency management, with the American Association of Airport

---

[1]Different reporting agencies have slightly different numbers for airline fatalities because of differences in what is considered a commercial operation. The Aviation Safety Network (ASN) has a threshold of 14 paying passengers for a flight to be considered commercial, while the Geneva-based Bureau of Aircraft Accidents Archives includes accidents of aircraft capable of carrying at least six passengers, besides the crew.

Executives (AAAE) starting an annual International Airport Emergency Management conference, and professional certifications for airport firefighters. While compared to other domains, the FAA requirements under Part 139 for airport emergency planning remain quite low, many airport operators have taken it upon themselves to incorporate better training, exercises, and planning of aircraft incidents.

PERSPECTIVES ON AIRCRAFT CRASHES AND AIRPORT RESPONSE

All airports are subject to emergencies and incidents. Additionally, airports are community assets during federal, state and local emergencies, so even when the airport is not experiencing an emergency it may play a critical role in the federal, state, regional, or local Disaster Management plans. An effective response to any emergency requires coordination, cooperation, and communication.

Airliner crashes may quickly overwhelm the limited assets available at any airport, and off-airport assets are often needed. Even large-hub airports that have significant levels of firefighting apparatus and personnel typically do not have the same levels of emergency medical service (EMS) personnel, or other personnel and resources on hand, that are necessary to effectively handle a large-scale incident. This perspective is scalable, as smaller, commercial service airports are required to have lower levels of firefighting capability. While the crash of a 19-seat aircraft at a large-hub airport may be well within the capability of the airport to respond to and effectively manage the incident with limited outside assistance and likely without even closing the airport, the same type of aircraft crash at a non-hub or small-hub airport would quickly overwhelm the airport's resources.

While a complete list of definitions can be found in Advisory Circular (AC) 150/5200-31C, *Airport Emergency Plan* (FAA, 2010a), a few are directly relevant to this section of the text:

1. An **Aircraft Accident** is any occurrence associated with the operation of an aircraft that takes place between the time the person boards the aircraft with the intention of flight and the time such person disembarks, in which a person suffers death or serious injury as a result of the occurrence, or in which the aircraft receives substantial damage.
2. An **Aircraft Incident** is any occurrence, other than an accident, associated with the operation of an aircraft that affects or could affect continued safe operation if not corrected. An aircraft incident does not result in serious injury to persons or substantial damage to aircraft.
3. An **Incident** is an occurrence or event, either natural or human-made, which requires a response to protect life or property. Incidents may, for example, include major disasters, emergencies, terrorist attacks, terrorist threats, civil unrest, wild and urban fires, floods, hazardous material spills, nuclear accidents, Aircraft Accidents, earthquakes, hurricanes, tornadoes, tropical storms, tsunamis, war-related disasters, public health and medical emergencies, and other occurrences requiring an emergency response (FAA, 2010a, p. 255).

In 2014, several plane crashes drew attention to airport safety, including the shooting down of Malaysia Airlines Flight 17 over the Ukraine that killed all 298 on board; the disappearance and presumed loss of 239 passengers and crew on board Malaysia Airlines Flight 370; the crash of TransAsia Airways Flight 222 while flying near the Indian Ocean, killing 48; the crash of Air Algerie Flight 5017 in Mali, killing 116 (presumed, only 113 bodies were recovered from the ocean); and the disappearance of AirAsia Flight 8501 between Indonesia and Singapore, killing 111. The number is extraordinary considering that in 2013 only 265 people were killed in commercial airline accidents (Yan & Marsh, 2014). The United States has not experienced a significant airline accident with massive loss of life since 2001, when American Airlines Flight 587 crashed into Queens, New York, killing all 260 people onboard, plus five people on the ground.

In all of the previously mentioned cases, the aircraft went down away from an airport. While aircraft overruns, sliding off the runway or taxiway, or landing with the gear still up are still considered accidents, the United States has not seen a large loss of life in the past decade (Tolan, Patterson, & Johnson, 2015). Recent U.S. events include:

1. Comair Flight 5191 with 50 passengers and crew onboard, crashed on takeoff in Lexington, Kentucky, in 2006, killing everyone except for the first officer. His miraculous survival was mostly the result of the rapid response of medical personnel;
2. Asiana Airlines Flight 214, which crashed at the San Francisco International Airport in 2013, resulting in three fatalities, with at least one possibly killed when she was run over by a fire truck responding to the accident[2] (Roberts, 2014). The National Transportation Safety Board (NTSB) Report made several references to the need for certificated airports to have qualified **Aircraft Rescue and Firefighting** (ARFF) personnel who meet the training requirements and to have conducted exercises on such events (NTSB, 2014);
3. On December 20, 2008, at 6:18 PM, Continental Flight 1404 slid off the runway while on takeoff at Denver International Airport. The initial report of the accident came to Denver Tower from another aircraft, and much confusion between air traffic control (ATC), Airport Operations, and ARFF personnel on the location of the accident caused a delay in response. The aircraft went off the west side of runway 34R, proceeded through the Runway Safety Area, and crossed a Vehicle Service Road a few hundred feet from ARFF Station 4, before coming to rest. Initially, response personnel headed away from the accident scene because of the wrong directions being provided by ATC (LiveLeak, 2009). The trucks were turned around quickly, but many of the passengers self-evacuated or were assisted by crew members by the time ARFF arrived.[3] All 115 on board survived, with only 38 people injured.

All three incidents provide lessons learned in responding to an Aircraft Accident that are addressed throughout this text. In addition to planning for Aircraft Accidents, airports are required to plan for a variety of other incidents that may occur, including hazardous material and fuel spills, natural disasters, Water Rescue, and security incidents, such as bomb threats and hijackings.

---

[2]While the final National Transportation Safety Board (NTSB) report noted that at least one victim was rolled over by an airport fire truck, and the coroner concluded that the girl was alive at the time, the City of San Francisco disputed the claim. Regardless, airport fire personnel should not run over any human, living or dead, during an Aircraft Rescue and Firefighting (ARFF) response. Regardless of the obvious moral issues with driving over the deceased, the corpse also represents evidence that may provide clues to the cause of an Aircraft Accident, or the cause of death, which could be from a design flaw in the aircrafts egress system, seat linkages, or a training issue on the part of the airline crew.
[3]This is not unusual in an airplane crash as flight attendants are taught that they are essentially *on their own* for the first 2 to 3 minutes of a plane crash, as it normally takes at least 3 to 4 minutes for ARFF personnel to arrive at an on-airport crash.

GENERAL AVIATION AIRPORTS

While general aviation (GA) airports are not required to adhere to Part 139 and are therefore not required by regulation to have an AEP, page one of AC 150/5200-31C, *Airport Emergency Plan* (FAA, 2010a), notes that noncertificated (GA) airports must follow the general guidelines prescribed by Homeland Security Presidential Directive (HSPD) 5, *Management of Domestic Incidents* (FEMA, n.d.a), and HSPD-8, *National Preparedness* (FEMA, n.d.b), related to emergency planning. These guidelines do not directly address airports, but they do address the requirements for state and local government agencies to have plans to respond to human-made and natural disasters. Also, the Stafford Act (2013) places the responsibility of emergency planning on the elected officials of a state or local government entity, which one can presume includes a federally funded public-use airport.

It is also good business to have emergency response capabilities, to attract tenants to base their operations at the airport, and potentially lower liability limits for those tenants with aircraft based at an airport with emergency response capabilities that meet Part 139. Also, the majority of Aircraft Accidents are in GA aircraft, with an average of nearly seven accidents per 100,000 flying hours, compared to commercial service, which has an average of 0.16 accidents per 100,000 flying hours (Fowler, 2014). Despite these inferred requirements and strong rationale, it is not unusual to find GA airports that do not have an emergency plan.

AIRPORT EMERGENCY MANAGEMENT PERSONNEL

A slow shift is occurring within the airport emergency management industry, from allowing the fire department sole domain over all incident responses except for security incidents to one of a professional airport emergency manager.

Throughout the 1980s and 1990s, depending on the nature of the incident, either airport firefighter or airport police personnel took over as Incident Commander (IC) at the majority of emergencies at airports, often despite of a lack of understanding of Airport Operations. At many airports, this occurrence is still the case, and on its face, the logic makes sense. One naturally assumes that police or firefighters will be better ICs since they have far more experience in managing emergency incidents and are more conditioned to experiencing life-threatening and extraordinary events. Other airports "split the difference" by having a fire or police officer, as appropriate, assigned as IC for the first phase of the emergency. Then, as soon as the initial response is over, police and fire personnel turn over Incident Command duties to Airport Operations. During a major accident, all operations stop, and the senior-ranking firefighter assumes Incident Command and performs the primary job of rescuing people and putting out the fire. A similar response occurs in a security incident, in which the senior police officer on duty at the airport assumes Incident Command, while the airport basically shuts down, and everyone waits for Incident Command to allow the airport to reopen.

Some other problems with this structure could occur. While shutting down a few streets, or even a radius of a few blocks, for a fire or police incident in the city may be practical, this practice is costly, and, in some cases, it is unnecessary to shut an airport down for the same reason. When an incident occurs, many of the issues important to Airport Operations are set aside while police or fire personnel handle the incident, which, depending on the duration of the shutdown, affects the entire National Airspace System.

How an airport addresses emergency management also depends on its size. Non-hub airports, small- and some medium-hub airports, along with many GA airports, do not have the personnel to maintain an emergency management department. Emergency management is often a collateral duty of an operations officer or manager, who is essentially in charge of drafting and ensuring compliance with the AEP.

Some larger airports have emergency management departments, with personnel who have undergone certification programs in emergency management and often also a variety of Federal Emergency Management Agency (FEMA) Incident Command courses. However, until recent years, even large-hub airports had small numbers of emergency management personnel, and at a few large-hub airports, as at smaller airports, one person would be assigned as the keeper of the AEP, with first responders shouldering the burden of implementing the AEP.

Up until the 2000s, few emergency management departments (much less personnel), and even fewer qualified[4] emergency managers, could be found at airports; this is still the case at many airports. In recent years, however, some airports have taken a new approach to emergency management by assigning the Incident Command function to the Airport Operations department and having individuals who are not fire or police be trained and certified in emergency management.

Under the NIMS and its Incident Command System (ICS) protocols, extinguishing a fire or neutralizing an active shooter are *functions* that must be performed. Police provide the *service* of law enforcement during an emergency; firefighters provide the *service* of firefighting and rescue during an incident. Incident Command is more than one function, and many airport operators argue that by having Airport Operations assume Incident Command, the functions of fire and rescue and law enforcement can be better executed. The senior fire officer on duty should be focused on rescue and firefighting and should not be worried about where the Salvation Army should set up its tents or where the airlines should set up a victim's assistance center. These decisions can be handled by an IC or, more accurately, an incident manager.

Regardless of the size or characteristics of an airport, at least one individual in airport management should be assigned the duties of maintaining the AEP and overall airport emergency management-related duties. Ideally, that individual should not only focus on keeping the AEP up-to-date but also should take a comprehensive approach to emergency management. The AEP is not a "one-and-done" plan. Rather, it is a living document that must change as incidents occur and as lessons are learned and applied.

For communities that place a heavy reliance on the airport during natural or human-made disasters, another consideration for airport operators is to take a lesson from the U.S. Coast Guard (USCG), which has established an **Emergency Preparedness Liaison Officer (EPLO)** program. The 9/11 terrorist attacks and Hurricane Katrina demonstrated the need for a more integrated and coordinated approach between federal, state, local, tribal, and private sector organizations to prepare for, prevent, respond to, and recover from terrorism, major natural and human-made disasters, and other major emergencies. EPLOs are assigned to foster the exchange of information, promote cooperation and communication, and coordinate the planning and implementation of contingency plans with federal, state, and local emergency preparedness partners (USCG, 2009). A designated airport emergency manager may be able to fill both roles, that of maintaining and updating the AEP and that of an airport preparedness Liaison Officer responsible for maintaining relationships

[4]The Certified Emergency Manager (CEM) program, managed by the International Association of Emergency Managers, is one of the certification processes for the industry. It is not aviation or domain specific.

with federal, state, local, tribal, and private sector organizations and coordinating the planning and implementation of contingency and incident management plans.

As more Airport Operations personnel become trained in incident management, and more police and fire personnel can trust that their core missions will not be compromised and will, in fact, be enhanced, the industry may see more "operations-centric" ICs. The role of Incident Command is explained more fully later in Chapter 11.

AIRPORT EMERGENCY MANAGEMENT PLANNING

All airports are subject to emergencies and incidents, and under Title 14 CFR Part 139.325, *Airport Emergency Plan*, each certificate holder must develop and maintain an emergency plan designed to minimize the possibility and extent of personal injury and property damage on the airport. The plan must include procedures for the prompt response to certain emergencies listed in 139.325(b) and have in place a communications network that includes methods of notifying response personnel of an emergency. The plan, known as the AEP, must contain enough detail to provide adequate guidance to each person who must implement the procedures and provide, to the extent practicable, an emergency response to the largest air carrier aircraft in the ARFF Index (FAA, 2010b).

Per AC 150-5200-31C (FAA, 2010a, p. 1), an airport emergency is any occasion or instance, natural or human-made, that warrants action to save lives and protects property and public health. The AEP should address those emergencies that occur on, or directly impact, an airport or adjacent property that are within the authority and responsibility of the airport to respond, may present a threat to the airport because of the proximity of the emergency to the airport, or when the airport has responsibilities under local/regional emergency plans and by mutual aid agreements (FAA, 2010a, p. 1). The AEP must include instructions for responding to:

1. Aircraft Accidents and incidents;
2. Bomb incidents;
3. Structural fires;
4. Fires at fuel farms or fuel storage areas;
5. Natural disasters (that occur in the region where the airport is located);
6. Hazardous materials/dangerous goods incidents;
7. Sabotage, hijack incidents, and other acts of unlawful interference with operations;
8. Failure of power to the movement area lighting system; and
9. Water Rescue, as appropriate.

In addition to the aforementioned items, the plan should also include any other significant emergencies and incidents as identified through a risk assessment. For example, for airports with underground passenger movement or transit systems, it is reasonable and the airport would be expected to have a plan for evacuation of personnel from the area during fire, flood, or other identified emergencies.

The AEP must also provide for an appropriate fire and medical response; describe facilities available for use during an emergency for such functions as a temporary hospital or morgue, Staging Areas, etc.; and address methods for crowd control. The plan must also address how various responders, such as police, Airport Operations, fire and rescue, EMS, and the principal tenants and off-airport responders should coordinate efforts to support the emergencies listed in the plan. Class I airports must test the effectiveness of their plans at least once every 3 years through an exercise, and all certificated airports (Classes I to IV) must review the plan on an annual basis.

FAA AC 150/5200-312C (2010a) provides guidance on the development of the AEP. An AEP consists of four sections, the Basic Plan, the Functional Sections, the Hazards Section, and the Standard Operating Procedures (SOPs). The AC is quite comprehensive but redundant.

In addition to establishing that elected officials are responsible for protecting people and property from the consequences of emergencies and disasters, the Stafford Act also requires that emergency plans must be developed within the **National Response Framework**.[5] The framework establishes the **all-hazards** approach to incident response, describes the federal government's resources and response plans, and describes how the federal government, tribes, states, and communities should respond to an incident. Plans must follow the NIMS, which provides standardization in vocabulary and structure of Incident Command functions. NIMS primarily focuses on:

1. Establishment and use of the **ICS**;
2. Multiagency coordination; and
3. Joint public information systems.

NIMS is applicable to all incidents and works across all disciplines. NIMS and its application are discussed in Chapter 11 and various other areas throughout.

COMPREHENSIVE EMERGENCY MANAGEMENT

Although no plan or SOP can address all of the incidents or emergencies an airport might experience, emergencies share several commonalities. These commonalities allow for an all-hazards approach to emergency management rather than an approach that attempts to predict and plan for all possibilities. All-hazards does not mean to literally prepare for all possible hazards but instead to be prepared for the foreseeable hazards that are typical to the community or airport. Preparation includes identifying necessary functions common to all hazards, such as fire and rescue, law enforcement and security, crowd control, emergency notification, and more. By identifying these functions, along with identifying their roles during the planned emergencies, the agencies should then be able to handle other unforeseen emergencies or incidents.

Comprehensive emergency management is structured around four separate actions: mitigation, preparedness, response, and recovery. While the AEP addresses most specifically the preparedness, response, and recovery section, the AEP is not all-inclusive to the actions and plans that should be addressed when planning for emergencies.

Mitigation actions involve lasting, often permanent, reduction of exposure to, probability of, or potential loss from hazardous events (FEMA, 1996). Mitigation measures are designed to prevent a hazard from occurring or to reduce its damaging effects. An example of a mitigation measure may

---

[5]The FEMA has published the *National Response Framework (NRF)*, NIMS, and the State and Local Guide (SLG 101), *Guide for All-Hazard Emergency Operations Planning*. NIMS and SLG 101 provide emergency managers and other emergency services providers with information regarding the FEMA concept for developing risk-based, all-hazards Emergency Operations Plans (EOPs) (FAA, 2010b, p. 3).

include zoning a parcel of land near the approach path to the airport to prevent the construction of homes, which would reduce the possibility of an aircraft crashing into the housing development on approach. Other approaches to mitigation can involve educating businesses and the public on measures they can take to reduce loss and injury during an incident. Some other mitigation examples in aviation may include:

1. Requiring window glazing on windows that face the terminal building near passenger pickup and dropoff points, to reduce the damaging effects of a vehicle-borne improvised explosive device or tornado;
2. Constructing tornado shelters and installing signage throughout the terminal directing passengers and employees where to go and what steps to take in the case of a tornado;
3. Reducing the size of a nearby hill to allow more room for arriving and departing aircraft;
4. Incorporating blast-resistant building materials in the terminal building (in some cases, a security benefit, such as blast-resistant building materials, also has a safety benefit of making the structure more resilient against natural disasters);
5. Providing training to airport tenants on the steps to take for a particular incident or disaster;
6. Conducting risk assessments; and
7. Inventorying existing structures and vulnerabilities.

Cost-effective mitigation measures are the key to reducing disaster losses in the long term (FEMA, 1996). FEMA occasionally uses the term **Prevention** within the National Preparedness Framework context (Prevention, Protection, Mitigation, Response, or Recovery), and many airport operators have also adopted this term to be used in conjunction with or in place of *mitigation*. The term *prevention* in the FEMA context addresses emergency management from a counter-terrorist perspective, and the term relates to those actions designed to prevent an attack on a facility. Prevention focuses on a facility or government agency developing core capabilities, including intelligence and information sharing, screening/search/detection, interdiction and disruption, forensics and attribution, planning, public information and warning, and operational coordination. Since an airport operator must prepare for emergencies as specified in Part 139.325, and for security incidents under Part 1542.307, prevention measures should be included in the airport incident planning process.

Preparedness measures are actions that enhance the abilities of emergency response agencies and include training, exercises, planning, and acquisition of materials needed in the event of an emergency. Typical airport preparedness measures include:

1. Revising the AEP;
2. Conducting an ARFF training exercise;
3. Conducting a full-scale, tabletop, functional, or other type of emergency exercise; and
4. Acquiring new fire trucks, hiring personnel, and equipment.

During the preparedness phase, the airport develops a plan of action to manage and counter risks and takes action to build the necessary capabilities needed to implement the plan.

Response elements are time-sensitive actions to save lives and property, reduce the possibility of initial and secondary damage, and accelerate recovery operations. Response elements also include initial incident notification, dispatch of rescue personnel, and those actions necessary to immediately address the incident, including firefighting, neutralization of an active shooter, or application of chemical coagulating agent to prevent a hazardous material (HAZMAT) spill from spreading into the storm water system. Response actions are sometimes referred to as *Priorities of Work.*

PRIORITIES OF WORK

All emergency planning is focused on the **Priorities of Work**, which are to:

1. Save lives:
2. Stabilize the scene;
3. Save property;
4. Save the environment; and, from an airport operator's perspective, the fifth and sixth priorities are to
5. Restore Airport Operations; and
6. Preserve the accident scene.

While saving lives is the top priority, in certain cases, the scene must first be stabilized before lifesaving functions can begin. A typical example is during a car accident when traffic may first have to be stopped in order to gain safe access to a victim in the road. For an aircraft fire, the fire may first have to be knocked down by the application of firefighting agents prior to rescue crews' injuring the fuselage to save lives.

First responders must make many rapid decisions during an incident and can generally follow these Priorities of Work to guide that decision making. Airport operators typically understand the importance of continuing flight operations during an emergency, if possible. Even during the active shooter incident at Los Angeles International Airport (LAX) in 2013, flight operations continued on certain parts of the airfield but not for economic reasons. Many aircraft using LAX are inbound international flights and are large aircraft, such as the Boeing 777, the Boeing Dreamliner, and the Airbus A380, that are short on fuel after flying over the Pacific Ocean and do not have other safe landing sites nearby.

Another important goal typically not shared by off-airport law enforcement investigators is to preserve the accident scene until the FAA or NTSB investigators arrive on scene. Once all of the lives that can be saved have been saved, the scene has been stabilized, property has been preserved, and environmental issues have been resolved, the NTSB desires that no one, includes local law enforcement homicide and arson investigators, be in the accident scene unless absolutely necessary. Unfortunately some criminal investigators do not understand that a plane crash is different from an automobile accident, so they will begin walking around the accident scene, taking pictures and collecting evidence. Airport management must make every effort to ensure that local investigators understand the NTSB's edicts to the fullest extent possible.[6]

Recovery actions include those that restore the airport to normal operations. Often the response and recovery phases of an emergency overlap. Components of recovery include short, medium, and long-term strategies to restore operations and assist those personnel who have been affected. Short-term needs may be to provide food, shelter, water, and restroom facilities to those injured in

---

[6]Scene management and security can become problematic, considering it is the responsibility of local law enforcement to preserve and control access to the scene and that these same officers also work for the same agency as the criminal investigators.

a plane crash. Medium- and long-term recovery items include restoring the runway to an operable condition, reopening the airport, and providing for family members who are arriving at the airport to be reunited with their loved ones. Long-term recovery actions may lead into measures that are more mitigation in their characteristics. These may include repairs to a runway, replacing airfield signs or obscured markings, and mental health care for victims and responders.

DRAFTING THE AIRPORT EMERGENCY PLAN

The fundamental goal of an AEP is to transition the airport from normal operations to emergency or irregular operations and back to normal operations, as quickly and effectively as possible. Also, recognizing that the airport plays an important role in community disaster planning, the AEP should be written with consideration given to state and regional disaster plans, as well as the Airport Security Program. In this way, the airport is prepared to handle its own emergencies, and it is better prepared to support community emergencies.

When drafting an emergency plan, airport management should understand the scope of the preparedness activity necessary to make the emergency plan more than a mere paper plan or a regulatory check in the box. The FAA provides airport operators and AEP template, but all too often, the individual responsible for drafting the plan becomes more focused on filling in the blanks rather than developing a plan that is workable and focused on the Priorities of Work. It is important also to understand that the AEP will drive the training and the exercise programs necessary to support the plan. Training helps to familiarize response personnel with their responsibilities and builds the skills necessary to perform the tasks (FEMA, 1996). Exercises provide a means to validate the plan, to identify errors in the plan, to validate or invalidate assumptions, and to identify critical gaps.

> "In preparing for battle I have always found that plans are useless, but planning is indispensable."
> **Dwight D. Eisenhower**

This oft-quoted phrase from former President Dwight Eisenhower captures the essence of the planning process. The process of planning is an essential element to planning, in that it can identify issues and solve problems ahead of time. Planning allows the department to determine its strategic objectives, along with the best tactical strategies to achieve those objectives. Planning provides insights into the organization's strengths, weaknesses, opportunities, and threats. It allows goals to be set ahead of time so that responders have a clear mission and a clear understanding of the materials, personnel, and actions that are necessary to achieve the goals. Planning can solve communication problems, resolve issues relating to chain of command, identify deficiencies in training, and determine the need for the amount and types of exercises needed to test the plan. Planning also helps to bring people on board with the plan.

While the AEP is a comprehensive document, the directives within the plan should be as clear, simple, and concise as each situation permits. Elaborate and long sentences or extreme detail are not characteristics of effective plans and action items. Short sentences are easily understood, but trivial phrases that create ambiguity and confusion should be avoided. Quite simply, when writing an AEP, write down what you want the agency to do—be specific. Also, when drafting the AEP, understand that there is no such thing as the perfect plan. The U.S. Marine Corps focuses on what is known as the 70% solution, which says: decisive actions based on 70% of the available information is better than slow decisions based on complete information (Hudson, 2013). The fact is, no one will ever have 100% of the information needed to make a decision or to develop a plan. Thus, moving forward with most of the information in a timely manner is better than waiting until it is too late.

> Sun Tzu once said: "A good solution applied with vigor now is better than a perfect solution applied ten minutes later."
>
> **Province, 1984, p. 165**

Remember that a plan is not a script to be followed to the letter but should be flexible and adaptable to the actual situation. An effective plan conveys the goals and objectives of the intended operation, along with the actions needed to achieve those goals and objectives, but leaves the implementation of the plan to the operator in the field. Planning must be community-based, representing the whole population in understanding the needs of the airport and community stakeholders.

One of the first steps in developing an AEP is to put together a **planning team**. Irrespective of the size of the Airport Operation, no AEP would be effective without input from those who are most affected by the plan—namely, the airport stakeholders, including airlines and tenants, and no AEP would be implementable without the buy-in and support of the first responders, including police, fire, and emergency medical personnel.

Team members, at a minimum, should consist of representatives from:

1. Airport Operations
2. Police
3. Fire
4. EMS
5. ATC
6. Major airlines or cargo operators serving the airport and/or major tenants with significant levels of flight operations
7. State, regional, and local emergency management personnel
8. Health and hospital agencies
9. Government agencies (Federal Bureau of Investigation [FBI], Transportation Security Administration [TSA], FAA)
10. Animal care/control
11. Military (if on or near a military base)
12. Coroner
13. Public information office

FAA AC 150/5200-31C (2010a) provides a comprehensive list of other individuals who could be part of the AEP planning team (a total of 37); however, a committee with 37 individual representatives may be difficult to manage. To develop a more effective plan, workgroups should be established to focus on various areas of the plan (typically within their field of expertise) and to look for areas of interdependence, where one entity relies on the work of another entity to achieve their core objectives. While having 37+ agencies serve on a committee may be impractical, any organization or entity with responsibilities under the AEP should at least be consulted and should provide their approval for their agencies, roles within the plan.

One approach to managing numerous agencies when creating or revising an AEP is to establish core members. A core member is an agency that has significant or primary responsibilities under the AEP, such as Airport Operations, police, fire, and EMS. Underneath each core agency are related functions (Figure 10.1). The lead representative from each core agency is responsible for coordinating the planning efforts for a particular subagency.

With regard to military facilities, if an airport is a joint-use airport, meaning that the U.S. government owns the facility and leases a parcel of land for civil air carrier and/or GA operations, the U.S. military usually takes the primary role for emergency management and Incident Command, even for civilian response. For a shared-use airport, where the U.S. government (i.e., military) owns one portion of the airport, while a civilian organization (city, county, or airport authority) owns another portion, and the runway/taxiway facilities are shared, the military commonly serves in the primary role for emergency response. However, two key considerations are important for

Airport Operations	Police	Fire	Emergency Medical Services	FAA/Airport District Office
FAA / ATCT Airlines Tenants Airport Sponsor Communications and Dispatch EPA Public Information Office Airlines or Major Tenants* Maintenance Public Works Engineering State Aviation Authority	FBI TSA Explosive Ordnance Disposal and local SWAT Military (if applicable—see note below)	HAZMAT Off-Airport Fire Response Local and Regional Emergency Management Agencies Red Cross Search and Rescue Civil Air Patrol Salvation Army Mutual Aid Agencies	Hospitals Coroner Mental health Animal care Clergy	NTSB FEMA National Weather Service U.S. Post Office

FIGURE 10.1 Example core members of an AEP.

Note: The U.S. military is often very responsive to emergency planning activities, and it may be desirable to designate them a core agency. Also, the above list is just a suggestion of one possible method of organization. Airport emergency managers should organize in a manner that makes sense for their operation.

*Air carriers and significant tenants (e.g., FBOs, major corporate operators) are significant part of the AEP team.

Airport Managers of joint- or shared-use facilities: (1) through base realignment and closures, the military organization on the airport may lose some or all of its firefighting and emergency response assets, or (2) the emergency assets may not meet the FAA requirements for response under the AEP or the ARFF Index. It is still the responsibility of the airport operator to ensure the airport can support the AEP in resources, personnel, and actions.

Another consideration is airports that do not have military stations on the airfield but may have military facilities nearby. Those installations may have resources, such as ARFF equipment or special operations teams, that can respond to a plane crash or incident of unlawful interference. In the case of armed response, some military bases have personnel on standby and may be able to respond more rapidly and with more force than local FBI or police assets. Even for military installations that do not have fire or rescue capabilities, there is a long history of military personnel, Air and Army National Guard personnel being mobilized on short notice to assist in an aircraft emergency. Probably one of the most notable instances took place when United Airlines Flight 232 crashed at the airport in Sioux City, Iowa, in 1989 (Gonzales, 2014, p. 71).

Another important step in developing the AEP is to **research** existing regulations, standards, and guidance. When developing an AEP, it is not necessary to start from scratch. As previously mentioned, the FAA offers a template for airport operators to use in building their plan. Airport operators should also seek the assistance of associates in the industry who work at airports of comparable size and characteristics and, if possible, review their AEP and get their counsel. The following documents should also be consulted:

1. NIMS
2. The National Response Framework (which replaced the National Response Plan)
3. SLG 101, *Guide for All-Hazard Emergency Operations Planning*
4. National Fire Protection Association (NFPA) 424, *Airport/Community Emergency Planning*
5. 14 CFR Part 139, *Certification of Airports*
6. Applicable state and local regulations
7. International Civil Aviation Organization (ICAO) technical instructions
8. International Air Transport Association, *Dangerous Goods Regulations Manual*
9. Department of Transportation, *The Public Transportation System Security and Emergency Preparedness Planning Guide*, 2003 as amended
10. National Response Team, NRT-1, *Hazardous Materials Emergency Planning Guide*

While the AC also advises reviewing the Airport Security regulations, including aircraft-operator and foreign air carrier regulations, this practice is of limited benefit. Most of the regulatory citations in the Transportation Security Regulations do not provide anything useful to an emergency manager. The action items, incident plans, and contingency plans, which are what an emergency manager would need, are contained in the Airport Security Program, the Aircraft Operator Standard Security Program (AOSSP), the Model Security Program (for foreign air carriers), and the Indirect Air Carrier Standard Security Program. Further complicating matters is that each of these programs is marked Sensitive Security Information (SSI) and shared on a need-to-know basis. The Airport Security Coordinator (ASC) may have access to the Airport Security Program, but not the airline's AOSSP, or the foreign air carrier or indirect air carrier security programs. For this reason, among others, the domestic airlines serving the airport, as well as any foreign air carriers or cargo operators, should be included as part of the AEP planning team, as they have access to their own security program requirements. Other programs and documents to review as part of the AEP development include:

1. *U.S. Coast Guard Addendum to the National SAR Supplement* (CGADD), COMDTINST M16130.2D, which establishes policy, guidelines, procedures, and general information for Coast Guard use in Search and Rescue (SAR) operations. This document would be relevant for operators of airports either with a Coast Guard Air Station or when the airport is located near international or intercostal waterways;

2. FAA Order 7210.3, *Facility Operation and Administration*, which addresses the operation of federal ATC facilities such as the control tower or radar facilities;

3. Any existing AEP;

4. The Airport Security Program;

5. Air Carrier Emergency Plan(s) with a focus on Air Carrier Aviation Disaster Family Assistance Act Plans;

6. Tenant Emergency Plan(s);

7. Local/regional Emergency Operations Plan(s);

8. Local Industry Occupational Safety and Health Administration (OSHA)/EPA Compliance Plans;

9. Existing mutual aid agreements/memoranda of understanding, airport agreements, local emergency response agreements, private sector organization agreements, and military installation agreements; and

10. Business continuity plans.

Risk Analysis

The next step in developing or revising an AEP is to conduct a hazard/risk analysis. If an airport has a robust safety management system and security management system in place, then a hazard or risk analysis has already been conducted. However, airport emergency managers should consider whether the risk analysis was conducted with the input from all of the agencies on the airport emergency planning team. If not, the agencies that were not involved in the initial risk assessment should be consulted.

Upon completion of the hazard or risk analysis, the planning team should develop hazard-specific plans and determine resource requirements. However, plans for every possible contingency do not have to be written. For example, a plan specific to an Aircraft Accident hazard that addresses the crash of a major airliner will work as well for a small-Aircraft Accident or incident. However, an aircraft crash on land differs from an aircraft crash on water or in frozen water under frigid conditions, such as occurred in 1982 when an Air Florida flight crashed into the Potomac River while taking off from Reagan National Airport. In some cases, two or more hazard-specific plans may be implemented rather than writing separate plans for separate scenarios. For example, rather than writing a hazard-specific plan for an airplane crash into a structure, if the incident were to occur in real life, elements of the Aircraft Accident hazard-specific plan can be combined with the structural fire hazard-specific plan. This is the nature of the all-hazards planning approach.

With changing weather patterns, researching hazard maps available through the U.S. Geological Survey and the National Weather Service, as well as any local floodplain maps or surveys, to determine the possibility and effects of natural disasters, is appropriate. Historical data is also available through federal, state, and county hazard analysis and Red Cross disaster records. Longtime residents of the area can also provide anecdotal information on potential hazardous weather events (FAA, 2010a). AEP planners should also take into account:

1. Individuals with functional needs (hearing impaired, sight impaired, etc.);
2. Special features of the airport, such as surrounding topography that may limit runway use;
3. Access requirements in the community and to the airport (i.e., Is there a single roadway or bridge that accesses the airport and that if flooded or damaged would significantly affect the airport's ability to implement aviation or emergency actions?);
4. Reduced staffing levels (many personnel may not be able to access the airport during a natural disaster, or the disaster may occur at night or on a weekend when airport staffing levels are usually lower, and it is more difficult to get high-level decision makers on scene);
5. Power or communications outages, which can occur during natural disasters, or during human-made disasters (on 9/11 and during other major events subsequent, cell phone towers were inundated with calls, making it nearly impossible to get a call out; however, many emergency responders have found that when calls cannot get through, text messages, Tweets, and Facebook postings can. Emergency planners should take into account whether response personnel have phones with text capability or other means of communicating with other agencies when the primary means of communications goes out).

Another critical component of airport emergency planning is consideration of resources. AC 150/5200-31C, *Airport Emergency Plan*, states that planning team members should know what resources are available for emergency response and recovery (FAA, 2010a). However, FEMA uses a much more effective model known as **Resource Typing and Readiness**.

Resource Management

Personnel, facilities, equipment, and supplies are the resources needed to respond to an incident. Resource typing, credentialing, training, and exercises enable the efficient and effective deployment of resources and ensure that personnel are prepared for their response roles. Resource typing assigns a designation to each resource that allows ICs to request and deploy resources, while **credentialing** ensures personnel can access the incident area (Figure 10.2).

Under NIMS, resources are first classified as Tier I or Tier II. Tier I consists of the current 120 resource-typing definitions. Tier II are resources defined and inventoried by the states, tribal, and local jurisdictions that are not Tier I resources but are specific and limited to intrastate and regional mutual-aid assistance. NIMS classifies 120 resources (FEMA, 2004), broken down into categories (Animal Health, Emergency Management Resources, Emergency Medical Services Resources, Fire/ HAZMAT Resources, Health and Medical Resources, Law Enforcement Resources, Public Works Resources, and Search and Rescue Resources).

Resources are classified by *Category* (i.e., function, such as firefighting, law enforcement, health and medical), by *Kind* (teams, personnel, equipment, supplies), and *Type* (measure of capability to perform its function). For example, a pumper fire truck is classified as Category: Firefighting, Kind: Equipment, and Type can either be I to VII, depending on the gallons per minute the unit is capable of pumping, its tank capacity, hose diameter, and number of personnel. Another component of resource typing is the response time of the asset under normal conditions.

RESOURCE: ENGINE, FIRE (PUMPER)							
CATEGORY: Firefighting (ESF #4)					**KIND:** Equipment		
MINIMUM CAPABILITIES:		TYPE I	TYPE II	TYPE III	TYPE IV	TYPE V	TYPE VI	TYPE VII
Component	**Metric**							
Pump capacity		1,000 GPM	500 GPM	120 GPM	70 GPM	50 GPM	50 GPM	50 GPM
Tank capacity		400 Gal.	400 Gal.	500 Gal.	750 Gal.	500 Gal.	200 Gal.	125 Gal.
Hose, 2.5 inch		1,200 ft.	1,000 ft.					
Hose, 1.5 inch		400 ft.	500 ft.	1,000 ft.	300 ft.	300 ft.	300 ft.	200 ft.
Hose, 1 inch		200 ft.	300 ft.	800 ft.	300 ft.	300 ft.	300 ft.	200 ft.
Personnel		4	3	3	2	2	2	2
COMMENTS: The engine typing needs to be taken out to type VII. Compromise between FIRESCOPE and NWCG is to use NWCG Standards for Engines and Crews. NWCG has seven engine types.								

FIGURE 10.2 FEMA resource typing.

Resource typing can be particularly important during a mass casualty incident in regard to the types and numbers of victims that area hospitals can handle. A Disaster Medical Assistance Team (DMAT) specifies the numbers of patients and the type of care available, denoting pediatric, burn unit, and trauma capabilities, response times of personnel, and how long the unit can function without resupply.

A comprehensive, well-researched, resource-typing document allows emergency managers to essentially "order off the menu" of emergency response capabilities. In numerous emergency exercises, available resources are usually not lacking, but often an inefficient use of resources, as ICs operated without an accurate resource-typing guide.

Training and Exercises

As the AEP nears completion, it should be checked for conformity with the applicable regulations and standards and to ensure the plan works as written or to the extent possible. Some of this validation may come by review with local community management officials and others who are part of the plan development, but the best way to test the plan, short of an actual emergency, is through training, drills, and exercises.

The most vital components of an AEP are the first responders, police, fire, emergency medical, and Airport Operations personnel. Training is essential to ensure that individuals know their roles, to identify gaps in the plan, and to ensure that personnel understand how to use the facilities, equipment, materials, and vehicles necessary to carry out their core functions. During an emergency, no first responder will have time to reference the AEP, at least within the first 30 minutes of a major incident. Certain actions must be done from memory and should be practiced so often that they are done subconsciously. Firefighters should be well trained to know how to perform the basic functions of attacking a fire and rescuing individuals from a fuselage. Police officers should be well trained to know how to respond to an active shooter event without having to consult the manual.

However, the AEP drives the drills, training, and exercises to ensure that all response personnel can carry out their basic functions.

All on- and off-airport personnel should familiarize themselves with the equipment and the facilities involved. On-airport personnel should have a grid map, training, and the ability to access any area on the airfield where an incident could occur. Training often includes airfield driver training, vehicle training for specific types of vehicles or apparatus, and how to communicate with the FAA on a VHF (very high frequency) radio. Off-airport responders should know where to respond during an emergency. Access routes and Staging Areas should be clearly delineated on response maps or grid maps, and these maps should be distributed to off-airport responders.

The initial training should be focused on SOPs. General training should be provided to all airport employees, along with emergency response personnel, and specialized training should be provided to personnel to perform their specific job functions (FAA, 2010a). On some occasions, because of a lack of personnel, certain personnel may be assigned to a function, such as maintenance or office administrative personnel assigned to be stretcher bearers—these individuals may also end up being "victims" as a result of the emotional trauma of a mass casualty incident. Once all personnel are familiar with and can confidently carry out the functions of their job, the next level of training should be on the hazard-specific sections of the AEP, so that responders understand their role in each particular emergency or incident. Facility layout, use of communications equipment, use of emergency equipment, and any specialized training depending on the job function should be included in these training sessions.

Training should also be conducted to familiarize first responders with the capabilities of others on the airport, such as ATC, and facilities that can be used in an emergency, such as a fixed base operator's hangar, corporate hangar, meeting and training rooms that may be used as command facilities, family gathering locations, or media Joint Information Center. This is also a good time to determine the locations for these types of functions, as well as any problems that may arise, such as putting the media center next to the family reunification center, although this practice is not advised.

As previously discussed, the airport operator should also provide emergency care training, which may include first aid and cardiopulmonary resuscitation (CPR) courses, first responder courses, independent first aid kit training, crowd control and panic prevention training, response to active shooter events, scene assessment and scene security, basic fire extinguisher operations, and evacuation and shelter-in-place contingencies, to appropriate personnel. Recertification and refresher training should be scheduled as needed, as skill sets diminish when not used. Training should be as realistic as possible. For instance, in the fire extinguisher class, the class should discharge various types of fire extinguishers and extinguish actual, controlled fires. Different extinguishers have various characteristics in the way they put out fires—failing to understand these characteristics can cause injury or death to the extinguisher operator.

Training should also include familiarizing all response personnel, including communications and dispatch personnel, on the capabilities of airport equipment, personnel, facilities, and facility access. Tours of the airport and participation in drills and exercises for all off- and on-airport response personnel are necessary. Certain personnel, such as police and fire, should be familiar with the various aircraft that operate at the airport, such as cargo versus passenger, small versus large, and turbine versus piston-engine planes.

Exercises help to determine the readiness of an agency or individual to handle an event, identify gaps between planning and execution, and allow personnel an opportunity to practice their skills in more realistic situations. A variety of exercises include orientation, drill, tabletop, functional, and full-scale.

Orientation

Orientation brings together responders and those with responsibilities in the AEP, to meet face-to-face, discuss upcoming drills, and become familiar with each others' various roles, procedures, and capabilities. Emergency managers often say you should not be exchanging business cards during an incident. The relationships among responders should be developed far in advance of an actual incident. Atul Gawande (2010) stresses the importance of surgical teams to introduce themselves at the beginning of a surgery, which subtly grants nurses the same standing as surgeons to speak up if a problem occurs.

Drill

A drill is the lowest level of exercise and is designed to test a single emergency procedure. A drill can be discussion based, as in two police officers having coffee in the terminal and discussing what they would do if they received a report of an active shooter in the terminal, right now. Or a drill can be action-oriented and involve an ARFF crew responding by truck to extinguish a fire on an aircraft fuselage fire-training device.

Tabletop Exercise

One of the most common forms of exercises is the tabletop exercise (TTX) A TTX is a higher level exercise than the drill or the orientation and is designed to provide training and evaluation of plans and procedures. A TTX can answer questions about which agency is responsible for which actions, clarify the actual time it takes for response units to arrive, or who is in charge, and how the incident management system will be established. The TTX is conducted usually in a conference room, and there is no movement of actual assets. Many airport operators conduct a TTX annually to meet the Part 139 requirement that the AEP be reviewed on an annual basis.

For a TTX, a Situation Manual (SitMan) is developed that includes the background of the airport and the purpose of the exercise. The SitMan also includes a scenario and a scope, along with the exercise objectives and assumptions. Note that this exercise typically simulates the first 30 minutes of a real-time response. The SitMan is typically shared with attendees in advance so that agencies can review their roles and game out their responses. A TTX is not about tossing in surprises and trying to catch agencies and personnel off guard. It is similar to a football practice, during which the airport and all other agencies with responsibilities under the AEP can determine if their plans are working. During a TTX exercise, facilitators often remind participants that this is not a *gotcha* game, where the facilitator attempts to embarrass the attendees: *test the plan, support the people* is a common mantra among exercise facilitators.

The TTX is conducted in a nonthreatening environment and provides the opportunity for agencies to discuss possible responses to scenarios, work out issues, determine limitations, and clarify expectations. A facilitator presents the scenario, walks the various agencies through their responses, and solicits feedback from the participants. The participants largely determine the effectiveness of the TTX, and each agency is expected to return to its home office and make adjustments to plans, training, and policies to fill identified gaps. All activities are conducted through discussion, no equipment is utilized, nor are personnel deployed. The mark of a successful TTX is that policies are actually changed, and gaps of capability are identified and subsequently addressed.

The FAA has determined that a TTX meets the requirements of the "AEP Review," but this determination has led to a common industry misconception that an annual TTX is required. However, no regulations of the *Airport Emergency Plan* AC require this practice—it has simply become urban legend. Per FAA Order 5280.5, *Airport Certification Program Handbook*, Section 419, Section 139.325, Airport Emergency Plan (a)(7), the certificate holder must: "Provide for an annual review of the AEP. This might be a tabletop exercise or a review meeting with each of the agencies with which the plan is coordinated. Correspondence about planning and outcomes should be retained" (p. 64). An "AEP review" means all entities meet, and their roles and responsibilities are reviewed on an annual basis. Regardless, since the TTX serves as a review, it's a good opportunity to get everyone together to practice likely scenarios.

Functional Exercise

A functional exercise (FE) exceeds the level of a TTX and is the highest level of exercise that does not involve the full activation of on- and off-airport personnel and facilities (FAA, 2010a). Although similar in nature to a TTX, a Master Scenario Events List (MSEL) is developed, which drives the exercise. The MSEL contains a chronological listing of scripted events and injects that generate activity in specific functional areas in support of exercise objectives. The MSEL sets up the scenario and preestablished prompts (actions), causing the participants to implement plans that the exercise is designed to test, or also inserts variables to determine how each agency will respond. Ideally, the agencies respond in the same way that is outlined in the AEP. If an agency responds differently, it must be determined by the facilitator whether the difference in response is (a) a misunderstanding of the agency's role, (b) a lack of capability of the agency, or (c) some other reason. As an example, if during an exercise, the AEP for an airport located near a large body of water calls for the USCG to be on scene within a specified time period to assist in the event of an aircraft crashing into the water, the expectation is for the agency to be able to accomplish that task within the time frame stated in the AEP. If the USCG representatives participating in the FE advise that their boats cannot be on scene within that time period or that some boats can be but only shallow draft vessels rather than larger vessels, then the AEP should be subsequently adjusted to fit this reality. The idea of an FE is to determine capability and compare the plan with reality.

A short MSEL lists the "inject" (prompt), its delivery time, a short description, the responsible controller, and the receiving player. A long MSEL contains a detailed description, exact quotes and formats, and a description of expected action. Some large FEs can contain dozens of MSELs for a variety of agencies. During a "functional" real-world exercise, assets may be moved, equipment used, and personnel deployed.[7] For example, if in the command center, the police commander says that he can have additional officers on scene within 10 minutes, he may be asked to call police dispatch and determine how many units are available right now, in real time. If possible, a police car may even be dispatched[8] from its present location to the location of the accident that is being

---

[7]"Functionals" are often conducted in the actual command center.

[8]When this tactic is used, often the police car responds code 1, which typically means no lights or sirens and obeying all traffic laws. In actual responses, code 1 and code 3 (lights and sirens) aren't often that far apart, based on traffic congestion and other factors.

simulated to test response time, to determine if the actual response time is close to what the police commander indicates it should be. FEs can be conducted in numerous ways, testing any and all elements of an AEP.

Full-Scale Exercise

The most comprehensive test of an AEP is the full-scale exercise. This exercise is intended to evaluate the operational capability of the emergency management system in a stress environment with actual mobilization and deployment to demonstrate coordination and response capability. The full-scale exercise uses all resources and requires reaction from equipment and personnel that would normally be available if the exercise were an actual emergency. The FAA requires Class I airports to conduct a full-scale airport exercise at least every 3 years (often called the "triennial"), and the exercise must simulate an airplane crash commensurate with the index of the airport (i.e., an airport that routinely has large aircraft, such as Boeing 777s and Airbus 320s, cannot likely get away with simulating an airplane crash of a Cessna 172). The full-scale exercise must ensure that all personnel having duties and responsibilities under the plan are familiar with assignments and are properly trained (FAA, 2010a).

A full-scale exercise uses an **Exercise Plan (ExPlan)**, which provides the scope, objectives, and synopsis of the exercise. The ExPlan includes tasks and responsibilities and is intended for use by players and observers. The ExPlan should not contain detailed scenario information or anticipated response options because participants might think through their responses ahead of time. Unlike the TTX, the full-scale exercise is designed to test the plan and the players for weaknesses and capability gaps. An MSEL is also developed, but more as a supplement to the active play, as the actual responses of agencies may render some injects moot or unnecessary. A Controller and Evaluator Handbook (C&E Handbook) is also created to supplement the ExPlan, except it contains more detailed information about the exercise, along with the roles and responsibilities of the player. Players should not view the C&E Handbook, as it contains detailed information about the scenarios players encounter.

An Exercise Evaluation Guide (EEG) is also part of a full-scale exercise. EEGs help evaluators to document exercise activities and to determine whether objectives are met. While there is some benefit to using outside observers, there should be an observer from every agency that has a role in the exercise. Objectives should be determined ahead of time, and the evaluator should "grade" the agency on how well its personnel met the objectives. There is generally one EEG for each of the capabilities in the FEMA Target Capabilities List (TCL).[9] Although they do list specific tasks and activities for observation during an exercise, the EEGs are guides meant to assist evaluators by prompting them to focus on specific events that may occur during an exercise (SETRAC, n.d.). The EEGs are not technically a report card but should be used as viewing guides to assist with exercise evaluation and as a resource for developing consistent After-Action Report/Plans and Improvement Plans (AAR/IP) (SETRAC, n.d.). In order to capture the most critical feedback, it is important to conduct the "immediate postbriefing" or **Hot-Wash** before the units demobilize and return to base. A subsequent "deep-dive analysis" and follow-up meetings to evaluate the exercise should be conducted at a later time.

---

[9]The TCL describes the capabilities related to the four homeland security mission areas: Prevent, Protect, Respond, and Recover.

The AAR/IP is a record of what happened during the exercise that is used to implement changes and improve capabilities, as well as to provide feedback to participating agencies on their performance. The AAR/IP analyzes performance of activities and demonstrated capability to accomplish the TCL and makes recommendations for improvement (SETRAC, n.d.). Immediately after an exercise a Hot-Wash is conducted, participants list their top three organizational strengths, their top three organizational improvements, and general remarks and comments.

A full-scale exercise at an operational airport comes with its own unique set of challenges, foremost is ensuring the safety of the participants while continuing flight operations. The most common hazards include access to the Air Operations Area (AOA), injuries caused by the movement of personnel during the exercise, particularly volunteer "victims" falling off backboards or stretchers, liability issues, vehicle collisions, and the most extreme circumstances, runway incursions.

As part of a full-scale exercise, a security amendment is typically required to cordon off areas of the airfield to be used for the exercise because of the high numbers of noncredentialed volunteers and off-airport responders that will be in the AOA. Additionally, access to the operational areas of the airfield should be restricted using barricades, checkpoints, and specific routes to and from the exercise site, and additional personnel should be assigned to monitor the movement of people and vehicles (FAA, 2010a).

A robust public notification process should also take place to prevent alarming passengers or the nearby community who may see smoke from practice fires or high levels of emergency activity on the airport. Typically, the media can be engaged as part of this public notification process, which can also serve a dual role to exercise the Public Information Officer functions in communicating through various conventional media and social media outlets.

A level of victim training should be conducted to ensure that volunteer victims display the proper behaviors and know the limitations of those behaviors. A system needs to be in place to determine if an injury is a simulated injury or an actual injury requiring a stoppage of play and how to respond to actual medical emergencies. Oftentimes, victims suffer from heat stroke, dehydration, or other ailments while performing their voluntary victim role. It is also important to train victims to display the appropriate behaviors for the injury they are simulating but also to not "take things too far," to the point where first responders may be injured by their behavior.

While the concept of conducting a full-scale exercise and simulating a plane crash every 3 years may seem to make sense, the disadvantage of this requirement is that airport operators rarely test other elements of their AEP, such as structural fire response, HAZMAT spills, natural disaster response, fuel farm fire, or other elements of an aircraft crash beyond the response phase. Also, 3 years is far too long between exercises to maintain proficiency.

Airports should conduct additional exercises, drills, and training, as identified through a Training and Exercise Planning Workshop (TEPW) and should go beyond the FAA standard of compliance by embracing and using FEMA's Homeland Security Exercise and Evaluation Program (HSEEP).

Homeland Security Exercise and Evaluation Program and the Training and Exercise Planning Workshop

The HSEEP provides a set of guiding principles for exercise programs, as well as a common approach to exercise program management, design and development, conduct, evaluation, and improvement planning (FEMA, 2015). HSEEP exercise and evaluation doctrine is flexible, adaptable, for use by stakeholders across the whole community, and applicable for exercises across all mission areas—prevention, protection, mitigation, response, and recovery.

Significant advances have been made in the field of emergency management since 9/11 and Hurricane Katrina. The FEMA has revised many Incident Command procedures, protocols, and documents and has created a substantial body of knowledge about the domain. Although the aviation industry has been slow to adopt these practices, several airport operators have led the way by deciding that mere compliance with the regulation does not adequately prepare their airport for real emergencies. Furthermore, several airport operators have decided that conducting an annual TTX, along with a full scale every 3 years, is just a "regulatory check in the box" and does not reflect the actual emergency management needs of an airport.

FEMA suggests that government agencies decide what drills, exercises, and training to conduct through the development of a Training and Exercise Plan (TEP), which is created through a TEPW. The workshop is typically a 1- or 2-day event where the agencies having responsibilities in the AEP get together to determine capabilities and shortfalls, in all areas of both the AEP and the Airport Security Program. A TEPW user guide, published by FEMA, provides guidance to organizations in conducting an annual TEPW and developing a multiyear TEP in line with the HSEEP.

The TEPW guides elected and appointed officials and responders to identify and set exercise program priorities, by developing a multiyear schedule of training and exercise events to meet those priorities. Stakeholders draw on jurisdiction-specific threats and hazards, identify areas for improvement, and determine core capabilities and external requirements and accreditation standards or regulations to develop or update the multiyear TEP. The TEPW establishes the strategy and structure for an exercise program and sets the foundation for the planning, conduct, and evaluation of individual exercises, rather than setting arbitrary objectives, like a full-scale plane crash every 3 years.

The TEPW identifies potential future exercises, such as the drills, functional, tabletop, and full-scale exercises, identifies training opportunities for training requirements that must be met, and often maximizes the exercises to address the regulatory requirements of not only the FAA but also the TSA or other federal, tribal, state, or local exercise requirements. The effectiveness of a TEPW is in setting the core capabilities and objectives, and then creating a plan of action with deadlines to achieve the specific goals and objectives to work toward meeting the desired standards.

HSEEP provides significant guidance on exercise design and development that is based on core capabilities such as Operational Coordination, Communications, Public Information and Warning, Planning, Forensics and Attribution, and Intelligence and Information Sharing, among others. A complete list can be found at www.fema.gov. Exercise facilitators should be trained in the use of HSEEP to ensure that the exercises are properly conducted. FEMA provides extensive online and live-classroom training opportunities, and many police and fire agencies also provide such training.

AIRPORT EMERGENCY PLAN: THE BASIC PLAN

Although the Airport Certification Manual (ACM) and the AEP may be physically separate documents, the AEP is considered to be part of the ACM. Like the ACM, the FAA must approve the AEP and any amendments using the same amendment process as the ACM. The Basic Plan provides an overview of the airport's approach to emergency operations. The Basic Plan generally defines policies, describes the responsibilities of the various organizations, and assigns key tasks. It establishes the authority of the airport to conduct emergency operations and describes the scope of the airport's emergency management responsibilities. It is also meant to provide a summary of the entire emergency plan, providing overall perspective but not specific details of each element of the plan. In addition to describing the elements required in an AEP, the AC also describes the process to create the plan and the format of the plan (FAA, 2010a). The AEP should be prefaced with the following six items: promulgation document, signature page, dated title page, record of changes, record of distribution, and table of contents.

The **Promulgation Document** is a letter signed by the airport sponsor that provides both the authority and the responsibility for the various organizations, including the airport management team, to perform the required emergency management tasks (FAA, 2010a). Depending on the contents of the letter, the document may also assign the responsibility to prepare and maintain SOPs, commit to training and exercise requirements, and commit to maintaining the emergency plan.

For major incidents, airport operators must rely on local community support Memorandums of Understanding (MOUs), Memorandums of Agreement (MOAs), and Letters of Agreement (LOAs). However, airports must guard against their own resources being used for all-local response. It is an unfortunate and unfair balance but a necessary one, that airport operators must ensure, to the extent possible, that adequate ARFF resources remain onsite to respond to airport emergencies.

The promulgation document may be used to provide general guidance about the airport operator's role during an off-airport accident. While the FAA requires an Aircraft Accident/incident response plan to be in place for on-airport incidents, it does not have specific requirements for an off-airport incident. Under the Robert T. Stafford Disaster Relief and Emergency Assistance Act, P.L. 93-288, the local jurisdiction is responsible for handling emergency events within its boundaries, including airplane accidents and incidents. In some cases, the airport may lie within the jurisdictional boundaries of the city or county in which the incident occurred, and policymakers may naturally assume that the airport is responsible for responding to any incident within the boundaries of the municipality. However, the FAA is stringent about meeting the Aircraft Rescue and Firefighting requirements for the airport during commercial operations. The FAA is hesitant to allow aircraft firefighting equipment and personnel offsite if doing so would drop the airport's ARFF Index and ability to respond to an onsite incident, regardless of the jurisdiction in which the accident/incident took place.

There are some instances when it makes sense to respond nonetheless, such as when the accident occurs a few hundred feet or a few hundred yards from the airport perimeter. Many airport operators establish a distance that airport fire and rescue equipment will respond away from the airport, with typical limits being 1 mile, out to a maximum of 5 miles. Other airport operators do not specify a distance but allow the Airport Operations Manager on duty to use personal judgment to make a decision about whether to dispatch airport fire trucks to an off-airport incident.

In an instance when a large, commercial service aircraft, either departing or arriving to the airport, crashes well away from the airport, the airport operator commonly sends an operations manager, Fire Chief, or other related support personnel to secure the accident scene and advise local fire and EMS personnel on responding to a large aircraft crash. First responders who are unfamiliar with aircraft operations often need assistance from individuals who do have such expertise, particularly in handling the accident scene, dealing with family members of victims, and the arrival of the NTSB investigation team.

A **Signature Page** contains the signatures of the league representatives of each agency with responsibilities under the plan, thus providing a legal obligation to support the AEP (FAA, 2010a). The signature page might also help fulfill the coordination requirements established under Part 139.325.

A **Dated Title Page** shows the date of the publication and its most recent revision.

A **Record of Changes** can be a chart with the number assigned to any change, a brief description of the change, and the signature or initials of the persons responsible for including the change in their organization's copy of the AEP (FAA, 2010a). Many airports now distribute the AEP electronically, so any method used to update the AEP electronically must be described within the plan.

A **Record of Distribution** is used to provide evidence that the individuals and organizations with responsibilities under the AEP have reviewed the AEP and understand their responsibilities (FAA, 2010a). Copies of the AEP should be numbered, showing a date of transmittal and a date of receipt by the agency or entity.

Prior to 9/11, AEPs were public documents, and by and large still are, as opposed to the Airport Security Program, which is considered SSI. A non-SSI AEP is more easily accessible by off-airport responders and makes management and distribution of the emergency plan much easier. The availability of the plan is based on the premise that during an emergency it is better to have access to all those available that can help. However, within the AEP are two sections that speak directly to security incidents, the *bomb threat and management* section and the *sabotage or other unlawful acts of interference with operations* section. Publicly available security response plans are not in the best interest in securing of the airport or the aircraft operator.

Part 139.325(i) states:

> Each airport subject to applicable FAA and Transportation Security Administration security regulations must ensure that instructions for response to paragraphs (b)(2) and (b)(7) of this section in the Airport Emergency Plan are consistent with its approved Airport Security Program.

The TSA requires the *bomb threat* and *unlawful interference* incident management plans to be considered SSI. However, under the rules of applying SSI, if only one page of a document is considered SSI, then the entire document must be considered SSI. Therefore, if the airport operator designates those two incident plans within their AEP, then the entire AEP becomes SSI. This classification makes distribution of the AEP much more difficult and potentially places the airport in a position to be fined by the TSA for failing to control SSI.

Some airport operators have moved forward to classify their entire AEP as SSI; however, this practice makes it more difficult for off-airport responders to understand their roles and responsibilities during an aircraft crash. To compensate for this lack of information to off-airport agencies, particularly those with MOUs or LOAs that articulate commitments to the airport during an accident or incident, extensive training and exercises should be conducted to better familiarize offsite personnel with their responsibilities.

Another option is much simpler as both the TSA and FAA allow for the security incident management sections of the AEP to be extracted from the AEP and placed in the Airport Security Program (ASP). The FAA only requires that within the AEP, the airport operator make reference that these procedures are available in the ASP. In this way the AEP can be maintained as a publicly accessible document, while the security-sensitive response procedures are protected under the ASP's SSI designation.

A **Table of Contents** makes it easier to find information and provides a brief overview of the document (FAA, 2010a). An electronic version of the AEP may also have the table of contents hyperlinked, which makes the retrieval of information even quicker. That said, it is unusual for anyone to have time to break out the AEP during an actual emergency at least for the first 30 to 60 minutes of the incident. However, when the plan must be referenced, efforts should be made to make this essential information readily accessible.

ADMINISTRATIVE ELEMENTS

The Basic Plan contains a description of the elements that are covered again in the Functional Annexes, along with an overview of the basic responsibilities for the key responders (Figure 10.3). The final key elements of the Basic Plan include:

1. **Purpose:** This statement within the Basic Plan describes what the AEP is meant to do.
2. **Situation and Assumptions:** This portion describes the hazards that AEP addresses, along with general assumptions (such as there will be confusion among passengers or there will be passengers with functional needs).
3. **Operations:** This section addresses the overall Concept of Operations (CONOPS) related to how each emergency situation will be approached.
4. **Organization and Assignment of Responsibilities:** This portion describes which agencies are to perform which tasks, without procedural details, which are usually covered in the hazard-specific section.
5. **Administration and Logistics:** This section addresses general support items such as mutual aid agreements, policies on record keeping, and resource tracking.
6. **Plan Development and Maintenance:** This portion addresses when to review the AEP, as well as when to conduct training, drills, and exercises, which should be covered in the FEMA-based TEP.
7. **Authorities and References:** This section provides the legal basis for emergency operations and lists formal agreements, laws, statutes, regulations, or ordinances, along with local emergency operations plans or other references that were used in the development of the plan.

The Administration and Logistics Section of the Basic Plan addresses the availability and support for all types of emergencies, contains the general policies for managing, reporting, and tracking resources, provides policies on issues such as staff augmentation and reassignment of public employees to conduct emergency operations, and describes the airport's financial record-keeping practices (FAA, 2010a).

The AEP must be reviewed at least once a year, specifically, every 12 consecutive calendar months. The review must ensure that all telephone numbers are up-to-date, radio frequencies have been tested, emergency resources have been routinely inspected, personnel assignments and training is up-to-date, and mutual aid agreements are still able to be fulfilled by off-airport agencies. Also, as training, drills, and exercises are conducted, a documented feedback loop should be in place to demonstrate where lessons learned were incorporated into the AEP.

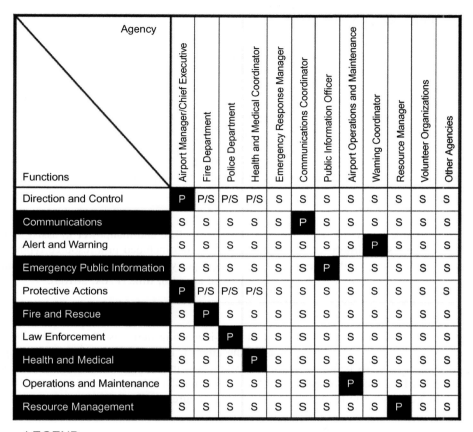

Functions	Airport Manager/Chief Executive	Fire Department	Police Department	Health and Medical Coordinator	Emergency Response Manager	Communications Coordinator	Public Information Officer	Airport Operations and Maintenance	Warning Coordinator	Resource Manager	Volunteer Organizations	Other Agencies
Direction and Control	P	P/S	P/S	P/S	S	S	S	S	S	S	S	S
Communications	S	S	S	S	S	P	S	S	S	S	S	S
Alert and Warning	S	S	S	S	S	S	S	S	P	S	S	S
Emergency Public Information	S	S	S	S	S	S	P	S	S	S	S	S
Protective Actions	P	P/S	P/S	P/S	S	S	S	S	S	S	S	S
Fire and Rescue	S	P	S	S	S	S	S	S	S	S	S	S
Law Enforcement	S	S	P	S	S	S	S	S	S	S	S	S
Health and Medical	S	S	S	P	S	S	S	S	S	S	S	S
Operations and Maintenance	S	S	S	S	S	S	S	P	S	S	S	S
Resource Management	S	S	S	S	S	S	S	S	S	P	S	S

LEGEND

P : Primary Responsibility

S : Support Responsibility

P/S : One of these may be in charge, depending on the nature and scope of emergency

FIGURE 10.3 Emergency response organization matrix.

Source: FAA, 2010a.

CORE FUNCTIONS OF RESPONSE AGENCIES

The core functions of each agency with responsibilities under the AEP are outlined both in the Basic Plan and in the Functional Annexes. Generally speaking, the responsibilities are as described in the following sections.

Airport Authority/Management

The airport operator is responsible for response and recovery operations. During response, the immediate priority is to assess and mitigate existing or potential threats to the safety of life and property. AC 150/5200-31C (FAA, 2010a) notes that the Fire Chief will be the IC, but as previously discussed, the industry is slowly recognizing the professionalism and capability of professional emergency managers, who may be in a better position to serve as an IC, thereby allowing the Fire Chief to focus on lifesaving operations. The AC was drafted several years before this trend when there was the natural assumption that the Fire Chief knew best how to manage an incident, and there was a distinct lack of certified emergency managers at airports.

The airport operator is also responsible for maintaining the AEP, closing the airport when necessary, and issuing Notices to Airmen (NOTAMs) about the condition of the airport.

Airport Tenants[10]

Tenants may be able to provide equipment, facilities, supplies, and manpower to assist in an emergency. The resources of airport tenants should be typed and included in a resource typing list, and any legal issues relating to the use of the tenant's property or personnel, including the safety of their personnel during a response, should be addressed ahead of time (FAA, 2010a).

Animal Care/Control

Animals are carried on commercial aircraft in ever-increasing numbers. Previously, most animals were shipped as cargo in pressurized areas of the aircraft, but the industry is seeing a significant trend toward more animals being carried in the cabin. It is important to include animal care professionals in the AEP to provide assistance and care for animal victims of an emergency and also the removal and care of wildlife involved in a collision with aircraft (FAA, 2010a).

Clergy

The primary mission of clergy during an incident is to provide comfort to casualties and relatives (FAA, 2010a). There is a rather long history of Aircraft Accidents where clergy have responded to the airport after seeing the accident or hearing about it in the media. Other agencies such as the airlines, the Red Cross, or the NTSB may also have made arrangements for clergy to be present. Unfortunately, some members of the general public or even the media may try to pose as clergy in order to access the accident site or the families of the victims' assistance center. The airport should implement a system to vet incoming clergy so that those who are truly clergy and are truly there to help can provide aid and comfort.

Coast Guard/Harbor Patrol

For airports located near bodies of water, the Coast Guard or local harbor patrol agencies can provide SAR services (FAA, 2010a).

---

[10]The role of the air carrier is significant in the response to an airline accident, but their responsibilities are addressed in Chapter 12, Air Carrier or Aircraft Owner/Operator section.

Communications Services

Communications are essential during any incident; thus, all private and public service agencies and the personnel, equipment, and facilities they can use to augment the airport's communication capabilities should be identified. Coordination should be conducted ahead of time to establish and identify the communication protocols, utilization of frequencies for emergency conditions, and repair capabilities for emergency conditions (FAA, 2010a). Drills are highly recommended for testing the interoperability of communications systems, deconflicting frequencies, and establishing radio networks or nets.

Coroner

The coroner is responsible for identifying bodies, reconciling personal belongings, and conducting related investigative activities (FAA, 2010a).

Emergency Management Agencies

These agencies include local, regional, and state emergency-planning agencies that the airport considers to have specific roles and responsibilities during regional disasters or national defense (FAA, 2010a).

Emergency Medical Services

EMS personnel provide medical services during an emergency including triage, initial trauma treatment and Basic Medical Care, patient stabilization and preparation for transport, and transport to hospitals or other medical facilities (FAA, 2010a). Unfortunately, the trend of urgent care–type facilities, so widely popular for most routine medical issues, has not yet been accepted into the AEP system. Several industry professionals, including firefighters and hospital and EMS personnel, have expressed the desire to include some of the urgent care facilities into the plan to receive certain personnel who have been injured in an airplane crash.

State or Local Environmental Agency

This agency responds and supports efforts to protect the environment from HAZMAT, including air cargo and fuel spills that may occur during an accident. The airport operator is used to primarily deal with fuel or oil spills as the primary form of HAZMAT; however, commercial aircraft carry a variety of HAZMAT substances, which may be released from their containment during an Aircraft Accident (FAA, 2010a).

Explosive Ordnance Disposal

Explosive Ordnance Disposal (EOD) personnel are called on as needed to handle potential Improvised Explosive Devices (IEDs).

Federal Aviation Administration

Personnel from the FAA Airport District Office are also trained as accident investigators. FAA personnel provide investigative services or support to the NTSB, as well as to ensure regulatory compliance.

Federal Bureau of Investigation

Regardless of cause, FBI personnel respond to major Aircraft Accidents. At one point, a directive went to local FBI offices that placed an assumption that all Aircraft Accidents are presumed to be caused by criminal or terrorist activity, unless or until otherwise determined, giving FBI the option of taking over Incident Command. However, the FBI has always had this option, and many FBI agents assigned to airports have an understanding with the airport operator that unless there is a substantial reason to believe that the accident was caused by sabotage or other criminal or terrorist activity, the FBI will allow the airport or the fire department to retain Incident Command authority, at least for the initial stages of the response (rescuing passengers, putting out the fire, triage, etc.). From an investigatory perspective, the FBI is required to take the lead (over NTSB) in any accident investigation in a criminal aviation disaster. Once the FBI has been notified, the agency deploys a "fly-team," which consists of an Investigator-in-Charge (IIC), along with other personnel who are on 24-hour alert (FBI, 2010). The Office for Victim Assistance (OVA) will also arrive on scene and establish a Family Assistance Center (FAC) to support family members of victims and a Joint Family Support Operations Center (JFSOC), which coordinates efforts among various federal agencies and local government emergency service providers (FBI, 2010).

Aircraft Rescue and Firefighting

These agents provide fire and rescue services.

Government Authorities

The roles and responsibilities of other government agencies with collateral, supporting, or secondary duties must also be addressed in the AEP to avoid conflict and confusion among agencies.

Hazardous Material Response Team

This team responds to HAZMAT emergencies.

Health and Medical Personnel

These personnel coordinate planning, response, and recovery efforts among local hospitals, EMS, fire and police departments, American Red Cross, the airport operator, and other agencies (FAA, 2010a).

Hospital(s)

Hospitals coordinate the hospital disaster plan with the airport and community emergency operations plans (FAA, 2010a).

Mental Health Agencies

These agencies provide mental health services for survivors, relatives, eyewitnesses, and responders to help deal with the effects of the emergency.

Military/National Guard

If the military is on or near the airport, military personnel support the AEP with personnel, supplies, and equipment. In some cases, such as at joint- or shared-use airports, the military is the primary responder.

Mutual Aid Agencies

These agencies support mutual aid agreements.

National Weather Service

The National Weather Service provides weather reporting and early alert of severe weather conditions.

National Transportation Safety Board

The NTSB conducts and controls all accident investigations involving civil aircraft, or civil and military aircraft, within the United States, its territories, and possessions. The NTSB is an independent federal agency, charged by Congress to investigate transportation accidents, including aviation-related accidents, to determine the probable cause and to make safety recommendations (Sumwalt & Dalton, n.d.). The NTSB is not a rule-making agency, nor does it determine fault or liability. However, the agency does track the status of its recommendations, with periodic follow-up required on those that have not been implemented (Sumwalt & Dalton, n.d.).

The NTSB has investigators stationed throughout the United States, and when an Aircraft Accident occurs, the airport operator (or local jurisdiction where the accident happened) notifies the NTSB, and an investigator is dispatched. For large-Aircraft Accidents, the Go-Team is launched from Washington, DC. The team numbers from two to four members, along with specialists from a variety of fields. For an Aircraft Accident, these specialties are **Operations** (history of the flight and crew members' duties prior to the accident); **Structures** (airframe wreckage, impact angles, preimpact course); **Power plants** (engines, propellers); **Systems** (hydraulic, electrical, pneumatic, and other flight control systems); **ATC** (reconstruction of ATC services, radar and radio transcripts); **Weather** (from National Weather Service and sometimes local TV); **Human Performance** (crew performance prior to the accident, such as medication, fatigue, alcohol, drugs, training, workload, equipment design, and work environment); **Survival Factors** (impact forces and injuries, evacuation, emergency equipment, community emergency planning, and all crash-fire-rescue incidents) (NTSB, n.d.). It is in the area of survival factors that the airport operator has the most influence on the outcome of an airplane accident.

The NTSB IIC assumes authority of the investigation once on site and retains the authority until relieved or authority is transferred to the FBI, the FAA, local police or fire investigators, or the airport operator. The NTSB may also delegate some accident investigations, typically nonfatal accidents in small aircraft, to the FAA. The NTSB publishes a guide[11] for police and public-safety personnel who respond to a transportation accident.

---

[11]National Transportation Safety Board. (n.d.). *Responding to a transportation accident*. Retrieved from: http://www.ntsb.gov/tda/TDADocuments/SPC0402.pdf.

The NTSB **Transportation Disaster Assistance Division (TDA)** provides information and assistance for family members and friends of accident victims and survivors in the immediate aftermath of an accident (NTSB, 2015). The TDA continues to provide information and support months and years later and tracks anniversaries or memorials related to the event, notifying the victims' family members.

Police/Security

Police/security provide the services of law enforcement and security, control access to the accident scene, direct traffic, and protect facilities, such as the FAC.

U.S. Post Office

The U.S. Post Office ensures the security of the mail, protects postal property, and restores service (FAA, 2010a).

Public Information/Media

Public Information/Media personnel gathers, coordinates, and releases factual information to the public, by way of various media outlets, such as traditional and social media.

Public Works/Engineering

Public Works/Engineering manages and directs public works resources and operations, including road and airfield maintenance, debris and trash removal, restoration of airfield lighting, and repair of signs and marking. It also provides essential services such as power, gas, water, and lavatory services to the scene and, if necessary, shuts down utilities (FAA, 2010a).

American Red Cross

The American Red Cross provides support services to victims, their families, and emergency responders. After the passage of the Aviation Disaster Family Assistance Act in 1996, which assigned the NTSB the responsibility of overseeing support services to families of passengers in commercial aviation disasters, the NTSB tasked the American Red Cross to coordinate emotional support services to those involved in airline crashes (Bowenkamp, 1999). The **Aviation Incident Response (AIR)** team of the Red Cross maintains the ability to travel anywhere in the United States within 4 hours of an airline incident. This team works with local clergy, local Red Cross personnel, and others to meet the needs of families, ensuring they have a private area in which to grieve, to await information about the crash, and to aid in the identification of loved ones (Bowenkamp, 1999). An airliner crash typically draws an outpouring of volunteers who wish to help; however, volunteers can quickly overwhelm response agencies. The Red Cross establishes a Staff Processing Center (SPC) to inspect the licenses and credentials of all volunteer and paid staff and to screen individuals for appropriate assignments. The Red Cross continues to work with response agencies as part of a Critical Incident Stress Management program (Bowenkamp, 1999).

Search and Rescue

This team provides SAR services usually for off-airport aircraft emergencies (FAA, 2010a).

All Tasked Individuals/Organizations

In addition to the above, all other individuals or organizations having responsibilities under the AEP must:

1. Ensure personnel notification rosters are up-to-date;
2. Maintain the capability to perform tasks in accordance with SOPs;
3. Determine resource (equipment, supplies) and communication requirements; and
4. Provide Continuity of Operations including lines of succession, the protection of records, facilities and equipment necessary for conducting and sustaining emergency operations, protect emergency response staff by providing proper clothing and equipment, ensure adequate training, provide security, rotate and provide for the refreshment of staff, and provide stress counseling (FAA, 2010a, p. 35).

SUMMARY

Although data shows that aviation is the safest mode of transportation, accidents still happen. When they do, certificated airports must have in place an AEP that addresses the largest commercial service aircraft serving the airport to the extent possible. The 9/11 terrorist attacks, along with significant natural disasters such as Hurricane Katrina, prompted the federal government to improve not only its own emergency management and response capabilities but also those of all tribal, state, and local organizations with emergency management responsibilities.

Through a series of executive orders and congressional acts, the National Response Framework was developed, promoting a system of comprehensive emergency management. Also, the ICS, which was first developed in the 1970s during California wildfire seasons, was formalized and set forth as a requirement under the NIMS. Airport operators are required to be NIMS trained and be able to implement NIMS effectively to manage a mass casualty incident or event.

Since a major airline crash would rapidly overwhelm the response and limited assets of even a major commercial service airport, the AEP not only must incorporate the use of NIMS but also must rely on off-airport responders, often through articulated MOAs, for additional support.

The AEP is expected to address aircraft crashes as well as a variety of other incidents that may occur on an airport. In all emergencies, the Priorities of Work remain first and foremost life safety and scene stability, followed by protection of property and the environment into the aviation domain and the restoration of aviation activities. AEPs should be developed in collaboration with all agencies having responsibilities within the plan. A risk analysis should be conducted to identify other hazards that could be experienced by the airport. Resources should be typed and classified so they are readily accessible during an incident.

Training on the AEP and conducting numerous exercises are essential to an effective emergency response. The Department of Homeland Security has developed the HSEEP to better help emergency management agencies plan and execute a comprehensive training and exercise program. However, no amount of training or exercises will improve the AEP unless lessons are learned, changes are made to the plans, and personnel are trained on the new procedures and exercises again.

Migrating to Agile Project Management in Exercise Design

by Jason Taussig
Manager of Training and Exercise Design at Denver International Airport

As emergency procedures and policies are developed in the absence of real events, a training and exercise program, if done correctly, is an excellent way to evaluate the emergency program. However, there is a caution. As Dr. Tony Kern notes, "It has long been assumed that when you train someone to do something right you are simultaneously training them not to do it wrong."[12] Effective training and exercise programs must then be able to ensure that the unintended consequences of negative learning and forming poor habits are minimized. As such, we need to ensure our training incorporates the existing plans and procedures and evaluations of the training. A well-developed and managed training and exercise program can provide the ability to combat this error, while providing an opportunity for continuous improvement of the plans and personnel performance. Emergency management personnel should develop the knowledge and abilities necessary to be effective training and exercise program managers.

FEMA provides the HSEEP as the "strategy and structure for an exercise program."[13] While HSEEP does provide an excellent framework, it does so under a more traditional project methodology in the creation of exercises. Life is moving at an ever-increasing pace. Social observers Tom Hayes and Michael Malone[14] have coined the term the "Ten-Year Century" to highlight this rapid changing world we live in. Emergency managers must become flexible and adaptable to the changing world. The systematic 5-year program has significant benefits, but it must be adaptable to the changing world and hazards. To effectively deal with these changes, HSEEP principles can be blended with Agile project methodologies (Wiley Publications, n.d.) to produce a significant benefit to the exercise program. This article looks at the primary advantages of Agile project methodology and how emergency management agencies can take advantage of them within an HSEEP construct. The paper uses a series of exercises at Denver International Airport (DEN) as a case study.

There are vast resources available that explore Agile project management and its variations. Space does not permit an extensive overview, so for the purposes of this article we look at the more significant aspects of Agile methodology. Agile methodology grew out of the software world where there was a significant need to accommodate the fast-paced evolution of the Internet.[15] The focus of Agile is to clarify objectives as you proceed by producing

(Continued)

---

[12]Kern, D. T. (2015). Loss Control Strategies That Work. Annual Aviation Insurance Association Conference, (p. 56 Slides). Retrieved December 14, 2015, from: https://aiaweb.org/PDF/2015AnnualConference/Kern_AIA%20Presentation_copyright %202015.pdf.

[13]Homeland Security. (April 2013). Homeland Security Exercise Evaluation Program (HSEEP) . Homeland Security. Retrieved December 14, 2015, from: https://www.fema.gov/media-library-data/20130726-1914-25045-8890/hseep_apr13_.pdf.

[14]Tom Hayes, M. S. (August 10, 2009). The Ten Year Century: As the Pace of Change Accelerates, Trust Becomes the Vital Currency. *Wall Street Journal*.

[15]ExecutiveBrief Staff. (October 2008). Which Life Cycle is Best for Your Project? Retrieved December 14, 2015, from: http://www.pmhut.com/which-life-cycle-is-best-for-your-project.

(Continued)

iterations rather traditional phases. Documentation becomes flexible, documenting what is necessary, and is focused on the team and the customer. In short, this method works very well in emergency exercise development.

Agile project management requires an empirical control method. This is a process of making decisions based on observed project realities rather than the project schedule defined at the beginning.[16] For this to be effective, the project requires three elements: (1) transparency— where everyone is kept up-to-date; (2) frequent inspection—where everyone invested in the process is able to evaluate the process; and (3) adaptation—where adjustments can be made based on the inspections. To do this effectively, the planning team must closely observe the daily formal and informal meetings with the customers.

This strategy blends nicely with HSEEP. The iterative Agile process correlates well with HSEEP's focus on building-block exercises. The documentation process outlined in HSEEP provides the flexibility for Agile. Finally, the empirical control method fosters the teamwork needed to build successful exercises that add values to the organization. It also ensures that the unintended consequences are accounted for, minimizing the impact of poor training and exercise fatigue.

We see how quickly DEN used this method in designing a series of exercises focused on an active-shooter threat. Extreme violence, such as that produced by active shooters, has been a long-time concern for airports and DEN. However, recent events elevated the risk and renewed an interest in managing the risk. DEN has increased its attention to this subject, and in mid-2014 the exercise staff began to plan for the exercise series.

A review of the literature[17] revealed that during active-shooter events, airports should focus on five significant areas: community resiliency, incident response, people management, command and control, and public communication. These five areas are important in all event phases and may offer the largest improvement opportunities. They became the loose framework for the series of exercises. The exercise team used a technique known as "mind mapping"[18] to further clarify the numbers and types of exercises needed to fully capture the event's complexity. This process allowed the team to further categorize the project into trainings, discussion-based exercises, and operational exercises. The resulting analysis revealed that it would take a minimum of four different trainings, seven discussion-based exercises, and two operational-based exercises.

(Continued)

---

[16]Layton, M. C. (2012). Comparing Agile Project Management and the Traditional Waterfall Method. In M. C. Layton, Agile Project Management for Dummies (pp. http://www.dummies.com/how-to/content/comparing-agile-project-management-and-the-traditi.html). John Wiley & Sons.

[17]FBI Report. (September 2013). A Study of Active Shooter Incidents In the United States Between 2000 and 2013. Retrieved December 14, 2015, from: https://www.fbi.gov/news/stories/2014/september/fbi-releases-study-on-active-shooter-incidents/pdfs/a-study-of-active-shooter-incidents-in-the-u.s.-between-2000-and-2013;

Los Angeles World Airport. (March, 18 2014). Active Shooter Incident and Resulting Airport Disruption: Overview of Response Operations. Retrieved December 14, 2015, from: https://www.lawa.org/uploadedFiles/LAX/LAWA%20T3%20After%20Action%20Report%20March%2018%202014.pdf.

[18]Buzan, T. (2015). About Mind Mapping. Retrieved December 14, 2015, from: http://www.tonybuzan.com/about/mind-mapping/.

(Continued)

To fully accomplish this using traditional sequential project management would have resulted in close to a 7-year project. The team was tasked with accomplishing this in 7 months. Utilizing the Agile methodology the team was able to plan and execute the training that was required and the requisite number of exercises, accommodating changing tactical protocols and identifying improvements during the process that could be incorporated before the exercise series was completed.

The planning team consisted of two full-time employees and about 12 part-time volunteers. The two full-time members facilitated regular formal meetings, but supplemented these with daily informal meetings to ensure the use of the empirical control method.[19]

At the time of this article more than 2,000 people have received training or have taken part in one of the DEN exercises. Currently, the data is being analyzed to offer up the real value associated with this practice, but the anecdotal feedback to this point is that the overall project was a success and the value of shrinking the timeline while not sacrificing quality allowed everyone involved to fully engage in the training and the practice it takes to improve.

In the face of evolving threats, shrinking budgets, and the dynamic nature of the aviation industry, emergency managers must continuously improve their preparedness capabilities and administrative processes. Facing a compressed timeline, the DEN team was able to explore options that used the HSEEP framework while maximizing the flexibility of the Agile project methodologies in a manner that is proving to be successful in emergency management at airports.

REFERENCES

Bowenkamp, C. (1999). The role of the American Red Cross in aviation disasters. *The Internet Journal of Rescue and Disaster Medicine*, *1*(2). http://dx.doi.org/10.5580/1496, available at http://ispub.com/IJRDM/1/2/8296.

Federal Aviation Administration (FAA), Airport Safety Standards. (2010a). AC 150/5200-31C, *Airport emergency plan*. Washington, DC: U.S. Department of Transportation.

Federal Aviation Administration (FAA). (2010b). Part 139 Airport Certification, Washington, DC [Online]. Available: http://www.faa.gov/airports/airport_safety/part139_cert/.

Federal Bureau of Investigation (FBI). (2010, May 21). *Criminal aviation investigations*. Retrieved December 13, 2015, from: https://www.fbi.gov/stats-services/victim_assistance/cid_aviation.

Federal Emergency Management Agency (FEMA). (2015, March 5). Homeland Security Exercise and Evaluation Program. FEMA.gov. Retrieved August 20, 2015, from https://www.fema.gov/media-library/assets/documents/32326.

Federal Emergency Management Agency (FEMA). (2004). *Resource definitions 120 resources (FEMA)*. Washington, DC: FEMA. Retrieved August 19, 2015, from http://www.bceoc.org/resource_typing.pdf.

Federal Emergency Management Agency (FEMA). (1996). *SLG101: Guide for all-hazard emergency operations planning*. Washington, DC: FEMA.

[19]It is a process control model used in Agile project planning.

Federal Emergency Management Agency (FEMA). Homeland Security. Retrieved December 13, 2015, from http://www.dhs.gov/publication/homeland-security-presidential-directive-5.

Federal Emergency Management Agency (FEMA). (n.d.b). Homeland Security. Retrieved December 13, 2015, from http://www.dhs.gov/presidential-policy-directive-8-national-preparedness.

Fowler, D. (2014, July 16). *The dangers of private planes.* Retrieved from http://www.nytimes.com/2014/07/17/opinion/The-Dangers-of-Private-Planes.html.

Gawande, A. (2010). *The checklist manifesto: how to get things right.* New York: Metropolitan Books.

Gonzales, L. (2014). *Flight 232: A story of disaster and survival.* New York: W.W. Norton.

Gresser, E. (2014, July 16). "Traffic accidents kill 1.24 million people a year worldwide; wars and murders, 0.44 million." *Progressive Economy.* Retrieved from http://www.progressive-economy.org/trade_facts/traffic-accidents-kill-1-24-million-people-a-year-worldwide-wars-and-murders-0-44-million/.

Hudson, P. (2013, April 28). *14 Marine Corps traits that translate to your success.* Retrieved from http://elitedaily.com/money/entrepreneurship/14-marine-corps-traits-that-translate-to-your-success/.

LiveLeak. (2009, February 27). *First dramatic moments of DIA (Denver) images/audio.* Retrieved August 16, 2015, from http://www.liveleak.com/view?i = 688_1235775507.

National Transportation Safety Board (NTSB). (2015, August 21). *Information for families, friends and survivors.* Retrieved from http://www.ntsb.gov/tda/family/pages/default.aspx.

National Transportation Safety Board (NTSB). (2014, June 24). *Board meeting: crash of Asiana flight 214 accident report summary.* Retrieved from http://www.ntsb.gov/news/events/Pages/2014_Asiana_BMG-Abstract.aspx.

National Transportation Safety Board (NTSB). (n.d.). *The Investigative Process.* Retrieved August 23, 2015, from http://www.ntsb.gov/investigations/process/pages/default.aspx.

Province, C. (1984). *The unknown Patton.* Bonanza Books.

Roberts, C. (2014, January 31). *SF claims Asiana crash victim was not killed by fire truck.* Retrieved August 16, 2015, from http://www.nbcbayarea.com/news/local/San-Francisco-Claims-Asiana-Victim-Was-Not-Killed-By-Fire-Truck-242850231.html.

The Robert T. Stafford Disaster Relief and Emergency Assistance Act, § PL 100-707 (2013).

SETRAC. (n.d.). *Exercise templates.* Retrieved August 20, 2015, from http://www.rhpc.us/go/doc/4207/1894222/Exercise-Templates.

Sumwalt, R., & Dalton, S. (n.d.). *The NTSB's role in aviation safety.* Retrieved August 21, 2015, from http://www.ntsb.gov/news/speeches/rsumwalt/Documents/Sumwalt_141020.pdf.

Tolan, C., Patterson, T., & Johnson, A. (2015, July 28). *Is 2014 the deadliest year for flights? Not even close.* Retrieved from http://www.cnn.com/interactive/2014/07/travel/aviation-data/.

U.S. Coast Guard (USCG). (2009, September 30). *USCG emergency preparedness liaison officer program.* Retrieved August 19, 2015, from https://www.uscg.mil/directives/ci/3000-3999/CI_3025_1.pdf.

Yan, H., & Marsh, R. (2014, December 30). *Missing plane and air disasters: how bad was 2014?* Retrieved from http://www.cnn.com/2014/12/29/travel/aviation-year-in-review/.

Wiley Publications. (n.d.). Agile Project Management For Dummies. Retrieved December 13, 2015, from <http://www.dummies.com/how-to/content/agile-project-management-for-dummies-cheat-sheet.html>.

AIRPORT EMERGENCY PLANNING, PART II: EMERGENCY MANAGEMENT FUNCTIONS

Airport communications control center Aspen-Pitkin County Regional Airport, CO.

Image by Shahn Sederberg, courtesy Colorado Division of Aeronautics, 2013.

Loading fire retardant on a Conair fire tanker at the U.S. Forest Service tanker base located at Rocky Mountain Metropolitan Airport, CO.

Image by Shahn Sederberg, courtesy Colorado Division of Aeronautics, 2012.

Airport Operations security team.

Courtesy Denver International Airport, CO [date unknown].

In revising Advisory Circular (AC) 150/5200-31C, *Airport Emergency Plan*, the Federal Aviation Administration (FAA) separated functional areas from the hazard-specific sections (FAA, 2010). This separation has created some confusion and more than a few redundancies in the AC. The Functional Section of the Airport Emergency Plan (AEP) is best understood by applying the term *function* literally, rather than connecting the function to a specific agency. The Functional Section addresses the *functions* that must be addressed in virtually *any* emergency, regardless of which individual or agency performs the function. According to the FAA (2010, pp. 37–38) the core functions of an aviation emergency are:

1. Command and control;
2. Communications;
3. Alert Notification and Warning;
4. Emergency Public Information;
5. Protective Actions;
6. Law enforcement/security;
7. Firefighting and rescue;
8. Health and medical;
9. Resource management; and
10. Airport Operations and maintenance.

Although not addressed in the AEP, other functions include: damage assessment, Search and Rescue, incident mitigation and recovery, mass care, and chemical, biological, radiological, nuclear, and high-yield explosive (CBRNE) protection (FAA, 2010, p. 37). Airport operators may wish to address security-related functions more thoroughly in the Airport Security Program (ASP) to protect the sensitive nature of that information.

As in all areas of Airport Operations and emergency management, the resources and staff on hand determine whether on- or off-airport responders, or some mix thereof, will handle these functions. Large, commercial service airports often have enough on-airport personnel, with the expertise and equipment to handle most or all of the core functions, at least for the initial response phase. Small, commercial service airports may have to rely heavily on off-airport personnel, through the use of Memorandums of Understanding (MOUs), and with their own personnel assuming multiple duties. Many Airport Operations and maintenance personnel at small airports are trained in Aircraft Rescue and Firefighting (ARFF), and some in Basic Medical Care or as Emergency Medical Technicians (EMTs).

ESSENTIAL FUNCTIONS FOR EMERGENCY OPERATIONS

The AC on airport emergency planning provides instructions to an airport operator on what should be included in the AEP. Each of the functional areas follows a format of: Purpose, Situation and Assumptions, Operations; Organization and Assignment of Responsibilities; Administration and Logistics; Plan Development and Maintenance; and Reference and Authorities. In this way, it is similar to the Basic Plan. In all the functional areas, sections relating to the Plan Development and Maintenance and Reference and Authorities generally note that the section should identify the responsible parties for keeping this section of the AEP up-to-date and that any references used in building the Functional Section should be noted in the AEP.

While each element of the Functional Sections includes Situations and Assumptions, there are several core situations and assumptions that are related to most every incident. First, it must be recognized that not all emergency situations can be anticipated. Joseph Pfeifer, Chief of Counterterrorism and Emergency Preparedness, Fire Department of New York (FDNY), notes that by its very nature, a crisis is often random, unexpected, and novel, requiring leaders to be prepared for a wide variety of urgent circumstances that demand quick decisions (Pfeifer, 2013, p. 2).

Decisions by leaders in an extreme event can also be challenged by the nature of the event, whether it is a *routine* emergency, or an extreme emergency, falling outside the parameters of what a police officer, firefighter, or Airport Operations officer is accustomed to seeing. Pfeifer classifies three types of extreme events: routine, crisis, and catastrophe. *Routine* emergencies use a single **Incident Commander (IC)** and have hierarchical command and control. One person is in charge and gives orders. In a *crisis*, which requires a multiagency response, the hierarchal structure divides into several leaders, each overseeing their own network, reporting to a central IC. If the incident becomes *catastrophic*, a formation of random networks haphazardly connected with no one central leader controlling the entire incident may form (Pfeifer, 2013, p. 9). It is important for both first responders and policy makers to understand that there will be an element of randomness and that not every situation can be controlled at all times.

Airport emergency management operates on a standard set of assumptions: first, hazards and incidents occur at airports, and for large-scale events outside assistance will likely be needed. Some incidents will have a long duration, several days or even weeks; unforeseen events will occur and the airport must still generate a response. Also, all personnel with responsibilities under the AEP should be knowledgeable and trained in their expected actions to be performed during an actual emergency and ensure that the materials and equipment necessary for the performance of those duties are available and in working order.

Although not typically noted in many AEPs, a realistic assumption should be that not all personnel will be available to respond to an emergency when it occurs, because of variations in staffing levels that occur throughout the day, week, and year. A well-written AEP should account for these variations and have other contingencies and alternate courses of action available. For long-duration incidents, personnel will have to rotate in and out of the command structure and will require relief, refreshment, and rest.

COMMAND AND CONTROL

Command and control is the largest of the Functional Sections, as it addresses many elements of managing an emergency incident and how the National Incident Management System (NIMS) integrates into the airport domain. Homeland Security Presidential Directive-5, *Management of Domestic Incidents*, directed the creation of the NIMS, which provides a template for federal, state, tribal, and local governments, nongovernmental organizations (NGOs), such as the American Red Cross, and private sector organizations to work together to prevent, prepare, respond to, and recover from emergency incidents (FEMA, 2008b).

The FAA argues that **Command and Control** is the most critical element of the emergency management function (FAA, 2010). The purpose of Command and Control is to provide the overall command structure, including a line of succession, and to establish the relationship between the **Emergency Operations Center (EOC)**, which is focused on overall centralized command and control, and the **Incident Command Post (ICP)**[1], which is focused on on-scene command and control. Relationships to outside agencies, such as state, regional, or local emergency management agencies or government structures, may also be part of the overall command structure and should be addressed in the AEP.

While the NIMS is supposed to be integrated into airport emergency management functions, aviation is rather unique compared to its transportation counterparts. In many incidents outside the aviation domain, such as in the local community, a standard, on-scene, single IC system is used, supported by emergency dispatchers and without the involvement of the local or regional EOC. The EOC is only activated for large-scale events when the on-scene assets are overwhelmed or when larger portions of the community are involved.

Many airports, however, have EOCs and communications and dispatch centers onsite. The EOCs get activated for most airport emergencies, and even some nonemergencies, such as snow removal, or for special events. Since an airport EOC is at the airport where most of the airport incidents occur, it is physically closer to the actual incident, and it is not unusual for the IC to be located in the EOC, using CCTV (closed circuit television) cameras or eyes on the incident (literally looking out the window of the EOC to the incident on the airfield) to direct and control operations. This model challenges a longstanding principle that the IC is always literally on-scene and thus in the best position to make decisions about how to manage the incident. While many airport operators easily make the distinction, off-airport personnel, mutual aid agencies, and those newly assigned to the airport that have come from other, more traditional command structures may have some adjustments to make. Frequent exercises and training with off-airport personnel can

---

[1]In emergency management, the terms Incident Command Post (ICP) and Incident Command Center (ICC) are often interchangeable.

help them better acclimate to the aviation structure, as airports bounce back and forth between *IC on-scene* and *IC in the EOC* structures. Airports have been known to use a blended structure, with the IC on-scene, and an EOC commander in the EOC. To avoid confusion, the EOC commander should be designated as a **Deputy IC.**

For a large-scale incident, the IC is almost always, initially, *on-scene.* Incident Command is established by the first responder on-scene until relieved by either a superior officer from the first responder's own organization or the first responding entity that has responsibility over the incident according to the line of succession. For example, Airport Operations officers are commonly first on-scene for an aircraft incident as they are typically in the airfield conducting their continuous self-inspections and other airfield related duties. Upon arrival at the incident scene, the Airport Operations officer will assume Incident Command and broadcast such over the airport's communication system. Regardless of the experience level of the first arriving officer or individual in the line of succession, that individual is in command until properly relieved. If the line of succession said that the first in command is airport fire, followed by airport police, then either the firefighting agency or the police department will take over Incident Command from the Airport Operations officer upon their arrival.

It is important to note that "in command" does not necessarily mean in an operating capacity to alleviate the problem. No one expects an Airport Operations officer, without the proper equipment and training, to run into the burning fuselage of an airplane. If an Airport Operations officer does not have firefighting responsibilities, training, or equipment, then their command function is to establish themselves as the IC (for now), set up an Incident Command Post, and ensure responding agencies are notified to the location of the incident and advised on accessible routes, if possible. The IC then ensures overall scene safety and security to the extent possible. Additionally, in some instances, such as an active shooter, any unarmed individual, including Airport Operations personnel, are usually advised to avoid the area entirely, to run away, or seek shelter, if necessary, until the shooter is neutralized. As additional units arrive, the Airport Operations person may retain IC duties, or IC duties may switch to then-appropriate personnel, based on the incident type, such as having ARFF personnel as Incident Command for an airplane crash, whereas airport police would serve as initial Incident Command for a sabotage, hijack, or bomb threat incident.

All those having command responsibilities under the AEP are listed in the Command and Control[2] section, along with key supporting agencies. The core responsibilities of each organization are:

1. **Chief Executive/Airport Manager:** Activates the EOC and provides overall direction of response and recovery operations, designating an IC as appropriate.
2. **ARFF:** Responds to the scene, establishes an ICP, and performs Incident Command duties as necessary. Conducts firefighting operations, handles hazardous materials, scene safety, and evacuation.
3. **Law Enforcement:** Responds to incidents and provides law enforcement services, including scene security, traffic control, and assists with evacuation. For security-related incidents, acts as the Incident Command, establishing an ICP and assigning personnel, as appropriate.

---

[2]Some early versions of the AEP AC referred to this section as Direction and Control, terms that are still used in some AEPs.

4. **Public Works:** Responds to incidents, as appropriate, directs public work operations, including debris collection and removal, provides damage assessments, as related to damage to public utilities, and provides emergency power generators with fuel, emergency lighting, and sanitation to emergency responders.
5. **Public Information Officer:** In addition to reporting to the EOC if necessary, handles all media functions.
6. **Health and Medical Coordinator:** Sends a representative to the EOC, if required, coordinates health and medical assistance, and provides critical stress-management counseling.
7. **Communications Coordinator:** Supports communication operations of the EOC.
8. **Animal Care and Control Agency:** May be required to send a representative to the EOC and is responsible for the rescuing and capture of animals that have escaped from confinement on the aircraft, providing care for injured, sick, and stray animals, and disposal of deceased animals.

The local coroner's office, National Transportation Safety Board (NTSB), Federal Bureau of Investigation (FBI), and the American Red Cross are also often included in the command and control section. Command and control and the NIMS are addressed later in the Command and Control and NIMS sections.

COMMUNICATIONS

Communication is a critical element in the ability to command resources and manage an incident. In addition to the day-to-day communications necessary to operate the airport, including police, fire, and emergency medical service (EMS) dispatch, maintenance and Airport Operations personnel, and air traffic control (ATC), any large-scale emergency operation will require communications beyond the normal capacities and equipment of a typical airport (FAA, 2010, p. 50). During an incident, Airport Operations personnel should assume that noise levels will be higher than normal, both on the airfield and in the terminal building; there may be areas on the airport where radios or cell phone coverage is sporadic or nonexistent; and during the emergency, communications equipment will be used for longer than the usual number of hours, resulting in the need for additional backup equipment and a ready supply of batteries. **Reliability** and **interoperability** are critical to the communications function. Reliability is the ability of the communications network or equipment to function when needed. Interoperability allows emergency management personnel to communicate across agencies through phone, text, email, video, or other means.

The Airport Manager must ensure that adequate communications systems are in place for normal and emergency operations. In extraordinary circumstances, such as a wide-scale community disaster, some organizations such as the **Radio Amateur Civil Emergency Service (RACES)** and the **Radio Emergency Associate Communications Team (REACT)** may be available to support emergency communications.

The **Communications Center Coordinator** ensures all necessary communications systems are available with proper redundancy, interoperability, and backups, where necessary. The coordinator also must support media communications and ensure the communications station in the EOC is properly staffed and able to function at full capacity.

An effective communications system should include recording devices with time/date capability, a sufficient number of landlines with both listed and unlisted numbers, and extra cell phones and batteries. Runners should also be assigned to the EOC and the Mobile Command Unit to augment other modes of communication (NFPA, 2013). During a power outage and resulting communications failure, runners are invaluable, as they are often the only means to communicate essential information.

Communications center personnel are also tasked with maintaining a chronological log of events and keeping the IC and other personnel apprised of events and activities related to the incident. AEPs often identify specific communications systems and frequencies to be used and by which agencies, including special radio codes such as discrete codes to notify all those on a frequency of an airplane crash, hijacking, bomb threat, or other incident that should not be broadcast in the clear on unsecure frequencies. All other agencies with emergency management responsibilities under the AEP must keep their communications equipment up-to-date and in working order, and the agencies must report to airport management any changes in procedures or personnel.

A core operating principle in the communications function is the ability for response agencies to be notified when there is an aircraft or other airport emergency. The emergency communications system explains how personnel are notified of an airplane or airport emergency, along with daily testing requirements of alarm equipment. Most notifications of an airplane emergency come first to the air traffic control tower (ATCT), which then activates a *crash phone* or similar alert system, to notify airport fire and operations personnel (Figure 11.1). However, the ATCT is not always aware an Aircraft Accident has occurred, and other situations necessitate a callout of fire, police, and other response personnel, so the notification system must address when an agency other than the ATCT becomes aware of an incident and how each agency will activate the crash alarm or emergency response process. Usually this is a call to Airport Operations, which can then activate the crash phone or alert system. According to the NFPA (2013), the following agencies should be immediately notified by alarm of an aircraft emergency: airport ARFF, airport police, medical service providers, and the airport operator. Additional agencies should be notified via telephone, or automated notification system, as needed.

Airport Operations personnel, in consultation with the Fire Chief, ATC, and sometimes the pilot, often determine the level of alert status. These functions cross over into the next functional area, Alert Notification and Warning.

ALERT NOTIFICATION AND WARNING

During an emergency, airport management must have a system in place to alert the public and to advise them on the actions to take, and also to alert first responders that an incident to which they should respond has occurred. Usually it is the job of the Communications Section to notify response agencies, tenants, and the public of any incidents or threats to the airport and to notify the public agencies, usually through the Public Information Officer (PIO), of what actions to take.

Airport operators must identify in their AEP methods and procedures to notify emergency response personnel and the airport population, including passengers, visitors, vendors, contractors, and tenants. Notifications to personnel on the airfield, particularly of inclement weather, such as tornadoes and lightning, are important and can be challenging because of the high noise levels on the airfield. Tornado sirens may not be heard over the noise of aircraft engines as planes start up, taxi, takeoff, and land. Some airports initiate a ringdown to their major tenants, who can then use their agency radios, or personnel, to communicate to those working in the Air Operations Area (AOA) of a hazard and of the appropriate actions to take.

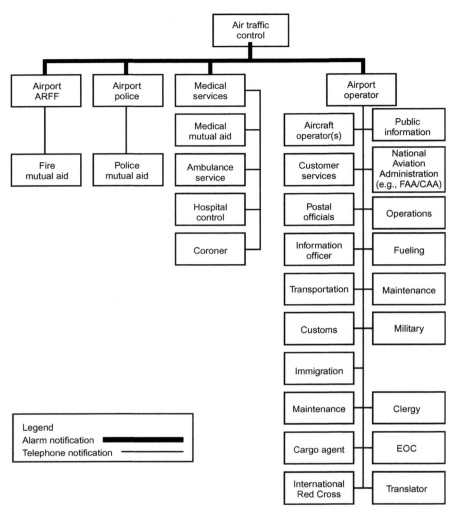

FIGURE 11.1

Sample incident notification chart.

Source: NFPA, 2013.

Inside the terminal, announcements compete for the public's attention; visitors to the airport are bombarded by gate announcements, paging announcements, and the endless warnings not to leave a bag unattended and to report suspicious persons to airport police. Airport management personnel must be aware that many passengers ignore announcements, requiring messages to be repeated, often several times, before the message begins to "sink in" (FAA, 2010, p. 54). Also, some passengers may have functional needs or may be unable to hear or understand the language. Airports can use a warning tone, similar to the FEMA Emergency Broadcast System tones used on local TVs, to capture the public's attention, along with Visual Paging systems. Airports with Ambassador programs have the ability to notify their Ambassadors, who can spread the word.

Airport paging systems should also have the ability to override any other public address systems in case of emergency. Elderly passengers, as well as some with functional needs, must be advised of evacuation routes or routes to shelter that are accessible by individuals with difficulty accessing stairs or escalators.

Emergency response personnel must also be notified during an airport incident or natural disaster. If the crash occurred at an airport with a control tower or an ARFF station, a ringdown line is used to notify the first responders. At the crudest level, notifications of emergency response personnel can be done through a notification list and a telephone. It is essential that the telephone list is always kept up-to-date, listing the primary point of contact, alternate point of contact, accurate phone numbers and emails, and whether the point of contact's phone can receive text messages. Most large- and medium-size airports have adopted automated notification and messaging systems, which can provide situational information to personnel via their phone or tablet. Similar to text alerts that individuals receive on their cell phones from The Weather Channel and other apps about the status and location of severe weather, automated notification systems provide a variety of services to an airport operator (Everbridge, 2015), including:

1. Automatic messaging during severe weather;
2. The ability to send messages in multiple formats and to multiple platforms (phone, tablet, text, etc.);
3. Immediate mass population notification allowing all response personnel to receive the information simultaneously, rather than when they are reached on the callout or phone-tree list;
4. Geographic information system (GIS) mapping noting the precise location of the incident or weather event;
5. Secure communications;
6. Verification of receipt of message.

Critical communications software reduces human error by ensuring the message that goes out is the same message to all parties and that the message has not been interpreted or paraphrased (Everbridge, 2015). Not only is uniformity of messaging important for incident response, but it also helps to defend legal claims after the fact.

The **Airport Manager** must also draft contingency plans to provide an alert and warning if the established communications systems fail to work, which can occur during natural disasters with the power grid offline and cell towers out of service. Backup plans usually include direct communication to Airport Operations, police, and maintenance personnel, who *spread the word* verbally. Transportation Security Administration (TSA) Transportation Security Officer personnel can also be extremely helpful in this capacity as all passenger traffic filters through the checkpoints and exit lanes.

Although the AEP AC does not specify a role for the Communications Center Coordinator under the Alert Notification and Warning section, it is usually communications center personnel who are directly responsible for carrying out the alert and notification functions. The Communications Center Coordinator should ensure that call lists and/or critical communications software are up-to-date and that all personnel know the conditions for activating various warnings and alerts.

Any other agencies with AEP responsibilities notify volunteers and other employees who may be part of a Community Emergency Response Team (CERT)[3] team or other internal response team to report to their duty stations and, if appropriate, send home nonessential personnel (or order to shelter-in-place) or recall essential personnel and determine whether to suspend normal business operations.

Airport grid maps should also be developed and used by all response personnel (Figure 11.2). Grid maps are helpful for on-airport responders who may have a difficult time deciphering airport-related signs and markings during an emergency, but are essential for off-airport responders. To provide an example, during an emergency, most off-airport (and some on-airport) responders would not know where the intersection of Charlie Four and Runway Three-Five Right is, but they can all look at a grid map and figure out where "B-4" is.

EMERGENCY PUBLIC NOTIFICATION

The Emergency Public Information section within the AEP AC has crossover with the Alert Notification and Warning and the Communications Sections, but more specifically addresses notifications to the community outside of the airport. The AEP must describe the methods used by the airport to notify the community at-large of an issue, emergency, or situation occurring at the airport that could affect the community or the operation of the airport. For most emergencies, the **Emergency Public Information (EPI)** organization (within the airport, it is usually the communications center) will initially focus on the dissemination of information to the public who are at-risk on the airport property (FAA, 2010), then to those outside its borders.

Prior to the advent of social media, the only means of addressing the public was through the mass communications abilities of the media. Social media now allows the airport to directly communicate with the populace, but social media also allows everyone else a community, or even worldwide, audience. This can cause confusion as passengers and others involved in or witnessing an event at the airport tweet, text, email, and post YouTube clips (often without context) of what they are seeing. During the November 1st active shooter event at LAX (Los Angeles International Airport), TSA personnel evacuating Terminal 3, where the shootings were occurring, texted coworkers in Terminals 1 and 2, causing both terminals to self-evacuate (when TSA shut down the checkpoint and ran, everyone followed). Many personnel evacuated to the ramp area where aircraft operations were taking place.

The airport operator must establish the lines of communication to be used in an emergency, listing the pathways, the organizations to be contacted, and specific means of contacting, along with contact information, hours of operation for radio/TV/cable stations, circulation (morning/evening, daily/weekly) of newspapers, and languages covered. Alternative methods should also be addressed if the primary pathways are unavailable (vehicle-mounted public address, door-to-door, etc.). The media generally cooperates with the airport's public notification process, and the media will be interested because of the nature of the story; however, the media can be fickle and may not transmit the information in the same way it was received from the airport and may not transmit it for long.

---

[3]While CERTs are a community-based entity, many airports have developed their own versions of CERTs using administrative and other nonoperational personnel to assist with implementing emergency plans, such as shelter-in-place, evacuation, and security breaches.

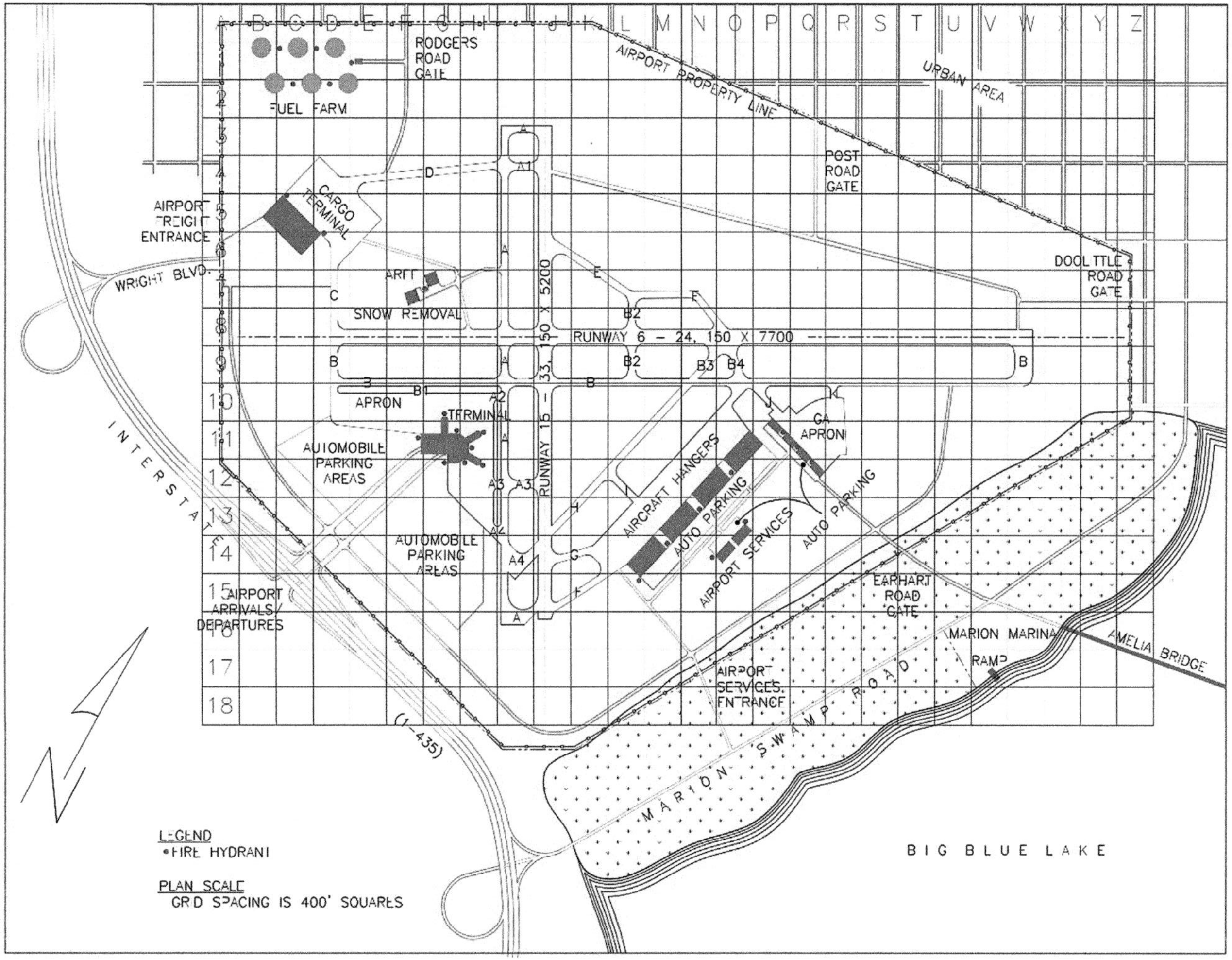

FIGURE 11.2

Sample airport grid map.

Source: FAA, 2010, p. 278.

Plus, during a natural disaster, dozens of response agencies and communities will attempt to use the media to push out information, and airport operators may find themselves competing for attention. Notifying landside operations personnel, others picking up and dropping off passengers, and those in the parking garage or outlying parking lots must also be addressed.

Many emergency public notifications relate to the status of the airport, particularly during inclement weather, such as snow and severe thunderstorms, and are fairly *routine*. Individuals want to know about flight delays, whether the airport is open or closed, and for how long. In the event of a plane crash, family members and friends of passengers want to know where to go for more information and assistance, while others want to know the status of the airport and whether their flight is affected.

For a mass weather event, such as a pending hurricane, along with associated flooding, tornadoes, and high winds, airports should have scripted messages noting the specific hazard; the estimated area and time of incident; priority protection measures (sandbagging, relocating aircraft, securing equipment); recommended content of disaster supply kits; evacuation instructions (coordinate with local emergency management); other "do's and don'ts"; and telephone or social media identifying information for specific kinds of inquiry. Other scripts can be prepared and given to airport paging or communications center personnel to be used depending on the emergency, such as what to do after an accident or natural disaster, whom to connect with for more information, and support for individuals that have loved ones who may have been involved in a plane crash. Part of the Emergency Public Notification process should be the simulation and practice of setting up the Joint Information Center, media center, and family assistance centers.

EPI should also be coordinated between the local government and the airport or other agencies, which rely on the same media sources. State laws often apply to how local and state agencies handle EPI, and there may be situations in which the federal government also becomes involved.

The Airport Director approves the release of information to the public, oftentimes working with the PIO, who consequently works with PIOs from other agencies, air carriers, tenants, and off-airport agencies. PIOs schedule news conferences, issue press releases, supervise the media center, and do their best to handle "rumor control." If available, voluntary organizations can staff phone lines and disseminate information to the public. Both during and after the incident, PIO staff will collect press clips and stories about the airport, assess the public's reaction, chase down false reports, and provide summaries to the Command Staff.

PROTECTIVE ACTIONS

Protective Actions are generally focused on protecting the health and safety of passengers and airport employees. The Airport Director must ensure that there is a policy on evacuation, along with policies on how to handle individuals who do not comply with evacuation or shelter-in-place orders. Primary methods of notification within an airport terminal typically include the fire alarm system and the public address or public announcement system. Airport police, fire, operations, and maintenance personnel are the primary individuals who facilitate evacuations or shelter-in-place actions.

Protective action plans typically focus on one of two options, **shelter-in-place** or **evacuation**. Evacuation plans and maps should be developed, along with routes and signs put into place throughout the airport. Airport and airline offices should also have evacuation plans with designated rally points outside of the structure. In some evacuations, personnel are simply looking to get away from the airport, such as for incoming natural disasters. However, for bomb threats, active shooter, or an actual detonation of an improvised explosive device, a designated rally point for personnel from each office or floor of an office building or personnel working in the terminal building, along with an appointed floor security manager who has a roster of personnel who are in the office that day, can help identify if individuals in the building are still in need of assistance.

For short-term incidents, such as severe thunderstorms or tornadoes, the shelter-in-place is typically the better option. In some cases, like tornadoes, evacuation may actually be more dangerous than staying inside the terminal building. Many airports, even small facilities, tend to be equipped with tunnels to accommodate baggage systems, in-line security baggage systems, or maintenance and utilities, making them relatively safe places of shelter during a tornado or high winds. However, in some cases these tunnel areas are in a Secured Area of the airport, so typically the airport will be closed for the duration of the storm and will stay closed until all passengers and unauthorized personnel are relocated back to the public areas and the Secured Areas have been searched.

Airport fire personnel should track the status of incoming severe weather and natural disasters, and they should prepare to render aid and assist the airport operator in taking Protective Actions. To protect personnel working on the ramp, airports experiencing severe thunderstorms accompanied by lightning routinely shut down ramp operations (which also shuts down flight operations), when there is lightning within a specified range[4] of the airport. In this case, the "evacuation" is not individuals from the terminal building to another location, but from the ramp areas to inside the terminal building and concourses.

In some situations, personnel who are warned of a threat may not take any action. One of several illogical reactions that people can have during an emergency is the failure to move out of harm's way. In her book, *The Unthinkable: Who Survives Disaster and Why*, Amanda Ripley posits that people respond better to warnings when they are told: (a) what specifically to do; (b) why they must do what is requested; and (c) the potential threats that could impact them (Ripley, 2009).

During the 9/11 evacuation of the World Trade Center towers, people waited an average of 6 minutes before heading down the stairs, with some waiting as long as 45 minutes. Failure to act in the face of a threat is a classic fight-or-flight response. Some individuals enter a temporary state of denial, saying to themselves, in effect, "this is not happening, it is not happening now, nor is it happening to me" (Ripley, 2009, p. 9). In 1960, an earthquake in Chile triggered a tsunami that headed for the Hawaiian Islands. Despite the warning sirens, which worked as advertised, most of the people who heard the siren did not evacuate, because they were not sure what the warning meant (Ripley, 2009, p. xiii).

If Ripley's research was applied to a tornado warning message sent to occupants of an airport terminal building, the message could say: "Attention all personnel in the airport terminal, a Tornado Warning is in effect, please proceed immediately to a tornado shelter. Look for signs labeled *Tornado Shelter* to prevent injury from shattering glass and flying debris. The airport is temporarily closed, and all flights are being held until the warning is canceled."

Any evacuation or shelter-in-place procedure must take into account individuals with functional needs. According to Dory Clark, Assistant Executive Director for The Arc, in Houston, Texas, it is illegal for a public-use airport to direct individuals with functional needs to use

---

[4]The range is variable by airport.

alternative evacuation points that do not provide the same level of protection and the same speed of egress as routes for those without functional needs (Clark, personal communication, 2015). It is also illegal for a public use airport to tell individuals with functional needs that they will have to wait until able-bodied individuals have evacuated before they can be evacuated (Clark, personal communication, 2015).

Individuals with functional needs or special needs include those with a hearing impairment, a visual impairment, physical disabilities, mental or emotional disabilities, unaccompanied children, elderly individuals, and even individuals with learning disabilities like dyslexia or the inability to read. It is also important to understand that passengers who do not have a clinical diagnosis for a particular condition may experience severe cases of anxiety in crowded or stressful situations or have other stress-induced health issues. Many passengers require access to medicines, and in some cases, medicines that require refrigeration. Some passengers may carry enough medicine to handle short-term shelter-in-place situations, but for extended situations, such as during a blizzard, that may shut down the airport for days and force thousands of passengers to stay in the terminal building, accommodations for refrigeration for medicines, and the need to evacuate some personnel because of medical needs, must be considered.

Not all personnel in the airport speak English, particularly at international airports, so public address announcements should also be scripted in other languages that are used in the region or that match up to the international carrier routes. For example, if Lufthansa flies out of the airport, prerecording a public address announcement in German would be logical. If Mexico is a primary service destination for airlines at the airport, it makes sense to have prerecorded announcements in Spanish. Also, apps are available that can help customer service personnel in translating various languages, and some services are also available by phone that allow an airport or airline customer service agent to call an interpreter, who can relay messages to passengers. Airport Ambassadors, or airport customer service personnel, should have these apps or phone numbers available.

For extended shelter-in-place situations, airports often keep extra supplies of blankets, pillows, and cots and have worked out contingency contracts with airline caterers to provide food. Many airport vendors and restaurants rely on daily deliveries of food and beverages to the airport, particularly refrigerated food, and cannot sustain operations for more than a day without resupply. Military meals-ready-to-eat (MREs) and a massive quantity of stored bottled water may be an option for some airport operators who desire to have sustenance options, particularly airports located in areas prone to hurricanes, where operations and community services may be shut down for days or weeks.

Another important component of Protective Actions is the protection of employees who are responsible for implementing the Protective Actions portion of the AEP. When hundreds or thousands of individuals are forced to shelter-in-place, disruptions, arguments, and fights can occur between passengers, placing Airport Operations personnel in harm's way. Therefore, adequate police coverage and proper deployment of law enforcement personnel to areas of concern should be addressed in the planning process.

For some large-scale disasters, such as hurricanes, or severe weather leading to numerous tornadoes, such as occurred in the storms of 2011 throughout the Midwest, Airport Operations are often forced to shut down completely. Airport employees who are responsible for implementing actions under the AEP also have families and homes they are worried about. Airport management must take these natural desires—to take care of one's family and home—into consideration in the AEP.

Personnel who are more worried about what's going on at home, and who have not been home for days or even heard if their family is okay, will not be effective at their job. The AEP should take into account reduced levels of operation because of personnel not showing up for work because of the inability to access the airport (damaged or washed-out roads, or community destruction that prevents them from getting to work) and allow the airport management to rotate essential personnel home to take care of personal needs.

When an entire community is affected by a power outage or natural disaster, a *get-home-kit* may be useful for getting employees home if they need to walk home or to another place of shelter (Anders, 2015, pp. 71–72). The kit should be a backpack, not a laptop or shoulder bag, as the individual may have to walk many miles. At a minimum, the kit should contain an adequate supply of bottled water, a lighter, a first aid kit, some high-calorie ration bars or protein bars, and a flashlight. If possible, a small knife, or a Swiss Army Knife or Leatherman, is useful, but may be prohibited in some workplaces. Some comfort items like a roll of toilet paper, an extra set of clothes, and a couple of pairs of socks and spare underwear are also advised, along with possibly a pair of sneakers or old comfortable boots, which can be tied to the outside of the bag to save space. A Mylar space blanket and hand-crank radio can also come in handy (Anders, 2015). Spare medicines when possible, along with any other essential item, such as batteries, a cell phone battery charger or backup battery, and a hat, gloves, and rain slicker, can also fit into a standard-sized backpack. While many personnel may not keep a kit at their desk all the time, they can be encouraged to create one if a hurricane or other foreseeable natural disaster is pending.

While the Protective Action section of the AEP AC says that this section of the emergency plan should address human-made and natural disasters, the AC was written in 2010, 3 years before the second active shooter incident since 9/11, at Los Angeles International Airport. Therefore, most of the AC focuses on natural, not human-made, disasters. An active shooter incident is significantly different from a pending natural disaster. Most natural disasters, such as a hurricane, tornado, severe thunderstorm, or blizzard, come with some advance warning. Some natural disasters, such as earthquakes, can occur with little to no warning, but airports located in areas known for the frequency of earthquakes typically have (or should have) contingency plans for such events, and the local populace often knows how to respond to an earthquake. However, active shooter situations are different.

An active shooter incident is not so much an evacuation as it is an escape. It is not so much a shelter-in-place as it is a "run-hide-fight." While some of the Protective Actions relevant to natural disasters can be used during an active shooter event, separate contingency plans should exist. Evacuations are usually somewhat orderly, following established evacuation routes with the assistance of airport personnel. Recovery from an evacuation is also rather orderly, compared to recovery from an active shooter escape. During an active shooter incident, there is no evacuation plan per se, as the primary goal is to escape from the line-of-fire as quickly and effectively as possible. During the Los Angeles International Airport active shooter event on November 1, 2013, thousands of passengers and airport employees streamed onto the ramp through fire alarm access doors as fast as possible. Recovery from such an escape will usually take much longer than recovery from a standard evacuation because of a pending storm as individuals do not follow established evacuation routes and are literally running for their lives. It is unreasonable to think people will follow standard evacuation protocols with someone shooting at them, so airport management should be less concerned with the methods of escape and focus on shutting down aircraft operations, notifying individuals who may be in harm's way that they need to run for cover or safety, and locating and neutralizing the shooter. Protective Actions, particularly during an active shooter event, reinforce the need for the airport operator to install panic alarms and have publicly posted phone numbers to call in the event of an emergency.

LAW ENFORCEMENT AND SECURITY

Title 14 CFR Part 139 does not have specific law enforcement requirements; however, many of the emergency plan's actions require police or some sort of security component. Additionally, commercial service airports that are regulated under Title 14 CFR Part 1542 require that the airport operator provide law enforcement to a level that is adequate to respond to the screening checkpoints, to support the ASP, including contingencies and incidents, and to respond to incidents of unlawful interference with civil aviation. The primary function of police on the airport is the enforcement of law, to support the ASP, and to support the contingencies and incident management plans within the AEP and the ASP.

Certain incidents such as bomb threats, active shooter, actual detonations of explosives, and hijackings will require immediate police response, and some situations may require additional support such as Explosive Ordnance Disposal (EOD) and K-9 teams or the FBI. During a natural disaster or airplane crash, law enforcement primarily is responsible for scene security and access control to the scene, Staging Areas, family assistance rooms, or in other areas where protection is needed (Figure 11.3).

Off-airport police or other law enforcement personnel may need to respond, depending on the situation. It is up to the police agency at the airport to ensure that off-airport responders know how to access the airport in a safe and proper manner. During some airport emergencies, local police and sheriff personnel have been known to access an airport by either driving through a gate or fence (knocking it down) and proceeding across aircraft movement areas without clearance, to respond to wherever they see smoke or perceive the incident to be (see Figure 11.4). These situations can cause runway incursions and potential collisions with aircraft. Offsite responders should be provided grid maps and simple instructions on where to respond at the airport and the importance of waiting for an escort to the incident site. Training with offsite responders is a way to reduce these safety incidents but still retain the benefit of police presence during an emergency.

Law enforcement personnel take the lead for any security incident at the airport and should be adequately trained and equipped to respond to any security issue, Aircraft Accident, structural fire, or other hazard in the AEP. During a hijacking or bomb threat, FBI hostage-response teams or special weapons response teams may take hours to get into position. Airport police are the first line of response and should know the procedures for securing the area in the event of a bomb threat, how to handle a bomb threat on an aircraft, and the procedures for handling a potentially hijacked aircraft that is on the airport or inbound to the airport. An important note: the TSA's Federal Security Director (FSD) has the authority to assume Incident Command for any security incident at an airport, but the FSD typically does not have any available armed response forces. TSA Transportation Security Officers and Transportation Security Inspectors are unarmed and are not trained in law enforcement response procedures.

FIGURE 11.3

Some airport police departments have mobile x-ray equipment and "Raider" vehicles, like this one pictured at left (Port Authority of New York and New Jersey). The Raider allows the rapid response and stable deployment of air-stairs to the access door of an airliner.

FIGURE 11.4

An ARFF truck responds during an emergency exercise at Centennial Airport, CO.

Although air marshals are TSA personnel and are armed and trained law enforcement officers, under Part 1542 it is still the airport operator's responsibility to respond to the threat using its own police force. Depending on the relationship between the air marshals based at the airport (if the airport is a Federal Air Marshal [FAM] base), local police may call on air marshals for assistance. If available, an Assistant Federal Security Director for Law Enforcement (AFSD-LEO) (a TSA law enforcement officer) may help facilitate federal agency response until the FBI is on-scene. However, AFSD-LEOs are very few and far between, so it's a good assumption for airport police to believe that they are on their own, at least for the first 30 to 60 minutes of an event. In some cases, airports are located on or near military bases and may have military special operations teams that can respond to an act of unlawful interference with aviation. This response option should be addressed in the ASP and familiarization training conducted with these off-airport response teams.

Airport law enforcement personnel should also work with local jurisdictions to provide additional support via air, land, and water, if appropriate, to respond to airport incidents. The airport law enforcement coordinator must ensure that a representative responds to the EOC or Incident Command center during an emergency and must ensure that all equipment, radios, and other materials are in proper and working order and ready to support the AEP and ASP.

Some airports use unarmed security officers to provide staffing for airfield vehicle gates, and general patrol of the airfield and terminal areas, to respond to security alarms, and watch for and respond to potential violations of the Airport Security regulations. While other security personnel cannot meet the TSA regulatory requirements for law enforcement personnel at an airport, they can be used as a force multiplier by enforcing the ASP and responding to alarms, freeing up police officers for other duties.

FIREFIGHTING AND RESCUE

Firefighting and rescue personnel provide emergency services to the airport that may affect life, property, and safety. While Part 139 requires a certain level of ARFF response to Aircraft Accidents and incidents, the AEP extends those responsibilities to structural fires and hazards, hazardous material (HAZMAT) incidents, and emergency medical response. The AEP must describe the level of firefighting capability, along with the number of personnel, the location and number of vehicles and support equipment, and outside agency support (FAA, 2010, p. 75). Although dedicated to ARFF response, some airport fire crews often provide response to the terminal building to provide emergency medical care, and at large airports, the fire department may have additional specific terminal (structural) and landside-response fire-rescue equipment (Figure 11.4).

Some airports maintain structural firefighting capabilities and on-scene paramedics or emergency medical personnel. At airports without such capabilities, the AEP must address how offsite responders will provide the services, including how they will be notified and how they will access the airport. As previously mentioned, some airports rely on military fire and rescue services, so the airport operator should ensure that military ARFF equipment and personnel meet the Part 139 requirements.

The ARFF chief must ensure compliance with all ACs related to ARFF training standards and regulations and HAZMAT standards and ensure the readiness of all necessary equipment.

ARFF personnel are required to participate in one live-burn exercise annually and to participate in the triennial emergency exercise.

At most airports, the Fire Chief or senior firefighter officer on duty will assume Incident Command for an airplane crash or other related incident. Fire and rescue personnel are responsible for the Priorities of Work (saving lives, scene stability, protect property, protect the environment), but once the incident is stabilized and recovery operations are underway, Incident Command typically shifts to Airport Operations or airport police. A representative from the fire department is expected to respond to the EOC, for most airport emergencies.

Fire and rescue personnel must also support HAZMAT issues, including fuel spills. Typically, only large airports have significant HAZMAT response capability. At smaller airports, HAZMAT response is often the responsibility of an off-airport unit. Fire personnel and equipment also support **security incidents** by providing lifesaving services, putting out fires, and managing any fire alarms that may have been activated during a security incident.

ARFF personnel that drive on the airfield must be trained and authorized to be in the AOA, and an airport grid map should be available in every fire and rescue vehicle. Specific duties for ARFF personnel and other fire and rescue personnel are addressed in the hazard-specific section of the AEP.

HEALTH AND MEDICAL

Airports often experience high levels of demand for health care services. Some passengers experience higher levels of anxiety during air travel, some passengers' preexisting medical conditions may be exacerbated by thinner air as a result of a pressurized airline cabin or as the result of traveling to a higher altitude, and some passengers may be sick or may become injured during travel. The airport operator should have available EMSs to treat conditions such as cardiac arrest, abdominal pains, burns, cuts, abrasions, and communicable diseases, as well as other medical problems (NFPA, 2013, pp. 424−28).

Today, it is normal for airport firefighters to also be trained as EMTs, or at least in Basic Medical Care, and many Airport Operations personnel are trained in first aid, and cardiopulmonary resuscitation (CPR), and critical trauma care. Some airports have first-aid treatment facilities with limited resources, but enough to treat most of the common injuries and ailments experienced by passengers (slip and falls, airsickness, headaches, etc.). **Automatic external defibrillators (AEDs)** are effective in certain cardiac events and should be positioned throughout the airport (NFPA, 2013, pp. 424−28).

The AEP must address how the airport operator will mobilize assets and respond to health and medical issues and the specific agency that is responsible for providing health and medical services. Any Part 139 certificated airport is required to have at least one individual on-duty, usually a firefighter, who is trained in Basic Medical Care. However, this training requirement is not equal to the level of Paramedic or **EMT**, and at any large commercial service airport, one medic will not be enough to handle the health and medical demands of the airport population.

Most airports cannot sustain health and medical capabilities beyond initial first aid and trauma care during a mass casualty incident and require assistance from outside entities. The AEP must describe the airport's ability to provide medical care, treatment, and transportation of victims during an aircraft crash or airport incident, describing also any public and private medical facilities and mortuary services available at the airport or in the community. Such entities should understand their role and requirements under the AEP, and the AEP should include the name, location, contact information, and emergency capability of each hospital and other medical facility that agrees to provide medical assistance or transportation (FAA, 2010).

The AEP should identify hangars or other buildings to be used for the staging of personnel, uninjured, injured, and deceased. The senior medical coordinator should ensure that a health and medical representative responds to the EOC (and the Incident Command Post), and that provisions are made for transportation of the wounded to proper medical facilities. All ambulances or other emergency medical vehicles should be equipped with a grid map of the airport and provided either with an escort to the accident site or a clearly marked pathway (using cones, barricades, and airport personnel) to ensure safe access to the site, particularly when the airport continues to be operational. The senior medical coordinator should also know the process for requesting support of the various **Disaster Medical Assistance Teams (DMATs)**, which are part of the resource typing categories in NIMS, and the **Disaster Mortuary Operational Response Teams (DMORTs)**.

Medical personnel are responsible for triage of the injured, transportation of critically injured to medical facilities as quickly as possible, ideally within 60 minutes, and identifying and arranging for the transport of the deceased.[5] During a HAZMAT incident, medical personnel are responsible for isolating, decontaminating, and treating victims as needed; however, airport fire personnel typically take on the role of initial decontamination of victims. **Environmental health officers** should also be appointed to monitor and evaluate health risks, inspect damaged buildings for health hazards or contamination, and ensure sanitary facilities in emergency shelters are available. Other key medical functions include coordinating with the **American Red Cross** and Salvation Army to provide food for both responders and patients, assist the air carrier in family member notifications, assist those with functional needs, and assist orphaned children and children separated from their parents, along with coordinating with veterinarians and animal hospitals to provide care as needed to those involved in the incident.

Communicable Diseases

As much as aviation allows us to travel the world in a matter of hours, it can spread a communicable disease from one side of the planet to the other just as quickly. Air travel reduces the time available for countries and airports to prepare interventions and stockpile antidotes. The primary goal of the airport operator is to protect the health of passengers, staff, and the general public. In 2009, Airports Council International (ACI) issued a communiqué on the responsibilities of airports to mitigate the effects of communicable diseases, health screening practices, and how to handle an inbound aircraft carrying a passenger with a suspected case of a communicable disease, which can pose a serious health risk (ACI, 2009).

Approximately 1.7 million passengers arrive daily in the United States on commercial passenger flights, with each large aircraft carrying more than 300 passengers and crew (ACI, 2009). This number does not take into account passengers and crews arriving on general aviation aircraft into the United States. The threat of pandemic flu, severe acute respiratory syndrome (SARS), Ebola, and other viruses spreading through the air transportation system has caused airport operators to

---

[5]Airplane accident fatalities are usually left in position until the NTSB allows the bodies to be recovered.

consider options for handling individuals who may be infected and require quarantine, or even quarantine of an aircraft or the entire airport population.

Many airports have installed hand cleaner dispensers in the rest rooms and throughout the terminal building, and signs encouraging passengers and employees to wash their hands to prevent the spread of infectious or communicable diseases.[6] To further reduce the risk of spreading communicable diseases, ACI encourages airports to develop an **Airport Preparedness Plan** that addresses how the airport will communicate with the public about the potential for a communicable disease outbreak or issue, the implementation of screening processes for communicable diseases, methods to transport passengers to health facilities, and having on hand the necessary equipment to conduct the screening along with **Personal Protective Equipment (PPE)** to reduce the risk of airport staff contracting a disease. Furthermore, airports should coordinate response plans with local, state, and federal public health authorities prior to an outbreak.

Communication is critical to preventing an outbreak or spread of communicable disease. Airports should leverage their notification processes that are already in place and outlined in their AEP to ensure that quick methods are available to get in touch with air carriers, tenants, vendors, contractors, and others working at the airport, along with passengers and the media. Information can be given to passengers prior to arrival at the airport through airport and airline websites, a dedicated telephone line that passengers can call to receive the latest information, and through normal mainstream media pathways (ACI, 2009).

The **World Health Organization (WHO)** says that screening for communicable diseases can reduce the opportunity for transmission or delay an international spread (ACI, 2009). A variety of screening methods are available, including visual inspection to look for obvious signs of illness or symptoms of particular diseases, and the use of thermal scanners or other suitable methods to take the temperature of inbound passengers from international destinations. Passenger interviews and questionnaires, along with identifying flights that have been routed through countries with known infectious disease outbreaks, are other methods of attempting to identify individuals with communicable diseases (ACI, 2009).

Health screening usually takes place at the Federal Inspection Areas of the airport. Airport operators should ensure at least one individual from the airport is appointed to keep up with the latest information coming out of the WHO and the U.S. **Centers for Disease Control (CDC)** on the latest epidemiological and virological findings, along with the geographical distribution of infected persons and suggested screening measures (ACI, 2009). In some circumstances, screening is conducted at the airport of departure, but that cannot always be counted upon. It's important that passengers are screened as soon as possible upon entering the airport and definitely before being allowed out of the Federal Inspection Service (FIS) area. A simulation model conducted as part of a study on U.S. airport entry screening in response to pandemic influenza (CDC, 2009) found that foreign shore exit screening significantly reduces the number of infected passengers while U.S. screening identifies 50% of the infected individuals.

---

[6]An infectious disease is caused by a virus or by bacteria that enter the body through one of a number of different transmission modes, such as harmful bacteria in food that is eaten and that then cause "food poisoning," or by inhalation of anthrax spores, which is an infectious disease but is not communicable. A communicable disease is an infectious illness that is spread from one person to another, such as smallpox, which is both infectious and communicable because it is spread from person-to-person (Stambaugh, Sensenig, Casagrande, Flagg, & Gerrity, 2008).

In 2014, approximately 80,000 passengers departed by air from the three countries most affected by Ebola: Guinea, Liberia, and Sierra Leone; approximately 12,000 of these passengers were en route to the United States. Procedures were implemented to deny boarding to ill persons and persons reporting a high risk of exposure to Ebola; however, no passengers who were denied boarding for fever or other symptoms or reported exposures were subsequently diagnosed with Ebola. Of those permitted to travel, none are known to have had Ebola symptoms during travel and none have been subsequently diagnosed with Ebola, but two passengers to the United States, who were not symptomatic during exit screening and travel, became ill with Ebola after arrival. CDC enhanced its procedures for detecting ill passengers entering the United States at airports by providing additional guidance and training to Customs and Border Protection (CBP) personnel, airlines, airport authorities, and EMS units at airports; the training covers recognizing possible signs of Ebola in travelers and reporting suspected cases to CDC (CDC, 2014).

If during the screening process a passenger is determined to be a health risk of having a communicable disease, they should immediately undergo a more extensive evaluation by a medical professional. Quarantine facilities should be previously designated, and protocols for handling potentially infected individuals should be in place.

If an inbound aircraft is carrying an individual that may have a communicable disease or an infectious disease, or an ill person[7] with an unknown cause, the pilot in command should be notified as soon as possible and advised of where to park the aircraft. The aircraft may even be diverted to another airport. Ideally, the aircraft should be parked away from the concourse or terminal building, on a remote stand or area of the airfield, and either with a separate passenger boarding bridge or air stairs (ACI, 2009). Passengers should be taken off the aircraft as soon as possible and provided with information about what is happening and what to do if they experience symptoms later on. The WHO publishes a **Passenger Locator Card** that can be used to track passengers who were on the affected flight (Figure 11.5). All passengers should be required to fill out the card. Methods should also be in place to handle screening of those arriving by general aviation aircraft into both commercial service and general aviation airports. Sick passengers should be taken to an isolation or quarantine area by personnel wearing the appropriate protective equipment, with procedures in place to obtain the passengers' bags and personal belongings, and provisions made for customs and immigration personnel to properly, and safely, process the individuals into the country.

The decision whether to quarantine an entire flight or airport population must be taken with great consideration. A large-scale quarantine will have a significant impact on flight operations at that airport and throughout the National Airspace System. Airport Cooperative Research Program (ACRP) Report 5 addressed the questions of deciding whether to quarantine and how to go about it (Stambaugh, Sensenig, Casagrande, Flagg, & Gerrity, 2008). The quarantine of an entire airport would involve a massive mobilization of community and federal resources, but the ACRP study was based on a more basic assumption, which would be to effectively quarantine up to

---

[7]An ill person is defined as a person who has a fever, defined as a temperature of 38°C or 100°F or greater, accompanied by one or more of the following: rash, jaundice, glandular swelling, or temperature persisting for 2 or more days, or diarrhea severe enough to interfere with normal activity or work (defined as three or more loose stools within 24 hours or a greater than normal number of loose stools) (Stambaugh et al., 2008).

Public Health Passenger Locator Form: To protect your health, public health officers need you to complete this form whenever they suspect a communicable disease onboard a flight. Your information will help public health officers to contact you if you were exposed to a communicable disease. It is important to fill out this form completely and accurately. Your information is intended to be held in accordance with applicable laws and used only for public health purposes.   *~Thank you for helping us to protect your health.*

One form should be completed by an adult member of each family. Print in capital (UPPERCASE) letters. Leave blank boxes for spaces.

FLIGHT INFORMATION: **1. Airline name**   **2. Flight number**   **3. Seat number**   **4. Date of arrival (yyyy/mm/dd)**

PERSONAL INFORMATION: 5. Last (Family) Name   **6. First (Given) Name**   **7. Middle Initial**   **8. Your sex**

Male ☐ Female ☐

PHONE NUMBER(S) where you can be reached if needed. Include country code and city code.

9. Mobile   **10. Business**

11. Home   **12. Other**

13. Email address

PERMANENT ADDRESS: **14. Number and street** *(Separate number and street with blank box)*   **15. Apartment number**

16. City   **17. State/Province**

18. Country   **19. ZIP/Postal code**

TEMPORARY ADDRESS: If you are a visitor, write only the first place where you will be staying.

20. Hotel name (if any)   **21. Number and street** *(Separate number and street with blank box)*   **22. Apartment number**

23. City   **24. State/Province**

25. Country   **26. ZIP/Postal code**

EMERGENCY CONTACT INFORMATION of someone who can reach you during the next 30 days

27. Last (Family) Name   **28. First (Given) Name**   **29. City**

30. Country   **31. Email**

32. Mobile phone   **33. Other phone**

34. TRAVEL COMPANIONS – FAMILY: Only include age if younger than 18 years

Last (Family) Name	First (Given) Name	Seat number	Age <18
(1)			
(2)			
(3)			
(4)			

35. TRAVEL COMPANIONS – NON-FAMILY: Also include name of group (if any)

Last (Family) Name	First (Given) Name	Group *(tour, team, business, other)*
(1)		
(2)		

FIGURE 11.5

Passenger Locator Card.

Source: World Health Organization.

200 passengers from an international flight for a period of 2 weeks. The study addressed the four phases of quarantine: (1) the decision to quarantine, (2) establishing quarantine, (3) quarantine operations, and (4) demobilization and recovery.

The study revealed the estimated cost to acquire and maintain the basic supplies to accomplish such a quarantine would exceed $100,000, a cost that does not take into account the cost of the space that would be needed for the quarantine, which was estimated to be $15,000 per month (depending on local variances) (Stambaugh et al., 2008). Quarantine operations would include establishing accommodations and renting showers and portable toilets, which could cost up to another $20,000 or more, plus another $150,000 or more to provide lodging, food, recreation, communications, sanitation, basic health services, security, and cleaning (Stambaugh et al., 2008).

However, the decision to impose a quarantine order on international travelers lies with the CDC, not the airport or an airline. Airlines have a duty to report certain illnesses, but only federal public health officials are authorized to implement a quarantine. The CDC may also choose less-extreme measures, such as a voluntary home quarantine, vaccinations, or collecting passenger information cards with follow-up by public health officials to determine if anyone develops symptoms, as occurred during the 2003 SARS outbreak (Stambaugh et al., 2008).

Once the decision is made to quarantine passengers, health officials must decide where individuals exhibiting symptoms will be taken, as well as how and where to put the remaining passengers. Keeping passengers on the aircraft for an extended period of time is not desirable. A site must be located, along with a method of transportation to get the passengers and crew from the aircraft to the facility. Vehicle operators and other personnel involved with moving the passengers and crew will also have to take protective measures (Stambaugh et al., 2008). Individuals with functional needs must also be accounted for; thus, wheelchairs and a lift service may be necessary to help some passengers off the aircraft into the quarantine facility.

The quarantine location should have accommodations for sleeping, bathing, entertainment, and communications, plus access to medical care, along with supplies and staffing for food preparation, cleaning, counseling, or additional considerations. If the quarantine facility is offsite, these responsibilities shift to the CDC or state and local health providers, but the airport operator still must ensure that the aircraft, along with any personnel involved with the quarantine, are properly taken care of. The aircraft must be cleaned, and airport and airline personnel involved in the quarantine operation must be screened for symptoms. From an airport operator perspective, one should conclude that these individuals would be out of commission and out of the work schedule for at least a few days.

If the quarantine facility is on the airport, the airport operator will likely be more involved with providing access to the facility and possibly providing support for the quarantine operation. Additionally, the CDC may only use an on-airport facility temporarily, which will necessitate another transfer of potentially affected passengers and crew, followed by a proper cleanup of the facility that was used. At the end of the quarantine, passengers and crew may still need to finish their journey, which may require providing transportation back to the airport to rebook passengers on other flights.

RESOURCE MANAGEMENT

The airport operator must ensure a list of resources is available to decision makers during an incident. Airport operators must assume that during an incident, particularly a natural disaster, there will be critical shortages of power, potable water, firefighting agents, and portable equipment, such as lights and generators, and further that emergencies will deplete the resources of responders quickly. Local transportation systems may also be affected by the disaster (bridges collapsed, highways blocked or damaged), making the replenishment of resources difficult or not possible for a period of time. However, airports do have a benefit in that they are not limited by highway transportation methods. Airports have historically accepted relief aircraft bringing in aid and resources to a community during a natural disaster by both Fixed-Wing aircraft and helicopters.

Resource typing is essential to ensuring that the necessary resources are identified and available for use when needed. Additionally, a resource manager should be appointed to ensure that all agencies are maintaining resources in a readiness state and that key points of contact, purchasing contracts, and other elements necessary to ordering up resources are in order.

A complete list of resources should be included in the appendix of the AEP that includes personnel (i.e., volunteers, off-airport responders), communications equipment, vehicles, heavy equipment, portable pumps and hoses, postincident recovery materials, such as tools, fuel, sandbags, and lumber, portable power generators, and mass care supplies (first aid, potable water, blankets, and lighting) (FAA, 2010, p. 90). Any resources that are not available at the airport that must be provided by a mutual aid organization should also be noted.

All response agencies should be self-sustainable for the first 24 hours of an incident; this standard helps to identify how many resources will be needed. Resource typing includes determining what is needed, why it is required, how much, who needs it, where it needs to be delivered, and when it is required. The **Supply Group** within the Incident Command structure will first try to fill resource needs with airport resources and then notify suppliers, negotiate terms, and arrange for transport of resources as necessary. The finance and administrative team should be kept aware of budget issues, with all transactions being properly recorded (FAA, 2010, p. 92).

After the emergency, the resource manager or the logistics unit within the Incident Command structure is responsible for disposing of excess stock, reimbursing owners for property or use of equipment, acknowledging suppliers, donors, and volunteer agencies, and exploring potential future agreements and contracts that will better facilitate resource needs in the future.

AIRPORT OPERATIONS AND MAINTENANCE

Even though the day-to-day roles of Operations and Maintenance are separate, the AEP AC treats them as a singular component in the emergency response context. However, many airports have very clear lines of distinction between the roles of Operations and Maintenance during an emergency. The Operations and Maintenance section of the AEP outlines the overall statement of capabilities and responsibilities of operations and maintenance personnel during an emergency.

The AC acknowledges that often Airport Operations or Airport Maintenance personnel are the first to respond to many airport emergencies, as a result of the nature of their duties, which requires them to be either in the airfield or in the terminal building most of the time. Airport Operations personnel represent airport management throughout the stages of an emergency, and they may have to establish Incident Command and act in the capacity as the IC either during the initial or other stages of the emergency. At some small non-hub airports, Airport Operations personnel are not onsite 24 hours a day, 7 days a week, so other arrangements must be made to notify Operations and Maintenance personnel of an emergency at the airport. Fixed Base Operators (FBOs), or air carriers operating at the airport after Operations and Maintenance personnel have completed their duty day, may have the responsibility for notifying an on-call airport representative, or local first responders may have to make the contact.

Primarily, the role of Airport Operations in an emergency is based on their assigned mission within the AEP and is airport-specific. Generally speaking, Operations ensures that all notifications have been made, will either assume Incident Command or support the IC by providing resources and communications services, and makes the initial determination regarding the issuance of a Notice to Airmen (NOTAM) to close a portion of or the entire airport.

Airport Maintenance personnel, if they are not required to be actively engaged in the emergency, will typically stand by and respond to requests for assistance from various response agencies. Many airfield maintenance personnel are trained in operating vehicles on the airport and can be highly effective at providing escorts for off-airport responders to get to an incident site. Maintenance personnel can also access supplies and equipment necessary for the support of the incident. A senior member of the maintenance department should also respond to the EOC in order to receive and coordinate requests for resources and assistance. A member of the maintenance department should also ensure that the command vehicle, mobile command centers, buses, and other vehicles are provided to the scene and are operational as soon as possible. All maintenance personnel who operate on the airfield should be provided with a grid map and should understand the procedures for notifying responders and other airport personnel during an emergency.

Maintenance personnel should maintain a resource list, ensure the safety of facilities during the recovery phase from a natural disaster, clear debris as necessary, provide sanitation services, potable water, and backup electrical power, transport portable emergency shelters to appropriate locations, and provide heavy equipment, cones, stakes, flags, and signs. Many large airports also keep buses equipped with body bags, blankets, cots, stretchers, and other items necessary to support an aircraft crash response.

Airport Operations personnel ensure compliance with regulations during and after emergency operations, noting any violations of regulations that occurred to facilitate the response. Operations personnel should follow up with any regulatory violation by properly notifying the FAA, TSA, Environmental Protection Agency (EPA), or other appropriate agency. During the recovery phase, Airport Operations, if they do not already have the Incident Command responsibility, will typically take over IC responsibilities and oversee the recovery phase to get the airport back to full operation.

THE AIRPORT EMERGENCY COMMAND CENTER AND OPERATIONS

It is often said that *all emergency management is local.* This statement reflects the approach taken by the United States when it comes to a local disaster. Initially, local response is supposed to handle the event, disaster, or incident, but when local resources are overwhelmed, the municipality calls on the state to assist. When the state's resources are overwhelmed, then a request is made to the federal government. This concept is reflected on an airport, where most emergencies are handled by Airport Operations personnel, firefighters, police, security, and emergency medical personnel and are supported by the airport's communications or dispatch center, without the need to activate a large, Incident Command structure beyond the single IC. A single Incident Command post is established on-scene, with the communications center providing logistical support, overall communications, and coordination. In essence, the communications center[8] functions as a lesser emergency command center for small-scale incidents.

However, for a large-scale emergency or natural disaster, the efforts of first-response agency personnel and others must be coordinated to ensure an effective response. In these situations, **EOCs** play a critical role in acquiring, allocating, and tracking resources; managing and distributing information; and setting response priorities among many incident sites (FEMA, 2008a). EOCs are a critical link in the emergency response chain, enabling ICs to focus on the needs of the incident and serve as a conduit of information between the Incident Command and higher levels of the **Multiagency Coordination System (MACS)**.

In a large-scale disaster, numerous government agencies activate their individual EOCs, so it is feasible that there will be more than a dozen different EOCs of various natures, such as airline, FBI, state, and Department of Homeland Security (DHS), involved in managing the incident. Some agencies set up their own local EOC and have a representative in the airport's EOC, while coordinating with their parent agency EOC located thousands of miles from the actual incident. Some good examples are the TSA, the FBI, and the air carrier. The TSA, in addition to setting up its own command structure and sending representatives to both the scene and the airport EOC, also coordinates and exchanges information with the Transportation Emergency Operations Center (TSOC), located in Virginia. The FBI will set up multiple incident centers and will also coordinate with the Strategic Information Operations Center (SIOC) in Washington, DC, while the airlines will set up a local emergency response center, provide a representative to the airport EOC, plus manage the family victim center, while still working with their Network Operations Center (NOC), which manages all airline activities, 24/7. With numerous EOCs, an Incident Command Post, Staging Areas, family assistance rooms, press rooms (along with dozens of PIOs, at least one from each major agency), and countless other moving parts, the MACS can help resolve differences among the various agencies (FEMA, 2008a) and provide a pool of resources.

The function of an EOC is to provide a physical location where multiagency response coordination can occur so as to form a common operating picture of the incident, obtain additional resources, and relieve on-scene command of the burden of external coordination (FEMA, 2010, p. 15). A **common operating picture** is an overview of the incident that provides incident information enabling either the IC or Unified Command to make effective, consistent, and timely decisions. Primarily, EOC personnel ensure that responders who are on-scene have the resources, including personnel, information, tools, and equipment, needed to respond to the incident. An EOC promotes problem solving at the lowest level and provides strategic direction and guidance to the incident management personnel, but an EOC does not typically "assume command" over the on-scene IC. The airport EOCs can facilitate multiagency communications and acquire and track resources, manage much of the Public Information requests, authorize emergency expenditures, and provide legal support.

EOCs are staffed by personnel representing multiple jurisdictions and functional disciplines with access to a wide variety of resources. The physical size, staffing, and equipping of an EOC

---

[8]In NIMS parlance, this would be referred to as a Department Emergency Operations Center (DEOC, or DOC).

will depend on the size of the incident management workload. An EOC should include the following core functions:

1. **Coordination** through the participation of multiple agencies.
2. **Communication** through extensive radio, telephone, and computer systems.
3. **Resource allocation** through resource typing and management.
4. **Tracking** by personnel who are not involved with on-scene management and can track the use of resources and costs.
5. **Information collection, analysis, and dissemination** through shared intelligence and information.

Once an EOC is activated, communication and coordination should be established between the EOC and the ICP, but the EOC, in most cases, does not command the on-scene, tactical level of the incident. EOCs should be both flexible and scalable, performing functions such as situational assessment, determining incident priorities, allocating resources, providing policy direction, coordinating with other regional response coordination centers, and providing Public Information through a Joint Information Center (JIC).

The EOC is a designated area on the airport used in supporting and coordinating operations for accidents and incidents, both safety and security in nature. The center should have the necessary communications equipment to communicate with all responsible agencies under the AEP and, most importantly, the ICP (NFPA, 2013, pp. 424−28). While the local, Incident Command structure directs on-scene incident management activities and maintains command and control, EOCs are activated as necessary to support the Incident Command effort (FEMA, 2010, p. 16).

Airport EOCs can be as simple as a desk in the Airport Operations office of a small, commercial service or general aviation airport, all the way up to an expansive multimillion-dollar, state-of-the-art dispatch, communications, and emergency coordination center. EOCs should be located away from the primary public areas of the airport, but they should still be accessible by off-airport responders, ideally without responders having to go through the screening checkpoint. Key personnel should be able to access the EOC within their required response times, and suppliers and support personnel should also be able to access the facility without undue delay. A separate entryway should be constructed for security purposes, as well as to allow a location for responding personnel to sign-in/sign-out. The entry should be protected by an armed law enforcement officer, who has no other duties other than the protection of the EOC. A separate individual should be responsible for the administrative processes so that the police officer guarding the EOC should not be distracted filling out paperwork and handing out identification badges.

The facility should be in an area that is resistant to blast pressures, either have no windows or windows that are glazed to reduce shattering, and should be away from identified areas of vulnerability for the airport (for instance, not next to the landside pickup and dropoff areas, which could make the EOC vulnerable to attack by a vehicle-borne improvised explosive device or active shooter). If the EOC is in the public area, it should not be labeled as the EOC but as another type of conference room, such as *Conference Room A* or some other label, so that off-airport personnel can easily locate the EOC, while ensuring the center is not an obvious target for attack. The EOC should have adequate heating, ventilation, and air conditioning, fresh water supplies, an Uninterruptible Power Supply in case of a power outage, backup generators and fuel, and working landlines. Backup power generators, potable water, coffee, and food may also be included in an

EOC to sustain personnel during long hours. For a sudden emergency, not everyone has time to stop for food, and the first personnel to reach the EOC could be there for an extended period of time.

Alternate EOCs can often be established should the primary EOC become nonoperational. Alternate EOCs can be set up as a hot site, warm site, or cold site. **Hot sites** can be used as soon as personnel arrive. They are the most expensive to maintain and require duplicate systems and equipment and the ongoing payment of utilities, but they are essentially ready to go when a responder enters the room. A **warm site** has critical systems and equipment in place, but equipment must be powered up, requiring several minutes to start up. A **cold site** is an empty shell, without any systems and equipment in place and no arrangements for utilities. Cold sites require the longest period of time for startup, and either responders must bring their own equipment, or Airport Maintenance must provide the equipment and materials to get the place operational. If an airport cannot afford an alternate facility, it may be practical to consider a mutual aid agreement with a neighboring jurisdiction to use its EOC, particularly during natural disasters that could affect the operation of the airport's EOC.

Some EOCs are combined with the airport's communications center, while others are separated, but usually within close proximity or adjacent to the communications center. It is logical to establish the EOC next to the communications center, as activating EOC is typically the responsibility of the communications center personnel. Communications center personnel are familiar with how to set up the various technologies, including computers, telephony, CCTV cameras and monitors, digital projectors, and other related equipment. Communications center personnel usually have at least one individual in the EOC to assist with technical functions, and often, if available, an additional person to enter significant occurrences during the event in the logbook. This running situational report is often projected onto a screen so that incoming personnel can see the latest information. Past information is usually printed and handed out, or it is consolidated into a briefing or summary sheet.

Additional breakout rooms can be used by various organizations and individuals to get away from the primary activity of the operations center and to coordinate and discuss information, policies, and plans. For a security response, while the FBI may leave one agent in the EOC, it is very common for the FBI to establish its own command center, away from the airport's EOC, and to utilize separate and secured office areas to conduct briefings, for hostage negotiations, and for staging for its response personnel. The air carrier involved in the incident will usually set up its own EOC, but should also have representatives in the airport EOC.

An EOC can also serve as a gathering area for local elected and appointed officials who may have primary responsibility for policy decisions. However, EOC commanders must guard against the EOC becoming a "hangout" for local officials and others who want to feel they are "part of the action," but have no jurisdictional responsibilities or authority. Some airport executives who understand this dynamic have designed EOCs with a variety of breakout rooms that are close to the functional areas of the EOC, often with glass partitions, CCTV access, and radio monitoring capabilities, so that various elected and appointed officials can observe the action, and still have a private location, where they can make decisions and discuss the incident.

A typical EOC table is equipped, at each station, with a computer and/or Internet and power plugins for laptops, a landline, and additional power outlets to keep personal electronic devices such as smartphones and tablets charged. A copy of the AEP may also be available online with phone directories. Some EOCs are designed with four primary tables representing the following functions: operational, logistical, planning, and administration/finance, while the command function is in an adjacent room. This design allows command personnel to be somewhat removed but still in close proximity to staff functions and personnel.

An EOC can be established using a series of large tables that serve as the five areas of Incident Command: command, operations, logistics, administration/finance, and planning. Or EOCs can be organized by function: police, fire, Airport Operations, airline, sheriff, etc. Regardless, the *right* method of establishing an EOC is what works best for that particular airport.

An example of a newer communications center and EOC is the **Airport Response Coordination Center (ARCC)** at the Los Angeles International Airport (LAX). The ARCC is staffed with personnel from LAX's airside, landside, police, maintenance, and government agencies (TSA) and provides basic communications center functionality. CCTV cameras capture much of the activity at the airport, and personnel can dispatch field operators to investigate issues and solve problems. During a major incident or airport emergency, LAX can activate the **Departmental Operations Center (DOC)**, which functions as the nerve center for dealing with critical incidents. The DOC uses a combination setup, with various areas around the center established by the **Incident Command System (ICS)** (operations, logistics, etc.) and specific positions within each area (PIO, TSA, police, etc.).

Many airport EOCs have standard stations, such as police, fire, operations, and PIO; however, not all personnel are needed during all incidents, and EOC commanders must also ensure that only necessary personnel are in the EOC. Factors to consider in staffing the EOC include the mission, the timeframe, the knowledge necessary to perform the critical tasks, and who has the authority to make decisions. The timeframe is also important to space requirements, as personnel must be relieved after a period of time, so there are double-staffing situations that take place as personnel rotate in and out.

The mission of the EOC is the desired outcome(s) of the particular emergency, but overall its function is to support Incident Command. Unless they can fulfill some other role, nonessential personnel do not belong in the EOC. Personnel who have the necessary knowledge, skill, and ability to perform the critical tasks may be in the EOC, and, ideally, these individuals will also have the authority to make the critical decisions (FEMA, 2008a). While many personnel are knowledgeable about a situation or may have an opinion on what should be done, few have the authority to enact policy. However, advisors with the technical expertise to provide counsel to the policy makers may be needed.

ORGANIZING THE EMERGENCY OPERATIONS CENTER

Unlike the ICS, which is governed by NIMS and has a specific organizational structure, NIMS does not require an EOC to organize under the ICS principles. FEMA notes that there are four ways to organize an EOC, and each structure comes with its own advantages and disadvantages. In some cases, the structure of an EOC may depend on state law or local policies. An EOC can be organized by Major Management Activities, around an ICS structure, by Emergency Support Functions (ESFs), or as a Multi-Agency Command (MAC) Group (FEMA, 2008a).

Organizing by **Major Management Activities** divides the EOC into four working groups: policy, resources, operations, and coordination. The **policy group** focuses on the overall strategy for the response, as well as overall response priorities and policy setting (FEMA, 2008a). The **resource group** includes representatives from any responding agency or organization that can provide resources such as transportation, utilities, and materials. The **operations group** includes representatives from each agency with responsibilities under the AEP and typically includes police, fire, Public Works, EMSs, and other agencies as dictated by the incident (FEMA, 2008a). The **coordination group** collects and analyzes data. The advantage of managing by activities is organization is relatively simple with straightforward lines of communication and a simple chain of command. However, linking to the ICS on-scene might be unclear because there is not a one-to-one match between the incident management personnel on-scene and the EOC.

Organizing around ICS is an attempt to align the EOC organizational structure with the on-scene Incident Command structure, but for this very reason, organizing around ICS may cause confusion about who has the command authority. However, large-incident logistical and financial support is often more easily coordinated from the EOC, rather than on-scene, and clear lines-of-connection are drawn between the functions of the EOC and the on-scene Incident Command. Organizing around ICS has five levels: Command, Operations, Planning, Logistics, and Finance/Administration. Important to remember is that the EOC command function is not the IC. Confusion can exist when organizing an EOC around ICS. The IC or Unified Command are on-scene command structures, whereas the EOC command function is more of a policy group that makes decisions and establishes the overall strategy of the response (FEMA, 2008a). The operations function coordinates with on-scene operations responders, which includes police, fire, Airport Operations, Airport Maintenance, and EMS personnel. The planning function serves the same purpose as it does at the incident scene, gathering and analyzing information, keeping decision makers informed, and tracking resources, along with developing **Incident Action Plans (IAPs)**. IAPs set forth specific goals and objectives to be obtained within a set timeframe. IAPs can derive from the Command function/group, which sets the strategic objectives. The planning function/group breaks down the strategic vision into measurable goals and then considers the operational challenges and the overall situation at hand to develop the IAP. Ideally, the Operations function/group then works toward achieving the goals and objectives of the IAP. The logistics function fundamentally serves as the grocery store for the incident, as these individuals have the purchasing authority, along with lists of the necessary resources and the authority to acquire them. The finance/administration function coordinates financial management processes for the incident, tracks personnel hours worked, including hours worked by off-airport responders (for potential reimbursement later), and, if an attorney is present, provides legal advice. In some cases, the on-scene Incident Command may retain certain roles at the incident site, while pushing other responsibilities, such as finance/administration, logistics, and planning, to their EOC counterparts.

Organizing by ESF provides similar structures to the ICS model, with each ESF assigned to a General Staff position. According to FEMA's IS-775 EOC Management and Operations course (FEMA, 2008a), the ESF agencies are organized as follows:

The **Operations** area includes:

1. Public Works/Emergency Engineering Branch
2. Firefighting Branch
3. Public Health and Medical Services Branch
4. Urban Search and Rescue Branch
5. Public Safety/Law Enforcement Branch

The **Planning** area includes:

1. Situation Analysis Unit
2. Documentation Unit
3. Advanced Planning Unit
4. Technical Services Unit
5. Damage Assessment
6. Resource Status Unit
7. GIS

The **Logistics** area includes:

1. Situation Analysis Unit
2. Communications Unit
3. Food Unit
4. Medical Unit
5. Transportation Unit
6. Supply Unit
7. Facilities Unit

The **Finance/Administration** area includes:

1. Compensation Claims Unit
2. Cost Unit
3. Purchasing/Procurement Unit
4. Time Unit
5. Disaster Financial Assistance

The advantage of organizing around an ESF is that it matches up well with the on-scene Incident Command organizations; however, it may not correspond directly with federal emergency support facilities. Additionally, personnel staffing the ESF require an enormous amount of additional training to ensure that they can perform their responsibilities.

Organizing Around a Multi-Agency Command Group

In this structure, a MAC Group is comprised of representatives from various organizations that are authorized to commit agency resources and funds. MAC Groups can often include organizations such as the local Chamber of Commerce, the Red Cross, and volunteer or other organizations with special expertise or knowledge that might be able to use their contacts, political influence, and technical expertise to aid in the management of an incident. The MAC Group Coordinator is in a position to provide supervision to the various units, such as the Situation Assessment Unit, the Resource Status Information Unit, and the JIC. The Situation Unit collects and assembles information needed for the MAC Group to accomplish the mission, and the Resource Unit helps determine the status of resources, as well as their availability and state of readiness.

The JIC is a Public Information unit that coordinates PIOs from a variety of agencies to push information to the media and, ultimately, to the public. A JIC is also a key component of other forms of EOC organizational structures and is not exclusive to the MAC Group. MACs work well to coordinate amongst other MAC entities to provide short-term, multiagency coordination and decision making when no other mechanisms exist, but they lack clearly defined and standardized relationships to other MAC entities.

As with all other forms of organizational structures in emergency management, ultimately, the airport operator should establish a system that works best for its operation in order to fulfill its critical tasks. However, airport ICs should be familiar with the variety of EOC structures that may be used by support agencies, as the airport operator may not get to dictate how a supporting EOC functions. Tabletop and orientation exercises are useful for learning how other agencies carry out their EOC functions and how the airport can integrate into larger-scale operations.

The core mission of an EOC is to provide overall coordination for a disaster or event. Essential to this coordination function is the ability to communicate with the various agencies in a real-time basis, in order to both build and share the common operating picture and to deploy assets and resources without delay. The basic requirements for communications under NIMS are that the systems be interoperable and redundant (FEMA, 2008b). Interoperability is the ability for first responders and those who support them to communicate with each other, specifically, the ability to exchange voice and/or data on demand and in real time.

A lack of redundant or interoperable communications can delay a response and put lives in jeopardy. Studies identify six key reasons for lack of interoperability: aging equipment; limited funding to update or replace equipment; different funding priorities and budget cycles; limited or fragmented planning; the reluctance of agencies to give up control over their communication systems; and limited radio-spectrum availability (FEMA, 2008b).

Many jurisdictions have not kept up with the times and still have older equipment with higher maintenance costs, reduced reliability, or that is obsolete and incompatible with newer digital communications systems. Even the newer digital systems are hampered by proprietary software, which may not effectively connect with proprietary systems installed for other government agencies.

A significant issue today is the ability of outside entities, such as hackers, or even curious citizens, to eavesdrop on essential emergency communications or, in extreme cases, to actually block communications. Thirty years ago, electronic supply stores sold police and fire radio scanners. Truncated radio systems eventually rendered many of the scanners useless, but then technology continued to advance, and now the scanner is obsolete, replaced with apps on tablets and smartphones. An unfortunate reality with cybersecurity is that the more security that is put into a software system, the less interoperable it becomes.

Some interoperability issues can be resolved or at least mitigated by identifying which agencies need to communicate with each other and how the information should be transmitted. A variety of information can now be sent in forms other than radio transmission; for example, routine information that is not time-sensitive can be sent by email. Time-sensitive information should still be sent by radio, while sensitive or classified information should be sent by landline. If necessary in an emergency, a cell phone can be used, with the understanding that cell phone transmissions can be intercepted. Text messaging, tweets, and message board postings are other methods used to communicate. However, procedures must be in place so that responders know to look at their text messages throughout the incident.

Communications is not the only area in which technology is changing the operations of an EOC or the function of emergency management. Today, a variety of software packages can assist with the emergency management process, including software that can conduct drills and improvised plans before, during, and after an event. Additionally, the software can set up incident communications; alert and notify responders via multiple mediums, including phone, email, text messaging, and Twitter accounts; integrate Global Positioning System (GPS) technology to enhance situational awareness; and be used to automatically build communication transcripts, to conduct electronic logbook activities, and to generate incident reports from an ICS database.

One of the most significant advancements in emergency management software is when it is combined with GIS technology, real-time photos provided by responders, or even posted via social media by individuals involved in the incident or observing the incident and, if available, cameras placed on Unmanned Aerial Vehicles (UAVs). Some software also includes hazard-modeling tools that can determine the spread rate of a chemical plume or the evacuation or standoff distance for an improvised explosive device and also suggest the locations of roadblocks.

Another component of EOC communications is pushing out information about the incident to the public. Prior to the invention of social media, the primary method by which an airport would get information to the public was through the media. Today, however, airports have complete capabilities (just as much as anyone else) to push information directly to the public, without being filtered by the media, through the use of websites, Facebook, Twitter, YouTube, and other forms of social media. The media still remains a primary source of information for the general public, as they can often provide context and can deliver their content via broadcast TV and social media. PIO functions are further addressed under the Public Information Officer section.

Activating the EOC is typically the call of the jurisdictional authority or can be at the behest of the IC as the IC sees the incident rapidly expanding or involving a cascading series of events. Imminent emergencies, such as hurricane warnings, pending flooding, or predictions of hazardous weather, can also trigger the activation of an EOC. The AEP should provide guidance about when the EOC should be activated, along with the personnel responsible for its activation. Opening the EOC in some situations is self-evident, such as the crash of a large airliner, an active shooter or hijack attempt, or a natural disaster occurring at the airport or in the nearby community.

THE INCIDENT COMMAND POST AND MOBILE COMMAND UNIT

The **ICP** is the on-scene location where the various Incident Command functions, such as the IC, Operations sector chief and response personnel, and others, are carried out. At an airport, the first responder on-scene to an airplane crash is usually either Airport Operations, airport police, or airport fire personnel. In most cases, the ICP is established by the first individual on-scene with Incident Command responsibilities. Normally, the vehicle driven by that individual is the *de facto* mobile, ICP. Airport fire and some police command vehicles, which are usually sport utility vehicles, come equipped with some Incident Command materials, such as extensive radio systems to talk to a variety of agencies, including the very high frequency (VHF) radios for talking to the ATCT and the pilots, whiteboards with placards to indicate the placement of response vehicles or to build the Incident Command organizational chart, and emergency response vests to readily identify key individuals on-scene. Essentially, the ICP is located wherever the on-scene commander sets it up.

Many large airports use **Mobile Command Units (MCUs)** for on-scene Incident Command. For a large-scale incident, it is not unusual to see what amounts to a recreational vehicle park, full of various MCUs from numerous agencies.

An MCU can act as a base of operations for a critical incident, providing communications, CCTV surveillance, and onsite, sheltered, miniature command centers. Many large-scale airports have their own MCU, while smaller airports typically rely on the MCUs from local police and fire departments. A variety of MCUs, both self-propelled and towed models, are commercially available *off-the-shelf*. Both versions have advantages and disadvantages. While the self-propelled version can be driven directly to the incident scene, it may not be large enough to meet the needs of the airport. A towed-trailer can keep personnel inside completely concealed from view, as well as out of the elements, if that is a desire, but may be less mobile should the situation call for its relocation. Even if the tow vehicle is still attached, there are usually electronic connections, antennas, and other items that may have to be disconnected prior to moving the post.

The type of MCU and its design, layout, and interior depend on the core functions of the command unit at the airport. If the MCU is to provide support for all of the various agencies that have core responsibilities, such as police, fire, EMS, and Airport Operations, then the needs of these agencies should be taken into consideration. However, since most off-airport fire and police agencies also have their own MCUs, airport management may wish to focus more on their core needs rather than trying to focus on all needs at once. For example, if the airport's MCU is also supposed to support EMS functions, then medical equipment and supplies should also be kept on board, but if EMS at the airport has its own unit, then the airport operator should use that space for something else.

Primarily, an airport MCU is a command and control center, so the inclusion of a small meeting space, along with essential communications equipment that mirrors equipment in the airport communications and EOCs, is essential. The NIMS includes Mobile Communications Centers (MCCs) in their resource typing catalog, listing capabilities, workstations, equipment, and personnel requirements. The NIMS Type IV MCU (MCC or Mobile EOC in NIMS vernacular) is typically a converted sport utility vehicle or travel trailer, with one to two workstations, standard radiofrequency (RF) communications, cellular phone systems (through individual user files), and a basic computer system. A full NIMS Type I MCU may be up to a 53-foot custom trailer or bus chassis, with six to 10 workstations, numerous RF transceivers, high-speed Internet access and satellite capability, PDX (phone data exchange) office-style phone and cellular systems, CCTV video, computer-aided dispatch, and Ethernet connections with 120V AC-protected receptacles.

All types of MCUs should be able to operate in an environment with little to no basic services, including electrical service, phone lines, or cell towers, for a period of time. MCUs should be able to provide their own power generation and fuel supply to operate a minimum of 3 to 4 days without refueling. Ideally, an MCU should require minimal setup time, operate as a forward EOC, facilitate communications between multiple agencies, and serve basic personnel needs such as a bathroom, mini refrigerator, microwave, and coffee maker (FEMA, 2005, pp. 26–28). While most airport emergencies do not require the MCU to operate independently for long periods of time, during a natural disaster, the airport may still be expected to maintain some level of minimal functionality, in which case an MCU can fulfill some of an airport's operational and communications requirements, until water, electricity, and other necessary resources can be restored.

When acquiring an MCU, airport operators should first determine the essential functions of the MCU while on-scene and how long it will take to carry out these functions. Then, other airports with MCUs should be researched to determine how those airports use their MCU and what they have found to be most important to be included, along with operational issues and challenges they did not foresee.

NATIONAL INCIDENT MANAGEMENT SYSTEM AND THE INCIDENT COMMAND SYSTEM

The organization of on-scene Incident Command is one of the most important elements of any effective response. Today, that response operates under the NIMS.

The **NIMS** can be a highly effective tool in managing an incident, although, in and of itself, it is neither an operational incident management plan nor a resource allocation plan. NIMS is a set of core doctrines, principles, terminology, and organizational processes that enable effective management of an incident (FEMA, 2008b, p. 3). It is most important to remember that NIMS is supposed to be flexible and adaptable to a particular situation. NIMS is designed to fit the situation and circumstances, not for the situation to fit into NIMS. Emergency management practitioners are cautioned from becoming *NIMS Disciples*, a slang term used in the industry to describe those individuals or agencies that are more focused on seeing that NIMS principles and processes are adhered to during an incident than on the actual outcome of the incident.

NIMS is not only a response plan to be used during large-scale incidents. It can be used to manage irregular operations, snow removal, and special events, such as an air show or a major sporting event such as an upcoming Super Bowl. NIMS is designed to be scalable to be used from day-to-day incidents all the way up to mass casualty or natural disasters. It is intended to standardize resource management procedures and emergency management vocabulary across all domains. During an airplane crash, it is not unusual to have a variety of federal, state, and local responders from numerous domains, including police, fire, and EMS, plus off-airport personnel from a variety of agencies, including the FAA, NTSB, FBI, and EPA. Additionally, even airport firefighting and police personnel must use slightly different terms than their city or county counterparts, but NIMS is designed to reduce the confusion to the extent possible.

A core principle of NIMS is that everyone is speaking the same language. A good example is seen in the change of language on the notification of an aircraft emergency. Previously, airports would use a variety of terms to describe an airplane incident or airplane crash, including terms such as yellow alert, red alert, local standby, and so forth. NIMS formalized, and the FAA standardized through the use of the AC AEP, that aircraft incidents would be referred to as Alert 1, Alert 2, Alert 3, etc. That said, there are still those in the aviation domain that have not embraced NIMS terminology and principles. Airline pilots do not use the terms *Alert 1*, *Alert 2*, and the like to describe the type of emergency they are experiencing, even though this is the same terminology that determines the level of Aircraft Rescue and Firefighting response. Pilots will describe the problem the aircraft is experiencing or they are having (e.g., "smoke in the cockpit," "can't get the landing gear down"), and it is up to either the FAA air traffic controller or the airport operator to determine the level of emergency response.

NATIONAL INCIDENT MANAGEMENT SYSTEM CORE COMPONENTS

The core components of NIMS are: Preparedness, Communications and Information Management, Resource Management, Command and Management, and Ongoing Management and Maintenance (FEMA, 2008b, p. 9).

1. **Preparedness** relates to the concept of building relationships between agencies having emergency management responsibilities, as well as having a unified approach to emergency management planning. Effective incident management begins long before an actual incident. Preparedness involves an integrated combination of planning, training, exercises, personnel qualification and certification standards, and equipment certification (FEMA, 2008b).
2. **Communications and Information Management** emphasizes the importance of having a *Common Operating Picture*, along with standardizing communications and information management systems. Communications and incident management are based on the interoperability, reliability, scalability, portability, resiliency, and redundancy of communications and information systems (FEMA, 2008b).
3. **Resource Management** is the process of identifying and typing resources and having a system in place to request, support, track, demobilize, and, ultimately, reimburse personnel and agencies. The flow of resources must be fluid and adaptable to the requirements of the incident, and NIMS defines standardized mechanisms and establishes the resource management process to identify requirements; order and acquire resources; mobilize, track, and report resource status; recover and demobilize resources; reimburse for resource use; and inventory resources (FEMA, 2008b).
4. **Command and Management** is one of the most important areas of NIMS and relates to three core principles: the *ICS*, *MACS*, and joint *Public Information* processes. Each concept is explained more fully later in this section.
5. **Ongoing Maintenance and Management** focuses on keeping NIMS and ICS relevant with revisions and the integration of technology into the incident management domain, such as the use of software-based notification systems and UAVs for surveillance, Search and Rescue (SAR), and other functions.

While a small-scale incident may have only one IC or incident manager, large-scale incidents have numerous command authorities from a variety of federal, state, and local agencies. NIMS promotes a unified approach to incident response and emergency management, commonly called **Unified Command**.

UNIFIED COMMAND

A significant challenge in a multiagency response is that the personnel from each agency tend only to take orders from personnel within their own leadership structure. For example, police may only listen to police supervisors and commanders, firefighters to their chiefs, and so forth (Pfeifer, 2013, p. 4). Rather than attempt to change the nature of first-response personnel, which is to respond to their superiors and peers within their own organizational structure, the concept of Unified Command instead recognizes and accounts for this reality.

Unified Command applies to incidents involving multiple jurisdictions or agencies, enabling them to coordinate and effectively interact across legal, geographic, and functional responsibilities. Unified Command consists of ICs from various jurisdictions, such as police, fire, Airport Operations, and EMS, operating together to form a single command structure. Within the Unified Command, ICs make joint decisions and speak as "one voice." Any differences are theoretically worked out within the Unified Command, and each responder continues to report to a single supervisor with the responder's area of expertise. Within Unified Command, a police officer would not tell firefighters how to do their job, but instead the key decisions would be made at the command level, with each jurisdictional entity (police, fire, etc.) issuing its orders through its appropriate chain of command (FEMA, 2008b, pp. 6–7). Another dynamic of responding to extreme events is that *crisis managers often limit their connectivity to their own network*, providing information to those within their group and limiting the amount of information provided to others outside the group (Pfeifer, 2013, p. 4). Unified Command features one set of incident objectives, a singular planning process, and one IAP. Other features of Unified Command include integrating multijurisdictional or multiagency General Staff personnel into other functional areas.

Much has already been written about several aspects of NIMS, including the importance of communications and information management and resource management. This section focuses on the Command and Management portion of NIMS—the ICS, MACS, and Public Information—the fundamental elements of incident management that together are the most visible elements of incident management (FEMA, 2008b).

INCIDENT COMMAND SYSTEM

Local communications dispatchers and a few emergency management or response personnel can handle the vast majority of incidents in the community and at an airport, but when an incident dictates a multijurisdictional, multidisciplinary, and multiagency response, ICS provides a flexible mechanism for a coordinated response. ICS was first developed over the course of several wildfire seasons in Southern California in the 1970s.

> Emergency management/response personnel include Federal, State, territorial, tribal, substate regional, and local governments, nongovernmental organizations, private-sector organizations, critical infrastructure owners and operators, and all other organizations and individuals who assume an emergency management role.
>
> **FEMA, 2008b, p. 45**

In *Introduction to Emergency Management*, Haddow, Bullock, and Coppola (2013) note that for ICS to work, it must provide effective operations at three levels of incident character: single jurisdiction and/or single agency, single jurisdiction with multiagency support, and multijurisdictional or multiagency support. Therefore, ICS must adapt to a wide variety of emergencies, from natural disasters to terrorist attacks to airplane crashes.

When implemented correctly, ICS maintains the autonomy of each agency, utilizes management-by-objectives, and maintains effective span of control. ICS is meant to resolve the issue common at many emergencies prior to the implementation of ICS, which was to have multiple agencies assigning their own commanders, resulting in power struggles, miscommunication, and duplication of efforts (Haddow et al., 2013, pp. 51–81). ICS features several characteristics, including common terminology, a modular organization that expands as the situation demands, reliance on IAPs, the complete accountability of personnel and resources, and information and intelligence management (Figure 11.6).

As noted previously, the five major functional areas within ICS are command, operations, planning, logistics, and finance/administration.

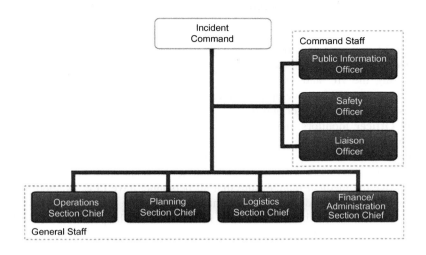

FIGURE 11.6

ICS structure.

Source: FEMA, 2008b.

Command

The command section includes directing and maintaining communication and collaboration with responders and multiple agencies, ensuring safety for those on-scene, and communicating with the public. The commander may be a single **IC** who is responsible for the command function at all times, or a unified **command staff**, which consists of the PIO, Safety Officer, and the Liaison Officer. If only a single IC is assigned, that individual is responsible for fulfilling the functions of the PIO, Safety Officer, and Liaison Officer.

In this section, the term *command* refers jointly to both the person and the function. The overall responsibilities of the IC include:

1. Naming the incident;
2. Establishing immediate priorities and an ICP;
3. Determining the incident's strategic goals and developing, approving, and implementing the IAP;
4. Developing the command structure appropriate for the incident;
5. Assessing resource needs and ordering resources;
6. Coordinating overall emergency activities while ensuring adequate safety measures are in place to protect responders and others;
7. Coordinating with outside agencies; and
8. Authorizing information released to the media.

The media plays a primary role in communicating with the public. Even in the age of social media, many people still look to mainstream media (TV and radio) and the daily print media (newspapers) for their information. The **PIO** gathers and releases information that has been approved by the IC or the Unified Command to the media and, when appropriate, through social media channels. The PIO must determine their own staffing needs (i.e., how many PIOs they will need to handle the incident) and monitor the public reaction to the information. In a multiagency response, a lead PIO must be designated and is part of the command staff. The lead PIO is responsible for operating the JIC and must coordinate the release of information with other agencies involved in the incident. PIOs develop press releases and arrange tours or interviews with key personnel, such as the Airport Director and IC.

The **Safety Officer** monitors incident operations to ensure the health and safety of emergency response personnel and to advise the IC on all matters related to operational safety. The Safety Officer also has the extraordinary authority, by way of the IC, to stop or prevent unsafe acts during the incident operations. Safety Officers must conduct a visual reconnaissance of the incident, review and approve the medical plan, ensure that all personnel have PPE, as appropriate, and investigate any accidents that occur during the incident.

The **Liaison Officer** (sometimes abbreviated LNO or LO) is the point of contact for representatives from other governmental, nongovernmental, and private entities that have responsibilities within the emergency plan. The Liaison Officer must maintain contact with all of the involved agencies and provide information to the Planning function about the agencies to prepare the IAP. The Liaison Officer must identify all of the agency representatives and have up-to-date and complete contact information. The Liaison Officer must keep the various agencies aware of the status of the incident and monitor the operations to identify potential interagency conflicts and issues.

The aforementioned personnel comprise the command staff. General Staff includes section chiefs from the Operations, Logistics, Planning, and Administration/Finance functional areas.

Operations

The Operations section is responsible for the tactical operations at the incident site. It can be easy to confuse the Operations section with the Airport Operations department; however, the Operations section is functional by nature, not agency specific. The Operations section includes personnel from police, fire, EMS, Airport Operations, Airport Maintenance, and, in some cases, airport communications personnel, but this is by no means a complete list of individuals that could comprise personnel within the Operations section. The **Operations Section Chief** (OSC) and the Operations Section focus on the *Priorities of Work (i.e., life, scene stability, property, environment, restoration operations)* and activate and supervise personnel in accordance with the IAP.

For Aircraft Accident response, firefighter personnel commonly fill the roles of the IC and the OSC, at least for the initial first few minutes of the incident. At airports where an Airport Operations emergency manager is always designated as the IC, the lead or chief firefighter is the OSC for the response phase. The OSC conducts a visual reconnaissance of the incident, briefs and assigns personnel their duties, and ensures safe tactical operations. They also help develop portions of the IAP and briefs personnel accordingly about their duties under the plan. OSC chiefs commonly change over when a normal shift changes or a shift in the mission. For example, during an aircraft crash, ARFF commonly assume the OSC role until the firefighting and lifesaving phases of the incident are over, then turn the OSC role over to Airport Operations, or if on-scene, the NTSB.

The NIMS recognizes that an effective span of control for an individual is about five to seven other individuals or groups. As the span of control expands, ICs have a variety of options, including branches, divisions and/or groups, task forces, strike teams, or single resources. Divisions or groups are established when the number of resources exceeds the manageable span of control of both the Incident Command and the OSC. *Divisions* are established to divide the incident into physical or geographical areas of operation, while *Groups* are used to divide the incident into functional areas (fire, police, EMS). *Branches* are established when the number of divisions or groups exceeds the recommended span of control (FEMA, 2008b, p. 55), and may be functional, geographic, or both, for instance, the multicasualty or fire branch director, which may have control over several divisions, plus a rapid intervention crew, a HAZMAT team, and a small boat team.

Single resources are individual personnel or equipment and any associated operators. *Task forces* are any combination of resources assembled for a specific mission or operational need, while *Strike Team* has a set number resources of the same kind. For example, a Task Force of police officers and EMS personnel may be created to enter an area of an active shooting, after the primary shooter has been neutralized, to perform tactical medical care. A Strike Team of three ARFF trucks may be assigned to attack one portion of a fire, in the case of an airplane crash where the fuselage has broken up and is lying in several locations of the airport.

The Operations Section can add branches to their organizational structure as necessary to manage the incident. Additional branches typically include fire, EMS, police, Public Works and Air Operations. Each branch director is responsible for implementing standard operating procedures (e.g., attack fire, respond to active shooter) and implementing pertinent sections of the IAP.

The Staging Area manager also reports to the OSC. The Staging Area manager identifies the location and establishes the boundaries of the Staging Area. Many airports already have predesignated Staging Areas that are located near airport access gates. In a mass casualty incident, multiple Staging Areas may have to be designated. Law enforcement personnel protect the Staging Area, control access, and ensure only authorized personnel are allowed onto the airfield. If Airport Operations continue during the incident, an Airport Operations representative should also be at the Staging Area to ensure that every vehicle accessing the airfield is properly escorted to the incident site.

Planning

The Planning section gathers information and works with the IC to develop the **IAP**. An IAP provides a concise and coherent means of capturing and communicating the overall priorities, objectives, strategies, and tactics of the incident both operational and support activities (FEMA, 2008b).

The **Planning Section Chief (PSC)** collects, evaluates, and disseminates information about the incident and the status of resources. The PSC must have a good understanding of the current situation, predict the probable course of future events, and prepare primary and alternative strategies to manage the incident moving forward. The PSC must work closely with the IC and the OSC to develop the common operating picture and to understand the overall objectives of the incident to develop a realistic IAP.

As the incident expands, the PSC can add additional branches, including the Situation Unit Leader, Resources Unit Leader, Documentation Unit Leader, Demobilization Unit Leader, and Technical Specialists. A variety of specialists often assist the PSC, including meteorologists, infectious disease specialists, radiological and HAZMAT specialists, and field observers. Plans are built around operational cycles, which are sometimes referred to as the "Planning P."

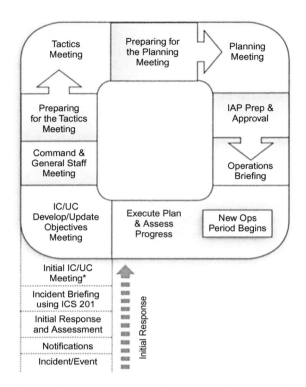

*During this timeframe a meeting with the agency Administrator/Executive can occur.

FIGURE 11.7

Planning workflow chart "Planning P".

Source: FEMA NIMS at https://training.fema.gov/emiweb/is/icsresource/assets/planningp.pdf.

The **Planning P** (Figure 11.7) is a guide used in the planning process that helps establish mission objectives that are measurable and achievable. Planning P is useful for both short-term and long-term planning of Incident Command. It engages the five levels of ICS such that each supports the operational elements of the plan. In the initial response phase, efforts are allocated to thoroughly understanding the situation (i.e., gaining situational awareness). During the initial response, an **Incident Briefing Form (ICS 201)** is used to document the incident name and time it started, along with a map or overview sketch and known resources available to the IC (and estimated time of arrival [ETA] if relevant). ICS 201 also contains a summary of current actions to date and other information relevant to the incident. The next phase in Planning P is to establish the incident objectives, through a meeting by the IC, command staff, and the General Staff (e.g., operations, planning, logistics, and administration section leaders). Once mission objectives are determined, the OSC reviews with the General Staff the tactics (i.e., tactical direction) the OSC is proposing to meet the response objectives in the established timeline and to makes resource allocations. The

OSC prepares the plan and delivers a briefing to the Command and General Staff; adjustments are made and a final plan is approved. Once the plan is executed, adjustments are made as directed by the OSC and personnel in the Operations section. The five phases in the planning process utilizing Planning P as a guide are:

1. **Understanding the situation** involves gathering, reporting, and analyzing information to get the most accurate picture of the incident;
2. **Establishing incident objectives** involves determining an effective strategy and prioritizing incident objectives and alternatives;
3. **Developing tactical direction and resource assignments** involves determining the tactical direction and resources needed to implement the strategy for one operation, which is typically 12 or 24 hours. Input and buy-in is sought from the command staff during this time;
4. **Preparing and approving the plan** involves the actual preparation of plans in the proper format and briefing operational personnel of the plan, along with associated assignments and orders; and
5. **Evaluating and revising the plan**, the fifth phase, involves comparing the planned progress with the actual progress and adjusting the plan, as necessary, either immediately or in preparation for the next operational period.

Logistics

The **Logistics Section** provides facilities, services, and materials in support of the incident. The **Logistics Section Chief (LSC)** participates in developing the IAP and activates the Service Branch and the Support Branch, as needed. The LSC has the necessary procurement cards, as well as the purchasing authority, to obtain needed items without delay. The Service Branch can include a communications unit, a medical unit, and a food unit. The Support Branch can include a supply unit, a facilities unit, and a ground support unit.

The LSC determines the level of service required to support the operations, anticipates needs, and coordinates with the OSC for the delivery of needed equipment. The LSC must also prioritize requests and work with a variety of private contractors and NGOs, such as the Salvation Army, to provide food and other necessary items to responders, passengers, and others involved with the incident.

Finance/Administration

The **Finance/Administration Section Chief (FSC)** must account for the funds used during the response and recovery phase of the disaster. The FSC is responsible for expanding the organizational structure to include a Time Unit Leader, a Procurement Unit Leader, a Cost Unit Leader, and a Compensation and Claims Unit Leader, or Workers Compensation specialist. On some occasions, the FSC branch may also include an attorney. An accurate tracking of how the money is spent is necessary, as citizens, politicians, and public officials are concerned about cost efficiencies related to the use of public funds. Also, after a disaster, insurance companies and FEMA, for federal disasters, may reimburse airports. The FSC should maintain contact with the airport executive staff on all financial matters. Some expenditures may be above the purchasing authority of those in the finance or logistics sections.

Information and Intelligence

Depending on the type of incident, an additional functional area, commonly called the **Intelligence** branch or division, may be established. This area is associated with security-related incidents. The Intelligence section is responsible for developing and managing information related to security plans and operations as directed by the IC. This responsibility could include the protection of Sensitive Security Information, information that is **For Official Use Only (FOUO)**, Law Enforcement Sensitive information (an FBI classification), or national security classified information. The intelligence branch must also coordinate with the OSC when the information may affect Operational Security, and the PIO particularly where the information affects public awareness.

The Intelligence function can also include additional branches, such as the Investigation Operations Group, which is responsible for the overall investigative effort; an Intelligence group responsible for obtaining intelligence at various levels, including unclassified, Sensitive Security Information, classified materials, and open source data; a Forensics group responsible for the collection of forensic evidence and maintaining the integrity of the crime scene; and an Investigative Support Group to ensure investigative personnel are available when needed and are provided with the necessary resources.

For a major security incident in which the intelligence and investigations function is part of the Incident Command structure, the airport operator acts in a support role, providing facilities, access to the site, and other necessities to support the investigative team. Airport management personnel should not expect to be included as part of any of the intelligence and investigation function, unless this function impacts the operational status of the airport.

INCIDENT MANAGEMENT TEAMS—SEADOG AND WESTDOG

Incident Management Teams (IMTs) are comprised of command staff and General Staff members and can be deployed as needed (FEMA, 2008b). The airport should establish an IMT to deploy to off-airport crashes to provide support to communities, responders, and other airports during natural disasters. While an IMT may not actually act as a command authority while deploying to an incident off-airport because of the jurisdictional responsibilities of the agency where the incident took place, an IMT can act in a support capacity, either as an ESF or to provide advice and resources, such as how to maintain the integrity of the accident scene until the NTSB arrives. Airports can also provide support to other airports during or after a natural disaster, by providing experts in airport management and operations, resources, materials, and equipment.

After Hurricane Ivan hit land at Pensacola, Florida, in 2004, causing widespread flooding, tornadoes, and damage to the airport and the community at large, two organizations were formed to assist airports during national disasters, **SEADOG** and **WESTDOG.**

SEADOG is the Southeast Airports Disaster Operations Group and **WESTDOG** is the Western Airports Disaster Operations Group. The organizations were created as a way for airports to assist other airports in their region during natural disasters. ACRP Report 73 (IEM et al., 2012) addressed the best practices in developing Airport-to-Airport Mutual Aid Programs (MAPs), related to logistical, financial, and legal considerations.

Airports routinely rely on mutual aid assistance during large-scale disasters; however, some disasters are so widespread mutual aid may be unavailable, and airports may not be the first priority for mutual aid responders. Many municipal and private nonaviation industries that provide power, sanitation, potable water, and other public utilities have mutual aid agreements with other municipalities. SEADOG and WESTDOG are based on the same principle. Municipalities operate by a general rule of thumb that outside aid should not be expected to reach their community sooner than 72 hours after a disaster, but airports may have to be back in business much more quickly in order to enable the arrival of outside aid and facilitate the evacuation of affected populations (IEM et al., 2012, p. 4).

Airports are excellent resources for other airports to call upon during disasters as they have the exact type of assets and knowledgeable human resources to assist in the unique operating requirements of airport systems (IEM et al., 2012, p. 5). Just as a police officer would understand the basics of law enforcement if redeployed to another jurisdiction, Airport Operations personnel understand the priorities of airport management and have the skills necessary to continue the operation of the airport (security, safety, maintenance, and other key functions that require a unique, airport-specific background).

Individuals from other commercial service airports will have the appropriate security clearances to operate in the Security Areas of an airport. However, individuals responding from general aviation airports will likely not have the same security clearance. General aviation personnel may not be allowed unescorted access to an active, commercial service airfield, but can perform other functions. If the airport is closed to commercial operations, then this may not be an issue until the airport reopens.

During some natural disasters, the airport will voluntarily not comply with Part 139 and cease commercial operations for several hours or several days. At this point, the airport is technically not a commercial service airport and may not be required to comply with Title 49 CFR Part 1542 (Airport Security). The Airport Security Coordinator should work with the local TSA senior official in charge to determine the exact status and requirements (if any) for regulatory security compliance during emergency operations.

Since 2004, both SEADOG and WESTDOG have demonstrated an ability to deliver aid to airports more effectively and earlier than the 72-hour window (IEM et al., 2012, p. 5). However, while many airports may be interested in forming or participating in such groups, there may be financial, legal, and logistical hurdles to overcome.

ACRP Report 73 classified six different categories of urgent needs where airports may need outside assistance, which are listed below (IEM et al., 2012, p. 10):

1. Category 1 is situations that started small, but grew in size to be too large for the airport to handle with its internal resources, and thus mutual aid agreements are activated;
2. Category 2 is situations, such as a power outage of the terminal or a shelter-in-place situation for a prolonged basis, the result of a community power outage or tornado outbreak, that may also affect the local community. Traditional mutual aid agreements typically serve in Category 2 situations as well;
3. Category 3 is a natural or a human-made disaster that damages or obstructs access to the airport, to the extent outside aid is required to return the airport to service. This is the level at which an airport-to-airport MAP can be most useful;

4. Category 4 is a regional disaster that does not damage the airport but puts extraordinary operational or unusual demands on the airport that exceed the capability of local staff and resources for a prolonged basis. An Airport-to-Airport MAP is recommended here as well;

5. Category 5 is an aviation disaster at the airport or in the vicinity of the airport that has a significant effect on the recovery of the airport to normal operations. Airport personnel who are part of the response to the disaster may be extraordinarily grief stricken and not able to return to work in the near-term. Airport-to-Airport MAPs may be useful in providing supplemental personnel from other airports to fulfill key operational, maintenance, or other roles. Other specialized services, such as grief counseling and assistance with PIO duties, may also be necessary and could be provided with a MAP, particularly at airports without a robust public affairs or Public Information system.

6. Category 6 is a situation where an essential piece of equipment has gone out-of-service, such as a fire truck causing the airport to fall below its ARFF index, or airfield lighting outages, where an Airport-to-Airport MAP could be able to loan essential vehicles or equipment in the interim.

In some cases, such as a large-scale disaster that effectively closes the airport for several days, a sort of *ad hoc* reverse-DOG, whereby personnel from the airport that has experienced the crash temporarily transfer to a nearby airport that has been designated to accept overflow or diverted air traffic during the investigation, may occur.

An example of a Category 5 airport need occurred at the Aspen/Pitkin County Airport, Colorado in 2001, when a charter flight crash resulted in multiple fatalities. Although aircraft operation was restored within 48 hours, the airport staff did not have the necessary expertise to deal with the recovery efforts, including the accident investigation, and working with the victims' families (IEM et al., 2012, p. 10). As a result, the Colorado Aviation Recovery Support Team (CARST) was created to provide mentoring, support, and guidance to assist an airport in the recovery from an aviation incident, including disseminating Public Information, infrastructure support and recovery, coordination with the FAA and NTSB, organizational, employee, and community care, and family/victim assistance. The program is funded through the Colorado Division of Aeronautics, the Colorado Aeronautical Board, the Colorado Airport Operators Association, and the Colorado airport agencies that have allowed their staff members to participate in this program (CARST, n.d.).

Setting up an Airport-to-Airport MAP requires several key elements. First is the notion that the affected Airport Manager must retain full control and that all incoming volunteers remember they are present to assist and supplement, not to take control (IEM et al., 2012, p. 26). Second, aid teams must be self-sustaining and not add to the burden of the local airport staff. They should bring their own food, water, and other necessities to support themselves for the duration of their stay (IEM et al., 2012, p. 28). Teams should also understand and be fluent in the use of NIMS and ICS. Any airport that provides mutual aid to another airport should assume that its cost will not be reimbursed. Although there might be mechanisms in place to reimburse the volunteers, those might not apply in an Airport-to-Airport MAP, or the agreement may not be recognized by some insurance agencies, or FEMA, depending on a variety of circumstances, including the nature of federal aid or declaration of disaster by the president.

Any airport operator considering whether to engage in an Airport-to-Airport MAP should explore the legalities and the liabilities involved with sending staff, airport equipment, and materials to another airport. However, any obstacles that arise in assisting another airport during a disaster should not be cause to avoid participation, but should be worked out, as the mutual benefit is worth the effort.

AREA COMMAND AND MULTIAGENCY COORDINATION

During a large-scale disaster affecting an entire community, the municipality may institute an **Area Command**. Area Commands oversee the management of large or evolving incidents with multiple IMTs or with numerous IMTs covering a large, geographical area. Area Commands are also used when a number of incidents of the same type, such as flooding, a wildfire, or hurricane, occur, causing multiple IMTs to compete for the same resources (FEMA, 2010).

MACSs allow various levels of governments to work together more effectively, by coordinating activities above the field level, and to prioritize the incident demands between critical or competing resources (FEMA, 2010). MACSs can be informal processes based on oral agreements between jurisdictions during an incident, or more formalized processes, which are laid out before an incident occurs. Whether formal or informal, a MACS can identify facilities, equipment, personnel, and procedures, integrating into a common system responsible for coordination and support of resources to emergency operations.

MACS facilities are often EOCs, communications centers, MCUs, or any location where activities can be coordinated. Some in the emergency management community at the state and regional levels see the airport EOC as a MACS, which may be accurate, but can be confusing when the term is used around airport personnel, who are generally unfamiliar with the concept.[9]

A MACS can also be certain personnel, such as agency administrators or executives who are authorized to commit agency resources and funds in a coordinated response effort, known as a MAC Group, and can also be procedures, such as business practices that define the activities, relationships, and functionality of the MACS (FEMA, 2010).

The primary functions of a MACS is to provide situational assessment, to determine incident priorities, to acquire and allocate resources, to support policy-level decisions, and to coordinate with other MACS elements and elected and appointed officials (FEMA, 2010).

The main difference between an Area Command and MACS is that a MACS provides off-scene coordination and support but does not have direct Incident Command authority, whereas Area Command has oversight and authority over the various IMTs. In a large-scale community disaster, the airport's emergency management personnel may be considered an IMT under a city or county Area Command.

PUBLIC INFORMATION OFFICER

The PIO plays an important part in the management of an emergency. Although not a *first responder* in the true sense of the term, the PIO performs numerous functions that facilitate an

---

[9]In the NIMS training, MACSs aren't given much attention, and most airport personnel are only required to complete the basic NIMS training, which are FEMA's Emergency Management Institute courses, ICS 100/200 and 700. More advanced training in NIMS and ICS, along with emergency exercises, is generally necessary to integrate some of the advanced concepts and terms.

effective response, such as distributing information to the public that reduces further casualties and keeps the public from obstructing police, fire, and EMS personnel. For a small, municipal-run airport, the PIO likely works for the city or county directly and represents the entire municipality, not only the airport operator. In this case, the PIO is unlikely to understand aviation terms and how things generally work. Whereas the PIO may have seen numerous police and fire-related incidents in the municipality, they often may not understand the differences in the aviation domain. The airport operator must ensure that the municipal PIO is fully educated on aviation incident management and that a knowledgeable airport staff member can assist the PIO.

Medium-size, commercial service and larger, general aviation airports may have a person on staff that is PIO as a collateral duty, whereas large, commercial service airports usually have a small staff that is dedicated to the PIO function. Traditionally, some of the PIO's main challenges have come from within the PIO's own organizational structure. Some in the command or political structure view the PIO as "the media" and seek to minimize the information given to this individual. This practice handicaps the PIO, disabling a powerful tool to assist with the response to, and recovery from, an emergency. The PIO may also experience distrust from the media who believe the PIO may be a gatekeeper, preventing them from getting the real story.

However, the PIO must develop a trusting relationship with those in the command structure, along with the media. That trust begins long before the emergency or natural disaster, and individuals who are assigned PIO functions should complete the NIMS PIO beginner and advanced training courses. Also, many PIOs are former news reporters and understand what the media needs—they know a good PIO learns quickly, has good people skills, and has integrity. A good PIO does not lie and projects integrity and credibility—reporters and photographers trust them (Jones, 2005, p. 92). However, one should never assume that the PIO function is somehow easy because it involves fewer hard skills (e.g., putting out fires, handling a firearm, applying a tourniquet to an injured passengers) and more soft skills, such as relationship building. Today's PIOs experience even more challenges with the advent of social media, citizen journalists, and UAV technology.

The Public Information Officer in Incident Management

The PIO is a member of the ICS command staff and is charged with advising the IC or Unified Command of all matters related to Public Information related to the incident (Walsh et al., 2012). The PIO is an important role for three key reasons: (a) to distribute essential information to the public about the event or crisis so the public knows what actions to take; (b) to keep the public and media informed so the public does not obstruct response and recovery operations, or, in some cases, so the public can support the recovery or response; (c) to create the narrative about the event (to the extent possible). How the story of how the airport handled an incident is told can affect the response actions in the short term, recovery actions in the near term, and future actions, through political and interagency fallout, in the long term. In their book *National Incident Management Systems: Principles and Practices*, Walsh et al. (2012) note that in addition to the primary role of the PIO (keeping the IC informed), the PIO also handles:

1. Inquiries from the media, the public, and elected and appointed officials;
2. EPI and warnings;
3. Rumor monitoring and responses;
4. General media relations;

5. Other functions, including gathering, verifying, coordinating, and disseminating accurate, accessible, and timely information related to the incident, particularly information concerning the public's health and safety, as well as public protection actions.

PIOs must be able to identify the key information that needs to be communicated to the public and craft messages that convey the information in a clear and understandable manner, which does not overwhelm the audience with too much at once (FEMA, 2008b). A top goal of the PIO is to reduce panic, by telling the public what actions to take, and to provide the public with enough information about the incident to act on the information, if appropriate, or to make informed decisions about what to do. For example, in an airplane crash, numerous audiences would require information from the PIO, and if no one in the Incident Command structure were designated and trained to handle these requests, the system would have to be developed *ad hoc*, and a responder or other person, who might not be trained in the job of the PIO, might be selected for the role. This situation could immediately have serious operational ramifications that hinder the overall response, as well as long-term political, bureaucratic, and legal impacts.

The list below is a sampling, based on a theoretical airplane crash, and crosses the functional lines between *Emergency Public Notification*, *Protective Actions*, and *communication*:

1. Family members of potential victims want to know where to go for more information about their loved ones;
2. Those with scheduled flights out of the airport want to know if the airport is open or if their flight is delayed;
3. Individuals who live near the incident want to know if there are HAZMATs on board, or if they should evacuate or shelter-in-place for any reason, and whether the accident has affected local transportation networks, such as shutting down highways or rail systems;
4. The IC or Unified Command will want to know any information about the incident that relates to the effectiveness of the response or the safety of the responders (e.g., a citizen is flying a UAV over the incident site, which poses a collision risk with medical evacuation helicopters);
5. Elected and appointed officials with responsibilities over the airport, the community, and/or the response want to know to which they should respond, and want to know that rescue personnel are on-scene and the situation is being handled;
6. Regulatory officials, such as the FAA and TSA, want to know what is happening. FAA officials are concerned with safety of the Airport Operations, safety of flight operations if the airport is staying open, and where the incident took place so they can respond. TSA officials want as much information as they can get in order to notify the Transportation Security Operation Center, to determine if this could be a terrorist event;
7. Off-airport responders, upon initial notification, will "tune-in" to the media channels to learn more about the event, to help form a common operating picture, as assets and personnel are deployed to the scene.

The above list includes the IC, elected and appointed officials, regulatory officials, and the general public, but the most important audience for PIOs are themselves. Like the *telephone game* that kids play, when one person whispers a phrase to someone, who then whispers it to someone else, and so on, the information changes each time it is passed to another person. Therefore, the original information must be as accurate as possible.

The process of gathering information is through the on-scene command and other PIOs from other agencies, monitoring the media, and working closely with elected and appointed officials, community leaders, and, most importantly, the IC/Unified Command. Information should be confirmed through multiple sources; even the IC may not have the accurate picture, and the PIO must ensure that if the IC says one thing that the PIO cannot verify, the PIO should advise the IC that the IC may not have the best information on which to act. The three basic categories of Public Information are: Narrative Information, Advisories and Warnings, and Action Messages (Walsh et al., 2012, p. 3888).

1. **Narrative Information** provides an overview of the incident. This type of information is usually sound bites or video clips, which paint a picture of what has happened, its magnitude, and the progress of the event. Examples of narrative messages may be, "an aircraft has crashed," "there has been a shooting at the airport," or "the airport announces the startup of service to Cancun." While all PIOs strive for accurate reporting of information, accuracy is not as important in the narrative information, as it is in Advisories and Warnings to the public. Also, in the beginning of an incident, information often comes to the IC piecemeal, and the initial information is not always as accurate as information that comes later, once the incident has matured.

2. **Advisories and Warnings** tell the public about a concern, along with specific action steps the public should take. Advisories and warnings are time-sensitive, and accuracy is important. These messages may also contain technical information, but should still be written using language most of the audience understands, minimizing acronyms and jargon. Examples of advisory or warning messages may be, "the airport is closed until further notice, call your airline to determine the status of your flight," "all traffic should avoid the frontage road north of the airport as it is reserved for emergency response equipment at this time," or "individuals are prohibited from operating drones[10] over the incident site, and citizens failing to obey, may be subject to arrest . . ."

3. **Action Messages** prompt the public to take immediate action, with timeliness and accuracy possibly being a matter of life and death. Action messages require an all-out media blitz during which local TV and radio broadcasts are interrupted, reverse 911 systems are used, and public warning systems, such as tornado sirens, are activated. Examples of Action Messages may be, "residents that live north of the airport should evacuate immediately" (and advise on the route of the evacuation), or "all personnel at the airport should immediately seek shelter in a designated tornado shelter location."

Just as social media has created additional challenges for PIOs, it has opened up new pathways for the airport to disseminate information directly to the public. Traditional methods included holding a press conference, issuing a press release, or giving direct interviews to media outlets. The challenge in these techniques is that the media outlet will then decide what information to disseminate to the public. While information related to emergency public notification or Protective Actions are often communicated directly and without a filter (the PIO must still ensure the media got the message right), the airport loses control of the overall *narrative*.

---

[10]Although we use the term Unmanned Aerial Vehicle (UAV) throughout the text, the term "drone" is used here as it's become more readily identifiable as to what it is, in the public eye.

The *narrative*, as it relates to an incident, is the story that is told of how the airport responded to the event. The term *narrative* is similar to the type of message that can be sent by a PIO (referenced above), but in this context, narrative relates to how airport management handled the entire event.

Within the PIO community, there is a general theme that agencies should aspire to achieve in telling the airport story. Regardless of the circumstances, airports and government agencies want to ensure that they acted responsibly and they were concerned for the safety and security of everyone involved; there were plans in place, and they were followed to the extent possible; and further, steps are being taken to either avoid or mitigate future problems (Hoffman, 2008).

Airport Managers, elected and appointed officials, and other responsible parties may need to defend their actions in managing an incident three or more times: once to their supervisors or electorate, a second time in the *court of public opinion*, and a third time in actual court, which may involve lawsuits, testimony, and depositions. An effective way of creating the narrative outlined above is to work the problems backward—in advance. This means to ensure risk assessments have been conducted, materials and equipment necessary to handle the identified threats and hazards have been acquired, plans were drafted to handle the problems, personnel received training on responding to the problem, and exercises were conducted with actual follow-up actions to identify capability and training gaps in the plan. If an agency has fallen short of these expectations, then much of the public messaging that says "the airport did the right thing" will be perceived as *spin*, instead of a sincere effort to be prepared.

With technology, the field of journalism is changing, and PIOs and government agencies must adopt strategies to change with it. Some of the most significant influences on journalism today are the invention and widespread use of social media, the emergence of the *citizen journalist*, and the advent of UAV, or drone, technology.

Social media allows anyone with access to the Internet to say whatever is on the individual's mind to a worldwide audience. The Merriam-Webster dictionary defines "social media" as: "forms of electronic communication (as Web sites for social networking and microblogging) through which users create online communities to share information, ideas, personal messages, and other content (as videos)" (Merriam-Webster, n.d.).

While thousands of social media avenues are available, a few are predominant. A few that have become standard are Twitter (a form of microblogging), Facebook (messaging, commentary, video and photo posting), YouTube (video posting), Periscope (live streaming), and websites. Other forms of social media become popular and unpopular on a yearly basis; consequently, part of the PIO's job is to keep up with the current trends and know what forms of social media people are paying attention to.

With social media, a passenger can be sending out tweets (messages with a 140-character limit) to thousands, hundreds of thousands, or millions of people, not only about what's going on at the incident, but also photos and links to video of the event. Even someone with a small social media following can have a message or video go viral, as it's reposted, retweeted, and re-sent through other social media outlets. During the active shooter incident at LAX on November 1, 2013, tens of thousands of passengers and others used their cell phones to videotape and photograph the scene of the shooting, uploading to their personal and professional social media outlets, all while evacuating the facility.

> "When the shooting happened, I suddenly had 20,000 amateur journalists on the airfield," noted John Kinney, director of emergency management at Los Angeles International Airport on November 1, 2013.
>
> **Kinney, J., personal interview, October 27, 2014, Denver, CO**

Another dynamic that has come about as a result of social media is the *citizen journalist*, or **blogger**. According to WordPress.org, a hosting site for many blogs:

> "Blog" is an abbreviated version of "weblog," a term used to describe websites that maintain an ongoing chronicle of information. A blog features diary-type commentary and links to articles on other websites, usually presented as a list of entries in reverse chronological order. Blogs range from the personal to the political, and can focus on one narrow subject or a whole range of subjects.
>
> **WordPress.org, n.d.**

Some blogs, like the Huffington Post, have expanded to legitimate news sources with staffs of professional reporters, photographers, and videographers. Blogs also crosslink to other blogs, which expands their reach, so that a posting on one blog may be reposted thousands of times over, reaching a global audience within a matter of minutes. Bloggers can make good investigative reporters and often work with mainstream investigative reporters, so their impact on what is said about the airport cannot be ignored by the PIO.

UAV technology allows aerial access to incident scenes that was previously only the domain of the news helicopter. For the media or public to see what was going on at an incident, either a helicopter or a very-long-range lens on a camera, or telescope, was needed. However, UAVs offer up-close access and are generally unaffected by police tape or an airport perimeter fence. News organizations are moving toward the use of UAVs, along with emergency management personnel and citizen journalists. CNN used a UAV to cover a story in Selma, Alabama, in 2015, and their use is beginning to spread throughout the nation. However, during an incident, UAVs operated by news agencies or private citizens can become a hazard to air navigation, violate the privacy of private citizens, and interfere with rescue operations.

PIOs must monitor mainstream media, but they must also monitor what is being said about the airport in the social media domain. The combination of social media, every citizen a journalist, and UAVs means that government entities must always operate with transparency, with the thought that everyone is watching and judging their actions.

Just as social media challenges PIOs, they also can use it as an effective tool to get information directly to the affected and interested populations, without a media filter. Many emergency exercises now have a social media component, and social media is also being used to communicate information during an incident to responders and other agencies (Raths, 2015).

Agencies can track road closures, power outages, needs of passengers in the terminal building, and other information, which can be uploaded and connected to GIS maps to help determine where first responders' assets should be deployed (Raths, 2015). Social media, including mass texting, can be used to communicate with volunteers so that they do not have to report to the EOC before being deployed (Raths, 2015). Also, volunteers can be used to help monitor and manage social media duties, and can do so from their own location, rather than an EOC or similar area.

Operational Security and Health Information

While PIOs are in the business of passing information along to the public, two areas of information must be protected from public disclosure. Operational Security, aka OPSEC, includes Sensitive Security Information and information about procedures; deployment of police, FBI, or other law enforcement assets during a security incident; discussions about tactics; videos of certain weapons or law enforcement surveillance tools; and tactical deployments that must be kept from public disclosure. Again, social media, UAVs, and citizen journalists may identify such information on their own, but airports should have policies restricting their own personnel from releasing such information via any method. Numerous cases of a family friend posting about the death of a friend or a loved one in Iraq or Afghanistan before the deceased family was formally notified have occurred.

Also, the **Health Insurance Portability and Accountability Act of 1996 (HIPPA)** addresses the privacy of an individual's health status and prohibits it from being publicly disclosed. Only certain personnel, such as law enforcement or clergy, will typically make a death notification; hospitals and health care professionals are required to adhere to HIPPA and can transmit information about the health status of an individual only under certain circumstances. The airport operator should not issue statements about the names and conditions of victims unless first cleared by medical professionals, the NTSB, or an other authorized entity. Furthermore, airlines are obligated to protect the identities of their passengers and crew and will likely not provide passenger manifests to the EOC.[11] However, while police, fire, and Airport Operations will not be provided the passenger manifest, the American Red Cross works with the air carriers and the health and hospitals section leader to coordinate the status and location of victims and others involved in the incident.

Joint Information Systems/Joint Information Center

A large-scale airport incident will rapidly expand beyond the capabilities of local responders, activating a mutual aid response and expanding the role of the PIO. Every agency should have its own Public Information process and personnel, and a key goal during the incident is to coordinate public communication efforts and not point the finger of blame at other agencies. Also, the public messaging should not interfere with the response and recovery operations, but should seek to enhance such operations.

The **Joint Information System (JIS)** is an organized, integrated, and coordinated mechanism to ensure the delivery of understandable, timely, accurate, and consistent information to the public, across multiple jurisdictions, during a crisis. The key elements of JIS are interagency coordination, gathering, verifying, coordinating, and disseminating consistent messages, providing information to decision makers, and staying flexible and adaptable to the situation (FEMA, 2008a). A **JIC** is a location that facilitates the JIS. It is where PIOs from various agencies meet and perform PIO functions, across jurisdictions, private sector agencies (such as the airlines), and NGOs (Walsh et al., 2012, p. 3086). A single JIC is preferable, but multiple JICs may be necessary to provide the adaptability and necessary coverage for the event or incident. While JIC personnel gather and coordinate information, the ultimate authority for releasing information rests with the IC/Unified Command.

---

[11]There is a significant difference of opinion in the industry about whether the air carrier has an obligation to provide the passenger manifest to entities other than the American Red Cross, or as requested by the FBI, but much to the consternation of local airport police, operations, and fire personnel, air carriers typically never release this list to them directly.

At an airport, JICs can be located near established media centers. A media center is a location to which media personnel are directed during an incident. The Birmingham/Shuttlesworth International Airport (Birmingham, Alabama), has a large meeting room that is set up to double as a media center, featuring a podium, effective lighting and seating, and a sound system, usable for press briefings, along with amenities for the press. Free access to the Internet, an abundance of AC/DC power outlets, a kitchen to provide coffee and snacks, a TV, and plug-ins for broadcast media personnel to pick up audio feeds are some elements of an effective media center. While the goal is to provide for the press during a situation, so they are less likely to interfere with Airport Operations, in no case should the media center be close to the family assistance area.

SUMMARY

Regardless of the type of incident, several core functions, including command and control, communications, police, fire, public notification, emergency medical, resource management, and Airport Operations and maintenance, must be addressed. Each function plays a particular role in an incident.

Essentially, the three core elements of an effective emergency response are command, control, and communications. Command and control are carried out in the aviation domain through the use of the NIMS. Command can be a single IC, often predetermined by airport policy or as determined by the nature of the incident. Command is the ability to effectively manage others, including those who do not work directly for the commander, and control is the ability to have a system of Incident Command in place that has been trained and tested and has the available resources it needs. An effective communications network that is interoperable and redundant is the key to carrying out the command function.

Many emergencies, including natural disasters, require emergency public notifications, and in some cases, Protective Actions, such as evacuation and shelter-in-place. Airport management should have in place procedures to notify the airport population, in the airside, landside, and terminal areas, and tell them what is going on and what actions to take.

Police, fire, and EMS are the core first responders to nearly any emergency, and these personnel have numerous responsibilities throughout the AEP. Airport Operations and maintenance personnel fill supporting or command roles during an emergency, and they are the experts on both the function of the airport and the national aviation system, but also have the access, vehicles, and training necessary to maneuver on the AOA.

The NIMS, created after 9/11, is the standard method of managing disasters, incidents, and other events in the United States. It is based on three principles: the ICS, multiagency coordination, and Public Information.

The five functions of ICS are command, operations, planning, logistics, and finance/administration. For some incidents, an intelligence/investigative function is added. Command includes the IC or Unified Command personnel, a Safety Officer, a PIO, and a Liaison Officer. Operations are personnel that execute the plans and policies; planning personnel develop IAPs, in an attempt to set and meet Incident Command objectives. Finance/Administrative personnel track the use of resources and personnel, and logistics personnel acquire needed personnel, materials, and vehicles to support the incident objectives.

Multiagency coordination enables the resources of numerous agencies to be pooled for use by response personnel. PIOs also play an important role in incident management, in both disseminating essential information to the public and to the command team, and in writing the airport's narrative on how the airport handled the event.

Creating Capabilities through the Homeland Security Exercise and Evaluation Program

by Justin J. Overholt, B.S., C.M., EMT-P, CFEI
Special Operations Training & Exercise Coordinator,
Denver Fire Department,
Denver International Airport, Denver, CO

It is well-known that a remote or even minor incident can have devastating consequences on the world's commercial aviation system. Whether it is a poorly placed stalled vehicle on a critical airport access route, a small fire in a communications center, or unprecedented terror attacks like those of 9/11, the continuity of commercial aviation operations is a delicate balance. So how do we do that in a consistent, effective, and measurable way?

All aviation professionals, regardless of role, are faced with the complex simplicity of an overriding mission of moving people safely. It's not enough to move them. It's not enough to keep them safe. This is best accomplished by developing, maintaining, and improving the overall flow of the Continuity of Operations of the entire aviation system. It is the noble intent of the required exercise cycles to develop, enhance, and evaluate the capabilities necessary to move people safely, which leads one to wonder: In the mire of annual tabletops, biannual Aviation Security Contingency (AVSEC) plans, and triannual crash exercises do we progress toward mastery of our overriding mission or simply check a box toward compliance? The truth is we do not really know.

Capabilities development is not a cryptic process. It is both intuitive and well accepted in any learning methodology that one must progress from the basics of individual skills through low-level coordination and into progressively more complex coordinations. How effective the higher levels of command, communications, and coordination are should be the focus of any capability development methodology.

In an ideal world, capability and compliance would be synonymous, with one simply being a measure of the other. However, in an industry governed by a plethora of standards and best practices, one glaringly neglected best practice is that of ensuring that our compliance with industry standards actually yields legitimate capabilities.

We are all overwhelmed with compliance and keeping the whirlwind of day-to-day operations running smoothly. The last thing any of us wants is to add more to our plates; however, if I told you that you could package everything, including day-to-day operations, into a beautifully simple system that would ensure your FAA inspector would leave your airport in awe of your amazing abilities, would you be interested in reading further? If I told you that you could obtain this amazing system not only free, but that it could potentially lead to increased profits and gazillions of dollars in grant funds, would this interest you? If so, read on.

(Continued)

(Continued)

First introduced in 2002, the Homeland Security Exercise and Evaluation Program (HSEEP) represents lessons learned and best practices from existing exercise programs and can be adapted to the full spectrum of scenarios and incidents. It is a proven methodology that, when properly applied, ensures capabilities are developed in a manner that supports local, state, and federal needs and is done so in a manner that is consistent with the National Response Plan and all its associated capabilities, standards, and best practices (e.g., NIMS/ ICS). If you do it right and keep it simple, it will simplify your life and dramatically improve your operations. Simply put: If you follow the system, you will check all of the boxes in a way that will make you look like a "rock star." The challenge is learning it and applying it consistently over time.

As with all processes, improvements come over time through regular evaluations, process reviews, and a commitment to implementing planned improvements. HSEEP is a progressive, building block approach used to identify existing core capabilities, determine target capabilities, and develop the knowledge, skills, and abilities necessary to achieve, improve, or sustain those core capabilities. It is scalable by design and elegantly simple *if* you utilize the key (i.e., progressive) steps. Unfortunately, I often find HSEEP users who throw their hands up in frustration over the massive amount of work before them because they've rushed to build intricate full-scale exercises without considering all the foundational building blocks first. Baby steps, Baby . . . baby steps.

HSEEP Basics

The fundamental HSEEP progression begins with individual skill development training and a progression from drills, tabletop, and functional exercises that lead up to a full-scale exercise (Figure 11.8).

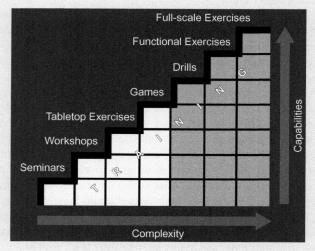

FIGURE 11.8

HSEEP program progression.

Courtesy Justin Overholt, 2015.
(Continued)

(Continued)

At each step there are evaluations and improvement planning processes. The key thing to understand about HSEEP is that training is for individuals, exercises are for teams (Figure 11.9). This is an important distinction as nothing mires an exercise cycle like attempting to train and/or evaluate individuals during an exercise or hindering operational coordination and flow because the requisite individual skill development process was neglected.

Exercises themselves are divided into two basic types: discussion based and operational based. One you talk through, the other you walk through. The Workshop and Tabletop Exercise (TTX) are the most commonly used discussion-based exercises. The main difference between the two is that workshops produce a plan and involve give-and-take to arrive at an end goal. A TTX should be a verbal demonstration of the player's knowledge of the plan as it's applied to a given scenario. A good TTX should be short, to the point, and reveal the strategic strengths and weaknesses of the plan being exercised. The workshop is where the plan was developed, the TTX is the talk through.

Operational-based exercises are the "walk through," made up of drills, functional exercises (FE), and full-scale exercises (FSE) (Figure 11.10). The more you move, the bigger the exercise. Individual group's drill (e.g., ARFF, EOC drills, EMS). A individual group drills (e.g., ARFF, EOC, EMS); a few groups practice working together towards better interoperability and interaction. These are FEs, limited in scope and focused on an interaction between groups.

When all groups work together in real time (e.g., EOC, ARFF, and EMS) it's considered a Full Scale Exercise, but these are not meant to be pomp-and-circumstance laden with unrealistic artificial timelines. These are capability-driven, objectively measured dress rehearsals of interoperability.

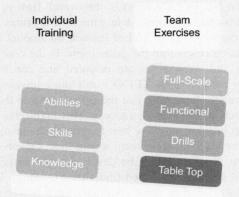

Individual Training — Team Exercises

Abilities / Skills / Knowledge — Full-Scale / Functional / Drills / Table Top

FIGURE 11.9

HSEEP training focus areas.

Courtesy Justin Overholt, 2015.

(Continued)

(Continued)

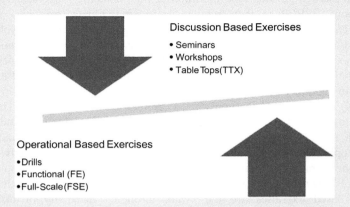

FIGURE 11.10

HSEEP "walk-through" exercises.

Courtesy Justin Overholt, 2015.

To put it into perspective, think of a kid's soccer team. The core capability any team wants to have is the ability to win games. To win games you must score points. To score points everyone on the field has specific duties and responsibilities to perform. The better each individual does their job, in the context of the overall flow of the play, the more likely the team will score points and, ultimately, win games. A lot rides on individual skill, but if it's unclear which goal the ball is to be kicked toward, no amount of mastery will overcome that ambiguity. The solution lies within the game itself. In the course of play, individual and organizational strengths and weaknesses are revealed and can be sustained or improved upon. Simply discussing the play book (TTX) won't show physical skills, but will improve understanding of the strategy. Practicing just the offense or just the defense creates an integrated functionality critical to the game's success. This highlights roles and responsibilities and gives the coach deep insights into how best to arrange the team.

An HSEEP process for a kid's soccer team would look something like this: The coaches determine what skill sets can reasonably be developed and sustained, and basic plays are written (workshop). Skill sets are developed (individual training). Everyone gathers to learn what the coaches have developed as plays (seminar), each player states their understanding of the play as it relates specifically to them (TTX). When everyone has a reasonable understanding (and can state that understanding), they head out to the field to work on low-level coordination (drills). When the small groups are comfortable about what's required of them, those groups are brought together and exercised (FEs). As capabilities grow, a

(Continued)

(Continued)

scrimmage is arranged and you pretend to play a real game in real time. This is the FSE. Throughout the process you evaluate progress, identify areas for improvement, and work those out—rinse and repeat.

It's important to note that all exercises—from TTX to FSE—are to run the plays as they are written and understood. These aren't the forums for bartering, criticism, or argument. The HSEEP evaluation and improvement planning process provides the tools to objectively evaluate performance based on the stated objectives and targeted capabilities. Those evaluations provide the information necessary to develop an improvement plan. The vast majority of progress will be made identifying and improving upon the little things that prevent a smooth operational flow. The magic is in the drills and FEs.

When you've done the preliminary work and are ready to tackle the FSE, it's easy to get sucked into the desire to evaluate too many objectives. After all, you're going to do a variety of things, why not evaluate them all? While this may seem reasonable at first, collecting too much data can quickly dilute and overwhelm even the most proactive improvement processes. With too much data we tend to lose sight of what is really important, and for us, it's Continuity of Operations. Every FSE conducted by a commercial airfield should focus squarely on Continuity of Operations. The things that will make the biggest improvements in safety, efficiency, and profitability all require Continuity of Operations. To keep things in perspective, I recommend using only three objectives for any FSE. Those objectives should be: Operational Communications, Operational Coordination, and EOC Operations. These objectives can be aligned with any target or core capability and will ensure the big picture is always in perspective.

The ability for ARFF firefighter's to make bubbly wet stuff come out of the big green machines is a training objective, *not* an exercise objective. The ability of paramedics to triage, treat, and transport is similarly evaluated and improved by skills and drills. However, the ability of EMS providers to perform their critical tasks in a coordinated and well-communicated manner as they transition from collecting evacuees from an aircraft on fire to receiving those rescued from the postfire control rescue efforts is an objective of a FSE. To put it simply, if you don't know how to put on your costume and don't know your lines, you're not ready for the show. What should be measured is how are all of those operations coordinated by the EOC, in support of Continuity of Operations, and is everything communicated in a consistent and effective manner.

Sadly, in the rush to satisfy the compliance box, progressive drills and FEs get neglected in hopes that the flash/wow factor of burning debris and moulaged patients garners the attention away from what should be the objectives. Just as operational flow is critical to the success of a commercial airfield, the operational flow of emergency response should be similarly scrutinized and aggressively improved.

HSEEP is an amazing tool and represents best practices for exercise conduct and design. By simply using the process you will ensure compliance with applicable standards *and* develop legitimate capabilities. Get the training, use the HSEEP templates, and keep it simple. Your training and exercise programs will give you the means to dramatically improve Continuity of Operations in ways you've never dreamed possible, all while putting a compliant smile on your FAA inspector's face.

REFERENCES

Airports Council International (ACI). (2009, April). *Airport preparedness guidelines for outbreaks of communicable disease.* Retrieved June 1, 2009, from: http://www.airports.org/aci/aci/file/ACI_Priorities/Health/Airport%20preparedness%20guidelines.pdf.

Anders, M. (2015). Office escape. *Off the Grid, 9,* 71–72.

Centers for Disease Control (CDC). (2009, March). *US public health entry screening of arriving international travelers at airports during an influenza pandemic.* Retrieved on June 3, 2009, from: http://ecfr.gpoaccess.gov/cgi/t/text/text-idx?c = ecfr&tpl = /ecfrbrowse/Title42/42cfr71_main_02.tpl.

Centers for Disease Control (CDC). (2014, December 12). *Airport exit and entry screening for Ebola—August–November 10, 2014.* Retrieved August 28, 2015, from: http://www.cdc.gov/mmwr/preview/mmwrhtml/mm6349a5.htm.

Colorado Aviation Recovery Support Team (CARST). (n.d.). *Colorado aviation recovery.* Retrieved August 28, 2015, from: http://www.coloradoaviationrecovery.org/#home.

Everbridge. (2015, August 26). *The Everbridge suite of products.* Retrieved from http://www.everbridge.com/products/.

Federal Aviation Administration (FAA). (2010). Airport safety standards. AC 150/5200-31C: *Airport emergency plan.* Washington, DC: U.S. Department of Transportation.

Federal Emergency Management Agency (FEMA) (2005). *Typed resource definitions* (pp. 26–28). Washington, DC: FEMA.

Federal Emergency Management Agency (FEMA). (2008a). *IS-774 EOC management and operations* (US, FEMA, EMI). Washington, DC: FEMA. Retrieved August 24, 2015, from: https://training.fema.gov/is/courseoverview.aspx?code = is-775.

Federal Emergency Management Agency (FEMA). (2008b). *National incident management system.* Washington, DC: FEMA.

Federal Emergency Management Agency (FEMA). (2010). *Considerations for fusion center and emergency operations center coordination.* Washington, DC: FEMA.

Haddow, G. D., Bullock, J. A., & Coppola, D. (2013). *Introduction to emergency management* (5th edn). Waltham, MA: Butterworth-Heinemann.

Hoffman, J. C. (2008). *Keeping cool on the hot seat: Dealing effectively with the media in times of crisis* (4th ed.). Highland Mills, NY: Four C's Pub.

IEM, Smith-Wooline, TransSolutions (2012). *Airport-to-airport mutual aid programs.* Washington, DC: Transportation Research Board (ACRP Report 73).

Jones, C. (2005). *Winning with the news media: A self-defense manual when you're the story* (8th ed.). Anna Maria, FL: Winning News Media.

Merriam-Webster. (n.d.). *Social media.* Retrieved August 30, 2015, from: http://www.merriam-webster.com/dictionary/social%20media.

National Fire Protection Association (NFPA). (2013). *NFPA 424, guide for airport/community emergency planning.* http://www.nfpa.org/codes-and-standards/document-information-pages?mode=code&code=424.

Pfeifer, J. (2013). Crisis leadership: The art of adapting to extreme events. *PCL Discussion Paper Series.*

Raths, D. (2015, July 23). *Social media: The next level.* Retrieved from: http://www.emergencymgmt.com/disaster/Social-Media-The-Next-Level.html.

Ripley, A. (2009). *The unthinkable: Who survives disaster and why.* New York, NY: Three Rivers Press.

Stambaugh, H., Sensenig, D., Casagrande, R., Flagg, S., & Gerrity, B. (2008). *Quarantine facilities for arriving air travelers: Identification of planning needs and costs.* Washington, DC: Transportation Research Board (ACRP Report 5).

Walsh, D. W., Christen, H., Callsen, C., Miller, G., Maniscalco, P., Lord, G., et al. (2012). *National incident management system: Principles and practice* (2nd ed.) [Kindle]. Retrieved August 30, 2015, from: http://www.amazon.com/National-Incident-Management-System-Principles/dp/0763781878.

WordPress.org. (n.d.). *What is a "blog"?* Retrieved August 30, 2015, from: https://codex.wordpress.org/Introduction_to_Blogging.

FURTHER READING

U.S., State of Michigan, Emergency management division. (2013). *Design recommendations and criteria for emergency operations centers.* http://www.michigan.gov/documents/MSPLocalEOCcriteriev2_03final_60263_7.pdf.

AIRPORT EMERGENCY PLANNING, PART III

Erickson Air Crane lands at the Rocky Mountain Metropolitan Airport, CO.

Image by Shahn Sederberg, courtesy Colorado Division of Aeronautics, 2012.

Self-serve fuel farm located at McElroy Field, Kremmling, CO.

Image by Shahn Sederberg, courtesy Colorado Division of Aeronautics, 2012.

On July 19, 1989, a United Airlines (UAL) DC-10, Flight 232, crashed while performing an emergency landing at the airport in Sioux City, Iowa. The actions of the pilots and air traffic controllers were extraordinary and contributed to saving the lives of some of the 296 passengers on board, and the response by emergency management personnel in Sioux City has become the case study on how to effectively respond to an aircraft crash. In all, 184 passengers and crew survived, many due to the professionalism and the forward thinking of the fire, police, sheriff, and emergency medical service (EMS) community in Sioux City.

The first responders humored their imagination and prepared for an event that was never supposed to happen. The Sioux City airport did not receive aircraft as large as the DC-10; however, newly appointed director of emergency management, Gary Brown, knew that the city was beneath a heavily traveled airway. Brown thought that the possibility existed that one day an airliner full of passengers would need Sioux City to be prepared for its emergency arrival (Gonzales, 2014, p. 115).

The crash of UAL 232 occurred in 1989, 15 years before the advent of the National Incident Management System (NIMS). However, Sioux City did nearly everything right, and what they didn't do well has been learned from and changed in the interim years. In 1992, the movie *A Thousand Heroes* told the story of both UAL 232 and the first responders. Many in the emergency management community use the movie as a teaching tool to teach others about how to respond to an airplane crash.

The "big one," the crash of a major airliner, is something that is often talked about within the airport emergency management community. Airport Operations professionals both hope it never happens, but then, privately, often wonder how they will perform if it does. It is far more likely though that airport personnel will be called to handle a variety of other airport incidents, and many will never be called upon to handle a large-scale plane crash. However, while the Airport

Emergency Plan (AEP) calls for a response to a variety of emergencies, airport first responders and emergency management personnel will judge themselves against their preparedness and response to the "big one."

An airplane crash is an extraordinary event. It is an occurrence that most people will never experience in their entire lives and, even for those in airport management, will not likely have to respond to. The crash of a major airliner can overwhelm the senses of even veteran fire and police officers, who are used to seeing death and severe injury at car accidents, homicides, and perhaps even an active shooter incident, but the number of casualties in an airline crash can be in the hundreds, and the physical forces involved in a plane crash contorts bodies and causes injuries in a way that only a high-speed collision of an airplane with the ground can create.

OVERVIEW OF THE HAZARD-SPECIFIC SECTIONS

The AEP Advisory Circular (AC) requires that Part 139 airports have hazard-specific plans to respond to certain events and also develop plans to respond to identified risks and hazards. The incidents spelled out in the AC 150/5200-31C (FAA, 2010a, p. 105) are:

1. Aircraft incidents and accidents;
2. Bomb incidents, including designated parking areas for the aircraft involved;[1]
3. Structural fires;
4. Fires at fuel farms or fuel storage areas;
5. Natural disasters;
6. Hazardous materials/Dangerous Goods incidents;
7. Sabotage, hijack incidents, and other unlawful interference with operations;
8. Failure of power for movement area lighting;
9. Water Rescue situations, as appropriate.

Additional hazards identified through a risk assessment are also included in the AEP and should include a description of the situation and assumptions pertinent to the incident. The hazard-specific section describes the operations related to the incident, including identifying the emergency phases and describing response and recovery actions and procedures, mutual aid agreements, and the organization and responsibilities of Airport Operations, air traffic control, fire rescue, police, EMS and communications. Administrative and logistical information, guidance to keep the plan up-to-date, are also included (FAA, 2010a, p. 106).

It is the responsibility of the Airport Manager vis-à-vis the airport emergency planning team to determine what to include in the hazard-specific section. Airport operators look at the unique operating characteristics of their airfield, historical weather conditions, and the history of natural disasters relevant to the area. The airport must also consider the needs and expectations of the community, federal, state, and local governments and their reliance on the airport during natural or human-made disasters, and adjacent facilities that may present a threat to the airport. Within the

---

[1]Bomb incidents and sabotage (#2 and #7 in the list) are listed separately in the AC, but are consolidated into one hazard-specific section, titled *Terrorism Incidents*, in the body of the AC.

AEP AC, the FAA has attempted to tie the Functional Section with the hazard-specific section topics by relating the hazard-specific appendices to the core functional sections, as shown in Figure 12.1.

As an overall matter of policy, in the event of any aircraft accident or significant incident that could compromise the safety and security of the airport, either the airport operator or FAA air traffic controllers should immediately close the airport.[2] The airport should not reopen until: (a) all aircraft operating areas are secure, (b) movement areas have been properly inspected and are safe for operation, and (c) Aircraft Rescue and Firefighting (ARFF) equipment, personnel, and materials are available for immediate response. Additionally, the airport operator must determine that rescue and evacuation activities will not be negatively impacted by resuming flight operations and that the accident or event does not pose a hazard to airfield operations. The closure may only be for a few minutes to provide time for the airport operator to determine the scope of the emergency, but when a large aircraft crashes, the airport typically remains closed until response operations are well underway.

AIRCRAFT INCIDENTS AND ACCIDENTS

Aircraft accidents and incidents are defined by the FAA as:

1. **Aircraft Accident.** Any occurrence associated with the operation of an aircraft that takes place between the time a person boards the aircraft with the intention of flight and the time such person has disembarked, in which a person suffers death or serious injury as a result of the occurrence or in which the aircraft, including cargo aircraft, receives substantial damage.
2. **Aircraft Incident.** An incident is an occurrence other than an accident that affects or could affect the safety of operations. (See 49 CFR Part 830, Definitions.[3])

Part 139 airport operators have an emergency preparedness plan for an aircraft accident or incident, including cargo aircraft, for both on and off the airport. The plan response usually extends to the adjacent property, as well as other areas within the responsibility of the airport to respond. The National Transportation Safety Board (NTSB) provides guidance to both on-airport and off-airport responders on how to respond to a transportation accident (NTSB, n.d.a). The brochure establishes the core *Priorities of Work* for any aviation or transportation incident.

The highest priorities are to save lives, and stabilize the scene, protect property and the environment, and mitigate hazardous material contamination. At an airport, the fifth priority is reopening the airport, because when an airport shuts down, it can affect the entire National Airspace System.

A secure perimeter should be established around the accident scene that allows public safety personnel to access the site to preserve life. Any ground scars or marks made by the aircraft should be protected and preserved, and all evidence must be documented and photographed prior to

Functional Section	Hazard-Specific Section Topics
Command and Control	✈ Response actions keyed to specific time periods and phases
	✈ HAZMAT assessment
	✈ Damage assessment
	✈ Debris removal
	✈ Facilities inspection
	✈ Protective equipment for emergency responders
	✈ Detection equipment and techniques
	✈ Utilities and lifeline repairs
	✈ Search and rescue
	✈ Actions to ensure the area is safe and secure for the return of evacuated populations of for scene investigation personnel
Communications	✈ Provisions that have been made to ensure that effects associated with a particular hazard do not prevent or impede the ability of response personnel to communicate with each other during response operations
Alert Notification and Warning	✈ Hazard-unique public alert and warning protocols
	✈ Required or recommended notifications of specific emergency response agencies, to include local, State, and Federal
Emergency Public Information	✈ Information the public (employee and transient) will need to know about the particular hazard (e.g. special evacuation routes, in-place sheltering)
	✈ Means that will be used to convey that information to the public
Protective Actions	✈ Evacuation or in-place sheltering options and their timing
	✈ Special exclusion zones for the particular hazard (e.g. down- and cross-wind areas for nearby nuclear power and major chemical plants; low-lying/coastal areas subject to flooding caused by storms, hurricane, tidal surge)
	✈ Evacuation routes
	✈ Transportation resources to support mass evacuations
Law Enforcement/Security	✈ Special traffic and/or access control requirements
	✈ Special or secure communications procedures
	✈ Special or unique resource, equipment, and/or supplies requirements
Firefighting and Rescue	✈ Special or unique response force (e.g. HAZMAT Team) requirements
	✈ Special or unique resource, equipment, and/or supplies requirements
Health and Medical	✈ Special or unique health consequences and treatment options for people exposed to the hazard
	✈ Environmental monitoring and decontamination requirements
	✈ Special or unique resource, equipment, and/or supplies requirements
Resource Management	✈ Provisions for purchasing, stockpiling, or otherwise obtaining special protective gear, equipment, medical supplies needed for response operations and to meet the immediate needs of disaster victims
Airport Operations and Maintenance	✈ Special or unique notification requirments (e.g. NOTAM, FAA, NTSB, etc.)
	✈ Provisions for conducting necessary facility inspections

FIGURE 12.1

Typical content of hazard-specific appendices as related to core functional sections.

Source: FAA.

reopening the airport (NTSB, n.d.a). A record of personnel who enter the accident scene should also be made, and the scene should be protected from tampering by those who may have motive to do so (e.g., aircraft operators). Any electronic data or video recorders that may have been dislodged during the accident should be secured, and a chain of custody should be established (NTSB, n.d.a).

Information about hospital patients and passengers is gathered; individuals involved are either tracked to a hospital or released on their own. Statements from witnesses are taken along with their point-of-contact information. Initial interviews of witnesses are conducted to determine their location relative to the accident site and what they saw (NTSB, n.d.a). Any videos or photos taken by bystanders should be acquired.

Any release of information related to the crash should be coordinated through the Public Information Officer (PIO); however, only the NTSB may release factual information on the investigation, and local agencies should not speculate on the cause (NTSB, n.d.a). The NTSB will not release the names of crew members, passengers, or other victims associated with the accident.

While the aforementioned procedures are specific to an off-airport response by local emergency management personnel, they also provide a **general context** for an on-airport response. The perspective of the brochure is for a highway accident, and the presumption is that the local government must get the highway open as soon as possible, which may be prior to the response by the NTSB. Both the FAA and the NTSB are often able to respond to an airport, so some of these guidelines are superseded by the AEP.

ALERT LEVELS

The AEP section on Aircraft Accidents should include the ARFF Index, the airport and ATCT hours of operation, the number of runways and their magnetic headings, a summary of daily operations by aircraft category, a summary of aircraft types that normally use the airport, and a summary of available first-response personnel (police, fire, etc.) (FAA, 2010a, p. 109). The AEP should also describe any prepositioning requirements for ARFF equipment during periods of low visibility, describe the airport's policy on activating the emergency operations center (EOC), and should make a standing assumption that all aircraft incidents or accidents could be a potential hazardous material (HAZMAT) incident (FAA, 2010a, p. 109). However, labeling an event a HAZMAT incident has a very specific meaning in the fire rescue community and may cause fire operations to shut down until a HAZMAT team arrives. It is safe to assume that an Aircraft Accident will involve HAZMAT, but that this may not be declared a HAZMAT event requiring a special response.

The AEP should also describe the incident/accident classifications used at the airport. However, the AEP AC provides several **response descriptions**, **categories of response,** and **classifications of the incident**, which can become confusing. The Airport Manager and the AEP planning team should agree upon which vernacular will be used in the AEP.

International Civil Aviation Organization (ICAO), *Airport Services Manual, Part 7, Airport Emergency Planning*, and National Fire Protection Association (NFPA) 424, *Guide for Airport Community Planning*, list three examples of incident/accident **classifications**:

1. **Alert I (Local Standby Alert):** An aircraft that is known or suspected to have an operational defect that should not normally cause serious difficulty in achieving a safe landing. This is notification only. No response is required. All units involved will be staffed and will stand by in quarters (FAA, 2010a, p. 110).

Although the FAA says, "no response required," NFPA 407 (pp. 424–37) notes that at least one ARFF vehicle should be staffed and positioned to permit its immediate use in the event of an incident. At some airports an Alert I response only requires ARFF personnel to stand by their equipment in the fire station or to put on their bunker gear and prepare the vehicle for movement. Other airports have eliminated Alert I entirely from their AEP—at these airports an aircraft emergency is either an Alert II or III.

2. **Alert II (Full Emergency Alert):** An aircraft that is known or is suspected to have an operational defect that affects normal flight operations to the extent that there is danger of an accident. All units respond to predesignated positions (FAA, 2010a, p. 110). NFPA 407 specifies that for an Alert II, a **full response** should be made with emergency equipment staffed and in position, engines running, and emergency lights operating in order to get to the accident site as fast as possible. Radio frequencies used by the pilot and air traffic control (ATC) are continuously monitored, and the ARFF vehicle should be able to initiate fire suppression as soon as the aircraft comes to rest (NFPA 407, pp. 424–37).

3. **Alert III (Aircraft Accident Alert):** An aircraft incident/accident has occurred on or in the vicinity of the airport. All designated emergency response units proceed to the scene in accordance with established plans and procedures (FAA, 2010a, p. 110). The NFPA further indicates that ARFF personnel should anticipate the worst situation possible and prepare accordingly. Incident Command can be established prior to the aircraft arrival, with a specific Incident Command Post (ICP) established but able to be relocated after the aircraft arrives.

Airport fire departments can respond to a variety of emergency situations including an **in-flight or airborne emergency**, a **medical situation** either on the aircraft or in the terminal, a **ground emergency**[4] that involves aircraft operations when the aircraft is on the ground, or a **structural emergency** at one of the facilities on the airport. Each one requires a different level and type of response. Additionally, the FAA includes an **Estimated Casualties** table, so that Incident Commanders (ICs) can determine how much equipment to send to a particular aircraft incident, based on the potential number of casualties (Figure 12.2).

The FAA describes three different phases of an emergency—**Response**, **Investigatory**, and **Recovery**—and recommends drafting the response to an aircraft emergency, which addresses the required actions for each phase. Activities in the response phase are focused on the **notification** and **dispatch** of the first responders, fire and rescue operations, and determining the status of HAZMATs. The investigatory phase may not begin until the recovery phase has already started, based on when the NTSB or FAA investigators arrive on scene. The recovery phase is focused on returning the airport to normal operational condition, which can sometimes be accomplished by cordoning off and protecting the area where the accident has taken place along with a reasonable perimeter and reopening other areas of the airfield for operation, issuing Notices to Airmen (NOTAMs) as appropriate.

An airport's ability to recover from an event is a measure of its **resiliency**, which is its ability to resist damage from a disaster and/or to recover quickly to an acceptable level of function afterward (Smith, Kenville, & Sawyer, 2015, p. 5).

---

[4]Some airports have established an Alert IV, describing it as a ground emergency involving an aircraft.

Aircraft Occupants	Number of Casualties	20% casualties Immediate Care Priority I	30% casualties Delayed Care Priority II	50% casualties Minor Care Priority III
500	375	75	113	187
450	338	68	101	169
400	300	60	90	150
350	263	53	79	131
300	225	45	68	112
250	188	38	56	94
200	150	30	45	75
150	113	23	34	56
100	75	15	23	37
50	38	8	11	19

These figures are based on the assumption that the maximum number of surviving casualties at an aircraft accident occurring on or in the vicinity of the airport is estimated to be about 75% of the aircraft occupants.

FIGURE 12.2

Estimated Casualties.

Source: FAA.

AGENCY RESPONSIBILITIES FOR AIRCRAFT ACCIDENTS

Often the first notification that there is an aircraft in trouble will come from the pilot of an aircraft experiencing trouble, via the ATCT, through the appropriate alarm notification system, which can be a ringdown line (i.e., crash phone), radio, or telephone notification. Otherwise, the initial notification that an airplane has crashed is from a member of the general public, an airport or airline employee who has witnessed the crash on the airfield, or even passengers who may have seen the crash out the terminal window or while driving past the airport. In periods of low visibility, or at night, sometimes an aircraft will simply disappear from radar, leaving the air traffic controller wondering what happened. During the interim time when the air traffic controller attempts to reestablish contact, someone else may have seen the aircraft go down and have called either the airport or, more commonly, 911. Unfortunately, when an individual dials 911 to report an airport incident, the emergency call may not come to the airport communications or dispatch centers, but instead to a municipal 911 call center. The call taker must then either relay the information to the airport or reroute the call; both options take additional time and delay the response. When the notification does reach any entity on the ringdown line, that entity should immediately activate the line to notify all other first responders.

Air Traffic Control

If ATC is advised by the pilots of a situation, there are a couple of important considerations with the initial notification. First, airline pilots do not use the vocabulary for an incident that is used in the AEP. They will not advise the control tower that they have an Alert I, Alert II, etc. Instead, they will describe the problem they are experiencing to the ATCT and may sometimes request that emergency equipment be standing by. The air traffic controller, or the airport operator, often upon consultation with the ARFF chief, usually determines the Alert level of an incident and decides whether to deploy response equipment. The Alert level, once determined, can also change as more information becomes available.

When an airliner is experiencing a problem it is likely that their flight operations center is already aware of the issue. This means that the Station Manager who represents the airline at that airport has also been notified that the aircraft is experiencing an issue and may already be activating their emergency response protocols. On some occasions, the airline operator may notify the airport operator of an emergency.

United Airlines Flight 232 was en route from Denver to Chicago when it first experienced flight control problems. While at cruise altitude, the pilots of UAL 232 heard a loud bang, followed by the loss of control of the aircraft. They quickly notified Minneapolis Air Route Traffic Control Center (ARTCC) that they were having problems and requested an altitude change, as they struggled to control the aircraft. Minneapolis Center then notified the control tower at Sioux City, Iowa, by radio. Upon being advised by Minneapolis Center of the Sioux City option for an emergency landing, UAL 232's captain, Al Haynes, contacted the controllers in the Sioux City tower, who notified the airport operator (Gonzales, 2014, pp. 8—9). The airport went to Alert II (the term used at the time and, ironically, today).

Upon experiencing an emergency, the ARFF and response personnel attempt to obtain the following information:

1. Type of aircraft and designation (call sign or tail number);
2. Number of passengers and crew on board (sometimes referred to as Souls on Board);
3. Type and amount of fuel (Fuel on Board);
4. Nature of the emergency;
5. Type, amount, and location of Dangerous Goods;
6. Number of nonambulatory passengers on board (if known); these are people with functional needs, such as needing a wheelchair to move.

The **type of aircraft** is relevant as it gives responders an idea of the scale of the incident. Many airport firefighters have trained on a variety of aircraft fuselages so knowing the aircraft type can let them know if this is a fuselage they are accustomed to, or they will be in unfamiliar territory. If the arrival of the aircraft is still far enough out, airport firefighters may attempt to find a similar airframe on the airport so they can study the door latching mechanisms and the interior, in order to become familiar with them.

The number of **Souls on Board** dictates the level of emergency medical response that should be expected and lets responders know how many people to look for. The amount of **Fuel on Board** can give ARFF personnel an idea of how much fire they can expect if the aircraft explodes or crashes. Aircraft that are experiencing emergencies will sometimes dump fuel in anticipation of a hard landing or in anticipation of a crash, in order to minimize the aircraft weight and to minimize the amount of fuel for a fire, should one start upon landing (Figure 12.3).

The **nature of the emergency** provides specifics and may provide some insight about the type of landing the aircraft may experience. For example, if the pilot cannot get the landing gear down and locked into position, it is likely the aircraft will slide a good distance down the runway but could otherwise be okay—many gear-up landings result in some damage to the aircraft, along with some bumps and bruises for the passengers, but rarely result in fire and explosion. However, if

FIGURE 12.3

An ARFF truck sprays water on a fire at an airport emergency exercise, as volunteer "victims" look on.

Source: Jeffrey Price, 2015.

only one or two of the landing gear are down asymmetrically, but not others, this increases the probability the aircraft will experience a **loss of directional control** on landing, as the aircraft might ground loop or cartwheel upon landing.

The number of **nonambulatory passengers**, and the type, amount, and location of **Dangerous Goods**, typically is not transmitted with the initial emergency notification. The pilots may be too busy or may not know this information offhand, but if it can be obtained it should be requested. An airline Station Manager may be available to access this data, which can be obtained onsite if the airline has a base-of-operations at the airport (i.e., this is not a diverted aircraft). Otherwise, a phone call to the airline may be necessary.

Controlling aircraft and ground operations, airspace in the vicinity of the airport, and notifying other FAA facilities is the responsibility of the ATCT (FAA, 2010a, p. 112). ATC may also arrange for the FAA, ARFF, the IC, and the emergency aircraft to use a discrete emergency frequency to facilitate secure communications.

Prior to the arrival of UAL 232, Gary Brown,[5] director of Woodbury County Disaster and Emergency Services (WCDES) in Iowa, escalated the incident above an **Alert III**, requesting even more equipment than the emergency plan called for. Notifications went out to surrounding responders,

---

[5]For many years before the crash, Gary Brown had lobbied for a disaster plan, specifically wanting to have a drill that simulated the crash of a large commercial airliner. People in the community rolled their eyes, referred to him as Chicken Little, and thought it made no sense (Gonzales, 2014, p. 115).

mutual aid agreements were activated, nongovernmental organizations (NGOs) and private agencies with responsibilities under the AEP were mobilized, and essentially everyone started heading to the airport. Also, Sioux City Airport is home to the 185th Tactical Fighter Wing of the Air National Guard (Gonzales, 2014), which staffed and maintained the airport's fire rescue equipment. ATC personnel ensured that they could communicate with UAL 232 on a separate frequency and begin moving personnel and equipment to or from the movement area, as appropriate. A flight of A-7 Corsair fighter jets had just landed and were relocating away from the movement area, while response personnel coordinated access the airfield with the control tower, to get into response-ready positions.

Unbeknownst at the time, Flight 232 had experienced a catastrophic failure of the Number 2 tail-mounted engine during cruise flight. Components of the stage 1 fan rotor assembly separated and fragmented, leading to the loss of the three hydraulic systems that powered the airplane's flight controls (NTSB, n.d.b). The flight crew had to maneuver the aircraft using differential thrust, as the flight controls were nearly useless. This caused the pilots to have to fly the aircraft in huge circles in order to change headings and to maintain some semblance of controlled flight. While the aircraft did make it to the airport, it landed far faster than it had been designed to land; the aircraft was also overweight as it was still carrying much of the fuel it was going to burn off during its normal route of flight. The wing dipped upon landing, causing the aircraft to cartwheel. Of the 285 passengers and 11 crew members on board, a flight attendant and 110 passengers were killed.

When the aircraft approached the airport, ARFF crews realized that the plane was set to land on a closed runway, but exactly where the fire rescue trucks had staged. The crews immediately scrambled off the runway as Flight 232 came in. Four A-7 Corsair fighter jets were also still in the vicinity of the runway so the possibility existed that if the DC-10 veered toward the pilots, they would have to execute a ground ejection to save themselves. It is assumed that during an emergency, while the FAA and others do their best to clear the area, other aircraft will still remain on and around the airport. Should an aircraft veer violently off-course upon landing, responders may have to respond to additional incidents.

Flight 232 was traveling nearly 50% faster than its normal landing speed, with a sink rate of 1,800-feet-per-minute toward the ground, three times in excess of the structural capacity of the landing gear. United flight instructor Denny Fitch, who had been commuting back home on the flight but had come up to help the flight crew, was controlling the thrust levers. He firewalled (pushed to the limit) the engines just shy of landing in order to get the sink rate under control (Gonzales, 2014); however, turbine engines take a few seconds to spool up and don't always cycle at the same rate.

As the aircraft came over the runway, the right wing dropped more than 20 degrees, causing the aircraft to cartwheel. The plane continued to break apart with large portions of the fuselage coming to rest from the impact point on the runway, to hundreds of feet away and into a cornfield at the edge of the airport. Fire and rescue personnel on scene believed that everyone on board had immediately perished (Gonzales, 2014).

FIREFIGHTING AND RESCUE

Firefighting and rescue crews are responsible for **initial response to an Aircraft Accident**, assuming Incident Command, beginning fire and rescue operations, and notifying mutual aid if necessary (FAAa, 2010). At the Sioux City Airport, emergency vehicles responded as soon as the aircraft and its various pieces came to rest, but were hampered by smoke from the fires, burning wreckage and debris from the crash, and by survivors wandering around in shock. Firefighters had to get out and walk in front of the trucks to move debris and allow the fire equipment to reach the main section of the fuselage. Temperatures reached 1,800°F from fuel fires inside the aircraft from ruptured fuel tanks. Pressurized oxygen bottles and fire extinguishers inside the aircraft exploded, which further endangered firefighters (Gonzales, 2014).

Firefighters initially began spraying foam on the fire trying to knock it down, and also were spraying passengers as they exited the rear of the aircraft, but they soon realized they would have to go into the fuselage in order to have any effect. Some passengers who could free themselves were self-evacuating, with many having to drop out of their seats 12 feet to the floor of the aircraft, which was actually the ceiling, as the fuselage was resting upside down. Rescue personnel were also affected by the horrifying scene before them, including seeing children who had been killed in the crash, and the realization that as the fire became so intense that the fuselage was melting around them, they would have to retreat, leaving those still inside to die (Gonzales, 2014).

Staff members at the nearby hospitals, which had already been alerted, were standing by preparing to receive casualties. Ironically, 2 years earlier, Gary Brown had convinced the Air National Guard, the two major area hospitals, and the local communities to conduct a full-scale exercise, simulating a plane crash with scores of injured people. The exercise was conducted on Runway 22, exactly where UAL 232 would crash 2 years later (Gonzales, 2014).

In any aircraft crash, it cannot be assumed that all have died. But responders must still take all necessary precautions in approaching the scene, and all debris should be checked. On Flight 232, the debris was spread across 3,500 feet of ground, beginning at the runway and extending off-airport into a cornfield. The cockpit on UAL 232 had balled up and was unrecognizable as the cockpit after the crash. Although the three pilots, along with the United Airlines flight instructor who was controlling the throttles on landing, were all alive but trapped inside the wreckage, several firefighters and responders passed right by it. What looked to most as just a crumpled up piece of the aircraft actually contained the living, still breathing, flight crew (Gonzales, 2014).

The four pilots would stay in the wreckage until discovered by a volunteer with WCDES, who was a local businessman flying his personal plane at the time; he landed at a nearby airport, caught a ride back to Sioux City, and reported to the incident site where he was dispatched by Gary Brown to check out a pile of wreckage. He saw firefighters and passengers standing around an unrecognizable pile of debris and asked "What's this?" A voice came out of the pile, "It's the cockpit, there are four of us in here" (Gonzales, 2014, p. 150).

The cockpit tumbled down the runway at over 100 miles an hour, wrapping itself in the numerous wires that connected the cockpit to the rest of the aircraft. A variety of tools, hydraulic clippers, and a forklift all had to be used to extract the pilots without causing further injury. It is important that fire personnel have an exact total of the number of passengers and flight crew on board so that all personnel can be accounted for before rescue operations shut down (Gonzales, 2014).

LAW ENFORCEMENT AND SECURITY

Police are charged with protecting the **security** of the accident scene. In Sioux City, after the response phase began moving to recovery, police had to set up a very large scene perimeter that caused the airport to be closed for days. A perimeter was created by plowing lines in the cornfield, around the wreckage, to make it easier for police to spot treasure seekers and curious citizens.

Protecting the incident site is not as easy as it seems, particularly at an airport, as there are numerous individuals other than police and fire personnel who may need legitimate access to the scene. Some entities that are normally authorized to be on the airfield, such as airline management personnel, typically must be kept away from the accident site during the initial stages. This is in conflict with many airline policies that advise their managers to get onsite as soon as possible. There may be a conflict of interest in having airline personnel at the site, but airline personnel, along with engine and airframe manufacturers, are also, eventually, part of the NTSB investigation teams. With the aircraft owner/operator on scene, the possibility exists that evidence may be tampered with, but there may also be a benefit to having airline personnel onsite to assist with passenger reconciliation, victim's assistance, and technical matters regarding the aircraft that affect the safety of first responders.

While no regulation exists that prohibits specific parties from accessing an accident site, FAA AC 150/5200-12C, *First Responders Responsibility in Protecting Evidence at the Scene of an Aircraft Accident*, recommends that no personnel should be in the area of the incident other than first responders and law enforcement authorities (FAA, 2009). Irrespective of the potential for tampering with wreckage, NFPA 424—13 notes that Aircraft Accident sites can be dangerous areas because of the possible presence of flammable fuels, Dangerous Goods, HAZMAT, biological hazards (blood-borne pathogens), and damaged and scattered pieces of aircraft wreckage (NFPA, 2013).

NFPA further recommends that under no circumstances should the media or other personnel not directly involved in firefighting, rescue, or emergency medical care be permitted inside security lines, until all rescue operations are completed and the area is declared safe by the IC (NFPA, 2013, p. 424—17). This is easier said than done sometimes, as there can be a tremendous amount of confusion during the initial stages of an emergency. Case in point is the media access to the Flight 232 accident scene.

Media personnel operate by a slightly different set of priorities than first responders. While media typically never desire to interfere with first responders or the saving of lives, they definitely want to be as close as possible to the action. Reporters are looking for the story, the video clip, the photograph, or the key interview. The normal barriers to keep the public off an airport, such as a fence or the police tape used to keep unauthorized personnel off an accident scene, are primarily visible barriers that can be easily defeated. Media personnel have been known to climb airport fences or look for other ways to access an incident scene, while removing any obvious signs they are press, such as issued credentials or cameras. While this may seem to be a serious concern, it does not preclude the saving of life, property, and so forth. First responders need to keep priorities focused on saving lives and putting out the fire, letting police and other personnel worry about reporters and other unauthorized personnel on scene, as staffing becomes available to handle such issues. In the initial stages of a crash, police officers responding to an aircraft crash are quickly recruited for stretcher-bearing and first aid duties and sometimes for emergency transportation to other medical facilities on or off the airport. These are priorities over removing reporters from a scene, unless they present an immediate hazard or threat to safety or security that is worth the possible loss of a human life.

During the crash of UAL 232, reporter Gary Anderson, who admits to driving through someone's front yard to get past a roadblock to access the airport, was standing with firefighters at the south end of the airport when the airplane crashed. He and another reporter used the shop doors to the Fixed Base Operator maintenance facility, which was unlocked, to access the airfield. Before being escorted off the airport by police, Anderson took the photo that came to epitomize the work of the people of Sioux City that day, when he snapped a photo of U.S. Air National Guard Colonel Dennis Nielsen carrying 3-year-old Spencer Bailey away from the accident scene. A bronze statue based on that photo sits on the Sioux City Riverwalk to this day to commemorate the crash (Gonzales, 2014).

Also on that day, a college intern, Shari Zenor, had been assigned to the fire department to write a feature story for the local paper. She was riding with one of the responders in an SUV and had a front-row seat to the crash and the rescue operations. The intern did as ordered and stayed in the SUV, but it's unlikely any other seasoned reporter would have obeyed those orders for what, to a reporter, would have been the story of a lifetime (Gonzales, 2014).

Another reporter, Mark Reinders, accessed the incident scene by climbing the airport fence and walking through the cornfield. At one point, rescue workers believed he was one of the passengers who had been involved in the accident and tried taking him to triage. Reinders was able to walk among the wreckage, see the dead, dying, and the living, so that he could tell their stories—their final stories in some cases; according to author Laurence Gonzales, Reinders became the official witness to the historic and tragic event (Gonzales, 2014).

Provided more pressing needs, such as rescue, are already being addressed, the first police officer arriving at the scene should establish traffic lanes for ingress and egress routes for emergency vehicles and notify the communications center of the location of the accident, along with the locations of the access and egress points. The accident site should be cordoned off as soon as possible and exclude any individuals not directly involved with rescue operations. Cones, police tape, and other visible barriers can be used, but flares should not be used within 300 feet of the accident site to prevent the ignition with fuel vapors. Flares should also not be used on grass areas of the airfield as they may start a fire (NFPA, 2013, p. 424—16).

Unlike an accident that takes place in the community or on a city street, there will be additional personnel who need to respond to the accident site, such as Airport Operations, management, and maintenance personnel. Unless these individuals have firefighting or emergency medical training and responsibilities, they should not be allowed to the area of the actual incident, but must be allowed access to areas surrounding the incident site, including the ICP. A system should be in place to have these essential personnel issued an armband, onsite passport **identification tag or badge** that indicates their authority to access the ICP or other relevant areas of the scene. This identification tag should be recognizable by both on- and off-airport police and sheriff personnel and only issued to those individuals who have duties at the ICP, Staging Area, EOC, or other essential areas during an incident.

At commercial service airports employees are issued **Security Identification Display Area (SIDA)** badges, and some airports have placed an icon on the badges for personnel who have authorized access to an incident scene. However, most off-airport personnel are not familiar with the SIDA badge and are unlikely to understand the access authority that the icon is supposed to grant. For an off-airport crash, or an airport incident that goes on for an extended period of time, supplemental law enforcement personnel may be brought onto the incident site to relieve other officers of their scene security duties. There are two concerns with this issue: first, off-airport police personnel responding to the Security Areas of an airport may not be allowed to have unescorted access to the airfield unless they have a SIDA badge, even during an emergency, and second, off-airport police personnel may not understand which entities on an airport (i.e., airport management or operations personnel) may have necessary duties at the incident site and could end up denying them access.

In the first instance, airport management personnel should coordinate with the Airport Security Coordinator, who should be working with the Transportation Security Administration's (TSA) Federal Security Director or designated official, to determine the security status of the airfield along with the identification requirements for **emergency worker personnel** during an incident. Some Airport Security Programs allow for an emergency worker **identification** to be "approved" identification in certain Security Areas of the airfield during an emergency.

To prevent off-airport police or sheriff personnel from denying access to the airport, the EOC, the ICP, or other areas that airport management or operations or maintenance personnel may need to access, they should be briefed during their shift changeover as to what the approved identification looks like (and a handout is helpful) and also equipped with a radio frequency or phone number to call to determine access authority if necessary.

Police personnel should be assigned to any Staging Area, media centers, medical facilities where drugs are stored, family assistance centers and holding areas for uninjured persons involved in the accident, and to the EOC. Security officers can be used at some locations, but at locations where there is the potential for violence, or a reason to believe that there is a threat to responders or the incident site, armed police personnel should be used.

Police duties may also include protecting members of the flight crew from physical assault by passengers who may be angered and responding violently to the accident, and may experience emotional outbursts, in essence blaming the pilot for the crash. Police may also be assigned to guard the Cockpit Voice Recorder and the Flight Data Recorders until the arrival of the NTSB, when custody is transferred to the investigators (NFPA, 2013).

Once firefighting personnel have stabilized the scene and scene security is set, anyone accessing the scene should be logged in and out, noting the time, their name, any specific identifying information (e.g., badge number), and agency represented. As part of the after-action, additional personnel who were part of the first response (i.e., firefighters and Airport Operations personnel who may have been first on scene before security was set) should be identified and estimates made as to their time of arrival on scene, and time of departure, along with a synopsis of actions taken.

A significant challenge for airports and for airport police officers in securing the accident site is the possibility that arson investigators or fire investigators from the local fire department, and homicide investigators from the local police department, will also arrive on scene, access the incident site, and began their own investigations. While it is unlikely that a police officer is going to prevent access to the incident site by what is in essence a superior officer, it may be helpful to remind local investigators of Section 830.10, *Notification and Reporting of Aircraft Accidents or Incidents and Overdue Aircraft, and Preservation of Aircraft Wreckage, Mail Cargo, and Records,* of the U.S. Code, which states:

Civil Aircraft Accident investigation is normally conducted by a number of investigators of the NTSB or their designees interested in establishing the probable cause. Federal or state governments are usually charged with the official responsibility but the operators, pilot groups, airport management, and others may be active in accident investigation work. Fire officials normally make their own investigation.

Normally, an investigation would not begin until firefighting and rescue operations are complete, at which point airport management would typically take over Incident Command functions and may be able to provide a better level of control to the accident location until the arrival of the NTSB or FAA.

EMERGENCY MEDICAL SERVICES

Emergency medical providers are responsible for triage and seeing to the initial treatment of casualties, patient tracking, and getting the injured to the appropriate treatment facilities as quickly as possible. The primary role of EMS is to provide the initial triage and treatment of casualties on scene and to stabilize and transport wounded to appropriate medical facilities. The FAA requirements under Part 139 and the AC on Airport Emergency Management for an airport to be prepared from an emergency medical perspective are rather vague (FAA, 2010a).

Although NFPA 424 provides guidance only, and airports are not required to meet the NFPA standard, NFPA 424 does provide a benchmark by which airports can measure their readiness from an emergency medical response perspective. Airports should have enough medical supplies to treat the capacity of the largest aircraft that normally uses the airport in addition to keeping materials and medical supplies on hand to deal with the routine medical emergencies associated with the day-to-day operation of an airport (NFPA, 2013).

Additional consideration should be given to geographical and topographical conditions at the airport; that is, airports located in traditionally colder climates should stock additional blankets for passengers and ensure that medical personnel are properly outfitted with coats, gloves, and hats so that they can operate outside for long periods of time. Additional generators and outdoor space heaters may also be beneficial. The airport should also have a bus or trailer (depending on the size of the commercial service aircraft typically using the airport) that can store stretchers, cervical collars, backboards, body bags, restraining straps, resuscitation equipment (to treat smoke inhalation victims), and other essential equipment to properly respond to an emergency (NFPA, 2013).

Getting medical personnel to the accident as soon as possible can reduce the loss of life, as the first minutes of a traumatic accident are critical to survival. The "Golden Hour," first described by R. Adams Cowley, MD, of the University of Maryland Medical Center in Baltimore, is an axiom that says a patient's survivability increases if the patient can reach definitive care within 60 minutes of being injured. Although over the years medical professionals have debated whether the Golden Hour is actually 60 minutes, the concept remains, and it is often used as a benchmark for medical personnel to get individuals to a definitive care facility (i.e., where surgery is possible) (Eisele, 2008).

As medical personnel access the incident scene, they immediately begin conducting triage, which is the sorting and classification of casualties to determine the priority for treatment and transport (NFPA, 2013, p. 424−22). Casualties are classified into one of four categories:

1. **Priority I, immediate care** (Red)—(a) major hemorrhages, (b) severe smoke inhalation, (c) asphyxiating thoracic and cervico-maxillo-facial injuries, (d) cranial trauma with coma and rapidly progressive shock, (e) open fractures and compound fractures, (f) extensive burns (more than 30%), (g) crush injuries including internal organs, (h) any type of shock, (i) spinal cord injuries (NFPA, 2013, p. 424−23).

2. **Priority II, delayed care** (Yellow)—which can include (a) nonasphyxiating thoracic trauma, (b) closed fractures of the extremities, (c) limited burns (less than 30%), (d) cranial trauma without coma or shock, (e) injuries to soft parts (NFPA, 2013, p. 424–23).
3. **Priority III, minor care** (Green)—which are either no injury or minor, non–life-threatening injuries; it's possible these individuals may not be transported to a hospital and may be cared for at the airport or on-scene.
4. **Priority 0, deceased** (Black).

A variety of **triage treatment cards** with varying levels of information, such as body outlines so medical personnel can indicate areas of concern and the type of injury, pulse, blood pressure, respirations, major injuries, destination, and personal information, if known, are available on the market. Triage decisions are made rather quickly and airport fire or medical personnel commonly issue a command to everyone at the accident site that if they can get up and move they should walk toward the firefighter or paramedic who is calling them. This quickly identifies those who may not be hurt, or at least the walking wounded who can be classified as green for now. It is possible that some personnel may not present injuries at the time, but injuries may become apparent later, so even those who do not appear to be hurt still need to be monitored for a period of time and eventually properly checked out by a medical professional (Figure 12.4).

Individuals with no respirations and individuals who do not begin respiring when the airway is cleared or the individual is repositioned are typically classified as deceased. If respirations do start, the individual is commonly immediately classified as red. Individuals who cannot follow simple commands are often also classified as red, as are individuals for whom bleeding cannot be readily controlled.

FIGURE 12.4

The walking wounded, photographed during an airport emergency exercise.

Source: Jeffrey Price, 2015.

Injured personnel should be stabilized at the accident scene and prepared for transport. The commander of the triage function is designated by the IC, until the medical group supervisor or a senior medical person arrives on scene and properly relieves the IC's designee. Uninjured individuals, or individuals with minor injuries that can be treated onsite, should be taken to appropriate shelter, and food and water should be provided along with access to telephones. Considering the number of individuals who carry cell phones today, it may seem that pay phones aren't necessary, but in an airplane crash, phones can be lost, left behind, or have lost battery power. A variety of cell phone chargers, power outlets, and Wi-Fi access (free-of-charge) should also be offered. While some people will make calls, others will prefer to text or email. Individuals behave differently after a traumatic event, and sometimes doing something "normal" can help with their emotional state. In an aircraft fire, NFPA recommends establishing the scene as shown in Figure 12.5.

The NFPA-recommended setup allows a consistent flow of personnel and vehicles into and out of the accident site, and because it's standardized, responders have an idea of where everything will be located during an incident. Early in an aircraft crash, however, there may not be time to formally set up this arrangement as the priority is first to save lives and get people to safety, then start sorting everything out. It may be awhile into the incident before this set up is finalized, and even then, certain elements may have to move if winds shift.

Injured personnel pass through four areas—the **collection**, **triage**, **decontamination**, and **care areas**—before being transported. The collection area is where most of the seriously injured have been taken once being removed from immediate danger at the accident site. It's recommended that the triage site be established at least 300 feet upwind from the accident site or smoke or fire sources and that, if necessary, more than one triage area be set up. The decontamination zone is where patients and others are processed to remove chemical, biological, etiological, or radioactive agents to prevent contamination of the ambulance or helicopter (NFPA, 2013).

The care area is divided into three categories related to the categories of the injured (e.g., priority I, priority II, and priority III, with each level indicating severity of injury and timeliness of triage required). Some fire rescue personnel carry large, colored blankets or cloths to designate these areas, but colored cones, flags, tape, and other objects can also be used. The **transportation area** is where personnel are sent to a hospital by ambulance, to the terminal building (or nearest first aid care facility) for minor injuries, to a victim assistance location for the uninjured, and by helicopter for those requiring the most urgent care. Uninjured passengers should also be interviewed as soon as possible to capture contact information and to notify relatives, friends, next of kin, or others. The American Red Cross will provide significant assistance in the care of survivors and for the family members of personnel who did not survive the crash (NFPA, 2013).

Just as being in an aircraft crash is an extraordinary event in the lives of most people, it is also extraordinary to those responding to an aircraft crash. Minor crashes are similar to car accidents in terms of the condition of fatalities, but large crashes can cause physical and emotional trauma in both victims and responders. In the case of UAL 232, responders reported numerous horrifying scenes, many of which have haunted them ever since. Additionally, victims of a plane crash can exhibit a variety of behaviors, many of them unusual and irrational. Here is a sampling of behaviors that passengers exhibited during Flight 232:

1. One of the children involved in the incident lying on the concrete repeatedly screaming his parents' address and phone number (Gonzales, 2014, p. 109);

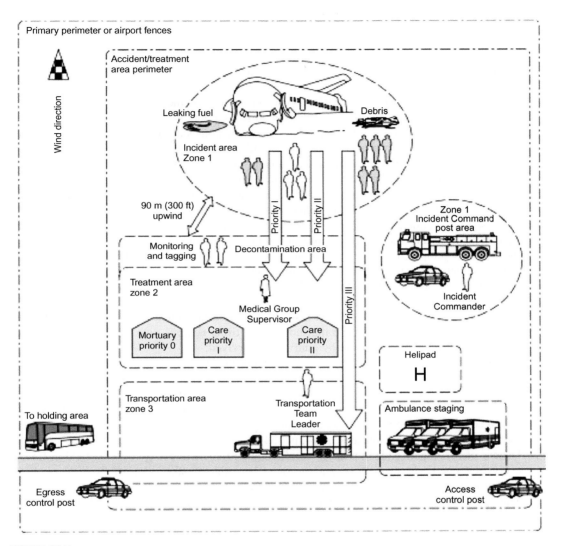

FIGURE 12.5

Triage and medical care at Aircraft Accident site.

Source: NFPA 424.

2. A mother who was hanging upside down in the wreckage next to her son released her seatbelt, fell to the ground, and even though her brain kept telling her to go back and get her son, inexplicably ran away from the wreckage to the safety outside (her son was assisted by another passenger and survived the incident) (Gonzales, 2014, p. 105);

3. Captain Al Haynes, who was caught up in the crumpled wreckage of the cockpit, remembered wailing, "Oh, I killed people!" (p. 94); Haynes later joked on the bumpy ambulance ride to the hospital, "Tell the driver to go back, I think he missed a pothole";[6]

4. As first responders approached the wreckage they saw bodies all over the ground, but then as if called by an invisible voice, many of them suddenly started sitting up and standing up, which astonished the first responders who thought they were all dead and that no one could have survived the crash they had witnessed (p. 131);

5. One passenger in a business suit stood up, looked around, found his luggage, and wandered off (p. 131). This phenomenon is not unusual; when Asiana Airlines Flight 214 crashed at San Francisco International Airport in 2013, several passengers collected their bags (if they could find them) from underneath the seat in front of them and from the overhead bins and took them as they jumped down the evacuation slides—even in cases where death is imminent unless the person escapes, some people cannot leave their belongings behind. This action may not be rational, but people often do irrational things when experiencing trauma. During the Los Angeles International Airport active shooter incident, one man at the Terminal 3 screening checkpoint continued to put his belt and shoes back on as TSA personnel and other passengers were running away and the shooter was firing nearby—two TSA employees who returned to help the man were hit by gunfire but survived;

6. For reasons that remain a mystery, UAL 232 had been carrying an exceptionally large amount of U.S. currency, and hundred dollar bills were flying everywhere. Gary Brown reported that many passengers and rescuers were bringing him handfuls of hundred dollar bills which he eventually had to lock up in his truck; however, one passenger who had enplaned with a laptop computer, video and still cameras, and a steel guitar only had his still camera and steel guitar returned to him[7] (Gonzales, 2014, p. 154);

7. Dozens of passengers ended up in the cornfield and rescuers had to go into the field to find everyone—one flight attendant tore a portion of her skirt to make a flag so rescuers could see her and several passengers who were in the field;

8. Many passengers who survived experienced violent injuries, and in one case a lady was literally scalped from her eyeballs back, yet was awake and talking to responders (p. 195);

9. Passengers had begun looking for lost relatives, but with nothing to write on, many passengers started writing their names and telephone numbers on the blouse of a surviving flight attendant (p. 196);

10. A priest who was heading to see a movie with his family responded to the incident and many people sought him out on scene to get a blessing from him (p. 203);

11. Even deceased victims with no visible injuries were disturbing to one Department of Criminal Investigations investigator, who, while assisting with morgue operations, noticed a beautiful

---

[6]It is very common for survivors and responders to use humor during a traumatic incident as a way to cope with the situation.

[7]Theft does still occur even during an airplane crash.

young woman, "perfect in every way and without a scratch on her", but she was deceased. It bothered him because in his mind, it shouldn't be that way (Gonzales, 2014, p. 251);

12. One man walked up to a rescuer and said: "Have you ever seen anything like this? I was on that plane. Is there a bar around here?" As the responder pointed at the terminal building, the man walked off as if nothing had happened and was found later drinking at the bar (p. 143).

Seeing the bodies of the deceased can also have a significant impact on the responders. Infants were found dead in the wreckage, which had a substantial effect on some personnel, particularly responders who also had children. A chaplain was particularly moved by the image of a large man embracing a young boy in a last ditch effort to protect them—both, father and son died. Another woman was screaming as she was hanging from her seatbelt, yet when a rescuer released the belt he found it was literally the only thing keeping her body together. She died at his feet (Gonzales, 2014). In any Aircraft Accident recovery, it is important to account for **posttraumatic stress** and to include mental health opportunities for first-responder personnel.

Once all uninjured and injured personnel have been transported away from an accident scene, recovery operations at the airport can proceed, but the accident site will have to be protected, with all wreckage, deceased persons and animals, and any other item that is part of the accident kept in place. If it is necessary to move human remains, wreckage, or personal effects, video and photos of the personnel or items in their original position should be taken prior to the move. It may be impractical to take such measures prior to moving items, particularly if an individual's life is in danger (e.g., trapped under the wreckage or the deceased), as the top priority is to save lives.

AIRPORT OPERATOR

Depending on the organizational structure in place at the airport, the airport operator is primarily responsible for supporting rescue and security operations, **activating the EOC**, moving the Mobile Command Unit to the ICP, and making all relevant notifications. Additionally, the airport operator should make ready available facilities to accommodate uninjured, injured, and deceased persons. Coordinating with the air carrier involved (or the tenant or Fixed Base Operator, if the aircraft crash involved a based tenant or a transient aircraft), ensuring access by response personnel to the incident site and Staging Areas, coordinating movement with the ATCT, and determining whether the airport is open or closed, or what part of the airport is open or closed, are also primary responsibilities of the airport operator. The airport operator will activate the Public Information component of the AEP, assist with media inquiries, designate a PIO (if one has not already been designated by the IC, or if Incident Command changes and the circumstances call for a change), and activate the Joint Information Center (JIC) (FAA, 2010a).

Prior to resuming flight operations, Airport Operations personnel inspect the airfield to ensure aircraft operating areas are safe and secure, conduct a Part 139−level inspection of the movement area, and ensure that ARFF equipment is ready to respond (i.e., trucks are refueled, extinguishing agent is replenished, and personnel are in place). Airport Maintenance personnel respond to the EOC and, usually, Staging Areas to assist with escorting response personnel to the incident scene, or ICP, and to provide whatever equipment and materials may be necessary such as portable lavatories, potable water, fuel removal materials, a portable public address system, cones, stakes, and flags (FAA, 2010a, p. 116).

Airport employees also should be prepared to assist with providing for the uninjured, those with minor injuries who are still onsite, and family members of victims. While care of the family members and passengers is legally the responsibility of the air carrier, the airline may take a long time to have sufficient personnel and resources in place to perform this function. In the meantime, people will look to the airport to handle these critical functions. When the airport engages early in the process to assist with care of family members, it reduces stress and trauma, it is considered the humane, and may avoid a poor public image of the airport.

While FAA AC 150/5200-31C recommends that the airport operator put together a coalition of air carriers that serve the airport who can respond and assist for the first 12 hours, many airlines already have such plans in place. The airport operator should ensure these plans are in place, and if not, provide for them. Some airports only have one small air carrier with limited personnel, and no other air carrier personnel available for hours or days, depending on how long it takes for them to mobilize and fly in. The airport operator also has an understanding (through the AEP) of what the airlines and investigators will require upon arrival and should use local emergency service resources for collecting passenger and crew contact information, particularly for passengers that do not receive medical attention (FAA, 2010a).

The airport can also predetermine (with the airlines) locations for key facilities, such as a "Friends and Relatives" reception area, and other areas where families may gather. One notable addition to many trauma treatment programs is the addition of therapy dogs to the family assistance centers, so airport personnel who are in charge of protecting or controlling access to family assistance areas should be briefed on the potential arrival of such teams.

It is natural for family members to go directly to an airline ticket counter or the screening checkpoint, upon arrival at the airport to seek information. Police and security officers are often used to respond to these locations and assist in getting family members to the right location and to prevent media and unauthorized personnel from entering the Friends and Relatives area. If the airport is closed, TSA personnel may occasionally be used to provide information to friends and relatives arriving at the airport. The IC should request such assistance from the senior TSA person at the airport at the time. The Assistant Federal Security Director-Screening (AFSD-Screening) is the senior official over the screening checkpoints; the checkpoints themselves are managed by Transportation Security Managers, who oversee screening operations for the airport overall. Transportation Security Supervisors or Lead Transportation Security Officers (TSOs) are usually assigned to specific checkpoints.

Once the response phase is over (or nearing completion), which is indicated by all personnel involved with the accident being transported away from the incident and, in some cases, a transfer of Incident Command to airport management, the airport must prepare for the arrival of investigators from the NTSB and the FAA.

AIR CARRIER OR AIRCRAFT OWNER/OPERATOR

The **Aviation Disaster Family Assistance Act (ADFAA)**, PL 104-264, Title VII, requires air carriers to have a plan in place to handle the families of victims involved in an Aircraft Accident. This requirement includes establishing a location for family assistance, arranging for passengers services such as the transport of uninjured personnel to holding facilities, arranging commissary items, telephone facilities, clothing, or additional medical services, and providing information to and reuniting with families and friends of the victims/passengers.

The air carriers will provide the airport operator with information about the number of individuals on board, any Dangerous Goods, and any other information relevant to the safety and security of the flight. In some cases, the TSA may provide information to the airport operator regarding the presence of individuals on the aircraft that may be on the Selectee list, prisoners on board, and law enforcement officers conducting prisoner escorts. The air carriers have this information as well, along with the location of any other armed law enforcement officer including Federal Air Marshals and Federal Flight Deck Officers.[8] Police and fire personnel on scene should be advised about the presence of firearms on passengers or flight crew members. As yet, there has not been a clear distinction on whether police officers should secure firearms found at the scene of an accident; ideally, all remnants of the wreckage should remain in place, unless there is a clear safety or security reason to move them. In some cases, the remnants of a firearm helped determine the cause of the accident, such as the case of Pacific Southwest Airlines (PSA) Flight 1771, where part of a pistol, which was used to shoot both pilots, was found with part of the perpetrator's finger lodged against the trigger.

Airlines are also required under ADFAA to track passengers and crew members, provide **Critical Incident Stress Management (CISM)** support, and coordinate Public Information activities with the airport operator by providing a PIO and staff members, if available, for the JIC. It is the responsibility of the air carrier to provide for the timely removal of the wreckage once clearance is authorized by the NTSB or FAA. Often the air carrier will have a contract with a local aircraft recovery service or can obtain services quickly. It is helpful if the airport maintains a list of such services in the area as it is in the best interest of the airport to have the debris cleared as quickly as possible. Airport Cooperative Research Program (ACRP) Synthesis 38, *Expediting Aircraft Recovery at Airports*,[9] by Dr. Daniel Prather, provides additional guidance and best practices on removing the aircraft from the airfield in a timely manner.

DIVERTS AND INCIDENTS AT GENERAL AVIATION AIRPORTS

In some cases, such as in United Flight 232, an airliner must divert to an airport where it does not have a base of operations. In this case, the supporting airline personnel may be hours from arriving at the airport to assist, leaving the responsibility of victim and survivor care in the hands of airport officials. In these instances, there are a variety of actions the air carrier can take to help with the situation until their personnel arrive.

If other airlines are based at the airport, airline officials from the diverted aircraft's company can reach out for their assistance. They can also reach out to local Fixed Base Operators for assistance in aircraft handling and for providing facilities and shelter, and work with the American Red Cross to assist in the interim, in addition to working with airport authorities. For an aircraft that is diverting, in most cases the airliner will be able to notify their operations centers, via radio or Aircraft Communications Addressing and Reporting System (ACARS) datalink, so that the airline can dispatch a response team to the diverted airport. In some cases, the destination airport may be

---

[8]Federal Flight Deck Officers are pilots who are authorized to carry firearms for the sole purpose of protecting the flight deck from intruders.
[9]http://onlinepubs.trb.org/onlinepubs/acrp/acrp_syn_038.pdf.

closed as a consequence of the crash, so a nearby commercial service or general aviation (GA) airport may serve as an alternate for the airlines "go-team." Others at the airline book rental cars and hotels[10] to accommodate their incoming personnel.

When the aircraft is not a commercial airliner, but is a GA aircraft, victim and survivor assistance is the de facto responsibility of the airport operator. Although GA airports are not required to have an FAA-approved AEP, any municipality must respond to emergency situations in their community, handling, to the extent possible, all aspects of the emergency. The diligent GA Airport Manager should be prepared for four types of situations: the crash of a GA aircraft that is **based** at the manager's airport, the crash of a GA aircraft that is not based at the manager's airport (i.e., **transient aircraft**), the crash of a **diverted** airliner that could not reach a commercial service airport, and the crash of a **military aircraft** not based at the manager's airport.[11]

When an aircraft crashes at its home GA airport, after the response phase is complete, handling of survivors and victims is similar to handling a car accident in the community. Local first responders (police, fire, EMS, clergy, coroner) can be asked to assist in handling family notifications and tracking of patients to hospitals. However, the airport operator will still be in the role of facilitating much of this activity, having facilities available for victims (first aid and temporary medical care of injured and temporary morgue facilities for the deceased) and as reunification locations for survivors. Survivors may also need assistance with media issues.

When an aircraft that is not based at the GA airport crashes, the response and initial recovery phases are similar to the based aircraft crash, but notifications and tracking down the aircraft owner or operator, or their business or family members, who may be located in another state or country, can be more difficult. Again, it is typically the responsibility of the municipality to handle these notifications, but the airport operator should be prepared to handle survivor and victim assistance (e.g., facilities, personal comfort such as food, water, phone access).

RECOVERY OF THE DECEASED

One of the most difficult things to do in any mass casualty or "crowd killer," as the NTSB informally refers to a crash of a large commercial airliner, is recovery of the deceased. The airport should have an adequate supply of body bags, along with smaller biohazard bags to contain body parts. Removal of the deceased takes place only after approval from the NTSB.

After the crash of United Flight 232, the approval to move the deceased did not take place for a few days. It is important that law enforcement secure the accident scene to keep out reporters, looters, and curiosity seekers, as well as wildlife that may come to prey on the deceased. From a moral perspective, airport management should take measures that they would like to see taken if it was their family member lying on the airfield. Generators and lights should be brought to the scene, along with posting an honor guard and allowing clergy access to the scene. If approved, the bodies may be able to be covered with a blanket or sheet. Airport operators should also be aware that

---

[10]Media agencies have been known to immediately book as many available hotel rooms as possible in the vicinity of an aircraft crash.

[11]The crash of a military aircraft based at the airport is not addressed as the military, in most cases, has the responsibility to respond to the accident. However, there may be instances where there is a small military presence at the airport that does not have ARFF capabilities, in which case the airport should be prepared for such an incident.

accidents such as this have significant impacts on Airport Operations personnel who are not accustomed to seeing such wide-scale tragedy. Even for seasoned firefighters and police officers, these tragedies can often evoke an emotional response as they are reminded of the other tragedies they have responded to (Gonzales, 2014).

A **Disaster Mortuary Operational Response Team (DMORT)** unit will be dispatched to assist with handling the deceased. DMORTs are comprised of volunteers who are specialists in temporary morgue facilities, victim identification, and forensic dental pathology and forensic anthropology methods. The team comes with its own "Morgue in a Box," known as a Disaster Portable Morgue Unit, which contains all the supplies needed to create a complete morgue, with workstations for each step in processing a body (Gonzales, 2014).

A temporary mortuary needs to be set up on scene, but remote from areas where relatives, media, or the general public have access. Strict security measures should be taken. The annex should contain electricity, running water, a closed drainage system, and enough floor space to accommodate morgue operations. NFPA recommends a facility of at least 4,000 square feet. The area will be used for victim identification and the collection, catalog, and storage of personal effects (NFPA, 2013, p. 424–25).

The lessons learned after UAL 232 contributed significantly to the process of identifying victims of a plane crash. After the deceased were documented as to their locations on the field, they were placed into body bags, moved to refrigerated trucks, and transported to a hangar on the airfield that was serving as a temporary morgue. Rather than allowing family members to come identify victims, even those whose faces were still in perfect condition, forensic dentists ended up removing the jaws from the faces of the victims and matching the teeth to dental records. Victim's fingertips were also cut off, making fingertip processing easier. The uproar and scandal that resulted from these techniques forced changes in the way fingerprinting methods and forensic dentistry are conducted. Today, digital x-rays can be taken without any disfigurement to the individual's face, and Federal Bureau of Investigation (FBI) technicians no longer routinely cut off people's fingers to obtain their fingerprints (Gonzales, 2014).

RECOVERY OPERATIONS AND INVESTIGATORY PHASE

Once the deceased have been removed from the accident site and the NTSB has cleared the airport air carrier to remove the wreckage, the airport operator will start taking actions to restore the airport to full operational capacity. The initial phases of the recovery ensure that all response personnel and any others that are on the airfield or in any of the Security Areas have been properly escorted back to the public areas. The airport operator will then conduct a comprehensive special self-inspection of all Air Operational Areas to ensure all the debris from the crash has been removed. Although large pieces of debris are easy to spot, and can be relocated with winches and other equipment, there will likely be paper, jewelry, personal belongings, pieces of pavement, dirt and mud, and possibly some pieces of the aircraft still left on the airfield.

After UAL 232, members of the Air National Guard, the Iowa Public Service Company, and 134th Infantry of the Iowa Army National Guard engaged in the cleanup of paper and other debris that still littered the airfield. They had to perform these duties among the pink spray-painted numbers that showed where bodies had been, bloodstains, and pavement scars from where banks of seats had skidded along the runway. According to Air National Guard Colonel Swanstrom, it took

10 days to get the last piece of paper picked up off the airfield. It was also reported that many small liquor bottles were also found among the debris, many of which were consumed on the spot, but it was important to Swanstrom that his Air Guard personnel be allowed to participate in the cleanup process. Swanstrom's theory was that by allowing his people to participate, they could get a feeling of having completed the job they had begun and, in some ways, of having purified the location where the crash occurred (Gonzales, 2014).

The Airport Director should take the time to personally thank all personnel who were involved in the response and recovery to an airplane crash. The role of the American Red Cross, along with numerous volunteers, including local lifeguards, who assisted with everything from triage and initial medical care, to assisting with autopsies and allowing themselves to be assigned as trackers, so that every deceased victim had a living volunteer who would stay with the body throughout the entire process, should not be forgotten. Steps should be taken to ensure that all personnel involved with the response received proper mental health support.

With a large Aircraft Accident, the NTSB *Go-Team* is dispatched to conduct the investigation, but for the investigatory phase to be successful and the NTSB to make the most accurate determinations about the probable cause. To make more effective recommendations to improve the safety of aviation, it is critical that the accident scene and the evidence be protected to the extent possible (FAA, 2010a).

Until the arrival of the NTSB or an authorized representative, the only time aircraft wreckage, **mail,**[12] or cargo may be disturbed or moved is to remove persons that are injured or trapped, to protect the wreckage from further damage, or to protect the public from injury. When it is necessary to move wreckage, mail, or cargo, sketches, descriptive notes, and photographs should be made if possible, noting the original condition and position of the wreckage and any significant impact marks (FAA, 2010a).

Protecting an Aircraft Accident scene is addressed in AC 150/5200-12C, *First Responders' Responsibility in Protecting Evidence at the Scene of an Aircraft Accident* (FAA, 2009), and accident/incident investigation procedures are addressed in Title 49 CFR Part 831, *Accident/ Investigation Procedures*. There are numerous additional documents related to ARFF standards, responders to HAZMAT incidents, and airport firefighter qualifications, in addition to military publications such as the U.S. Air Force Fire Emergency Service Technical Order 00-105E-9, *Aerospace Emergency Rescue and Mishap Response Information*, which provides guidance and a variety of criteria for responding to an Aircraft Accident. The complete list is available in AC 150/ 5200-12.

Saving the lives of the aircraft occupants is the primary consideration over all other activities, including the preservation of wreckage. However, once life safety actions have been taken and the incident is moving to the final stages of response, care should be taken to not unduly disturb any evidence that may help determine the cause of the accident or incident. Of vital importance are the **Cockpit Voice Recorders** and the **Flight Data Recorders** (Figures 12.6 and 12.7), which can help determine the probable cause of the accident. These items should not be moved or disturbed, except to prevent them from further damage. If moved, their location should be noted and, if possible, photographed (FAA, 2009).

---

[12]Most commercial aircraft carry mail—on UAL 232, 900 pounds of mail were scattered across the airfield. The postmaster is always on the notification list for Aircraft Accidents or incidents.

FIGURE 12.6

Representative Flight Data Recorders.

Source: FAA.

FIGURE 12.7

Representative Cockpit Voice Recorder.

Source: FAA.

While UAL 232 has been the case study to provide context and to attempt to provide a heavy dose of reality about what it is like to respond to an actual aircraft crash, the authors understand that every airplane crash is slightly different. However, much of what has been noted can be found in many major airline accidents, as there have been similarities in the crash of UAL 232, in passenger and responder behaviors, that can also be seen in some of the most recent crashes, such as Asiana Airlines Flight 214 at San Francisco International Airport in 2013, Continental Airlines

Flight 1404 at Denver International Airport, which ran off the runway (no fatalities), and the crash of U.S. Airways Flight 1549 into the Hudson River in New York.

TERRORISM INCIDENTS

Within the AEP, not many details explain how to respond to terrorist incidents such as the explosion of an improvised explosive device (IED) or vehicle-borne IED, hijackings, or active shooters. The specific incident response plans for these events are marked as Sensitive Security Information (SSI) and are contained in the **Airport Security Program**.[13]

From a Part 139 regulatory perspective, the AEP notes that all terror threats should be taken seriously until the validity of the threat can be determined, and airports should have on-call **Explosive Ordnance Disposal** personnel and equipment and bomb threat mitigation programs in place. Personnel should also be trained on the procedures to take if there was a bomb threat at the airport, and anyone in a call center capacity should be trained in how to handle a bomb threat. A **bomb threat call procedures checklist** is available in the AC and online through the Department of Homeland Security (FAA, 2010a).

Any aircraft that may be experiencing an act of unlawful interference should be directed to an isolated position on the airfield, commonly called the **Isolated Parking Position (IPP)**. However, just like the terminology used in an aircraft incident (Alert I, Alert II, Alert III) is not known to pilots, pilots are also typically not familiar with the term "IPP," or "Isolated Parking Position." Air traffic controllers (who are familiar with the term and the location of the IPP) will advise the pilot to taxi to a location on the airfield; pilots typically refer to this as the **penalty box** or the **holding area.** Airport police will respond to the location and initiate the appropriate procedures based on the threat: potential hijacking, potential bomb, etc.

On September 18, 2012, two aircraft at JFK Airport in New York were suspected of having terrorists hiding in the wheel wells and of having explosives on board. Both aircraft were directed to the IPP (what the controller called a "safe area"), but one of the pilots became increasingly agitated when he was not being told why the aircraft was being surrounded by police forces. He threatened that unless he was given an answer, he was going to stop the aircraft and evacuate the plane using the slides. When the air traffic controller offered to provide a better explanation over a different line, the pilot said "negative" and demanded that the controller give the information now, and over an open frequency (Associated Press, 2012).

The unfortunate reality for the pilot and passengers is that the proper protocols were being followed by law enforcement, who will continue to approach similar incidents in the same manner in the future. When there is a potential hijacking, there is an assumption that the pilot or the individual on the radio may not actually be the **Pilot-in-Command (PIC)**, or maybe the PIC, but under duress from the hijackers,[14] so information to the cockpit will be limited until such time as authorities can determine the actual identity and the condition of the individual on the radio. This is a source of anguish for many commercial-airline pilots, who are all trained with the understanding

---

[13]Some additional Public Information can be found in the authors' companion book, *Practical Aviation Security: Predicting and Preventing Future Threats*, 2nd edition (2013). Elsevier.

[14]That is, a gun to their head or other type of threat.

that the PIC should be made aware of all aspects of the flight—security, safety, or other important issues affecting the operational requirements of the flight.

In this case, the threatening tone from the pilot and the unwillingness to discuss the issue over a discrete frequency (or cell phone call from the tower) suggests that he may not be under positive control of the aircraft, that is, he may be under heavy duress. A better solution for the PIC may be to allow the situation to develop before taking extreme action or making the situation worse. The aircraft is on the ground and will be kept there until law enforcement believes it is safe to depart. Situations in the air may be handled differently as there is the possibility the aircraft can become a weapon, and there are no police surrounding the aircraft. The reports of hijackers and explosives turned out to be false, and the pilot never gave the order to evacuate the plane. Had the pilot evacuated the aircraft that action would have further delayed the flight and subjected passengers to injuries from sliding down the evacuation slides.

Despite this incident, responding law enforcement personnel will continue to treat such circumstances as a potential hostage situation, but Airport Operations personnel may need to assist in such circumstances by being ready to respond to law enforcement requests for additional personnel for crowd control, buses, and other personnel and equipment that would be necessary to help resolve a similar situation.

STRUCTURAL FIRES, FUEL FARM, AND FUEL STORAGE AREAS

Part 139 requires airports to meet minimum capabilities in ARFF, but does not specify the minimum requirements for structural fires. The airport operator conducts a risk assessment, working closely with the local fire department, to determine the types of equipment and the amount of personnel necessary to respond to structural fires on the airport or in adjacent supporting facilities (Figure 12.8).

Procedures for responding to structural fires on the airport vary widely throughout the nation. Even notification procedures can vary from jurisdiction to jurisdiction. For some airports, fire alarms in the terminal building or concourses go to a central dispatch facility, instead of to the airport's communications center, and a truck or engine will be dispatched from a local station and will require access to the airport. Some airports have on-airport structural firefighting capability, while other airports rely on an off-airport response.

The AEP describes how the airport is prepared to handle structural fires and describes the sprinkler and alarm systems, the location of the response agency, identifies the dispatching agency, along with the approximate response time of fire departments tasked with structural or fuel fire support. It also describes the water supply system, hydrant locations, and supporting structural fire response operations (FAA, 2010a).

Notifications for structural fires are similar to those for aircraft fire, but may come from a variety of sources including the ATCT, a fire alarm in a structure on the airport, a phone call to the communications center, or other means. Once any agency has been notified of a structural fire, the notification system is engaged through the approved means. Some airports are hesitant to use the aircraft "ringdown line" or "crash-phone," preferring that this phone only be used for an airplane crash or an Alert I to Alert III.

FIGURE 12.8

Structural firefighting unit on an airport.

Source: Jeffrey Price, 2015.

Upon notification, control tower personnel facilitate the movement of response equipment across the airfield to the location of the incident and may have to divert aircraft traffic away from the structure because of smoke reducing visibility. The airport operator takes Protective Actions for the public and employees, while off-airport, and sometimes on-airport, fire personnel respond to the incident. Police and security personnel provide crowd and traffic control as needed, while EMS personnel provide emergency medical services. The airport operator may decide to activate the EOC for a large-scale event, such as a fuel farm fire or major structural fire. The Fire Chief is often the initial IC and is responsible for fire suppression, as well as activating any mutual aid agreements.

Airport Maintenance personnel provide utility support, such as cutting off fuel supplies or ensuring an uninterrupted flow of water, if necessary. Maintenance personnel can also assist in safety inspections and restoring the facility. The airport Public Information office may issue a news release (to the media, plus message postings on the website, tweets, and other public notification methods) and may do public notifications throughout the terminal building to let passengers know what is happening, how it affects them, and what Protective Actions to take. Putting out the incident via both conventional and social media can also reduce inquiries to the airport, because when people see smoke at the airport they think there might be an aircraft crash.

STAPLETON FUEL FARM FIRE

On November 25, 1990, a fire erupted at the fuel storage facility 1.8 miles from the main terminal of Stapleton International Airport[15] in Denver, Colorado. The fire burned for approximately 48 hours with a total of 634 firefighters, 47 fire units, four contract personnel, 56,000,000 gallons of water, and 28,000 gallons of foam concentrate being used before the fire was extinguished. Of 5,185,000 gallons of fuel stored in the tanks, 3,000,000 gallons were consumed by fire or lost as a result of leakage from the tanks, with damage totaling between $15 and $20 million dollars (between $28 million and $38 million in 2015 dollars) (NTSB, 1990).

Flight operations were disrupted, because of both the smoke and the response operations involved in fighting the fire, with United Airlines experiencing significant disruptions as a result of the lack of fuel for their aircraft. The NTSB (1990) determined the probable cause of the fire was the failure of a contractor to detect loose motor bolts, which permitted the motor pump of unit three to become misaligned; the subsequent damage resulted in leakage and ignition of the fuel.

The report also provides valuable lessons-learned for airport operators who may experience fuel farm or large, structural fires. A catering employee first noticed smoke coming from the facility, but the employee did not notify the fire department for at least 20 minutes, at which time numerous personnel on the airport, including security officers and the tower, all noticed the smoke. The fire department notified Colorado's public utility company and requested electrical power to the farm be terminated, but it took approximately 45 minutes to complete the work about an hour after the fire was called in (NTSB, 1990, p. 2).

ARFF personnel quickly deployed a foam concentrate mixed with water, yet because of fuel spraying from a ruptured fuel line, the foam layer quickly washed away, and the fuel reignited. Within 3 minutes of the initial attack, the airport firefighters depleted their entire water supply and started to replenish it from a nearby hydrant (NTSB, 1990, p. 3).

City firefighting units arrived on scene within the first 10 minutes and sprayed water on adjacent exposed fuel tanks to protect them from fire and explosion. As firefighting efforts continued into the evening, all foam concentrate supplies were depleted except for the amount reserved to keep the airport in compliance with FAA requirements. Additional foam concentrate was flown to Denver from fire departments in Seattle, Houston, Philadelphia, and Chicago (NTSB, 1990, p. 4).

Gusting winds and a cold front caused changes in wind direction, repeatedly disrupting the foam blanket and forcing firefighters to continually readjust tactics. On November 27, representatives from Williams, Boots and Coots, Inc. (WBC), a private company that specializes in large-scale fuel fires, arrived on-scene, and received permission from the Denver Fire Department to attack the fire. The private company assumed responsibility for firefighting operations. Continental Airlines called and ultimately paid for the company's services as Continental was concerned that the fire might reach its holding tanks that were also located at the fuel farm. Within 45 minutes of taking over fire-suppression operations and through the use of its special foam/concentrate water proportioners, WBC extinguished the fire (NTSB, 1990, pp. 4−6).

At the time, Part 139 did not require the fire department inspector who performs the quarterly inspections to be trained in the inspection process, only that the certificate-holder (i.e., the airport operator) maintain *sufficient qualified personnel* to comply with the requirements in the Airport Certification

---

[15]Now closed and replaced by Denver International Airport.

Manual (NTSB, 1990, p. 41). Also at the time, FAA regulations addressed fuel storage, fire protection, training, and inspection for airport operators related to fueling operations, but there were no equivalent regulations under Parts 121 and 135 to require air carriers to meet the same standards.

Additionally, the FAA was uncertain which office, Airport Districts Office or Flight Standards District Office, should be responsible for inspecting air carrier−operated fuel operations. The FAA subsequently issued a policy memorandum in an attempt to resolve the issue and clarify which organization within the FAA is responsible for inspection and oversight of fuel storage facilities. The FAA Airport District Office conducted a certification inspection of Stapleton International Airport in June 1990 and noted that the airport was not in compliance with Part 139.321, which requires the airport to adhere to fueling standards for protection against fire and explosion, to conduct quarterly inspections of fuel storage facilities, and to maintain yearly training[16] certification of fueling tenants (NTSB, 1990).

The NTSB further concluded that while airport and local firefighters could not be expected to have a sufficient supply of foam concentrate to fight a fire of this magnitude, the Board was concerned that the City of Denver and the fire department had not contemplated a fire of this type and did not have procedures or contingency plans in place. Arrangements for WBC to provide onsite experience were made only after Continental Airlines became concerned that its fuel tanks were in jeopardy. In their conclusions, the Board cited Denver's lack of procedures or a contingency plan for responding to a fire of this magnitude as prolonging the duration of the emergency and also called out the FAA for failing to specify the responsibility for the inspection of fuel farms located on airport property when such installations are operated by air carriers. The NTSB also noted that the airport did not allocate sufficient resources to perform thorough quarterly inspections of fueling operators on the airport (NTSB, 1990).

NATURAL DISASTERS

Airports play a vital role in emergency management. It is often said that an airport can be many things, but only an airport can be an airport. During human-made and natural disasters, airports have served as hospitals, shelters, evacuation areas, medivac sites, Staging Areas,[17] an ICP, an EOC, a Base[18] or Camp,[19] a helispot, helibase, or Air Base to receive casualties or to receive outside aid, a **Point of Distribution (POD)**,[20] a morgue, a church, and the center of government.

---

[16]Part 139 required training for fueling operators, but at the time did not require training for the fire inspectors to conduct the inspections. The fire department inspector who performed the quarterly inspections attended a one-week course in 1988 on the requirement of Part 139.321, which, according to the inspector, he paid for himself.

[17]This is an Incident Command System (ICS) term. Staging Areas are locations set up at an incident where resources can be placed while awaiting a tactical assignment.

[18]This is an ICS term. A Base is the location at which primary logistics functions for an incident are coordinated and administered. There is only one Base per incident. (Incident name or other designator will be added to the term *Base*.) The ICP may be colocated with the Base.

[19]This is an ICS term. A Camp is a geographical site, within the general incident area, separate from the Incident Base, equipped and staffed to provide sleeping, food, water, and sanitary services to incident personnel.

[20]A POD is a Federal Emergency Management Agency (FEMA) term that describes the area where the public goes to pick up emergency supplies following a disaster.

The AEP lists five separate natural disasters including hurricanes, earthquakes, tornadoes, volcanoes, and floods. Airports are not only required to have a section in their AEP that addresses natural hazards that are relevant to their area, but should also include plans to address other natural disasters that are not listed in the AEP AC but that occur locally. Other natural disasters can include:

1. Severe thunderstorms and lightning
2. Winter storms, extreme cold, and blizzards
3. Extreme heat
4. Landslides and debris flow
5. Tsunamis
6. Wildfires

A natural disaster can involve a large geographical area, can impact a sizable population, and frequently requires the implementation of mass evacuations or sheltering-in-place, along with mass-care operations. A natural disaster will often have more than one IC, and resources such as transportation facilities, including the airport, may come under the direct control of federal, state, or local government. The airport operator should be prepared with contingency plans so that the airport can survive a natural disaster, including mitigation steps, preparedness efforts, and a response-and-recovery plan, but should also understand the airport's role in the community during the various natural disasters likely to occur in the area.

HURRICANE

A hurricane is a severe Tropical Storm, sometimes referred to as a *tropical cyclone*, which forms over tropical or subtropical waters, with sustained winds of 74 miles per hour or greater, occurring primarily along the Atlantic seaboard, the United States Gulf Coast, the Pacific West Coast, Hawaii, and the Caribbean (FAA, 2010a). Hurricanes in the Pacific are often called *typhoons*, but are the same as a hurricane in all other definitions. A hurricane can be up to 600 miles wide with wind speeds of up to 200 miles an hour. It moves between 10 and 20 miles an hour over the open ocean gathering heat and energy through contact with warm ocean waters, but it loses its energy as it makes landfall.

"Hurricane season" typically begins on June 1 and ends on November 30, although hurricanes have occurred outside this timeframe. The National Hurricane Center tracks, on average, 12 hurricanes per year in the Atlantic Ocean. A hurricane begins as a Tropical Depression, which is an organized system of clouds and thunderstorms with a defined surface circulation and maximum sustained winds of 38 miles an hour or less. It becomes a Tropical Storm when the maximum sustained winds exceed 39 miles an hour up to 73 miles an hour. A hurricane is rated using the Saffir-Simpson scale, which is a rating from 1 to 5 based on the sustained wind speed and estimated potential property damage (National Oceanic and Atmospheric Administration (NOAA), 2015a) (Figure 12.9).

A **storm surge** is defined by the NOAA as an abnormal rise of water generated by a storm, over and above the predicted astronomical tide; more simply put, a storm surge occurs when water from the ocean is pushed toward the shore by the force of the hurricane's winds. A storm surge can increase the water level by more than 30 feet and as it moves farther inland and can cause lakes

Category	Sustained Winds	Types of Damage Due to Hurricane Winds
1	74-95 mph 64-82 kt 119-153 km/h	**Very dangerous winds will produce some damage:** Well-constructed frame homes could have damage to roof, shingles, vinyl siding and gutters. Large branches of trees will snap and shallowly rooted trees may be toppled. Extensive damage to power lines and poles likely will result in power outages that could last a few to several days.
2	96-110 mph 83-95 kt 154-177 km/h	**Extremely dangerous winds will cause extensive damage:** Well-constructed frame homes could sustain major roof and siding damage. Many shallowly rooted trees will be snapped or uprooted and block numerous roads. Near-total power loss is expected with outages that could last from several days to weeks.
3 (major)	111-129 mph 96-112 kt 178-208 km/h	**Devastating damage will occur:** Well-built framed homes may incur major damage or removal of roof decking and gable ends. Many trees will be snapped or uprooted, blocking numerous roads. Electricity and water will be unavailable for several days to weeks after the storm passes.
4 (major)	130-156 mph 113-136 kt 209-251 km/h	**Catastrophic damage will occur:** Well-built framed homes can sustain severe damage with loss of most of the roof structure and/or some exterior walls. Most trees will be snapped or uprooted and power poles downed. Fallen trees and power poles will isolated residential areas. Power outages will last weeks to possibly months. Most of the area will be uninhabitable for weeks or months.
5 (major)	157 mph or higher 137 kt or higher 252 km/h or higher	**Catastrophic damage will occur:** A high percentage of framed homes will be destroyed, with total roof failure and wall collapse. Fallen trees and power poles will isolate residential areas. Power outages will last for weeks to possibly months. Most of the area will be uninhabitable for weeks or months.

FIGURE 12.9

Saffir-Simpson scale.

Source: NOAA.

and rivers to also flood. The highest surge is near the "radius of maximum winds," or where the strongest winds of the hurricane occur. Storm surge should not be confused with **storm tide**, which is a rise of the water level during a storm caused by a combination of a storm surge and the astronomical tide (NOAA, n.d.b).

A storm surge is often the greatest threat to life and property during a hurricane, beyond the damage done by the high winds of the hurricane, the associated tornadoes, and other related damage. During Hurricane Katrina in 2005, at least 1,500 people lost their lives, with many of the deaths attributed to the storm surge. Many areas along the Gulf Coast are susceptible to a storm surge, and the surge is more devastating where the ocean floor slopes gradually into beach areas, as opposed to a cliff side or sea wall. (NOAA, n.d.c).

Previously, the Saffir-Simpson scale, used to measure the force of a hurricane, was also associated with storm surges; however, in several recent hurricanes the wind speed did not have a direct correlation to the size of the storm surge, so now the terms are no longer related. Forecasters at the National Hurricane Center use a computer model known as **SLOSH (Sea, Lake, and Overland**

Surges from Hurricanes) to predict storm surge heights. The model assesses the hurricane's track, intensity, and size, and uses water depths, land elevations, and barriers to determine which areas may need to be evacuated (NOAA, n.d.a).

Hurricanes also produce tornadoes, which can cause significant damage to the community and the airport. Tornadoes are covered in a separate contingency plan, but airports may have to implement elements of their hurricane, tornado, and flood contingency plans to prepare for, respond to, and recover from a hurricane.

AIRPORT HURRICANE PREPAREDNESS, RESPONSE, AND RECOVERY

Airport operators should conduct a risk assessment that determines if the airport is vulnerable to hurricanes and to determine the hurricane category that is typical to the area and for which the airport should prepare. **Flood maps** should be prepared to show those areas of the airport that may be subject to flooding and identify any facilities that may be at risk. Terminal buildings and concourses often feature large panes of glass, which can become shrapnel in a hurricane. Essential equipment, tools, and vital records should be stored in a safe location that is not susceptible to flooding. The airport operator should also identify any facilities that should be evacuated during the hurricane. The airport should determine the availability of an **Uninterruptible Power Supply (UPS)** and should also have on hand auxiliary generators to provide power to essential equipment and key facilities (FAA, 2010a).

Major hurricanes will impact wide geographic areas that can restrict the availability of resources such as generators, plywood, and truck buckets (sometimes called *Cherry Picker Trucks*), along with food, fresh water, and other essential items. Airport access may also be affected from flooding, trees, and downed power lines, restricting access to the airport by the airport's own personnel, so the contingency plan for a hurricane should include consideration for when to send staff home, how to operate at minimal staffing levels (and who essential staff are), when to shut down the airport to commercial operations, and when to shut down the airport completely.

A variety of definitions of "airport closed" should be articulated in the AEP. While some smaller airports may completely close, some large airports claim they are never "closed," even though they may have ceased flight operations. Other activities, such as concessions, aircraft services, Airport Maintenance, and snow removal operations, may still be taking place. Emergency public notification messaging should clearly explain what is meant by the status of a closed airport (Smith et al., 2015). These definitions are particularly relevant to a natural disaster. Most airport "closures" imply that commercial-aircraft operations have ceased, but during a natural disaster, "airport closed" may mean that all personnel are being evacuated from the airport and told not to return until the airport has been reopened for public use.

The airport operator should have experts complete a review on the airport's structures to certify the wind loads that each structure is capable of withstanding; to identify communication capabilities along with alternate communication plans with the assumption that radio towers, cell phone towers, and other normal forms of communication may not be available; and to entertain the worst-case scenarios. Hurricanes never happen without warning. They take days to form and to move toward shore, giving airport operators plenty of time to implement contingency plans, but these assessments should be conducted months or years in advance.

The track of the storm can change within a short period of time so that an airport operator that thought the hurricane was missing its airport can suddenly experience its full force. Airport operators may only have a few hours to implement some of the last-minute contingency plans, such as closing the airport's commercial operations and evacuating all passengers and nonessential personnel.

The airport operator also must consider that many of the passengers may be transferring between flights and may not have Ground Transportation to get away from the airport. Local hotels may already be fully booked or also in the process of evacuating. Contingency plans should include procedures for moving transient personnel to local evacuation centers. Prior to the arrival of the hurricane, firefighting, and law enforcement personnel can respond to calls of emergency medical assistance, petroleum leaks, and other HAZMAT issues. Airport Maintenance personnel can assist in sandbagging operations, turning off gas, electricity, and water systems when necessary, and ensuring all communications equipment has been tested and is ready to go. Emergency medical personnel may experience higher call volumes because of passenger stress. Passengers with functional needs should also be considered in the evacuation plans. Air traffic controllers, along with Airport Operations personnel, should continue to issue NOTAMS about the status of the airport (FAA, 2010a).

For a commercial service airport, several days before the arrival of the storm the airport operator should begin to hold meetings with the air carriers and with key tenants. Air carriers will typically begin canceling flights to the airport a day or two prior to the arrival of the storm, depending on the storm track, weather forecasts, and management's best judgment. It is important for the airport operator to know when the air carriers plan on canceling all of their operations, as it may relieve the airport from its Part 139 responsibilities and better enable airport staff to prepare for the arrival of the storm.

Many airport tenants also want to save their own personal aircraft so there may be a rush of aircraft attempting to depart in a short period of time. However, one unique circumstance that can occur is that some base aircraft owners will leave their aircraft at the airport in the hopes that it will be damaged so they can collect insurance money. Many airports that are susceptible to hurricanes will develop a weather disaster plan that is separate from the Airport Certification Manual. This plan is more flexible as it does not require FAA approval to change it or make modifications. Provided that the airport operator has put the minimum information into the AEP that is required by the FAA to demonstrate that plans are in place to handle a hurricane, other plans can also be used. In fact, the FAA's own AC advises that the airport produce a **Hurricane Response Schedule** that establishes phases for the approaching hurricane and activities (by priority) to be completed during each phase (FAA, 2010a).

While it may go by different names from airport to airport, the Hurricane Response Schedule can be broken down into long timelines based on the estimated time of arrival of the hurricane. The plan should include four elements:

1. **Awareness:** occurs 3 to 5 days in advance of the arrival of gale force winds (35 to 54 mph) and describes actions to be taken by the various airport entities. A Tropical Storm Watch is usually issued around this time or before.
2. **Standby:** occurs 48 to 60 hours before the arrival of gale force winds. A Tropical Storm Watch may be issued, or a full hurricane may have already formed.
3. **Response:** occurs within 48 hours of the arrival of gale force winds and addresses the actions taken by the airport operator, fire and rescue personnel, ATCT, law enforcement, the air carriers, and others.

4. **Recovery:** occurs after the passage of the storm and addresses the recovery actions and timelines by all airport entities.

Key decisions to be made at the airport in preparation for during and after a hurricane include:

1. When will the airport activate its Disaster Operations Plan/Hurricane Response Schedule?
2. When will the airport close to commercial operations?
3. When will the airport close to all operations?
4. When will the terminal be evacuated and the airport go to minimal staffing?
5. When will the ATCT close?
6. When will the EOC be activated?
7. What procedures are in place for the protection of essential airport personnel who must remain onsite?
8. What is the minimum level of staffing the airport needs in order to operate enough to begin recovery operations and to act as a Staging Area or logistics coordination center for the arrival of incoming resources? Note: This is not the same as restoring commercial service operations.

After the storm passes, recovery operations include rescuing any personnel who are trapped or injured from collapsing structures, clearing debris, surveying the airport for damage, and determining the status of key facilities such as the control tower, fire stations, and utilities. Timelines can then be established for the restoration of aircraft operations and commercial service. Airport personnel should also anticipate that the airport will turn into an "Air Base" to serve the community recovery efforts and can expect the arrival of a variety of civilian and military aircraft.

Both commercial service and GA airports should expect the arrival of GA aircraft from companies that have businesses in the area. If precoordinated, many of these GA aircraft can bring in relief personnel and supplies, as well as evacuate their own personnel or conduct medical evacuations. Helicopters from the Coast Guard, Air and Army National Guard, and local medical service providers may also look to the airport as a location point to bring casualties and to refuel their aircraft. Helicopters do not need large areas of land in which to operate and will likely arrive earlier than Fixed-Wing assets. As soon as a runway can be cleared, inspected, and readied for use, larger Fixed-Wing relief aircraft can arrive. Note: The runway does not have to meet the Part 139 standard for use by military and GA aircraft, but the airport operator should note this via NOTAM.

Outside assistance from Air National Guard and Army National Guard units will also likely respond to the airport and set up a Camp[21] on airport property. The National Guard units are highly self-sustaining and bring their own food, water, sanitation services, and other essential needs so as to not burden the community any further. Airport operators should be prepared, through training, drills, and exercises, on how to run their airport as a disaster and relief facility for a period of time, which will increase the effectiveness of all response personnel.

Airport operators should also expect a higher use of Unmanned Aerial Vehicles (UAVs or drones) in the area as news agencies, private citizens, businesses, and rescue personnel use UAVs to assess damage, film damage for news reports, and search for lost personnel. There will also be UAV users who just want to look at the damage for no other purpose than curiosity. These operators may cause hazards to navigable airspace for rescue and recovery aircraft operations. Airports

---

[21]This is an ICS term.

may wish to obtain their own UAVs for similar use. Drones can also be used as messengers, delivering physical, handwritten messages (i.e., message in a bottle) and video imagery to other response-and-recovery personnel, via internal SD chips. The FAA may, or the airport operator may ask to, declare a **Temporary Flight Restriction (TFR)** over the area during relief operations and establish a system to approve aircraft that desire to use the airport.

HURRICANE IVAN, PENSACOLA, FLORIDA, 2004

On September 16, 2004, Hurricane Ivan made landfall in Alabama and Northwest Florida, striking the city of Pensacola with full force (Hurricane Ivan, 2005). Although the eye of the hurricane went ashore west of Pensacola, near Mobile, Alabama, the city caught the worst part of the storm because it was struck by the hurricane's front-right quadrant, which always carries the strongest winds. The hurricane eliminated a quarter-of-a-mile section of the east-bound Interstate 10 bridge over Escambia Bay, and swept away homes and businesses. Tornado damage as a result of the storm, and flooding, caused millions in damage to the city.

The storm began several days earlier, moving its way up the Gulf of Mexico, and at one point reached Category 5 on the Saffir-Simpson scale. It made landfall as a Category 3 hurricane, bringing sustained 120 mph winds and a historic storm surge. The storm killed more than 60 people, including eight people in the Florida panhandle,[22] and the damage estimate was nearly $14 billion dollars. While Hurricane Katrina resulted in far more deaths and more destruction, the actions of the staff at Pensacola Gulf Coast Regional Airport (now Pensacola International Airport) set the standard in tactics and strategies airports can implement in handling such storms.

Preparations for the arrival of the hurricane begin with tenant briefings on Friday, September 10, 2004. Airport staff were focused on keeping the airport open as long as possible to get those who needed to get out of Pensacola out of town. Airport staff worked closely with airline managers to determine when the airlines would cease flight operations. Some airport staff also took advantage of the opportunity to evacuate their own family members from town, so they could concentrate on operations at the airport. The airport also was concerned about the terminal building becoming an impromptu shelter, and they were not set up to handle and sustain the needs of a large number of evacuees. An unexpected occurrence, however, was the rush of rental car returns prior to the storm as people sought to relieve themselves of liability damages for their vehicles (Price, 2005).

On September 13th, the airport implemented its **Destructive Weather Plan (DWP)**. The Plan is separate from the Airport Certification Manual (ACM) so that it can be modified on-the-fly, without waiting for FAA approval. The primary purposes of the DWP are to address notification procedures for airport staff and the general public about the status of the airport, to establish the readiness conditions in anticipation of hazardous and destructive weather, and to set forth the responsibilities for safeguarding personnel and property at the airport. The DWP designates a **Storm Preparedness Coordinator** within the Airport Operations Center, which is staffed 24 hours a day and AOC is responsible for all communications and monitoring activities at the airport including disseminating destructive weather warnings and the airport's status (G. Donovan, personal communication, April 1, 2005).

[22]The majority of deaths were throughout the Caribbean up to Massachusetts, as the storm moved up through the Gulf Coast and made landfall, continuing as a severe storm throughout the United States.

On September 15, the terminal building was closed to all public and nonessential personnel, with concrete barricades deployed at all roadways and police staffing checkpoints to control access. Weather conditions deteriorated to the point that Part 139 standards could not be maintained. However, aircraft operations continued as many GA pilots continued to ferry aircraft out of the storm's path, and continued to operate even after the ATCT and the FAA's Terminal Radar Approach Control center (TRACON) closed because of high winds. At 3:30 PM, the airport, through NOTAM, was indicated as closed because of massive flooding and flying debris. Maintenance personnel were needed early on to secure jet bridges, rewire emergency generators, and clear debris from clogging the storm water system, but were sent home prior to the arrival of the actual storm. Airport police were called in to provide facility security (Price, 2005).

As the storm approached in the evening hours, the terminal building's roof started leaking, two hangars on the airfield collapsed, and three small aircraft were destroyed, likely by tornadoes that were a result of the storm. Unexpectedly, the Airport Operations Center received a frantic call from the TRACON, which was located at the base of the ATCT. Airport personnel believed the facility to have been evacuated hours ago, but some controllers thought the building to be sturdy enough to handle the storm, so they had brought in their families, spouses, kids, and pets and had chosen to shelter-in-place in the TRACON, unbeknownst to airport management. Despite attempts by the assistant Airport Director and airport police to reach the personnel in the facility, 114 mph winds prevented any rescue attempts—controllers and their families rode out the storm as air conditioning units ripped away from the roof and sections of the TRACON collapsed (Price, 2005).

The storm arrived on shore shortly before 2:00 AM on September 16. Numerous tornadoes and fierce winds whipped through the city; at the airport, portions of the terminal roof collapsed and a 30-foot section of a terminal wall collapsed onto the ramp. Operations personnel put trash cans beneath the leaks as glass and metal doors blew off their hinges, while outside, signs, light posts, and even roof gravel became airborne projectiles on the airfield. By the following morning, there was extensive damage to two corporate hangars and four T-hangars, and airfield directional signs were damaged or destroyed, as were large portions of the perimeter fence. All cell phone lines were down and the airport radio communications system was sporadic (Price, 2005).

The City of Pensacola was without power, and causeways and bridges were washed out, effectively cutting off access to Pensacola Beach and Gulf Breeze. With debris spread across roadways throughout the city, for a period of time the airport was the only way into or out of town. At the time, city plans called for Naval Air Station Pensacola to be used as the Primary Air Base and Staging Area to receive recovery assets and from which to coordinate disaster recovery efforts. However, there was extensive damage to the Navy base and a number of other nearby smaller military facilities, leaving the regional airport to fulfill the role. A member of the airport staff traveled by vehicle to the Escambia County EOC, which did not previously have an airport representative as part of the response plan. County administrators ordered the airport to reopen as soon as possible in order to facilitate relief operations (Price, 2005).

In the early morning hours of September 16, the airport was able to open the helicopter landing pads, as Coast Guard helicopters begin arriving with their first loads of evacuees. The next wave of aircraft included military C-17s and C-130s bringing food, water, and supplies, along with 300 soldiers to assist with the relief effort. The airport was able to use portions of a previously closed runway to accommodate the inbound aircraft (Price, 2005).

An important consideration for Airport Managers is that some military aircraft have short-field takeoff and landing capabilities and may not need the full length of a commercial service runway in order to operate. Airport Operations personnel should work with military personnel to determine the airfield needs in advance, as well as the needs of personnel who are coming to help (do they have their own food supplies, water, shelter, etc.).

The airport continued to serve as a Staging Area for hundreds of semi-tractor—trailer rigs, forcing airport staff to find food, water, and toilet facilities for the drivers and workers. Gates had to be taken down to accommodate the semi-truck operations, as 150 National Guard and Air Force personnel staffed the offload area and camped on closed runways. Stalls in the airport bathroom were without water, and food was eventually provided by airport concessionaires, but not until 3 days later (G. Donovan, personal communication, April 1, 2005).

Air traffic controllers went back to work coordinating the inbound relief aircraft as the airport reopened for essential aircraft operations only. An unexpected wave of relief aircraft arrived from corporate America, as Albertsons, Walmart, and other major companies started bringing in relief supplies. A TFR was established and airport staff had to generate a system to decide which aircraft would be allowed in and which would not. Additionally, seven other airports sent personnel and equipment to assist the staff at Pensacola—an act that was the genesis of SEADOG and WESTDOG (Price, 2005).

More than 70 members of the Virginia Air National Guard arrived with heavy equipment and began clearing debris from the airfield and landside. Florida National Guard units, along with statewide law enforcement personnel, arrived to maintain and guard the airport's 9-mile perimeter, as most of the fence was damaged. Emergency generators were deployed to power the fuel farm. Because the airport had an operational runway, had established helicopter-landing zones, had available fuel and ground support, and had a secure perimeter, the airport quickly became the logistical hub for all disaster relief materials by both air and ground for the City of Pensacola (G. Donovan, personal communication, April 1, 2005).

As part of the recovery operations, teams of structural, mechanical, electrical, and civil engineers and roofing specialists from the airport's contract engineering firm mobilized from Jacksonville and began a comprehensive damage evaluation, just one day after the storm. The team worked around-the-clock for 2 days to verify that the terminal building, TRACON, fire station, and maintenance buildings were structurally safe for occupancy. The airport was losing nearly $50,000 a day in revenue while taking on the full weight of the expense of the recovery operations. A recovery plan was quickly put into place to begin commercial operations on September 24. By September 20 people who left their vehicles parked in the garage were able to retrieve them, the airfield was reopened to GA operations on September 21, and the airport was back up to Part 139 standards. Cargo flights began arriving on September 22. By September 24, restaurants and gift shops resumed normal schedules, and TSA, which had deployed additional contingency staffing, had all screening equipment functional and passengers experienced no delays (G. Donovan, personal communication, April 1, 2005). Some of the key lessons learned from the Hurricane Ivan case include (Price, 2005, p. 23):

1. Have a DWP (or similarly named plan) and review it frequently; ensure the plan is developed with stakeholder input and that it includes the airport's role in regional EOC operations;
2. Be prepared to be self-sustaining for several days, with stored food, potable water, and sanitation facilities;

3. Don't assume that everyone will do what they are supposed to do—e.g., the unexpected traffic jam that resulted from everyone returning the rental cars at the same time, FAA personnel ignoring the evacuation order;
4. Have backup communication capabilities, such as satellite phones (or drones[23]);
5. Keep track of all costs, personnel, vehicles, and equipment. U.S. Department of Transportation (DOT) Secretary Mineta arrived a few days after the storm with a $2.5 million discretionary grant to help pay for parts of the recovery effort that were not covered by insurance or the Federal Emergency Management Agency (FEMA);
6. Consider personnel needs—not all personnel are needed the entire time. Send nonessential personnel home and rotate (if possible) essential personnel;
7. Extend letters of agreement beyond government agencies to local businesses to provide supplies and equipment on a priority basis; plywood became a precious commodity in the days leading up to and after the storm.

The destruction caused by Hurricane Katrina in 2005 continued to push the operational capabilities and versatility of airports even farther, with the Louis Armstrong New Orleans International Airport and others becoming field hospitals, temporary morgues, and EOCs for the continuity of government. Another lessons learned on incident planning for a hurricane is to assume the local police that typically provide law enforcement coverage at the airport may be redeployed to the city, but some law enforcement presence is still needed at the airport as it is probably one of the places with some power and shelter (Broderick, 2005). EMS personnel may also be in short supply. The airport itself may be in a situation where it is a disaster zone, without water or shelter for its own personnel, much less for incoming response personnel, so the airport should be prepared with at least a 3-day supply of nonperishable food and potable water. It is important to prioritize the recovery tasks, and getting runways, taxiways, and roadways cleared is usually at the top of the priority list. This will enable personnel to access the airport by land and by air (Broderick, 2005).

If some things can be done in advance to minimize the damage, those items should be identified and completed far in advance. Mitigation and preparedness steps can include moving key vehicles inside areas of strong shelter, stockpiling equipment and tools that will be needed later (such as extra perimeter fencing, hammers and screwdrivers, roofing material, wire and fuel for vehicles), and securing the items in one or more trailers that can be immediately accessed and deployed when needed. Other items to ensure self-sufficiency include nonperishable food, work gloves, sleeping bags, backup power generators, gravity-fed ice machines, and a mobile command center that can serve as a shelter in a pinch (Broderick, 2005).

The airport operator needs to have a "seat at the table" in regional EOC operations and plans. During Hurricane Rita, which hit Beaumont, Texas, city officials had not considered the airport's role in early planning sessions. As the storm approached, the Airport Director had closed the airport and sent home staff, but then received a call from a county official telling him to reopen the airport in order to receive medical evacuees. The airport was able to reopen quickly as it had just several

---

[23]Although UAV capabilities did not exist at the airport operational level at the time, they can be used for messaging functions.

weeks earlier received 15,000 people who were displaced by Hurricane Katrina. Within the next day, the airport moved 1,500 nonambulatory and 6,000 ambulatory people through the facility. This reinforces the notion that airport disaster response and evacuation should be taken seriously, and the airport should conduct tabletop exercises on evacuation scenarios and potential regional emergencies (Broderick, 2005).

EARTHQUAKES

An earthquake is a sudden shaking of the ground caused by the sudden breaking and movement of the tectonic plates of the earth's rocky outermost crust. It can occur anywhere in the world, but there are areas that are subject to frequent earthquakes (see www.earthquake.usgs.gov). In the United States, earthquakes are most common in California, Alaska, and in the central part of the United States (Figure 12.10). However, in 2011, an earthquake registering a magnitude of 5.8 occurred in Virginia. Flights were delayed at airports up and down the eastern seaboard, including JFK International, Newark Liberty International Airport, Ronald Reagan National Airport, and Dulles International Airport (McDonnell & Rossier, 2011).

Primary hazards of earthquakes are the effects of the ground shaking, which can damage buildings, either through the shaking or by sinking the building itself. During an earthquake, **liquefaction** can occur, through the mixing of sand or soil and groundwater, causing the soil to behave like quicksand (the soil hardens up after the quake has stopped but may be deformed). The second main hazard of an earthquake is **ground displacement** along a fault, which can cause a building to rip apart. Additional hazards can include fire, the release of HAZMATs, landslides, dam failure, and flooding (UPSeis, n.d.).

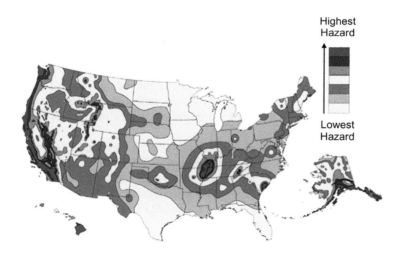

FIGURE 12.10

Earthquake hazards in the United States.

Source: FEMA.

Earthquakes are measured in a variety of ways, including the **Richter Scale** and the **Modified Mercalli Intensity Scale**. The Richter Scale measures the **magnitude** of the earthquake, which is *determined from the logarithm of the amplitude of waves recorded by seismographs* and is expressed in whole numbers and decimal fractions. A magnitude 5.3 might be computed for a moderate earthquake, and a strong earthquake might be rated as magnitude 6.3 (United States Geological Survey (USGS), n.d.a).

The Modified Mercalli Intensity Scale measures the **intensity** of an earthquake. The scale consists of a series of certain key responses, such as people awakening, movement of furniture, damage to chimneys, or total destruction. The Mercalli scale values are assigned to a specific site after an earthquake and are a more meaningful measure of severity to the nonscientist than the magnitude because intensity refers to the effects actually experienced at that place (USGS, n.d.c) (Figure 12.11).

According to the FAA, 39 states face the threat of a damaging earthquake and are considered to be earthquake hazard areas. Airport risk assessments should include a hazard analysis to determine if the airport is located within one of these areas, as well as to identify the facilities, properties, equipment, and so forth that may be vulnerable to an earthquake. The risk assessment should also identify airport facilities that may be more susceptible to earthquake damage, such as the ATCT (FAA, 2010a).

Intensity	Shaking	Description/Damage
I	Not felt	Not felt except by a very few under especially favorable conditions.
II	Weak	Felt only by a few persons at rest, especially on upper floors of buildings.
III	Weak	Felt quite noticeably by persons indoors, especially on upper floors of buildings. Many people do not recognize it as an earthquake. Standing motor cars may rock slightly. Vibrations similar to the passing of a truck. Duration estimated.
IV	Light	Felt indoors by many, outdoors by few during the day. At night, some awakened. Dishes, windows, doors disturbed; walls make cracking sound. Sensation like heavy truck striking building. Standing motor cars rocked noticeably.
V	Moderate	Felt by nearly everyone; many awakened. Some dishes, windows broken. Unstable objects overturned. Pendulum clocks may stop.
VI	Strong	Felt by all, many frightened. Some heavy furniture moved: a few instances of fallen plaster. Damage slight.
VII	Very strong	Damage negligible in buildings of good design and construction; slight to moderate in well-built ordinary structures; considerable damage in poorly built or badly designed structures; some chimneys broken.
VIII	Severe	Damage slight in specially designed structures; considerable damage in ordinary substantial buildings with partial collapse. Damage great in poorly built structures. Fall of chimneys, factory stacks, columns, monuments, walls. Heavy furniture overturned.
IX	Violent	Damage considerable in specially designed structures; well-designed frame structures thrown out of plumb. Damage great in substantial buildings, with partial collapse. Buildings shifted off foundations.
X	Extreme	Some well-built wooden structures destroyed; most masonry and frame structures destroyed with foundations. Rails bent.

FIGURE 12.11

Modified Mercalli intensity scale.

Source: United States Geological Survey.

Unlike a hurricane, earthquakes occur without warning, and the effects are highly variable from one earthquake to the next. Most of the casualties that result from an earthquake are not as a result of the earth movement, but of falling debris and partial or complete building collapses. As with any natural disaster, more than the airport is likely to be affected, and airport personnel should expect the airport would be used as a critical element in the community's recovery. While individuals who live in areas that experience frequent earthquakes typically know what actions to take in the event of an earthquake, airports are filled with transient passengers who may not be familiar with the basic safety procedures. Passengers can be informed with signs to a certain extent, and all airport personnel should be fully informed and trained on the actions to take during an earthquake.

Personnel who are outside should move away from buildings, tall lights, and utilities. Personnel who are inside should take cover under a sturdy desk, table, or bench or against an inside wall. If there is no cover, individuals should cover their face and head with their arms and crouch in an inside corner of a building. No one should move from their position of cover until the shaking stops or if they must move to avoid falling debris. Vehicles on the airfield or landside should pull over and stop until the movement of the earth stops. Flight operations should cease until the shaking stops and it is determined that the airport is safe for operations. After the initial earthquake, personnel should be aware of aftershocks, which are a follow-up to the actual event and can still be of a high enough magnitude to cause damage. Once the event is over, it is possible that utilities will be damaged—gas leaks, for example, can occur—so individuals should not light matches, sewer lines may backup, and personnel may be caught underneath debris, injured and unable to call for help.

Airports should take the usual steps to prepare for an emergency, including consideration of vulnerability of access roads and bridges to earthquake damage and what would be the impact if some or all were rendered unusable. Airport contingency plans should also address the function of the airport if an earthquake should occur during the airport's peak period, during nighttime operations, or during periods of low staffing. An airport should also have communication backup plans in case antenna facilities are rendered inoperable. The functions carried out by Airport Operations personnel, airport fire and police personnel, Public Information office personnel, and airport tenants are similar to those functions in preparation, response, or recovery from a hurricane or other natural disaster (respond to the EOC, ensure equipment and supplies are available, etc.) (FAA, 2010a).

Post event, Airport Maintenance personnel should conduct assessments to determine what elements of the terminal and airfield need to be restored. These elements include power, sanitation, water, airfield lighting, and radio communication systems. Debris may have to be cleared, and Search and Rescue operations and fire suppression may have to be conducted, particularly if a building collapses. Public warnings should go out about the continuing threat of fire, unsafe areas, and aftershocks, along with the status of drinking water, use of utilities, and overall sanitary conditions (FAA, 2010a).

The airport operator should develop a **personnel accountability standard operating procedure** and encourage airport tenants to do the same, so that individuals can be located or accounted for after an earthquake. The airport should also maintain emergency generators, fill special storage lockers with disaster supplies, and conduct earthquake-specific training, drills, and exercises (FAA, 2010a). In the recovery period, all personnel should be accounted for, and all facilities should be assessed for damage, including photos and videos, when appropriate. The condition of the FAA control tower should be assessed as soon as possible and personnel returned to the facility as soon as it is declared safe for use. A special self-inspection should be conducted to determine whether the airport is safe for operation, with personnel paying particular attention to the pavement conditions and the conditions of airfield signs, markings, and lighting. If the earthquake occurred during the day, additional inspections should be conducted as evening approaches to determine the status of lights and lighted airfield signs.

It can be assumed from several recent disasters that these airport facility inspections can delay Airport Operations, even if no damage has occurred, and that airport runways, terminals, and other facilities will be affected, particularly the ATCT, which is highly vulnerable to damage. In a large-scale emergency that has affected the community, airport operators can expect to experience demand from four types of operations: air cargo, airline passenger carriers, disaster service providers (military and off-airport response), and business users (GA) (Perkins, 2013).

Earthquakes and Airports: Historical Review and Lessons Learned

On October 17, 1989, the Loma Prieta earthquake occurred in the San Francisco Bay and the Monterey Bay areas. It measured 6.9 (Richter Scale) and lasted approximately 15 seconds, killing 63 people and injuring more than 3,700. The earthquake caused massive power outages throughout the region, along with damage to several natural gas pipelines (more than 500 gas line leaks in the region), and Ground Transportation was disrupted as roads and bridges were closed (Perkins, 2013, pp. 33–34).

At slightly over 35 miles from the fault line, San Francisco International Airport (SFO) halted operations for one evening. The airport experienced no significant damage to the facilities or the runway. However, the tower had window and nonstructural damage. The primary reason for the shutdown, however, was that not enough controllers were available to operate the tower safely as a consequence of the closure of the San Francisco–Oakland Bay Bridge. General gridlock was exacerbated by individuals leaving the San Francisco Giants vs. Oakland A's World Series baseball game at Candlestick Park, near the airport, making it difficult for airport personnel to commute to work. On the airport, there was some damage to an air cargo building and a power transformer, but there were no problems with access roads or freeway closures in the immediate vicinity of the airport (Perkins, 2013).

At the Oakland International Airport, despite being 40 miles from the fault point, the airport's main 10,000-foot runway was severely damaged by liquefaction; 3,000 feet of the runway sustained cracks, some a foot wide and a foot deep. Large sand boils appeared on the runway and adjacent taxiway, some as wide as 40 feet. Recovery operations were hindered as both telephone service and usable radio frequencies became quickly overloaded. The control tower lost three windows, a walkway between terminals was damaged, and a water main rupture caused a service road collapse (Perkins, 2013). While cellular technology was available at the time, it was not widely used. Today, during most natural disasters, cellular phone operation is still heavily restricted because of either damage to the cell phone towers or too many people trying to use the system simultaneously. However, text messaging does tend to work more effectively during times when the cell phone's voice function does not.

The San Jose International Airport was only 15 miles from the fault source of the earthquake. The airport was immediately closed, and all facilities, runways, taxiways, the tower, and navigational aids (NAVAIDs), along with parking garages and landside access routes, were inspected. The airport was fully operational 40 minutes after the earthquake, having experienced only some cosmetic damage. Commercial power was lost, but backup generators continued to function (Perkins, 2013).

As a result of the earthquakes, terminal facilities, concourses, and the ATCT at SFO were brought up to compliance to meet current seismic code. At SFO, the airport conducted a Shoreline Protection Feasibility Study to assess its vulnerability to flooding, sea level rise, and tsunami events. At Oakland, the airport improved the perimeter dike system to prevent inundation by water from San Francisco Bay and to reduce earthquake-induced liquefaction. At San Jose, liquefaction is a hazard because of ancient, naturally occurring, stream-channel deposits and localized fills under-lying the runways. The airport has since made significant physical improvements, reconstructing and extending both runways, and including design elements within the runway to mitigate underly-ing soil conditions from liquefaction. Terminal facilities were also improved, and a new fuel farm, with 10 times the storage capacity as the original, was completed, reducing the airport's reliance on tanker truck deliveries (Perkins, 2013).

Jeanne Perkins, under contract with the Association of Bay Area Governments, conducted an anal-ysis of several other earthquakes and noted that typical earthquake damage at an airport ranged from broken glass, particularly in the control towers, power loss, and fallen ceiling tiles and light fixtures, to runway and pavement damage caused by liquefaction. When the Nisqually earthquake occurred in Seattle in 2001, the control tower suffered serious enough damage that it was evacuated, and tempo-rary towers (provided by the FAA) mounted on trucks were established. As a result of the earthquake, SeaTac airport created positions in the Emergency Coordination Center that are unique, including a Continuity of Operations (COOP) position and a second for Recovery of Operations. SeaTac has also shared its experience with WESTDOG as part of the voluntary mutual aid agreement (Perkins, 2013).

Other impacts of an earthquake include damage to the airport perimeter fence, the loss of power to the airport access control and credentialing system, and a loss of power that can affect screening equipment and other essential security and safety systems necessary for the operation of the airport.

While airports have played a lesser role in assisting with community recovery during an earthquake in the United States, airports were critical to the recovery efforts following several earthquakes that occurred around the world, including the 2009 Samoa earthquake and tsunami and the 2010 Haiti earthquake. Earthquakes cause considerable disruptions, particularly at international airports, due to more stringent timetables. Flight delays or cancellations at international airports have extensive reverberating effects throughout the worldwide airspace system. In 2011, the Tohoku, Japan, earthquake and tsunami temporarily shut down both Tokyo's Narita International Airport and the Tokyo International Airport, causing a major disruption of passenger flights, includ-ing the diversion of at least 11 flights to the nearby Yokota Air Base. Approximately 13,000 pas-sengers were stranded at Narita airport when flights were stopped; more than 290 flights were canceled, impacting more than 60,000 passengers (Perkins, 2013).

While Perkins' (2013) report focused on the five commercial service airports in the San Francisco Bay Area, the recommendations are relevant for any commercial service or GA airport. The report noted that an airport's revenues can decrease significantly as a result of the drop in reve-nue from canceled traffic and the expenses associated with repairs. The report encourages all air-ports to work to have support from elected officials and regional organizations and to conduct more frequent **training, drills**, and **exercises** with transit districts; water, wastewater, and power utility companies; the American Red Cross; the U.S. Coast Guard; and other related organizations. One interesting point that was redacted from the final report was that "AEPs are best utilized if openly shared on the Internet to promote transparency and provide opportunities for the public and compa-nies to contribute to the improvement of the plan" (Perkins, 2013).

AEPs are not required to be labeled as SSI,[24] and both the FAA and the TSA have provided a procedure for the AEP to remain a public document and achieve the benefits noted, while TSA and airport security-related procedures can be addressed in the SSI-protected Airport Security Program. Another interesting note from the Perkins report is that GA airports would benefit by examining the AEPs from commercial airports in their region and should participate in municipal training and exercises to enhance their understanding of what is expected of their airport following a disaster, as well as to test their emergency plans on a regular basis (Perkins, 2013).

TORNADOES

Tornadoes are violent storms consisting of a vortex of low atmospheric pressure, accompanied by a funnel-shaped cloud. They are usually associated with severe weather such as thunderstorms and hurricanes. They can be extremely destructive, with the average width of a tornado being between 300 and 500 yards (the largest measured at 2.5 miles wide), and their path can extend up to 50 miles, with a ground speed between 10 and 50 miles an hour. Wind speeds within the funnel have been estimated to be between 100 and 500 miles an hour. Approximately 2% of all tornadoes are classified as "violent," with wind speeds exceeding 300 miles an hour, an average width of 425 yards or more, and an average length of 26 miles. Tornadoes can occur in any state within the United States, but occur most frequently in Texas, Oklahoma, Florida, Kansas, Nebraska, Iowa, South Dakota, Illinois, Missouri, Mississippi, Louisiana, Colorado, Wisconsin, Arkansas, Georgia, North Dakota, Minnesota, Indiana, and Michigan (FAA, 2010a, p. 160).

On average, 75 people a year are killed by tornadoes. The year 2011 was exceptional with 553 deaths, making it the deadliest year for tornadoes since recordkeeping began in 1950. That total includes the 158 people killed in the Joplin, Missouri, tornado (Weather.com, n.d.). In the United States, tornadoes can occur year-round, but tornado season typically runs from March to August, with peak activity between April and June. The Enhanced Fujita Scale is widely recognized and accepted as the measurement of the destructive power of a tornado. F-scale winds are estimated from structural and/or tree damage. The system was enhanced to incorporate 28 damage indicators and classifies tornadoes into six categories based on wind speed and damage (FAA, 2010a, p. 160).

For a vortex to be classified as a tornado, it must be in contact with the ground and the cloud base; otherwise, the vortex is typically considered a funnel cloud. Funnel clouds are still hazardous to aircraft operations and serve as warnings to Airport Operations personnel that a tornado may soon be present. While hurricanes provide several days' advance notice of their potential arrival and earthquakes provide no notice, tornadoes may also provide some notice. Tornadoes do not occur without some sort of prior phenomenon, such as a severe thunderstorm or a hurricane. Hail, rain, wind, and lightning may accompany tornadoes, making both aircraft and ramp operations hazardous.

As with all other natural disasters, an airport should conduct risk assessments to determine the airport's vulnerability to tornadoes, identify essential equipment, tools, and vital records that may need to be moved to a safe area, and identify any facilities that should be evacuated. Furthermore, the airport should identify structures and locations that are suitable to serve as tornado shelters and

---

[24]Some in the aviation emergency management community argue that AEPs should be marked as Sensitive Security Information (SSI). This topic was previously addressed in this text.

prepare signage and protective action public messaging to alert passengers about an impending tornado. Personnel at the airport should also be trained in Protective Actions so that they can not only protect themselves, but assist with passenger evacuations, or shelter in place operations (FAA, 2010a, pp. 160−161). Responsibilities of Airport Operations and maintenance, fire, police, EMS, air carriers, and tenant personnel are fundamentally the same as those responsibilities and actions that should be taken in preparation for a hurricane. Tornado recovery operations are similar to earthquake recovery operations and may include a damage assessment, Search and Rescue to identify areas of building collapse and trapped individuals, access control systems to the airport, clearance of debris, and a special self-inspection of the airfield prior to reopening to Airport Operations (FAA, 2010a, pp. 162−166).

Joplin Tornado, 2011

On May 22, 2011, the city of Joplin, Missouri, experienced an EF-5 tornado, resulting in 158 deaths and more than 1,000 injuries. Wind speeds were in excess of 200 miles an hour, and the tornado was on the ground for slightly more than 22 miles, lasting an estimated 38 minutes from start to finish. Seven thousand homes were destroyed with extensive damage to businesses and public buildings. St. John's Hospital was severely damaged, steel reinforced concrete porches and driveways were lifted and tossed, and some vehicles were tossed into homes or crushed completely. Franklin Technical Center, along with a newer section of Joplin High School, and a bank, all except for the vault, were destroyed (Wheatley, 2013).

The tornado also eliminated one of two medical flight helicopters in the town, and with the loss of one of the hospitals, temporary medical facilities were set up at a local community center, with doctors performing surgery on the basketball floor. Ninety-five percent of the primary and secondary streets in the destruction area were impassable, and with the elimination of landmarks, personnel and workers did not know what streets they were on. First responders also experienced health and safety hazards trying to get to persons in need (Stockam, 2015).

The Joplin Regional Airport found itself in an unusual position, as its industrial park became a FEMA temporary housing facility, providing 586 families with temporary housing—all of which were moved to permanent housing within 3 years. About the only form of communication that worked immediately after the tornado was text messaging; however, the airport worked with local radio stations to inform the general public (Stockam, 2015).

As part of the recovery operations, the airport ran eight helipad locations, along with numerous jet aircraft operations, moving people to hospitals outside of the damaged areas. As with other natural disasters, something unexpected usually occurs, and in the case of the Joplin airport, GA pilots returned to the airport soon after the tornado to go flying to see the damage for themselves—not in an official capacity but for personal edification. The airport had the FAA establish a no-fly zone to help handle all of the essential air traffic (Stockam, 2015).

After the storm, the airport revised its tornado siren warning testing process from daily to monthly. The daily testing had become ineffective as people had become immune to it. The airport also added public safe rooms to handle airport and passenger populations and changed its ARFF off-airport response procedures to allow for taking ARFF equipment and personnel offsite in order to assist the community (Stockam, 2015).

After major natural disasters, VIPs (very important persons), such as politicians and public officials, often desire to visit the damaged areas. The Joplin Airport had to be ready to receive Air

Force One within a few days of the tornado. Bleachers had to be set up at the airport and security coordinated with the U.S. Secret Service. The airport asked if the president would be willing to fly into Springfield, Missouri's airport, but the request was declined. Decisions about where to take the president of the United States are sometimes politically driven, but in other cases are driven by security issues, and the U.S. Secret Service determined at the time that it was more secure to land at Joplin than at an adjacent airport, and then have the president transported either by vehicle or by the Marine One helicopter. Airport operators must be willing to stay flexible and make the best of any situation, as they do not always have control of decisions that are made related to community and federal needs.

VOLCANOES

Approximately 70 active volcanoes are located in the United States, mostly on the West Coast, from California to Washington State, along with Alaska and Hawaii. Volcanoes are formed when magma rises up from below the Earth's surface, gathering in a reservoir called the magma chamber. Sometimes, the magma erupts onto the surface. Volcanoes can trigger earthquakes, and they can spew volcanic ash more than 100,000 feet into the atmosphere, impacting areas for thousands of miles.

Airport procedures during and after a volcanic event are addressed in the ICAO Document 9691 *Manual on Volcanic Ash, Radioactive Material and Toxic Chemical Clouds* (ICAO, 2001). Ash fall is the primary hazard from volcanic activity, and accumulations of only a few millimeters are sufficient to force airports to close temporarily (Guffanti, Mayberry, Casadevall, & Wunderman, 2008). Volcanic ash is especially harmful to aircraft operations because of its small grain size, hardness, and abrasive nature, its ability to hold an electrostatic charge, and its ability to absorb water, which also contains droplets of corrosive acid. As with all other natural hazards, airports should conduct risk assessments to determine if they are in an area affected by volcanic activity (FAA, 2010a).

Volcanic activity has caused significant hazards to airports throughout the world. On average, five airports per year have been affected by volcanic activity since 1990. The majority of incidents have been caused by ash in the airspace in the vicinity of airports, but in a few circumstances, the airport itself has been impacted by lava flow, gas emissions, steam eruptions without lava ejective, and pyroclastic flow, a fast moving current of hot gas and rock that can reach speeds of 450 mph as it blasts away from the volcano. In the United States, the Ted Stevens Anchorage International Airport is among the most vulnerable to continued nearby volcanic activity, and the United States overall hosts the second highest number of volcanoes that have caused airport disruptions (Guffanti et al., 2008).

While the majority of threats to aircraft are from airborne volcanic ash clouds, volcanic activity causing physical damage to the airport is also a significant threat to Airport Operations. The primary hazard to airports is ash fall, which can reduce visibility, create slippery runways, affect communication and electrical systems, interrupt ground services, and damage buildings and parked airplanes. Volcanic ash contains small bits of glass, jagged pieces of rocks, and minerals. It is a mistake to assume that a volcanic ash cloud is harmless smoke. Unlike smoke, which is the product of combustion, such as burning wood, leaves, or paper, volcanic ash is hard, does not dissolve in water, and is extremely abrasive and mildly corrosive (USGS, n.d.b). Accumulations of less than a few centimeters can cause temporary airport closures. Ash accumulations must be removed before the airport can resume full operation, and, unlike snow, ash does not melt or blow away, but must be disposed of in a manner that prevents it from blowing back onto the airport during the cleanup process (Guffanti et al., 2008).

Volcanic ash easily penetrates all the most tightly sealed areas, including small electronic components, hangars and maintenance areas, and cooling, lubrication, and filter systems. In extreme cases, wet ash has the consistency of wet cement, and when deposited on top of an aircraft hangar can cause the building to collapse, as happened at Clark Air Force Base in the Philippines during the Mt. Pinatubo eruption, in 1991. The heavy wet ash can also tip aircraft onto their wings or horizontal stabilizer (tail) (ICAO, 2001).

Volcanic activity is routinely measured by a variety of agencies throughout the world, and there is usually a notification of the pending eruption, allowing the airport operator time to take mitigation measures. All agencies having airport operational responsibilities, including Airport Operations, police, firefighters, Airport Maintenance, ATC, EMS, and airline operators and tenants, have similar responsibilities under the volcanic contingency plan as under other contingency plans (e.g., EOC representation, ensuring equipment is tested and ready to go, training and exercises, testing of alert systems and radio systems, etc.) (FAA, 2010a). Additionally, the airport should have stockpiled duct tape and plastic sheeting to cover and seal openings on aircraft and vehicle engines, strategic buildings, and electronic equipment, along with heavy equipment for collecting and dumping volcanic ash, and a designated area for dumping and covering ash, away from the airport (ICAO, 2001).

Prior to the eruption, it may be possible to remove aircraft from the airport to avoid damage, which also reduces the number of passengers that may be stuck at the airport. Remaining aircraft and all ground vehicles and equipment should be sheltered to the extent possible, with essential components covered and sealed. Upon eruption, airport management and ATC personnel must make decisions about continuing Airport Operations. Aircraft landing after an eruption should limit the use of reverse thrust, which may ingest ash into the engines and contribute to reduced visibility, and Aircraft Operations should avoid operations in visible airborne ash (ICAO, 2001).

At some point, ground vehicles will have to reenter the airfield to remove the ash. No single technique is completely effective in removing ash; a combination of techniques has been found to provide the best results for managing and removing volcanic ash. Some in the industry believe that water should be used to assist in removing the ash, whereas other note that water causes the ash to harden (ICAO, 2001, App A-2). ICAO DOC 9691-AN/954 (ICAO, 2001) includes some basic removal techniques:

1. Wet the ash with water trucks;
2. Blade into windrows;
3. Pick up with belt or frontend loaders;
4. Haul to dump areas;
5. Sweep and flush residue;
6. Sweep/vacuum ash first, then flush with water (best for ramps, etc.);
7. Push ash to runway edge and plow under or cover with binder such as Coherex or liquid lignin;
8. Install sprinklers along edges of runway to control resuspension of ash from aircraft engine blast or wingtip vortices; and
9. Keep residue wet on taxiways and ramps.

Ground support equipment will need constant cleaning and maintenance. Equipment should be vacuumed, with oil and other filters changed more frequently, but equipment should not be washed as the water turns ash to sludge, which then washes into the equipment. Computer systems and radar and optical systems must also be protected and then cleaned up posteruption (ICAO, 2001, App A-4).

An important step in mitigating and reducing vulnerability to volcanic hazards is to form airport-specific operational plans, describing methods and available equipment for cleanup, procedures for incorporating up-to-date information from volcanological reporting agencies into operational decisions, and establishing protocols to close the airport (Guffanti et al., 2008). ICAO DOC 9691-AN/954 (ICAO, 2001) includes the Emergency Plan for Volcanic Eruptions in Alaskan Airspace, which provides guidance for other airports and states that may be affected by volcanic activity.

FLOODING

Flooding occurs when normally dry land becomes inundated with water, usually as the result of natural bodies of water overflowing their banks, dam breakages, a storm surge as the result of a hurricane, or earthquake-caused tsunamis (FAA, 2010a). Floods can also occur when large amounts of rain fall in a short period of time, overwhelming the ability of the stormwater system to handle the increased flow. Floods are capable of undermining buildings and bridges, eroding shorelines and riverbanks, washing out access roads, and causing loss of life and injuries. Floods are very prevalent in the United States because of the prevalence of human development in floodplains (Haddow, Bullock, & Coppola, 2013).

As with other natural disasters, airport operators should conduct a risk assessment to determine the risk of flooding at the airport and take mitigation measures. The **National Weather Service (NWS)** maintains a list of communities with potential flash flood problems; additionally the National Flood Insurance program has Flood Insurance Rate Maps and Flood Hazard Boundary maps (FAA, 2010a).

All agencies having airport operational responsibilities, including Airport Operations, police, firefighters, Airport Maintenance, ATC, EMS, and airline operators and tenants, have similar responsibilities under the flood contingency plan as under other contingency plans (e.g., EOC representation, ensuring equipment is tested and ready to go, training and exercises, testing of alert systems and radio systems, etc.). In addition, the airport should determine the impact of a flood on the community and the airport's potential role in assisting with mitigation efforts. Major floods can impact utilities, including electricity and water and sewer facilities. Mitigation efforts should include mapping areas likely to be flooded, identifying potential locations for the placement of temporary levees, and arranging for a labor force to perform flood fighting tasks such as filling sandbags (FAA, 2010a, pp. 170−182).

The **NWS** is responsible for most flood warnings in the United States; for large river systems, hydrological models are used by **River Forecast Centers**. For many small river systems the NWS has developed a system called **ALERT (Automated Local Evaluation in Real Time)**. ALERT is a flood-warning system for a local agency (city or county) that includes a sensor and a bucket. Each time the bucket is tipped, it sends a line-of-sight-dependent radio signal to the base station to provide real-time precipitation accumulations. The airport operator should be aware of flood warnings in the local area and, of course, any flooding that could directly affect the airport (FAA, 2010a).

When floods develop slowly, the airport operator should have enough time to determine the impact on the airport and decide whether to evacuate or shelter-in-place the airport population. In a rapidly developing flood, protective action decisions must be made quickly, and when an evacuation is not feasible, directions to high ground facilities should be provided. As in all natural disasters, airport operators should take into account basic personal needs such as food, water, sanitation, and moving those individuals with functional needs. Health and medical professionals should provide information to people on the health and sanitary hazards that can be created by floodwaters including untreated sewage, dead animals, disinterred bodies, and HAZMAT (FAA, 2010a).

The airport should stockpile essential flood-fighting items such as sandbags, fill, polyethylene sheeting, and pumps, with necessary fuel, setup personnel, operators, and tubing/pipes. Water supplies should be monitored for potability, fire hydrants should be monitored for water pressure, and food and dry clothing should also be acquired and stored for airport emergency workers. The airport should also conduct just-in-time flood-specific training programs, drills, and exercises. As in all natural disasters, NOTAMs should be issued to notify users of the status of the airfield, and public notifications should be issued through the PIO to advise the local community about the status of the airport (FAA, 2010a).

HAZARDOUS MATERIAL INCIDENTS

The variety of HAZMATs used in everyday life has increased the need for emergency preparedness at all points throughout the HAZMAT distribution system. A HAZMAT spill or release poses a significant risk to life, health, or property and could affect a few people or an entire community. The DOT's *Emergency Response Guide* (USDOT, 2012) is the primary guide for first responders in identifying the specific or generic classification of the HAZMAT involved in an incident and protective measures during the initial response phase (FAA, 2010a).

> Hazardous material is defined as any substance or material that when involved in an accident and released in sufficient quantities poses a risk to people's health, safety, and/or property. These substances and materials include explosives, radioactive materials, flammable liquids or solids, combustible liquids or solids, poisons, oxidizers, toxins, and corrosive materials.
> **FAA, 2010a, p. 187**

The *Emergency Response Guide* contains descriptions of the materials considered hazardous, along with the material's physical description, synonyms and trade names, the level of danger (e.g., poison, flammable, toxic to aquatic life, etc.), isolation distances, exposure/protection, relevant shipping regulations, and the level of the hazard presented (e.g., extreme hazard, noxious, corrosive). The *Emergency Response Guide* also lists symptoms from exposure to hazards, precautionary measures such as isolating a spill, protective clothing, evacuation distances, and first aid for a particular substance (USDOT, 2012). Placards help identify the type of HAZMAT:

- Class 1 Explosives
- Class 2 Compressed Gasses
- Class 3 Flammable Liquids (flammable, combustible, gasoline, etc.)
- Class 4 Flammable Solids
- Class 5 Oxidizers
- Class 6 Poisons (inhalation hazard, poison, toxic, etc.)
- Class 7 Radioactive Materials

- Class 8 Corrosive Liquid
- Class 9 Miscellaneous

UN/NA numbers (the four-digit number) found on bulk placards refer to specific chemicals or groups of chemicals and are assigned by the United Nations and/or the DOT (Environmentalchemistry .com, n.d.). Both the ICAO and the International Air Transportation Association (IATA) have instructions related to HAZMAT (called *Dangerous Goods* in both instances). The majority of HAZMAT at an airport is handled by the airlines, with the exception of aviation fuel. Airport operators should also be aware of criminal/terrorist use of chemical, biological, and radiological agents, and any circumstance that involves **Boiling Liquid Expanding Vapor Explosion (BLEVE)**, which can occur if the HAZMAT is Liquefied Petroleum Gases (butane, butylene, isobutylene, propylene, isobutane, and propane) (USDOT, 2012).

In addition to aviation fuel, packages with hazardous goods can be found in airport cargo buildings, on aircraft loading ramps, and in aircraft cargo compartments. As with all other emergency management contingencies, the airport operator should conduct a risk assessment to determine the types of HAZMAT that can be shipped by air, HAZMATs that may already be in use on the airport, and any facilities within the vicinity of the airport that use, store, or transport HAZMAT that may present a threat to the airport. Common HAZMATs that can be shipped by air include explosives, compressed or liquefied gases, which may be flammable or toxic, flammable liquids or solids, oxidizers, poisonous substances, infectious substances, radioactive material, and corrosives. Air cargo can also include numerous other items, such as food, human remains, and live animals— air cargo regulations specify which substances can and cannot be carried with other substances, and which substances can be carried on an aircraft but not next to another substance. Areas that present a threat should be mapped out and appropriate contingency measures taken (FAA, 2010a).

There are some HAZMATs that cannot be shipped by air (Class 1 explosives, infectious substances, poison gas, lithium batteries, car batteries, etc.), and some that can only be shipped in all-cargo aircraft (i.e., not passenger aircraft). The airport operator should refer to Title 29 CFR Part 1910, *Hazardous Waste Operations and Emergency Response* (OSHA 1910.120—HAZWOPER), and Title 40 CFR Part 311, *Worker Protection*, for guidance on the protection, safety, and health of employees involved in emergency response to HAZMAT incidents.

Any individual who is likely to encounter or witness a hazardous substance release should be trained to initiate an emergency response by notifying the proper authorities. Personnel who respond to releases should be trained to respond in a defensive fashion without actually trying to stop the release. **HAZMAT technicians** and specialists are specially trained to try to stop the release. The primary responsibility of fire personnel is containment without exposing themselves unnecessarily (FAA, 2010a, pp. 188—89).

INDICATIONS OF A CHEMICAL, BIOLOGICAL, RADIOLOGICAL, NUCLEAR/EXPLOSIVES (CBRN/E) ATTACK

Note: indicators of a possible chemical incident include (USDOT, 2012):

1. Unexplained odors;
2. Large numbers of dead animals, birds or fish;

(*Continued*)

(Continued)

3. Lack of insect life;
4. Unusual numbers of dying or sick people, particularly if there is a pattern, such as downwind from a certain location;
5. Blisters/rashes;
6. Illness in a confined area;
7. Unusual liquid droplets;
8. Low-lying cloud not consistent with existing weather patterns;
9. Unusual metal debris (i.e., bomb-like munitions).

Indicators of a possible biological release include (USDOT, 2012):

1. Unusual numbers of sick or dying people and animals;
2. Unscheduled and unusual spray being disseminated;
3. Abandoned spray devices.

Indicators of a possible radiological release include (USDOT, 2012):

1. Radiation symbols on a nearby container;
2. Unusual metal debris (i.e., bomb-like munitions).

The airport's vulnerability assessment should include the description of the substances located on or near the airport that are considered HAZMATs, transportation corridors in the vicinity of the airport, the name and location of the **HAZMATs Response Team** designated to respond to the airport, the level of training provided to airport personnel, and the emergency response to a HAZMAT incident on an aircraft (FAA, 2010a). Airports should work with air carriers on training, drills, and exercises related to responding to a HAZMAT incident.

In a HAZMAT incident, the Incident Command center operations (i.e., the ICP) may be modified for the protection of response personnel. All unnecessary personnel should be moved away from the ICP, and only qualified personnel should be involved in the response effort. Response personnel should have and wear the appropriate proximity protective gear and clothing—typically, a **Protective Action Zone** is established where people can be assumed to be at risk of harmful exposure. The airport operator should work closely with the airport fire command, the air carriers, and ATC to make decisions about whether to continue Airport Operations during the incident (FAA, 2010a).

Airport operators can assume a variety of Control Zones will be established around the incident site. **Control Zone** areas at a HAZMAT incident are designated based upon safety and the degree of hazard and are defined as the hot, warm, and cold zones. The **Cold Zone**, also referred to as the support zone, is a contamination-free zone established around the Warm Zone where emergency operations are directed and supported. The Cold Zone is normally established in an area where radiation levels are at natural background levels. The **Warm Zone**, also referred to as the contamination-reduction zone, is established around the Hot Zone to provide a buffer between the hot and cold zones and is where **decontamination** often takes place. The **Hot Zone**, or exclusion zone in some jurisdictions, is set up in the area immediately surrounding the spilled material or incident scene. Access to the Hot Zone must be controlled for accountability, safety, and contamination control (USDOE, n.d.).

Maintaining site security includes identifying the direction of the wind, locations of the command post, Staging Area, rehabilitation[25] area, and access control points. All areas should be located upwind from the Hot Zone, and accommodation should be made for access of the HAZMAT response team to the airfield. Evacuation routes may also be established by the response team and emergency evacuation procedures, which may require additional support from airport fire and rescue personnel.

Airport operators must establish emergency Public Information messaging and consider evacuation or shelter-in-place options based on the nature of the HAZMAT risk. Materials to respond to HAZMAT incidents can also be stockpiled and maintained at the airport. Airport operators should understand that a HAZMAT incident is unlike many other incidents that can occur at the airport. A HAZMAT incident can significantly disrupt Aircraft Operations for hours or days, and depending on the severity of the incident, may render certain areas of the airport inoperative for a considerable length of time. Also, HAZMAT incidents are not confined to air cargo areas, as passengers have been known to carry HAZMATs in their checked or carry-on bags sometimes illegally or, otherwise, unknowingly. Therefore, training, drills, and exercises should also be conducted for HAZMAT incidents that could occur in the terminal building, checked bag screening areas, and bag storage and sorting areas.

FAILURE OF POWER FOR MOVEMENT AREA LIGHTING

Airports are required to have a contingency for failure of power to the movement area lighting systems. All pilots are trained to land at night, and they are even trained in emergency situations to land just by using the landing lights on the aircraft itself; landing, however, is a far safer operation when the pilot can actually see the runway lighting. Runway lighting provides more than just the location of the runway; it also contains information related to the distance of available pavement that remains for landing and the location of taxiway exits. The primary power supplier for movement area lighting should be identified in the AEP, along with the description of any secondary or alternate power sources, emergency backup power generators, and how soon after failure of primary lighting the backup generator will engage (FAA, 2010a).

The AEP includes the procedures in place for tower or airport operator notification of the failure of the airfield lighting system, and notifications to FAA maintenance and Airport Maintenance personnel. Inspection of the airfield lighting system takes place daily as part of the Airport Safety Self-Inspection, with primary and backup power inspections taking place periodically.

WATER RESCUE

Airports that are located on or near major bodies of water, or with inbound and outbound flight paths that must cross significant bodies of water or marsh lands, must have a Water Rescue contingency plan. According to the FAA (2010b, p. 203), a body of water or marshland is significant if the area exceeds one-quarter square mile and cannot be traversed by conventional land rescue vehicles. Significant bodies of water as defined above located within at least 2 miles of the end of an airport runway should be included in the emergency plan area of response. The airport operator should also

---

[25]An area established for fire and rescue personnel to hydrate, rest, and receive minor medical attention, if necessary, during the response.

assume that if the significant body of water is off-airport property, the airport might not be the primary response agency. Primary response could be the responsibility of the U.S. Coast Guard, Harbor Patrol, or another federal, state, or local law enforcement agency having Water Rescue Capabilities.

The airport should plan to provide rescue vehicles with a combined capacity that equals the maximum number of individuals that can be carried on board, the largest air carrier aircraft that the airport can reasonably be expected to serve. Additionally, AC 150/5210-13, *Water Rescue Plans, Facilities, and Equipment*, provides requirements for airports located near water bodies (FAA, 2010b). In many ways, the Water Rescue plan is similar to the aircraft-accident contingency plan, with similar responsibilities for all responding organizations, except that the incident occurs on water. Airports may still have to assume roles related to family assistance, NTSB support, and other activities not directly related to the response to the incident.

The AEP contains information related to the types of bodies of water around the airport (ocean, river, lake, marsh, etc.), tidal conditions, the average size, depth, water temperatures, icing conditions, wave height, and prevailing winds. The AEP AC advises that response to an Aircraft Accident involving water should take the same precautions as a HAZMAT response. Spilled fuel is a primary source of HAZMAT when an aircraft goes down in the water (FAA, 2010b).

Responsibilities of Airport Operations, Airport Maintenance, fire and rescue, police, and EMS personnel are similar to those of an Aircraft Accident. The airport fire department should conduct an assessment to determine what types of equipment and training are necessary to enable its response to an aircraft crash on frozen lakes and rivers, and in water. Mutual aid agreements should be created with other agencies having Water Rescue capabilities, such as federal, state, and local harbor police and fire personnel, and privately contracted boating and helicopter operators. Training, drills, and exercises should also be conducted with all mutual response partners.

The time it takes for responders to get to an aircraft in the water can be substantially increased over the time it would take to respond to a land incident, so historically, the "first responders" on scene to an aircraft that has crashed in the water have been local citizens. These include recreational boaters and civilians that witnessed the crash, sailing over or pulling over and swimming out to meet victims of the accident, or pulling them to shore. Maximum use of aerial resources such as helicopters that have the capability of responding to an incident quickly should be engaged. Also, the airport should focus on methods of getting information to recreational boaters and others who are already on scene, about where to take rescued individuals for triage and treatment or to a designated Staging Area. Emergency Public Information functions may switch from one of notifying the public about the status of the airport, to one of attempting to put the word out to civilians involved in search and recovery of an aircraft that has gone down in the water.

The ICP for a water incident may not be near the scene of the crash, but near the location of the scene, on shore, providing access to the incident and access to hospital response routes. If the accident occurs next to the airport, in the water, then the ICP may be located on the airfield, or adjacent to the airport, depending on the location of the crash. The airport operator will have to consider whether to continue flight operations based on the availability of ARFF personnel to respond to another incident on the airport, and whether the response activities would be hampered by continued flight operations.

Other agencies, including the **U.S. Coast Guard**, the **U.S. Coast Guard Auxiliary**, and the **Civil Air Patrol (CAP)**, should be included in the response to any Water Rescue plan. All three agencies have Water Rescue and/or search capabilities. Another element to consider in a Water Rescue is whether the aircraft is a domestic or international flight. Domestic air carriers typically only have inflatable seat cushions and slide/raft flotation devices, whereas international flights carry inflatable life vests, large rafts, and other flotation devices. In both cases, the flotation devices are useful if there is some advance notification to passengers of a potential ditching. However, a 1985 in-house study by the NTSB *Air Carrier Over Water Emergency Equipment and Procedures* (NTSB Report SS-85/02) (NTSB, n.d.) noted that a review of air carrier water contact accidents between 1959 and 1984 shows that most water-related accidents were inadvertent, with no preparation time, substantial aircraft damage occurred, and there was a high chance of occupant injury. Most Water Rescue accidents did not occur on extended flights over water but close to an airport, during approach and departure, with many accidents occurring between the outer marker and the physical end of the runway. These areas should be a primary focus in Water Rescue planning (FAA, 2010b).

Individuals in an aircraft that crashes into the water may be threatened by fires as a result of the impact, fuel or vapor inhalation, ingestion of water, hypothermia, further injury from debris, drowning, and attack by marine life. **Survivability** in a water environment depends on the deceleration forces at the point of crash, the ability of seatbelts and seat structures to remain intact, occupied areas remaining relatively intact to prevent ejection and provide living space for the occupants, the rapid response of trained rescue personnel, and the availability of rescue craft (FAA, 2010b).

Water temperatures play a significant role in survivability because of the onset of **hypothermia** from being in the water and increased body-cooling rates from evaporating fuel. Rescue personnel should assume that all survivors are suffering from hypothermia until medical personnel determine otherwise. The Water Rescue plan should include provisions to remove fuel from survivors, particularly from their eyes, and all Water Rescue craft should carry an adequate supply of wool blankets. Other complicating factors may include frozen rivers or lakes, swift currents, and marine life, such as alligators, poisonous snakes, and sharks (FAA, 2010b).

In Water Rescue operations, emergency planners must take into account the designation of the ICP and the location of the Staging Areas and passenger/crew collection areas. Collection areas must take into account the height of the docks, and ensure waterways are of sufficient depth to accommodate the draft[26] of the watercraft used in rescue operations. There should also be a rescue accountability system established to keep track of divers in the "Hot Zone," (which is near the aircraft), and divers that have entered the fuselage. AC 150/5210-13, *Water Rescue Plans, Facilities, and Equipment*, contains additional guidance on boat operations and training, rescue swimming training, hypothermia and cold water drowning, ocean dynamics near aircraft, and additional sources of information on communications systems and rescue craft and capabilities (FAA, 2010b).

Whether or not the airport has Water Rescue boating capability, it is important for airport operators and ICs to understand the capabilities of the variety of boats that are used by recreational boaters and first-response agencies.

1. **Conventional boats** are useful for transporting rescue personnel and equipment to the scene, deploying floatation equipment, and picking up survivors. Some may have firefighting capabilities (FAA, 2010b, p. 12).
2. **Rescue boats** are fiberglass or aluminum-hulled with inboard or outboard engines capable of speeds up to 60 mph. Some have removable freeboard to provide easy access into or out

---

[26]Draft is a measurement of how far below the waterline a vessels hull extends. If there is inadequate depth available for a particular vessel, the vessel will become grounded (i.e., stuck).

of the water, along with enclosed accommodations to protect survivors from the elements (FAA, 2010b, p. 13).

3. **Rafts/flotation platforms** are large inflatable rafts with netting draped over the side and can keep 10 to 45 people afloat until rescue equipment can arrive (FAA, 2010b, p. 13).

4. **Inflatable boats** are shallow draft vessels with a rigid or inflatable boat, and jet propulsion capabilities. They can accommodate up to 15 people and can be swamped and still support survivors (FAA, 2010b, p. 13).

5. **Shallow draft "air boats"** are propelled by aircraft or auto engines driving aircraft-like propellers. Large models can carry more than 2,000 pounds of people and/or Water Rescue and medical equipment, and they can operate at speeds up to 50 miles an hour. They can operate in shallow water, tidal flats, marshes, and snow; however, they will sink if swamped. They cannot go into reverse and can never be fully stopped to maintain station (FAA, 2010b, p. 13).

6. **Air cushion vehicles ("hovercraft")** are amphibious vehicles that can be used on ground, water, and mud. They are especially useful in very shallow water and on mud flats, but tend to push out jet fuel from the vessel, which can cause an explosive mixture when combined with fuel from the plane crash (FAA, 2010b, p. 13).

7. **Helicopters** and some Fixed-Wing aircraft are useful for transporting and deploying rescue personnel, providing spotlights, and conducting area searches. Some are equipped with infrared capability, CCTV (closed circuit television), and video downlink capabilities. The rotor noise and downwash, however, can disorient and frighten survivors and cause debris to become airborne. Helicopter operations may also be dangerous in narrow rivers constrained by obstructions, trees, bridges, and power lines. Some amphibious aircraft can land on calm waters to provide rescue operations (FAA, 2010b, p. 14).

8. **UAVs** can be used for rapid response to the area of the accident, as a search-and-rescue platform, and, using video capabilities, may be able to scout out locations for casualty collection points, ICPs, and Staging Areas. They may also be useful in helping to establish the operating picture for the Incident Command or the Unified Command.

The airport should also have stockpiled, available, and readily accessible area maps and navigation charts, bailing buckets, water pumps, blankets, bullhorns, communications equipment, emergency lights, flares, forcible entry tools, marine night vision binoculars, life rafts (with oars or paddles), medical kits, navigational equipment, medical equipment, portable 500-watt or greater floodlights, rescue nets, stretchers/litters, rescue throwing bags, and anchors. A sample Water Rescue plan is available in the AC (FAA, 2010b), and airports should include water rescues into their training, drills, and exercise programs.

Air Florida Flight 90

The Miracle on the Hudson, as the 2009 crash of U.S. Airways Flight 1549 into the Hudson River is referred to, is an excellent example of the likeliness of an off-airport Water Rescue needing to be conducted in the future. The first individuals on-scene were mostly civilians, and the survivability of the passengers was initially largely dependent on the actions of the flight crew and other passengers. The initial official responders were harbor police from the Port Authority of New York and New Jersey and the U.S. Coast Guard. However, the incident that set forth the precedence and the significance of airports having Water Rescue plans was the crash of Air Florida Flight 90.

On January 13, 1982, Air Florida Flight 90, also known as *Palm 90*, a Boeing 737, crashed while on takeoff from Washington's National Airport.[27] The aircraft came down directly on the 14th Street Bridge, which spans the Potomac River, crushing four automobiles and killing five people. The aircraft then impacted the icy water and quickly sank. Only four passengers and a flight attendant were pulled alive from the icy waters (Kilroy, n.d.).

Civilians, who were driving by and witnessed the accident, pulled over and jumped into the water to rescue some of the passengers. A police helicopter, the pilot navigating largely following the road because of low visibility, helped pull out more survivors. The investigation of the crash concluded that the crew had used the thrust reverser to back out of the plane's gate[28] and failed to activate the engine anti-ice system, which allowed large amounts of snow and ice to be sucked into the engines and remain there (Kilroy, n.d.).

Including the individuals on the bridge, 74 people were killed in the crash, but the incident served as an industry reminder that airports should have Water Rescue capabilities. Today, Ronald Reagan Washington National Airport houses the River Rescue Section of the Special Operations Division, which is responsible for all aspects of Water Rescue. The unit currently has six boats and a boat support unit, an inventory of Ice Commander dry suits, Mustang cold-water exposure suits, and personal flotation devices for River Rescue personnel, as well as additional responders. Also, the division has twelve 10-person life rafts and four 30-foot life ramps, plus hand tools, EMS equipment, rescue blankets, and basic aircraft and watercraft recovery equipment (Metropolitan Washington Airports Authority, 2015).

Personnel assigned to the unit undergo an 80-hour in-house training program, which teaches maritime navigation rules and aids to navigation, use of personal flotation devices and other Personal Protective Equipment, nautical rope skills, basic water survival, boat launching and recovery, boat trailering operations, vessel maneuvering, navigation, radar operations, chart plotting and reading, victim recovery, vessel towing, and area waterway familiarization (Metropolitan Washington Airports Authority, 2015).

CROWD CONTROL

Crowds gather at airports for a variety of reasons: to conduct peaceful assemblies, as the result of an accident or natural disaster, or for hostile reasons. Crowds are a natural part of many other incidents, such as an aircraft crash, security breach, the arrival of a VIP or celebrity to the airport, or holiday passenger overflow in the terminal building. To the extent that crowds can inadvertently or deliberately disrupt Airport Operations, the AEP contains a section to address crowd control.

Methods of control fluctuate based on the nature of the assembly. Peaceful assemblies could be impromptu, such as when a VIP, celebrity, or well-known athlete or other public figure is recognized at an airport. Other examples of peaceful assemblies include welcoming a new air carrier to the airport, community airshows, and airport open houses featuring static displays of aircraft or public viewing. Crowds may also gather for disruptive or hostile reasons, such as when a

---

[27]The airport was later renamed Ronald Reagan National Airport.
[28]The attempt was unsuccessful and the aircraft was eventually pushed back via a tug, but the attempt had already managed to suck large amounts of debris into the engine intake.

controversial person or group arrives at the airport, during a period of civil unrest nationally, regionally, or locally, or during labor- or union-supported strikes (FAA, 2010a).

For a friendly crowd, particularly when the airport operator knows in advance, proper measures can be taken to minimize airport efforts to control the crowd, such as designated access and viewing locations and cordoning off areas for the crowd to observe the event or activity. For hostile situations, it may be difficult to determine the degree of the disturbance to landside, terminal, or aircraft operations. Some individuals are trained or have experience dealing with civil disorder, and they may operate with secrecy among the airport population and/or the local population. Advanced intelligence information developed by law enforcement may help the airport operator prepare for such disturbances (FAA, 2010a).

Even though disturbances can disrupt passenger operations in the terminal, the priority is to keep unauthorized personnel out of Security Areas and off the airfield. This can be difficult if the disruptive individuals are also employees at the airport and have active SIDA badges. Vulnerable areas that should receive additional attention during a period of civil disturbance include access points to the airfield, the fuel farm, areas between the parking lots in the terminal, emergency entrances, and airfield gates (FAA, 2010a).

Some airports choose to activate their EOC during the period of the disturbance (friendly or hostile). Airport police assume the primary responsibility for crowd-control actions and activate any mutual aid agreements to support the efforts (FAA, 2010a). Airports also employ unarmed security personnel to provide higher levels of security during these periods of time. Fire, EMS, and other response agencies should be aware that airport access roads might be closed or blocked, either by the airport operator in an attempt to control crowds or deny access to a Security Area, or by protesters themselves.

SUMMARY

All commercial service airports in the United States that have an approved ACM are required to have an AEP as part of the manual. The AEP includes the hazard-specific section, which addresses the required response to a set of particular emergencies and incidents, including airplane crashes that occur off- and on-airport, natural disasters, fires, crowd control, and HAZMAT occurrences.

Key responders to the hazards are ATC, Airport Operations and maintenance, fire, police, and EMS. Airport tenants and air carriers may also have roles, depending on the incident. Airports should have enough emergency capability to handle the largest commercial service aircraft that uses the airport on a regular basis. While the ARFF Index addresses the requirements in terms of firefighting apparatus and personnel, the AEP should include EMS requirements related to the number of passengers on the largest aircraft.

During an aircraft crash, the Priorities of Work are saving lives, scene stability, saving property, saving the environment, and restoring aircraft operations. Upon initial response to an aircraft crash, fire and rescue personnel have the primary responsibility of rescuing survivors and putting out the fire. Police are responsible for scene security and controlling access to the incident, while Airport Operations and maintenance personnel are focused on supporting the response effort and preparing to take over recovery operations. Air carriers have the legal responsibility to take care of the family members of victims of the accident, but will likely need the assistance of the airport in the early hours.

Airports should be prepared for a variety of natural disasters that could occur in their geographic region. Many of the steps to prepare for a hurricane or earthquake are similar to preparing for other natural disasters, and the roles and responsibilities of agencies remain largely the same. Airport operators should prepare for the range of hazards that can occur, and they should conduct drills, training, and exercises on all possible contingencies.

Lessons Learned from Recent Airport Emergencies

by John Paczkowski
Senior Vice President, Project Management Professional,
ICF International

The terrorist attacks of September 11, 2001, rocked the world of aviation public safety and put a laser-like focus on airport security and emergency management. Since then, there has been growing awareness among airport executives concerning a range of risks beyond what had been an almost myopic concentration on aircraft-related emergencies. The legacy of 9/11 is that airports now operate in a more complex external public safety framework, and with greater awareness of the risks, comes a growing responsibility to help ensure public safety in what is a highly charged fishbowl of increasing expectations and accountability.

Though most operators have put considerable effort into airport emergency readiness, two distinctly different emergencies at two world-class airports should give senior airport executives pause to consider how effective their own preparedness efforts have been and whether a more critical review of disaster readiness at their facilities may be warranted. Those events seem to highlight the wisdom that simple conformance with TSA and FAA mandates is not enough to effectively manage airport risks.

Emergency management programs must be tailored to address the most likely threats and hazards and be well integrated among airport partners. Plans, processes, equipment, and people must be tested to the point of failure since interagency relationships, training, and performance under pressure are more vital than the planning documents themselves. The tie that binds such programs is strong executive leadership, interest, and ongoing support as a major operational priority.

Asiana Flight 214 Crash at San Francisco International Airport—July 6, 2013

An Asiana Airlines Boeing 747 crashed on approach to runway 28L at San Francisco International (SFO) following a flight from Seoul, Korea. The aircraft cartwheeled on impact, losing its engines and tail section and coming to rest in the runway median. A fire erupted as evacuation was underway, resulting in scores of injuries and one postcrash fatality. All runways were closed for 4 hours and flights diverted to other West Coast airports. Though the airport was partially reopened within just hours after the crash and runway 10R/28L reopened just 6 days later, questions concerning the management of the response prompted airport leadership to conduct a candid review with all responding agencies and airport community stakeholders.

The review found that, as a function of prior efforts at emergency preparedness, quite a few things went right. On-scene cooperation among agencies was effective, largely based on

(Continued)

(Continued)
collegial relationships among Airport Operations and first responders. Police, firefighters, and EMS executed individual missions well, enabling a speedy response. Airfield recovery began early, was well planned, and was conducted in a way that minimized airport downtime. There was a proactive public communications campaign across all media with good use of social networking. Senior airport leadership were highly engaged throughout, and a strong management culture and can-do attitude was a contributing factor to identifying and solving problems early.

The review also found that there were challenges, indicating a need to more carefully assess the airport's ability to mobilize and coordinate responses to complex emergencies. The first area of concern was operational communications. Initial alerts and notification to first-responder agencies were fragmented and incomplete. Though a major investment in radio communications was made by the airport, local agencies had yet to upgrade their systems, and as a result there was a lack of communications interoperability. Moreover, the sharing of on-scene information was stove-piped within individual agencies. Incident Command did not fully evolve, nor did the airport EOC fulfill its potential in supporting the ICP or enabling leadership decision making. EMS was not well integrated within the Incident Command structure, there was a lack of a standard system of victim triage, and survivor accountability following transportation to area hospitals was problematic.

Active Shooter Incident at Los Angeles International Airport—November 1, 2013
A TSA officer was murdered and three others wounded by a lone gunman at Los Angeles International Airport (LAX) Terminal 3, triggering one of the largest multijurisdictional law enforcement operations in the history of the Los Angeles region. Approximately 4,500 people self-evacuated from the scene, and another 20,000 sheltered in place during the initial hours of the emergency. Though Airport Operations partially resumed 7 hours later and central terminal roadway access reopened in 9 hours, the entire event lasted almost 2 days, impacting 1,500 flights and nearly 171,000 passengers.

As with the Asiana crash at SFO, LAX management was quick to initiate a comprehensive third-party review of all aspects of the emergency response with all public safety agencies, facility management, and airport partners participating. Here, too, there was much that went right with the coordination of response operations. LAX had the advantage of a well-established emergency management governance and planning framework that included all relevant stakeholders. Both Airport Police and their Los Angeles Police Department (LAPD) partners responded heroically and with great tactical skill having jointly conducted active shooter tactics training. There was an immediate and substantial response from public safety agencies across the region and a unified multiagency command was established and maintained throughout.

Like the response to the Asiana crash at SFO, initial alert and notification was disjointed. LAX had also invested in advanced radio communications yet still lacked interoperability with responding agencies, and, like SFO, it too lacked an interagency communications plan that mitigated that gap. Though Unified Command was established despite some initial

(Continued)

(Continued)

delay, the Incident Command structure was not fully built out sufficiently to support a dynamic emergency situation. Though the airport had invested in a state of the art EOC, there was no interface with the IC at any point during the event, so it did not fulfill its intended role. Challenges in incident management, communications interoperability, and the EOC/ICP interface had a negative impact on response operations. Perimeter security was not flexible enough to adapt to changing conditions, terminal clearing conducted by law enforcement lacked coordination with airport civilian personnel, and passenger assistance and information was slow and incomplete.

General Observations from the SFO and LAX Emergencies

The Incident Command System (ICS) works but requires training and a collegial partnership. Airport civilian staff, tenants, and partners must be integrated into the ICS framework through training and realistic exercises. Visible personal leadership, or the lack thereof, plays a key role in success or failure in a major emergency. Don't assume that systems and processes (alert, radios, etc.) will function as advertised. Challenges are typically at the seams between agencies and system interfaces. Though the use of ICS is steadily improving across the airport community, issues around integration, joint operations, and crisis decision making remain. Information sharing, interoperable communications, and leveraging the investments made in large airport EOCs still require attention.

Airport executives can no longer be complacent and simply rely on the assumption that local public safety agencies have these issues covered. They may not. Higher public and political expectations put these executives squarely in the crosshairs of accountability as the leadership at LAX and SFO were wise to understand. Executive stewardship of airport public safety begins with sound governance, focused preparedness, and ongoing risk management.

An Airport CEO's Checklist for Emergency Readiness

Airport executives can do much to advance the cause of emergency preparedness by just taking a few basic steps:

1. Demonstrate emergency management is a leadership priority and shared responsibility. Emphasize an integrated approach to public safety and remove functional walls or silos.
2. Communicate that meeting regulations is not sufficient and critically look for weaknesses. Challenge yourself as to whether you are personally ready and know your role, asking the same of others.
3. Determine whether subordinate accountability is clearly assigned for emergency management and whether a strong, collaborative, and ongoing preparedness framework is in place.
4. Encourage the engagement of all airport partners in preparedness activities and ensure that there are enough trained personnel to scale Incident Command to meet a range of emergency situations.
5. Stress partnerships and collaboration and find common ground in shared appreciation of risk. Critically test and evaluate response systems and processes to point of failure and drive continuous improvement to fill any gaps identified.

Emergency Management at General Aviation Airports

by Rosemary Rizzo
Airport Operations Supervisor at DM AIRPORTS LTD

On a beautiful summer morning, the sun is shining, the air is calm, and then the unthinkable happens. You hear a sound so loud and unusual that all you can think of is a tool chest full of wrenches being poured into a giant whirring blender. You look around and see that a Learjet that had started its takeoff roll down the runway for departure has struck a flock of Canadian geese. The aircraft has damage to the windscreen and the leading edge of the wing, and it also ingested some birds, causing catastrophic engine failure. Fortunately, the aircraft is able to stop before reaching the end of the runway, but you as an airport employee are left with 3,000 feet of engine debris and goose remains strewn about the runway. The aircraft leaked oil from the damaged engine all the way from the runway while it was being towed to the ramp, almost a half mile. This is just one example of an airport emergency that I experienced as an entry-level employee at a GA airport.

As you respond to an event such as the one I described, a million questions will be racing through your mind. Was there something you could have done to prevent this from happening? Do you have a plan for emergencies? What resources do you have available? Who can you call? Making quick decisions with or without direction is key in an emergency situation, because as the airport representative onsite what you do next could save lives and ensure business and operating continuity for your airport. If you were in this situation, what would you do?

GA airports can see a broad range of traffic depending upon their size and location. The facility may accommodate aircraft of various sizes and operating capabilities, from gliders to the Boeing Business Jet. Thus emergencies can vary widely, based upon many factors, such as the type of emergency, aircraft involved, the severity, the type of responders arriving, and the level of involvement by stakeholders. You may be the only airport representative onsite or the first to respond, and knowing what you have and the best way to work with it is the key to success in making a bad situation manageable.

Always remember that your airport is a vital component of the community. You may require assistance from resources such as firefighters, police, or EMS during an emergency at your facility, but, in turn, your airport may be the location of an emergency operating center or shelter during a community or regional emergency. Returning to normal operations as safely and efficiently as possible is very important as a community resource.

GA airports are not as heavily regulated as airports certified under Federal Aviation Regulation (FAR) Part 139. Those airports are required to have AEPs, among other plans, to conduct day-to-day operations. The opening example alone speaks volumes of the importance of taking the time to prepare for potential emergencies. Although not every emergency can be anticipated, having a plan in place and the ability to implement it can save lives, limit your airport's liability, and ensure a safe and efficient return to normal operations.

One of the benefits of being a GA airport is that you can use the guidance provided for certificated airports, such as regulations, ACs, and industry-accepted practices. This allows you to maintain flexibility that you might not otherwise have. You also have the added

(Continued)

(Continued)

resources from the NTRB ACRP and the NIMS, as well as other state and local resources, at your fingertips. By using a combination of all of these resources, you can create an AEP that fits your airport's needs. Many of the questions that raced through your head from the scenario provided would have already been answered in the AEP, if your airport had one.

Some important parts of a basic AEP for a GA airport include communications (including contact lists and notification and alert procedures), command and control, a list of resources including equipment and personnel who can respond, and any pertinent airport maps. You essentially want to know: Who is part of your team, how will they talk to each other, and where will they be going? You will also want to think about external communications with airport users and the media. If you are able to make response procedures to specific types of accidents and incidents your plan will be even better. The AEP could include topics such as: Aircraft Accidents, natural disasters like hurricanes and tornadoes, and terrorist events. Also included should be a way to actually test your plan and then incorporate any revisions as needed.

Even though different airports must comply with many of the same rules and regulations, they will meet the requirements in a variety of ways, causing every airport to be different. It is also important to educate stakeholders and get them involved so they understand your operations and planning. Some of the stakeholders that you may want to include could be local politicians, the airport board, local first responders or Community Emergency Response Teams (CERTs), any tenant or user associations, state or local community groups, and the FAA. Using meetings or setting up committees will create an airport team that focuses on safety, saving lives, Continuity of Operations, and liability in your AEP. It will help you to make a plan that meets the needs of the airport, first responders, airport users, and the community.

Creating this airport group to plan for emergencies will create an understanding and safer environment for all. You should also test the AEP with this group and other responders, whether by a live exercise or a tabletop exercise. Doing this allows everyone to meet each other and practice their individual roles, as well as how to communicate effectively for when an emergency or incident happens.

There is one last element to consider in emergency management at any airport: prevention. This refers back to the question, "Was there something you or someone else could have done to prevent this from happening?" Not only is having an AEP important, but having plans and procedures for airport inspections, wildlife management, and general safety and security can help prevent an emergency situation altogether. You can even use some of the same group member stakeholders used to create the AEP in planning for other aspects of the airport.

Even though the runway had been inspected less than a half hour before the bird strike, the incident still occurred. What saved the day and allowed us to reopen the airport under a safe set of conditions was that we had a plan. The appropriate personnel were notified and responded to the incident, and we used all the resources available to clean up the debris and engine oil in a timely manner. Afterward we were able to take this incident and evaluate it as a team and learn from it, and this is an ever-important step in being prepared.

(Continued)

(Continued)

Although GA airports may not have all of the regulations and resources of an airport certificated under FAR Part 139, they are still a vital part of the National Transportation System and local communities. Unfortunately, incidents and emergencies can happen any day at any time, and the airport can be responsible for responding to it onsite or supporting a response locally or regionally. Creating a plan and being able to successfully implement it can make all the difference in saving lives and returning to normal operations in a safe and efficient manner, no matter how large or small an airport.

REFERENCES

Associated Press (AP). (2012, September 18). *Pilot threatens to evacuate plane at JFK after not being told about threat [VIDEO]*. Retrieved from: <http://nj1015.com/pilot-threatens-to-evcauate-plane-at-jfk-after-not-being-told-about-threat-video/>.

Broderick, S. (2005, November/December). Mission: Possible. *Airport Magazine*.

Eisele, C. (2008, August 31). *The golden hour*. Retrieved from: <http://www.jems.com/articles/2008/08/golden-hour.html>.

Environmentalchemistry.com. (n.d.). *U.S. DOT hazmat placards*. Retrieved September 7, 2015, from: <http://environmentalchemistry.com/yogi/hazmat/placards/>.

Federal Aviation Administration (FAA). (2009). Advisory Circular 150/5200-12C, *First responders responsibility in protecting evidence at the scene of an aircraft accident*. Washington, DC: Federal Aviation Administration.

Federal Aviation Administration (FAA). (2010a). Airport safety standards. *AC 150/5200-31C: Airport emergency plan*. Washington, DC: U.S. Department of Transportation, Federal Aviation Administration.

Federal Aviation Administration (FAA). (2010b). Advisory Circular 150/5210-13, *Water rescue plans, facilities, and equipment*. Washington, DC: Federal Aviation Administration.

Gonzales, L. (2014). *Flight 232: A story of disaster and survival*. New York, NY: W.W. Norton & Company.

Guffanti, M., Mayberry, G., Casadevall, T., & Wunderman, R. (2008, March 7). *Volcanic hazards to airports*. Retrieved September 7, 2015, from: <http://pubs.er.usgs.gov/publication/70035662>.

Hurricane Ivan [Telephone interview]. (2005, April 1).

Haddow, G. D., Bullock, J. A., & Coppola, D. (2013). *Introduction to emergency management* (5th edn). Waltham, MA: Butterworth-Heinemann.

International Civil Aviation Organization (ICAO). (2001). *Manual on volcanic ash, radioactive material, and toxic chemical clouds*. DOC 9691-AN/954. Montreal, Canada: ICAO.

Kilroy, C. (n.d.). *AirDisaster.Com: Special report: Air Florida Flight 90*. Retrieved September 7, 2015, from: <http://www.airdisaster.com/special/special-af90.shtml>.

McDonnell, T., & Rossier, A. (2011, August 23). *The great east coast earthquake of 2011 explained*. Retrieved September 6, 2015, from: <http://www.motherjones.com/blue-marble/2011/08/earthquake-dc-explainer>.

Metropolitan Washington Airports Authority. (2015, July 30). *River rescue*. Retrieved September 7, 2015, from: <http://prod.mwaa.com/about/river-rescue>.

National Fire Protection Association (NFPA). (2013). NFPA 424, Guide for airport/community emergency planning. <http://www.nfpa.org/codes-and-standards/document-information-pages?mode=code&code=424>.

National Oceanic and Atmospheric Administration (NOAA). (2015a, September 4). *Saffir-Simpson hurricane wind scale*. Retrieved from: <http://www.nhc.noaa.gov/aboutsshws.php>.

National Oceanic and Atmospheric Administration (NOAA). (n.d.a). *Hurricane storm surge*. Retrieved September 5, 2015, from: <http://oceantoday.noaa.gov/hurricanestormsurge/>.

National Oceanic and Atmospheric Administration (NOAA). (n.d.b). *Introduction to storm surge: What is storm surge?* Retrieved September 5, 2015, from: <http://www.nws.noaa.gov/om/hurricane/resources/surge_intro.pdf>.

National Oceanic and Atmospheric Administration (NOAA). (n.d.c). *Storm surge overview*. Retrieved September 5, 2015, from: <http://www.nhc.noaa.gov/surge/>.

National Transportation Safety Board (NTSB). (1990). Rep. No. AAR-91-07, *Fuel farm fire at Stapleton International Airport*. Washington, DC: National Transportation Safety Board.

National Transportation Safety Board (NTSB). (n.d.a). *How to respond to an aviation accident*. Retrieved August 31, 2015, from: <http://www.ntsb.gov/tda/TDADocuments/SPC0402.pdf>.

National Transportation Safety Board (NTSB). (n.d.b). *United Airlines Flight 232 McDonnell Douglas DC-10-10*. Retrieved August 31, 2015, from: <http://www.ntsb.gov/investigations/AccidentReports/Pages/AAR9006.aspx>.

National Transportation Safety Board (NTSB). Air Carrier Overwater Emergency Equipment and Procedures. Retrieved December 13, 2015, from: < http://www.ntsb.gov/safety/safety-studies/Pages/SS8502.aspx >.

Perkins, J. B. (2013, January 13). *Roles of airports in regional disasters (Rep.)*. Retrieved September 6, 2015, from Association of Bay Area Governments website: <http://resilience.abag.ca.gov/wp-content/documents/Cascading_Failures/Role-of-Airports-in-Disasters_2015.pdf>.

Price, J. C. (2005, July/August). Ivan the terrible: Lessons in disaster. *Airport Magazine*.

Smith, J., Kenville, K., & Sawyer, J. (2015). ACRP Synthesis 60: *Airport emergency post-event recovery practices* (U.S., Federal Aviation Administration, TRB). Washington, DC: Airport Cooperative Research Program (ACRP).

Stockam, S. (2015, June 23). Aviation disaster planning for off-airport events. Speech presented at the American Association of Airport Executives (AAAE) International Airport Emergency Preparedness Conference in Westin Oaks Houston at the Galleria Hotel, Houston.

United States Department of Energy (USDOE). (n.d.). *Model procedure hazardous materials incident response* (United States Department of Energy, Office of Transportation and Emergency Management). Retrieved September 7, 2015, from: <http://energy.gov/sites/prod/files/em/TEPP/2-b-2HazardousMaterialsIncidentResponse.pdf>.

United States Department of Transportation (USDOT). (2012). *Emergency response guidebook* (United States Department of Transportation, Pipeline and Hazardous Materials Safety Administration). Washington, DC: Department of Transportation.

United States Geological Survey (USGS). (n.d.a). *Measuring the size of an earthquake*. Retrieved September 6, 2015, from: <http://earthquake.usgs.gov/learn/topics/measure.php>.

United States Geological Survey (USGS). (n.d.b). *Properties of volcanic ash: Volcanic ash hazards and ways to minimize them*. Retrieved September 7, 2015, from: <http://volcanoes.usgs.gov/ash/properties.html>.

United States Geological Survey (USGS). (n.d.c). *The modified Mercalli intensity scale*. Retrieved September 6, 2015, from: <http://earthquake.usgs.gov/learn/topics/mercalli.php>.

UPSeis. (n.d.). *What are earthquake hazards?* Retrieved September 6, 2015, from: <http://www.geo.mtu.edu/UPSeis/hazards.html>.

Weather.com. (n.d.). *States with the most tornado deaths in 2014*. Retrieved September 7, 2015, from: <http://www.weather.com/news/news/tornado-deaths-2014-vilonia-pilger>.

Wheatley, K. (2013, May 22). *The May 22, 2011 Joplin, Missouri EF5 tornado*. Retrieved September 6, 2015, from: <http://www.ustornadoes.com/2013/05/22/joplin-missouri-ef5-tornado-may-22-2011/>.

FURTHER READING

National Oceanic and Atmospheric Administration (NOAA). (2015b, September 4). *What is a hurricane?* Retrieved from: <http://oceanservice.noaa.gov/facts/hurricane.html>.

EMERGING ISSUES IN AIRPORT OPERATIONS, SAFETY, AND EMERGENCY MANAGEMENT

"Falcon Hover" UAV with camera manufactured by Falcon Unmanned.

Image by Shahn Sederberg, courtesy Colorado Division of Aeronautics, 2015.

MULTIROTOR G4 Surveying-Robot with camera manufactured by Multirotor.

Virgin Galactic SpaceShipTwo, which was designed for the advent of space tourism.

In 2014, SpaceShipTwo suffered an in-flight breakup, resulting in the fatality of one pilot. The National Transportation Safety Board (NTSB) ruled the case as an accident. Virgin Galactic is underway with testing of the second SpaceShipTwo. In response to this accident, National Aeronautics and Space Administration (NASA) Administrator Charles Bolden stated "Space flight is incredibly difficult, and we commend the passion of all in the space community who take on risk to push the boundaries of human achievement" ("Statement from NASA Administrator on Virgin Galactic SpaceShipTwo Mishap," October 31, 2014. Available at: http://www.nasa.gov/press/2014/october/statement-from-nasa-administrator-on-virgin-galactic-spaceshiptwo-mishap/).

Airport Operations personnel are challenged with a variety of new technologies and issues, including the operation of Unmanned Aerial Vehicles (UAVs), Vertical Takeoff and Landing (VTOL) aircraft, commercial spaceport operations, hypersonic aircraft, and the practical realities of implementing regulatory procedures. Aircraft are likely to become both larger, like the A380, and smaller, like very-light business jets, but with more capabilities to operate in commercial airspace above 18,000 feet. The combination of these technological developments will also further congest airspace. Cybersecurity will also be a primary concern as the industry shifts from a land-based to a satellite-based navigation system.

Natural disasters continue to occur, along with new threats to safety and security, such as lasers being flashed into the eyes of pilots while on approach and the possible use of UAVs outfitted with improvised explosive devices. Despite a stellar safety record, aircraft still crash from time to time, and other issues must be addressed for an airport operator to be effective, including embracing the realities involved with implementing Incident Command at a multiagency or multijurisdictional level, the psychological impact on emergency operations personnel who are not accustomed to traumatic situations, and more scrutiny and litigation after every accident. Airport operators will need to increase training and put added emphasis on exercises and drills if they hope to keep the airport protected from liability claims, as well as provide the services that are expected by air travelers, air carriers, tenants, and other stakeholders.

Today, airport operators deal with problems that will likely be amplified with the increase in UAV and spaceport operations; however, the most significant challenge is that most airport operators do not yet know what those challenges will be. Decisions must be made that may have a negative impact on future operations that may later prove to be irrevocable or too costly to fix. Additionally, many of the shared practices that go on in the aviation community have not yet made it to the commercial space industry. Space operations companies are keeping their proprietary information to themselves, making it difficult to establish best practices, or even to learn what those practices are.

This chapter provides an overview of some of the key issues in the industry related to airport safety, operations, and emergency management as they stand today, with a fair warning that information and breakthroughs are being made, literally, overnight. Airport operators should continue to stay informed about the industry and its impacts as the next decade of Airport Operations begins.

THE PSYCHOLOGY OF EMERGENCY RESPONSE: RESPONDERS AND VICTIMS

An often-overlooked component of emergency response is the psychological impact an emergency may have on the first responder. Another important issue is the need for training response personnel on dealing with the emotions of those involved in a traumatic event. When individuals respond to an emergency, a variety of psychological factors are at play, both with the individuals that are involved in the emergency, such as passengers and crew members, as well as with first responders. Additional challenges arise when Incident Commanders ignore the dynamics between differing first-responder agencies that reduce the effectiveness of the overall response. Airport first-responder personnel may have widely varying levels of experience with emergencies and traumatic events, making coordination difficult.

It is not a safe assumption that Airport Operations personnel, compared to police and fire personnel, typically have less day-to-day experience with emergencies. This depends on how the airport's police and fire personnel departments are structured. Fire and police personnel who come from city fire and police departments likely have high levels of experience with emergencies, whereas fire and police personnel who have only worked at an airport may have less-extensive experience with emergencies or traumatic events. However, even this assumption may not be true in all cases: Los Angeles International Airport (LAX) is a classic example of the saying, "If you've seen one airport, you've seen one airport," because at LAX, airport police are assigned only to the airport, yet they patrol the high-crime areas around the airport and experience a variety of "city"-related police emergencies. The Los Angeles Fire Department staffs the Aircraft Rescue and Firefighting (ARFF) stations, so firefighters have a variety of experiences they bring to the airport. Airport Managers and Incident Commanders must understand that just as each airport's circumstance is unique, so are the psychological responses of the response team members.

EFFECTIVE INCIDENT COMMAND

The military has a saying: "no plan survives first contact with the enemy (because the enemy gets a *vote* too)." Even though this is a military saying, it is just as relevant in the emergency management domain, except that the "enemy" is numerous variables, many of which cannot be accounted for prior to the incident. Even the most carefully designed and best laid plans may not be executed to perfection because of variables, including misinterpretation of procedures; a lack of training, exercises, or drills, or a lack of follow-up to a previous incident or exercise; communication or equipment failures; weather; key personnel being unavailable when the incident occurs; and numerous unexpected circumstances, that can plague an incident. Many organizations incorrectly assume they are prepared for an extreme event—that existing hierarchical systems, standard operating procedures, and adequate time to allocate resources are adequate to handle any circumstance (Pfeifer, 2013, p. 11).

Incident Commanders (ICs) and emergency planners must recognize the psychological issues at work in a multiagency, multijurisdictional response, mass casualty incident. Effective ICs and planners account for actions that individuals and organizations naturally take when under a stressful, dynamic, and novel situation and make the plan fit the people rather than attempt to make the people fit the plan.

Although this section focuses on effectiveness during an extreme incident, the information can also be used in the day-to-day operational management of an airport. There are many correlations, such as the sudden onset of a crisis, which, at the airport operator level, may not be something that endangers life and property, but affects the operational flow of the airport for aircraft. An inadvertent breach of the screening checkpoint; a temporary closure of the airfield while operations personnel chase wildlife off the Air Operations Area (AOA), while 30 aircraft sit, awaiting takeoff, until the critter has been properly spooked; or the shelter-in-place of several thousand passengers during a tornado warning, may all cause a mini-crisis situation in the world of Airport Operations.

In *Crisis Leadership: The Art of Adapting to Extreme Events*, Chief of Counterterrorism and Emergency Preparedness Joseph Pfeifer of the Fire Department of New York (FDNY) defined an **extreme event** as one that is multijurisdictional and overwhelms a single organization's capacity to manage the incident alone (Pfeifer, 2013, p. 1). Many police, fire, emergency medical service

(EMS), and airport operational personnel are accustomed to handling routine emergencies. Routine emergencies are characterized by a single IC, hierarchical command and control structure, good access to information, and the use of standard operating procedures (Pfeifer, 2013, p. 5). Not all are experienced in handling an extreme event.

The Department of Homeland Security's (DHS) *National Response Framework* (DHS, n.d.) defines an extreme event as: "any natural or manmade incident, including terrorism, that results in extraordinary levels of mass casualties, damage or disruption severely affecting the population, infrastructure, environment, economy, national morale and/or government function" (DHS, n.d.). Extreme emergencies push organizations past their capabilities, requiring more skills than a single agency can provide; past their capacity, requiring more resources than the agency has access to; and beyond their capability of delivering resources as rapidly as needed. Without an understanding of these operational limitations, leadership during a crisis will not be effective (Pfeifer, 2013, pp. 5–6).

Extreme crises often happen without advance warning, at any time of day or night, and every instance has its own unique circumstances. Even first responders, such as police and fire personnel, who generally have more experience in emergencies, can be psychologically overwhelmed by the event. While they are used to responding to a range of "normal" emergencies, what they are experiencing is an abnormal event. When individuals are confronted with a new situation, they attempt to fit the situation into their normal range of experiences. This phenomenon is known as the *normalcy bias*, which may inhibit the effectiveness of their response (Kahneman, 2011).

To be effective, ICs must understand that first responders are faced with the physical challenges of the environment, such as a fire or active shooter, along with environmental conditions, such as fire personnel wearing bunker gear or working outside during extreme heat or cold. Other factors that are at work during an incident include each responder's social structure. For example, responders may have the tendency to keep information "in-house" rather than share it with other response groups; political factors are also at play, as response agencies differ on how to handle the crisis (Pfeifer, 2013). Numerous agencies are typically involved in a large-scale airplane crash or disaster, and humans have a natural tendency to avoid liability (it is not our fault) and improve perception in the public eye. The agendas of various personnel and agencies may conflict with each other and hamper operations.

When United Flight 232 crashed, several executives from United Airlines arrived later in the evening and demanded that recovery of the deceased begin immediately.[1] The executives were told no. At the Incident Command Center, emergency management director Gary Brown was hearing the same thing from his bosses and the county administrator, telling him that *someone named Stephen Wolf* (CEO of United Airlines at the time) was insisting the bodies be removed. According to Lawrence Gonzales, author of *Flight 232*, Brown stormed into a room in the terminal building where the UAL executives were set up and demanded to know who Stephen Wolf was. Wolf identified himself, and Brown said, "You're making my life miserable, and you need to stop" at which point Wolf assigned an employee to be a liaison for United in the Incident Command Post. "And it was very smooth after that," according to Brown (Gonzales, 2014, p. 124). Having the right people

---

[1]There is a history of attempting to protect the company brand. Prior to Flight 232, airline employees were often sent out to obscure the logos on wrecked aircraft, but as far back as 1912, when the survivors of the *Titanic* were brought to New York along with the lifeboats, the White Star Line sent personnel to sand out the name Titanic from the bows of the lifeboats (Lord, 1955/1987, p. 163).

in the Incident Command Center can help to resolve peer-to-peer conflict between operators in the field and to establish relationships ahead of any incident, whenever possible.

In the airport domain, first responders are police officers, firefighters, EMS personnel, and airside and landside Airport Operations or terminal managers. People look to first responders to solve their problems. Whether that means to save their lives or the lives of a loved one, to find a lost child, or to track down their missing luggage they believe has been stolen, first responders are supposed to know what to do. Most day-to-day, or routine, situations and emergencies, much of what first responders are challenged with, is well within their span of control; however, during a natural or human-made disaster, first responders may often work long hours and under stressful conditions, witnessing the physical destruction, the psychological devastation, and the violent injuries and sometimes death that can occur in a plane crash or natural disaster (Rutkow, Gable, & Links, 2011, p. 56).

The U.S. Department of Health and Human Services (DHHS), Substance Abuse and Mental Health Services Administration distributes a brochure that can assist first responders when working with individuals who have experienced a traumatic event. The brochure can be found on its website, but, in general, responders should (DHHS, n.d.):

1. Speak calmly and in a relaxed manner; use eye contact and stand or sit next to, not directly in front of, the person;
2. Use a soft tone of voice, smile as appropriate, and allow the person to dictate the amount of personal space he or she is comfortable with;
3. Introduce yourself and ask what they would like to be called—do not shorten the individual's name or use the first name without permission;
4. Speak to the person with respect.

Individuals in an evacuation may also experience some level of fear. Responders should not give evacuees complex directions and should stick to basic commands or directives. Remember that individuals need food, water, shelter, and sanitation to satisfy their basic needs. Responders should work to provide those. People also want accurate information and periodic updates, even if the information has not changed or no further information has been gathered. People should not be forced to share their personal stories unless they want to, nor give simple reassurances, like, "everything's going to be okay" (DHHS, n.d.).

First responders can also experience psychological stress, by seeing those who are injured or killed during the response, or having significant psychological challenges in dealing with the incident afterward. Studies have demonstrated that first responders experience elevated rates of depression, stress disorder, and posttraumatic stress disorder for months and sometimes years after the incident. Unlike some skills-based training, such as fighting a fire or shooting a pistol, extreme incident training cannot truly replicate a disaster, and most training that attempts to address the issue does not include sufficient content regarding mental health and self-aid (Rutkow et al., 2011, p. 56).

Mental health conditions are often difficult to identify, and first responders are often reluctant to seek help on their own. Doing so may reduce legal and liability issues in the future. While many agencies conduct mental health screening prior to employment, first responders should also have access to mental health screenings during the disaster response, or in the recovery phase, as screening increases the chance for a timely diagnosis and treatment (Rutkow et al., 2011, p. 56).

During an emergency, licensed health care providers should be provided, even if they have to come from an outside jurisdiction. Airport Managers should ensure that waivers and reciprocity agreements are in place prior to the incident, or at least immediately after the incident enters its recovery phase (Rutkow et al., 2011, p. 57). Finally, workers compensation for mental health treatment should be extended to include personnel who have volunteered their services during the disaster or incident. Other means to support first responders can include enacting legal protections in areas relevant to responder's mental health and establishing priority mental health access for first responders.

First responders also experience fear: fear of injury or death from threats in their physical environment (e.g., fire, bullets, building collapse), fear of reprisals for wrong actions or bad decisions, and fear of the unknown. Many secretly fear how they will react during an **extreme** circumstance, such as seeing dozens of dead and disfigured bodies amidst aircraft wreckage. ICs must understand that nearly everyone, even highly trained military special operations personnel, police officers, and firefighters, experience fear, and that people deal with that fear in different ways.

Fear is a primal instinct meant to protect us from harm. When the brain experiences fear, it prepares the body for action, often by reducing focus to seeing the threat object or area through tunnel vision. The body protects itself when it experiences fear. Blood chemistry changes; blood coagulates more easily so the person will bleed less if injured, and cortisol and adrenaline surge through the system to give gross-motor skills a sort of *bionic* boost of strength (Ripley, 2009, p. 57). ICs must understand that local police, fire, and other first-response personnel rushing to an incident, many times because they are wired to chase the excitement and the adrenaline rush that comes with saving a life or performing similar functions, are also fighting back fear.

Ripley (2009, pp. 60—61) posits that for everything that fear gives a person, it takes one away, such as reducing our ability to reason and perceive our surroundings, reducing our complex abilities, reducing the use of fine motor skills, or, in some cases, causing the loss of bladder or sphincter control. Many individuals involved in a traumatic situation feel a dissociation from the event, such as *time slowing down*, or viewing the incident from afar, as if they are watching themselves from on high. In airplane crashes, people have reported forgetting how to operate their seat belt, and many forget to inflate their life vest prior to stepping out of the plane and into the water (Ripley, 2009, p. 63). One study cited by Ripley (2009, pp. 92—94) discovered that individuals who can stay more lucid (i.e., who are not disassociating) perform better in life or death situations and remain more resilient afterward. Many U.S. Navy SEALS and others in the military special operations community often talk about *putting their fears, their thoughts of home, their doubts, in a box*, which they mentally lock up when on a mission to more effectively focus on the task at hand. Members of the Navy SEALS are trained to increase their mental toughness with the ultimate purpose of controlling their fears and being able to appropriately respond in panicking situations (Act of Valor). It also turns out that this type of resiliency can be built up over time, not by "nature over nurture," but rather *confidence comes from the practice of doing*.

Many individuals who experience fear will avoid the source of the fear altogether and find creative ways to *not be around* when the incident occurs. Others may be present at the disaster or incident, but not be as effective because they are too worried about controlling their own fears rather than working the problem. When people become frightened or angry, they stop thinking with their forebrain (their *mind*) and start thinking with their midbrain, sometimes called their *monkey brain*, because it operates at a level that is indistinguishable from an animal's brain. They become literally *scared out of their wits*, says Dave Grossman, author of several books on the brain's reaction to fear and overwhelming circumstances (Grossman, 1996, p. xviii).

To a "normal" person, when an abnormal incident occurs, there is a moment of, *What's happening here?*, as the brain tries to fit the event into a past known circumstance. Then there is a moment of, *Is this really happening?*, as the brain tries to verify that it is seeing something unique; then a moment of, *This is happening, and what should I do about it?*, during which the brain tries to figure out what orders to give to the body. Reducing the time this *loop* takes to cycle is essential to an effective first response. Veteran police, fire, and Airport Operations personnel can quickly identify a threat situation. In the 19th century, Carl von Clausewitz, author of the first modern scholarly studies on military strategy, used the French term, *coup d'oeil*, to describe the intuition great commanders use to recognize how to win a battle in advance. Clausewitz (1832) says the expression means "the rapid discovery of a truth that, to the ordinary mind, either is not visible at all or only becomes so after long examination and reflection" (p. 142). It turns out that with experience, intuition improves.

> This "glance" is the moment of insight during which commanders intuitively make sense of a situation by quickly envisioning a plausible course of action with its possible outcomes before developing a plan of action.
>
> **Pfeifer, 2013, p. 7.**

Firefighters and others in similar capacities, who must make decisions within a short timeframe, do so by using cues, including visual, auditory, kinesthetic, to recognize that a situation is occurring or about to occur, as well as to determine what to do based on prior experience. They do not stop to compare all possible options, but rather choose the first course of action that makes sense to them. If that option does not work, another is immediately chosen, as most sudden occurrences do not afford someone the luxury of time to think longingly about it or to assess the options. This enables personnel to quickly adapt and not suffer from what is commonly called "paralysis by analysis" (Pfeifer, 2013, p. 7). The unfortunate side effect of this process is the *Monday morning quarterback* effect where the person's actions are judged by those who have the time to assess other options and the knowledge of the actual outcome based on the decisions made by the responder. To reduce the fear experienced, or at least allow the brain to make better decisions when faced with a situation that produces fear, the individual must be subjected to similar situations, repeatedly—a disaster training session, of sorts. Grossman (1996, p. xviii) posits that the only thing that influences the midbrain is the same thing that influences a dog: classic operant conditioning.

However, many police officers, military special operations personnel, and others in the first-response field have developed methods to reduce the fear response. **Operant conditioning** is already used as a training tool in aviation, law enforcement, EMS, and firefighting. In the aviation domain, operant conditioning is used to train pilots to handle life-threatening emergencies, such as when the engine quits. Student pilots are not allowed to fly solo until they can prove that they understand these basic emergency procedures from memory and demonstrate them properly. The premise of operant conditioning is: the more people do something, the more it is ingrained into their *psyche* or *muscle memory*. After a period of time, the individual can literally perform the technique without conscious thought.

Police officers spend time on the range firing their weapon and are encouraged to spend more hours dry firing it (without ammunition inside); firefighters practice fighting actual fires in a controlled environment and study fires that others have experienced; military special operations personnel practice urban assault skills, entering a room where there may be hostages, bad guys, or both; when pilots first learn to fly, they are taught several emergency procedures, such as how to configure the aircraft for the best glide speed and angle when the engine quits, what to do in the case of an in-flight fire, and what they are supposed to do if they lose radio communications.

For some, simply thinking through a situation could help during the actual response. Such is the premise of the *coffee shop drills*, during which responders sit around talking about situations and events that could occur and determine the appropriate action to take. The more vivid the response visualization (participants literally envision themselves performing the task, with all the sights and sounds engaged), the better the person may react during an actual response. A study conducted by Dwight Kearns and Jane Grossman, *Effects of a Cognitive Intervention Package on the Free-Throw Performance of Varsity Basketball Players*, showed that visualization combined with relaxation techniques can improve performance over the performance of those that only train physically. Also, relaxation techniques provide the individual with better arousal control, which results in better concentration on the task (Kearns & Grossman, 1992).

The airlines make extensive use of flight simulators to drill emergency procedures into pilots. Airline pilots are given a set of emergencies for which they have to demonstrate the proper response. Pilots must memorize several items, known as "memory items," and be able to perform without referencing the Pilot Operating Handbook or emergency procedures guide. The procedures are drilled into pilots over and over and over, until their response becomes automatic. When an emergency occurs, pilots perform the required tasks to keep the plane flying, and then they may have time to reference the emergency procedures manual and notify their airline operations base or air traffic control (ATC) for further assistance. Pilots call it *aviate, navigate, communicate*—fly the plane first, navigate to the closest airport or reasonable place to land, and then tell everyone that you are experiencing a problem.

The way to train Airport Operations personnel and other first responders is to use **games, simulations, training, and exercises**—the more realistic, the better. Also, the training, games, and exercises must be conducted frequently. Once every 3 years for a full-scale exercise is not frequent enough that everyone will remember what to do and how to do it. Airport Training and Exercise department personnel (or those charged with overseeing training and exercises) should use Homeland Security Exercise and Evaluation Program (HSEEP) models to establish a schedule of drills, tabletop, full-scale, and functional exercises, that keep proficiency above the regulatory standard. Denver International Airport has pioneered some methods using Agile project management planning to conduct dozens of exercises throughout the year, with little cost and little impact to Airport Operations. The key is breaking the mold of what a traditional exercise looks like and learning how to conduct an exercise in new and more effective ways.

Two other considerations for ICs during an incident are, first, to recognize that in a large-scale incidents, groups of responders will put together **hastily formed networks**—essentially impromptu teams—comprised of various response personnel. The key, effective leader is one who can link together the responders on scene, along with the Emergency Operations Center (EOC) and government officials, toward a common purpose, and can also leverage technology. This was demonstrated during the U.S. Airways crash into the Hudson River when fire and police departments, health care personnel, the U.S. Coast Guard, and even private citizens developed their own work groups to collaborate and coordinate the rescue effort (Pfeifer, 2013).

Second, leaders cannot allow themselves to get microscopically fixated on the problem that they are most associated with or have the most experience with. If the IC is a fire chief, the commander has a tendency to only focus on fire-related problems and to ignore other issues, such as access control to the site, security and law enforcement challenges, and other challenges outside of the traditional firefighting realm. If the IC is a police chief, the commander may have a tendency to focus only on law enforcement—related challenges. ICs must take the big-picture view of the entire incident, staying in close proximity to other key decision makers and using technology such as video to enhance situational awareness and form a common operating picture.

The overall solution to an effective response is to identify the gaps: Are there training issues, technology issues, or a lack of resources or personnel? Develop a budget to acquire the needed resources, and develop a training schedule to build the skills responders will need during an incident. Unfortunately, training is often one of the first things cut when budgets get tight—personnel furloughs typically follow, and soon, too few individuals are doing the job of too many, which can be a recipe that turns an accident or natural disaster into a major tragedy.

UNMANNED AERIAL VEHICLES

The sudden growth of the UAV industry presents challenges to airport and aircraft operators and to regulators. Going by a variety of names, such as drones, **UAVs**, **Unmanned Aerial Systems (UASs)**, and **Remotely Piloted Vehicles (RPVs)**, the technology and availability of UAVs is rapidly outpacing the ability of regulatory agencies to keep up, and airport operators are not yet sure what this will mean for their facilities. This section provides an overview of UAV technologies and what they may mean to the airport operator. It is not a detailed look at all the various types of technologies that exist and how they function.

Any explanation of UAVs should establish a common vocabulary and a clear understanding of the similarities and differences between a drone, a UAV, a UAS, and an RPV. According to Falhlstrom and Gleason, writing in *Introduction to UAV Systems*, the three kinds of unpiloted aircraft, excluding missiles, are (2012, p. 28):

1. UAVs
2. RPVs
3. Drones

While many people use the terms *UAV* and *RPV* interchangeably, the strictest definition of a RPV is when an operator at a remote site actually **pilots a "true" RPV**; a "UAV" may be both piloted and programmed to perform autonomous missions. The UAV purist uses the term **drone** to describe something that flies in a dull, monotonous, and indifferent manner, such as a target drone. The term *UAV* describes the actual vehicle that flies, whereas the term *UAS* describes all the components that are required to operate the UAV, such as a Ground Control Station, payload, a datalink, and the vehicle. The word *drone*, however, has been widely adopted by the general public and the media, both of which will likely continue to use it. However, to an airport operator, understanding the differences in UAV technology is important as it relates to the impact of UAVs on Airport Operations (Falhstrom & Gleason, 2012, p. 28).

While the vast majority of the American public and the world became aware of UAVs through the wars in Afghanistan and Iraq, where UAVs have primarily been used as surveillance and weapons platforms, some of the first UAVs can be traced back to World War I. Charles Kettering developed a biplane UAV for the Army Signal Corps, called the Kettering Aerial Torpedo. The UAV carried 180 pounds of high explosives, was guided to a target by preset controls, and had detachable wings that were released when the aircraft was over the target, converting the airplane to a gravity bomb. Throughout the 1930s and 1940s, both the United States and Great Britain developed various forms of UAVs, as did Germany in the form of their lethal V1 and V2 rockets (Fahlstrom & Gleason, 2012, pp. 24−25).

By the 1960s, UAVs were used extensively in combat, but for reconnaissance only, and only by the Central Intelligence Agency (CIA). The CIA first developed the D-21 drone, which rode atop the SR-71 Blackbird and could achieve speeds exceeding Mach 3. Drones have also routinely been used by the U.S. military for target practice, and a few pilot projects were conducted throughout the late 1970s and 1980s. By Desert Storm in 1991, five UAV systems were in use, three by U.S. forces, one by the French, and one helicopter UAV by the British. Desert Storm helped prove the need for UAVs as potential weapons systems, and they have since seen widespread use throughout Iraq and Afghanistan and in the "war on terror" (Fahlstrom & Gleason, 2012, pp. 24−25). By 2011, the U.S. Air Force (USAF) had trained more RPV pilots[2] than fighter and bomber pilots combined (Benjamin, 2013, p. 87).

Remote-controlled aircraft are not an entirely new concept on the civilian side. Model airplane operators have been building and flying scaled replica aircraft for decades, even putting still and movie cameras on them in some cases. However, the industry was largely self-limited—to fly a remote-controlled aircraft one had to build it, or at the very least master the skill of flying the plane remotely. Model aircraft were also limited by the distance away from the operator they could travel. Too far away and the pilot could either lose sight of the plane (or helicopter), or lose the radio frequency connection. Many of today's UAVs are incredibly easy to fly, and they can be operated by anyone that has a tablet-computer.

UNMANNED AERIAL VEHICLE CATEGORIES AND EXEMPTIONS

The three classes of unmanned aircraft system operations are: (a) Civil, (b) Public, and (c) Model Aircraft. Each of these classes has its own waiver or exemption programs. The first exemption was made available to people operating **Model Aircraft**. In June 1981, the Federal Aviation Administration (FAA) issued Operating Standards in Advisory Circular (AC) 91-57, (Forrest, Cozart, White, & Ormen, 2015, p. 12). The AC set safety standards, which have since been modified (FAA, 2015b):[3]

1. Fly below 400 feet and remain clear of surrounding obstacles;
2. Keep the aircraft within visual line of sight at all times;
3. Remain well clear of and do not interfere with manned aircraft operations;
4. Do not fly within 5 miles of an airport unless you contact the airport and control tower before flying;

---

[2]There is still debate throughout the industry whether UAV operators are actual pilots or "operators." This text will not attempt to settle the debate.

[3]http://www.faa.gov/documentLibrary/media/Advisory_Circular/AC_91-57A.pdf

5. Do not fly near people or stadiums;

6. Do not fly an aircraft that weighs more than 55 lb;

7. Do not be careless or reckless with your unmanned aircraft—you could be fined for endangering people or other aircraft.

The FAA does not make a technological distinction between model aircraft and unmanned aircraft under 55 pounds, therefore, it is possible for individuals to operate small, unmanned aircraft under these rules, if they are not being operated for a commercial purpose (Forrest et al., 2015, p. 12). The FAA was charged by Congress to develop rulemaking to address the use of UAVs by 2015. The FAA has also established "Know before you fly," a website for UAV operators that provides information on how to operate the UAV safely (FAA, 2015a). On February 15, 2015, the FAA released its Notice of Proposed Rulemaking (NPRM) for small, unmanned aircraft. An NPRM is a public notice issued by law when an independent agency wishes to add, remove, or change a rule or regulation as part of the rulemaking process. It does not change any existing guidelines, rules, regulations, or policy that may be in place, but it opens the door for public comment and the beginning of the rulemaking process (FAA, 2015a).

The next exemption was made for **civil aircraft operations**. Civil operators are nongovernmental entities that are typically operating a UAV for some commercial purpose. There are two possible exemptions in this class of operations: a Special Airworthiness Certificate and the Section 333 exemption (Section 333 of the *FAA Modernization and Reform Act of 2012* [FMRA]). Operators can obtain a Special Airworthiness Certificate by having an aircraft tested by the FAA or by a Designated Airworthiness Representative at a test site (Forrest, et al., 2015, p 12).

Currently, Special Airworthiness Certificates are only available in the experimental category. This only allows UAS makers to conduct research and development, demonstrate the system, and train flight crews. The specific rules governing operation are determined through an application and discussion with the FAA. When the final rules are established for all small UAS in the National Airspace, it is likely that the Section 333 exemption will go away (Forrest et al., 2015, p. 12).

Public, or governmental aircraft, organizations are permitted to fly UAVs for research purposes for up to 2 years through a **Certificate of Waiver or Authorization (COA).** Because the COA will be operated by a public organization, this is the most relevant exemption. The FAA grants COAs through an online application process in which the organization asks for permission to fly a particular aircraft, for a particular purpose, and in a particular area. The FAA works with organizations to develop additional parameters for the COA (Forrest et al., 2015, p. 13). There are already several success stories of law enforcement and other first-responder agencies using UAVs.

Additional parameters include:

1. The UAS must be designated as a public aircraft, with an N-number, and cannot be used for any commercial purpose.

2. The public organization is required to conduct its own Airworthiness process and certify to the FAA that the UAS is Airworthy. The Airworthiness testing must be based on one of four military standards, and the Airworthiness Statement must include a detailed description of the UAS components and their maintenance schedule.

3. Operations can technically be granted in areas outside of Class B airspace. However, most public organizations are restricted to Classes D, E, and G.

4. The COA will name certain individuals who will have the authority to operate the UAS. Usually, the operation of a UAV will require three people: a Pilot-in-Command, a Visual Observer, and a Ground Control Operator. In some cases, operators may be required to pass the FAA ground school or have Private Pilot Certificates.
5. Depending on the area of operations and its proximity to an active airport, the COA may require that the operator communicate with the FAA or airport operators prior to conducting any flight. It might also entail issuing a Notice to Airmen (NOTAM).
6. All COA programs must incorporate a Safety Management System for Aviation Service Providers outlined in AC 120-92. While it is not technically required, the COA program should develop policies that describe its own requirements for Hull and Liability insurance.

UNMANNED AERIAL VEHICLE USES

Uses of UAVs are seemingly endless, with companies and individuals figuring out new ways to use UAVs nearly every day, including (UAVSA, 2015):

1. Security and law enforcement
   a. Security patrol
   b. Surveillance and reconnaissance
   c. Suspect or vehicle search
   d. Monitoring crowds
   e. Traffic watch
   f. Drug and illegal alien interdiction[4]
   g. Customs and Border Patrol
   h. Detection of chemical/biological/radiological, and nuclear elements
2. Firefighting, Search and Rescue
   a. Maritime and Mountain Search and Rescue
   b. Life raft, water pump deployments
   c. Rescue point marking
   d. Search and Rescue
   e. Wildland firefighting and patrol for wild fires
3. Research
   a. Atmospheric research
4. Commercial
   a. News reporting
   b. Product delivery
   c. Real estate sales
   d. Aerial photography

---

[4]During a 2-week U.S. Coast Guard demonstration of UAV capabilities, a ScanEagle UAV aided in the interdiction of nearly 600 kilograms of cocaine, the first time the Coast Guard has used UAVs in an interdiction operation. The ScanEagle, which was in the air for more than 90 hours, was deployed by the U.S. Coast Guard Cutter *Bertholf* to monitor a suspected go-fast vessel. When the UAV located the vessel, it maintained constant on-scene surveillance until the MH-65D Short Range Recovery helicopter and Over the Horizon cutter boats arrived to interdict and apprehend the vessel's crew (Carroll, 2013).

5. Monitoring
   a. Civil engineering sites
   b. Waterways and shipping
   c. Oil and gas pipeline
   d. Forestry
   e. Power line and phone line monitoring
   f. Fishery Protection
   g. Pollution Control and Air Sampling
   h. Litter on beaches and in parks
   i. Wildlife and wildlife research
   j. Environmental compliance
   k. Rail lines
6. Disaster Management
   a. Disaster effects management
   b. Rescue and cleanup effort supervision
   c. Disaster damage estimation
7. Crop Management
   a. Countryside and agriculture
   b. Agricultural activities
   c. Crop dusting
   d. Crop performance
8. Communications
   a. Telecommunications
   b. Telecom relay and signal coverage survey
9. Survey
   a. Oil and gas exploration and production
   b. Mineral exploration
   c. Geophysical surveys
   d. Suburban planning
   e. Remote sensing

Airport operators will likely discover that UAVs can create challenges for the safe and secure operation of an airport, but may also find uses for UAVs, such as:

1. Perimeter patrol using Unmanned Ground Vehicle (UGV) technology;
2. Wildlife management, similar to the way birds of prey are used at some airports today;
3. Disaster Management—able to provide a visual of the scene to be transmitted back to the Emergency Operations Center.

The two major flight categories are Fixed-Wing and VTOL. UAVs are divided into broad categories based on gross takeoff weight and airframe type. The U.S. military has categorized UAVs into tiers to better describe their function, physical size, takeoff weight, ceiling (how high they can fly) and range (how far they can fly). Figure 13.1 below presents a representative example of categories and tiers of common UAVs. The tier system applies primarily to fixed-wing UAVs.

Category/tier	Sample UAV/UAS & mission	Specifications	UAV type
Small/micro UAS	**AirVironment-Raven** California Intelligence Surveillance Mop-up Visual/thermal	Length: 3 ft Wingspan: 4.5 ft Duration: 60 min Ceiling: 15,000 ft MSL (mean sea-level) Cruise Speed: 35 mph Weight: 4.2 max Payload: ~ 6.5 oz Power: Electric Range: 6.2 mi	Fixed-Wing 
Small/micro UAS	**Precision Hawk** Raleigh, NC Intelligence Surveillance Reconnaissance Mop-up Visual/thermal Multispectral Hyperspectral Light Detection and Ranging (LiDAR)	Length: 3.5 ft Wingspan: 4 ft Duration: 50 min Ceiling: unpublished Cruise Speed: 60 mph Weight: 3 lb Payload: 2.2 lb Power: Electric Range: unpublished	Fixed-Wing
Small UAS	**MLB-Super Bat** Santa Clara, CA Intelligence Surveillance RT Infrared Fire-line mapping Wind velocity/direction Night operations	Length: 5.3 ft Wingspan: 8.5 ft Duration: 10 hr Ceiling: 10,000 ft MSL Cruise Speed: 60 mph Weight: 35 lb max Payload: 5 lb Power: 26 cc–2 stroke Range: 400 mi	Fixed-Wing
Tier I (Also grouped in Tier II)	**Insitu-Scan Eagle** Bingen, WA Intelligence Surveillance Reconnaissance Mop-up	Length: 5.6 ft Wingspan: 10.3 ft Duration: 24hr + Ceiling: 19,500 ft MSL Cruise Speed: 69 mph Weight: 48.5 lb max Power: Piston engine	Fixed-Wing 

FIGURE 13.1

Example category and tier UAVs.

Source: Forrest, Cozart, White, & Ormen, 2015.

Tier II (Also grouped in Tier I)	**Textron-Shadow M2 Intelligence** Surveillance Reconnaissance Mop-up Night operations	Length: 12 ft Wingspan: 25 ft Duration: 14 hr Ceiling: 15,000 ft MSL Cruise Speed: 69 mph Weight: 493 max Power: Piston engine	Fixed-Wing 
Tier III	**General Atomics-ERMP** (Predator – A, B) NASA (National Aeronautics and Space Administration) – Ikhana Intelligence Surveillance Reconnaissance Mop-up Night operations	Length: 28 ft Wingspan: 56 ft Duration: 30 hr Ceiling: 29,000 ft MSL Cruise Speed: 170 mph Weight: 1,075 lb max Power: Piston engine–jet fuel	Fixed-Wing 
Small/Micro UAS	**Aeryon-Sky Ranger** Waterloo, ON Canada Quad Copter Intelligence Surveillance Mop-up Backpack version	Diameter: 3.5 ft Duration: 50 min Ceiling: Unspecified Power: Electric Wind tolerance: 40 mph, 55 mph gusts Payload: EO/IR High-resolution camera	VTOL
Small	**Pulse Aerospace-Vapor** Lawrence, KS Intelligence Surveillance Reconnaissance Mop-up	Rotor Diameter: 65 in. Duration: 1 hr Ceiling: 15,000 ft MSL Range: 5 mi Weight: 30 lb Power: Electric Payload: 12 lb Varied, EO/IR +, LiDAR, multi- and hyperspectral, thermal	VTOL

FIGURE 13.1

Continued

CybAero-APID 60 Intelligence Surveillance Reconnaissance Suppression Mop-up Payload delivery	Rotor Diameter: 27 ft Duration: 6 hr Ceiling: Unspecified Range: 115 mi Weight: 400 lb max Power: Jet engine Payload: 110 lb Varied, EO/IR +	VTOL	
Northrop Grumman United States, Global MQ-8B FIRE SCOUT Intelligence Surveillance Reconnaissance Suppression Mop-up Payload delivery	Rotor Diameter: 27 ft Duration: 5+ hr Ceiling: 20,000 ft MSL Range: 130 mi Weight: 3,150 lb Power: Jet engine Payload: Varied, EO, IR, LRF, + heavy lift, payload delivery	VTOL 	
Lockheed Martin United States, Global K-Max Autonomous flight capability Intelligence Surveillance Reconnaissance Suppression Mop-up Heavy lift **NOTE: can be autonomous or piloted**	Duration: 2.75 hr Ceiling: 15,000 ft MSL Range: 112 mi Weight: 5,145 lb Power: Jet engine Payload: Cargo (6,000 lb), Utility focus	VTOL 	

FIGURE 13.1

Continued

The U.S. Department of Defense has also developed an unofficial classification of UAVs based on maximum takeoff weight, normal operating altitude, and speed (Figure 13.2).

UNMANNED AERIAL SYSTEMS AND AIRPORT OPERATIONS

While it is unlikely that UAVs will soon be operating out of busy, commercial service airports, it is very likely that they will soon be operating out of general aviation facilities, particularly airports

UAS Groups	Maximum Weight (lbs) (MGTOW)	Normal Operating Altitude (ft)	Speed (kts)	Representative UAS	
Group 1	0–20	<1,200 AGL	100	Raven (RQ-11) WASP	 Raven
Group 2	21–55	<3,500 AGL	<250	ScanEagle	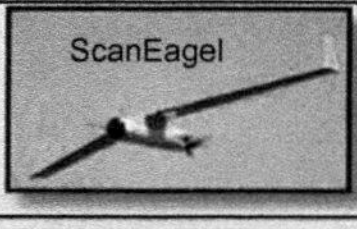 ScanEagel
Group 3	< 1,320	<FL 180		Shadow (RQ-7B) Tier II/STUAS	 Shadow
Group 4	> 1,320		Any Airspeed	Fire Scout (MQ-8B, RQ-8B) Predator (MQ-1A/B), Sky Warrior ERMP (MQ-1C)	 MQ-1/Predator
Group 5		<FL 180		Reaper (MQ-9A) Global Hawl (RQ-4) BAMS (RQ-4N)	 RQ-4/Global Hawk

FIGURE 13.2

U.S. Department of Defense UAS group descriptions.

Source: U.S. Department of Defense, 2011.

with low levels of activity. In 2013, the FAA completed a 10-month selection process to pick six test sites for UAV application—all are general aviation airports. Each airport was selected to participate in a particular component of the research including: (a) standards for unmanned aircraft categories, (b) traffic control procedures and NextGen, (c) sense and avoid technologies and airspace integration, (d) differing climates, Airworthiness, and reliable data links, and (f) UAS failure mode testing.

The vast majority of UAV users operate UAVs under the 55-lb limit, and these users are therefore considered model aircraft users. These are not the types of UAV operators that will be approaching airports in which to base operations. The small UAVs do not need a long runway, or in some cases any runway, in which to operate, and they can be stored in a small space when not in use. The UAV operators that will soon approach airport operators, looking for hangar and maintenance space, payload storage facilities, and access to the runway/taxiway system, are those operating UAVs that require a runway of sufficient width and length and that meets certain safety standards.

Reports of UAS operating in the vicinity of airports around the country are on the increase, and even with FAA regulations, the increasing numbers of UAVs and inevitable proximity to manned aircraft require significant attention and evaluation of systems and methods that will ensure the safe operation of both manned and unmanned aircraft. The best chance for conflict is near an airport. Conversely, airports also offer the opportunity to develop operational concepts and technology to integrate UAS vehicles into the National Airspace System. Airport operators should help promote safe UAV operations in the community by conducting as much outreach as possible, in a variety of forms—social media, community meetings, press releases, and holding "safe UAV operations" courses.

For a large UAV to operate at an airport, several factors must be taken into consideration, such as payload type (hazardous materials?), the launch-and-recovery process, and the ATC and safety clearances necessary to keep the UAV from conflicting with manned aircraft. To a certain extent, at general aviation airports with low levels of operation, or at low-level, commercial service airports when commercial service aircraft are not operating, it may be possible to incorporate UAV operations, similar to how skydiving operations are handled at some airports. There are specific drop zones, and the skydiving operation announces over UNICOM (Universal Communications) when skydivers are in the air. For airports with higher levels of flight operations, it may be better to incorporate a separate UAV runway, the same way many airports with glider operations have built and designated a separate runway for gliders. Separate runways keep UAV operators off the active runways that are in use by manned aircraft. From a design perspective, the USAF publishes Engineering Technical Letter (ETL) 09-1: *Airfield Planning and Design Criteria for Unmanned Aircraft Systems (UAS)*, which lays out basic design guidance for building a UAV runway, and which also supplements UFC 3-260-01, *Airfield and Heliport Planning and Design*.

Airport operators who are considering UAV operations should establish a base of support within the local aircraft operator community and ensure the concerns are understood and addressed. While grant assurances prevent an airport operator from denying the aeronautical use of the airport to a user, the industry is on untested ground with respect to the use of UAVs. A precedent has been established that certain aeronautical operations (such as ultralights or skydiving at a busy commercial-service or general aviation airport) can be restricted if, upon an airspace study conducted by the FAA, the aeronautical use is not compatible with the airport's operations from a safety perspective. However, the question of UAV compatibility is yet to be answered.

In addition to the operation of the UAV, airport operators should take into consideration the amount of ground personnel that are necessary to launch and recover the UAV; interference with airport or air traffic communications by UAV datalink systems; payloads that may have hazardous materials on board, and how the UAV will be handled if it crashes at the airport. Will special response procedures be in place for responding to a UAV crash rather than an aircraft crash? Will it still be considered an Alert III, or will a different designation be made as the element of human life at risk is not an issue in a UAV crash, unless it hits a building on the airport or collides with another aircraft or vehicle.

Failure testing is a critical component of UAV operations—when the datalink breaks between the UAV and the Ground Control Station, most UAVs have a *run-home* function, where the UAV will return to its launch point. Some questions to be considered are: Would the airport operator have any liability for the crash if a UAV loses signal and goes down in a populated area? How would the flight of this now essentially uncontrolled aircraft affect other airport or aircraft operations? What are the minimum standards for UAV operations at an airport? What are the rules and regulations? How will the definition of *aeronautical use* apply to property leases? And most importantly, what questions are there that have not yet been asked that will be relevant to UAV operations at airports and in the National Airspace System in the future? Perhaps the option is to take the UAV operations away from the airport and to construct a special **"UAVport"** or **"Droneport."**

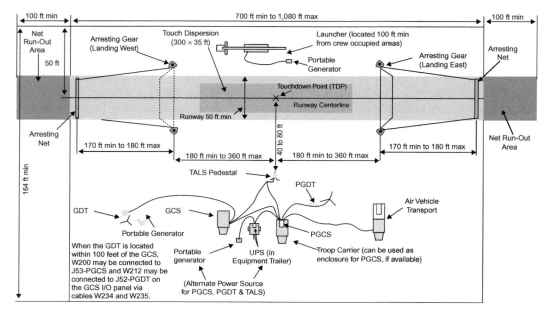

FIGURE 13.3 Launch and Recovery Site for Shadow 200, UAV.

Key: GDT, ground data terminal; GCS, Ground Control Station; PGCS, portable ground control station; PGDT, portable ground data terminal; TALS, tactical automated landing system.

Source: United States Air Force.

Droneports or UAVports

In 2014, the U.S. Army announced that it would build a special airport for the Grey Eagle and Shadow, UAVs at the Fort Bliss Army base in El Paso, Texas. The drone airport will have two runways, a 5,000-foot paved runway and a smaller 1,000-foot paved runway, and a 50,000 square-foot hangar with office and support buildings, a command and control center, a hot loading facility for munitions, and a hazardous materials building. The drone airport will have a 1,000-foot cleared and graded, dirt, safety, run-out zone at each end of the 5,000-foot runway (i.e., safety area), with security lighting and fencing around the perimeter (Keller, 2014).

According to the USAF planning criteria for UAV operations, the size and length of the runway depends on the size and flight characteristics of the UAV that will use the facility—i.e., the "Design UAV." Wingspan, wheel base,[5] weight, landing speed, takeoff distance, turning radii, and recovery method are all taken into account (Figure 13.3).

Figure 13.3 shows that operating a larger UAS takes more than a tablet PC. The mission planning and control functions (Ground Control Station) of a UAS incorporate the launch, the flight, and the recovery of the vehicle, which receives (and sends) data from its internal sensors of the flight system and payloads. Launch and recovery can be the most difficult phases of the flight,

---

[5]UAV's are also given an Aircraft Classification Number (ACN) pavement rating number.

particularly during turbulence, as the pilot can only determine what the UAV is doing based on instrumentation, rather than on feel (Fahlstrom & Gleason, 2012, p. 264). The operator is not inside the plane and can't feel the aircraft pitching and rolling as it approaches its landing site. Some automated systems handle the landing function, but an operator should still be ready to take over the controls to activate a "run-home" function, or a parachute in cases when the UAV threatens passenger aircraft, buildings, or people.

Launching a UAV depends on the type of UAV. Some UAVs are simple; others are very complex and require several personnel. The simplest method is hand-launched, sometimes referred to as "chuck-a-drone." This method is practical for smaller drones weighing less than 10 lb. For any wheeled takeoff, a prepared surface, such as a paved runway, is necessary. Some larger UAVs, particularly those that are too heavy for hand launch and those that require a higher takeoff speed, can be truck launched. Bungee-powered launchers, rail launchers, and pneumatic launchers, which rely on compressed gas, can all launch relatively small UAVs, while hydraulic/pneumatic launchers have been successful at launching UAVs up to 1,225 lb (Fahlstrom & Gleason, 2012, pp. 270−72). VTOL UAVs need little in the way of launch or recovery equipment.

Recovery of a UAV can be done via a conventional landing provided the UAV has landing gear or skids. Arresting gear can be used with a tail hook similar to the way aircraft are recovered on an aircraft carrier. Skid landings have been made on unimproved surfaces. Other forms of recovery include vertical net systems, basically a net strung between two poles into which the UAV is flown. Parachute recovery has a long history of use with UAVs and target drones and is a feasible alternative to other forms of landing, provided the UAV has space inside to hold the parachute and cord system. Gliding parachutes have also been used (Fahlstrom & Gleason, 2012).

The FAA continues to work with commercial partners in industry on a variety of programs to determine how best to regulate and integrate UAVs into the National Airspace System. It is safe to say that UAV's are here to stay and that soon, airport operators will have to make decisions about how to best integrate their operations into the airport environment.

SPACEPORTS

In the movie *2001: A Space Odyssey*, filmmaker Stanley Kubrick and author Arthur C. Clarke envisioned what they believed to be the next level of air travel—the space plane. The movie debuted in May 1968, only 2 months before Apollo 11 landed at Tranquility Base on the Moon.

The space plane concept predated the film as Pan Am, in 1964, went so far as to take reservations for the airline's first passenger visit to the moon (SunSentinel, 1989). However, it would be nearly 40 years later when the concept of a commercial space transport would be considered feasible and affordable. When NASA (National Aeronautics and Space Administration) ended the Space Shuttle program, the way was paved for commercial, space-launch operations. NASA is still in the business of launching satellites and payloads into orbit, and work continues on deep space missions, such as Lockheed's Orion crew space exploration vehicle, but the lower Earth work is slowly becoming the domain of the private space launch industry.

Author Chis Impey, in his book *Beyond: Our Future in Space* (Impey, 2015), argues that we are at an important time in history, when technology will soon enable us to make space travel routine.

While some in the airport industry claim that we are still 15 to 20 years away from routine commercial space tourism operations, over a dozen airport operators throughout the country already have a spaceport license or application filed with the FAA. Today, several pioneers in the industry, including Burt Rutan, Richard Branson, Peter Diamandis, and Elon Musk, are making great strides in the commercial space domain. It is fitting that some of these men, who are billionaires, got their start in the Internet, because to a certain extent, while the beginnings of commercial space have certain parallels to the beginnings of commercial aviation, a more accurate comparison is the birth of the Internet.

Like the space program, the Internet depended on investment by the military—industrial complex in order to mature. The military needed a way to maintain communications between key bases in the event of a nuclear attack. Soon, DARPANET[6] was created by the Department of Defense and served as the technical core and de facto test lab for what would eventually become the Internet. In the 1980s, the National Science Foundation and the academic community continued to mature the technology, and by the 1990s, with the advent of the private Internet Service Providers (ISPs), individuals could have an email account and the fledgling Internet was available to the general public. By 1995, the National Science Foundation (NSF) dropped all restrictions on Internet commerce, which also was the year that Yahoo, eBay, and Amazon were founded (Impey, 2015, pp. 78—79).

In 1993 the Internet accounted for 1% of telecommunication traffic, but today it accounts for 99%. Impey (2015, p. 80) believes that space travel will follow the same trajectory, becoming demilitarized and then massively commercialized. One of the first major successes for the private sector came when the Dragon spacecraft, built by billionaire Elon Musk's company, SpaceX, docked with the International Space Station in 2012. The Dragon is made by a company with 3,000 employees, compared to NASA's 18,000 employees and 60,000 contractors.

WHAT HAPPENED TO THE SPACE SHUTTLE?

Shortly after President John F. Kennedy's national goal of going to the moon was achieved in 1968, funding for NASA slowly started to decrease. The primary objective of the moon missions was part of the Cold War space race between the United States and the Soviet Union. Once the United States achieved the high ground of space, even the Soviets gave up on going to the moon. When the final moon mission, Apollo 17, returned to Earth, future missions were canceled and funding switched to the Skylab space station, using up the remaining Saturn V rockets (Impey, 2015, p. 54). Soon funding would switch to America's next big endeavor in space, the Space Shuttle.

The first flight of the Space Shuttle occurred on April 12, 1981. Launched atop two solid rocket boosters centered over an external fuel tank, the Space Shuttle would go on to fly 135 times between 1981 and 2011, sending 300 astronauts into space. The Shuttle had several key flights, including the launch and service of the Hubble Space Telescope, Spacelab, numerous space walks, service to the International Space Station, and taking America's first woman into space, Sally Ride. Unfortunately, the launch rate ended up 10 times lower than originally planned, two of the five

[6]The name is a derivative of the Defense Advanced Research Projects Agency, which established the first real-time "Internet" link.

orbiters suffered catastrophic failures with the loss of all personnel on board, and the cost to use the Shuttle for most routine launches exceeded that of other options (Impey, 2015, p. 55).

Over the course of the Shuttle program, the cost of each launch averaged approximately $1 billion, which works out to $80,000 per kilogram placed into orbit. Most commercial entities were only able to use the Shuttle with massive subsidies from the government, and instead of the one flight per week that was originally planned by NASA, the Shuttle managed about one flight every 2 or 3 months. The U.S. military's launch demands exceeded what the Shuttle could provide, so it eventually started developing their own heavy lift capabilities (launching out of Vandenberg Air Force Base in California) and its own unmanned version of the Shuttle, the diminutive X-37 (Impey, 2015, p. 55).

The Shuttle program experienced two major losses, *Challenger* in 1986 and *Columbia* in 2003. The loss of *Challenger* on liftoff in January 1986 also took with it America's first teacher in space, Christa McAuliffe. This quickly and quietly ended NASA's program to send civilians, such as teachers, artists, and poets, into space, although her backup did eventually fly. When *Columbia* broke up upon reentry in 2003 it signaled the end of the program; all remaining Shuttle flights focused on finishing the International Space Station, while many scientific missions were canceled (Impey, 2015, p. 75).

On July 8, 2011, Space Shuttle *Atlantis* lifted off over Florida's Space Coast from NASA's Kennedy Space Center to make a delivery to the International Space Station. *Atlantis* landed at Kennedy's Shuttle Landing Facility on Runway 15, on July 21, 2011, which ended America's Space Shuttle program. Prior to the final flight, NASA had already issued the layoff notices, and only one day after *Atlantis* landed, NASA issued them in the thousands. Today, NASA's focus is primarily on robotic probes sent to explore the solar system, asteroids, and planets nearest to Earth, along with training astronauts to go to the International Space Station, on Russian rockets.

In 1968, only two countries could put people into space: the United States and the Soviet Union. In 2015, only two countries can put people into space: the Russian Federation and China. While U.S. astronauts now hitch rides (paid for by the U.S. government) on Russian rockets, and Russian rockets and engines are used on some U.S. spacecraft, this relationship is tenuous. The Air Force's X-37 uses a Russian RD-180 engine for its first stage, and in 2014, amid tensions over the situation in the Ukraine, the Russian defense minister announced that Russia would no longer supply rocket engines for U.S. military launches.[7] Besides NASA's Space Shuttle, and its Russian counterpart Buran, which only flew once in 1988, the most frequent visitor to space is Burt Rutan's privately built and funded SpaceShipOne, which flew to space 17 times between 2003 and 2004 (Impey, 2015, p. 72).

THE NEW PIONEERS

Burt Rutan, a former civilian test engineer for the USAF, has led the way in unconventional aircraft designs. Today, his Voyager aircraft, which was the first to circumnavigate the world without refueling, sits in the Smithsonian National Air and Space Museum, next to the Apollo 11 capsule and Lindberg's Spirit of St. Louis, along with four other aircraft of his design. In June 2004, Rutan launched SpaceShipOne, becoming the first manned civilian vehicle to reach an altitude of

---

[7]The Boeing-built X-37 is changing to the American-made Delta family of rockets to boost the X-37 into space.

100 km.[8] Three months later, Rutan won the Ansari X-prize with SpaceShipOne by flying it to the required 100 km height twice in a 2-week window.

Media mogul (and billionaire) **Richard Branson**, founder of the Virgin Group, which is made up of more than 400 companies, started Virgin Galactic in 2004. Branson commissioned Rutan to scale up his SpaceShipOne to be ready for space tourism. SpaceShipTwo can carry two pilots and six passengers. Unlike all other versions of shuttles to lower Earth orbit, which are launched vertically on top of a rocket ship and glide to a landing, SpaceShipTwo rides aboard a carrier aircraft, White Night II, to an altitude of 52,000 feet, at which point the two craft separate with SpaceShipTwo rocketing upward to just over 100 km, or 60 miles. Total flight time is expected to be 2.5 hours, with 6 minutes of weightlessness, and the ability to see the curvature of the Earth. Rides on SpaceShipTwo are selling for $250,000, and as of 2013, more than 650 people have signed up, including actors Brad Pitt and Tom Hanks, singer Katy Perry, and renowned physicist Stephen Hawking (Impey, 2015, pp. 88–89).

As with any risky endeavor, there is always the potential for disaster. In 2007, three people were killed and another three were injured in an explosion at Rutan's Scaled Composites factory. In October 2014, a pilot was killed and another was seriously injured when SpaceShipTwo malfunctioned during flight (Impey, 2015, p. 89).

Peter Diamandis once read Charles Lindbergh's memoir and was inspired by the famous pilot. Lindbergh went from being a barnstormer crisscrossing the country, giving joyrides in a biplane, to spending a year as a pilot for the U.S. Army flying mail, and then, finally, became the first to successfully fly solo nonstop across the Atlantic, winning the Orteig prize, which was offered for the first pilot to complete such a feat. Six other aviators died trying to win the prize. However, within 3 years of Lindberg winning the prize, passenger air traffic increased 30-fold, and upon reading about Lindbergh, Diamandis found his business model. He eventually persuaded the Ansari family to fund a $10 million prize[9] to spur innovation, which eventually became the X prize won by Burt Rutan (Impey, 2015, pp. 90–91).

Elon Musk, another Internet billionaire (building the PayPal brand among other things), is a visionary and the founder of Tesla Motors, SolarCity, and SpaceX. Musk's company landed the contract from NASA to become the first privately funded company to put a satellite in Earth orbit and the first commercial company to dock with the International Space Station. Musk has a slightly darker, dystopian vision of the future and believes humanity should hedge their bets against threats to our survival, including an asteroid hitting the Earth, or super volcano, an engineered virus, global warming, or some as yet unknown threat.[10] SpaceX also constructs the Falcon 9 and Falcon 1

---

[8]There is no clear delineation where the Earth's atmosphere ends and space begins; it is a gradual transition, so at 100 km (62.13 miles) above mean sea-level is the Karman line, which is the common definition of space. The Karman line is also where U.S. pilots earn their astronaut wings—several X-15 test pilots earned their Astronaut Wings by flying higher than 100 km, even though some never went on a rocket or the Space Shuttle.

[9]Diamandis eventually approached Larry Page, CEO of Google, to extend the X prize into areas of health, energy, and the environment.

[10]Author Andrew Krepinevich explored several end-times disasters that could befall us in his book, *7 Deadly Scenarios: A Military Futurist Explores War in the Twenty-First Century*. Some of the top scenarios include a pandemic virus, the collapse of Pakistan and who will control the country's 100 + nuclear weapons, nuclear explosions within the United States, and a war with China (Krepinevich, 2010).

rockets, which are capable of carrying 15 tons to low Earth orbit and 5 tons to a geostationary transfer orbit.

These men, and other entrepreneurs, such as Amazon founder Jeff Bezos (who is also pushing the FAA on UAV regulations so that UAVs can be used to deliver products), are determined to make commercial space travel not only a reality, but also a way of life, as quickly as possible. There are even plans for commercial lunar flybys starting in the near future. As NASA's share of the federal budget has shrunk from 5% to 0.05%, power is shifting to private and commercial organizations vying for government contracts, but eventually the government may be reduced to regulatory control only, as it is with the aviation industry (Impey, 2015, p. 100).

It appears that much of what is holding back the development of the commercial space industry is not technology or capability, but bureaucracy. Starting with the **International Traffic in Arms Regulation (ITAR)**, which requires a license for the export of rocket systems, and licenses if rockets are worked on by a non–U.S. citizen or even shown to a non–U.S. citizen. Burt Rutan notes that export regulations (including ITAR) resulted in cost overruns, increased the risk for test pilots, did not reduce the risk to the general public, actually removed opportunities for innovative safety solutions, and delayed SpaceShipTwo's development by several years (Impey, 2015, p. 103).

Another difficult issue is **insurance**. Insurance is not calculated for the exact risk of traveling to space, and the unfortunate reality is that people have died in space travel, and will continue to die. By 2013, an estimated 540 people have been in space and 21 have died, which is a mortality rate of 3.9%. Compare this to commercial aviation, with 1.3 deaths per 100,000,000 miles flown in 2008 alone, meaning the likelihood of dying on an airplane is one in 20,000, or 0.005%. However, the mortality rate in 1938 in aviation was 10 times higher than it is today (Impey, 2015).

"Don't believe anyone who tells you the safety will be the same as a modern airliner's," says Burt Rutan. SpaceShipTwo reaches a top speed of 2,500 miles an hour; passengers experience six Gs of acceleration; and passengers wear helmetless spacesuits. If the spacecraft loses pressure, death, or at the very least, brain damage, could happen within a short period of time (Impey, 2015, p. 89). The very thought of a spacecraft returning from a suborbital flight gone wrong, delivering several permanently brain-damaged passengers back to an airport, is just one example of how spaceport operations will differ significantly from Airport Operations.

THE FEDERAL AVIATION ADMINISTRATION'S ROLE IN COMMERCIAL SPACE

The mission of the FAA's **Office of Commercial Space Transportation (AST)** is to ensure protection of the public, property, and the national security and foreign policy interests of the United States during commercial launch or reentry activities and to encourage, facilitate, and promote U.S. commercial space transportation (FAA, 2015c).

AST[11] was established in 1984, with the passage of the **Commercial Space Launch Act** of that same year. The office regulates launch sites, issues launch licenses, and recommends rulemaking and other policy changes related to the commercial space industry. Since 1984, the majority of launches has been vertical launch with expendable launch vehicles. Vertical launch is loud, dangerous, expensive, and not particularly neighbor-friendly to have at a local airport. However, recent

---

[11]Note that the FAA is responsible for regulating commercial space, not NASA. NASA is a civil research and development agency of the federal government and does not have regulatory responsibilities.

developments in technology have enabled horizontal-takeoff to low Earth orbit operations, making Pan Am's original vision a soon-to-be reality.[12] The U.S. space transportation industry operates in almost half the states in the United States, with several companies around the world offering orbital commercial launch services or suborbital services for paying passengers. In recent years, commercial launches have comprised about one-third of all launches conducted worldwide (FAA, 2013).

Until recently, only a few spaceports operated in the United States, the most notable being Cape Canaveral,[13] Florida, home of the Space Shuttle and site of the civilian launches of manned, and many unmanned, spacecraft. Several communities, though, are at the vanguard of developing private or state-operated launch, reentry, and processing sites known as commercial spaceports. As of 2010, additional spaceports were approved in Alaska, California, Texas, New Mexico, Oklahoma, Virginia, and Florida (Cecil Field in Jacksonville). Two other spaceports are located in the Pacific Ocean, one in the Marshall Islands, and another at the Equatorial Pacific Ocean (a sea launch platform). These spaceports provide alternatives to government launch sites operated by the USAF or NASA. Other launch sites and spaceports have been proposed by: Alabama, Colorado, Florida (multiple locations), Georgia, Hawaii, Indiana, Texas (multiple locations), Washington, Wisconsin, and Wyoming (FAA, 2013). There remains tremendous uncertainty in exactly how spaceports are going to develop, what they will look like, and how they will be operated. It is natural to attempt to make parallels between airports and spaceports, but significant differences remain unidentified.

The Spaceport Application Process

For an airport to apply to be a launch site, the airport must submit an application to the FAA. The process is covered under the **Commercial Space Launch Act**, 51 U.S.C. Ch. 509, §§ 50901-23-2011, and Title 14 CFR Parts 401, 417, and 420. FAA AC AC 413-1 (1999, August 16) addresses License Application Procedures.

The process begins with a preapplication consultation with the FAA to allow the applicant and the FAA to identify potential issues, to familiarize the applicant with the licensing process, and to familiarize the FAA with the applicant. There is not a formal structure to this process, but the FAA advises that the applicant should consult with the FAA early in the process to avoid significant delays or costs later. Consultation may be made by telephone, email, in person, or other means. Upon submission of the application, the FAA will review it and may require more documentation. It is important for applicants to remember that they are responsible for the accuracy and completeness of the information provided to the FAA, with any material changes provided to the FAA in a timely manner. After review, the FAA will either issue a license or reject the application.

The application process goes through several phases, including a policy review, a safety review, an environmental review, and, upon issuance of the license, compliance monitoring. As part of the policy review, the FAA will review the license to determine whether any issues might affect the national security of the United States, U.S. foreign policy interests, or international obligations of the United States. The FAA also consults with the Department of Defense, the Department of State, NASA, and other federal agencies (FAA, 2006).

---

[12]Pan Am declared bankruptcy in 1991, in part because of the 1988 bombing of Pan Am Flight 103 over Lockerbie, Scotland.
[13]Cape Canaveral includes the Kennedy Space Center and Cape Canaveral Air Force Station.

The safety review determines whether the operator can safely conduct the proposed operation, demonstrating that the operator has a clear understanding of the hazards involved, and explaining how operations will be safely performed. One of the analyses that must be performed as part of the safety review is an **Expected Casualty Calculations for Commercial Space Launch and Reentry Missions**. The loss of Space Shuttle Challenger in 1986 during launch, and the loss of Space Shuttle Columbia on reentry in 2003, sadly demonstrates the need for this type of study. A primary objective of the licensing process is to limit the risk to the public's health and safety, and the safety of property. As a consequence of the altitudes and the speeds involved, the crash, disintegration, or explosion of a spacecraft in the upper atmosphere can result in far more widespread damage than the crash of a commercial airplane.[14]

Compared to commercial aviation, spaceflight is still immature in its development, so it is somewhat understandable that suborbital flight possesses more variables and risk than commercial air, but individuals traveling on commercial space missions want to know that all reasonable safety precautions have been taken (FAA, 2006). The term **expected casualty** is used in the space transportation industry as a measure of risk to public safety from a specific mission and is used to determine if the mission may proceed or a license should be granted. Expected casualty is the expected average number of human casualties per commercial space mission and is defined as a fatality or serious injury (FAA, 2006, p. 2).

Additional documentation includes documentation related to **Casualty Areas from Impacting Inert Debris for People in the Open**. Missile or space vehicle risk studies show that a significant portion of the risk is from falling inert debris. A USAF report presents methods and procedures for estimating the casualty areas for debris falling onto people in the open, but not for people in houses, office buildings, or other structures. The report is based on breakups of Atlas IIAS and Delta-GEM vehicles and was produced prior to the 2003 crash of the Columbia Space Shuttle, but essentially, factors such as the cross-section of the vehicle, the path-angle, and the impact velocity are the primary factors that influence the amount of casualties (Montgomery, 1995).

The National Environmental Policy Act (NEPA, 1969) forms the basis for the applications environmental review requirement. Under the **Environmental Review for Licensed/Permitted Commercial Space Transportation Activities**, the FAA analyzes the environmental impacts of proposed licensed and permitted actions, including the licensing of launch and reentry activities, the operation of launch and reentry sites, and the issuing of permits for suborbital reusable rockets. It then takes the appropriate action required under NEPA. Once all environmental requirements are satisfied, the FAA prepares an environmental determination, for example, a Finding of No Significant Impact (FONSI) or a Record of Decision (ROD), which becomes a part of the license or experimental permit evaluation (FAA, 2006).

Considerations in Becoming a Spaceport

Unfortunately, because of the tremendous amount of secrecy surrounding these commercial space operations—that is, SpaceX, SpaceAdventures, and so forth—very little has been learned or shared about how an airport will become a spaceport. Much is known about vertical launch facilities, as they have been the primary method of getting to space since the days of Sputnik. However, little is

---

[14]On one crash of an X-15, the plane went into a hypersonic spin at 60,000 feet and broke apart; the debris was spread over 50 square miles. Debris from the Shuttle Columbia spread from Texas to Louisiana.

known, or published, about how a horizontal takeoff to low Earth, suborbital craft, gliding back down from more than 100 km, through commercial airspace and back to an airport, safely and securely will work. The whole concept and its challenges may be an excellent example of a dance, where you learn it as you go.

Since it is difficult to predict what problems will occur with something that has not yet even been developed, this text uses a Part 139 perspective to approach the potential challenges to an airport operating as a spaceport. It is generally understood that spaceports for suborbital flights will most likely be general aviation airports, which are not required to adhere to Part 139, but Part 139 does provide a basis for a safety standard.

The key to becoming a good spaceport is to first become a good airport. In addition to applying for a spaceport license, the airport should strive to adhere to Part 139 standards. Additionally, there may be significant security threats to spaceport operations, so the airport operator should also strive to adhere to Part 1542 Airport Security regulations. Although no transportation security regulations presently address spaceport operations, the regulations are likely to do so in the future, once the programs near reality. The Department of Defense or NASA should assume that certain levels of security will be necessary for some of the initial launches, particularly at some spaceports that are not already airports, such as Richard Branson's Spaceport America in New Mexico.

It is safe to assume that whatever airport regulations are in existence will be amplified and increased for spaceport operations. An airport operator that is seriously considering becoming a spaceport should begin by educating themselves on the commercial space industry by attending seminars and conferences, reading periodicals and texts, and meeting with industry leaders.

The airport should have a solid set of minimum standards for aviation operations, and rules and regulations that are enforced to the extent that any interested party desiring to conduct commercial space operations feels that the airport is both safe and secure. Routine violations of safety procedures, such as runway incursions or unauthorized personnel on the ramp, or security incidents, such as individuals accessing the AOA, must be resolved. The implementation of both Safety Management Systems and Security Management Systems can help inculcate a culture of safety and security, which can better provide assurances to potential spaceport clients.

Airport pavement should be in excellent condition, and if possible, funding for pavement strengthening and other related projects to accommodate spacecraft operations, included within the Airport Master Plan. All airfield signs, markings, and lighting, navigational aids, and traffic and wind direction indicators should be in good condition, with regular maintenance performed. The airport should have ARFF capabilities to meet the existing aircraft that typically use the airport, and up-to-date snow removal, wildlife, vehicle and pedestrian, and Airport Emergency Plans.

Unfortunately, many general aviation airports do not have fencing or gates, and this will surely be a minimum requirement for spaceport operations. Another area where the airport will likely have to greatly improve is response to hazardous material releases, as many of the spacecraft carry a variety of propellants and hazardous materials as part of their construction and operation that go beyond standard aviation fuel. Airport operators may also need to increase their ARFF capabilities, along with their medical response capabilities, particularly to respond to the scenario of a rapid decompression taking place at high altitude, resulting in individuals with severe brain damage upon landing (assuming that somehow the pilots are able to return the aircraft to the spaceport).

Key design considerations for spaceport operations include: a guarantee that the launch activity will be long-term; the potential to expand; the safety of persons and property; the protection of public's health and the environment; security of the facilities, the absence of danger to other facilities (so that a disaster or explosion in one facility does not trigger such calamity in other facilities, or cause damage to critical networks such as—nearby roadways, railways, and critical facilities such as chemical or power plants, or the airport (Sgobba, Allahdadi, Rongier, & Wilde, 2013, loc. 1245).

Many of these assurances will be difficult for airport operators, particularly for any airport that is within a populated area or that has significant noise abatement issues, which may result in threats to close the airport or restrict flight operations, including spacecraft operations. From an operational perspective, the launch of a commercial spacecraft, at least in the initial years, will likely cause temporary airport shutdowns, possibly for the entire duration of the flight. As commercial space operations become more routine, shutdowns will likely not be necessary, but any airport operator considering spaceport status should understand that even temporarily shutting down the airport may cause consternation with existing airport tenants.

Commercial spacecraft may also have a variety of effects, such as thermal heat from the skin of the spacecraft or the engines, toxic chemical emissions from reaching suborbital flight, aerodynamic effects (sound barrier), or other issues, depending on the type of spacecraft and its operating characteristics. In addition to the operation of the spacecraft, there may be payload issues as one's commercial operations move beyond space tourism to more routine flights carrying satellites or other materials such as scientific experiments. Even the leasing of space to a spaceport tenant will be different than an airport tenant. Additional facilities may be required for training individuals to go into space, mission control facilities, meteorology and range safety facilities and personnel, observation facilities, larger aircraft hangars and maintenance facilities, and even additional security systems separate from the Airport Security Program. Lastly, intermodal connections will be important so that payloads and passengers can easily access the facility, particularly for space tourists that arrive at a nearby commercial service airport.

Additional challenges before spaceports can become a reality will be the integration of suborbital flights with commercial air traffic. While the Space Shuttle dropping out of orbit on a periodic basis was not that difficult for ATC to handle, the challenge would be magnified greatly when several operations occur per day, throughout the United States and the world. However, some of these challenges are not within the control of the airport operator. The FAA, the commercial space pioneers, and others will have to solve many of these problems before spacecraft operations can become routine. To that end, the airport operator should focus on becoming a first-class airport, with an eye on their master plan so that they can incorporate spaceport planning and operational principles as they become known.

EMERGING AIRPORT SAFETY AND SECURITY CHALLENGES

In addition to UAV operations, airport operators are challenged by a variety of other issues, including the use of lasers around airports, protecting the network that runs the facility from cyberattacks, and developing response plans when a cyberattack leverages NextGen technologies to affect the operation of an aircraft, navigational system, or the airport. Irregular operations and tarmac delay issues will also continue to challenge the smooth and efficient operation of the airport.

Other challenges to Airport Operations include the use of personal lasers around airports, which can be a blinding hazard and definitely a safety hazard to pilots. New aircraft, such as VTOL planes and hypersonic corporate jets, will continue to push the airport to accommodate these unique aeronautical operations.

SUMMARY

The field of Airport Operations, safety, and emergency management continues to grow and expand. While technology brings new aeronautical uses in the form of UAVs and commercial space, the continuing growth of the emergency management field continues to bring new ways of handling incidents that airport operators must become aware of if they are to successfully manage an incident, while reducing liability to the airport.

Much of the text has been dedicated to the skills and knowledge required to respond to an airport emergency, but success all hinges on one critical component—the human factor. To be effective, ICs must understand the psychological dynamics at the individual, group, and organizational levels that are at work during an extreme crisis. First responders are people, too—they experience fear, and they see things that most in the general population would never see. Their fear response may not have previously been triggered, but could be triggered in an extreme event. Consistent training and exercises help responders to reduce the fear response, so that it is manageable. These practices can reduce liability claims after an incident, thereby saving the airport money and possibly helping responders to better cope with the aftermath of an incident.

In the past few years, UAVs have literally flooded U.S. airspace, at a rate far faster than the industry can regulate. While UAVs may represent a hazard to aviation, their uses are highly versatile, and their operating costs are incredibly low; thus, there is no denying that UAVs are here to stay.

Airport operators will see both challenges and opportunities with UAV operations. Challenges will come in the form of small UAVs operated near an airport by individuals that do not understand, or abide by, the regulations on such operations. These types of UAVs present a collision hazard, but could also be useful to the airport operator for certain airport functions, such as wildlife control, or to improve the common operating picture of an incident. Larger UAVs also represent operational challenges to airports and aircraft, but also potential future revenue sources for airports. Large UAV operators will need a place to store their craft and the associated hardware that is required to fly the vehicle. Some airports may be able to accommodate UAVs with existing runways, others may construct or designate separate runways only for UAV operations, and there may even be the potential for commercial UAVports in the near future.

Technology and the cessation of the Space Shuttle have left the door open for the commercial industry to take over space. Several airports and facilities have already been designated as spaceports, and there have been several flight tests of craft designed to take space tourists on suborbital flights. Commercial launch facilities have already been successful at servicing the International Space Station, and despite the occasional setback, the industry continues to grow.

Airport operators also see both challenges and opportunities in the commercial space industry. Challenges come in the form of new types of craft that can go beyond Earth's atmosphere, but may return with hazardous materials, or individuals with medical challenges, that are beyond what is normally seen at an airport. Opportunity comes in the form of accommodating the new generation of horizontal-takeoff to low Earth orbit industry.

Other challenges, such as safety issues from lasers fired at airplanes, cyberattack on the NextGen ATC systems, and numerous other as yet unseen issues, will continue to confront the industry, especially global Airport Operations.

Spaceports and Unmanned Vehicles
Spaceports and Airports

by David Ruppel
Manager, Front Range Airport, CO

A typical space launch requires you to shutdown 30 to 50 miles of airspace around the launch site. Right? A space launch implies using a launch vehicle similar to the Atlas V. Right? Well not exactly—and there is much more to the misperceptions of a public spaceport and how spaceports are truly evolving. Traditionally, a space launch has required powerful vertical-lift rockets requiring the closure of extensive airspace. But now other options and technologies, such as horizontal launch spacecraft, are within a few years of commercial licensing. That an airport could become a spaceport and see these vehicles operating from the same runways and facilities that currently host conventional aircraft is gaining acceptance as a long-term strategy. These vehicles present hazards similar to conventional aircraft, normally require flight corridors very similar to conventional aircraft, do not require large areas of airspace to be closed, and are able to operate safely within the NAS—all from the same runways that currently host conventional aircraft.

According to the Commercial Space Launch Act of 2011 (51 U.S.C. Subtitle V, ch. 509, §§ 50901–50923) and Title 14 CFR Chapter III—Commercial Space Transportation, Federal Aviation Administration, Part 420—License to Operate a Launch Site, and Part 431—Launch and Reentry of a Reusable Launch Vehicle (RLV), Spaceport and Spacecraft Licensing is happening and the FAA is charged with supporting these efforts. Unfortunately, not all of the FAA looks at this opportunity in the same way. The FAA Office of Commercial Space is charged with Licensing Spaceports and Space Vehicles and works hard to help applicants move through the process. The FAA Office of Airports and the Air Traffic Organization, charged with the safety of conventional airports and the NAS, respectively, see these changes as a threat to the limited funding available to airports and a hazard to the NAS. Many of the airport and airspace officials still see all space launch activities as presenting the same hazards as the old Atlas V and have an extremely hard time accepting the way the world is changing. This division is illustrated by the unwillingness of FAA departments to agree on a common definition Spaceport and Space Launch, much less as aeronautical activities.

So the Horizontal Space Launch Vehicle that takes off from the airport's runway and flies very much like an airplane through most of its flight profile, then returns and lands on the

(Continued)

(Continued)

airport's runway just like an airplane, is considered a nonaeronautical activity by most of the FAA. It is not surprising that the process of obtaining a Spaceport License is challenging.

The FAA divides Horizontal Launch Vehicles into three types—Concept X, Concept Y, and Concept Z—and refers to these vehicles as RLVs. Concept X vehicles make use of both air-breathing jet engines and rocket engines. Concept Y vehicles use rocket engines only and are referred to as "single-stage-to-space" vehicles. Concept Z vehicles use a "captive carry" system, depending on a conventional aircraft to carry the rocket vehicle as high as possible prior to the rocket plane engaging its rockets and flying away from the airplane into space. All three can launch and recover from a conventional airport with little or no alteration, and all three represent the future of horizontal launch space access.

For Front Range Airport, when we look at opportunities for bringing in revenue in addition to ways to expand operations on our airport, the Spaceport License is an exciting and interesting additional line of business. Front Range Airport was selected to be Spaceport Colorado by the Governor of Colorado, and not every airport will have that opportunity. The Commercial Space Industry is a multi-trillion dollar industry and, along with other aerospace-related businesses, is an outstanding fit for association with an airport. For Front Range Airport, which has exceptional access to Denver International, easy proximity to a major metropolitan city with one of the strongest Aerospace and Commercial Space economies in the United States, and the ability to safely handle Horizontal Space Launch activity, Spaceport Colorado is a logical extension and an important addition to the growing Commercial Launch Industry.

Unmanned Aircraft Systems and Airports

UASs present another dilemma of sorts for airports. There is a growing crossover between conventional aircraft systems, commercial space systems, and UASs. With the UAS industry becoming one of the fastest growing industries in the world, and one that will impact airports for better or worse, it is an industry that Airport Managers need to be aware of. *Presidential Memorandum: Promoting Economic Competitiveness While Safeguarding Privacy, Civil Rights, and Civil Liberties in Domestic Use of Unmanned Aircraft Systems* and Public Law 112-95, Title III, Subtitle B—Unmanned Aircraft Systems (FAA, Modernization and Reform Act of 2012) establish the FAA's responsibility to figure out how UASs will operate on and around airports. It is the responsibility of Airport Managers to engage in this debate and make sure that UAS operations occur in a way that makes sense for our airports and that we can support and benefit from.

The challenges are clear: rapid proliferation of UAS both in the United States and overseas; wide variation in the training and knowledge level of operators; and how to develop healthy, viable interaction on and around airports and around conventional aircraft. No easy answers here, but lots of opportunity. Mostly it comes back to education—not only for ourselves but also for our communities. Airports tend to be a source for information about anything that people see flying and we want to keep it that way, so we need to be prepared to talk about UAS operations and how they affect our airports and our communities.

(Continued)

(Continued)

Additionally, there are a lot of very smart people involved with the development and management of UASs and if we work with them to find solutions, UASs can become a legitimate and safe part of the aeronautical business of airports.

Airport Directors should be involved with the local industry groups such as, in Colorado, UAS Colorado and the Colorado Airport Operators Association, as well as the national groups like American Association of Airport Executives (AAAE). When the FAA puts out guidance on UASs make sure you comment and engage constructively with all airport users including UAV operators every chance you get. Place links on your airport's website to the section of the FAA website that addresses UAS operations and to the FAA B4UFLY[15] application that addresses UAS operating rules. Make it as easy as possible for operators to contact you, and help them understand the requirements for operating UASs, especially near airports. This is fascinating technology that, if handled correctly, can operate safely with the other legitimate users of the NAS.

Conclusions

Spaceports and UASs both present challenges for airport operators, but if properly understood and handled correctly offer an exciting addition to traditional airport activities as well as a significant source of potential revenue. As burgeoning industries that will very likely affect our airports whether we pursue them or not, we need to make certain that we are engaged and seeking every chance to influence how our airports will interact with these technologies. As with most of the things we do as airports, if we develop appropriate procedures, consider carefully how we can deal with these operations in ways that take into account not only their hazards but their benefits, and educate ourselves, our staffs, and our communities, we will be able to handle these exciting technologies and operations safely and securely and have an effective place in this next great advance for aviation and aeronautics.

REFERENCES

Act of Valor. Dir. Mike McCoy and Scott Waugh. Perf. Roarke Denver and Alex Veadov. Eagle Pictures, 2012. Film.

Benjamin, M. (2013). *Drone warfare: Killing by remote control*. London, UK: Verso.

Carroll, J. (2013, December 6). The future is here: Five applications of UAV technology. Retrieved September 10, 2015, from: http://www.vision-systems.com/articles/2013/12/the-future-is-here-five-applications-of-uav-technology.html.

Clausewitz, C. (1968 [1832]). *On war*. London, UK: Penguin Press.

Fahlstrom, P. G., & Gleason, T. J. (2012). *Introduction* to UAV systems [Nook]. http://www.barnesandnoble.com/w/introduction-to-uav-systems-paul-fahlstrom/1119704934.

Federal Aviation Administration (FAA). (2006, November 17). *Office of Commercial Space Transportation*. Retrieved September 11, 2015, from: https://www.faa.gov/about/office_org/headquarters_offices/ast/licenses_permits/.

---

[15]See https://www.faa.gov/uas/b4ufly/

Federal Aviation Administration (FAA). (2013, February 12). *Office of Commercial Space Transportation.* Retrieved September 11, 2015, from: http://www.faa.gov/about/office_org/headquarters_offices/ast/industry/.

Federal Aviation Administration (FAA). (2015a). *Know before you fly.* Retrieved September 10, 2015, from: http://knowbeforeyoufly.org/.

Federal Aviation Administration (FAA). (2015b, March 4). *Model aircraft operations.* Retrieved September 10, 2015, from: https://www.faa.gov/uas/model_aircraft/.

Federal Aviation Administration (FAA). (2015c, April 25). *Office of Commercial Space Transportation.* Retrieved September 11, 2015, from: http://www.faa.gov/about/office_org/headquarters_offices/ast/.

FEMA. (n.d.). National Response Framework. Retrieved December 13, 2015, from: http://www.fema.gov/national-response-framework.

Forrest, J., Cozart, J., White, D., & Ormen, M. (2015). *A technical assessment & feasibility analysis for UAV/UAS operations based in Garfield County & serving as a COE in aerial firefighting (Rep.).* Denver, CO: MSU Denver.

Gonzales, L. (2014). *Flight 232: A story of disaster and survival.* New York, NY: W.W. Norton & Company.

Grossman, D. (1996). *On killing.* New York, NY: Back Bay Books.

Impey, C. (2015). *Beyond: Our future in space.* New York, NY: W.W. Norton & Company.

Kahneman, D. (2011). *Thinking fast and slow.* New York, NY: Farrar, Straus and Giroux.

Kearns, D. W., & Grossman, J. (1992). Effects of a cognitive intervention package on the free-throw performance of varsity basketball players during practice and competition. *Perceptual and Motor Skills*, 75(3f), 1243−1253. Available from: http://dx.doi.org/10.2466/pms.1992.75.3f.1243.

Keller, J. (2014, December 9). *Army to build special UAV airport at Fort Bliss for Grey Eagle and Shadow unmanned aircraft.* Retrieved September 10, 2015, from: http://www.militaryaerospace.com/articles/2014/12/bliss-uav-airport.html.

Krepinevich, A. F. (2010). *7 Deadly scenarios: A military futurist explores war in the twenty-first century.* New York, NY: Bantam Books.

Lord, W. (1955). *A night to remember.* New York, NY: Holt.

Montgomery, R. (1995, April 13). *Casualty areas from impacting inert debris for people in the open.* (Rep.). Retrieved September 11, 2015, from USAF website: https://www.faa.gov/about/office_org/headquarters_offices/ast/licenses_permits/media/99may_inert_rpt.pdf.

Pfeifer, J. (2013). Crisis leadership: The art of adapting to extreme events. *PCL Discussion Paper Series.* http://www.hks.harvard.edu/programs/crisisleadership/publications/articles.

Ripley, A. (2009). *The unthinkable: Who survives disaster and why.* New York, NY: Three Rivers Press.

Rutkow, L., Gable, L., & Links, J. M. (2011). Protecting the mental health of first responders: Legal and ethical considerations. *Journal of Law, Medicine & Ethics*, 39, 56−59. Available from: http://dx.doi.org/10.1111/j.1748-720x.2011.00567.x.

Sgobba, T., Allahdadi, F. A., Rongier, I., & Wilde, P. D. (2013). *Safety design for space operations* [Kindle]. http://www.amazon.com/Safety-Design-Operations-Firooz-Allahdadi/dp/0080969216.

SunSentinel. (1989, September 3). *93,000 Passengers waiting for First Pan Am moon flight.* Retrieved September 11, 2015, from: http://articles.sun-sentinel.com/1989-09-03/features/8903010181_1_moon-flight-requests.

Unmanned Aerial Vehicle Systems Association (UAVSA). (2015). *Unmanned Aerial Vehicle Systems Association commercial applications.* Retrieved September 10, 2015, from: https://www.uavs.org/commercial.

U.S. Department of Defense (DoD). (2011). *Unmanned Aircraft System Airspace Integration Plan.* Retrieved September 16, 2015, from: http://www.acq.osd.mil/sts/docs/DoD_UAS_Airspace_Integ_Plan_v2_%28signed%29.pdf.

U.S. Department of Health and Human Services (DHHS). (n.d.). *Psychological aid for first responders* [Brochure]. Washington, DC: Author.

Appendix: Coda

*"The FAA has to wait for harm to occur or almost occur before it can improve restrictions,"
FAA's commentary on rulemaking for commercial space travel* (Yates, 2008).

Throughout the history of aviation, we frequently observe disaster or significant loss occurring prior to the issuance of regulations designed to prevent or mitigate these instances. Unfortunately, far too many people believe that regulations represent the highest standard of safety (or security) for uniformly addressing risk. Instead, regulations are usually minimum standards designed to help prevent the reoccurrence of specific types of risks. Regulations are useful, in that for those specific areas of jeopardy we can use them for determining noncompliance and exposure to potential loss. Nevertheless, a narrow boundary usually separates being "compliant" with being "unsafe." Compliance, without a conscious effort to continuously seek improved safety and operational best practice, does not guarantee safety. To be proactive and exceed levels of required safety compliance, it is essential for the Airport Operations Manager to (a) stay informed through continuous learning, (b) sustain innovation in the practice of safety and operations, and (c) create a safety culture that motivates all stakeholders to exceed minimum regulatory and operational process requirements.

We understand that budgets for operating an airport are tight—they always will be. In these fiscal conditions, it can be difficult to convince your board, your manager, or your elected officials to take an extra step in safety beyond what is required in the regulations or is minimally acceptable to the public. However, our goal for this textbook has been to provide the reader with the knowledge to make convincing arguments for going beyond regulatory requirements in safety and operational processes. In Airport Operations, sustaining a safety culture that advocates effective and safe operational air transportation service requires a belief of *doing what is right, for the sake of it being the right thing to do*—regardless of the degree of regulatory compliance.

An airport can represent many values to the public, but "only an airport can be an airport," and it is critical to the infrastructure of the United States that our system of airports operate safely, securely, and effectively. Some may suggest that the adverb *efficiently* should be added to these requirements. However, we believe that effectiveness in Airport Operations is inclusive of efficiency. As Dr. Stephen Covey, author of *The 7 Habits of Highly Effective People*, has suggested, we must be efficient with things, but effective with people. In Airport Operations, efficiency is born from effective relationships with all stakeholders of the airport and surrounding community.

The aviation industry has a long history of being reactive rather than proactive in managing safety and operational effectiveness. For this reason, we believe Safety Management Systems (SMS) and Security Management Systems (SeMS) should become the new standards of proactive operational process at all airports. SMS and SeMS are already in use throughout numerous U.S. aviation agencies, including the airline and corporate aircraft industries, the U.S. military, and in many other settings throughout the world. However, adoption of SMS and SeMS by the field of airport management and operations has been slow. Modern airport management should recognize and embrace SMS and SeMS as two of the most proactive means for making safety, security, and operational effectiveness the highest priority in air transportation.

REFERENCE

Yates, R. A. (2008). Informal regulation of space activities. *Nebraska Law Review, 87*(2). Available at: <http://digitalcommons.unl.edu/nlr/vol87/iss2/8>.

Index